CASPIAN SEA

ARAL SEA

R. Jaxartes

(Syr Daria)

CHORASMIA

SACAE

Tashkend (FERGHANA)

MASSAGETAE

Alexandreschate (Chodjend)

Polytimetus R (Zarafshan) Cyropolis

(Bokhara) Marakanda (Samarcand)

R. Oxus

(Amu Daria) SOGDIANA PARA

DAHAE TACENE

Alexandria (Merv)

Bactra-Zariaspa (Balkh) BACTRIA Drapsaka

R Arius (Heri Rud) HINDU KUSH

Zadracarta (Astrabad) SADAE

HYRCANIA (Meshed) Alexandria PAROP ASPASII (SWAT) ASSACENI

Hecatompylos (Damghan) ad Caucasum Massaga

Rhagae (Kabul) Peukelaotis Ca Aornos

Caspian PARTHIA ARIA Artacoana (Attock) Taxila NDHARA (CASH-

Gates Alexandria Areion Alexandria Bucephala MIR)

Ecbatana KAVIR (Herat) (Ghazni) (Jhelum)

(Hamadan) PARAETACENE (Salt desert) PUNJAB

(Ispahan) Farah R Akesines (Ravi)

GABIENE DRANGIANA Alexandria Lahore R Hydraotes (Ravi)

UXII Prophthasia Arachoton R Hydaspes R) Hyphasis

Pasargadae ARIASPAE (Candahar) (Sutlej) OXYDRACAE

Charax R.Helmund Craterus route

Persepolis (Kerman) (Quetta) Alexandria

(L.Niriz) Bolan Pass (Ootch) (DESERT)

Habil Rud R. Mulla Pass

CARMANIA Alexandria Shikarpore INDIA

(Gulashkird)

(Bender Abbas) Bampur Patala

Harmozia Pura GEDROSIA SIND

TYLOS R. Bampur (Fahraj) old mouth of Indus

(Bahrein) Gwadur Pasni Taloi ocala

PERSIAN GULF Range old coastline

INDIAN OCEAN (approximate)

E. Raisz

50   55   60   65   70

This book
belongs
to

Melissa
Kett

ANCIENT HISTORY

ANCIENT HISTORY

from
PREHISTORIC TIMES
to the
DEATH OF JUSTINIAN

William G. Sinnigen

Professor of History,
Hunter College of the City University of New York

Charles Alexander Robinson, Jr.

Late David Benedict Professor of
Brown University

THIRD EDITION

Macmillan Publishing Co., Inc.
NEW YORK
Collier Macmillan Publishers
LONDON

COPYRIGHT © 1981, MACMILLAN PUBLISHING CO., INC.

PRINTED IN THE UNITED STATES OF AMERICA

Earlier edition(s) copyright © 1951 and 1967 by Macmillan Publishing Co., Inc.

MACMILLAN PUBLISHING CO., INC.
866 THIRD AVENUE, NEW YORK, NEW YORK 10022

COLLIER MACMILLAN CANADA, LTD.

Illustrations on pp. 1, 23, 95, 273, 321, and 411: Granger Collection

Library of Congress Cataloging in Publication Data

Robinson, Charles Alexander, 1900–1965.
Ancient history, from prehistoric times to the death
of Justinian.

Bibliography: p.
Includes index.
1. History, Ancient. I. Sinnigen, William Gurnee,
(date) joint author. II. Title.
D59.R64   1981   930   80-13472
ISBN 0-02-410810-3

Printing: 5 6 7 8   Year: 7 8

ISBN   0-02-410810-3

Clarissimae et Carissimae
Universitati Brunensi

Preface
to the Third Edition

In preparing the third edition of Professor Robinson's *Ancient History,* I have tried to correct such errors of fact that existed in the first and second, to bring the interpretive sections up to date, and in general to tighten up the organization. The result has been a shorter book than the previous editions. Revisions throughout the entire text are extensive. In particular, I should like to draw the reader's attention to chapters 16, 17, 18, 19, and 20, which have been completely rewritten. Most of the illustrations and many of the maps are new. Wherever possible the latter have been simplified for the sake of clarity. Abbreviated versions of the prefaces to the first two editions are given in the pages following.

I should like to thank Mrs. Celia Sachs Robinson Stilwell for her support of this edition of her late husband's textbook. I owe a special debt of gratitude to Professors Donald Kagan (Yale University), Charles Robert Phillips III (Lehigh University), Roger A. de Laix (University of Arizona), and John A. Brinkman (The Oriental Institute, University of Chicago), who read and criticized either parts or all of the manuscript, suggested many improvements, and saved me from errors and inconsistencies. Members of the staff of the Macmillan Company supervised the editing and production of this book with their usual efficiency. I should also like to thank Signora Karen Einaudi of the Fototeca Unione (Rome) and especially the staff of the Granger Collection (New York) for their help in supplying the new illustrations, under which the appropriate credit lines appear.

Naturally, errors of conception, fact, or judgment in this edition of *Ancient History* are my own responsibility.

William G. Sinnigen

New York City

Preface
to the Second Edition

When Mrs. C. A. Robinson, Jr., asked me to revise her husband's *Ancient History* not long after his untimely death, I was glad to agree because Professor Robinson had been a colleague and friend. Only a few months of an unusually busy academic year could be given to the revision, but I have done what I could to incorporate the results of continuing historical research in the new edition in that time.

In preparing this revision, I have *inter alia* considered the useful reviews of R. S. Rogers in the 1952 *Classical Weekly,* M. Cary in the 1953 *Classical Review,* and C. J. Cadoux in the 1954 *Journal of Hellenic Studies.*

Alan L. Boegehold

Preface
to the First Edition

If we take ancient history to be the story of Western civilization from its earliest beginnings to Justinian's death in 565 A.D., it is obvious that we have to deal not only with an enormous span of time and space, but with many and very different societies as well. Once the complicated millennia of prehistory are left behind, the study of the past does not become a relatively simple one of examining isolated worlds of Semites and Greeks, Egyptians, Iranians and Indians, Italians, Spaniards, Gauls, Germans and Britons, for their civilizations were inextricably mixed. It has been remarked that the method of natural science—where a botanist examines a sufficient number of plants and obtains uniformities—will not yield, as Toynbee seems to think it will, a better understanding of the subject. Civilizations cannot be handled arbitrarily in the manner of plants, for they consist of men and more particularly of the achievements of the mind and spirit. The history of mankind, we must insist, is primarily a record of ideas, particularly ideas that caused particular growths. These were rarely conceived in the mind of a genius and more often were produced by a wide body of factors. In order to work through to an idea and understand it, it is necessary to grasp those factors—dates and names, wars and institutions, the struggle for daily bread no less than for justice, man's environment and inheritance, and his relation to himself, his fellows, and his God.

The facts and forces that make up ancient history are numerous enough to fill several volumes. I have limited myself to one volume in the belief that it should be possible to present most of the essential points within a reasonable compass. Instead of developing these at greater length—and a second volume could do little more than that—the next task, I believe, should consist of special studies, including art, philosophy, and literature (though not in mere snippets).

One of the most fascinating features of studying the ancients is the profusion of new material that accumulates year by year. There are, nevertheless, both large gaps in our knowledge and considerable uncertainty about every year and every event and institution and personality of antiquity. I have not known how to indicate this, except for a few words of warning in the text, for it would be unbearable to qualify each sentence with "probably" or "perhaps." The well-informed general reader and the student, on the other hand, may find it a positive advantage, as I have already intimated, to have in one volume a connected account of those important matters that seem likely.

I should like to thank my colleagues for their support and criticism. My deepest debt of all, to Celia Sachs Robinson, must remain, save for this brief mention, unexpressed, but I would ask her to join with me in dedicating this book to the great university which has been regarded for almost two centuries as a center of classical studies.

C. A. Robinson, Jr.

Providence, Rhode Island

Contents

PART I
HISTORY AND PREHISTORY

1. Ancient History   3
2. Prehistoric Man   10
   The food gatherers, 11.   The food-producing revolution, 17.

PART II
THE ANCIENT NEAR EAST

3. Sumer, Akkad, and Babylon   25
   The Tigris–Euphrates Valley, 25.   The land of Sumer and Akkad, 27.   Babylon, 35.   Babylonian civilization, 36.
4. Egypt   42
   The Valley of the Nile, 42.   The Archaic (3100–2685 B.C.) and Old Kingdoms (ca. 2685–2180 B.C.), 46.   The Middle Kingdom (2040–1785 B.C.), 54.   The Second Intermediate Period (ca. 1785–1560 B.C.), 58.   The New Kingdom (1560–1085 B.C.), 58.
5. Asia Minor, Syria, and Palestine   69
   The Hittites, 69.   The Phoenicians, 72.   The Hebrews, 75.
6. The Assyrian Empire and Its Successors   81
   The supremacy of Assyria, 81.   Assyrian Civilization, 87.   The new states of the Near East, 89.

PART III
HELLAS

7. The Aegean Age   97
   Introduction, 97.   Minoan civilization, 99.   Mycenae, 106.   Troy, 109.
8. The Greek Middle Age and Renaissance   111
   The Dorian Invasion, 111.   Homer, 113.   The city-state, 114.   Colonization, 116.   Tyranny, 121.
9. Sparta and Athens   124
   Sparta, 124.   The Peloponnesian League, 127.   Athens, 127.   Democracy, 131.

10. The Civilization of Archaic Greece   133
     Religion, 133.   Literature, 134.   Art, 138.

11. The Persian Empire   146
     Europe and Asia, 146.   The reign of Darius I (522–486 B.C.), 149.

12. The Persian Wars   154
     The Ionian Revolt (499–493 B.C.), 154.   Marathon (490 B.C.), 156.   Thermopylae (480 B.C.), 160.   Salamis (480 B.C.), 167. Plataea and Mycale (479 B.C.), 168.   The Carthaginian invasion of Sicily, 169.

13. The Athenian Empire   171
     The Delian League, 171.   The Greek world after Plataea, 173. The Athenian democratic constitution, 177.   The land empire, 181.   The Thirty Years' Peace, 183.

14. The Peloponnesian War (431–404 B.C.)   185
     The causes of the Panhellenic conflict, 185.   The Archidamian War (431–421 B.C.), 187.   The Peace of Nicias, 194.   The Sicilian expedition, 195.   Oligarchical revolution in Athens, 202. The fall of Athens, 203.

15. The Periclean Age   206
     Social and economic life, 206.   Art, 209.   Literature, 213.

16. The Era of Hegemonies and Persia (404–336 B.C.)   226
     Introduction, 226.   Economy and Society, 227.   Theban Hegemony, 232.   The Western Greeks, 233.   The Rise of Macedonia, 234.

17. The Civilization of the Fourth Century B.C.   241
     Introduction, 241.   Cyrenaics and Cynics, 242.   Plato, 243. Aristotle, 245.   Xenophon, 246.   Isocrates, 247.   Demosthenes, 249.   Art and Architecture, 251.

18. Alexander the Great   255
     Source Problems, 255.   Alexander's Youth, 256.   Macedonia Versus Persia, 258.   The Campaign Against Persia, 260.   The Period of Crisis (330–327 B.C.), 263.   The Indian Campaign and Its Aftermath, 264.   The Purges, 266.   The Unity of Humankind, 267.   The Last Year, 268.   Alexander and History, 270.

PART IV
THE HELLENISTIC AGE

19. The Hellenistic World   275
     The Break-Up of Alexander's Empire (323–275 B.C.), 275.   The Hellenistic State System, 279.   Hellenistic Greece, 283.   Hellenistic Asia, 289.   Hellenistic Egypt, 294.

20. Hellenistic Civilization   300
     Introduction, 300.   Economy and Society, 300.   Hellenistic Culture, 303.

PART V

THE ROMAN REPUBLIC

21. Early Italy   323
    The land and its people, 323.   The Etruscans, 327.   Latium, 329.   The kings of Rome, 334.

22. The Expansion and Development of Rome to 265 B.C.   337
    The early Republic, 337.   The Latin and Samnite Wars, 338. The conquest of southern Italy, 340.   The organization of Roman rule in Italy, 342.   The magistracy, senate, and assembly, 344.   The great laws, 348.   Social progress, 351.

23. Rome and the Mediterranean (264-133 B.C.)   353
    The First Punic War (264-241 B.C.), 353.   The Illyrian and Gallic Wars (229-219 B.C.), 355.   The Second Punic War (218-201 B.C.), 356.   The Greek East (200-133 B.C.), 361.   The West, 364.

24. Roman Government and Society (264-133 B.C.)   366
    Government at Rome, 366.   Provincial administration, 368. Intellectual development, 370.

25. The Beginning of the Roman Revolution (133-78 B.C.)   373
    The Gracchi, 373.   Gaius Marius, 377.   The Allied War (90-88 B.C.), 379.   The First Mithridatic War (89-85 B.C.), 380.   The dictatorship of Sulla, 381.

26. The End of the Republic (78-27 B.C.)   384
    The rise of Pompey, 384.   Rome during Pompey's absence, 387. The First Triumvirate, 390.   The end of the First Triumvirate, 394.   The dictatorship of Caesar, 397.   The Second Triumvirate, 399.

27. The Society and Civilization of the Late Republic   403
    The social and economic background, 403.   Philosophy and law, 407.   Literature and art, 408.

PART VI

THE ROMAN EMPIRE

28. The Principate of Augustus (27 B.C.-A.D. 14)   413
    The foundation of the principate, 413.   The princeps, senate, *equestrians, and plebs, 415.   The provinces and frontiers, 418. Religion, literature, and art, 421.   The succession, 425.*

29. The Early Empire (A.D. 14-192)   427
    The Julio-Claudian emperors (A.D. 14-68), 427.   The year of the four emperors (A.D. 68-69), 433.   The Flavian dynasty (A.D. 69-96), 434.   Nerva, Trajan, and Hadrian (A.D. 96-138), 438.   The Antonines (A.D. 138-192), 443.

30. The Greco-Roman World During the Early Empire   446
      Weakness amid strength, 446.   Art and literature, 450.   Law,
      458.   Religion, 462.

31. The Imperial Crisis and Recovery (A.D. 193–395)   467
      The militarization of government: the Severi (A.D. 193–235), 467.
      Military anarchy (A.D. 235–285), 473.   Autocracy: Diocletian
      and Constantine (A.D. 285–337), 476.   The last years of the
      united empire (A.D. 337–395), 485.

32. The Transition to the Middle Ages (A.D. 395–565)   488
      The Germanic invasions of the West (A.D. 395–476), 488.   The
      Germanic kingdoms of the West (A.D. 476–526), 492.   The East-
      ern Empire (A.D. 395–527), 494.   Justinian (A.D. 527–565), 496.

33. The Civilization of the Latin Empire   502
      Art, 502.   Literature, 504.   The Christian Church, 509.   Epi-
      logue, 511.

Chronological Tables   513
List of Roman Emperors   527
Genealogical Tables   529
Select Bibliography   530
Index   545

Illustrations

1.	Stone age cave painting of bison bull, Altimira	15
2.	Cave painting of horse, Dordogne	16
3.	Neolithic skull found at Jericho	19
4.	Stonehenge, England	21
5.	Sumerian standing figure	30
6.	Sumerian statuette of Gudea	33
7.	Bull-head harp pillar from Ur	34
8.	Ziggurat at Ur	35
9.	Stele of Laws of Hammurabi	40
10.	Narmer Pallette	48
11.	Step pyramid of King Djoser	52
12.	Great Sphinx at Gizeh	53
13.	Portrait head of Prince Rahotep	55
14.	Queen Hatshepsut as a Sphinx	61
15.	Portrait of Amenhotep IV (Akhenaten)	62
16.	Portrait head of Nefertiti	63
17.	Akhenaten and his family	64
18.	Death mask of Tutankhamen	65
19.	Egyptian tomb painting of maidens at a banquet	66
20.	Egyptian tomb painting of peasants cultivating wheat	67
21.	Ashurnasirpal II of Assyria	85
22.	Minoan painting of libation procession	102
23.	Cretan ivory figure of snake goddess	105
24.	The "Treasury of Atreus"	107
25.	Athenian jar with geometric ornament	115
26.	Corinthian wine jug with animal ornamentation	139
27.	Warriors arming, from Attic red figured vase	140
28.	Hera of Samos	143
29.	Archaic Greek marble Kouros	144
30.	Glazed brick panel from palace of Darius	151
31.	"Charioteer of Delphi"	176
32.	Discobolus	177
33.	Present-day appearance of the Agora, Athens	208
34.	The Acropolis of Athens	210
35.	Temple of Athena Nike	212
36.	Centaur and Lapinth from the Parthenon	213
37.	Greek coin of Athena	214
38.	Pericles	215
39.	Socrates	221

40.	Demosthenes	250
41.	The Palaestra at Olympia	253
42.	Alexander	257
43.	Hellenistic statuettes of women playing knucklebones	311
44.	Hellenistic boxer	312
45.	Winged Victory of Samothrace	313
46.	Laocoön	314
47.	Etruscan statuette of a warrior	328
48.	Etruscan horse and rider	329
49.	Wall painting from Tarquinia	330
50.	Etruscan chimera from Arretium	331
51.	Etrusco-Italian rhyton	332
52.	The Via Latina as it appears today	358
53.	Cicero	386
54.	Julius Caesar	391
55.	Augustus	414
56.	The Roman Forum	423
57.	Relief from the *Ara Pacis*	424
58.	The "Gemma Augustea"	425
59.	Roman coins showing Claudius and M. Junius Brutus	429
60.	Agrippina the Younger	432
61.	Wall painting from Pompeii	436
62.	Street scene, Herculanaeum	437
63.	Remains of Roman amphitheater near Naples	450
64.	Roman street in modern Libya	451
65.	Roman apartment houses, Ostia	452
66.	The Pantheon	453
67.	Roman relief of sacrifice to Mithra	464
68.	The Tetrarchs of Diocletian, St. Marks, Venice	477
69.	Byzantine mosaic of Justinian	497
70.	Santa Sophia, interior	504

Maps and Diagrams

1. Alexander's Empire   Front Endpaper
2. Land-Type Map of Europe, Northern Africa, and Western Asia   6
3. The Descendants of *Australopithecus afarensis*   12
4. Tools and Implements: 70,000 B.C.   14
5. The Earliest Villages, ca. 7,000 B.C.   18
6. Assyria and Babylonia   28
7. Ancient Egypt   43
8. Palestine, Syria, and Hittite Empire; Kingdom of David and Solomon   70
9. Early Alphabets   74
10. The Assyrian Empire, 7th Century B.C.   82
11. Lydian, Chaldean, and Median Kingdoms, 6th century B.C.   90
12. Reference Map of Ancient Greece   98
13. Greece in the Bronze Age; Boeotia, Attica, Argolis   100
14. Palace of Minos at Cnossus   104
15. Greek Colonization   118
16. The Peloponnesus; Plan of the Olympia   125
17. Orders of Greek Architecture   142
18. Persian Empire about 500 B.C.   148
19. Marathon   157
20. Artemisium and Thermopylae   161
21. Plan of the Acropolis   211
22. The Hellenistic World about 275 B.C.   280
23. Hellenistic Egypt   295
24. Italy in the Sixth Century B.C.   326
25. Site of Rome   333
26. Acquisition of Rome and Allies, 500–265 B.C.   341
27. Growth of the Roman Empire, 265–44 B.C.   389
28. Roman Gaul   392
29. The Roman Empire Under Trajan   441
30. Orders of Roman Architecture   454
31. Roman Germany and the Limes   469
32. Roman Empire in the Fourth Century A.D.   480
33. The Roman Empire and the Germanic Kingdoms, A.D. 527   493
34. The Roman Empire, A.D. 565   498
35. The Roman Empire at the death of Augustus   Rear Endpaper

PART I
HISTORY AND PREHISTORY

1

Ancient History

The earth, scientists tell us, is three billion years old, perhaps much older. Life on earth has existed for at least a tenth of that period, while the development of man is still much more recent, perhaps beginning some 3.5 million years ago. Recorded history—and with it, civilization—has existed for only about five thousand years, an awesomely short period when compared with the age of our planet and of humankind.

Ancient history—the story of our own foundations from the earliest beginnings to that borderland where antiquity ends (the sixth century of our era, let us say)—is far longer than the subsequent periods of European history: the medieval and the modern. But of much greater importance is the fact that ancient history provides the opportunity to consider most human experience at every level—literature, art, religion, philosophy, science, and government—in a constant process of development and change. It is obvious that ancient history has long since ended; it has run its course; many of the passions that fired humanity in ancient times are dead. Now we can perhaps view the issues with some perspective. No other period of history is sufficiently long or complete to provide quite this opportunity.

Antiquity should be studied simply because it is a fascinating subject concerning human beings who faced, solved, or avoided problems basic to living in any epoch, yet also in many ways different from those of our highly industrialized twentieth century. Students of antiquity, whether beginners or professionals, rightly develop their own "philosophy" of history. They choose to emphasize that phase of ancient development—economic, political, military, social, or cultural—that seems to them most significant in terms of their own, contemporary situation.

Thus every generation of historians reinterprets the past, no matter what the period, by emphasizing elements in it that seem to relate to contemporary problems. It is accordingly no accident that the first great works of social and economic history dealing with classical Greece and Rome were written by scholars who personally experienced the social and economic upheavals of the West in the period between the two world wars. Similarly, thoughtful historians of the late 1930s began to rewrite Roman imperial history, particularly the reign of the first Augustus, in the light of their new observation of the bases of political power butressing the authoritarian regimes in Germany and Italy. Perhaps the most striking developments in current scholarship involve a growing interest in social classes previously neglected, like slaves, peasants, and women. This interest surely reflects the increasing egalitarianism of our twentieth-century civilization, as well as the central position occupied by history in the social sciences.

If we are to examine the driving force of history, we may begin by saying that there is no "law of progress" that compels the human race to "improve" against its own will and effort. Historical experience suggests that the political welfare of a state can be dependent on the condition of the lowest class within its borders. It also suggests that among the conditions that have got civilizations into trouble in various ages are a flight from rationality, loss of individual and local community freedom, unresponsive government, the unplanned growth of cities to the injury of rural life (as in ancient Rome and modern Iran), and the neglect of literature, art, and science, and perhaps also of patriotism, justice, and religion, as one seriously conceives of these. Our problem here is to discover, if we can, what it was that carried the ancients to high peaks and conversely how it happened that at times they failed and were ultimately overwhelmed by disaster. Put in this way, the value of ancient history clearly consists of both inspiration and warning.

The history of Rome—superficially, at least—can be readily understood and provides much food for thought. On balance, it is the story of a remarkable city-state, which seemed to pile success on monumental success and yet, perhaps because of its failure to identify and solve some of its most crucial problems, finally enmeshed itself in catastrophe. The history of Greece, on the other hand, is not for those who must read on the run, for it is subtler and is, in essence, a story of ideas, important ideas developing through the centuries and at every point hotly debated. If we now select from each of these peoples—the Greeks and the Romans—the centuries of their history that have the most to teach us, we may be able to suggest some of the very human problems they faced.

Of all the pre-Christian periods, it is the fifth and fourth centuries B.C. that probably speak to us most loudly. This is the period of the great Athenian dramatists and of classical art, of Socrates, Plato, and Aristotle. Nevertheless, the picture is darkened by frequent warfare, the decline of the city-state system, and its ultimate demise in a kind of political universalism temporarily imposed on the Greek world by Alexander the Great. And of all the centuries after Christ, it is surely the second that provides us with the greatest food for thought. Humankind had never been so prosperous, nor had peace ever been so long and profound. Yet this century, conspicuous for its lack of initiative (as the years had increasingly been since Augustus had won the principate of Rome, 27 B.C.), produced few great books, few new ideas in government, no new principle in art or science, no significant technological advance; and collapse lay immediately ahead. These apparent contradictions are further complicated by the simultaneous rise of Christianity. Many Romans were bewildered by the early Christians. How could people seemingly plot to create a state within a state? Now, from the second century onward, pagan letters declined because they stressed form rather than substance and were addressed to a narrow, educated circle, whereas Christian literature carried its message to all and was full of vitality because the Christians were engaged in competition or, as we might express it more exactly, in confrontation with government, pagans, and heretics.

The transformation of imperial Rome, that is to say, can apparently be matched by simultaneous growth on the part of those people who had faith in themselves and their cause. Here, too, is a major key to an understanding of the achievements of the Greek city-state and indeed of any institution. Call it what one will—the search for new ideas, or intellectually productive strife at a high level, or the opportunity of initiative to solve one's own problems and hence society's—ancient history suggests that great success stems from faith based on man's confidence that he can improve himself.

Thus far, in the course of suggesting a point, we have drawn our parallels from the experience of the Greeks and the Romans, but another great department of ancient history includes the Near East—the Orient, as it is often called for the sake of convenience, though what we generally mean by the Orient (India, China, and Japan) lay outside the growth of ancient European history. The Near East has its own peculiar, and very great, lessons for us, not only in religious development and imperialism but also in its striking cultural achievements. The Near East, moreover, stimulated the growth of Greek civilization and then was brought within the orbit of the Greeks by the conquests of Alexander the Great. The political unity of the entire ancient world was achieved, however, by other Westerners, the Romans. Thus ancient history is a unit, chronologically, politically, and geographically, for the area concerned is the Mediterranean coast and its neighboring lands, Mesopotamia and Iran to the east and the interior of Europe to the north and west (the front and rear endpapers show the area). The map on page 6 suggests, moreover, how the ancient world was inevitably destined to receive not only waves of invaders from its hinterland of plains and deserts, but also cultural and commercial stimuli from far beyond its political limits.

Here is the world, here are the institutions, from which modern society has in part developed. Back of that world lie its own foundations, buried in the vast span of prehistory. To attempt an account of antiquity in one volume requires some temerity, just as the reader is as surely called on to exercise vigilance toward what he reads. After all, the first edition of the monumental *Cambridge Ancient History* (currently being rewritten) runs to twelve volumes of text and five of plates, stops two and a quarter centuries short of this book, and contains hardly a page that cannot be questioned. The purpose of this book, however, is not to provide encyclopedic knowledge but to stimulate further reading and debate.

The word *history,* in its original Greek sense, it should be said, means inquiry, investigation, an activity that best describes the work of the historian. The first duty of the historian, in other words, is to gather together the facts that bear on the past and then try to interpret them, in the hope that people will be able to learn by past experience. It would be catastrophic if every individual had to begin at the beginning and tackle each problem afresh. The career of Charles Evans Hughes, the great American Secretary of State and Chief Justice of the Supreme Court, is a case in point, for it has been said that his omnivorous reading habits while an undergraduate at Brown gave him "vicarious experience upon which he was able to draw throughout his life. He did not have to grope through every problem himself and learn every lesson at first hand; he could recall the issues and situations historical and fictional characters had faced before and he knew the consequences of their choices."

The facts available to historians are of the most varied kind, for historians must

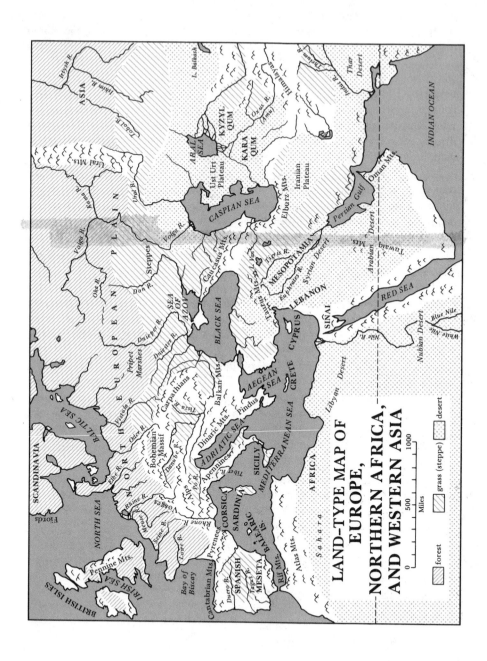

LAND–TYPE MAP OF
EUROPE,
NORTHERN AFRICA,
AND WESTERN ASIA

0   500   1000
        Miles

forest

grass (steppe)

desert

6

re-create not only political, economic, and military history but also social customs and institutions, philosophy, literature and religion, art, and technology. Despite the overwhelming evidence, there are frequently total, or almost total, blanks to fill that require all the historian's ingenuity. Finally, historians have two tasks that test their judgment. In the first place, they must evaluate their evidence and see what it is worth for its own sake and in its relation to other matters; this task is particularly difficult when the chief source for an event is known to be untrustworthy. And, second, historians must give the proper emphasis to their story: Periclean Athens, let us say, must loom larger than certain other periods of Hellenic (Greek) history, without, however, preempting the field. This striking of a certain balance even means, in the case of a one-volume history whose aim is to give the story of ancient Western civilization, that certain epochs, periods, and civilizations are here, but only here, more important than others. It would be unwise, for example, to devote more space to the millennia of the Stone Ages than to the succeeding centuries, and it would be similarly unwise to pretend that the various periods of civilization have equal significance for our stated purpose. It seems hardly necessary to suggest again that a reader's first duty is to guard against the presentation and conclusions drawn by the historian; nor are any two persons likely to agree on what constitutes proper emphasis.

It seems clear, however, at least to the classicists, that the history of Greece and Rome should loom largest in the study of antiquity, a statement with which some ancient Near Eastern specialists will not entirely agree. Many of the great achievements of the ancient Near East—those of Babylonia, for example, in science—have entered our life chiefly through the medium of Greece and Rome. More germane, probably, is the Hellenist Toynbee's remark that "the Hellenic Civilization is perhaps the finest flower of the species that has ever yet come to bloom . . . [it] still outshines every other civilization that has ever come into existence up to the present." To quote Toynbee again, the perhaps unarguably decisive factor is that "the surviving materials for a study of Graeco-Roman history are not only manageable in quantity and select in quality; they are also well balanced in their character." This cannot be said of any other ancient civilization.

By far the most important source of information available to the ancient historian consists of written records. These fall into three broad classes. The most reliable records, because contemporary and subject to public scrutiny, are inscriptions, thousands of clay tablets and stones on which were recorded economic information, decrees, treaties, and the like. Tons of papyri, the ancient writing paper, form a second class; these, too, are often contemporary and are chiefly valuable for the social and economic history of Egypt (the principal place of finding). The preservation of inscriptions and papyri is due to accident, whereas the literature of antiquity has been preserved—in part, at least—because the monks of the Middle Ages, who engaged in the labor of copying books as an ascetic exercise and thereby incidentally preserved ancient culture, preferred this or that work. These copies on vellum or parchment—*manuscripts,* as they are called—obviously are not contemporary and often have mistakes, but together with inscriptions and papyri the medieval manuscripts constitute our chief written evidence for antiquity, even though they represent only a small fraction of the original total. The restricted scope of the available evidence and its fragmentary character are part of the challenging fascination of studying ancient history.

In recent years, however, our knowledge has been immeasurably increased by the new science of archaeology. Buildings, statues, utensils, and documents are multiplied annually by many excavations in various lands, and the information they yield not only adds to our knowledge but often also unsettles previous opinions that we had considered true and opens up unsuspected vistas as well. The fact that the study of ancient history is far from static is another of its most fascinating features. When all is said and done, however, archaeology's chief contribution is an enrichment of our knowledge of the artistic and social life of the ancients, for it cannot hope to do more than supplement the written records. For some periods, nevertheless, archaeology provides the only surviving evidence for important periods, and the historian must accordingly be wary in writing the "history" of such epochs without a contemporary ancient historical narrative.

In ancient times, as generally now in the Near East, people built their houses of sun-dried bricks on foundations of field stones. The field stones remain to tell us about the evolution of domestic and public architecture, but with the passage of time, the bricks disintegrated into earth again, and instead of the debris being carried away, the old house was leveled off and a new one built on top of it. Thus a mound might rise, and in the various layers, houses, palaces, jewelry, and other objects might be buried. Since clay pots were an ordinary household article, great quantities of pottery are always found on ancient sites, generally in broken fragments called *potsherds,* which enable us to give relative dates to all the other objects. By a careful study of the pottery, its fabric and decoration, and the stratum in which it is found, as well as by comparison with other sites, a relative and fairly accurate dating has been worked out for it and thus for all the objects found with it. The presence of Egyptian objects, for example, in Minoan Crete, and vice versa, enables us, with the help of the Egyptian calendar, to speak approximately in terms of years B.C. for one period of antiquity. The absolute chronology is often more difficult to establish than the relative, but it is facilitated by synchronisms of astronomical phenomena like eclipses with regnal dates (mentioned, for example, in king lists or chronicles for Egypt and Mesopotamia), by the habit of dating years by officials (as by archons in Athens), by the ultimate Greek fashion of dating by Olympiads (the first Olympic games were reputedly held in 776 B.C.), and by the Roman custom of dating from the supposed foundation of their city (753 B.C.).

By a definition that has become conventional, a period is spoken of as historical when it has left records that can be read and understood. Thus we have been correct in speaking of written documents and archaeology as providing the evidence for the historical past, but obviously for prehistory the evidence is more restricted. A prehistoric period, by definition, is one that has left no written records or, at any rate, no written records that can be read and understood. The only things we have to go by are the objects made, or cultivated, by humans, and consequently for prehistoric periods archaeology is history. Especially for very remote prehistoric periods back to about 60,000 B.C. (but only infrequently for the period postdating the first literate civilizations, ca. 3000 B.C.), the analysis of traces of carbon 14 in once live tissues has facilitated absolute dating of ancient sites within certain limits. Carbon 14 (also called *radiocarbon*) is present in the atmosphere at all times and is absorbed by plants, trees, and animals. Once these living organisms die, carbon 14, rather like uranium, decays at a fixed rate with a measurable half-life of 5,730 years. That is to say, "X amount" of carbon 14 found in bones, wood, or charcoal can lead a chemist to deduce the approximate ultimate age of the archaeological specimen, providing that the chemist knows the amount of carbon 14 in the atmosphere when the specimen was alive and absorbing the isotope. Until recently, it was thought that the level of carbon 14 in the air was stable throughout many millennia. This is now known not to be the case; the variable carbon-14 factor thus complicates prehistoric dating. Certain other chemical controls, however (e.g., the use of dendrochronology, the study of rings in long-lived trees attesting to yearly variations of the isotope in the atmosphere) show that the carbon-14 method of dating remains very useful.

2

Prehistoric Man

Beginning more than two million years ago, and during most of the time since—until about 7000 B.C.—people gathered their food wherever they found it, but a great revolution occurred some nine thousand years ago, when prehistoric man learned how to produce his own food. The two periods, preceding and following the revolution, are frequently called the Paleolithic (Old Stone) and Neolithic (New Stone) Ages, because of the different treatment of the stone tools and weapons, but it is merely a convention; what mattered was the domestication of plants and animals, or its absence. Another turning point followed very quickly (not long before 3000 B.C.), when humans gradually attained a kind of life conveniently called *civilized.* They had had metal for some time, and the new epoch, at its beginning, is generally called the Bronze Age; but again this is only a convention, for what counts is the presence of cities. It was at this time that humans learned how to write, and with this achievement we have moved into the historical period. To put it another way, almost 100 per cent of human existence on earth was spent in the prehistoric period.

At least one thing that marks the difference between apes and humans is culture—the possession of a common body of beliefs and habits, which in earliest days was practically equivalent to no more than the use of tools, fire, and language. Our evidence for tools and fire goes back hundreds of thousands of years, and probably language is just as ancient, because the use of tools and fire could hardly be taught by one generation to the next without it. We may say, then, that culture is a distinguishing mark of humankind.

Equipped with tools, fire, and language, humans began to dominate their environment, instead of having to accept whatever circumstances brought them. To fit itself into a new situation, an animal has to go through the development of appropriate anatomical structures or physiological adaptations by means of natural selection, a process that may take thousands of generations. Humans, if they are smart enough, can figure out the problem in a few days, months, or years, and come through with a perfect adaptation, conceived in the brain and executed with the hands. Though human progress was very slow in the Paleolithic period, it was nevertheless much faster, and more versatile, than the progress of the quadrupeds.

We can understand that man's lot was far more secure when he learned to domesticate plants and animals (ca. 9000 B.C.) and to live in villages (ca. 7000 B.C.), but we cannot yet call him civilized. This sort of relatively simple life—and the description might fit the North American Indian—can be led under the guidance of custom, with little need for decisive individual leadership. To explain the rise of civilization—or at any rate, European civilization—we have to go to the Near East, where it had its roots. The Near East—Egypt and Mesopotamia—is dominated by great rivers, which can be, through their floods, either a disaster or a blessing. It is not too much to say that the necessity of irrigation was a prime factor in the rise of European civilization, for if the floods were to be controlled, people had to live and work together. Irrigation works require planning, coordinated efforts, orders that are carried out. The bigger the works, the more necessary this kind of organization becomes; and it can function only when some capable person is in command and makes the decisions, without having to debate each point with all the old people in the village. This is the explanation—in part, at least—for early monarchies. Monarchies, in turn, needed records and specialists, and so the whole cumulative apparatus of civilization—cities, manufactures, trade—came into being. It took humans approximately two million years to learn to produce food, and reach the stage of village life (see the map, p. 18), and at least four more millennia to become civilized.

THE FOOD GATHERERS

The study of the origins of humankind is a very controversial subject, involving as it does religious and scientific beliefs, which some people continue to regard as incompatible. Even within the scientific community, there is disagreement among scholars as new prehuman fossils are continually unearthed, requiring redating and reinterpretation of previous finds. The following is a very tentative outline of the most recent (1980) viewpoints of anthropologists and geologists who have traced the biological evolution of modern man from remote antecedents.

Most controversial are theories concerning the date of the evolutionary split between apelike creatures (pongids) and manlike ones (hominids). Some scholars still hold that an animal called *Ramapithecus,* inhabiting west Europe, East Africa, India, and south China some 14 million years ago, was the first hominid. It seems more likely, however, that he was a pongid, a creature existing before the actual split between the two groups. *Ramapithecus,* in any case, was quadrapedal and had dental development enabling him to chew plants and meat.

Perhaps by four million years ago, the split between hominids and pongids had occurred, our own very remote ancestors having evolved into bipedal beings. Bipedal locomotion, rather than brain development, has been called "the great permutation in human evolution." Fossils recently found in east-central Africa (Tanzania and Ethiopia) lend support to this view. Called *Australopithecus afarensis (africanus),* this bipedal creature stood some three to four feet high and had a brain capacity of some 500 cubic centimeters, 100 more than a modern chimpanzee. He did not belong, it appears, to genus *Homo,* but himself underwent a twofold evolution involving the ultimate emergence of our genus. On the one hand, the descendants of australopithecines did not experience enlargement of the brain; they became heavier and developed massive teeth and a correspondingly thick skull to support pow-

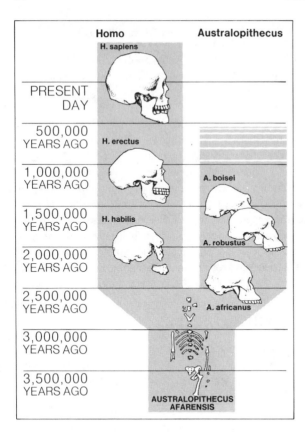

The descendants of *Australopithecus afarensis.*

erful chewing muscles. This branch of *Australopithecus* apparently became extinct between one and two million years ago. The second branch developed lithe and slender bodies, larger brains, and smaller teeth.

Some of these so-called gracile australopithecines may well have evolved into the first known representatives of the genus *Homo* in the east African savannah more than 3.5 million years ago. They are called *Homo habilis,* "able (i.e., tool-making) man." They were somewhat larger and heavier than the coexisting gracile australopithecines but shared with them the same ratio of brain to body weight. The opposable thumb was well developed, and the lobes of the brain were apparently connected with the powers of speech. These creatures may already have constructed primitive houses of wood, grass, and stone; they have left tools of stone, bone, horns, and teeth, sometimes very carefully made, and at least two million years old. With the conscious creation of the first tools, we enter that period of prehistory known culturally as the Old Stone or Paleolithic Age.

The development of Paleolithic man took place during three worldwide and four Alpine periods of glaciation between 3 million and 10,000 B.C., called by geologists the Pleistocene period. It would seem that *Homo habilis* evolved into *Homo erectus* some two million years ago. Traces of this man have been found in Europe, Java, Kenya, and China. His brain capacity averaged 1,000 cubic centimeters and sometimes overlapped that of modern man. He was taller than his predecessors and had a smaller face and smaller teeth. Females of this species had notably large pelvises, permitting the birth of larger-brained babies. The tool-making technology of *Homo erectus*—the production of rather standardized hand axes by striking one stone against another—was widely spread, and there is some evidence of cooperative hunting. This, in turn, suggests a rather high ability to communicate and the further development of language skills. His greatest discovery—made, it seems, ca. 500,000 B.C.—was the use of fire.

Neanderthal Man. The biological relationship between *Homo erectus* and his successor, Neanderthal man (so-called from the Neander River Valley in Germany, where his remains were first discovered in 1856), is obscure. Suffice it to say that Neanderthal man flourished just before and during the last glaciation, ca. 86,000–40,000 B.C., at first inhabiting a band across Europe and Eurasia, roughly between 30 and 50 degrees north latitude. Neanderthal man experienced an important breakthrough in stone technology by creating a much finer cutting edge and thereby new varieties of stone tools. In some areas, he flaked one side of a stone to produce a kind of axe; in others, he shaped hand axes all around by flaking or prepared them from carefully flared cores. He also made pointed cleavers with sharp, straight edges. Differently shaped stone tools might exist side by side at the same sites.

Neanderthal man lived in open camps and, after the coming of the glacier, in the mouths of caves. He used fire and clothing and, moreover, buried his dead, along with tools, in the floor of the caves, from which we conclude that he had a primitive religion or belief in spirits and an afterlife. It is conventional to speak of his culture as Mousterian, since so many of his tools were found at the French site, but this must be regarded as a very loose designation, for the culture, like the men themselves, was greatly mixed.

Aurignacian Moderns. *Homo sapiens*—the "wise man," the modern human—existed at the latest about seventy thousand years ago during the last glaciation and is broadly described as Aurignacian, after the cave of Aurignac on the Upper Garonne River in France. The relationship of the coexisting Aurignacian and Neanderthal species is obscure. Aurignacian man may have both exterminated the Neanderthals physically and absorbed them biologically and genetically. For whatever reasons, the Neanderthals gradually disappeared from their original northern habitat and left their last traces in more southerly latitudes around the Mediterranean and in Africa. Cave sites in Iran and at Mount Carmel in Palestine, yielding skeletons and remains of both types, suggest that they could interbreed and produce fertile offspring. If that was the case, *Homo sapiens,* as we know him today, probably has some Neanderthal ancestry and an even larger share of Aurignacian *Homo sapiens.* Aurignacian man was of lighter build than Neanderthal man, but taller (about five feet six inches), and had a higher skull. His arms were very long, the nose broad, the jaw prominent, the chin weak. Probably the most famous branch of the Aurignacians was the Cro-Magnon people so called after the cave of that name in the Dordogne district of France, but other breeds of men shared the world with them. The Late Paleolithic period witnessed the evolution of the races of *Homo sapiens* known today. One such was an apparently negroid people who are represented by skeletons from the Grimaldi cave on the northern Italian coast.

Life.   The Aurignacians ate wild fruits and vegetables, bison, reindeer, and other meat, and varieties of fish that they caught with harpoons of horn or bone. The reindeer provided them with bone and horn; the mammoth, which is now extinct, with ivory. In their career of killing animals and other humans, they were aided by throwing sticks for spears (see illustration). With bone needles, the women sewed clothing of skins and furs and occasionally adorned themselves with necklaces and other jewelry of shell and ivory; animal fat was burned in stone lamps; fire gave these people warmth. Beneath their hearths they might bury their dead with implements of this life for use in the next, and occasionally they painted red ocher on the dead body, the idea doubtless being to suggest blood and the hope of life's returning to the deceased. In cold weather they lived in the openings of caves, but during warm spells they moved outside and scooped out holes in the earth and built huts of brush and skins.

Tools.   One localized Aurignacian culture—the Solutrean—developed a remarkable tool industry. Fine, sharp blade tools were struck from flint and obsidian, a natural volcanic glass. Among their stone and bone implements are knives, chisels, drills, scrapers, daggers, spears, arrowheads, pins, fishhooks, harpoons, and beads.

Art.   Another localized Aurignacian culture, the so-called Magdalenian, is notable for its great achievements in art. In point of time the Magdalenian extends approximately from 30,000 to 17,000 B.C. Occasionally the artists made sculptures of people, especially of seemingly pregnant women, who represent, perhaps, goddesses of fertility. The figures are not very successful as works of art, but the geometrical designs and engravings of animals on bone, horn, and ivory show skill and taste and a real feeling for the essential quality of the particular animal. Even more extraordinary, however, are the amazingly realistic paintings of bisons, bulls, mammoths, reindeer, bears, boars, the woolly rhinoceros, wild goats, horses, birds, and fish on the walls and ceilings of their caves. The most famous of these caves are in the Dordogne district of France—particularly those of Font-de-Gaume and Lascaux—

Tools and implements ca. 70,000 B.C. except as noted.

Arrowhead
ca. 8000 B.C.

Antler spear thrower

Antler harpoon

Flint drill

Arrowhead

Scraper

Obsidian Blade

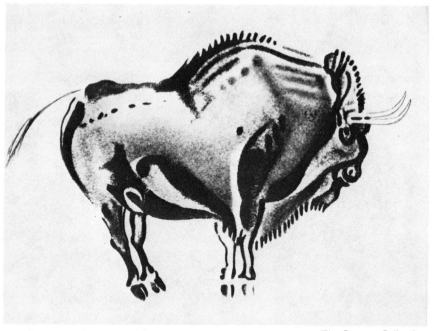

FIGURE 1. Cave painting of bison bull from Old Stone Age in the Altamira caverns of Northern Spain.

and at Atlamira in Spain. The artists of these wonderfully naturalistic animals, which are so full of life and energy, frequently engraved the outline with a sharp instrument and then filled in the picture with various colors that are still well preserved (see Figs. 1 and 2). Though the people lived in the front of the caves, they made the pictures far to the rear, where it was dark and mysterious. Lamps gave them light in their work, but even so, they often deliberately drew one picture over another. Because of this, and the curious location, it has been suggested that it was not the picture but the act of painting that counted to create sympathetic magic. That is to say, the people believed that by painting pictures they might ward off dangerous animals or have good luck in increasing their food supply.

The Forest Folk. When the last glacier began to slack off in Europe (ca. 14,000 B.C.), the continents and climate of the earth soon became as they are today. The growth of the thick, continental forest, however, caused life in western Europe to decline. Hunting was so difficult that many people made their homes along the Atlantic coast from Portugal to Scotland and Denmark. The sea became the chief source of food, and as a result the coasts (particularly in Denmark) are strewn for miles with ridges full of oyster shells and bones. The people who left these heaps of rubbish are sometimes called the *kitchen-midden people,* after the Danish word for *kitchen leavings,* but the expression *forest folk* better describes the inhabitants of Europe at this time. One of their summer camps, the Maglemosear

FIGURE 2. Cave painting of horse, about 5 feet long, from Dordogne, France.

area in Denmark (ca. 8000 B.C.), was a huge peat swamp, which has fortunately preserved many of the objects dropped into it, including even wooden paddles and sled runners. Meanwhile, the friendly and helpful dog had been domesticated. Somehow, too, probably by accident, people learned that the clay lining, which was placed inside a crude basket or leather bowl to prevent it from leaking, would harden when set over a fire, and the all-important discovery of pottery was made.

End of the Paleolithic Era.   At the same time, an advance in the manufacture of stone tools was taking place. The new fact in human life, however, was far more fundamental than that. Hitherto humans had obtained their food by gathering it where they could. They were soon to learn to produce it. How this revolution occurred cannot be stated precisely, but it first took place in southwest Asia. Thereafter agriculture was discovered independently in certain other so-called nuclear areas, in sub-Saharan Africa, southeast Asia, China, Middle America, and the Andes highlands in South America. It was once thought that climatic changes caused by the retreat of the last glacier and the consequent desiccation of the Near East and north Africa caused humans and animals to retreat to river valleys and oases, where they found edible plants. This migration might have set the stage for the agricultural revolution.

Such a theory would not, however, explain the later, independent agricultural revolutions occurring elsewhere and under much different climatic conditions. More probably, the discovery of agriculture in all nuclear areas depended on a certain atmosphere of experimentation in a natural environment that encouraged a stable population with sufficient water, proper soil constituents, and enough arable land to sustain domesticated edible plants and animals. Such conditions were first exploited by humankind in the piedmonts and watered grassy uplands of what are today Iran, Iraq, Syria, Palestine, and Turkey. These areas were well supplied with wild wheats—emmer, einkorn, and barley—and wild goats, sheep, and pigs.

THE FOOD-PRODUCING REVOLUTION

The Stocks of Mankind.   Nothing whatever can be said about the racial origin of man, except that all men belong to the human species. Mixed from the very beginning, the human race evolved three main stocks, each of which was further mixed: the Caucasoids, the Negroids, and the Mongoloids. At the opening of the new era in man's development, the Caucasoids were certainly the chief stock in Europe. These, in turn, may be divided into three large groups who, hopelessly mixed at the beginning and increasingly so with the years, still dominate Europe. The Nordics—a tall, blond, long-headed people—occupied northwestern Europe. The Alpines—a stocky, brunette, round-headed people, represented today by Celts and Slavs—made their home in the center of the continent. The Mediterraneans—a short, dark, long-headed people—settled in the Mediterranean basin and beyond, as far as the British Isles. It was probably the Mediterraneans who produced the first food and built the first villages.

Mesolithic Period in the Near East. Ca. 10,000-7,000 B.C.   The discovery of agriculture did not take place overnight, and for a long time in the Near East humankind first merely intensified food collection by reaping wild grains with flint sickles without sowing and cultivating crops. Evidence for such practice has been found in the Natufian caves near Mount Carmel in Palestine, in open-air camps and incipient villages in the Kurdish hill country of northeastern Iraq, and along stretches of the Middle Euphrates. The settlers of the latter seem already to have domesticated the sheep and the goat. All these places probably originated ca. 9000 B.C. and were certainly inhabited intermittently for many centuries by people who were gradually becoming sedentary.

The Effects of the Neolithic Revolution. Ca. 7000-3000 B.C.   The discovery in the Near East of agriculture and herding inaugurated a revolution of far-reaching proportions (ca. 8000-7000 B.C.). It was not enough to drop seeds into rich soil at the right time, for if one wished the harvest, one had to remain in the same place. For a roaming existence, accordingly, was substituted a sedentary one. The first known farming villages that fully domesticated both plants and animals originated somewhat earlier than 7000 B.C. and are found at Jarmo (Iraqi Kurdistan), Jericho

(Palestine), and Catal Hüyük (western Turkey) (see map below and illustration p. 19). Similar communities arose later on Cyprus and in the Balkans and in Mesopotamia. Scores of such Neolithic sites have been excavated in and around the so-called Fertile Crescent, that stretch of easily cultivated land that arches upward from Palestine, through Syria, and down into Mesopotamia.

The best-preserved and perhaps most interesting Neolithic village, which also shows some features of incipient urbanization, is found at Catal Hüyük in south-central Turkey (ca. 5750 B.C.). The settlement was built in a circle 32 acres in area, covered with 16 blocks of 1,000 mud-brick houses; these houses consisted normally of one large room with partitions and a hearth in one corner. They were all contiguous and were entered by a ladder reaching an opening in the roof. Some forty rooms, apparently religious shrines of some sort, were discovered on the site. They were decorated with wall paintings of human beings, deer, vultures, wierd headless creatures, and even, it appears, an erupting volcano. Figurines of bulls and a female figure that may represent Mother Nature suggest the cults that the inhabitants practiced.

Such settlements led to the concept of property—at least to family or village holdings—and at the same time there arose the need of customs, rules, and laws to regulate conflicting claims and interests. Someone had to settle disputes and admin-

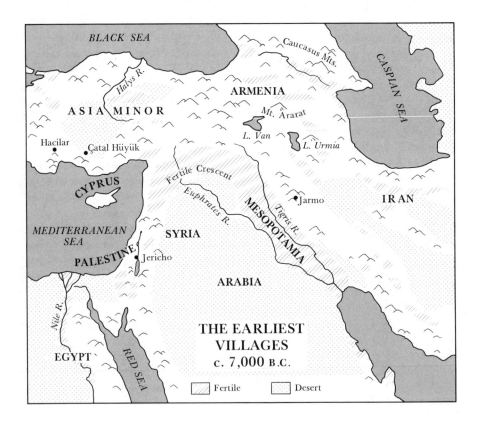

THE EARLIEST
VILLAGES
c. 7,000 B.C.

FIGURE 3. Skull found at Jericho with living features affixed in plaster, 7th millennium B.C.

ister things in general, and since a fertile community was eyed enviously by others, it was only natural to select one person as the leader. Moreover it was found that the old hunting deities and their priests did not suffice for the problems of agriculture. Sunshine was necessary and a drought was to be avoided if the planting and cultivation of crops were to be brought to a successful harvest. New gods must be found and buildings must be built for them; new priests, too, were required to propitiate by sacrifice and festival the dark forces of nature that held human beings in their grip. These were clever, able persons—these priests and headmen—and they were important to their communities.

Life. The Neolithic period, with its discovery of agriculture, clearly made life more complex. At first, it was probably the duty of women to take a crude hoe and cultivate a small patch of land, but the domestication of the ox changed this, for many women were not strong enough to handle a plow. That is to say, though wheat and barley were apparently first cultivated by women with a hoe, the domestication of the ox and the invention of the plow created a new job for men, who now had to abandon hunting for the life of a farmer. The domestication of other animals—the sheep, goat, and pig, and later, the donkey and camel (the horse, perhaps, was domesticated later still; the dog, long before)—provided people with milk, meat, clothing, and fat for fuel and allowed some to become nomadic shepherds. More seeds were planted, and before long people were cultivating not only wheat and barley but also oats, rye, millet, lentils, fruit trees, the olive, and the grape. The more certain and greater food supply caused a population explosion and permitted

humans to pursue different careers. Neolithic communities were able to get on with
very little specialization, and yet not everyone needed to be a farmer. Some worked
stones into finished articles and bartered them for food. Ultimately the axes,
knives, hammers, chisels, and hoes were ground and polished on a whetstone. The
old-time flint axe was too brittle to chop much wood, whereas the ground stone
axe led to carpentry.

Trade. To provide and exhange these necessities, humans learned to make a boat
and then a sled, which developed into a wheeled cart. Regular overland routes grew
up, while before the end of the Neolithic age, boats plied the Mediterranean, the
Red Sea, and the Persian Gulf. Amber from the Baltic and obsidian from the Aegean island of Melos testify to widespread trade.

Pottery and Textiles. The idea of making pottery was probably hit upon independently in different places, but this discovery, which ranks in importance next to
agriculture and the taming of animals, was carried to a high peak during the Neolithic period. At first, to be sure, the pottery was very crude, and during the entire
period it was shaped by hand, for the invention of the potter's wheel was to occur
in the succeeding Bronze Age. Gradually, however, finer shapes and textures were
obtained, especially after it was learned that it was better to bake a pot in an oven
than in an open fire. The decoration also improved, from incised or painted linear
designs to spiral and geometrical motifs. Closely allied with the manufacture of pottery was another great development of the Neolithic period, the textile industry.
The ability to spin and weave flax and wool meant better clothing, baskets, and
fishnets.

The Swiss Lake Villages. From the Near East, the idea of food production and
villages spread to western Europe, where the lake villages of Switzerland have a
particular interest, because of both their peculiar construction and the abundant
evidence. In the winter of 1853-1854, during a severe dry spell, the lakes of Switzerland reached a very low level, and thousands of piles, or stakes, were exposed. At
Wangen alone, fifty thousand piles have been counted. Between 4500 and 2500 B.C.,
when these villages flourished, people sought the safety of the Swiss lakes and, at a
distance from the shore, drove wooden piles, 20 feet long, into the bottom; on
these piles they built wooden platforms for their square houses. Cloth and grain,
stone tools in wooden and antler hafts, and other objects that were dropped into
the lakes became water-logged and so were preserved. The houses were often near
enough to land so that a bridge would connect, but the bridges were removable and
doubtless were taken up at night. The people also had boats. With hooks of bone
and in nets, they caught fish from the boats or through trapdoors in their houses;
on the shore, they had their gardens.

Megaliths. Even more imposing—indeed, among the most imposing monuments
in the world—are the huge stone remains (*megaliths,* as they are collectively called)
belonging to New Stone Age cultures. These are found especially in France, England, and Scandinavia, but also in Ireland, Spain, Malta, Syria, and elsewhere. They
apparently range in date from ca. 3500 to 2000 B.C. Huge stones, set on end, are
known by the name of *menhirs* and are a dramatic tribute to the transportation and
engineering skill of the day. Some of the menhirs in Brittany stand 35 feet high,

The Granger Collection

FIGURE 4. Stonehenge: Sarsen (left) and Bluestone Circles.

although one that has fallen down and is broken measures 65 feet. The most famous example of stones set in a circle (cromlech) is at Stonehenge (ca. 2000 B.C.)
in England and is 100 feet across (see Fig. 4 above). Nearby is what appears to
be an avenue, two miles long. At Carnac, in Brittany, is a famous example of parallel rows of 3,000 stones, over two miles in length. Powerful people were buried in
great chambers known as *dolmens,* stones set vertically and capped by a huge horizontal slab. One can only speculate on the purpose of these megaliths. The Maltese
examples were perhaps temples; the menhirs and even Stonehenge may have had
some astronomical significance. In any case, they suggest a Stone Age society organized in chiefdoms, each competing to build more grandiose monuments.

Civilization. As the Neolithic period progressed, someone in the Near East,
about 5000 B.C., first beat copper out of its ore. The copper was hardened by being
hammered cold; this process caused crystallization and gave a better cutting edge.
Still, it was relatively soft for general use, and stone tools, therefore, continued to
be popular. The transitional period of copper and stone is sometimes spoken of as
the Chalcolithic Age. The Bronze Age began when people learned to mix tin with
copper, thus obtaining bronze, a metal far superior to stone. Bronze was in widespread use in the Near East just before ca. 3000 B.C., the date that may conveniently
be taken as the beginning of the Bronze Age. The discovery and working of metals
were, however, of secondary importance for the development of humankind. What
really mattered was that in the river valleys of Egypt and Mesopotamia people had
to build dikes and irrigation canals to live. It is very interesting that it was in irri-

gated river valleys that the Neolithic culture developed into civilization, while people remained barbarians, though village farmers, in many other parts of the world. The necessity for large-scale political organization to handle big irrigation projects explains—at least, in part—the rise of civilization. Government, specialized manufactures, trade, and cities grew from the need of cooperative living. Before the end of the fourth millennium B.C., moreover, Sumerians in Mesopotamia were learning to draw a picture for an object, then to make a picture for an idea and finally for a sound or syllable. The Sumerians wrote their symbols on clay tablets with a rectangular stylus, producing wedge-shaped or cuneiform writing. Slightly later, Egyptians were incising writing on stone and other objects and writing in ink with a reed stylus on strips of papyrus.

The rise of government and cities, accompanied by the use of bronze and writing and the potter's wheel, meant the rapid development of civilization in the Near East ca. 3000 B.C. Western Europe, with its forests and swamps, fell far behind and remained in a much more primitive Neolithic state of development for many centuries.

PART II

THE
ANCIENT
NEAR EAST

3

Sumer, Akkad, and Babylon

THE TIGRIS–EUPHRATES VALLEY

While the forests and swamps were bringing progress in western Europe to a stop at the close of the Neolithic Age, the fertility of the river valleys of the Near East accelerated cultural development. In one of those valleys, the Tigris–Euphrates, civilized life first began.

Geographical Features. Across the Red Sea from Egypt is the sandy desert of Arabia, bounded on the northwest by the hills and mountains of Syria, and on the northeast by the Persian Gulf and the Valley of the Tigris and Euphrates Rivers (cf. map, front endpaper). In the south this valley is separated from Syria by the northern end of the Arabian desert (here called the Syrian Desert). In the north, however, the Tigris–Euphrates Valley and Syria are joined by arable land—forming a semicircle or, as it has been called, a Fertile Crescent (cf. map, p. 18)—that extends from the head of the Persian Gulf northward through Nineveh, one of the capitals of ancient Assyria, and then bends westward until it reaches the Mediterranean coast, thence it continues south through Syria and Palestine toward Egypt. It will be seen from the map that this Fertile Crescent has mountains behind it to the north and that it is open to the south, facing a region of grasslands, desert, and oases. From immemorial times the mountaineers to the north and the desert nomads to the south have struggled for possession of the Fertile Crescent. And from early days much of this area—Fertile Crescent, desert, mountains, and river valley—has been occupied by the Semites. These were linguistically and culturally related peoples, who in the historical period played important roles during various eras. They were the Arabs in the south; the Phoenicians, Canaanites, Hebrews, and Moabites in the west; the Aramaeans, or Syrians, in the north; and the Akkadians, Babylonians, and Assyrians in the east.

The Tigris and Euphrates Rivers rise in the northern Anatolian mountains and, after a westerly course, turn southeastward to flow a thousand miles and more to the Persian Gulf. Along the middle course of the Tigris, chiefly on the west side, was the undulating plain of Assyria (with the Zagros Mountains to the east). Farther down the river, on its east side, lay the mountainous land of Elam around the plain of Susa (in the modern province of Khuzistan in Iran). On both sides of the lower Euphrates, however, the valley is uniformly flat. It covers some ten thousand square miles and presents severe environmental challenges to settlement. Wind-swept, hot, and dry, and also subject to violent storms, it is naturally unproductive. To be sure, the life-giving waters of the Tigris and the Euphrates, with their sus-pended alluvial silt, could then as now be exploited by farmers, but even the rivers were a mixed blessing. They normally flooded each spring, but at a bad time, inun-dating already planted fields. Dikes were required to protect tender crops, and canals and water courses were needed to lead the floodwaters to reservoirs, where they could be stored until they were needed to fill irrigation ditches. These ditches, in turn, needed constant cleaning and repair as they were continuously clogged with suspended mud. The river water itself was slightly saline and deposited salt in the soil when the water evaporated in the dry climate. Salinization of the earth even-tually became an acute problem in many parts of southern Mesopotamia as the affected land became unproductive. The creation and maintenance of extensive waterworks, plus the need for occasional resettlement due to salinization, were the stimuli for strong government. On the other hand, the very flatness of the land in the south and the ease of river transport facilitated trade, especially northward and then westward overland along the Fertile Crescent to Syria. While the absence of natural barriers along the frontiers enabled influences of one kind or another to travel far beyond Mesopotamia, at the same time it invited invasion, warfare, and unification.

Historical Sources.   Today this country is desolate, for it has had little care for centuries. It is seamed with the ruins of ancient canals and dotted over with mounds (tells). Before the middle of the nineteenth century, archaeologists began to excavate these heaps and found them to be the ruins of ancient cities; and ever since that time, archaeological exploration has continued to add vastly to our knowledge of the land. Since Mesopotamia had no stone in the south or suitable timber, the people in ancient days were compelled to use brick almost exclusively for building houses, walls, palaces, and temples. Eventually the bricks crumbled and formed a mound; the debris covered not only the buildings but also the other mate-rial remains of ancient life. For example, libraries have been found, consisting of books whose pages are thin clay tablets (the fine local clay was used for many pur-poses, obviously). Many other documents are on clay cylinders.

The recovery of the civilization of ancient Mesopotamia has been very largely dependent, of course, on our ability to read its various languages, and this monu-mental task was achieved in the nineteenth century, chiefly by the German scholar Georg Grotefend and by the Englishman Sir Henry Rawlinson. Their work was facilitated by the fact that Darius I of Persia once cut on the Behistun Rock in his country a long inscription, not only in Persian, but also in the Babylonian and Elamite languages. When the signs for certain proper names in the Persian text had been established, it was discovered that ancient Persian was akin to the language of the sacred *Avesta,* a collection of hymns and prayers that was put together early in our era and is still read. This discovery made possible the eventual translation of the Persian inscription and, in turn, a translation of the two other texts. Because the languages of the Tigris–Euphrates Valley have now been deciphered, it has become possible, with the additional aid of archaeology, to write the history of the country.

THE LAND OF SUMER AND AKKAD

The Sumerians. About 3500 B.C. a gifted people known as the Sumerians moved into the southernmost part of the Euphrates Valley, at the head of the Persian Gulf. The region became known as Sumer, and the country immediately to the north, where the Tigris and Euphrates nearly come together, was called Akkad. The ancient land of Sumer and Akkad was in time called Babylonia.

The original homeland of the Sumerians is unknown. They themselves believed that they came from the "land of the rising sun," which may have been in the direction of India. Another theory holds that they came from the north, possibly from an area near the Caspian Sea. There is some indication that at the time of their settlement in lower Mesopotamia they were culturally influenced by the Semites, but their own language was not Semitic.

In the period ca. 3500–2800 B.C., at the very dawn of history, the Sumerians created the first civilized, urban life, as far as we know. Not only did they invent cuneiform writing, a calendar, and a system of weights and measures, but they also planned large-scale irrigation by means of canals, plowed the land, organized religious and political institutions, and carried on trade with India, Syria, and Egypt. As a result, the population of Sumer increased, and villages grew into proud cities, such as Eridu, Ur, Lagash, Umma, Larsa, Erech, Isin, Nippur, and Kish. The cities strove to maintain their independence and to remain sovereign, each under its own ruler. At Uruk a priest-king *(en)* was in charge. Elsewhere, cities were under the control of an *ensi,* a kind of secretary of agriculture, or a *lugal,* a general of the army. The power of these rulers—technically, at least—was not absolute. They were apparently advised by a council of elders, and Sumerian tradition even knew of citizen assemblies, whose functions, however, are unknown. Organized life made possible the construction of large temples, which, because of the danger of floods, were often reared on artificial mounds or ziggurats (see p. 35). In addition to copper alloys and bronze, the Sumerians used gold and silver, and they shaped their pottery on a wheel and baked it in an oven.

It seems rather extraordinary that when we first meet the Sumerians, they already have a developed idea about themselves, their government, and the universe. The Sumerians believed that the universe was governed by intangible forces more powerful than humans. As the Gilgamesh epic puts it: "Mere man—his days are numbered; whatever he may do, he is but wind." People had been created to serve the gods, and since the only sovereign state in the universe consisted of the assembly of the gods, it naturally followed that man's state on earth served the gods. The Sumerians apparently accepted it as self-evident that the gods should own most of the land, even though there was also room for privately owned property; in particular, they must have temples and temple lands. Just as most of the people labored on behalf of the gods, in order to give them leisure, so the priests, the special servants of the gods, ranked high in the people's estimation.

At the very beginning of history, then, the Sumerians had created city-states in which religion permeated all phases of government and life in general. All human beings and animals, as well as inanimate objects, natural phenomena, and even ab-

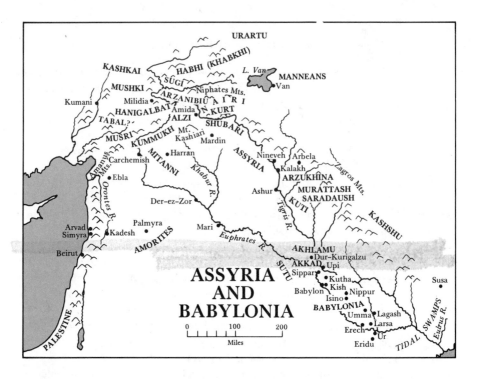

stract ideas constituted the state. Difficult as it is to grasp the Sumerian conception of the state, it becomes clearer when we recall that early human beings regarded inanimate substances, such as salt and grain, as being full of life, each with its own personality.

From this concept of the state, servant of the gods as it was, there followed the notion that the only citizens of the universe were the gods. It was the assembly of the gods that discussed all human questions and reached fateful decisions. The chief god, and therefore the head of the assembly, was Anu, the sky god; all other gods derived their authority from him, and consequently the affairs of men followed a pattern, anarchic though they might seem to human eyes. As Anu represented authority, so Enlil, god of the air and the second most important god, stood for force. It was Enlil who carried out the decisions of the gods; the thunder and lightning over the Mesopotamian plain was Enlil, and also (somewhat more difficult to comprehend) it was Enlil, not simply barbarian mountaineers, who destroyed a city. Next to these two gods of sky and storm stood Mother Earth (Innana) and the active force of creation, water (Enki). These and other gods governed the world state. Man had no power over them but stood in the same relation to them as slaves did to free men in human society. Nevertheless, it was possible, and indeed important, to pray to the gods, especially to minor deities whom one might claim as one's own. For this reason, by about 1900 B.C. every house had its own chapel. In the relationship with one's own personal god, the chief thing was to be obedient, for one who served him well would be rewarded. In other words, justice was bestowed as a favor, not as a right.

As the state became larger and more complex, however, there developed the idea that human beings had a right to justice. Law codes answered this demand, but only in part, for injustice remained. The Sumerian explains to us that the ways of the gods are strange, and the most we can do is to hope.

The city-state, we have remarked, had as its purpose the service of a god. But just as one god gained power over other gods, so rulers on earth might conquer others—when the assembly of gods willed that one of their number should govern a wider realm. This happened, normally under a successful lugal, and the god of his city became the chief god of the land, though he did not supplant the other deities. The land of Sumer during the third millennium B.C. saw much warfare between the city-states, normally over water rights, punctuated by periods of relative peace when one city or another had conquered its neighbors.

Early Dynastic Sumeria (Ca. 2800-2350 B.C.). By the beginning of the third millennium, kingship in the city-states had become dynastic following what later Sumerians believed to have been an epochal flood that inundated the entire land. This was the so-called heroic age of Sumerian history, a period of great warrior kings dimly remembered, some of them, but by no means all, being mythical figures. Gilgamesh, king of Uruk (ca. 2700), subject of the famous epic poem, was a historical figure; tradition holds that he repaired a famous sanctuary at Nippur.

At about the same time (ca. 2750-2650) a wealthy and powerful dynasty ruled at Ur, known for its tombs, which were excavated in the 1920s. The royalty were buried with jewelry and other rich objects, as well as with their courtiers and servants, who were ceremoniously killed to attend their masters and mistresses beyond the grave.

Eannatum. More is known about Eannatum, a ruler (c. 2500) of Sumerian Lagash. Eannatum conquered Ur, Kish, and perhaps Elam, but apparently he was especially pleased by his defeat of the people of Umma, hereditary foes who lived just across a canal, the "Lion of the Plain," as it was called. To commemorate his victory, Eannatum set up a boundary stone (a stele or sculptured slab of stone), which is known from its tragic subject matter as the Vulture Stele; on it we see the king and his troops setting off to war, and the ensuing destruction of the enemy, with vultures or eagles carrying away their dead: this is probably the first example of a story in the history of art. Precisely how much of the land of Sumer and Akkad was conquered by Eannatum is unknown, but there is no doubt that this early ruler created a large empire for the time, albeit a temporary one. The people of Umma were not denied their revenge, however, and ultimately they overthrew the humiliating Vulture Stele.

Uruinimgina. A successor of Eannatum at Lagash, Uruinimgina, (ca. 2355 B.C.) stands out in this age as a social reformer who tried to protect his people from the civil and military officials and the priests. Calling himself "King of Lagash and Sumer," Uruinimgina brought to his state a brief period of prosperity and power. In addition to building temples, canals, and reservoirs, he created perhaps the oldest known prototype of a code of laws, which is remarkable for its spirit of justice. For example, the high priest of a temple estate could no longer tax a widow or an orphan. It was the business of government, moreover, to provide the dead with food and drink in their graves, so that their souls might journey successfully to the lower

FIGURE 5. Male figure
from Tell Asmar, Iraq;
Sumerian, c. 2600 B.C.,
about 11 inches high.

The Granger Collection

world. And if a rich man wished to buy something belonging to a poor man, he had
to "pay in silver" as much as was demanded, or not be angry if his offer was refused. Thus Uruinimgina gave the inhabitants of Lagash a measure of freedom and
security.

Lugal Zaggisi. It is possible that Uruinimgina's reforms produced discord and
weakened his position. In any case, he was overthrown not much later by Lugal
Zaggisi of Umma. The historical tablet that tells how Lagash was despoiled con-
cludes, "But as to Lugal Zaggisi, the ensi of Umma, may his personal diety bear this
crime on her neck." Lugal Zaggisi, now a powerful king, transferred his capital to

Erech, a city famous for its temple to Eanna, the "house of heaven." Many gods were recognized, in a systematic pantheon, but it was the cult of Inanna, goddess of love and war and the Sumerian counterpart of Ishtar, that dominated the religious life. Under Lugal Zaggisi, Sumerian influences continued to travel far and wide; in fact, he even boasted that his empire extended to the Mediterranean.

The Akkadians. Sargon (Ca. 2340 B.C.).   Probably it was inevitable that in time the Sumerians should be overwhelmed by their numerous Semitic Akkadian neighbors to the north. The land of Akkad boasted many cities, in particular Kish and Sippar. About 2340 B.C. a remarkable man of humble origin, Sargon (or Sharrukin), seized power in Kish. Various romantic stories have survived concerning his origin, which at least tell us something of what people liked to believe at that time. It is said that Sargon's mother was a lowly woman and that he never knew his father. He was born in concealment, was cast adrift by his mother on the Euphrates in a reed basket, was rescued by an irrigator, and was reared as a gardener. But Ishtar, the great Semitic goddess, loved Sargon, and he became king for fifty-five years.

In any case, after becoming king of Kish, Sargon extended his sway over all Akkad and conquered Sumer and as far east as Susa in Elam. For his capital he founded Agade, just below Sippar. The Babylonian Chronicle tells us that the new "king of universal dominion crossed the sea of the west," which may mean that he crossed the Mediterranean to Cyprus. One of Sargon's inscriptions states that he conquered "as far as the cedar forests and the silver mountains." The cedar forests are the Lebanon mountains in Syria; and the silver mountains refer to the Taurus range, especially the region near the Cilician Gates (cf. map, front endpaper). Sargon's long and glorious reign over this great empire caused Sumerian influences to travel widely, for the civilization of Akkad was based on that of Sumer. Thus backward Syria and far-off Cyprus benefited, and the products of the two areas were exchanged. At home Sargon built temples to the gods and a great palace for himself; after death he was regarded by the people as a deity.

Naram Sin.   Every king of Akkad, like those of Sumer, had constant rebellions to suppress during his lifetime, and upon his death it often happened that his conquests fell apart. Sargon, however, was able to bequeath his empire, if somewhat contracted, to his successors. One of these, Naram Sin (ca. 2250 B.C.), "the beloved of the moon god" and probably Sargon's grandson, built an empire that extended perhaps from Armenia to the Persian Gulf and the Red Sea, from Elam and the Zagros Mountains to the Mediterranean coast. One of his conquests was the city of Ebla in Syria, which he destroyed. The site of Ebla, rediscovered in 1964, has yielded thousands of cuneiform tablets written in a previously unknown dialect of the northwest group of Semitic languages. The documents—in the main, administrative records, business inventories, and diplomatic correspondence—also seem to contain rather enigmatic proper names, like Abraham, which some scholars believe may have biblical connotations. The continuing Ebla excavations promise to revise our conception of the transmission of civilization in the northwest Fertile Crescent. The role of Ebla seems to have been basic in transmitting Sumerian culture to the west and in adapting, apparently for the first time anywhere, the cuneiform syllabary to the writing of a Semitic tongue.

Styling himself "King of the Four Regions of the Earth," Naram Sin set up a remarkable stele, which has been found in Susa, the capital of Elam. On the stele, the king has just won a great victory and in his military habit is climbing a mountain, followed by his soldiers. The enemy have been slaughtered; one is pulling a spear from his throat, another begs for mercy. Terrible though the subject matter is, the stele must be admired, for it is full of movement. Naram Sin gained a great repuation as a builder of temples, but probably the most striking remains of his reign are beautifully engraved cylinder seals.

The Guti, Gudea. Not long after 2150 B.C., the land of Sumer and Akkad was invaded by the Guti, warlike nomads from the Zagros Mountains. For a time, Mesopotamia was thrown into anarchy, and contemporary records plaintively ask, "Who was king? Who was not king?" Certainly the Gutians controlled at least part of the lower valley, while some cities merely paid them tribute. A shadowy Sumerian dynasty seems to have controlled Ur, while one Gudea, ensi of Lagash (see illustration p. 33), clearly achieved total independence; supported art, literature, and religion; and achieved fame and posthumous deification for piety as a temple builder. His reign marks a transition to revived Sumerian power.

The Third Dynasty of Ur (Ur III) (Ca. 2135-2027 B.C.). Ur-Nammu. It was the Sumerian city of Erech, however, that took the initiative in driving out the Guti. Their expulsion led to a renewal of Sumerian political power and to the highest achievements of Sumerian civilization. For more than a century, Sumer led the surrounding lands in the arts, in trade and commerce, and in the promotion of agriculture by well-regulated irrigation. The leading city was Ur, where a new dynasty had been established by Ur-Nammu, "King of Ur, King of Sumer and Akkad."

This period of Sumerian history is better documented than any other. Hundreds of thousands of cuneiform tablets have survived from Ur III, 99 per cent of them dealing with economic transactions. This and particularly later periods are illuminated by texts from the kingdom of Mari on the west bank of the Euphrates and an ally of Ur-Nammu. Mari was a busy place, a kind of Near Eastern Chicago, an important crossing point on the river on a first-rate trade route leading to the Levant. The Mari texts mention people flowing in and out of this part of the Near East: Amorites, Hurrians, and even Hittites and Assyrians. They attest to the importation into Mesopotamia of copper and wool from Anatolia and of luxury goods like oils, perfumes, ivory, and glass from Egypt.

Ur-Nammu was a successful warrior, conquering all the other city-states and unifying Mesopotamia, but he was also famous for more peaceful pursuits. He repaired old harbors and built new ones, refurbished canals neglected in the period of anarchy during the Guti invasions, and achieved even greater fame for his temples at Ur and Nippur and for his ziggurat at Uruk. He also laid the groundwork of the Sumerian code of laws, thus pursuing a development that had had its earliest roots in the reforms of Uruinimgina (see p. 29). The Sumerian code was not as well thought out as the later Babylonian code, but it was more humane. For example, according to Sumerian law, if a woman committed adultery, her husband did not even divorce her; he was allowed to marry a second wife, and the first wife lost her position. By Hammurabi's Code, however, she and the corespondent were slain.

Beginning with Ur-Nammu, Sumerian culture had a marked renaissance in many

FIGURE 6. Diorite statuette of Gudea
from the temple of his god Ningizzida in
Girsu (Telloh), Iraq. Neo-Sumerian, c.
2150 B.C., about 17 inches high.

The Granger Collection

fields, especially architecture, as evidenced by impressive suriving remains of sculpture, temples, and palaces. The Sumerians also cultivated literature, especially
religious writings. Their liturgical literature produced the elaborate daily services of
a formal and musically intricate religion. Drum, flute, or lyre accompanied the
hymns, which generally contained a lamentation on some specific calamity or on
ordinary human troubles. Probably the most profound idea in the liturgies is that of
the great mother goddess, the sorrowful mother who grieves for the woes of humanity and is its suppliant before the angry gods.

Shulgi. Ur-Nammu's son and successor, Shulgi (ca. 2094–2047) was a warrior
equal to his father. After twenty-one years of peace, he conducted numerous campaigns in Assyria and against the Guti and beyond the Zagros Mountains into what
is today Kurdistan. He was a very conspicuous figure, saluted in a series of royal
hymns by court poets as an almost divine personality. Indeed, the priests of Nippur
deified him in his own lifetime. He also was interested in internal reforms, devel-

FIGURE 7. Harp pillar in the form of the head of a bull from Royal Tombs of Ur, 3rd millenium B.C.

University Museum, University of Pennsylvania

FIGURE 8. Ziggurat at Ur (third dynasty, ca. 2100 B.C.).

oped his father's law code, standardized the calendar, and instituted accurate weights and measures.

Shulgi's successors were confronted with problems that ultimately caused the downfall of Ur III. The last king of the dynasty, Ibbi-Sin (ca. 2028-2004), proved unequal to controlling rebellion by his vassal states and to confronting invasions of his kingdom by Elamites and Amorites. The latter, Semites from the deserts to the west of Mesopotamia, had at first infiltrated Sumer peacefully as immigrants. About 2000 B.C., however, that infiltration became a violent invasion. Ur was destroyed, the dynasty fell, and Sumer never again played an active role in history. The Sumerians were overwhelmed by the flood of Semites into the valley. Their spoken language was replaced by Akkadian, although it survived as a written scholarly tongue. The Amorites set up petty kingdoms of their own in Issin, Larsa, Mari, Babylon, and Erech.

BABYLON

Hammurabi (Ca. 1792-1750 B.C.). The sixth Amorite king of the first Babylonian dynasty was one of the remarkable rulers of history, the famous lawgiver Hammurabi. Among his achievements were the defeat of Rim Sin, king of Larsa, and the incorporation of Sumer into his realm; with the years, he steadily advanced his political dominion, until it included Assyria. So powerful and influential was the rich new empire that the land about its capital, Babylon—the former land of Sumer and Akkad—became known as Babylonia. Babylonian culture, however, was largely an adaptation and elaboration of the Sumerian culture. Herein lay both its strength and its weakness. Sumer's literature had long since been translated; her writing, calendar, and other ways of civilized life had also been adopted. In short, Babylonian civilization—partly original, partly an adaptation—was the most vital yet produced in the lower Tigris–Euphrates Valley. Moreover, it was Babylonia's destiny to pass elements of her civilization on to other ancient peoples, some immediate neighbors, others more indirectly and farther afield. The Sumerians were dead, or at any rate, they had been absorbed by the newcomers, and the basis of their life had been destroyed.

Babylon's Decline. The First Dynasty of Babylon, as it is called, lasted about three hundred years. During the course of the seventeenth century, however, it lacked the vitality to ward off its enemies: first, certain raiders from the Land of the Sea (as they were described) who seized the southern part of their country, and then the northern Hittites from Asia Minor. The devastating Hittite incursion (ca. 1595), although brief, effectively ended Hammurabi's dynasty at Babylon. The Hittites then withdrew into Asia Minor. The chief beneficiaries of their destruction of Babylonian power were another people, the Kassites, who drifted in from their homes in the middle Euphrates and then made themselves supreme in the valley. The leader of the Kassite invasion seized Babylon and set up a dynasty, which endured for almost five hundred years. The new state was smaller than Hammurabi's and contributed little to the development of civilization. Not until the rise of the strong Assyrian Empire in the ninth century B.C. did the Tigris–Euphrates Valley again play a dominant role in world politics.

BABYLONIAN CIVILIZATION

Europe derived many of the essential elements of civilization from the Near East, and the greater number of these came from Babylonia. Through their trade and commerce, the Babylonians spread their science, art, and beliefs over a large part of the ancient world. The Syrians adopted from Babylonia most of their ideas and arts, including the cuneiform script, and the Babylonian language became the language of diplomacy, not only over all Syria but even at the Egyptian court in the fourteenth century B.C. From Syria the culture of the Babylonians was carried to Asia Minor and to Europe. Thus, for example, the use of the arch and of the practice of divination, hallmarks of later Etruscan and Roman culture, originally derived from Babylonia. The Greeks borrowed their system of weights, their calendar, and some of their astronomy. The Hebrews received many elements from their religion. The division of the day into twelve double hours and the twelve signs of the zodiac are theirs. Babylon, quite obviously, ranks very high in the history of civilization.

Babylonian culture, based on the Sumerian, was an elaboration of a way of life that had been built up slowly through the centuries. Since there was a remarkable continuity to that life, it is probably often correct to fill gaps in our knowledge for one period with survivals in another and thus obtain a reasonably full picture of the whole. On the other hand, it was Babylon's triumph—and more specifically, Hammurabi's—not only to bring this civilization to a great height but also to protect it and nourish it by political stability.

Government. At the head of the state stood the king, an autocrat who ruled with the blessing of the gods. His capital was Babylon, the Gate of the Gods, and the city's patron god, Marduk, was the chief deity of Babylon. The king was surrounded by a large bureaucracy: ministers, judges, and various officials for the collection of taxes and tribute, for the maintenance and control of canals, and for the regulation of business matters. Business agreements of every kind had to be in writing to be valid, and since thousands of these have survived, we have a detailed picture of economic life in those days. Another group surrounding the king consisted of both citizen soldiers and professionals; the latter received land lots from the king, which they could bequeath to their sons on condition that the sons also render military service—a practice followed by certain other ancient peoples as well.

Society. The king and his civil and military officials, the priests, the landed proprietors, the rich merchants, and the manufacturers formed one of the three classes recognized by Babylonian law. The second class consisted of laborers and farmers; many of the latter were tenants who paid a share (perhaps a third) of their produce to the owner. The lowest class in Babylonian society was made up of slaves, persons who had been captured in war or had lost their freedom through debt. The law protected them carefully. Though the slaves were chattels, they could own property and eventually buy their freedom; a male slave was also allowed to marry a free woman, and the offspring of such a union were free.

The basis of this society was the family, and the position of women was better than in many subsequent periods. The courts recognized women as free individuals who could own property, legally marry, and even obtain divorce. Divorce was easier for a man, but if a man was rich enough to afford concubines, his wife took precedence over them, and on his death the concubines became free.

Agriculture. Agriculture provided the chief means of livelihood in Babylonia. Much of the land was owned by the king and his officials and by the "gods"; that is to say, the temples, or rather the priests of the temples, actually held large areas in the name of the gods. Small freeholders and tenants were required to keep nearby canals in order, for these were necessary for both irrigation and transport. If a landlord failed in his duty, he or she was fined for any harm caused his or her neighbor; on the other hand, if a debtor's land was unavoidably flooded, he was excused from paying his debt that year. On the farms, large and small, were grown various fruit trees—especially the date palm—vegetables, wheat, barley, and spelt. The common animals were oxen, cattle, pigs, goats, sheep, and donkeys; camels and horses were not yet known in Hammurabi's Babylon.

Industry and Art. Skilled industry was carried on by craftsmen and their apprentices. The law regulated their wages and the prices of their manufactures. From their shops came finely woven and brilliantly colored linens, muslins, and woolens; gold, silver, glass, and bronze wares; and excellent furniture. Probably the chief industry was brickmaking, but the Babylonians also became famous for their ivory carvings and for beautiful objects of lapis lazuli. Because official correspondence, business agreements, sales, and wills were voluminous, it was customary to sign documents with engraved cylinders of semiprecious stones, a practice learned from the Sumerians; thousands of these seals, often of exquisite beauty, have survived. Large sculpture in stone, on the other hand, is rather timid in execution—the artists were relatively unfamiliar with stone, as it had to be imported—and shows squat, unlifelike figures.

Trade. In Babylonia, as elsewhere in the Near East, goods were exchanged by barter or on the standard of established weights of metals. The standard weight was the talent, which was divided into sixty minas. The mina weighed about a pound and contained sixty shekels. The notation chiefly used was sexagesimal (based on 60 as a unit), although the decimal system was also known. Both numerical systems derived originally from the Sumerians. Rich merchants and priests acted as bankers, arranged credits and loans, and charged interest as high as 25 per cent a month. Partnerships were formed to carry on an extensive trade with Syria.

Architecture. A great city such as Babylon was a teeming metropolis. Beside the narrow streets rose the houses of ordinary people. They presented a drab, monotonous stuccoed exterior to the passerby, but within they were comfortable. Each house was built around an open court and was often two stories high; in that event, the bedrooms were in the upper floor, while below were located the living rooms and a chapel, with its burial vault. The houses were constructed of brick and normally had flat roofs resting on cedar beams. Larger buildings, such as a palace or a temple, were imposing. The Babylonian architects knew the column, the true arch, and the vault; they reared any large structure on a huge platform or terrace, often covering several acres, in order to protect the building from floods. A temple—such as that of Marduk at Babylon or of Nanna, the moon god, at Ur—was constructed of baked and unbaked brick, with a facing of colorful glazed bricks, and was dedicated to the city's chief god. It contained a school and rooms for worship, but its striking feature was the ziggurat, also derived from Sumer. This was a series of terraces, reaching a height of perhaps seventy feet, at the very top of which was the god's sanctuary.

Religion. The Babylonians had a gloomy view of the next world, which they imagined as a cave full of dead persons leading an unhappy, colorless existence. Although they believed that proper burial and sacrifices could ease the lot of the dead, their religious practices were chiefly directed to this world. To secure a happy and prosperous long life, it was necessary to perform certain sacrifices and celebrate festivals. Various forms and rules had to be observed, and for that reason priests, who were wise in such matters, were indispensable. Everywhere were spirits, demons, and gods, some friendly, some not, but all needing attention. Every locality and every association had its gods. More important was the leading deity of a city-state, and greatest of all was the god of the imperial capital, Babylon. The gods had female consorts; just as Marduk, the patron deity of Babylon, was the greatest of gods, so the Semitic mother goddess, Ishtar, a goddess of fertility, became the chief female deity and was identified with the planet known to us as Venus.

A large literature, written by scribes and stored in libraries, dealt with religion. It prescribed in detail the ceremonies of worship, the forms of magic for repelling evil spirits, and the prayers for soothing the anger of the gods and for winning their favor. All strange occurrences and all abnormalities had to be explained, for they might contain a message from the gods. Many ways were invented to discover the will of the gods (*divination,* as it is called). Most important was the examination of the liver of an animal offered in sacrifice. The liver was marked off into parts and searched for irregularities; its study became in time an elaborate and complicated system. Dreams also had to be explained, and the actions of birds and animals. Moreover, the Babylonians believed that the will of the gods could be discovered and the future foretold by the study of the heavenly bodies, especially of the sun, the moon, and the five known planets. Thus they created astrology.

Literature.   Many of the religious texts were composed in Sumerian, which, because of its antiquity, had an appeal for the educated. Sumerian, however, was now a "dead language," and grammars and dictionaries were necessary for its study. Schools were conducted in the temples, where boys learned reading and writing, arithmetic and geometry. Mathematical and medical texts were written; indeed, Hammurabi's Code regulated the fees a surgeon might charge and prescribed severe penalties for gross negligence. Babylonians interested in geography drew maps and city plans on clay tablets, several of which have survived. It is, however, by the protests of reforming spirits and the striking conceptions of introspective minds that we gain understanding of a people. Here we must rely chiefly on the religious texts, the myths, prayers, hymns, and psalms, which emphasize the necessity of being good and hold out practical rewards in this life.

Much of Babylonian poetry is epic in nature; that is to say, the poems are of considerable length and celebrate in narrative form the deeds of real or legendary heroes. The famous Epic of Gilgamesh, which was composed about 2000 B.C. from earlier stories, tells how a Sumerian king of Uruk sought immortal life. Gilgamesh was a Mesopotamian Odysseus, who journeyed far and endured much. Although he allegedly ruled 126 years according to an ancient king list, he did not want to die and sought the secret of immortality. The poem is essentially a protest against death. If indeed this is a world of justice, how does it happen that one must die, even though one has done no wrong? The epic provides no answer to this question. The poets also delighted to tell of the creation of the world by one of their gods, and of a great flood and the building of the ship in which one human family alone was saved. Some of these stories are also told in the Bible, but we should note that the Babylonian hero of the flood is characteristically saved by the favoritism of a god, whereas according to Genesis, Noah was delivered by his own merits.

Science.   By 1800 B.C. the Babylonians had a highly developed algebra and had made significant advances in astronomy. They divided the lunar year into twelve months of 29 and 30 days each. This gave them a year of only 354 days, and they made the correction by inserting an additional (intercalary) month whenever necessary. The day they divided into twelve double hours, each 120 minutes long; to measure the hours, they invented water clocks and sundials.

Hammurabi's Code.   Probably the most important achievement of the Babylo-

FIGURE 9. Stele inscribed with Hammurabi's Code, c. 1792–1750 B.C.

nians was the creation of a written law, which governed people's relations with each other and with the state. The developed law as we know it in Hammurabi's famous code shows a high sense of justice, though many punishments were more severe than the Sumerians'. Our knowledge of the law derives chiefly from an inscribed slab of black diorite, about eight feet high. It was found by the French archaeologist De Morgan in 1901 at Susa, where it had been brought by an Elamite king in the twelfth century B.C.; it is now in the Louvre Museum in Paris. The code consists of more than thirty-six hundred lines, which go around the slab. At the top, King Hammurabi stands in an attitude of adoration before Shamash—the rays behind his shoulders proclaim him the great sun god. Shamash is handing the symbols of kingship to Hammurabi, which serve to emphasize the divine origin of the laws.

The civil and criminal laws of Hammurabi regulated practically everything in life. The laws applied to personal property, real estate, business, trade, agriculture, inheritances, and adoption; they controlled the price of labor and animals, purchases, sales, contracts, leases. The rights of women, children, and slaves were carefully protected, and, as we have seen, women were able to marry, transact business, and inherit and bequeath property. There were penalties for injuries to property and to the body; in general, the law made a distinction between the three classes of society, so that a poor person hurting a noble received a more severe penalty than in the opposite case. The basis of criminal law was that of retaliation *(lex talionis)* or, as we might express it, "an eye for an eye, and a tooth for a tooth." For example, we read in Hammurabi's Code that if a man destroys the eye of another man, his own eye must be destroyed. At first the courts administering the law had been located in temples, but by Hammurabi's day civil courts had almost supplanted the priestly courts. Cases were tried in their local communities of origin, but appeals to the king were allowed.

The Tigris-Euphrates Valley had created a rich and complex civilization. Another river valley, that of the Nile, could make a similar claim.

4

Egypt

THE VALLEY OF THE NILE

The Land and Its People.   The Nile River, on which the life of Egypt has always depended, rises in central Africa and the mountains of Ethiopia. After a northward journey of several hundred miles it passes through southernmost Egypt and Sudanese Nubia, where its course is interrupted by six cataracts or rapids. The northernmost of these cataracts is counted as the first, and it is here that Egypt begins. From this point—the site of Syene (modern Asswân)—to ancient Memphis (near modern Cairo) it is more than six hundred miles. For most of this distance the valley is less than ten miles wide, though at places the limestone hills, which hem the river in, recede and the valley attains a width of thirty miles. The whole area, from Syene almost to Memphis, is known as Upper Egypt.

Below Memphis the character of the Nile changes, for it divides itself into several channels, through which it flows one hundred miles to the Mediterranean Sea. This land, which is swampy near the coast, is known as Lower Egypt; in appearance it is a triangle, resembling the fourth letter of the Greek alphabet, and hence it is also called the Delta. The total habitable land of Upper and Lower Egypt is very small—only about 3.5 per cent of the land will support population—and doubtless in antiquity, as today, over 99 per cent of the population were compressed into the Nile River Valley. Today, at any rate, there are more people to the square mile in Egypt than in either Belgium, the most densely populated nation of Europe, or Java.

The Delta enjoys some rainfall, but it almost never rains in the rest of Egypt. The land would have been a desert, were it not for the fact that each summer the Nile, swollen by monsoon rains and melting mountain snows, overflowed the valley before the recent construction of the Asswân High Dam. When the water returned to its channel in early December, it left the land fertilized with a rich coat of earth. The silt that was deposited enabled a farmer to raise each year one or two crops of grain, grasses, flax, and vegetables, provided that he continued to irrigate the land. To do this, it was necessary for the ancient Egyptian to lift water from the Nile or wells and carry it across the fields by a complex system of canals. Our picture, it must be said, is an ideal one, for in certain years the Nile's overflow might be very small, bringing famine in its wake; or it might be a rushing flood, destroying canals, dams, and even villages.

Important as the Nile has always been to Egypt, the ancient Egyptian regarded

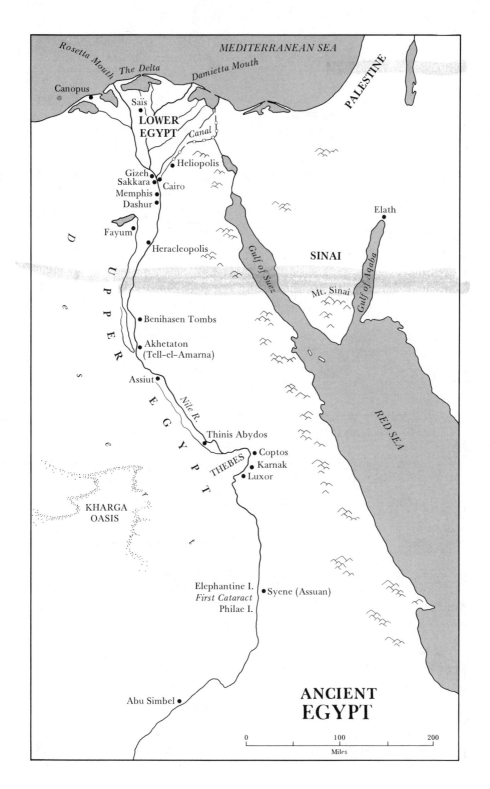

ANCIENT EGYPT

MEDITERRANEAN SEA

Rosetta Mouth
The Delta
Damietta Mouth
PALESTINE

Canopus

Saïs

LOWER
EGYPT

Canal

Heliopolis

Gizeh
Sakkara
Cairo
Memphis
Dashur

Fayum

Elath

Heracleopolis

SINAI

Gulf of Suez

Mt. Sinai

Gulf of Aqaba

Benihasen Tombs

Akhetaton
(Tell-el-Amarna)

Assiut

Nile R.

RED SEA

Thinis Abydos

Coptos

THEBES
Karnak
Luxor

KHARGA
OASIS

Elephantine I.
First Cataract
Philae I.

Syene (Assuan)

Abu Simbel

0   100   200
Miles

43

the sun as even more vital. Here was the true source of life. Each day, after an absence that seemed to resemble death, the sun rose again in the region of rebirth and
renewed life, just as the river itself renewed life every year. Renewal of life could
constantly be seen, and inevitably, perhaps, it suggested to the Egyptian the idea of
victory over death. The uniformity of the landscape made its own impression on
the people, too. Here were the river and its two banks, exactly the same, the green
cultivated fields stretching away, then the desert and finally the mountains to east
and west. It gave the Egyptian a sense of symmetry and balance that is noticeable,
for example, in Egyptian art. Moreover, anything that was different in this monotonous scene—such as a crocodile on the mudflats—immediately became inordinately
full of life and helped the Egyptians acquire a totemistic outlook on nature. They
were ready to personify anything, not as a great god, to be sure, but at least as a
force to be reckoned with.

   As in the case of the Tigris and the Euphrates, the Nile was a mighty factor in the
unification of the country and in the growth of domestic trade. Unlike Mesopotamia, however, Egypt is relatively isolated and protected from invasion. The cataracts of the river—and beyond them, the tropical jungles—impede invasions from
the south, while to the east and west of the mountain ranges that line the Nile are
large deserts. To the north, of course, is the Mediterranean. Cut off by sea and deserts from other people, the Egyptians tended to be culturally conservative; they
looked upon themselves as a race apart and took an isolationist pride in their country. Though an invasion from the north, across the sea, might succeed, a strong,
centralized government could usually defend the land with considerable ease. The
mountains, moreover, produced an abundance of building stone, and gold could be
had in Nubia and copper there and in the Sinai Peninsula; the one conspicuous lack
was wood. Protected by nature from enemies and blessed with varied resources, the
ancient Egyptians were more self-contained than most people have been, but the
need for the "cedars of Lebanon" brought them to Syria and consequently into the
stream of influences emanating from Mesopotamia.

   Historical Sources.   Egypt's dry climate has preserved the works of the ancients.
The modern traveler in this hot and sunny land is astonished at the great number
and size of the Egyptian monuments: obelisks, colossal statues, vast temples, and
pyramids. Nowhere else did the ancients build so magnificently, and nowhere have
their works been so well preserved. Archaeological excavations have recovered
further quantities of ancient remains, including many papyri. The archaeological
evidence, together with the writing—not only on papyri, but also on the walls of
monuments—provides us with an intimate knowledge of everyday life in Egypt.

   The key to the Egyptian language dates back to 1799, during Napoleon's campaign in Egypt, when some of his men, who were digging the foundation of a fort
near the westernmost or Rosetta mouth of the Nile, found a stone of black basalt
three feet nine inches long, two feet four inches wide, and eleven inches thick. The
officer in charge saw that one side of the stone had Greek letters on it and also
some lines of characters that might be writing. When Napoleon heard of this stone,
he turned it over to the body of learned men who had accompanied him to Egypt.
Then, after the successful military operation of Sir Ralph Abercromby against the

French in Egypt in the spring of 1801, the Rosetta Stone, as it has always been known, was sent to the British Museum in London.

The inscription on the Rosetta Stone is written in two languages, Egyptian and Greek. The Egyptian portion consists of hieroglyphic and demotic characters. The hieroglyphic characters were the old priestly picture writing that was employed from the earliest dynasties in nearly all state and ceremonial documents intended to be seen by the public. The demotic characters were the popular, abbreviated, and modified form of the hieratic or cursive form of hieroglyphic writing. The presence of Greek on the stone is to be explained by the fact that the inscription dates from the time of the Macedonian conquest. It represents a decree by the ruler, Ptolemy V Epiphanes (196 B.C.), who employed both the Greek and the Egyptian languages so that all his subjects might read it.

A significant step in deciphering Egyptian was taken when it was noted that the ovals, or cartouches, in the hieroglyphic inscription occupied a position analogous to those portions of the Greek inscription that contained the name of Ptolemy. The same seemed to be true of another bilingual inscription, an obelisk from Philae, where both Ptolemy and Cleopatra are mentioned in the Greek. The two names, Ptolemy and Cleopatra, have enough characters in common to prove that the cartouches of the hieroglyphic inscriptions contain the royal names written phonetically. This proved to be the decisive discovery in the decipherment of the Egyptian language. After many years of labor, chiefly by a French scholar named Champollion, it became possible to give the correct alphabetic values of other Egyptian signs. A knowledge of Coptic then made possible the translation of the ancient Egyptian language. *Coptic* is a name meaning "Egyptian." The Egyptians who became Christians after the preaching of Mark in Alexandria were called Copts by the Arabs, and knowledge of their language has never been lost.

In their earliest writing, the Egyptians represented objects by pictures; a disk, for example, stood for the sun, a crescent for the moon. From pictographic script they developed ideographic and phonogramic stages, and before 3000 B.C. they had invented alphabetic letters each representing a single sound. But they were too conservative to adopt an alphabet exclusively and continued to use pictographs and phonograms in hieroglyphic, hieratic, and the late form of writing known as *demotic*. At an early date, moreover, the Egyptians developed a lunar calendar, but at some time during the first three dynasties, a calendar of 365 days was introduced. The relative accuracy of the Egyptian calendar, combined with the vast amount of writing and the archaeological remains, accounts for our detailed knowledge of ancient Egypt. Finally, we also have accounts of Egypt from Greek historians and, more particularly, from Manetho (early third century B.C.), an Egyptian who wrote in Greek. Manetho's valuable history is lost, but parts of it were incorporated in the works of later writers; it has become conventional to follow his division of Egyptian history into dynasties or families of kings. [1]

---

[1] The chief dynasties were as follows: Dynasties I-II (3100-2685 B.C.) were formative and are spoken of as archaic. Dynasties III-VI are equivalent to the Old Kingdom (2685-2180 B.C.), followed by disorder (Dynasties VII-X, 2180-2040 B.C.). Egypt was reunited during Dynasty

Predynastic Egypt. A strongly unified Egypt, as we have said, made invasion difficult, but in early prehistoric days the country consisted of communities of an apparently mixed population, although this is a very controversial point. Libyans from the northwest, Semites from the northeast, and Nubians from the south entered the Valley of the Nile during that dim past to form the mixed, though distinctive Egyptian race. Remains from the Paleolithic Period are numerous, and human traces exist there dating from about one million B.C. For the Neolithic Period, which began in Egypt about 5000 B.C., we have mounting evidence of an increasingly complex culture. The people lived in houses of mud bricks and reeds, at first on bluffs above the Nile because the valley was still filled with jungle. They worshiped deities, and when they buried their dead they put objects of daily use into the graves with them. The chief settlement thus far excavated, at Nakadeh (near Thebes), has produced flint tools, sculptured figures, and remarkably fine alabaster and steatite vases. Though the wheel was unknown, the potter was able to mold clay into beautiful forms, which were decorated with geometrical and later pictorial designs and burnished. Rudimentary hieroglyphs appeared late in the predynastic period. Copper and gold implements are also found, for predynastic Egypt was on the threshold of the age of metals.

We may suppose that the people of the predynastic period fished in the Nile and hunted on the desert and in the marshes of the Nile Valley, independently of one another. The gradual desiccation of the country, however, probably compelled the inhabitants to congregate in the valley in considerable numbers, and to resort to farming and stock raising. They could not take this step without clearing the land and irrigating the fields, but for such enterprises cooperation was necessary. It was this need that brought a centralized state into being. The necessity of enforcing strict cooperation among the people in reclamation and irrigation projects, mineral exploitation, and trade gave the government great power and correspondingly reduced the freedom of the subjects; centralization of government was ultimately responsible for the organization of the people.

THE ARCHAIC (CA. 3100–2685 B.C.)
AND OLD KINGDOMS (CA. 2685–2180 B.C.)

The Archaic Kingdom. Dynasties I-II. The little chiefdoms of predynastic Egypt and Nubia competed and warred with each other until finally two large kingdoms were created from them sometime after 3150 B.C. One of these comprised Upper Egypt, and the other, Lower Egypt (the Delta). Eventually the kings of Upper Egypt, who had their capital at Hierakonpolis, conquered the Delta and unified the

---

XI, and this dynasty, together with the twelfth, is equivalent to the Middle Kingdom (2040–1785 B.C.). This was followed by the invasion of the Hyksos. Dynasties XVII–XX are equivalent to the New Kingdom or Empire (1560-1085 B.C.). This was followed by foreign invasions and conquests. Dynasty XXVI was the last independent, native dynasty; this was the period of Saite Egypt (663-525 B.C.) and is connected with Assyrian and subsequent history.

Nile Valley. According to tradition, this important task was accomplished by one king, Narmer, who may be represented on a famous palette (see page 48). Narmer was apparently succeeded by Menes, perhaps his son, who established the First Dynasty and founded Memphis, his capital city.

The first two dynasties created the basic institutions that characterized Egyptian civilization for the next three thousand years. Interestingly enough, the rather fast evolution of that civilization during the late predynastic period may have been stimulated by influences from Sumer. The appearance of cylinder seals, artistic motifs like winged griffins and intertwined snakes, and building in mud brick rather than stone all suggest important borrowings from Mesopotamia. Even the idea of writing appeared somewhat abruptly, and the characteristically hieroglyphic system with its ideograms, phonograms, phonetic signs and its determinatives may have been inspired by early cuneiform.

The Old Kingdom. Dynasties III–IV. The kings of the Third Dynasty continued to rule from Memphis, which was conveniently located between Upper and Lower Egypt. Though the king was ultimately referred to as the "Great House" (peraa or pharaoh), Egypt's ancient division was never forgotten, and among the royal titles was "King of Upper and Lower Egypt." Egypt now entered on a prolonged and productive period of peace and prosperity. Noteworthy in this early period is the reign of Djoser of the Third Dynasty (ca. 2650), under whom the famous architect Imhotep created a step pyramid that still survives and that at the time was the largest monument built entirely of stone in the world. Even more stupendous were the Great Pyramids created by kings of the Fourth Dynasty (ca. 2613-2494 B.C.): Here, at the peak of the Old Kingdom's power and wealth, the Egyptians were an independent, self-reliant people, full of vigor and zest for action and accomplishment.

Egyptian administration was based on the nome, which in the dim past had probably represented an independent state; there were twenty nomes in Lower Egypt, twenty-two in Upper Egypt. The governors of the nomes (nomarchs) were responsible to the king, and during the Third and Fourth Dynasties their power was strictly limited by the strong, centralized government. Under the Fifth Dynasty ca. 2492-2345 B.C.), however, the power of the nobility began to increase in the nomes, and decentralization was carried so far under the Sixth Dynasty (ca. 2345-2181 B.C.) that the governors were able to challenge the throne. The hereditary nobility were now practically independent in their nomes. The king, nevertheless, remained supreme in overall policy, and under Pepi I and his son, Pepi II (ca. 2275), Egypt's influence reached beyond the first cataract. Expeditions were also sent to Punt (Somaliland) to secure gold, incense, and other riches, and to Sinai for its turquoise. Following the long reign of Pepi II, however, the nobles and decentralization won out, the Old Kingdom fell, and Egypt was again torn by strife between contending nobles.

Government. The Egyptian pharaoh of the Archaic and Old Kingdoms was a living god, an autocrat with almost unlimited power. His prime duty was to preserve the right order of things and to ensure justice, a duty expressed in the ultimately untranslatable Egyptian word *ma'at.* The concept of *ma'at* was essential to the nature of Egyptian kingship, confirming as it did the stable and unchanging continuity

FIGURE 10. Egyptian
schist tablet commemo-
rating a victory of King
Narmer, the "palette of
Narmer." From Hierako-
nopolis, 1st dynasty;
about 25 inches high.

The Granger Collection

of pharaoh's rule. The opposite of *ma'at* was the notion of falsehood or deceit;
therefore *ma'at* itself also approximated the concept of *good*. The king had a five-
fold titulary and wore two crowns in token of his kingship over Upper and Lower
Egypt. The Fifth Dynasty had as its patron deity Re, the sun god, whom it established as the most important god in Egypt. Beginning in the Sixth Dynasty, the king
himself was Re, in order that he might rule Re's chief concern, Egypt. He embodied, moreover, the deities of both Upper and Lower Egypt and was also Horus,
the falcon god. Despite this picture of unapproachable absolutism, the Egyptians
regarded their pharaoh as an ideal ruler, composed necessarily of power as well as
graciousness, a balance, so to speak, between force and a loving care for his people.
Officials could dispense only his law, but the king was able to exercise discretion
and add justice to the law. In short, he was a divine ruler, vested with the obligation
to guard his people and to act as deputy of the gods on earth. Not only was the
king the chief priest of all the gods, but he also could command the army, administered justice, and controlled the economic life of the country. He theoretically
owned all the land of Egypt, directed the planting of crops and every major activity.

To carry out their will, the early kings had a bureaucracy that gradually grew in size. Offices were multiplied, some of them becoming sinecures with high rewards and leading to large-scale corruption. The higher officials formed a nobility, which was in large part hereditary, and was often related to the king. The officials had some education, so that they could help the king administer justice and supervise the erection and care of public works. It was also necessary for them to make a biennial census, assess property throughout the kingdom, and collect and manage the revenue. At first, nomarchs were appointed by the king. By the time of the Fifth Dynasty, the office of district governor tended to be hereditary, as were many other offices; it was the ensuing decentralization under the next dynasty that helped lead to a feudal period. The royal law court sat at Memphis. This court was in the charge of the vizier, who helped govern Egypt and was the most important individual in the realm after the king. The vizier, through the time of the Fourth Dynasty, was generally the crown prince. Among his many administrative duties was the government of both Upper and Lower Egypt; from the end of the Old Kingdom there were two viziers, one for each of the major divisions of the country.

Classes of Society. The members of the royal family, the officials and nobles, and the priests formed the upper class of Egyptian society. Egyptian society at this time was highly stratified, and there was little possibility for a person to rise from one class to another. Scanty evidence from the Old Kingdom suggests that an intermediate class consisted of the city dwellers: those engaged in trade and commerce, professional people such as scribes, and artisans. The largest class was made up of the peasants; and at the bottom of society were the slaves.

Throughout ancient Egyptian history, most of the people were poor. They lived in mud huts, crowded closely together along narrow, crooked lanes. Food was simple, beer the favorite drink. A single linen garment sufficed for dress. While the women carried water, ground meal between two stones, baked bread in the ashes, sewed, spun, and wove, the men worked all day in the fields or at their trade. They toiled under an overseer who could, and often did, beat them for a mistake, inattention to duty, or nonpayment of taxes. Nevertheless, the poor as well as the rich had a lively imagination, a ready wit, and strong social qualities. They were a patient people who were obedient to their superiors and reverenced their god-king. Under these circumstances, no other government than absolute monarchy seemed credible.

Busy as the nobles might be in the government or on their estates, their life by contrast with that of the poor was one of ease and refinement. They lived in roomy houses of mud bricks, furnished with comfortable furniture. Their meals were large and varied; the drinks they enjoyed most were wine and beer. The men wore linen loincloths and shaved their heads and faces; the women clothed themselves in long dresses. Both sexes wore wigs and jewelry and used cosmetics. Monogamy generally was practiced, though concubines were common. The house of a rich noble was often set amid beautiful gardens, with a pond full of lilies and fish. Boating, water sports, fishing, hunting, storytellers, and musicians occupied his time. Birds were brought down with throwing sticks, lions and hippopotami with spears.

Economic Life. Agriculture was the basis of economic life in Egypt. Because the strictest cooperation was necessary if the maximum amount of food was to be raised, the peasant apparently found himself regimented more and more; he ultimately became little better than a serf, though he remained legally free.

Theoretically the king owned all Egypt, but in practice he made large grants to the nobles and priests. There was not a temple that did not have rich lands for its support; they were taxed, however, in the Old Kingdom. The small landowner, accordingly, paid taxes or rents in kind on his farm and possessions.

Prisoners and criminals were subject to forced labor, in the mines and quarries, on irrigation and building projects, and in the manufacture of bricks. It was the duty of the peasant, as well as the government, to maintain the irrigation ditches and canals. Since the entire life of the Nile Valley depended on the proper regulation of the annual overflow, scribes kept a record of the river's rise and fall. The overflow, of course, destroyed landmarks, and on the recession of the floods the land was again surveyed.

The farmer plowed his land and planted wheat, barley, and other grains, flax for its linen, sesame plants for their fats, beans, lentils, and other vegetables. Flowers and date palms dotted the landscape; bees were kept for their honey. At the proper time the farmer cut his grain with a sickle; drove cattle over it by way of threshing, and finally threw it into the wind to separate out the chaff. Cattle, sheep, goats, pigs, donkeys, oxen, ducks, and geese demanded the farmer's attention; the camel and horse were still unknown, and desert travelers used donkeys.

The Egyptian "middle class" lived in the towns and cities. A large section of this class consisted of artisans, many of whom worked for the king and the nobles or at Memphis near the temple of Ptah, the god of artisans. The artisans produced beautiful jewelry and other work in copper, gold, and silver; wonderfully thin, translucent stone vases; exquisite furniture; and linen tapestries.

The chief imports were spices and incense from Punt; ebony, ivory, and gold from Nubia; and timber from Syria and Nubia.

Religion. Like other ancient peoples, the Egyptians were totally immersed in nature, respecting its forces, which so closely affected their lives. Dominated by totemism and animism, they viewed the world illogically as a continuum of substance shared by a bewildering variety of beings, which they regarded as deities that sometimes had the same attributes. The deities had the forms not only of men and women but also of birds, fish, crocodiles, hippopotamuses, jackals, cats, dogs, and cattle; the local gods in animal form were best loved by the people at large, and festivals in their honor provided the chief popular recreation. Each village, city, and nome had its own deities, but in time certain gods won national recognition, such as Horus, the god of kingship who had a falcon's head and a human body; the Fifth Dynasty added their own patron god, Re, the sun god, although the pharaohs remained Horus kings until the Sixth Dynasty. Ptah, the god of artisans, and Nut, the sky goddess, were also national deities. The gods were very human, with human weaknesses. In general, the Egyptians regarded the world as being full of many humans and many gods, all of whom, however, were ultimately of one nature. In other words, the Egyptians were pantheistic rather than monotheistic, for they insisted that, though there were many different beings, all were of the same substance.

Egyptian life was so delightful, at least for the powerful, that they hoped to pro-long it after death. The early Egyptians looked upon death as a kind of second life, a projection of life into a better world, although, strictly speaking, at first only the kings—who were, after all, gods in their own right—could expect immortality. Even though the nobles during the Old Kingdom were not as yet assured of an afterlife; they constructed their tombs as close to the kings' as possible, in the hope that their services would still be needed in the next world and thus guarantee their con-tinued existence beyond the grave. There is no good evidence that the lower classes in this same period expected life after death, but this was to come. The belief that an afterlife could exist was encouraged by the dry climate, which preserved dead bodies remarkably well. As it was important to preserve the body indefinitely, for the sake of the soul, the body was mummified and placed in a tomb. Within the tomb, which served as a bridge, so to speak, between two existences, were stored food and drink for the dead; and cheerful pictures of the daily routine adorned the walls of the kings' sepulchers. The paintings show us what values the early Egyp-tians attached to this life; the emphasis is on action, on the material world. A gay and lusty people, full of the love of living, they insisted with an aggressive optimism on bringing into the next world the merry life of this. Pictures of food and drink were of necessity painted on the walls of the tombs, to guard against the exhaustion of the real provisions; in the absence of either, the soul would be forced to leave the tomb.

The eventual popularization of the cult of Osiris and his wife-sister, Isis, in the Sixth Dynasty and later led to the further idea that the body was the home of a "vital force" known as *ka*. At the judgment seat of Osiris, king of the dead and god of immortality, *ka*, who preceded one in death to bring about one's successful exis-tence in the next world, was called upon to account for his actions on earth. Had he murdered, stolen, coveted the property of others, blasphemed the gods, given false testimony, or ill-treated his parents? If so, he was devoured by a monster; if not, he was admitted to eternal happiness.

The Pyramids. The kings and nobles were first buried in rectangular tombs, first made of brick and later of stone, called *mastabas,* the modern Arabic word for "benches," since their above-ground superstructure resembles benches. Royal tombs tended to become more elaborate as *mastaba* was piled on *mastaba,* a process that culminated (ca. 2650) in the famous step pyramid of Djoser's architect, Imho-tep. Within a century thereafter, having perfected their stone technique, and using primitive technology but lots of manpower and time, the Egyptians were producing the Great Pyramids near Memphis, at Gizeh, the work of kings of the Fourth Dy-nasty: Khufu, whom Herodotus, the Greek historian, called Cheops; Khafre; and Menkaure. Herodotus tells us that 100,000 men spent twenty years building the largest of the three pyramids, that of Khufu. It was erected during the pharaoh's life-time, for he wished to be certain of his soul's resting place. Even if Herodotus' statis-tics are exaggerated, the building of the Great Pyramid was a gigantic undertaking.

The pyramid covers thirteen acres, measures 755 feet square at the base, and is 481 feet high. Almost 2.5 million blocks, each weighing about two and a half tons, were quarried locally and east of the Nile, ferried across the river, and by means of

The Granger Collection

FIGURE 11. Step Pyramid of King Djoser, near Sakkara, Egypt; 3rd Dynasty.

ramps and cranes moved into place. Within the pyramid a long passage winds and climbs to the actual tomb. Nearby is the famous Sphinx, with a human head and a lion's body, currently fighting a losing battle against the desert sands. It is clear that the Egyptian kings spent much time thinking about the next world; they also used human and natural resources on a prodigious scale in making ready for it. The kings of the Fourth Dynasty commanded the necessary wealth and power, but they drained the country, and none of their successors was able to compete with them.

Art.   The Egyptian artist made useful and decorative objects with extraordinarily fine taste. Indeed, Egyptian art in general was worthy of appreciation by that nation of connoisseurs, the Greeks. Plato in particular admired Egyptian art for what he thought was its "rational" quality. The jewelry and other work in gold, silver, and copper, the translucent stone vases and the beautiful pottery, and the furniture—all point to exceptional skill and feeling. But certain conventional standards for art as a whole, and particularly perhaps for sculpture and painting, were set during the Old Kingdom and persisted for centuries. This amazing conservatism is probably to be explained by the fact that Egyptian art was concerned primarily with religion, and it was accordingly more important to perpetuate religious customs than to experiment with new artistic ideas. In painting, for example, figures in the same plane are shown in successive rows; there was little interest in perspective

The Granger Collection

FIGURE 12. The Great Sphinx at Gizeh, Egypt, 4th Dynasty.

or shading; objects of different size are usually shown as if they were the same size. For centuries the Egyptian artist painted the human face in profile and the eye in full view, the legs in profile and the shoulders forward. And for centuries the sculptor carved figures in a frontal pose, arms to the side, one leg advanced. It was religious conservatism that tied the artist to these canons.

For all its conventions, Egyptian art is full of vitality. It strove to duplicate reality and to preserve personality. Fidelity of proportion, together with a careful counterpoising of elements, gave their work a harmonious balance. The tempera paintings on walls give a realistic and lively impression of daily life. The sculptures—in wood, copper, bronze, gold, and stone—are powerful, and so exact is the marvelous portraiture that the statue of a man and his mummy often bear a strong resemblance. It would be difficult to imagine a more realistic portrayal than that of Prince Rahotep (p. 55).

Literature and Science. Standardizing conventions for literature, as for art, were set during the days of the Old Kingdom. Once again, the influence of religion can be detected, but the keen desire of the Egyptians for practical knowledge also channeled the normal growth of a gifted people. A book of etiquette, the Precepts of Ptahhotep (Fifth Dynasty), has survived that explains how to get on in this world. Be an official and learn the rules, especially how to treat your superiors, equals, and inferiors. If you are smart enough and follow common-sense principles, you are sure to be a success. Education, accordingly, had as its primary aim the preparation of young men for a post in the bureaucracy. The Egyptians apparently kept a record, sometimes in duplicate and triplicate, of almost every conceivable transaction. The first task before an ambitious and gifted boy was to learn to read and write, with reed pens and ink on paper made from strips of the papyrus plant. He learned proverbs and maxims that were considered beneficial for his development; and he was taught to write model letters and petitions such as he might have to use later on. All this he learned from a scribe, and it was his hope that in time he too might become a scribe and occupy an enviable position in official life. In that event he would need a knowledge of arithmetic and geometry as well, in order, for example, to keep the tax lists and to survey and record land and boundaries after the Nile's annual overflow.

Science, too emphasized the useful and sought practical knowledge. Though fractions gave difficulty, arithmetic, geometry, and surveying were understood, and they made possible the measuring of land and the drawing of boundary lines. A complex system of canals and ditches controlled the Nile's waters. Engineering was studied for the erection of pyramids and other large structures. There were great achievements in these fields, but little formulating of general principles. Religion— and more particularly the task of arranging the calendar of festivals—encouraged the growth of astronomy. The Egyptians also possessed a limited knowledge of medicine and surgery, as a remarkable surgical papyrus makes clear, but an unwillingness to experiment and theorize left them with the belief that evil spirits caused disease. In general, they had little sense of causation; they could arrange knowledge, but not systematize it.

THE MIDDLE KINGDOM (2040–1785 B.C.)

First Intermediate Period. The increasing power of the nobles under the Sixth Dynasty produced an individualism so strong that shortly after the end of the dynasty (2180 B.C.), the Old Kingdom fell. Once again Egypt became disunited, and a prolonged period of civil strife ensued (2180-2040 B.C.), marked by drought and famine. Misery and poverty stalked the land. Life was further unsettled by invasions of Nubians and by incursions of Libyans and Semites into the Delta. Three rival families in particular—those of Memphis, Heracleopolis, and Thebes—contended for

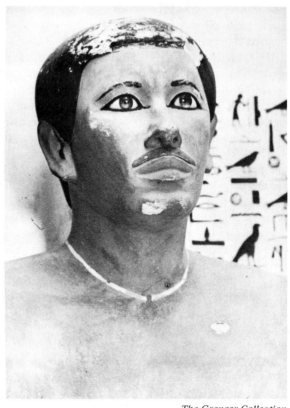

FIGURE 13. Egyptian
painted head of Prince
Rahotep, son of King
Snefru; 4th Dynasty.

The Granger Collection

supremacy, until finally the rulers of Thebes conquered the north and made Lisht, south of Memphis, the capital of the kingdom.

The chaos that ensued, called the First Intermediate Period, profoundly affected the Egyptian outlook, which never thereafter quite recaptured its complacently optimistic view of the world. This change is reflected in contemporary literature like the *Dialogue of the Despairing Man with His Soul,* with its gently pessimistic agnosticism and its discovery of higher, nonmaterialistic values. Other writers poignantly expressed their shock and grief at the violence and ruthlessness in a world gone topsy-turvy, whose *ma'at* had been replaced by chaos. It was also a period of leveling, when even pharaoh was proved to be humanly fallible and could be blamed for his evident shortcomings. Curiously enough, the nobles now claimed immortality for themselves independent of the kings, as evidenced by the inclusion in their coffins of documents like the pyramid texts. These were passports to the other world that had previously been used only by kings. In fact, the funeral ritual of the kings could theoretically be used by any good person, perhaps even the lowest peasant. In any case, the dead had to be judged righteous by the court of the dead, presided over by Osiris. For a time, it even seemed as if Egypt might move toward a kind of social equality emphasizing humanitarian justice, but this ultimately was not to be.

Dynasties XI-XII. The reunion of Egypt under one dynasty, the Eleventh, marks the beginning of the Middle Kingdom (2040 B.C.). Under the following dynasty, the Twelfth, ruling from Lisht, the government realistically adjusted itself to the experiences of the past and consolidated its position. The brilliant first king of the dynasty, Amenhemhet I, was a nonroyal ex-vizier who bolstered his reign by sponsoring and disseminating a kind of propaganda literature asserting the legitimacy of his rule. The nobles recognized the advantage of a single ruler, a system that during the Old Kingdom had prevented civil war and foreign invasion. Yet the king did not at first attempt to destroy the power of the nobles (until Sesostris III), (1878-1843), and thus there was a certain degree of feudalism. The nomarchs still had great authority within their nomes and over the villages, although their power was gradually curbed as they were rotated in office. The judges were appointed by the king, and appeals were permitted to the royal judicial court at the capital. The nomarchs were required to remit the royal share of the taxes to the king promptly. The king also had agents—known as the "Eyes and Ears of the King"—who traveled throughout the realm, enforced his will, and reported to him.

Under the Middle Kingdom, Egypt rose to a peak of power and prosperity. Kings of the Twelfth Dynasty beautified Thebes and Lisht, supported the economic life of the country, and slowly curtailed the power of the nobles, and centralization of power depending on the pharaoh culminated under Sesostris III. Under this dynasty Nubia was conquered and annexed. The land was policed by a series of fortresses, and the rule was harsh; a boundary stone has been found that prohibited the immigration of Nubians into Egypt except for purposes of trade.

The Middle Kingdom witnessed an unparalleled expansion of foreign commerce throughout the Near East and elsewhere. In particular, trade with Punt, Syria, Cyprus, and Crete enriched the royal treasury. The mines of Sinai, gold from Nubia, revenues from the quarries and lands of Egypt were other important sources of the pharaoh's immense income. The army that now protected Egypt was made up of troops in the nomes.

The Fayum. The new era of prosperity enabled the kings of the Twelfth Dynasty to inaugurate a large reclamation program. Of lasting value to Egypt was the addition of thousands of acres of arable land in an oasis just west of the Nile and south of Memphis. This area is now known as the Fayum. The overflow of the Nile each year passed through a natural cut into the Fayum but receded as the river fell. Dams and irrigation canals were built, with a twofold result: the overflow could be kept and used for irrigating the land; and the surplus could be stored and released during the driest months for use along the Nile farther north. The Fayum became one of the most fertile and popular areas of Egypt. A great temple within it—consisting of a pyramid amid colonnades and halls—was known to the Greeks as the Labyrinth; and the natural lake that had been there since prehistoric times was called by them Lake Moeris. The Twelfth Dynasty carefully regulated its in- and out-flow.

Art. Heliopolis, the City of the Sun, grew rapidly at this time, but unfortunately its great temples, including the famous Temple of the Sun, have not survived. The construction of pyramids was renewed; the fabric could not approach the splendor of the Old Kingdom, although the chambers were carved with even greater skill. The Middle Kingdom is known as the classical period of Egyptian art and literature, and yet the achievements were uneven, when compared with those of the past. Ever greater colossal statues were made, remarkable for size, for a new spirit of realism, and for new conceptions; on the whole, sculpture and painting, like architecture, were tied to the past. The minor arts, and especially jewelry, were a notable exception and proclaim the ability and taste of the Egyptian craftsman, as do the fine chests, beds, and chairs. The tombs differ from those of the Old Kingdom, for instead of clustering around a pharaoh's pyramid (in the hope of sharing his immortality), they are confidently cut in the cliffs on both sides of the Nile; Abydos, a short distance down the river from Thebes, was a veritable necropolis. The painted reliefs continued to stress merrymaking, hunting, and the abundance of life.

Literature.   Egyptian literature during the Middle Kingdom tried to recapture some of the complacency and optimism characteristic of the Old Kingdom. Once again the good life was equated with royal favor rather than with self-sufficiency, indicating the prizing of peace and law more than individual human life. The literature reflects a sense of assurance and special election in the world. It is both introspective and cheerfully urbane. A continuing feature of literature and art is the display of the Egyptian sense of humor. Puns abound in the hieroglyphics of the period; humor appears even in the pyramid texts, and there is laughter among the gods. In short, the literature reflects a cheerful refusal to be absolutely rigorous and dogmatic, the feeling that Egyptians were, after all, God's chosen people.

Many of the religious texts, rituals, and magic spells of the Middle Kingdom were later brought together in a collection known as the Book of the Dead. Kings took pleasure in having their achievements and virtues recorded on temple walls and columns; private persons, according to their means, had such inscriptions carved on their own tombs and on stelae.

There were also simple songs of shepherds, threshers, and other classes of laborers; religious poems; hymns to the gods; and songs of love. To the collections of stories that taught some useful or moral lesson were added entertaining tales of travel and adventure—such as the famous story of the shipwrecked sailor, Sinuhe—historical accounts of military campaigns, and records of important events.

Religion.   The Middle Kingdom also saw a marked development in religion. Hitherto the national deity had been Re, the sun god, whose winged disk was so conspicuous in art. The Twelfth Dynasty, however, elevated its own patron god to the headship of the national religion; this was Amon, the ram-headed god of Thebes. The two gods were united, and in the future the chief god of the state was Amon-Re. Egyptian religion had always encouraged justice and honesty, but now, following the experience of the First Intermediate Period, religion was democratized. Paralleling the ethical theme that runs through the literature, everyone was allowed to hope for immortality. During the Old Kingdom, the dead king became Osiris; under the Middle Kingdom, however, every deceased Egyptian became Osiris.

The kings of the Twelfth Dynasty, who protected and fostered this extraordinary civilization, were followed by weak rulers. There were, after all, still basic weaknesses in the Egyptian government, and the Thirteenth Dynasty could not cope

with harem conspiracies, a reassertion of local independence by the nomarchs, and
the usurpation of pharaonic authority by viziers. Upper and Lower Egypt split
apart and were ruled by rival dynasties, the Thirteenth and Fourteenth. This situation invited attack by the Libyans and even more importantly by certain Asians to
the northeast, bringing about the era generally known as the Second Intermediate
Period.

THE SECOND INTERMEDIATE PERIOD (CA. 1785-1560 B.C.)

The Hyksos. The term *Hikau-Khasut,* or *Hyksos,* means "chieftains of a foreign
hill country" and thus designates not a race of people but their rulers. They apparently were a mixed bag of displaced persons, largely Semitic (primarily Amoritic,
but possibly also numbering some Hebrews), from Syria and Palestine. They were
pressed south by other invaders to their own north, the Hurrians. They entered
Egypt in about 1674 B.C., conquered Lisht in about 1640, and established the Fifteenth and Sixteenth Dynasties with their capital in the eastern Delta region at
Avaris/Tanis, where traces of their large camps survive. Hyksos rulers assumed
pharaonic regalia and viewed the traditional "legal" Egyptian kings—restricted to
Thebes and Upper Egypt in what was to become the Seventeenth Dynasty—as
merely chieftains. The Hyksos owed their success to the following factors: they
were more mobile than their enemy, since they had learned from Indo-Europeans
to use horses and chariots; they also used a very strong, composite-laminated bow
and had a new type of bronze sword and new fortification techniques.

The Hyksos occupation was remembered by subsequent generations of Egyptians
as a period of their own most abject national humiliation. Later Egyptian tradition
consistently portrayed the Hyksos as bloody, uncouth savages who "ruled without
Re." Actually things were not as disastrous as all that, and the Second Intermediate
Period was probably not as bad as the First. Egyptian bureaucracy remained intact,
and famine was apparently not as widespread. The Hyksos may even have tried to
win over the Egyptians; their kings at least used *Re* elements in their names, which
suggests an accommodation to Egyptian religion. The Hyksos flourished on commerce, and the ubiquity of their pottery and weapons in Egypt indicates that their
rather lively trade continued. What the Hyksos wanted above all was tribute; most
nomarchs gave it to them, including the nomarch of Thebes.

The nomarchs of Thebes became the Seventeenth Dynasty (ca. 1650-1558).
Learning how to use the new military techniques against the Hyksos themselves and
securing the aid of Nubian auxiliaries, they made outstanding progress under their
last king, Kamoses, who pushed the Hyksos back to the vicinity of Memphis itself.
He did not totally drive them out before his death, however.

THE NEW KINGDOM (1560-1085 B.C.)

Dynasties XVIII-XX. The final expulsion of the Hyksos was accomplished by
Kamoses' brother, Ahmose, founder of the Eighteenth Dynasty, Egypt's most bril-

liant. The Eighteenth Dynasty began where the Twelfth had left off, with a much publicized reversion to *ma'at*. But now there was a new vision of creating effective frontiers far abroad, a vision no longer limited to the Nile Valley. Inscriptions and literature refer constantly to "our army"; they also express a desire to revenge recent humiliation by attaining domination over foreign peoples and taking loot, at first through punitive raids beyond the frontiers and then through direct incorporation of foreign lands into an Egyptian empire. One of the by-products of this imperialism was the first emergence of a significantly large class of slaves, made up of prisoners of war.

The Eighteenth Dynasty could embark on such ambitious schemes because the administrative machinery had survived the Hyksos. For the first time, a standing professional army was created, incidentally creating another avenue for the social advancement of the lower classes. The kings, now first called pharaohs by their contemporaries, were great generals, and proud of it. Their inscriptions brag ingenuously of their physical strength and of their skill as archers and hunters. Generally speaking, Egyptian imperialism created vested interests within the state that supported continued militarism, as much loot went to the soldiers and to support the priesthood of Amon-Re.

Ahmose, the reuniter of Egypt, expelled the Hyksos and pushed as far north as Sharvhen. He had to stop there and turn south to crush a revolt in Nubia, where he appointed a special viceroy. During the reign of Ahmose, the influx of booty and tribute and the collection of duties on foreign trade pumped wealth into the country and effected a marked rise in the Egyptian standard of living. Increasing influence was exercised over Ahmose by the chief priest of Amon-Re. Indeed, beginning with his reign, the power of that priesthood began to increase markedly, as evidenced by the growing size of that cult's temples. The economic power of the cult was to become a problem, eventually threatening the stability of the dynasty itself.

Amenhotep I (1533-1512) succeeded Ahmose and continued his father's policy of internal consolidation. He patronized the priesthood of the Amon-Re cult by recommencing the building of the temple at Karnak on a grand scale. He was the first to separate his tomb from his mortuary chapel to hide his true burial place.

The first daughter of Amenhotep I married his leading general, who through her succeeded to the kingship as Thutmosis I (1512-1500). His reign was notable for a campaign up to the Euphrates against the Mitanni, who fled at his approach, so great was the reputation of the Egyptian war machine. He also fought against Nubia as far as the fifth cataract. (At about this time, central African Negroes appear for the first time in the sources.) There is clearer evidence under his reign than previously for the emergence of a military-priestly complex that put pressure on pharaoh to continue his conquests.

The short reign of Thutmosis II (1500-1490) is interesting chiefly as a prelude to subsequent events. Thutmosis II, like his predecessor, was not a royal son but a general, married to pharaoh's first daughter, in this case the famous Hatshepsut.

The next pharaoh was Thutmosis III (1490-1436), Egypt's greatest militarist of any epoch, sometimes called the "Egyptian Napoleon." Son of one of his father's minor wives and a child at his accession, he was completely dominated by the ambitious Hatshepsut for over twenty years. She first acted as his regent but then claimed to be pharaoh in her own right, Thutmosis III becoming junior co-regent. She was depicted wearing the double crown of Upper and Lower Egypt, in male attire, and wearing a beard (see p. 61). Her chief adviser, and possibly her lover, was the architect Senmut. Some have seen in her policies a conflict with the imperialist "party" and a return to the "internal" policies characteristic of the Twelfth and earlier dynasties. If so, she presumably alienated factions in the bureaucracy and the army. In any case, her peaceful reign was characterized by the fostering of foreign trade and a notable expedition to Punt. She did much building and restoring, especially at Karnak. Her mortuary temple at Deir el Bahri, built under Senmut's guidance, is generally recognized as a consummate example of Egyptian architecture.

In the meantime, Thutmosis III had been in training as a soldier for about twenty years and was surely as ambitious as Hatshepsut. In 1469 he asserted himself, and Hatshepsut fell. Her fate is unknown, but her inscriptions were eventually mutilated and she became a nonperson. Within two months of taking over, Thutmosis III had his army mobilized for the first of a series of mighty military expeditions, which were repeated every summer for many years, chiefly in the Levant. It would appear that Hatshepsut's pacific foreign policy had been interpreted by Syrian and other princes as a sign of Egyptian weakness, and her rule in that area seemed threatened. In 1468 Thutmosis defeated the opposing coalition at Megiddo and demanded treaties promising fealty and tribute from the vanquished rulers. Egyptian garrisons and military governors were established throughout the Levant. Thutmosis allegedly took back to Egypt 330 princely sons as hostages to be educated and then eventually returned to rule their homeland as future puppet kings. His claim that he also took a like number of princely daughters as wives strains credulity, but in any case his harem probably did swell as part of the diplomatic aftermath of the war. By the end of his reign, he could boast that there were 500 kings "on Egypt's water"—that is to say, paying tribute—an exaggerated number, no doubt, but an indication of his claims to imperial glory.

His son and successor, Amenhotep II (1436-1412) is known as the "Sporting King," since he emphasized his ability as an archer, a rower, and a horseman. He conducted several Asian campaigns, including one against a mysterious people called the Khapiru, who were apparently outcasts or bandits belonging to no particular ethnic group.

The Egyptian Empire reached its political and military height under Amenhotep II's son, Thutmosis IV (1412-1402). The existence of a kind of *Pax Egyptica* existed in the southwestern Near East is indicated by the fact that Egypt's power went unchallenged during this peaceful decade.

The economic prosperity of Egypt apparently peaked under Amenhotep III (1402-1363), whose reign was almost as peaceful, although subtle changes in the political balance of power were taking place beyond the frontiers. Notable were his buildings at Karnak and Luxor, as well as certain changes in art, foreshadowing by a generation the so-called Amarna revolution. This newer art had more vivacity and movement than was normal to the Egyptian tradition, and it may reflect the many cosmopolitan influences that the kingdom experienced during its imperial heyday.

FIGURE 14. Hatshepsut, Pharaoh of Egypt, bearded, in the form of a sphinx. From her temple at Deir el Bahri, Thebes. 18th Dynasty.

Indeed, the Egyptian imperial period in general has sometimes been called an age of internationalism, which modified Egyptian culture in many ways. The influx of thousands of slaves, especially Semites, helped change the classical Middle Egyptian language. The presence of so many foreigners at court and elsewhere largely accounts, no doubt, for the development of a new and lively vernacular language replete with many Semitic loan words. The greater ease of communication and commercial intercourse, as well as the prolonged residence abroad of Egyptians in military and other capacities, also produced a widespread syncretism of Egyptian and foreign, especially Canaanite, gods.

By the early fourteenth century, although Egyptian power was at its height, one senses an underlying flux and instability. These movements were to surface dramatically under the next pharaoh, Amenhotep IV.

The Amarna Period. Almost everything about Amenhotep IV (soon to become Akhenaten), including his regnal dates (1378-1362? or 1364-1347?) is controversial. He was pharaoh's son by Queen Tiye, herself of a military family; he married Nefertiti, probably the daughter of a general of the chariotry. He *may,* according to one regnal dating, have held a co-regency with his father during the latter's last years, when he was ailing. He *may* have been pathological and subject to Froehlich's Syndrome, which results in infantile genitals, fatness, feminine body shape, and a grotesque lantern jaw, for he is depicted that way on monuments in the new art style.

In his fourth regnal year, he rejected the cult of Amon-Re and embraced that of

FIGURE 15. Fragment of
a pillar of Amenhotep IV
(Akhenaten) found at
Karnak.

The Granger Collection

the sun disk or aten, changing his name to Akhenaten ("serviceable to the sun
disk") and shortly thereafter removing his residence to a remote, virgin area on the
Nile, which he christened Akhataten ("horizon of the sun disk"), now known by its
modern name, Tell-el-Amarna. Much has been made of this "monotheism," yet in
truth Egyptian gods had always easily changed names and shapes, as in the case of
Amon-Re himself. Furthermore, since the Fourteenth Dynasty, priests had interpreted the solar cult universally, as the "sole god who has made himself for eter-
nity," and already under Amenhotep III, the aten had been worshiped in similar
terms. Akhenaten's Atenism, if religious "reform" it was, was thus by no means
unprecedented.

   The traditional view sees Akhenaten's dismissing the priests of Amon-Re, worshiping the aten as the universal lord and creator, and emphasizing to an unprecedented degree the practice of *ma'at*. Again, according to this view, Akhenaten
sought to destroy polytheism by hacking out the names of the gods and was, in

FIGURE 16. Portrait of Nefertiti, wife of Akhenaten; 14th century B.C.

FIGURE 17. Polychrome
limestone stele of Amen-
hotep IV (Akhenaten)
with Nefertiti and their
three eldest daughters, c.
1364 B.C.

The Granger Collection

short, the first monotheist in history. A pacifist solely interested in his religious
reforms, he neglected foreign policy, which meant that Egypt's control over her
empire weakened.

Recent scholarship suggests that this view can be drastically modified. There were
actually two gods in the Amarna period. Akhenaten and his family worshiped the
sun disk; everybody else worshiped Akhenaten, the son of the sun disk. There is no
indication that Atenism penetrated beneath the royal family and the royal court.
Akhenaten's own famous "Hymn to the Solar Disk," sometimes cited as the first
"monotheistic" document in history, with putative influence on the much later
development of Hebrew monotheism and even on the conception of Psalm 104,
seems actually to have been nothing of the sort.

Atenism, whatever its precise nature, seems to have lacked an ethical content;
the hymn suggests that the rewards of its worship were solely physical and life-
sustaining. The artistic innovations, which grotesquely caricature the king, seem to
have been limited to the royal family and the court. They may be explained simply
by pharaoh's wanting his deformities depicted to distinguish him from common
humanity.

FIGURE 18. King Tutankhamen's death mask from his tomb, c. 1338 B.C.

Possibly, Akhenaten receives too much blame for the difficulties then being experienced by Egyptian foreign policy. The evidence comes from the so-called Amarna letters, some 350 tablets consisting mainly of dispatches from Levantine puppet rulers to the Egyptian court, many of them requesting defense or complaining that none has been given them. Some of these complaints actually predate Akhenaten's reign. Perhaps the most that can be said is that he should have undertaken a Syrian expedition at some point. But his foreign policy was surely passive, rather than pacifist as a point of religious doctrine, and thus was little different ethically from that of his two immediate predecessors.

Atenism was abandoned and the old cults restored in the fourth year of the reign of the boy king, Tutankhamen (1347–1338), immortalized by the discovery in 1922 of his virtually intact tomb. After the brief reign of Nefertiti's father, Aye, the kingship went to the general Horemhab (1333–1303), who established the Nineteenth Dynasty. Horemhab especially favored the traditional establishment by lavishing tax-exempt lands on temples. He in turn was followed by Ramses I and his son, Seti I, who, as a vigorous general, repelled Libyan invaders and won back southern Syria.

Ramses II (1298-1232 B.C.). Magnificence on a grand scale returned to Egypt with the long reign of the great Ramses II. It was a magnificence that cared little for

FIGURE 19. Fresco of maid-servants attending ladies at a banquet. From tomb of Vizier Rekhmiré, 18th Dynasty.

The Granger Collection

taste and understood it less; rather, as under some earlier kings also, it loved the grandiose and the colossal. The omnipotent and divine pharaoh, in his conceit, put his name on ancient statues, occasionally reworking the face to resemble himself. Buildings were restored, others ransacked for his own structures. At Thebes he built an enormous temple known as the Ramesseum; at Karnak he completed one of the largest buildings in the world, where one hundred people can stand on the capital of a column in the great hypostyle hall.

Ramses II was, withal, a man of personal bravery. It was this quality that saved an Egyptian army from annihilation in 1287, when the Hittites ambushed him at Kadesh on the Orontes. Ramses had hoped to win back Syria from the Hittites, but it was a vain hope, and he and the Hittite king, Hattushil, drew up a famous mutual defense treaty dividing Syria between them in 1267 (see page 71).

Ramses II's son and successor, Merneptah, himself something of a military genius, was able to crush both the Lybians and the Sea Peoples. Thereafter the Nineteenth Dynasty collapsed because of internal squabbling among Merneptah's descendants.

Ramses III. The last important pharaoh of ancient Egypt, Ramses III, the second king of the Twentieth Dynasty, reigned from 1198 to 1167 B.C. He was both a builder and a warrior. He repelled continuing attacks by the Lybians and the Sea

FIGURE 20. The cultivation of wheat; from an Egyptian tomb painting, 18th Dynasty.

The Granger Collection

Peoples (originating, perhaps, in the Aegean area) and enlisted his defeated foes in the Egyptian army as mercenaries. After his death in 1167 B.C., Egypt's internal difficulties increased. Under the later kings of the Twentieth Dynasty, new feuding within the royal family was increasingly decentralizing, since it permitted the priests of Amon-Re to increase their power at the expense of the pharaoh. Renewed Libyan invasion and, possibly, failure of the Nile brought on economic crises and severe inflation, which were complicated by widespread corruption in the government. Ultimately, the loss of Egypt's Asian domains, especially the mines in the Sinai, and the continued disruptions of international trade by the Sea Peoples transformed economic crisis to economic collapse. With the fall of the Twentieth Dynasty (ca. 1085), the New Kingdom came to an end. Thereafter the Ramessid military policy based on foreign empire and international cooperation was generally abandoned, and ultimately Egypt was overrun by Libyans and other foreigners (ca. 945 B.C.). Egypt's great chapter in history was concluded. On the neighboring continent of Asia, meanwhile, momentous developments had been taking place.

5

Asia Minor, Syria, and Palestine

THE HITTITES

The Indo-Europeans. It seems likely that invaders known as Indo-Europeans settled in large parts of the world from the Atlantic to India about 2000 B.C. Racially they were as thoroughly mixed as any people can be, but the languages they spoke had a common ancestor. Thus, for example, our word *father* is *pitar* in both Sanskrit (the classical language of India) and ancient Persian, πατήρ *(pater)* in Greek, *pater* in Latin, *Vater* in German, and similarly through kindred tongues. It is clear that once upon a time the so-called Indo-Europeans had a common home— whether it was in eastern Europe, central Asia, or the steppes of Russia is unknown—and that as they separated they kept many of the essential elements of their speech, though not their ethnic entity. Nomads worshiping a great god of the sky, they had the horse and wheeled cart, which was destined to develop into the war chariot. Their society was patriarchal and monogamous.

Asia Minor. Before 2000 B.C. a group of Indo-Europeans known as Hittites overran much of Asia Minor. This part of Hither Asia—or Anatolia, as it is sometimes called—consists of a great plateau rimmed by high mountains. Though the Taurus Mountains and the Armenian highlands hindered access to Syria, Mesopotamia, and Iran, there were passes (especially by way of the Cicilian Gates) that facilitated trade; and Asia Minor became, in a sense, a bridge between the East and the worlds of the Aegean Sea and the Danube River (cf. map, rear endpaper). Gold and silver mines, more notably iron mines, were its chief natural assets. Long before the arrival of the Hittites, Asia Minor and Mesopotamia had been in communication with each other, but the distinctive civilization of Asia Minor and neighboring Armenia dates from the Hittite invasion.

Hittite Expansion. The capital of the kingdom that the Hittites created in Galatia in Asia Minor was located at Hattusha (modern Boghazkhy or Bogazköy), a bleak spot not far from the Halys, the great river that rises in eastern Anatolia and after a westward sweep flows into the Black Sea (see map, p. 70). In the beginning the political expansion of the Hittites into Syria was resisted by the Egyptians, and into Mesopotamia by the Mitanni, who were in eastern Syria and Western Mesopotamia. Shortly after 1600 B.C., the Hittites descended briefly upon Babylon, sacked the

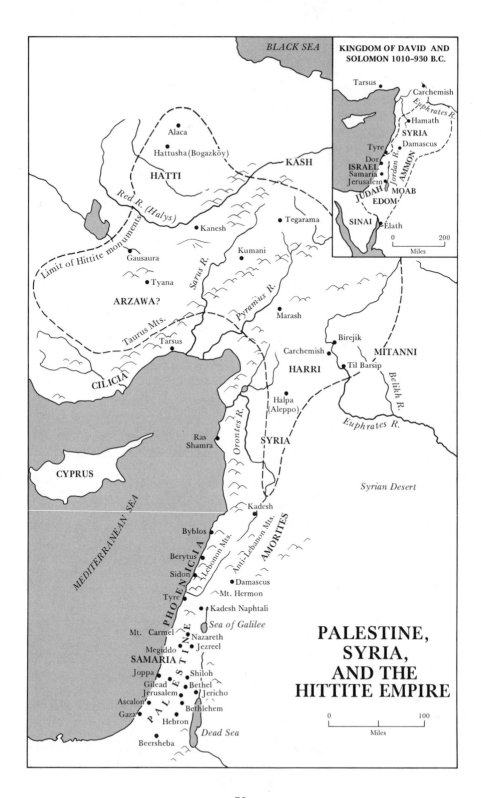

BLACK SEA

KINGDOM OF DAVID AND
SOLOMON 1010–930 B.C.

Tarsus

Carchemish

Euphrates R.

Hamath

SYRIA

Tyre
Dor
Damascus
ISRAEL
Samaria
Jerusalem
AMMON
JUDAH
MOAB
EDOM
Jordan R.
SINAI
Elath

0   200
Miles

Alaca

Hattusha (Bogazköy)

KASH

HATTI

Red R. (Halys)

Limit of Hittite monuments

Kanesh

Tegarama

ARZAWA?

Gausaura

Tyana

Kumani

Sarus R.

Pyramus R.

Marash

Taurus Mts.

Tarsus

Birejik

Carchemish

MITANNI

Til Barsip

HARRI

CILICIA

Halpa
(Aleppo)

SYRIA

Euphrates R.

Belikh R.

Ras
Shamra

Orontes R.

CYPRUS

Syrian Desert

MEDITERRANEAN SEA

Kadesh

Byblos

AMORITES

Berytus

Lebanon Mts.

Anti-Lebanon Mts.

Sidon

Damascus

Tyre

Mt. Hermon

PHOENICIA

Kadesh Naphtali

Sea of Galilee

Mt. Carmel

Nazareth

Megiddo

Jezreel

SAMARIA

Joppa

Shiloh

Gilead

Bethel

PALESTINE

Jerusalem

Jericho

Ascalon

Gaza

Bethlehem

Hebron

Dead Sea

Beersheba

PALESTINE,
SYRIA,
AND THE
HITTITE EMPIRE

0   100
Miles

city, and withdrew; it was then that other invaders, the Kassites, created their own Babylonian dynasty. Our information allows us to follow the varying fortunes of the Hittites in some detail until 1400 B.C., when their kingdom became a strong power. The archives from Boghazkhy emphasize the large size of the contemporary world and its domination by important states, whose rulers corresponded with one another, drew up treaties, and intermarried. From the far-off Agean, Minoan Crete and subsequently Mycenaean Greece (see map, p. 100) sent their ships and wares eastward; strong Mycenaean influences, for example, mingled with Sumerian culture on the Phoenician coast at Ras Shamra (ancient Ugarit). Hittite relations with the rather distant Egyptian pharaohs were not infrequently cordial.

Nearer home the Mitanni—and especially their important vassal cities of Carchemish and Aleppo—sought peace with the Hittite king. The Mitanni, who had an Indo-European ruling class, were important neighbors of the Hittites. They controlled the arch of the Fertile Crescent, which they occupied in about 1600 B.C. They ruled over both Semites and a people called Hurrians, who were neither Semites nor Indo-Europeans. Mitanni culture was essentially Mesopotamian. Something of their history can be reconstructed, since they appear so frequently in Hittite records.

Soon after 1400 B.C., however, Shuppiluliuma, greatest of Hittite conquerors, crossed the Taurus Mountains, overwhelmed the Mitanni, and incorporated Carchemish and Aleppo into his empire. He even wrested northern Syria from Egypt during Akhenaten's reign. Later on Ramses II tried to win northern Syria from Egypt but failed at the battle of Kadesh (1287 B.C.). The destruction of the kingdom of the Mitanni, however, exposed the eastern frontier of the Hittites to the growing power of Assyria, and the new Hittite king, Hattushili III, wisely sought and obtained a treaty of permanent peace and alliance with Ramses (1267 B.C.). The treaty, which called the thousand gods to witness, divided Syria between them, reaffirmed previous treaties, and provided for a defensive alliance and for the extradition of political refugees and immigrants, who, however, were to be treated humanely. Two copies of this treaty have been found in Egypt, and another was found among the cuneiform archives of Boghazkhy, a remarkable achievement of modern archaeological scholarship.

Some time after the treaty, however, the Hittites declined. They faced incursions of the same Sea Peoples who were attacking Egypt. Except in southeastern Anatolia and Syria, where traces of their civilization lingered on for some centuries, the Hittite kingdom was wiped out completely by about 1200 B.C.

Government. The Hittite kingdom was an empire consisting of the Hittite core in Cappadocia and of vassals and temple, or priestly, states elsewhere in Asia Minor or at a distance. The dependent states enjoyed local government but had no voice in foreign policy; they were united to the central government by treaties that contained long and, for us, very valuable historical preambles. At the top of the government stood the king. As the Hittite power increased, however, the kings adopted the ways of their eastern neighbors and became despotic. From 1400 B.C. the king was an absolute ruler, whose sacred nature was symbolized by the winged Egyptian sun disk. He had a harem, though his queen had considerable authority. Surrounding the king were nobles and priests; the soldiers enjoyed a privileged position, and beneath them were the artisans and peasants, many of whom were serfs.

Economy. Agriculture was vital to the Hittites, but probably the grazing of flocks and herds formed the economic basis of their life. Mining, including iron, gave the Hittite economy its peculiar stamp. In the archives of Boghazkhy are many pleas from Egyptian and other rulers for more, ever more, iron weapons. The products of the Hittites traveled far and wide, southward across the Taurus and westward beyond the Bosporus. Horses were used not only for transport but also for military purposes.

Culture. The Hittites adopted Babylonian cuneiform writing. Their code of laws, however, was not as severe as the Babylonian code and stipulated, more often than not, a monetary fine instead of the death penalty. Hittite religion included a multiplicity of gods, including the Great Mother goddess, an earth goddess of fertility, whose worship was indigenous to Asia Minor. A weather god (Teshub, as he was called) and deities of the sun and the moon were other important deities in the pantheon. The German excavations at Boghazkhy show that the temples and palaces, while exhibiting skill in masonry, were ruder and far less luxurious than other contemporary palaces, as we should expect from the simple social apparatus of the Hittites as a whole. The sculptures of gods, people, and animals are in both relief and the round. They are frequently of large size and are portentously solemn and heavy, and they give us a good idea of the appearance of the Hittites, a people with high foreheads and hooked noses, dressed in conical caps and boots with upturned toes. Iron weapons, horses, and chariots were their special delight, and they enclosed their spacious imperial capital, as they did all their cities, with massive fortifications.

THE PHOENICIANS

Syria and Palestine. The land of Syria and Palestine has an average breadth of less than a hundred miles and stretches along the eastern coast of the Mediterranean, from the Taurus Mountains in the north to the desert just above the Egyptian Delta, for a distance of approximately four hundred miles (see map, p. 70). To the northeast, across the Fertile Crescent, is the Euphrates, to the east the Syrian Desert. Syria occupies the northern and larger part of this area, Palestine (or Canaan, as it was first called) the southern. In northern Syria the Lebanon Mountains, which attain a height of more than ten thousand feet, come very close to the sea, and the narrow coastal plain was known in antiquity as Phoenicia. East of the Lebanon Mountains is another, parallel range, the Antilebanon, and beyond it, commanding a trade route to Mesopotamia, Damascus. The Jordan River rises in the Antilebanon, flows southward to the Sea of Galilee, and thereafter, at a level below the Mediterranean, empties into the Dead Sea, which has no outlet. The coastal plain is broader in Palestine than in Syria, but the mountains so crowded the ancient inhabitants of both areas against the sea that it was inevitable that they should take to trade and commerce. The soil, north and south, is not fertile; indeed, except for the famous cedars of Lebanon, the natural assets of Syria and Palestine are poor. The Egyptians, Babylonians, and Hittites, nevertheless, fought over this land, both for its wood and for the control of its coast and important trade routes. Conquest was relatively easy for them, because the mountains divided the people into small communities, but as a result of the marching armies, and the traders who came with or without them, foreign influences poured into Syria and Palestine.

Rise of Phoenicia. At an early date Semitic tribes left their homes in the desert for the Mediterranean coast. Some of these nomads were Amorites, who came to Syria before their subsequent invasion of Mesopotamia, where Hammurabi was to create his empire. Other tribes settling in Syria and Palestine became known to history as Canaanites, Aramaeans, and Hebrews. The Greeks called the Semites who occupied the coastal strip in the north Phoenicians, "redskins," because of their swarthy complexions. The opportunity for the Phoenicians to play a dominant role in history derived from the fact that the Minoan–Mycenaean civilization collapsed at approximately the same time that the eastern empires lost their power. This collapse left the Mediterranean without a commercial leader, but by 1000 B.C., when the entire ancient world was entering the Iron Age, the Phoenicians filled that role on the sea. They maintained their leadership until the eighth century B.C., when they lost their freedom to the Assyrians and some of their trade to the Greeks.

All the Phoenician cities—such as Sidon, Tyre, Beirut, and Byblos—were small, monarchical city-states, though in defense of their country they often acted together. One of their oldest cities was Sidon, but after 1000 B.C., Tyre became the most important. It was safely located on an island a few hundred yards offshore, had excellent harbors and boasted fine temples and palaces. Hiram, Tyre's king in the tenth century B.C., was an ally of Solomon.

Culture. The Phoenicians had a considerable literature of their own. They were also masters at imitation. Not only was their culture influenced by the Egyptians and Babylonians, but the products of their workshops were copied from others. These products, nevertheless, were very fine and were eagerly bought by the outside world: bronze armor and weapons, war chariots, gold and silver vessels, inlaid furniture, glass, and brightly colored pottery. Most famous were their purple dyes and textiles. The slopes of the coastal plain sufficed for pasturage but yielded little grain. The Phoenicians cut the cedars on the mountains behind their cities, used some of the wood for their own houses and ships, and exported the rest to Egypt and Mesopotamia. It was this lack of natural resources that forced the Phoenicians to industry and trade.

Trade. Phoenician merchants traveled far and wide—we meet them, for example, in the pages of Homer—but the Phoenician colonies were unusual in that they were primarily trading stations, founded for the exploitation of natural resources rather than as true settlements; where circumstances favored, they grew into cities. Thus the Phoenicians were attracted to Cyprus by its rich mines of copper, to Spain for its mineral wealth, to Gaul for hides, by Baltic amber, by British tin, and by other products that traveled down the valley of the Rhone. Ultimately these skillful sailors passed through Gibraltar and continued to the northern coast of Spain. Of all the Phoenician settlements in the Mediterranean—Gades (Cadiz), Utica, and

1	2	3	4	5
𐤀	A	A	A	A
9	B	B	8	B
⌐	Λ	⟨	⟩	C
◿	Δ	D	◁	D
⧢	E	E	⧢	E
Y	F	F	⅄	F
⊥	I	I	I	Z
目	日	日	目	H
⊕	⊕	⊕	⊗	
₹				
⅄	K	K	⅄	K
∟	L	L	∟	L
⧢	M	M	⧢	M
⅄	⌐	⌐	∨	N
∓			⊞	X
O	O	O	O	O
⌐	Γ	Γ	⌐	P
⌐			M	(S)
φ	φ	φ	φ	Q
◁	P	R	◁	R
W	S	S	S	S
✝	T	T	✝	T
	Υ	Y	V	V
	φ	φ	φ	
	X	✝	✝	

Early alphabets. 1: a schematic representation of a North Semitic alphabet; 2: early Attic Greek; 3: western Euboic colonies; 4: Etruscan; and 5: Roman. Roman C and F were pronounced differently from similarly shaped letters in their horizontal rows; Roman Y and Z are late additions from Greek, and G is a Latin innovation. Not all details of the development of the alphabet are precisely fixed, but the progression as a whole is from North Semitic to Greek generally, and then from Western Greek to Etruscan and Roman. There were also variations of certain letter shapes and sounds within the alphabets shown here. The earliest known Greek was written in the syllabary which is called Linear B.

others—none was so favored by nature as Carthage. This colony was founded in the eighth century B.C. on the northern coast of Africa across from Sicily. Enjoying a large harbor and a remarkably fertile hinterland, Carthage was midway between Spain and Phoenicia and within an easy sail of Sicily, Sardinia, Spain, and elsewhere. These activities ultimately brought Carthage into rivalry and conflict, first with the Greeks and then with the Romans.

The Alphabet. Wherever the Phoenicians went, they carried the products of eastern industry, the Babylonian system of weights and measures, and other useful knowledge. Middlemen though they were, they may be described as the propagators of civilization. Their most valuable gift to Europe was the alphabet; they did not invent it, but they did spread a knowledge of it, as they did of Egyptian papyrus, pen, and ink. The new alphabet and writing materials, so very superior in their simplicity to cuneiform script and heavy clay tablets, quickened intellectual life.

The origin and development of the alphabet that the Phoenicians spread are still shrouded in mystery, but our earliest significant evidence consists of Semitic inscriptions cut in the mines of the Sinai Peninsula, perhaps in the nineteenth century B.C. These signs—Egyptian hieroglyphics and other symbols were adopted—were developed in Phoenicia during the succeeding centuries, until by the eleventh century B.C. the alphabet consisted of twenty-two letters, each representing a Semitic consonant. Probably in the eighth century B.C. the Greeks adopted the new alphabet from the Phoenicians; they changed it somewhat to suit their own language and chose certain consonants by which to indicate the vowels. The Etruscans and the Romans made slight changes in the Greek alphabet, which in its Roman form has come down to us (see the chart, p. 74).

The Aramaeans. The alphabet and other achievements of Eastern civilization, which the Phoenicians spread across the sea, were carried overland by the Aramaeans. The Aramaeans were Semites from the desert who settled in northern Mesopotamia, Syria, and Palestine. Damascus was their most important city. Because of their control of ancient trade routes, the Aramaeans were able to become merchants. Wherever they went, they took the alphabet and their language with them. Long after their conquest by the Assyrians in the eighth century B.C., they remained traders, and their language became an international tongue for the Semitic world. It was Aramaic that Christ and his disciples spoke, though the Hebrew writers of the New Testament wrote in the new international language of their day, Greek.

THE HEBREWS

The Old Testament. The Old Testament, on the other hand, was composed in Hebrew over a long period of time, perhaps from the thirteenth to the third centuries B.C. It is, so to speak, a national library of tradition, history, proverbs, songs, and prophecy, written to glorify Yahweh and to show the plan of his dealings with men. Composed in magnificent prose and poetry by a creative and intellectual people, the Old Testament reveals Israel's deep religious insight and her high standards of ethics. Perhaps it is astonishing that such profound thought, which stood head and shoulders above any other literature of the Near East, should have come from the Hebrews, a people materially and militarily inferior, who were late arrivals in a small and poor, though already an ancient, land. Equally surprising, perhaps, is the optimism and hope of a people who at some times suffered greatly and at others were almost obliterated by Assyria and Babylon.

The Old Testament describes Israel's career in a world setting; that is to say, its central theme is history on a grand scale, which begins with nothing less than Creation. The narrators of early Hebrew history sought those principles that determine events and hence act as guides in contemporary life. First, they ascertained the facts and explained them, and then they gave them significance by fitting them into a general scheme. They found two principles at work in history. One was the will and purpose of God. Against him, however, is man, with his varied purposes and independence. History, the Hebrews believed, was to be explained in the ebb and flow of these forces. The Old Testament sees as the end of history that human life is a progress to better things.

Early History.   The Old Testament moves on many levels. It is part poetry; part assertion of miracle, or divine intervention in human affairs; part rule of law; and part history. It is therefore very difficult to use as a historical source, although we are frequently able to correct and supplement our information through archaeological discoveries. Unfortunately, however, this does not hold for the early period, because, despite the vast amount of labor by many scholars, little that is certain can be said about the Hebrews' early history.

At least the world of Abraham and the patriarchs depicted in the Bible fits the historical situation otherwise known in the Fertile Crescent in the period before Hammurabi (ca. 2000-1700 B.C.). According to the tradition, Abraham left his home at Ur and is supposed to have discovered his God at Harran in northern Mesopotamia, which we know was occupied by Amorites. Perhaps we must imagine him as a prosperous Amoritic shepherd nomad, wandering up and down the Fertile Crescent in search of pasturage. We know that northwestern Semites were settling in Palestine about 2000-1750, and the migration of Israel's ancestors to the area was undoubtedly part of the movement. The tradition of the patriarchs cannot be proved or disproved; at least their names—Jacob, Benjamin, Levi, Ishmael—are akin to Amoritic, and their marriage, adoption, and inheritance customs correspond to those of contemporary Semitic sheikhs.

According to tradition, the Hebrew tribe of Levi, which was oppressed by famine, subsequently invaded Egypt and settled in the land of Goshen, east of the Delta. This makes sense if these Hebrews were part of the Hyksos invasion of the seventeenth century B.C. If Joseph existed, he then served a Hyksos pharaoh of the Fifteenth or Sixteenth Dynasty. Presumably enslaved when the Hyksos were expelled, the tribe of Levi lived in bondage, probably until the reign of Ramses II in the thirteenth century. Their leader, Moses, then brought his people into the desert of Sinai in Exodus. On top of the mountain, we are told, Moses received a body of laws— among them the Ten Commandments—from Yahweh, (Jehovah), a God who became the patron of the wandering people.

This was the most important moment in the history of developing Judaism, but the significance of the Yahwehists' Covenant is obscure. *Yahweh* apparently means "the Creator"; he has no special abode, stands alone, and cannot be represented artistically. In the Covenant there is no explicit denial that other gods exist beside

Yahweh, which makes it possible that the Hebrews from the beginning were not monotheists but henotheists, ideally worshiping Yahweh exclusively, but admitting that there were other deities. During their years in the desert, the Hebrews acquired the qualities characteristic of nomadic life: group solidarity, blood covenant, blood revenge, and hospitality. Eventually they continued to Canaan, where, in addition to their social solidarity, they took on the individualistic ways of farmers.

At least in later times, the Hebrews liked to believe that their forebears had looked upon themselves as forming twelve tribes. In the south of Canaan dwelled the tribe of Judah, a name that came to apply to this district. Northward the land eventually became known as Israel. In between the two areas was the important Canaanite city of Jerusalem, on its commanding summit. The only government the early Hebrews had was in the hands of leaders called *judges,* but nevertheless they fought with one another and with the Canaanites.

The Philistines. During the twelfth century B.C., in the reign of Ramses III, one of the Sea Peoples known as the Peleset, after a rebuff in Egypt, descended on Canaan and seized the southern coast. The Peleset were not Semites; they may have been Indo-Europeans. The designs on their pottery and armor, no less than their athletic habits, suggest that they had been in contact earlier with the Minoan–Mycenaean world, perhaps in Asia Minor. The Peleset gave their name to Palestine, but they themselves became known to history as Philistines, and the coastal district in which they actually settled was called Philistia. Their most important city was Gaza.

Saul. Well organized and using iron weapons, the Philistines extended their sway over the Hebrews. Toward the middle of the eleventh century, the great judge Samuel, of the northern tribe of Benjamin, urged his people to unite and revolt against their oppressors. At Samuel's instigation they chose (ca. 1040) as king of Israel Saul, a strong impetuous leader of armies, who displayed great energy in uniting the Hebrews, even those in southern Judah, under his rule. Saul humbled the Philistines but in the end was killed by them at Mount Gilboa.

David, King of Israel and Judah (Ca. 1000–961 B.C.). Saul's successor was his son-in-law David of Bethlehem, son of Jesse of the tribe of Judah. Beginning life as a shepherd boy and poet, David came to the front through personal bravery and ability to command. His accession as king marked the firm establishment of a united Hebrew state. One of David's most important acts was the capture of Jerusalem, which to this time had remained in the hands of the Canaanites, and which he now made the capital and the religious center of his realm. He also overwhelmed the Philistines, who were destined to be absorbed by the Hebrews, and various small tribes, such as the Edomites, the Moabites, and the Ammonites. Aramaean Damascus was taken. These successes enabled David to extend his kingdom northward to the Euphrates and southward to the Red Sea and Egypt.

David established in Jerusalem the Ark of the Covenant, the portable shrine of Yahweh that the Hebrews had carried with them in their nomadic life. The cult of Yahweh prospered and developed by its enshrinement at the city that the northern and southern tribes had chosen as their capital. Not that the worship of Yahweh was everywhere accepted. Indeed, the masses of Hebrews worshiped many gods.

Some of their religious customs and ideas they had brought with them from the desert; others they adopted from the Canaanites and the Babylonians. They took over from Canaan the cults of agricultural gods, such as that of Baal, and from Tyre the earth-mother goddess, Ishtar. Magic and religious prostitution were practiced. Yahweh was only one of many gods worshiped in high places, for the religion of the Hebrews, clearly, was a mixture derived from various backgrounds. The followers of Yahweh, however, though few in number, were exceedingly zealous and aggressive. The priests of Yahweh insisted on the intense, exclusive interpretation of their religion and preached the commandment, "Thou shalt worship no other god: for the Lord, whose name is Jealous, is a jealous God." To keep his worship they emphasized another commandment, against idolatry. Thus they sought to uproot paganism; future events were to show how Yahweh, worshiped already in Israel and Judah, could be the God of his people no matter where they were, for he could be universal.

Under David, then, Jerusalem became both a holy city and the seat of the central government for his united kingdom. A tendency toward urbanization throughout Palestine, and with it the luxury of city life, began to transform Hebrew society. With the help of workmen lent him by Hiram, the friendly king of Tyre, with the cedars of Lebanon and the arts of Phoenicia, David built and adorned his city. He was now an Oriental king, with his hand in the politics of the world, living magnificently in a palace filled with wives and slaves. The extensive wars, forced labor, and heavy taxes oppressed the people, however, and they followed David's favorite son, Absalom, in a revolt against him. But the son fell, and David continued to rule. After his death his oppression, caprices, and violence were soon forgotten, and the people, remembering only his service to a united kingdom and to Yahweh, looked back to him as their ideal king and their national hero.

Solomon (Ca. 961-922 B.C.). After David's death Solomon succeeded to the throne. He was the son of David and the beautiful Bathsheba, David's favorite wife. Devoting himself to the ways of peace, Solomon built on the summit of Jerusalem a magnificent temple to Yahweh. He added even stronger walls to the fortifications that David had erected and made for himself splendid palaces. Cedars from Lebanon and gold and bronze objects from Tyre were used in his buildings. Thirty thousand men were engaged in cutting stone and hewing wood. The copper mines of the Sinai peninsula added to his wealth; in the stables at Megiddo, which have been excavated, were kept his famous horses. In short, Solomon surrounded himself with all the luxury and brilliance of an Oriental despot; his favorite wife, an Egyptian princess, was one of many foreigners in a harem of one thousand. A commercial alliance was formed with Hiram of Tyre; together their ships sailed the Mediterranean and Red seas and brought home the products of distant lands. In administration and diplomacy, as well as in the practical affairs of life, Solomon displayed a shrewdness that gained for him, though with little reason, the reputation of being the wisest man in the world.

Kingdoms of Israel and Judah. All this glory meant heavy taxes and forced labor for the people, and they chafed under the yoke. Therefore, when Solomon's son attempted to continue Solomon's policy after his death, the northern tribes rebelled. Henceforth Palestine was divided into two weak states. In the north was the kingdom of Israel, under the rebel Jeroboam. Israel was the larger and richer of the two states, and ultimately Samaria was selected as its capital. The other state, to the south, was the kingdom of Judah, with Solomon's son, Rehoboam, as its king; Jerusalem continued to be the capital. Both kingdoms were afflicted with internal strife and were nearly always at war with one another. The significant fact for history, however, was that the two states had once formed a united kingdom where, for some, Yahweh was the one and only God. Now that the united kingdom had divided into its component parts, Yahweh continued to be worshiped in both north and south.

God and Man. Many Hebrews, of course, continued to worship other gods. Because of this and other problems—the rich, for example, oppressed the poor—there arose in Palestine during the ninth and eighth centuries a series of teachers, or prophets, such as Elijah, Elisha, Isaiah, Jeremiah, and Amos, who preached obedience to God and the necessity of right conduct. In these generations before the Babylonian captivity (sixth century B.C.), no less than during it and afterward, Israel was moving toward the conception of an ethical monotheism. Surrounded by a world of callous might and barbarities, the Hebrews nevertheless insisted on the moral righteousness of God and declared that people could confidently walk the earth as children in their father's house. The center of the Hebrews' world, however, was neither a blind force nor a sun god—nor a group of gods involved in their own affairs, who only by special effort could turn to the world of mortals—but a God who punished the erring but who also had loving kindness and tender mercy. He was a personal God, invisible and omnipresent, who demanded of his followers decency, honor, and human compassion.

But what, we may ask, is the place of tiny, yet significant, humans in this huge, and often inexplicable, universe? The Hebrew answer to this critical question is that God made man in his own image and that man is in his nature but little lower than God. Man, moreover, is infused and impelled by the wisdom of God himself, the difference between men, between the wise man and the fool, being the measure with which the individual has heard and then obeyed the appeals of wisdom.

The Hebrew writers concluded that the divine in us is slowly overcoming the bestial and that, because of the guidance of divine wisdom, we are climbing from savagery to a civilized life. On the other hand, how can we account for sin in a world created by God? Genesis gives the answer in the story of the Fall: "But of the fruit of the tree which is in the midst of the garden, God hath said, Ye shall not eat of it, neither shall ye touch it, lest ye die." In spite of this, and knowing the penalty, Adam and Eve did eat the fruit, and yet they had the power to do otherwise. Human freedom exists, though a divine purpose runs through history, and God reveals to mortals as much of the ultimate nature of things as is good for them. The individual can hear the voice of God deep in his own consciousness, and if he chooses, he can lead the good life. The good life was basically and supremely the religious life. The Lord "hath shewed thee, O man, what is good; and what doth the Lord require of thee, but to do justly, and to love mercy, and to walk humbly with thy God?" Attainment of this life brought salvation.

Destruction of Jerusalem (586 B.C.). The Hebrew thinkers got a view of the world—of one God of the universe who is a God of both wrath and love—that still shapes our outlook. The wrathful side of God's nature was emphasized by the last prophets, who fulminated against a backsliding Israel and confidently predicted God's intervention in Hebrew affairs as a punishing father. In the event, they were proved right. In 732 B.C., Tiglath-pileser III, the Assyrian king, captured Damascus and made both Israel and Judah tributary. A decade later Israel revolted, where-upon Sargon II, the new Assyrian king, destroyed Samaria, its capital, and trans-planted much of the population to the country beyond the Euphrates. They were soon absorbed among the natives of that region (the so-called Ten Lost Tribes). The lands of the rebels were assigned to colonists from the banks of the Tigris and the Euphrates and were incorporated in a province of the Assyrian Empire. Eventually that empire fell, but the rise of the new Babylonian Empire meant for Palestine merely a change of masters. To punish Jerusalem for rebellion, Nebuchadnezzar, the Babylonian king, besieged and captured the city (586 B.C.). He had already deported many of the inhabitants on a former occasion of disobedience, but now he destroyed Jerusalem and carried into captivity the rest of the people, excepting the poorest.

For fifty years the Hebrews remained in exile. Their long stay abroad tended to strengthen the tie of blood, and more particularly the family bond. The Babylonian captivity chastened them and made of them a new Jewish community adhering to tradition and law with emphasis on certain modes of behavior and ritual, a cultic rather than a national entity. Perhaps most important was the final working out of their monotheism in captivity. An unknown prophet, the "Second Isaiah," was the first to express this concept unequivocally. God, he insisted, would redeem his people, having purged them. Yahweh is the sole god, no other existed. His rule was universal over Jews and gentiles; the latter were invited to accept him, even though the Jews would retain a special place in his favor.

When Cyrus, the king of Persia, conquered Babylon in 539 B.C., he restored the Hebrews to their native land and permitted them to rebuild their temple. Naturally, he was enthusiastically accepted by them as God's instrument of redemption. Jeru-salem rose from its ruins, but Palestine remained a province of the Persian Empire. Restored Jerusalem honored Yahweh, who continued to demand of his worshipers moral as well as ceremonial holiness. Throughout the centuries Judaism continued to insist on strict obedience to the religious law, and from this faith sprang both Christianity and Islam. Probably no other single contribution to history can equal in its effect Israel's influence through these two religions and her own thinkers.

6

The Assyrian Empire and Its Successors

THE SUPREMACY OF ASSYRIA

The Land and the People. Assyria is a rolling hill country on the Upper Tigris some seventy-five thousand square miles in area, with an invigorating climate in contrast to the enervating heat of the Mesopotamian plain southward, in the direction of Babylonia. It is a compact, fertile land, productive of good crops even when not irrigated; its hills, moreover, contain building stone like marble, alabaster, and limestone. To the east are the Zagros Mountains, to the north is Armenia (Urartu). Since the trade routes between Babylonia and Armenia followed the course of the Tigris, it was inevitable that Assyria should be the scene of many struggles. Indeed, the early history of the land consisted in large part of wars against apparently omnipresent enemies, but from the wars and the long periods of submission, the independent, hardy farmers and shepherds emerged a fierce nation of fighters. (Cf. map, p. 82.)

Mitanni and Hittites, Babylonians and Elamites long prevented Assyria's expansion. The simultaneous decline of the Kassite dynasty at Babylon and of the Hittite and Egyptian Empires gave Assyria, as well as the small states of Syria and Palestine, the opportunity of independent growth. In the course of centuries the Assyrians built the mightiest empire the world had thus far seen, stretching from Media in the east to the Halys River in Asia Minor and to Egypt in the south. It is possible that they owed this remarkable achievement to the unity of their nation, to the vigorous character of the ordinary Assyrian, to the skill of the imperial officials, and to a long line of able kings, lists of whom have been discovered in the capital of Sargon II at Khorsabad. To speak generally, the many campaigns of the Assyrians were undertaken as a policy of defense of its expanded empire; for example, the expeditions against Egypt were necessary to prevent the pharaoh from interfering in Palestine, the possession of which was vital to Assyria if she was to hold the commercially important Syrian coast and the passes over the Taurus Mountains into Cilicia.

Assyria has acquired a reputation for cruelty almost without parallel in history. There is no denying that the Assyrians flayed their enemies alive, impaled them, and butchered them. The difference between them and their contemporaries, how-

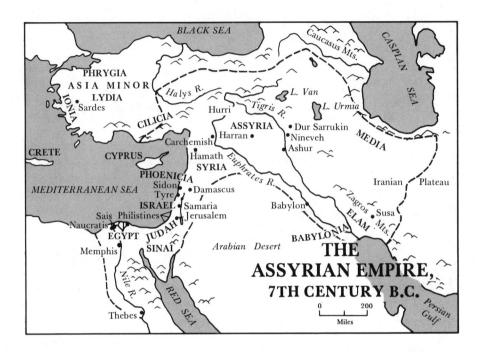

ever, did not lie in the fact of barbarous acts, which have been practiced by all states of all periods. Perhaps they do not quite deserve the reputation they acquired. Modern observers are often biased against the Assyrians because they tend to have pro-Hebrew, antiimperialist views and thus overemphasize Assyrian atrocities. The Assyrians were by no means universally condemned by their contemporaries; some Hebrew prophets, for example, actually approved of them as the rod of God's anger. Certainly their invasion and plunder were neither wanton nor unpredictable, and they never interfered with faithful vassals. On balance, they probably served a positive historical role as one of the bulwarks defending the civilized Near East against incursions by barbaric nomads to the north, and they were also efficient administrators. The Assyrian policy of transplanting entire populations from one area to another stemmed not from sheer delight in the heartless but from a determination to break stubborn national resistance and to discourage the restive from rebellion. On the other hand, the great constructive achievement of the Assyrians was the creation of the abiding type of polity known as the *Oriental monarchy*. It was they, too, who developed a system of provincial administration that became the basis of the Persian Empire.

Early History. The desert Semitic tribes who constituted, essentially, the Assyrian people had as their center the small town of Ashur—home of the local god, Ashur—on the west bank of the Tigris. Sumerian and Babylonian influences permeated their culture. The site was first occupied in about 3000 B.C. and later fell under the sway of Sargon of Akkad (ca. 2350) and Ur III (2100). Shortly thereafter (ca. 1950) an independent Assyrian commercial kingdom is documented, one that traded with Mesopotamia and across the Taurus Mountains in Cilicia, where it had a commercial outpost. It was characteristic of Assyrian power to rise and fall periodically. In subsequent centuries, Assyria was a vassal state to the Hurrian kingdom and previously to Hammurabi's Babylon, whose law code Assyria took as a model. Independent in the fourteenth century, she was important enough for her king to assume equality with Akhenaten, but thereafter her power declined in the wake of Aramaean attacks in about 1100 B.C. The first notable Assyrian attempt at expansion occurred at the end of the twelfth century B.C. under the king Tiglath-pileser I (1114-1076), but two hundred years were to pass before the Assyrians were able to pursue a successfully aggressive policy. The Aramaeans, by their possession of Damascus and Aleppo, blocked the routes to the Mediterranean. The Chaldaeans constituted a hostile element in southern Mesopotamia. Northward, around Lake Van, tribes of unknown origin formed the kingdom of Van or, as it is called in the Assyrian records, Urartu (a name that survives in Mount Ararat). The Vannic kingdom, which had its capital at Van on the southeastern shore of Lake Van, came to embrace the area later known as Armenia. The relations between Assyria and Van illustrate the international character of this age, when an event in the national history of one country was likely to have importance for other countries through its international connections. While the Assyrians longed to put an end to Van's menacing ambitions and to capture its iron and copper mines, Van, by its very position, acted as a buffer against northern barbarians, especially the Cimmerians, keeping them from overwhelming Assyria, a fate earnestly desired in Babylonia and Egypt, Syria, and Palestine.

Assyria's military successes began with Ashurnasirpal II (884-859 B.C.), who carried his conquests as far as the frontiers of Van and to the Mediterranean. Deliberate frightfulness was part of his policy, and he was rewarded with numerous prisoners and spoils. His successor, Shalmaneser III, spent most of his thirty-five years as king on military campaigns, not infrequently against Van, but also against Syria and Israel. Shalmaneser campaigned in Babylon to aid his ally, the Babylonian king. As Assyria subdued other states, it became the practice to reestablish the native rulers as vassal princes and to impose an annual tribute. Though he failed to capture Damascus, Shalmaneser did gain the passes over the Taurus and the province of Cilicia, with its vitally important metal trade. The wealth that poured into Assyria enabled Shalmaneser to beautify his capital, Calah (modern Nimrud), with a magnificence becoming its new position in the world.

Tiglath-Pileser III (Ca. 745-727 B.C.). The increasing power of Van, reinforced by that of the Phrygian kingdom in Asia Minor, meant troubled days for Assyria in the decades following Shalmaneser's death, but by the middle of the next century a usurper had restored and increased his country's fortunes. This was Tiglath-pileser III (ca. 745-727 B.C.), with whom the greatest military period in Assyria's history commenced. Tiglath-pileser developed a disciplined army constituted, in part, of professional soldiers and, in part, of a national militia. In addition to the cavalry and chariots and the heavy infantry equipped with fine iron weapons, there were light-armed troops, such as the famous archers and slingers, and a siege train with sappers and battering rams to undermine and knock down the mud-brick walls of an enemy. There were also platforms on wheels, with defenses against arrows, that could be moved against a wall to place the attackers on the same level as the defenders. The troops were organized in small fighting units; fortified camps served as safe bases from which to launch an attack; the whole science of warfare was studied.

Babylonia, which constituted a perpetual problem for Assyria, was now reconquered, and the troops of Van were decisively beaten, though it proved impossible to take the capital. Of first importance, however, was Tiglath-pileser's capture of Aramaean Damascus (732 B.C.). Henceforth many Aramaeans engaged themselves in trade, to Assyria's benefit as well as their own. The fall of Damascus was quickly followed by the submission of Ahaz, the king of Judah, and Hoshea, the king of Israel. The two kings were set up as vassals, and their states became tributary. On the whole, however, the scheme of vassal states was modified in favor of a system of imperial provinces, under regular governors and lesser officials, whose duty it was to dispense justice and collect the taxes. This was a milestone in the history of imperial administration and was to be elaborated upon by the Persians.

Sargon II (722-705 B.C.).   The Sargonid dynasty, which endured until the fall of Nineveh (612 B.C.), was established soon after Tiglath-pileser's death by Sargon II (722-705 B.C.). His immediate predecessor, Shalmaneser V, had undertaken the seige of Samaria, and in the last year of Shalmaneser's reign the capital of Israel fell. Thirty thousand Israelites (the so-called Ten Lost Tribes) were transplanted to the interior of the empire, and their place was taken by foreign colonists. Israel was made an Assyrian province. Later Sargon met the troops of Egypt, now ruled by an Ethiopian dynasty, at Raphia in southern Palestine. He inflicted a sufficient defeat on the Egyptians to persuade them of the advisability of presenting him with gifts, which he was pleased to regard as tribute. He then made a demonstration in the Arabian peninsula with the purpose of restoring order along the trade route to Yemen. In Babylonia, where a hostile Chaldaean dynasty was entrenched, Sargon met continued resistance, as had his predecessors. The situation was complicated by a Babylonian alliance with Elam, but Sargon was able to take Babylon and reduce Elam to impotence.

Early in his reign Sargon founded a new capital north of Nineveh, at Dur-Sharrukin (Khorsabad). Built at great cost, with a palace and a library, the city was abandoned by his successors. Nevertheless, from the city named in his honor—"Sharrukin's (Sargon's) fortress"—Sargon was able to undertake decisive campaigns against both the kingdom of Van and the Cimmerians, northern barbarians who had overrun much of Asia Minor, slaughtering Greeks and Lydians. Had they been allowed to continue unchecked, they would doubtless have conquered all of western Aisa. It was Sargon's achievement to check them and, on his death, to leave Assyria stronger along its northern frontiers than ever before. As we look back on this monarch, who knew how to be both cruel and kindly, we see that his aggressive campaigns, like those of the Roman Empire, had as their primary object the defense of the realm.

Sennacherib.   Sargon was succeeded by his son, Sennacherib (705-681 B.C.), an experienced general and governor. So firmly had Sargon laid the foundations of peace that Sennacherib was able to spend his first two years rebuilding Nineveh as

FIGURE 21. Statue of Ashurnasirpal II, King of
Assyria. From Nimrud (Calah), 884–859 B.C.;
height: 3 feet 6 inches.

The Granger Collection

the splendid capital of the empire. Its great library has yielded a nearly complete set
of cylinders, which in vivid language and with an accurate regard for details recount
the activities of his reign. As long as danger threatened on his northern border,
Sennacherib wisely limited the commitments of Assyria elsewhere. This must be the
explanation of his tolerant attitude toward Babylonia, where he hoped that a
friendly kingdom might provide sufficient security for Assyria in the south. But
when the northern danger passed, and the Chaldaeans in Babylon continued hostile,
Sennacherib captured Babylon. The provinces along the Mediterranean presented a
more difficult problem. Piankhi, the Ethiopian king of Egypt, did not feel strong
enough to attack Assyria himself but hoped to raise a successful rebellion within
the empire. With this end in view, he schemed with Judah and the Phoenician cities
to throw off the Assyrian yoke. Sennacherib immediately marched west, persuaded

Tyre to capitulate, captured Sidon, and by ravaging Judah caused the king, Hezekiah, to submit before Jerusalem was destroyed. A demonstration in Egypt proceeded only as far as Pelusium, in the eastern Delta, for apparently a plague decimated Sennacherib's army and forced its return. While the details of the campaign are obscure, it is certain that Sennacherib did not plan the conquest of Egypt.

Esarhaddon.   In 681 B.C., Sennacherib was murdered by a son and, after a period of civil strife, was succeeded by a younger son, Esarhaddon (681-669 B.C.). The significance of Esarhaddon's reign is that by continuing the policy of choosing able provincial governors, he was able to maintain the security of the empire—this at a time when Media, to the east, and a reappearance of the Cimmerians in the north confronted him with very real dangers. With an equity that is rare in an enemy, Esarhaddon rebuilt Babylon, which had been damaged during Sennacherib's siege, and restored its population. It is accordingly somewhat surprising that during his efforts to consolidate the empire, Esarhaddon should have undertaken the conquest of Egypt (671 B.C.). Such a venture had always been avoided by his predecessors and was now unwise, for the northern and eastern dangers should have occupied him exclusively; he was probably motivated by a desire to be rid of Egyptian intrigue in Palestine and Syria. The conquest of Egypt proved successful, for the moment at least, and a prince of Saïs in the western Delta (Necho), was established as a vassal.

Ashurbanipal (669-626 B.C.).   Esarhaddon's successor, the famous Ashurbanipal, ruled Assyria forty-three years (669 -626 B.C.). He was the best educated and last effective Assyrian king. Three-quarters of a century had elapsed since Tiglathpileser III had inaugurated (745 B.C.) the unbroken period of Assyrian supremacy, and during this time of internal peace Assyria had reached a high level of culture. Enemies confronted Ashurbanipal at the opening of his reign, but enemies had never thwarted Assyria before, and nothing seemed more likely than that Assyria's glorious age would continue. The danger to Assyria, however, was the possibility of nationalistic revolt, which always existed, but with an ever-increasing chance of success, for the many military campaigns over a period of several generations had slowly sapped Assyria's manpower. To obtain an adequate supply of soldiers, therefore, Assyria relied more and more on mercenaries, drawn from the conquered peoples of her empire, but the zeal of such troops could hardly be expected to equal that of the native Assyrian.

On his accession Ashurbanipal found that he and his generals would be fully occupied by the Indo-European Medes of the Iranian plateau and by the Cimmerians, who now threatened Cilicia. Accordingly, he established a brother on the Babylonian throne in the hope that peaceful relations might endure between them. The arrangement worked well enough, until the brother schemed with Elam to rebel. There thus began a long and terrible war, during which Babylon was captured, though not sacked; this was followed by the conquest of Elam and the complete destruction of its capital, Susa (ca. 639 B.C.). Tyre, too, was punished for its share in the revolt.

These activities explain Ashurbanipal's attitude toward Egypt. Early in his reign he had recognized that Egypt, because of its distance, required more garrisons than

Esarhaddon had felt necessary. Despite the extra garrisons and the vassals that Ashurbanipal proceeded to install, Egypt revolted under the leadership of Psammetichus of Saïs. Psammetichus received help at this juncture from his ally Gyges, the king of Lydia, who sent him mercenaries; probably other mercenaries from Asia Minor (Ionian Greeks) also served him. With very little trouble Psammetichus cleared the Assyrian garrisons out of Egypt (651 B.C.), for Ashurbanipal was not only fully occupied elsewhere but saw the unimportance of Egypt to Assyria. Now that Egypt was free, its relations with Assyria became cordial, and under the twenty-sixth, or Saïte, dynasty, it entered on a century of prosperous independence, until the coming of the Persians. Not that Saïte Egypt ever recovered its old vigor, but it did attract Greek soldiers and merchants and thus contributed to the intellectual awakening of a distant land.

Destruction of Nineveh (612 B.C.). The last years of Ashurbanipal were troubled by incursions of wild northern nomads, known as Scythians. Then, when at last the great king died, the enemies of Assyria set upon her. In Babylon the upstart king, Nabopolassar, plotted his attack; so did Cyaxares, the able organizer of the Median tribes. Scythians stood ready to help, and the Indo-European Persian tribes from southern Iran moved into devestated Elam. In 612 B.C. the allies—Nabopolassar, Cyaxares, and the Scythians—captured Nineveh. The capital of the empire was utterly sacked; the palaces and temples were obliterated; the thousands of clay tablets in the library were broken and scattered; the works of art, the parks, and the people themselves were destroyed. The remnants of the Assyrians made a final stand at Carchemish. They were aided by the Egyptian Necho II, successor of Psammetichus, who thought he saw in a surviving Assyria Egypt's best chance for control of Palestine. He therefore marched north, defeated Josiah, the king of Judah, at Megiddo and then joined the Assyrians at Carchemish. But Nebuchadnezzar, the brilliant son of the aging Nabopolassar, overwhelmed them (605 B.C.).

The fall of the Assyrian Empire was a stunning event. The Assyrians had nurtured Babylonian civilization at a time when Babylon itself was no longer creative and had passed it on to the Chaldaeans, while to the Persians they bequeathed a developed system of provincial administration.

ASSYRIAN CIVILIZATION

Society and Government. The unity of the Assyrian people, to which the kingdom partly owed its supremacy, derived from the fact that Assyria was not a collection of tribes or city-states but a nation. In theory, this nation of hardy fighters was ruled by a king with absolute power. In practice, however, the king customarily consulted oracles—especially that of Ishtar at Arbela—on matters of importance, and consequently the priests who controlled the oracles constituted an effective check on the king. From the nobility came the generals of the armies and the governors of the provinces. These aristocratic officials were capable and loyal to the king. In one case, toward the end of the ninth century, the whole empire may have been ruled by a queen regent, the famous Semiramis.

The majority of Assyrians were peasants, many of whom owned their farms. There was also a middle class of professional men and craftsmen. These were the bankers, merchants, scribes, carpenters, weavers, and metalworkers, who lived in their own quarters of the city. Compared with the masses elsewhere, the lowest class in Assyria was reasonably well off. Since trade and industry were largely in the hands of foreigners, agriculture ranked next to war as the main activity of the Assyrians. Serfs were a normal sight in the country, just as slaves were in the city. In the great age of Ashurbanipal, Nineveh, the imperial capital, was a meeting place of various races, where foreigners were perhaps actually in the majority. Assyrian was the official language, but Aramaic was widely spoken.

The Assyrian Empire brought to the Near East the advantages of comparative peace and unity and increased trade. The military roads promoted the economic welfare of a large area, and at the same time caravans crossed the deserts in relative security. Certain cities, because of their commercial importance, received charters defining their rights, and often they were exempted from taxes. Beginning with Tiglath-pileser III, the large territories that were conquered were divided into small districts, or provinces, each a reflection of the central government, and each liable to taxes or tribute. At the head of the province was a governor, directly responsible to the king and controlled by him. The governor passed on to the king information concerning his province, which he had gathered through an intelligence corps. In effect, however, the Assyrian system of provincial administration meant that distant provinces were ordinarily ruled less firmly than those nearer the capital.

Culture.   Although Assyrian civilization was permeated by Sumerian and Babylonian influences, the debt to Babylon was particularly great in the realm of religion. The gods of the two peoples were much the same, except for the chief god. In Assyria the supreme deity was not Babylonian Marduk, but Ashur. Ashur was a warlike god, represented by a winged disk (within which the god himself was shown); his symbol was placed on standards, which were carried by the Assyrian armies, and rebellious provinces had reason to dread his vengeance. So fierce a god befitted the nature of the Assyrians, who were a superstitious people seemingly confronted by a multitude of powerful forces. In the never-ending struggle with them it was necessary to invoke charms and the aid of priests. Solar and lunar eclipses were watched for their religious implications, and thus the Assyrian interest in the heavens was directed to astrology rather than astronomy.

Although we know something about Assyrian law for the early period of the country, nothing has survived from the time of the empire. The only Assyrian documents we possess for the later period concern economic matters, while the thousands of tablets dealing with other subjects are copies of the Babylonian. And yet, though the Assyrians were not remarkable for original, creative thinking, they have put posterity in their debt through their ability to preserve and arrange knowledge. Both Sargon and Sennacherib had libraries, but it remained for Ashurbanipal to bring together two huge collections at Nineveh, consisting of thousands of copies of Babylonian cuneiform tablets. In this way Babylonian literature was copied and edited, and much of our own knowledge of it, such as the Gilgamesh Epic, has been preserved in its Assyrian form. Assyrian literature, as an independent genre, consisted chiefly of oracles, predictions by omens, and historical texts. On clay and stone the scribes described in chronological order the exploits of the kings, and, needless to say, their inscriptions are of immense value to us.

Many of the royal exploits in hunting and warfare were recorded by text and picture on the walls of palaces. The reliefs are delicately carved and show good pictorial sense; there is a striving, too, for individual representation. The best of these reliefs come from Ashurbanipal's palace. Though the human figures are not done as well as the animals, few sculptors in history have been so successful in showing the pathos of a wounded beast. Many sculptures, in both relief and the round, were carved in stone. Because of the plentiful supply in the neighboring hills, stone was widely used in architecture, particularly for foundations and columns, but it was customary to build walls of brick. Precious woods and metals were also popular. Colossal human-headed bulls have survived in stone; these were placed before the gateways of palaces and temples. The Assyrian artists also excelled in small, detailed workmanship, such as the art of seal cutting.

THE NEW STATES OF THE NEAR EAST

Chaldaeans, Medes, and Scythians had joined in the attack on Nineveh (612 B.C.), and the first two of these peoples were destined to be the principal successors of the Assyrian Empire. The Scythians disappeared from the local picture—having been absorbed or driven out—but the Chaldaeans took lower Mesopotamia and Syria, while the Medes occupied eastern Assyria.

The Chaldaean Empire.   The short-lived state that the Chaldaeans now created is called the Chaldaean or New Babylonian Empire. Its founder was Nabopolassar, one of the captors of Nineveh, but its architect and the only king of distinction was his son, Nebuchadnezzar. After his victory over the Egyptian Necho at Carchemish (605 B.C.), Nebuchadnezzar won most of Syria and Palestine, but his father's death soon recalled him to Babylon. Harking back to the ancient past, which was his particular delight, he became king as Nebuchadnezzar II, and during a long reign (604–562 B.C.) extended his frontiers to the Persian Gulf, the Taurus Mountains, and the border of Egypt (map, p. 90). Chaldaean relations with Media were friendly, but within the empire opposition at Jerusalem caused much unrest. Finally this flared into open revolt, and after taking Jerusalem (597 B.C.), Nebuchadnezzar deported the upper classes to Babylon. The king, Zedekiah, was left as his vassal in Judah. A decade later, however, Judah and Phoenicia, with Egyptian aid, rose in rebellion. Nebuchadnezzar defeated an Egyptian army in Syria, reconquered all Phoenicia, except Tyre, which submitted after a siege of thirteen years, and captured Jerusalem (586 B.C.). This time he destroyed the temple and the city and carried off most of the remaining inhabitants into their famous Babylonian captivity.

The city of Babylon prospered under Nebuchadnezzar, for he was determined to bring back the memories of a wonderful past. Imposing fortification walls were thrown around the city; inspiring temples, particularly that of Marduk, were erected; a broad street for processions, with the magnificent Gate of Ishtar, was

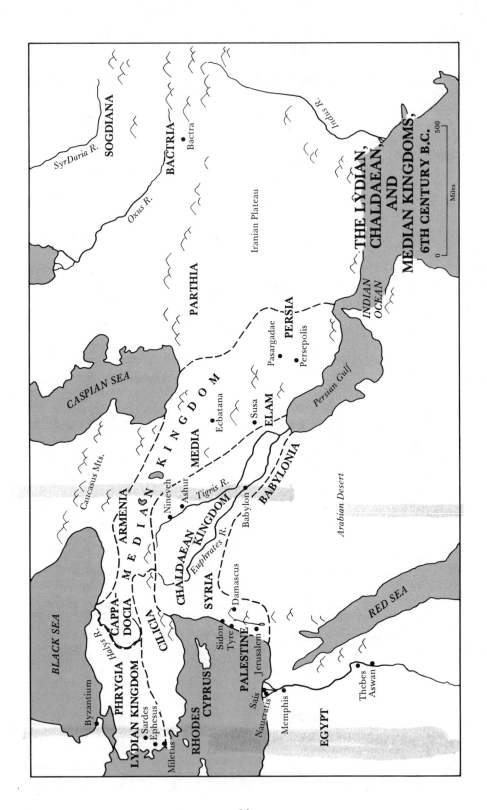

THE LYDIAN, CHALDAEAN, AND MEDIAN KINGDOMS, 6TH CENTURY B.C.

SOGDIANA

BACTRIA

Bactra

SyrDaria R.

Oxus R.

Indus R.

Iranian Plateau

PARTHIA

PERSIA

Pasargadae

Persepolis

INDIAN OCEAN

CASPIAN SEA

Persian Gulf

MEDIA

ELAM

Ecbatana

Susa

M E D I A N   K I N G D O M

ARMENIA

Caucasus Mts.

Nineveh

Ashur

Tigris R.

BABYLONIA

CHALDAEAN KINGDOM

Babylon

Euphrates R.

Arabian Desert

CAPPADOCIA

SYRIA

Damascus

RED SEA

BLACK SEA

PHRYGIA

Halys R.

CILICIA

LYDIAN KINGDOM

Byzantium

Sardes

Ephesus

Miletus

RHODES

CYPRUS

PALESTINE

Sidon

Tyre

Jerusalem

Sais

Naucratis

Memphis

Thebes

Aswan

EGYPT

500

0

Miles

built; the royal palace was rebuilt. Because his Median wife was homesick for the mountains of the north, Nebuchadnezzar reared a great palace and planted trees and bushes on its terraces; this became known as the Hanging Gardens of Babylon and was counted as one of the Seven Wonders of the ancient world. Most of these structures had walls of brick, faced with colorful glazed tiles of lions, bulls, griffins, and other animals.

Saite Egypt. Another state obsessed with re-creating the past, and caught therefore in cultural and political stagnation, was Saïte Egypt. The twenty-sixth Dynasty—founded by Psammetichus and carried on by Necho—had succeeded in reestablishing absolute rule, but the whole tendency in art and other activities was to restore the glories of the Old Kingdom. In a modernizing vein, however, Amasis (569-526 B.C.) welcomed Greek mercenaries and merchants, settling them in a city in the Delta, Naucratis.

Lydia. Impressions of ancient Egypt inevitably filtered back to Greece, to the great benefit of the Greeks, but of course few of them knew the land of the pharaohs at first hand. It was far otherwise in the case of Asia Minor, for we must remember that the Greeks settled not only in Greece but also along the Aegean coast of Asia Minor (see map, p. 98). Here they met, and were eventually subdued by, Lydia. The Lydians were a mixture of Indo-Europeans and Asiatics, whose expansion commenced in the eighth century after the Cimmerian barbarians had overthrown the kingdoms of Van and Phrygia, successors to Hittite power. The ultimate fate of the Cimmerians was absorption, but not before they had attacked the Lydians and killed their king, Gyges (ca. 685-652 B.C.), in battle.

It was another Lydian king, Alyattes, who set the Lydians on an active career of imperialism, which was to result in a rich and powerful kingdom, with its capital at Sardes (map, p. 90). Preparatory to a westward thrust at the Greek cities along the coast, Alyattes pressed east, an action that brought him into conflict with the Median Empire. An eclipse of the sun forestalled the decisive battle, and with the aid of Nebuchadnezzar, the Lydian and Median kings concluded a treaty and alliance (585 B.C.). The Halys River, whose waters form a historic landmark of Asia Minor, was chosen as the dividing line between the two states; and the daughter of Alyattes was given in marriage to Astyages, son of the Median king, Cyaxares.

The Median Empire. The weakening and the downfall of the Assyrian Empire, quite obviously, were accompanied by independent development not only in Egypt and Asia Minor but in Mesopotamia as well. Here, as we have observed, the Neo-Babylonians and Medes were the successors to Assyria. The ancestors of the Medes and the Persians seem to have been Indo-European tribes that migrated from the Caucasus into the western Iranian plateau in about 1000 B.C. In 836 an Assyrian king recorded that he had received tribute from the "Parsua and Mada," and in the eighth century some of their personal names turn up in Assyrian tablets. We do not have much information concerning their government and life. According to tradition, however, the Median dynasty was founded by Deioces (ca. 708-675 B.C.), who established his capital at Ecbatana (Hamadan). His successor, Phaortes (675-653 B.C.), became a vassal of the Assyrians.

The vigorous nature of the Medes and the development of mounted archers enabled their king, Cyaxares (633–584 B.C.), to join with Nabopolassar in the attack on Nineveh. As his share of the spoils, Cyaxares took eastern Assyria and the provinces north and east of the Tigris. The Persians in southern Iran became his vassals. The northward and westward expansion of Cyaxares brought him the region around Lake Van, henceforth known as Armenia, and Cappadocia, but it ended, as a result of his treaty with Lydia, at the Halys River. During the first half of the sixth century, the Medes, under Cyaxares and Astyages, created a large empire that stretched from the Halys to the frontier of India (map, p. 90).

The Persians.   About the middle of the sixth century the Persians revolted. The Persians were Indo-Europeans akin to the Medes. It was Achaemenes, according to tradition, who founded the famous Achaemenid dynasty by uniting the various Persian tribes under him, and though the Persians were then vassals of the Medes, they seized control of Elam from the Chaldaeans. This step was taken under a king who became known to history as Cyrus the Great, a skillful, merciful conqueror and a genius in organization. Cyrus maintained the old capital of Pasargadae in Persia, but he styled himself "King of Anshan." Anshan was the district of Elam that was adjacent to Susa, the future administrative capital of the Persian Empire. In 550 B.C., Cyrus invaded Media, and during the following year he occupied Ecbatana. Astyages' subjects, apparently, were not devoted to him and were ready to welcome what amounted, in effect, to little more than a change in dynasty.

Croesus.   The implications of the developments in Iran were not lost on Croesus, the king of Lydia (ca. 560-546 B.C.). Prevented by the treaty with Media from expanding beyond the Halys, Croesus had turned his energies westward and had incorporated the Greek cities of the coast in his kingdom; the sole exception was the city of Miletus, which was powerful enough to maintain the status of independent ally. The new situation was not as difficult for the Greeks as might be imagined, for Lydia had become Hellenized to a large degree, and Croesus was a conspicuous philhellene, who delighted in making gifts to ancient sites on the Greek mainland. The Greeks, moreover, benefited economically by their union with Lydia—sufficiently, at least, to offset their tribute—for they were now tied in with the great trade routes that ran from the Aegean coast through central Asia Minor to Mesopotamia and Iran. Since the Anatolian plateau was well suited to sheep raising, the textile factories of the Greeks prospered. Advantageous as all this was, the Greeks resented a foreign rule that governed them through local tyrannies and aristocracies.

Astride important trade routes and drawing tribute from the Greeks, Croesus became rich; indeed, the Lydians were credited with having invented the first coined money. Accordingly, when Croesus learned of the revolution in Iran that had put a fresh and ambitious people at the head of a powerful state, he feared for his kingdom and allied himself with Amasis, king of Egypt; Nabonidus, the new king of Babylon; and Sparta on the Greek mainland. He then marched across the Halys in order to secure Cappadocia and a better frontier against the Persians. An indecisive battle with Cyrus followed, and since it was now winter, Croesus returned leisurely to Sardis. Cyrus was not bound by the conventional rules of warfare, and much earlier in the year than might have been expected, he descended on Sardis, burned the city, and captured Croesus (546 B.C.). His lieutenant, Harpagus, then took over the Greek cities of the coast, though once again Miletus was able to retain the status of ally. Cyrus led his victorious armies eastward and overran the lands around the Caspian Sea, Parthia, Bactria-Sogdiana to the Jaxartes River, and the frontiers of India; it was only a matter of time before Egypt would be brought within this framework, though actually it was accomplished after his death (530 B.C.) by his son Cambyses.

The Fall of Babylon (539 B.C.). Meanwhile, there was the Chaldaean Empire. Nabonidus, the archaeologist-king, was interested, as some of his predecessors had been, in reviving ancient religious festivals and in studying Sumerian texts. His partiality for other gods offended the priests of Marduk, who secretly urged Cyrus to invade Babylonia. In 539 B.C. Cyrus was able to take Babylon without a struggle. With the same religious tolerance for which his immediate successors were to be noted, Cyrus respected and restored the worship of Marduk and allowed those Hebrews who wished to return to Jerusalem.

The year 539 B.C. is one of the decisive dates in the history of the ancient Near East. For many centuries Semitic power and influences had dominated Mesopotamia and adjoining lands. Akkad, Phoenicia and Palestine, Assyria, and finally Babylon had had their day. Now their place was taken by a new force, a mighty world state, which was to solidify Asia in the first *Pax Orientalis*. Stretching at its greatest extent from European Thrace to India (see map, p. 148), the Achaemenid Dynasty was to endure for more than two centuries, until the coming of Alexander the Great. Inevitably, perhaps, the Persians longed to conquer the Greeks of the mainland, as they had already those along the coast of Asia Minor, and eventually the great issue of East versus West was decided by immortal battles at Marathon, Thermopylae, and Salamis. The stage of history was then to contain both East and West, but by the time these battles were fought, the Greeks and their forerunners had gone through a long and remarkable development. Accordingly, we must turn to Greece before we follow the expansion of the Persian Empire.

PART III
HELLAS

7

The Aegean Age

INTRODUCTION

It was not until the opening of the great classical century of Greece, the fifth before Christ, that a mighty empire of the Near East (the Persian) and the city-states of Greece became locked in combat. In spite of many contacts between East and West before that time, the development of Greece and her civilization is best understood as a continuous entity.

The Significance of Ancient Greece. The challenge of the Greeks to posterity is not simply that they were the first people in history to place humanity in the center of things, as Israel had God, but that they carried their discovery to the point where at least some few of them established the ideal of the dignity of the individual and, as a natural corollary, the institution of democracy. It is true that the Greeks, with none of our scientific instruments and few of our comforts, bequeathed to humanity profound and sensible thought, noble poetry, and beautiful art, but it is probably of greater significance to history that they loved truth for its own sake and that some of them were even passionately devoted to reason. A people of mixed origin and speech, full of contradictions and paradoxes, and apparently bent at times on deliberate ethnic suicide, the Greeks at their best built a civilization based on experience and knowledge, sometimes free of religious and political oppression.

It is also true that in a very real sense the Greek *polis,* or city-state, is merely Western civilization in miniature and that Greek history portrays the birth, growth, and decay of a civilized society that we are able to understand. In spite of vital and illuminating differences, Greek society, composed as it was of the people's ideals of moderation, self-restraint, and an eagerness to know oneself, can be readily comprehended. The smallness of the Greek political unit, however, had ambivalent meaning. We have the particularism and jealousy of the various city-states, but also the fact that in a small state so many duties fell on the individual that he received an exceptional training in the art of civic life. This made for versatility, just as it also made every Greek a politician. It was, in part, at least, the combination of these factors that gave birth to intense local patriotism, a sense of responsibility, and a love of liberty, which in turn engendered a fearlessness that in time of war produced good fighters and in time of peace an inquisitive spirit willing to experiment.

The Physical Features of Greece. The Greeks were influenced, as any people must be, by the land in which they lived. Smallness was the essence of their country, as it was of their political unit. From Mount Olympus, on the northern border

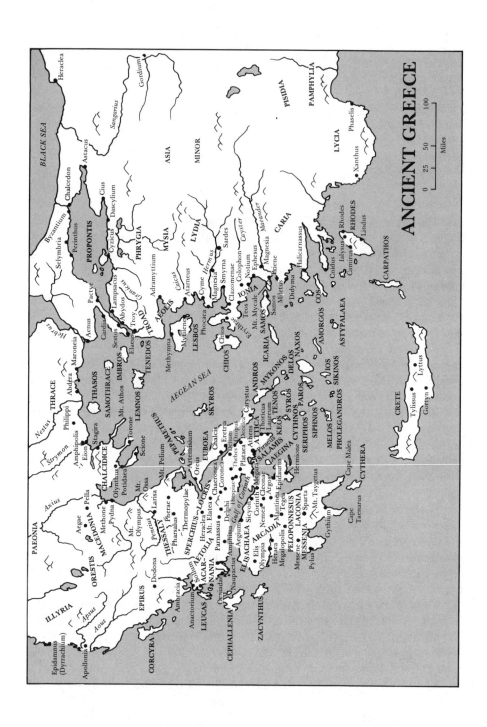

ANCIENT GREECE

Miles

0   25   50   100

BLACK SEA

Heraclea

Gordium

PISIDIA

PAMPHYLIA

Phaselis

Sangerius

Astacus

Chalcedon

Byzantium

Selymbria

Perinthus

PROPONTIS

Cius

Dascylium

Cyzicus

ASIA

MINOR

LYCIA

Xanthus

Pactye

Lampsacus

Abydos

Cardia

Sestos

Elaeus

Troy

TROAD

Adramyttium

PHRYGIA

MYSIA

LYDIA

Sardes

Hermus

Smyrna

Colophon

Notium

Ephesus

IONIA

Magnesia

Priene

Miletus

Didyma

CARIA

Halicarnassus

Cnidus

Camirus

Ialysus

Lindus

RHODES

CARPATHOS

Caicus

Arneus

Cyme

Phocaea

Clazomenae

Teos

Chios

Mt. Mycale

Samos

SAMOS

ICARIA

Erythrae

Maeander

Magnesia

Cayster

AEOLIS

TENEDOS

Methymna

Mytilene

LESBOS

CHIOS

AMORGOS

ASTYPALAEA

COS

Aenus

Maronia

Abdera

THRACE

Nestus

Philippi

Hebrus

THASOS

SAMOTHRACE

IMBROS

Mt. Athos

LEMNOS

SKYROS

AEGEAN SEA

SCIONE

Torone

SEPARETHUS

Mt. Pelium

Artemisium

EUBOEA

Chalcis

Eretria

Carystus

ANDROS

TENOS

MYKONOS

DELOS

NAXOS

SYROS

KEOS

PAROS

IOS

SIKINOS

CYTHNOS

SERIPHOS

SIPHNOS

MELOS

PHOLEGANDROS

CRETE

Tylissus

Lyttus

Gortyn

PAEONIA

Axius

Aegae

Pella

MACEDONIA

Pydna

Methone

ORESTIS

Mt. Olympus

Ossa

Larisa

Peneus

Mt. Pelium

CHALCIDICE

Amphipolis

Eion

Stagira

Strymon

Olynthus

Potidaea

Mt. Athos

ILLYRIA

Apsus

Aous

Epidamnus
(Dyrrachium)

Apollonia

CORCYRA

EPIRUS

Dodona

Ambracia

Anactorium

ACAR-

NANIA

LEUCAS

Oeniadae

CEPHALLENIA

ZACYNTHUS

THESSALY

Pharsalus

Pherae

SPERCHIUS

Thermopylae

LOCRIS

Heraclea

Mt. Elatea

Parnassus

Delphi

Chaeronea

Coronea

Thebes

Thespiae

Plataea

BOEOTIA

Tanagra

Decelea

ATTICA

Athens

Piraeus

Eleusis

Laureum

Thoricus

Marathon

SALAMIS

AEGINA

Megara

Eleutherae

AETOLIA

Naupactus

Amphissa

Calydon

Gulf of Corinth

Sicyon

Corinth

Cleonae

Nemea

Mycenae

Argos

ELIS

ACHAEA

Aegium

Olympia

Elis

ARCADIA

Mantinea

Tegea

Megalopolis

Heraea

PELOPONNESUS

Messene

MESSENIA

LACONIA

Sparta

Mt. Taygetus

Pylos

Gythium

Cape
Taenarus

Cape Malea

CYTHERA

Hermione

Epidaurus

Troezen

98

of Thessaly, to the tip of the Peloponnesus, where in the valley of the Eurotas lies Sparta, is only 240 miles. This area—though it excludes Macedonia, which achieved importance relatively late in history, and Thrace—is half the size of New York State, while Attica, the home of the nimble-witted Athenians, is not as large as Rhode Island. Overland communication was difficult. The imposing Pindus Mountains, which everywhere throw off long ranges hem in little boxlike valleys and shut one off from the next. This helps to explain why a nation or empire did not develop in ancient Greece; rather, a smaller political unit, the city-state, developed, with its center in the chief town of each valley.

The varied beauty of Greece is famous in song and story. Partly central European and partly subtropical in climate, this land of hill and plain has countless inlets and bays, which provided, especially on the long eastern coast, harbors adequate for the boats of antiquity. In much of southern Greece, olive groves and vineyards cover the countryside, and orange trees grow in the south; in the spring a profusion of wild flowers are a riot of color, softened by the blossoms of the almond trees and the hues of the mountains, which change in color with the brilliance of the sun. In summer it is hot, in winter, during the prolonged rainy season, cold and wet. These seasonal changes make for activity, especially since on the Mediterranean shores, where men need less food and shelter than elsewhere, the struggle for existence is not all-absorbing. Simplicity and even poverty mark the life, and there is leisure for thought and the interchange and clarification of ideas.

Ancient Greece—Hellas, as it is called—extended beyond the Balkan peninsula, for at an early time the Greeks and their forerunners also settled along the western coast of Asia Minor and on the islands of the intervening Aegean Sea, those beautiful and colorful stepping stones that invited ancient mariners ever onward. This little world is not so much a part of Europe as of the Mediterranean basin, and since it juts in the direction of the ancient civilizations of Egypt and Asia, it was inevitable that Crete, its farthest island outpost, should first have fallen under important influences that led to the brilliant Bronze Age of Greece. This entire period, with its various subdivisions, can be described more exactly as the Aegean Age, because it centered on the Aegean Sea.

The Earliest Inhabitants. Neanderthal remains attest to the presence of humans in Greece since Paleolithic times. Greece experienced the Neolithic revolution slightly after other places in the Near East. Neolithic sites in Macedonia (Nea Nicomedia) and the Argolid date from about 6500-6000 B.C. and, while showing local variations, suggest a population of farmers and husbandsmen who also hunted. Having no flint, the people imported obsidian to use as a cutting edge. Similar village cultures existed on the Aegean islands (the Cyclades) and at the site of the later palace at Knossos on Crete.

MINOAN CIVILIZATION

The Discovery of Bronze. Knowledge of how to mix copper with tin, which the Cretans acquired about 3000 B.C., marks at last the beginning of civilization in

GREECE IN THE BRONZE AGE

MACEDONIA

THRACE

Axius R.

Stryman R.

Thessalonica

Olynthus

Sestos

IMBROS

LEMNOS

Abydos

Troy

Scamander R.

Haliacman R.

Mt. Olympus

Peneus R.

Mt. Ossa

TENEDOS

Ida Mt.

ASIA MINOR

Dodona

Pindus Mts.

Larissa

THESSALY

Mt. Pelion

Dimini

LESBOS

Hermus R.

Pharsalus

Lianokladi

Achelous R.

Spercheus R.

AETOLIA

PHOCIS

EUBOEA

CHIOS

Thermon

Delphi

Calydon

BOEOTIA

Chalcis

Thebes

ATTICA

Aegium

SALAMIS

Athens

Mt. Mycale

Maeander R.

LEUCAS

ITHACA

CEPHALLENIA

ZACYNTHUS

ARCADIA

Corinth

Alpheus R.

Mycenae

AEGINA

Thoricus

DELOS

Miletus

CARIA

Olympia

ARGOLIS

SYROS

PAROS

CALYMNUS

PELOPONNESUS

Sparta

LACONIA

NAXOS

AMORGOS

Pylos

Vaphio

C Y C L A D E S

MELOS

THERA

RHODES

CYTHERA

AEGEAN SEA

CRETE

Rethymnos

Candia

Knossos

Mallia

Gournia

Palaikastro

Mt. Ida

Messara

Kamares

Cave

Hagia Triada

Phaestos

Hierapetra

Dictaean

Cave

Zakro

**GREECE
IN THE
BRONZE AGE**

0   100

Miles

BOEOTIA, ATTICA, ARGOLIS

Orchomenus

Gla

Delphi

L. Copais

Chalcis

Eretria

CORINTHIAN GULF

Thebes

Thisbe

Eutresis

Aphidna

Menidi

Eleusis

Spata

Athens

Korakou

Corinth

Zygouries

SALAMIS

Thoricus

Mycenae

Prosymna

AEGINA

Argos

Dendra

Tiryns

Lerna

**BOEOTIA,
ATTICA, ARGOLIS**

0   100

Miles

100

Europe. The early Bronze Age, moreover, is prehistoric, since the Cretans, as yet, were illiterate. This means that we are thrown back on the evidence of archaeology, the dramatic excavations of Schliemann, Evans, and others. This early chapter in civilized life is significant not only for itself but for its contributions to the later historical period of Greece as well. Crete underwent a notable population increase at the beginning of the Bronze Age, receiving immigrants from southwestern Asia Minor and, perhaps, from Libya. The island then entered an age of small towns with three areas of rather distinct cultures, in which the arts of pottery and engraving underwent significant development. The working of gold jewelry—bracelets, pins, and necklaces—is striking.

Knossos. After hundreds of years of slow progress (2900-2100 B.C.), during which the potter's wheel had been introduced (an invention that rendered easier both the manufacture of pottery and the expression of the artist's sense of line), the civilization of the Aegean age blossomed at Knossos on the northern coast of Crete. Sir Arthur Evans, the excavator of Knossos, has called this civilization, so long as its center remained in Crete, Minoan, after the legendary king Minos, whereas the term *Helladic* has been adopted for the mainland culture. [1]

The Palace of Minos. Soon after about 2000 B.C. isolated buildings, which had stood around a public square of Knossos, were probably consolidated to form a palace. Several hundred years later (before 1600 B.C.), the palace was damaged by an earthquake and was rebuilt. The rebuilding of the palace ushered in the greatest period of Minoan civilization. Here was the residence of King Minos; centuries later, when Greek invasions brought the Aegean age to an end, legend turned the palace into a labyrinth, the home of a fearful monster known as the Minotaur.

Minoan Art. The visitor to Knossos today senses at once that the palace was a self-contained village, with its own olive press, arsenal, workshops, and storerooms, while the long corridors, with their vivid frescoes, the stately rooms, the broad staircases, the bathrooms, latrines, and various appointments appear to have been comfortable and tasteful. Perhaps more than anything else, the frescoes give an insight to the artistic genius of the people. They were executed with a brush on a wall while the plaster was still wet, and rapid work was necessary. We can see the artists' passion for nature, for vivid color and movement and action, their desire to give the effect of the whole rather than to labor a detail. There are frescoes of blue monkeys peering through papyrus flowers, of partridges and hoopoes, of a simple blue bird

[1] Minoan and Helladic are divided into three periods, Early, Middle, and Late, and each of these is subdivided into three sections, approximately as follows:

Early Minoan, 2900-2100.	Late Minoan III, 1400-1100.
Middle Minoan I, 2100-1950.	Early Helladic, 2700-1900.
Middle Minoan II, 1950-1800.	Middle Helladic, 1900-1600.
Middle Minoan III, 1800-1600.	Late Helladic I, 1600-1500.
Late Minoan I, 1600-1500.	Late Helladic II, 1500-1400.
Late Minoan II, 1500-1400.	Late Helladic III, 1400-1100.

The civilization in Crete reached its height at Knossos in Middle Minoan III and Late Minoan I; on the mainland the peak was reached in the Late Helladic period at Mycenae, which thereafter dominated the eastern Mediterranean.

FIGURE 22. Libation procession. Detail of painted limestone sarcophagus from Hagia Triada, 1500–1400 B.C.

amid rocks and roses. From Hagia Triada, on the southern coast of Crete, comes the picture of a lifelike cat creeping through the rushes toward an unsuspecting pheasant. The palace at Phylakopi on the island of Melos has yielded a fresco of flying fish. Probably executed by a Cretan artist, it creates rhythm and balance as the fish rise and fall amid the rocks and sea.

Animals and fish, white lilies and green foliage waving against a red ground, and a close and sympathetic observation of nature characterize this free and imaginative art. The artist never hesitated to alter the true colors for effect. In spite of the interest in nature and in the use of rich and brilliant colors, the artist could give the impression, when he wished, of crowds of people or of an individual marching in a procession, such as in the fresco of the cupbearer, a tall, refined youth. By an artistic convention, the men are generally painted red or dark and the women white, and the waists of both sexes are very narrow.

The major art of mural decoration inevitably influenced the pottery. Manufactured so splendidly that some of it is called eggshell, the emphasis of the design is on an almost uncontrolled polychromy, with abstract patterns in white, yellow, orange, and cherry red, such as we see in the vases from Kamares. In time, naturalistic designs were used almost exclusively. Here again, the interest is not primarily in the actual forms but in things in space—branches, flowers, leaves blown by the wind, crocuses, lilies—and various marine motives, such as cuttlefish, sea anemones, and reeds. A Late Minoan vase, in which pattern and shape seem perfectly suited to each other, comes from Gournia and shows two dark brown octopuses floating across the light surface amid drifting seaweed and cuttlefish.

Architecture. The palace of Minos at Knossos, where so many of these frescoes and vases were first enjoyed, was constructed of unburnt brick or rubble, in a timber frame; the lower courses consisted generally of a dado of gypsum or limestone blocks. The palace covers more than six acres and, being built on the slope of a hill, is several stories high in parts.

The palace was built around a central court, approximately two hundred feet long and eighty-five feet wide, with the official state rooms on the west side. Here, for example, was located the throne room; but since another room, with a lustral basin for acts of purification, is connected with it, it is doubtless correct, in the light of other evidence as well, to regard the king as a priest-king who represented the Great Goddess. Behind the throne room and opening on a long corridor are the magazines where stood immense jars filled with olive oil, wine, and cereals (taxes, perhaps, paid in kind to the king). Across the court, on the east side, were the private dwelling rooms of the family. North of the Hall of the Double Axes, it will be noted on the plan (see p. 104), the long east-west corridor leads to the Hall of the Colonnades and the impressive grand staircase, with five flights of broad, easy steps, while to the south is the Queen's Megaron, with its own bath and toilet and private staircase.

The Dominion of Minos. From the fact that Knossos, like the rest of Crete, was practically devoid of defenses and that later legend speaks of a Cretan thalassocracy (sea rule), we infer that the priest-kings of Knossos feared neither domestic nor foreign foe. Certainly such a palace implies a long period of peace and prosperity, but it is difficult to say whether the king ruled the entire island, or, as seems more likely, merely exercised a lordship over vassal princes. The Italian excavations at Phaestos, on the southern coast, have revealed a similar but smaller palace of a prince who was rich and mighty enough to maintain an informal summer residence at neighboring Hagia Triada as well. French excavations have revealed another palace at Mallia, and Greek excavations yet another at Kato Zakro. There are other notable ruins—such as those at Palaikastro, Gournia, and Tylissos—that show that town life was widespread in Crete at this time. Since 1967, excavations on the island of Santorini (Thera) have revealed the extensive remains of another city, complete with striking frescoes done in the Minoan style and depicting a fleet.

Writing. The Cretans eventually became literate—some of them, at least—and developed several modes of writing. Their earliest form was a system of hieroglyphs, and later they began to use a syllabary, which is now called Linear A. The language of Linear A has not been identified; that of its successor, another syllabary, which is called Linear B, has been shown by the inspired discovery of Michael Ventris to be Greek. The Cretan syllabary (Linear A) was apparently taken over, modified, and augmented by the Greeks who came to rule Knossos and who used Linear B writing in the implementation of their highly developed bureaucracy.

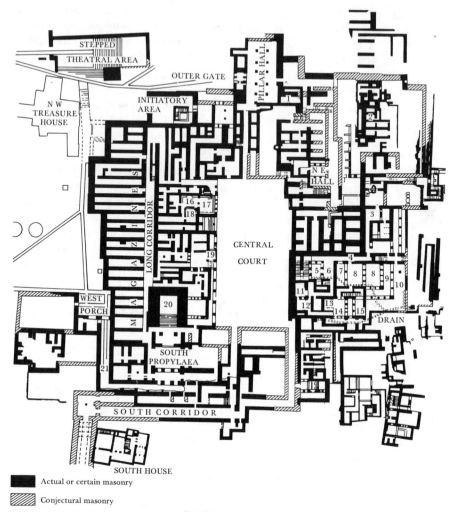

STEPPED
THEATRAL AREA

OUTER GATE

N W
TREASURE
HOUSE

INITIATORY
AREA

PILLAR HALL

1

2

N E
HALL

3

CENTRAL

COURT

4

5 6 7 8 8 9

10

11

12 13

14 15

DRAIN

N E
HALL

16 · 17

18

19

20

WEST
PORCH

21

SOUTH
PROPYLAEA

LONG CORRIDOR

M A G A Z I N E S

SOUTH CORRIDOR

SOUTH HOUSE

Actual or certain masonry

Conjectural masonry

PLAN OF THE
PALACE OF MINOS AT KNOSSOS

0   50

Meters

1. Guard room
2. Royal pottery stores
3. School room
4. Lower east-west corridor
5. Light area
6. Hall of the Colonnades
7. Light area
8. Hall of the Double Axes
9 Portico
10. Light area
11. Court of the Distaffs

12. w.c.
13. Bath
14. Queen's Megaron
15. Light area
16. Room of the Throne
17. Ante-room
18. Lustral basin
19. Shrine
20. Grand Staircase up to Piano Nobile
21. Corridor of the Procession

104

FIGURE 23. Gold and ivory
figure of a snake goddess from
Crete, c. 1600 B.C.

The Granger Collection

Customs.   The so-called Little Palace and Royal Villa and other imposing private
houses at Knossos suggest an aristocratic bureaucracy. The central government was
sufficiently enlightened to provide the people with paved roads, bridges, and aqueducts. The men wore simple loin cloths with an apron, the women long flounced
skirts, with bodices open in the front and high collars at the back. There is evidence
that their life was gay and carefree, for they had not only a fine artistic sense but a
love of sports, particularly boxing, wrestling, and bull vaulting. No great temples are
known; worship seems to have been carried on in small chapels in the palaces and
houses and at mountain shrines, such as those on Mount Juktas, the Dictaean cave
at Psychro, and Kamares on Mount Ida. The principal cult was that of the Mother
Goddess, whose symbol, the double axe (originally sacrificial), presumably placed a
building or object under her protection. Various snake goddesses have been found,
for example, the one in Boston, about a foot high, which is carved in ivory, with
gold snakes in her hands and gold ornamentation on her dress. It shows a goddess of
austerity and breeding, as it does also a long tradition in sculpture. The snake may
have represented the soul of the deceased, or it may have been, as in modern
Greece, a protector of the household.

Sequence of Events.   The history of Minoan civilization can be called that of
Knossos, its ruling city. But the evidence from which such a history is constructed
is not unambiguous, and scholars disagree, for example, on the circumstances sur-

rounding the end of Knossos. The following reflects what appears to be the majority view. It seems that Knossos was richest and most potent during the one hundred years (ca. 1600–1500) or so preceding its conquest in the fifteenth century. If there ever was a King Minos and a Cretan thalassocracy, it was then. About 1500 B.C., however, many scholars believe that a cataclysmic eruption of the volcano on Thera buried parts of Crete in ash and destroyed ports and the fleet in seismic waves, thereby weakening the Minoans. In any case, about 1480 B.C. the mainland Greeks, whose art and mode of life Knossos had long and profoundly influenced, apparently gained control of Knossos itself. They maintained control until shortly after 1400 B.C., when, on an April day, Knossos burned. A number of other Minoan centers also burned at about the same time, and Minoan civilization came to a close.

MYCENAE

Beginning about 2200 B.C., Indo-Europeans began arriving in Greece from, it would seem, Asia Minor, speaking a language that was the ancestor to the classical and modern Greek tongues. Their presence is attested to archaeologically by remains of their megaron houses and of the horses they introduced and by the pottery (Minyan ware) that they used, often soapy to the touch, and gray or yellow in color. The most famous of these Bronze Age Greek sites is Mycenae.

The greatness of Mycenae was due partly to its location a few miles distant from the sea and possible pirates, with its citadel hill, or acropolis, dominating the broad Argive plain and the trade routes to Corinth and the western sea. The origin of Mycenae's rulers and their wealth, however, is not wholly certain, though it is reasonable to assume that we have here not a Cretan outpost but a strong native power under Minoan influence. The people themselves were Greeks, speaking a Greek dialect.

Mycenae's Influence. In the fifteenth century the mighty Tholos Tomb Dynasty, as it is known from its tombs, came into power. This was the dynasty that perhaps occupied Knossos and set about the economic domination of the Aegean. Mycenae's trade extended as far as Sicily, Egypt, Palestine, Cyprus, Troy, and Macedonia, while her leadership, if not actual dominion, may have been recognized in Athens, in Thessaly and Aetolia, in most of the islands of the Ionian and Aegean Seas, and in central and southern Greece. From Korakou, on the Corinthian Gulf, communications were maintained with Orchomenus, Thebes (the traditional home of Cadmus), and other great cities of Boeotia.

The Acropolis at Mycenae. The Mycenaean acropolis was reconstructed at this time. On the top was built the king's palace, in stepped terraces, with sumptuous apartments, halls, and courts, while an immense wall was built around the entire hill. At one point, near the famed Lion Gate when the perimeter of defense was enlarged in the thirteenth century, the wall was made to include seven graves, apparently the most important, of a cemetery of the previous dynasty (ca. 1650–1500). These are the famous shaft graves, where Schliemann found one of the greatest gold treasures from any Bronze Age site in the world: gold bracelets, sig-

nets, diadems, breastplates, beads, cups, death masks, and bronze daggers with in-
lays in dark and light gold showing scenes from life, such as lion hunts.

A second grave circle, discovered recently, lay well outside the walls of the citadel. Its graves have yielded among other treasures an exquisite crystal duck whose
work shows Egyptian influence. Although it is now called Grave Circle B to distinguish it from Schliemann's find, it is the older of the two.

Tombs. As already intimated, however, the greatest architectural wonders from
the days of Mycenae's glory are the circular or tholos tombs, which are popularly
called *beehive tombs* (ca. 1500-1200). The most magnificent of these, with many
decades of development behind it, is the so-called Treasury of Atreus. It is approached by a passage, or *dromos,* cut into the side of the hill and approximately
115 feet long by 20 feet wide. The *dromos* is lined with well-cut conglomerate
blocks set in regular courses (ashlar construction), and at the end is the impressive

FIGURE 24. Entrance to a beehive tomb, the so-called "Treasury of Atreus."

The Granger Collection

doorway, eighteen feet high and capped by two lintel blocks, the inner of which weighs more than one hundred tons. Green breccia columns stood on either side of the doorway, and above the lintels the empty space, known as the *relieving triangle,* was originally filled with red porphyry slabs carved with spirals. Within the doorway is the circular chamber, fifty feet in diameter and crowned by a dome of about the same height, which resembles a beehive in appearance. Each course of the chamber projects slightly beyond the one immediately below, until finally the whole is arched over (the corbel dome). Off this chamber is a small room, probably for burials.

The nine tholos tombs at Mycenae have long since been robbed, but a similar tomb at Vaphio, near Sparta, has yielded beautiful gold cups, with embossed scenes showing the capture and taming of wild bulls. At Dendra near Midea, in the Argolid, the Swedish excavators found a tomb containing, among other things, an exquisite gold cup with octopuses in relief, a gold-lined silver cup with bulls in relief, and another gold-lined silver cup decorated with bulls' heads, knives, gems, and beads. Apparently people felt that in the next world the dead needed equipment reminiscent of that which they had enjoyed during life. Care for the dead, however, apparently ended with interment, for families would reopen tombs, cast aside the old dead, sometimes into the very *dromos,* and install the new, again properly equipped.

Houses. Just as ordinary folk had graves that were simpler than those of kings and nobles, so too their houses were far less elaborate. The typical house, or megaron, was deep and narrow, with a flat roof and a porch in front; the main room was directly to the rear and had columns down its axis to hold up the ceiling. Here was the hearth, around which the family held its gatherings, and farther back was a small bedroom.

Pylos. In southwestern Peloponnese, on a low hill called Epano Englianos, overlooking the Bay of Navarino, Greek and American excavations have uncovered remains of a Mycenaean palace. It is now generally recognized as the site of Homeric Pylos, important later on in classical times. An extensive complex, its outer walls of limestone, heavy timbers throughout, it was clearly the residence of a king. A throne room, reception halls, separate living suites, decorative tiles, brightly colored frescoes—all testify to opulence. An archive within the palace has yielded hundreds of clay tablets that preserve the writing known as Linear B. The king was careful of what he owned; the tablets are mostly inventories of possessions. They also show an extraordinary division of labor among his subjects and an extremely detailed bureaucratic control over all facets of the kingdom's society and economy. Thus it seems that Mycenaean kingdoms like Pylos resembled closely in their organization contemporary Bronze Age states in the Near East and that they had little in common with the classical Greek city-states of a much later epoch.

Houses of private persons, as at Mycenae, were built near the palace. Presumably others were clustered in hamlets in the neighborhood. Royal and private burials were in tholos tombs at a little distance from the palace. No defensive fortifications have been found.

The complex was built early in the thirteenth century and burned down in a great fire around 1200 B.C., as did many other Mycenaean centers. The founder of Pylos may have been Neleus, whose son, Nestor, ruled through three generations of men. Pylos, to judge from Homeric poems, was an independent state whose rulers, at least during the expedition to Troy, recognized the higher authority of Mycenae. Members of the ruling family, after the destruction of Pylos, found refuge in Athens, which was not devastated by the Dorians. Some Neleids remained there until historical times; others settled in Asia Minor. But Pylos itself was never resettled.

Tiryns.   The plan of the megaron was incorporated into the mainland palaces, the best example of which can today be seen at Mycenae's dependency in the Argive plain, Tiryns. The whole hill was protected by an immense wall, fifty-seven feet thick in places, formed of huge roughly hewn blocks, with small stones in the interstices ("Cyclopean" construction).

The art that adorned these palaces is filled with epic scenes, such as boar hunts and battles, but though it was essentially Cretan in style, Mycenaean technique and spirit were inferior. Art had now become an industry and played its own role in bringing something of a common culture to the Aegean basin. Comparative peace, it is clear, reigned in at least the first centuries of Mycenaean Greece. People cultivated their fields and traveled by land and sea, but by the end of the thirteenth century the need for land and the pressure of restless northern tribes allegedly caused many of the princes to undertake an expedition, concerning which one of the greatest of all poems was written.

TROY

Troy, the scene of Homer's famous war, was not so much a city as a citadel or royal stronghold located near the Hellespont. Troy's wealth, it seems, was derived from the exportation of woolen goods and perhaps horses. In any case, she looked economically to the West and seems not to have had significant commercial contacts with her Anatolian hinterland. Otherwise, in certain ways—such as in the practice of cremation, which was characteristic of the Sixth City—Troy stood somewhat apart from the Aegean culture.

Today Troy is marked by a mound, known as Hissarlik, where in the last century Heinrich Schliemann, a merchant prince of Germany who later became the father of archaeology, discovered nine successive cities. With his typical enthusiasm Schliemann called the Second City and its vast hoard of gold and silver pins, earrings, vases, and weapons the Homeric Troy. After this conjecture had been proved wrong, it was long thought that the important Sixth City was the city of the Trojan War, until Carl Blegen and his University of Cincinnati excavations showed that an earthquake had destroyed the place about 1300 B.C. Troy VIIa, as it is known, was immediately constructed of the material of the previous city. Historians who believe in the historicity of the Trojan War think that Troy VIIa must be the Homeric city; it was destroyed by fire in what was evidently a war in about 1250 B.C., a date that corresponds remarkably well with the legendary date of the fall of Troy, 1184 B.C.

But things are not that simple. One school of skeptical scholars would deny that there ever was a Trojan War pitting a united Greece against an Asian power. For them the Trojan War was "once upon a time," a "timeless event floating in a timeless world." They say that there were undoubtedly many Trojan wars, conflicts by Trojans with enemies unknown to us, and one of these would account for the destruction of Troy VIIa in ca. 1250 B.C. Other scholars believe that they have found Troy and Mycenaean Greeks in Hittite documents of the thirteenth century B.C. They would at least posit a war involving some Mycenaean Greeks with Troy and perhaps other west Anatolian cities, jockeying for power and attempting to fill the power vacuum brought about by the collapse of the Hittites in the period 1250–1200 B.C.

8

The Greek Middle Age and Renaissance

THE DORIAN INVASION

The Greek Migrations. During the transition from the Bronze Age to the so-called Middle or Dark Age of Greek history, Greece was in a state of flux. During the twelfth century, written tradition, not, however, supported by archaeological evidence, holds that Greece was invaded from the northwest by Dorians, a warlike Greek people living at a much more simple level than their civilized Mycenaean cousins. Many Greeks sought refuge from the "Dorian Invasion" by emigration. Those of Thessaly and Boeotia, the Aeolians, moved eastward across the Aegean Sea and colonized the island of Lesbos as well as the adjoining Asiatic mainland, which then became known as Aeolis. Similarly, from central Greece, especially from Attica and Euboea, there was a movement of other Greeks—Ionians, as they are called—to the Cyclades Islands and the rich central littoral of Asia Minor, to be known to history as Ionia.

Though Attica remained untouched by the invasion, some of the newcomers settled in Thessaly and Boeotia. The majority of Dorians passed into the Peloponnesus and by about 1000 B.C. overwhelmed the entire country, with the exception of the interior highlands of Arcadia, whose people managed to maintain their original language and ethnic character. Dorian emigrants from the Peloponnesus also crossed to Melos, Thera, and Crete and eventually to Rhodes and the southwestern coast of Asia Minor.

The New Era. The Dorians and Ionians occupied the area once most thoroughly permeated with Minoan-Mycenaean culture and were its principal heirs. In material civilization, religion, government, and social structure, these two great branches of the Greek people were essentially alike. Their later differences, which so mark the historical period, must be explained in the light of developments immediately following the Dorian Invasion, particularly the growth of industry, commerce, and intellectual life among the Ionians. The collapse of the Mycenaean world was a catastrophe. The arrival of many northerners, the attendant breaking up of Mycenaean kingdoms, and the destruction of great sites, which entailed dissolution of

111

the palace bureaucracies, set the stage for a new and simpler day. This was the Greek Dark Age, and it bears some analogies to the later European Middle Ages, in that both periods were characterized not only by invasions of less civilized peoples but also by a decline and an incipient recovery of culture. Knowledge of writing seems to have disappeared altogether. The clay tablets with Linear B inscriptions that Blegen found at Pylos were baked (and so preserved) in the fire that destroyed the palace in about 1200 B.C. The first written Greek thereafter is in an alphabet that derives from the Phoenician (see p. 74) and arrived on the mainland about 725 B.C.

The State.   The strong tribal organization of the Dorians and the superiority of their iron weapons made conquest relatively easy. Though the closing of the lines of communication fostered local variations, life slowly became settled and order prevailed. Small and rudely fortified cities were built, ruled by petty kings who boasted descent from a god and the ability to win divine favor. Thus arose the king's priestly character; the need of protecting the state from domestic foes gave him judicial power, as the duty of warding off foreign enemies made him a general. The state was a crude, undeveloped institution, and in point of fact the king, whose power was limited in practice by his council of elders, was little better than a noble.

The economy of this period was preeminently agricultural; industry, as we understand it, was practically nonexistent, and communication with the outside world, in particular with the civilized Near East, was almost totally cut off. The great fifth-century historian, Thucydides, was not far wrong when he remarked that during this time the Greeks had no mercantile traffic and mixed little with one another without fear, either on land or sea, and that each man tilled his land only enough to procure a livelihood from it, having no surplus wealth.

Religion.   The religious beliefs of the Greeks also had the humblest origin, but from primitive fetish worship and fear of the unseen there evolved the immortals of Olympus, who represent a blending of Indo-European and Minoan beliefs. Certain cult places of the Aegean age continued in use, such as Delphi, Delos, and Eleusis, and the Minoan house goddess became Athena. By the eighth century B.C. Greek regard for the gods could be very sophisticated.

The gods of the Greeks had human form and differed from mortals only in their superior stature, strength, and physical perfection; in the character of their food and drink (ambrosia and nectar); in their dwelling place and life of ease; and in their immortality. They lived together as a family on the summit of snowy Olympus, under the presidency of Zeus, father of gods and mortals, and there they sat in council on the destinies of humankind. Their society was an idealized reflection of that of earth, yet freer from moral restraint, and in their capricious dealings with humans they helped those whom they loved and brought misfortune to their enemies. They were so close to humans that no priestly caste was needed, and each individual prayed directly to them. The ceremonies in honor of the gods were performed on sacred land, but eventually small temples were built for them. These were placed under the care of a priest who was no better than his fellows.

HOMER

Homer. Among those who want to know the history of Mycenaean Greece, the available evidence is likened to a series of pictures without captions or texts. The Linear B tablets, mostly inventories, have helped some; it has seemed to some that Homer, if the crucial questions concerning his existence and his work could be answered, might also help. But we do not know who he was, where or when he lived, whether he wrote or sang, upon what traditions he could draw—we do not even know what he composed, for there is no unanimous agreement as to the authorship of the works that have been attributed to Homer.

A Greek of the fifth century B.C. thought of Homer as the blind bard who originated two or more great epic poems and certain old hymns to gods as well. A number of islands and Ionian cities claimed his birth, and a class or guild of Homeridai (descendants of Homer) sang and interpreted his works. The central works, the *Iliad* and the *Odyssey,* claim to present in their general outlines the Mycenaean world. Homer represented Mycenae and Pylos as preeminent, for instance, and archaeological research has shown that these cities did in fact dominate that era. We also now know that Troy did exist. But there are anachronisms and inconsistencies in the poems that would not exist in homogeneous creations of a single era.

Bards were conceivably singing in Mycenaean palaces as early as the fifteenth century B.C., and the lays that they composed could, because they were in meter, be accurately reproduced by succeeding generations of illiterate singers, who were trained in the same skill. The tales endured through the Dark Age, not without change, and at some point, a great poet united selected elements of this traditional material in composing two great epics. He lived at or toward the end of the oral tradition, say, about 725-700 B.C., for soon after he had created his poems, they were committed to writing, and the text thereafter resisted change. This last great singer, perhaps the very one who recited his works to an amanuensis, can conveniently be called Homer. He received stories of long ago with the accretions of their long lives and made them into the complicated, and powerful epics that continue to fascinate the world today. We seldom know precisely, however, to what era a particular episode belongs, although the general atmosphere of the *Iliad* and the *Odyssey* seems to be that of the Dark Age rather than the Mycenaean age.

The Iliad and Odyssey. The *Iliad* was apparently constructed before the *Odyssey,* and although it deals with only a few weeks in the tenth year of the Trojan War, we are made to feel the whole background and environment. The poet sings of the tragedy of a city and of a man, of how Achilles' temper led him to degradation and disaster. The wrath of Achilles is the central theme of the *Iliad* and holds the poem together, lending it its most dramatic developments. The poet occasionally gives his hearers an indication of what is to come, but in order that the end may not be reached too quickly, the gods are used to delay the action. The deeds of other heroes, of Patroclus and Hector, are also sung, but Achilles, who symbolizes for some readers the destiny of humanity, is the real hero. The *Odyssey,* on the other hand, is an epic romance and blends in one artistic whole a number of folklore motives and deep-sea tales. The goal, though not the end of the poem, is to reunite Odysseus with his wife, Penelope, who has faithfully waited for him on the island of Ithaca during his absence at Troy and his subsequent wanderings.

Art. It is remarkable that at the outset of its history and amid the simplest surroundings, Greece was able to produce one of the greatest poets who has ever lived, and yet it must not be imagined that the period that Homer illumined was otherwise wholly dark culturally. The remaining evidence consists chiefly of pottery, and concerning its artistic merits opinions vary, as is bound to be the case with anything that is subjective. Some students consider the pottery primitive and crude, while others see in it a beautifully simple style, a little naive perhaps, but charming and complete in itself. The style is geometric and employs angular patterns, zigazags, rows of dots, swastikas, triangles, crosses, and meanders, set in horizontal bands, row over row. Scenes from everyday life, such as battles and funerals, are placed in the main zone, and the figures of men and animals are stylized silhouettes. Some new shapes were introduced; the profile was sharpened and the neck lengthened, due, as the composition itself, to a tectonic principle that seems to have been innate in the people themselves. This can be seen in the splendidly manufactured amphoras from the Dipylon quarter of Athens (p. 115). It has seemed to some that this geometric ware is the first Greek statement of the canons of classical beauty, which were mathematical and stressed balance and proportional harmony.

The Greek People. The other material remains of the period—small bronzes and ivories and light architectural ruins—are not of great significance. Indeed, the Greek Middle Age, an interesting and complete though simple chapter in human existence, is chiefly important as being the prelude to historic Greece. During this period, moreover, the fusion of population elements—aborigines, some Mycenaeans, and Dorians—occurred, an amalgamation that by 900 B.C. produced the classical Hellenes.

It has been pointed out that the process of biological blending, rather than the dominance by any single racial type, that preceded the classical culture climax shows that genetic mixture is one of the real and probably indispensable factors that help to produce a great people and that underlie the whole history of civilization.

THE CITY-STATE

From the close of the Greek Dark Age (ca. 750 B.C.), Hellenism—Greek civilization—developed very fast and produced results that no other people can claim. This extraordinary achievement was due primarily to the city-state (*polis*), an institution whose character inevitably combined good and bad features. The constitutions of the city-states varied, being in each case determined by special factors, for they did not function *in vacuo;* but we may make the generalization that the city-state, ideally, was small and independent in all its affairs, even though this status was not everywhere attained by the fifth century.

Urban Life. Probably it was the example of urban life in the Bronze Age, no less

FIGURE 25. Athenian jar from a grave with geometric ornament and funeral scene, c. 9th century B.C. Height: about 60 inches.

The Granger Collection

than the feeling of kinship that the new settlers, who were grouped in clans, felt for one another, that first led the Greeks of the Dark Age to occupy the old sites or new ones nearby. The low, fortified hilltop, or *asylum,* to which the common people of the surrounding villages might flee with their flocks and belongings in time of danger, eventually became a convenient spot for sacrifices to the gods and the exchange of goods, and it was only natural that the king and his retainers should live within it. There was thus created a settlement that actually had a political center, but at the very outset we can see both its virtue and its failing. Group life was intimate and intense and capable of boundless versatility, but it was also the exclusive possession of the person born to it, who was bound to his family and fellows by blood and worship. The inhabitants not only considered themselves descended from a common ancestry, but each citizen was also a member of a brotherhood, originally an association of kinsmen who fought in battle together. Several of these brotherhoods formed a tribe. The inability of Greeks in later years to envisage a broader citizenship, not one so inextricably bound up with parents and place, perhaps their greatest fault, sprang from these narrow beginnings.

Aristocracy. During the Dark Age there had been steady pressure against the

kings, and by the eighth century the nobles had everywhere, except at Sparta, succeeded in superseding the monarchy, either through outright usurpation or by reducing it to an elective office, with functions exclusively priestly or judicial. At the
same time other offices were created, until at last the city became a complicated
organism. Although the assembly of citizens seems not to have been a potent body
in this process, aristocratic governments did codify and write down laws, a step that
was in the interest of the people generally. The tendency was to establish law as
supreme over all citizens in the regulation of public and private life. The body of
civil law remained, even when the constitution, which was unwritten, changed overnight with a change of party. The Greek, however, never lost his awareness of the
possibility of revolution, and a persistent issue in his political life was the struggle
of the few against the many.

Leagues.   The motive that first led groups of neighboring states to combine in a
league, as not infrequently happened, lay far anterior to recorded history and might
have been the existence of a border market, the need of allies, the desire for frontier security, or a consciousness of kindred blood. In any case, such groups chose a
sanctuary of a god, conveniently situated, in which to worship or to hold a fair for
the interchange of goods. Such a union was termed an *amphictyony;* that of Delos,
centering in the shrine of Apollo and celebrated in the Homeric "Hymn to the Delian Apollo," was originally a union of insular neighbors but came to include all the
Ionians. Another amphictyony comprised twelve states in the neighborhood of
Thermopylae, with its earliest seat of worship at the shrine of Demeter at Anthela.
In time it acquired a second and more important center in the temple of Apollo at
Delphi and hence came to be known as the Delphic Amphictyony. The object of
the league was the protection of shrines, especially the temple and oracle of Apollo,
but one of its earliest resolutions attempted to lessen the primitive rigors of war by
imposing an oath on the members not to destroy an amphictyonic city or cut it off
from running water in war or peace.

A religious union tended to become political when it contained a state of superior
power and secular ambition, as in the case of Thebes in Boeotia, but on the whole,
federation was a mark of political and intellectual backwardness and was popular
with people such as the Aetolians and Acarnanians. The amphictyony mitigated in
part the particularism of the city-state, while other factors—such as a common language, art, and literature, and general meeting places such as Olympia and Delphi—
tended further to remind the Greeks that they were one people. The city-state,
which the Greek continued to look upon as normal, was the driving force in the
development of Greece. Not least among its achievements was the period of colonization inaugurated shortly after 750 B.C.

COLONIZATION

The two centuries after 750 B.C. are among the most interesting in history. With
reasonably adequate information at hand, Greece takes on for the first time real
flesh and blood. The Greek world, it will be recalled, was now governed by aristoc-

racies. Yet in another century the aristocrats were succeeded by tyrants, who in turn sometimes yielded to popular rule. Meanwhile the Greek people embarked on a second phase of colonial expansion and dotted the Mediterranean and Black seas with their new settlements. The invention of coinage, the rise of industry, and stimulating ideas from the East further altered the scene, a veritable renaissance in literature and art occurred, but violence, class hatred, and poverty remained.

As a rule people do not willingly leave home, and if the land for which they are headed is unknown, perhaps a wilderness or inhabited by unfriendly natives, then it becomes clear that the motivating force—discontent of some sort, probably—must be especially strong. Hesiod of Ascra, the influential Boeotian poet who lived in the early seventh century B.C., complained bitterly in his *Works and Days* against the greedy nobles who seized the best land, while the poor farmers had to be content with a stony and barren soil. By 750 B.C. the condition in certain areas was worse: some farms were heavily mortgaged, and many farmers had become debt slaves.

Growth of Industry. As the nobles accumulated wealth, there arose a demand for better wares than could be supplied by unskilled hands. To meet this need, some of the poor, who felt cramped on their little farms or had been made homeless by economic oppression, began manufacturing on a small scale. Perhaps they bought a slave or two, and eventually, as business grew, they rivaled the nobles in wealth and could contend with them for political supremacy. The growth of industry was accordingly interwoven with the political and constitutional development of Greece, although agriculture was always the overwhelmingly predominant occupation of the Greeks.

The industries of the new age had their principal origin in Ionia and her neighbor, Lydia. The great plateau of Asia Minor was especially adapted to sheep raising, which enabled the textile industry to develop quickly in the cities of the coast. Here Miletus won fame for her finely woven woolens of rich violet, saffron, purple, and scarlet colors, and her embroideries for the decoration of hats and robes. As skilled industry expanded, Aegina, together with Chalcis on the island of Euboea, became noted for her bronze work. Corinth, under the leadership of the Bacchiadae, the ruling aristocracy, took advantage of her two harbors, on the Saronic and Corinthian gulfs, to become a thriving mart and a center of industry. Immediately to the north of Corinth was Megara, a little city-state whose stony soil forced the people to manufacture, with their scant means, coarse woolens and heavy potteries. Attica was still essentially agricultural, though she ultimately exported oil and wine and beautifully decorated vases.

Discontent. By the middle of the eighth century the Aegean world presented a complex and contradictory picture of wealth and poverty existing side by side, of rich nobles, slaves, a laboring class, and a new vestigial class of merchants. Perhaps the most important underlying reason for discontent was a burgeoning population and an inadequate amount of land to support the numerous and growing peasantry, which, after all, comprised the vast bulk of the population. Thriving, growing cities demanded not only an increased food supply but also raw materials from distant countries and markets for manufactured products. The nobles, moreover, made matters worse by denying political rights to the masses, so that class consciousness

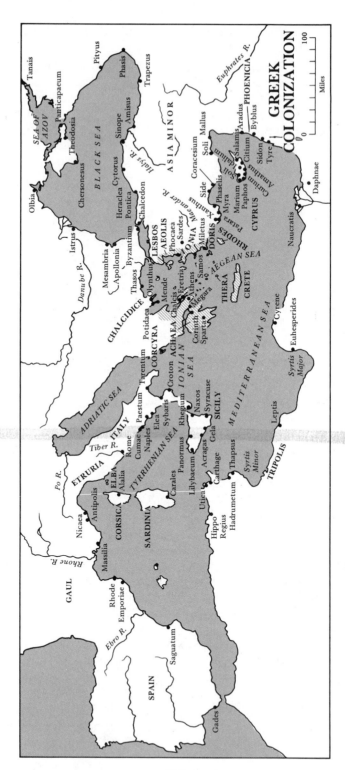

GREEK COLONIZATION

Miles
0   100

and class hatred developed. In some places, especially around the Corinthian Isthmus, there was bitter ethnic feeling between Dorian lords and non-Dorian serfs; the pages of the poet Theognis show how bitter a noble could be when the tables were turned. The one thing uniform to the Aegean world was discontent, which varied in its cause from district to district, but it was clear that revolution might be forestalled if ambitious nobles and troublesome poor could be persuaded to satisfy their yearnings in a new country. Being an adventurous people, many Greeks decided on emigration as the best solution of their difficulties.

Colonization.   The two centuries from 750 to 550 B.C. were the period of colonial expansion. Generally speaking, the founding city, after obtaining the sanction of the Delphic Apollo and perhaps inviting friendly neighbors to take part, appointed a noble as founder to conduct the colonists to their new home, establish the government, and after death receive worship as a hero. A charter of incorporation was drawn up, which constituted the proposed settlement as a community, named the founder, provided for the assignment of lands and for other necessary matters, and regulated the relations between the mother and daughter cities. Decentralizing tendencies were so powerful that distant colonies became sovereign states; yet a strong bond of filial sentiment remained and showed itself in the general continuity of the religious, social, and political usages and institutions of the old city in the new.

Westward Expansion.   The general direction taken by these new colonies was to the north Aegean, the Black Sea and its approaches, North Africa,[1] Sicily, Italy, southern France, and Spain. Colonists from Chalcis were the first to go to Italy, and about 750 B.C. they planted a colony on an island of Pithecusae (Ischia) in the Bay of Naples, and then on the mainland at Cumae and nearby Neapolis (Naples). The Cumaeans had rich fields and manufactured vases and metal wares for trade with the native Latins farther north. Their city was the first Greek center of culture with which the Romans came into touch. It was from the Graii, who had gone out with the Chalcidians as colonists, that the Romans derived the word by which to designate the whole Greek people, though the Greeks, whenever they thought of themselves as one people, called themselves Hellenes.

Among the other Chalcidian colonies were Himera, on the north coast of Sicily, and Zancle, which in later years, when refugees fleeing before the Spartan conquest of Messenia settled there, came to be called Messene (Messana). The acquisition of Messenia so satisfied Sparta's need for land that she founded only one colony, Tarentum in the instep of Italy, which developed a great export industry in weaving and dyeing woolens and in vase making. Meanwhile Achaeans from the northern Peloponnesus founded Sybaris in the instep of the Italian peninsula and Posidonia (Paestum) on the west coast, below Cumae, which is famous for its temple to Poseidon. In all, so many Greeks settled in southern Italy that it was called Magna Graecia (see map, p. 118).

---

[1] Cyrene was the only important Greek colony there, because of Phoenician opposition.

One of the greatest colonizing states was Dorian Corinth, and among her founda-tions the greatest was Syracuse. After seizing the island of Corcyra (Corfu), which was a convenient halting place for boats traveling to the West, the colonists pro-ceeded to Sicily, and in 734 B.C. they founded Syracuse on the island of Ortygia. Soon the city expanded to the mainland, where the surrounding country was worked by the native Sicels. Through other colonies Greeks nearly encircled Sicily, a process that ultimately brought them into conflict, in the west, with colonies of Carthage, the most famous of all Phoenician foundations.

As the ships of the Greeks developed from small round-bottomed boats to a somewhat longer type, with flatter bottoms, furnished with fifty oars and armed with a bronze beak for attack, navigation even further west became easy. The Sa-mians, and more especially the Phocaeans, voyaged from Asia Minor to Spain for gold, silver, and copper, and perhaps even beyond the Pillars of Heracles. The Phoe-nicians resisted Greek penetration beyond Gibraltar, and the Phocaeans confined themselves to Spain and southern Gaul, where one of their colonies, Massilia (Mar-seilles), became the chief center of Greek culture in the western Mediterranean. Ionian laws and the cult of Ephesian Artemis became common, and we must ac-cordingly regard the Phocaeans as the forerunners of Rome in the work of civilizing southwestern Europe.

The Chalcidice and Black Sea. A somewhat different interest attaches to colo-nial movements in other directions, for the founding of settlements along the north-ern Aegean, the Hellespont, and Propontis served merely to expand Aegean Greece to its natural limits. In the occupation of the Chalcidic peninsula[2] the name itself suggests that Chalcis took the lead, though Eretria and Corinth also participated. It was from these colonies that the Macedonians of the interior, a backward Greek people, slowly acquired the civilization of their progressive southern kinsmen. Meanwhile the Ionians, and particularly the citizens of Miletus, which is said to have founded eighty colonies, were sailing through the Hellespont and the Propon-tis and along the coasts of the Black Sea to catch the tunny fish, to trade with the natives, and to plant settlements on all the shores. Although Greek colonies sur-rounded the Black Sea in a nearly unbroken chain and sent back to Greece many useful products, such as fish, timber, dyes, wheat, metals, cattle, and slaves, the settlers were far too few to affect materially the civilization of the natives. On the strategic Bosporus, however, rose a colony of Dorian Megara, Byzantium, which a thousand years after its founding became, under the name of Constantinople, the capital of the Roman Empire.

Syria and Egypt. In another direction Greek enterprise was to bear rich intellec-tual fruit. A Greek colony or trading post existed in northern Syria in the seventh century B.C.; it may have been very important in opening up an avenue for Oriental influence coming into Greece. About the middle of the seventh century Psammeti-chus, with Ionian and Carian aid, made himself master of Egypt. Being friendly to the Greeks, he permitted a settlement of Ionian traders, at Naucratis on the Cano-

---

[2] The most important colonies here of Chalcis were Olynthus and Torone; of Eretria, Mende, Methone, and Scione; and of Corinth, Potidaea. See map, p. 118.

pic channel of the Nile, to grow into a great trading post. As a result papyrus was imported into Greece, while the elementary facts of geometry and astronomy were brought home by inquisitive tourists and stimulated the birth of Greek science and philosopy. To the opening of Egypt, therefore, we may trace in part the intellectual awakening of Greece.

Results of Colonization.   Colonization meant that surplus population found an outlet, that the needy gained land, and that trade increased. It meant, too, a broadening of the Greek horizon and the steady penetration into Greece of new ideas from other countries. Inevitably Greek culture was bestowed in a varying degree on the peoples of the Mediterranean basin; in the west, for example, the Sicilian and Italian Greeks were a mighty factor in the civilization of Italy, and through Italy of central and western Europe.

TYRANNY

The nobles had encouraged colonization as a safety valve. In spite of the many benefits, dissatisfaction remained and had been further increased, during the seventh century, by two additional factors. In the first place, the old aristocratic cavalry had been outmoded by the growth of the hoplite force, those heavy-armed foot soldiers of the nonnoble landholders of means and some merchants, who now demanded a voice in the government. And, second, the Lydians invented a metallic coinage, consisting at first of striated pieces of electrum, a natural amalgam of gold and silver. The date for the invention of metallic coinage in Lydia is debatable. Some numismatists believe that it was invented toward the end of the seventh century B.C. But this view contradicts the evidence of ancient historians. Most probably the first coins appeared early in that same century. The use of coins passed quickly to Ionia and the West and created a new form of wealth, independent of land. People of humble origin might now acquire money and challenge the political exclusiveness of the noble landed proprietors.

Revolution.   The enslaved farmer, the landless factory worker, the new hoplite class, the budding merchant, the ethnic hatred between Dorian and non-Dorian on the Corinthian Isthmus, the knowledge of a larger world—these were the people and the forces that confronted the aristocracies on many fronts in the seventh century B.C. As a specific crisis arose here and there, such as the growth of Lydia in Asia Minor, and as the nobles frequently were incompetent, the old system of aristocracy fell. The procedure that the people generally followed was to rally round an individual, who was frequently an ambitious noble, for in the days before the democratic process had been worked out, the only apparent solution was to destroy the present government. Later on, as the general level of the masses was raised, it was easy enough to get rid of the new ruler or his successor and to govern in his stead. Accordingly it is proper to look on one-man rule, which characterized Greece in the seventh and sixth centuries, as a necessary, albeit an unconscious, step in some city-states on the road to democracy.

Tyranny.   A person who thus seized the reins of government illegally was known as a *tyrant,* in its origin a word imported from Lydia, where the example of tyranny had first been set by Gyges. In the beginning the word *tyrant* carried no opprobrium; it was only when the sons and grandsons of the tyrants became corrupted by wealth and power that the word gained its present meaning. The first tyrants, at least, ruled like modern political bosses in the interest of the people, the ultimate source of their power. Through the support of public works and the patronage of poets and artists they advertised themselves and incidentally contributed to cultural progress and introduced a critical age of questioning. Rhapsodists recited the Homeric poems at popular gatherings; at festivals in honor of the god Dionysus, song and recitation—the germ of drama—celebrated the sufferings and joys he experienced among humankind. The consequent growth of interest in letters had a part in preparing people for self-government.

Corinth. One tyrant, Thrasybulus of Miletus, is now unfortunately an obscure figure, but since his rise was due to the growth of Lydia, and people were needed at home to combat it, we understand why, under certain tyrants, there was a lessening of colonization. Among the earliest tyrannies on the Greek mainland was that of Cypselus at Corinth (ca. 655–625 B.C.), the son of a non-Dorian father but related on his mother's side to the Bacchiad nobles. He came to power on the threat of Argos and Megara and the mishandling of Corcyra; under him Corinth became the greatest sea power in Greece. His son, Periander (ca. 625–550 B.C.), was instrumental in founding an important colony in the Chalcidice, Potidaea, and in raising Corinth itself to a level of luxury, power and brilliance. Three years after his long reign a band of conspirators overthrew the tyranny.

Sicyon. Next in brilliance among the early Greek tyrannies was that at Sicyon, founded by the non-Dorian Orthagoras (ca. 656 B.C.). Sicyon lay northwest of Corinth in the narrow but fertile valley of the Asopus and was as famous for its garden and orchard products as for bronze wares and potteries. Of the descendants of Orthagoras it was Cleisthenes (ca. 600–560 B.C.) who made Sicyon one of the most magnificent cities in Greece. In a successful war he freed Sicyon from the political control of Argos and expelled from the city the cult of an Argive hero, Adrastus, an incident that illuminates the importance of hero cults among the early Greeks. Another picture of Cleisthenes, drawn from the historian Herodotus, sheds a pleasant light on the genial elegance of the tyrant, on his wide interstate connections, and on the social relations and intermarriage of the great nobles of Greece. According to the story, the hand of his daughter, Agariste, was sought by many young nobles, and it was only after a year's entertainment and competition that the lucky suitor, Megacles of the illustrious Alcmeonid family at Athens, was chosen; Cleisthenes of Athens (who framed the democratic constitution of that city), Pericles, and Alcibiades were descendants of this union.

On the whole, tyrannies were short-lived, though in Asia Minor, Persia, as she advanced to the seaboard, found tyranny a surer method of controlling the Greeks. The service that the tyrants performed was very great, for despite harsh treatment of the nobles, they maintained the civil law as they found it, destroyed aristocracy as a political institution, broadened the base of wealth, and extended an intelligent patronage to the arts. A few states were now ready for democracy, but in the never-ending struggle between the few and the many, more states returned to oligarchy, albeit a more liberally constituted oligarchy than the earlier aristocracy. In this absorbing period of colonial expansion, industrial development, and social and political change, two states, Sparta and Athens, stand out as special cases. Sparta scarcely participated in the colonial movement, and Athens began to colonize only at a very late date; Sparta never experienced tyranny, and Athens produced its famous one, the Peisistratid, only after tyranny had begun to disappear elsewhere. To them we must now turn in order to understand better the meaning of the city-state.

9

Sparta and Athens

SPARTA

Sparta is situated near the center of Laconia; beside the banks of the Eurotas River, with the sea to the south and, immediately to the west, the range of Mount Taÿgetus, beyond which lay non-Dorian Messenia. Here came, in the days around 700 B.C., Terpander from Lesbos to play his lyre; Thaletas of Gortyn introduced choral song and dance; and here, too, the great Alcman, who perhaps was a Lydian from Sardis, sang verses of peace and pleasure and love, poems that give us a glimpse of a Spartan life of contentment. The British excavations at the Sanctuary of Artemis Orthia, moreover, illustrate the fine taste of the early Spartans, and pottery finds, in general, prove Sparta's commercial relations with the Greeks of Asia.

There was every reason, then, for Sparta to develop as other states, for, in spite of its peculiar structure, each state had its own individuality. And yet, Sparta's history shows how a rigorous training can turn a people, no braver than the rest, into an invincible force and, indeed, how conservatism can stagnate until it becomes a force determined to maintain a system at whatever cost. The price exacted was high, but Sparta did become the most powerful state in Greece.

Helots and Perioeci.   The invading Dorians, at the outset of the Middle Age, reduced the population of Laconia to a state of serfdom, known as *helotry*, while those natives who had managed to flee to the mountains were allowed to remain there in a semi-independent condition and became known as *perioeci* or "dwellers around." Then, about 730 B.C., the Spartans reached across Mount Taÿgetus and after a bitter struggle of twenty years conquered Messenia and made helots of its people. This conquest, together with the founding of Tarentum, at least satisfied Sparta's need of land, but political tensions, as elsewhere, still existed because of aristocratic domination of the government. That government was also weak, and Sparta suffered a stinging defeat by Pheidon of Argos at Hysiae (669?). The Messenians, aided by Argives, Arcadians, and Pisatans, revolted soon after 650 B.C. Led by Tyrtaeus, their official poet laureate or propagandist, the Spartans finally put the revolt down.

The Spartans were quick to see the significance of the Messenian revolt. Could they hope to lead an ordinary life devoted to commerce, agriculture, and the arts, but indefinitely keep in subjection a population ten times their size, and if not, would it not be better to keep the easy helot system? They decided on the latter

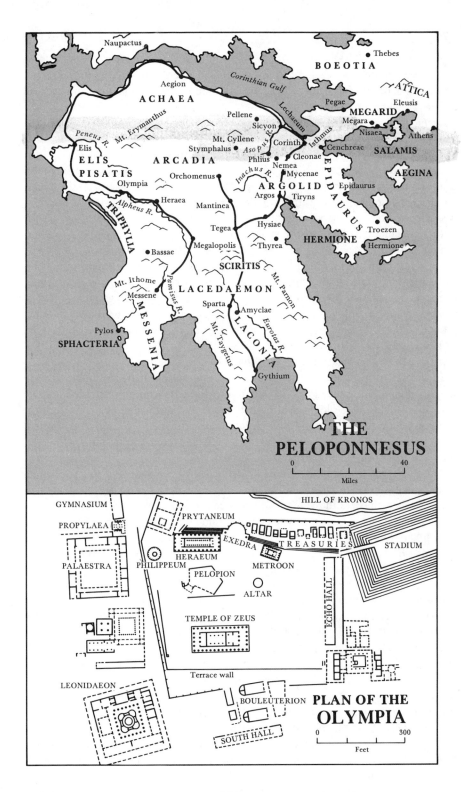

THE
PELOPONNESUS

0   40

Miles

PLAN OF THE
OLYMPIA

0   300

Feet

course, though, as they realized, this entailed a deliberate reordering of their lives, and a gradual abandonment of the pursuit of culture and commerce, and even all currency except iron money.

Regimentation. In order to keep the helots in their place and to make all citizens, in essence, hoplites, the Spartans now constituted themselves a perpetual army and occupied their entire life with training. In other states of Greece, for example, custom gave the father the option of rearing his child or putting it to death immediately after birth, but in Sparta this function was usurped by a board, which might order the exposure of a weak infant on Mount Taÿgetus. If the child was allowed to live, he was taken from his mother at the age of seven and placed directly under the control of the state until he was twenty, when he became a citizen liable for military service in the field. Though he could now marry, he did not enjoy a real home but passed his life in military drill, eating and sleeping in the barracks. Here he joined a mess of fifteen persons known as a *syssition,* each of whose members contributed his monthly share of barley, wine, cheese, figs, and meat. The women, however, enjoyed comparative luxury at home and accumulated so much property, through dowries and inheritances, that in the time of Aristotle they owned nearly two-fifths of the land. In Sparta all lived alike under a system that sacrificed the individual to the ideal good of the state.

To guarantee his status in the mess, every full-fledged Spartan hoplite received the use of land lots, divided equally, worked by the serfs who supplied their masters with subsistence. These lots could be withdrawn and reassigned by the state if for any reason the tenant failed in his military duties. Other land was privately owned, so that there were always disparities of wealth and even social status at Sparta, some families always being recognized as noble.

Although, strictly speaking, the helots belonged to the state and not to an individual, they lived with their families in cottages on the lots assigned them and rendered to their masters the amount of produce fixed by law. This requirement was rigidly insisted upon, for a Spartan master falling behind in his contribution was suspended from his *syssition.* The helots were liable to military service in time of war and received freedom as a reward for bravery. Nevertheless they were subjected to many indignities and were spied on by a kind of secret police force, known as the *crypteia.* The towns of the perioeci, which ringed Laconia, hedged the helots in and served further as a bulwark of the land. These people, by now a mixture of pre-Dorians and Dorians, were personally free, formed the business community of Laconia, and, with the Spartans, constituted the "Lacedaemonians."

Government. Sparta had two kings, drawn from the royal families of the Agiads and the Eurypontids, and these, together with twenty-eight elders past the age of sixty, formed the *gerousia* or council, which had the task of considering measures to be presented to the assembly of citizens. The latter, called the *apella,* was given technically sovereign powers when the state was reformed after the Messenian revolt. Actually it simply passed or rejected the proposals brought before it, for it could neither initiate nor debate measures, except the vital ones touching peace and war. It also elected the magistrates, the board of five ephors, who, depending on personalities, could be more powerful than the kings.

The reform that we have just described was attributed in antiquity to Lycurgus, but it seems likely that Lycurgus was a hero to whose protection the reform was entrusted when it was effected, probably just after the Messenian revolt. In any case, the constitution, so far as it affected the citizens, was essentially democratic, but in view of the great masses whom she ruled, Sparta must be considered an oligarchy.

THE PELOPONNESIAN LEAGUE

Sparta used her military might during the sixth century to humble Tegea in Arcadia (ca. 550) and to make it Sparta's first dependent ally in the Peloponnesus. Then she united all the states of the Peloponnesus, excepting Argos, her ancient enemy, and some of Achaea, into an alliance concerned solely with foreign affairs. This so-called Peloponnesian League thus began to develop about 550 B.C., and consisted of a separate treaty between each state and Sparta, in which the members pledged themselves to furnish military forces for the wars waged by the league and to serve under the command of the Lacedaemonian kings. The all-important body, the Assembly, met at either Sparta or Corinth, and though the members were free to manage their own affairs, Sparta, being an oligarchy herself, upheld oligarchy among her allies. The significance of the Peloponnesian League for history, however, is that a well-centralized military force was receiving its finishing touches at the very time when the danger of Persian conquest threatened Greece, though there was another state, Athens, that made an equal contribution to the common cause.

ATHENS

Precisely why Athens became a democracy is of course as important a study as the democratic constitution itself, for the road from monarchy to democracy was long and hard, and the first step could not have been taken with any conscious knowledge of the ultimate goal.

The Athenians were Ionian Greeks; they did not inherit from the migrations the curse of serfdom, with all the hatred and fear that it engendered. In place of the Dorian Invasion, Attic tradition points to a steady, even development, a fact that archaeology, and particularly the continuous series of pottery, helps to confirm.

Attica. Attica, a peninsula of about a thousand square miles jutting into the Aegean Sea, is cut off from central Greece by mountains, which perhaps explains why the various communities were spared the shock of overwhelming invasion at the end of the Bronze Age. Its relative isolation is compensated for by good harbors at Marathon and, nearer Athens, at Phaleron and Piraeus. The marble quarries on Mount Pentelicus, the silver mines at Laurium, the clay, and the wheat, olive groves, and vineyards of the plain were among Attica's chief natural assets.

Early Athens. The outstanding fact in the early history of Attica is the gradual growth, from ca. 1000 to 700 B.C., of a community of interest among the inhabitants, until finally the people transferred their allegiance and their sovereignty to one city, Athens, and called themselves Athenians, never Atticans. This is the *syn-*

oikismos that legend attributed to the hero Theseus; we do know, in spite of the obscurity of all details in this early period, that it was the last regal dynasty—that of the Medontidae—that annexed nearby Eleusis and the Thriasian plain, thus rounding out the city-state.

Like other Greek states, early Athens had a king and an aristocratic council with administrative, judicial, and religious functions; this was the Areopagus and was a development of the Homeric council of elders. There was also an ineffective assembly of the people, who were grouped in their four Ionian tribes (*phylae*). Each tribe was divided into three phratries, originally brotherhoods of fighting comrades but now small administrative units, closely connected with religion. Membership in a phratry was necessary for citizenship, which could be won only through birth. This law was to become troublesome as Athens became less isolated. The aristocratic clan (*genos*), whose purpose was to serve the interest of the landed nobility, called Eupatrids, would be a further cause of friction.

Archons.   The monarchy at Athens was first weakened by the creation of other offices—the *polemarch,* or commander in chief, and the *archon eponymos,* who gave his name to the year—with the result that the kingship was left with so little power that it was thrown open to annual election. The *archon basileus,* or king archon, now became the official responsible for religious matters. The archons, then, were the magistrates and were supervised by the Areopagus, and on the expiration of their year of office they joined that council. At some time thereafter the number of archons grew to nine, with the creation of six *thesmothetai,* officials concerned originally with the administration of justice. Later they supervised court calendars and procedure for certain kinds of trials, as did the three senior archons.

The Army.   At the same time a reorganization of the military forces of the state was to bring about a more liberal conception of government, powerful enough to challenge the aristocracy, since it had a new and broader base, that of wealth rather than birth. When the hoplite phalanx was introduced, it was found that the aristocrats were too few in number to constitute it, as they once had the cavalry. Accordingly it was necessary to recruit the heavy infantry from the common landowners and others whose income would enable them to equip themselves with a panoply. To determine those liable for service and their duties, the entire population was divided by census into three classes based on property.[1]

Attempted Tyranny.   Athens experienced some aspects of the economic depression common to archaic city-states. The plight of the tenant farmers, who had to pay one-sixth of their produce to the great landowners, emboldened an ambitious noble, Cylon (ca. 632), to attempt a tyranny, with the aid of his father-in-law, the Megarian tyrant Theagenes. His bid for power failed, which suggests the condition of the peasants was not yet so depressed as to lend grass-roots support to tyranny. In the course of putting it down, the archon, Megacles, was accused of having commited an impious act, and he and his clan, the Alcmeonidae, were exiled.

---

[1] The *hippeis,* or horsemen, who were the wealthiest; the *zeugitae* who were the heavy infantry; and the poorest people, called *thetes.* Attica was divided into forty-eight districts, or naucraries, to facilitate the raising of troops and their maintenance by land and sea.

Draco. The Athenians saw that if another attempt at tyranny was to be fore-stalled, stability must be achieved. Therefore, about 621 B.C., they commissioned Draco to codify the law. Little is known about his reforms, but it is clear that they marked a great advance in the field of homicide. In spite of the fact that the nearest of kin, assisted by the phratry, were still permitted to prosecute, the state now assumed its responsibility for the public welfare by asserting its power over the accused, to punish or acquit.

Solon. Since Draco's code was harsh and favored the landowners, it could not be expected to settle primarily economic problems. In the hope of relieving over-population, the Athenians conquered Salamis, a neighboring island, and Sigeum in the Troad. The domestic situation still pressed for solution, however, and in 594 B.C. Solon, a moderately rich noble, a merchant and poet, was appointed ar-chon with extraordinary powers to reform the consitution.

Economic Reforms. Solon had to give his attention to economics, the constitu-tion, and law in order to reconcile conflicting interests and make possible future security and stability. He did not intend to set up a democracy, for he would not have understood the word. His first act, known as the *seisachtheia* or "shaking off of burdens," was to abolish all securities on land and person, to free those who had fallen into slavery, and to forbid anyone in the future to become a debt slave. To make it easier to pay one's debts, Solon shifted from the Aeginetan standard to the Euboic, which was lighter by a third. This currency reform also facilitated trade with Corinth, Chalcis, Eretria, and their many colonies, who used the Euboic stan-dard. To pay for the importation of wheat from the Black Sea, Solon developed the export abroad of Athenian olive oil in beautiful but serviceable pots. He also opened up the silver mines of Laurium, a step that was to prove momentous in Ath-ens' history, for her fine silver coinage was essential to her power and prosperity.

If agrarian Athens were to grow rapidly, it was necessary to attract residents from abroad. This Solon accomplished by promising them citizenship, an action that stamps him as one of the most liberal statesmen in early Greek history. He con-vinced the Athenians that people could win citizenship even though they had not been born in Athens and had not undertaken the religious obligations that went with membership in a phratry. He then proceeded to form religious societies for the new citizens—who came from other states, with their wives and children, to pursue their jobs—in order that they might join the state on the same terms as others.

Reform of the Constitution. An amnesty to political exiles, including the Alc-meonidae; the revision of the calendar and the system of weights and measures; the regulation of wills; a limitation on the amount of land one person might own, and a lightening of penalties—these were some of Solon's other moderate reforms, which pleased neither the very rich nor the very poor. His reforms tried to free individuals from family and religious associations and to attach them more closely to the state. In his revision of the constitution, wealth became the sole qualification for office; Athens thus ceased to be an aristocracy and became a timocracy.

In his new constitution, Solon kept the old property classes, except that the rich-est were put into a special class known as "500-measure men" (*pentacosiomedimni*); below them were the horsemen (*hippeis*), those whose estates produced annually

300-500 *medimni* or measures of produce—from these two classes the magistrates, including the nine archons, were annually elected. Next came the *zeugitae* with 200-300 measures, who were now eligible for membership in a new Council of Four Hundred; and finally the *thetes,* the laborers who produced under 200 measures, and who were admitted to the assembly, though barred from office. The popular nature of the assembly was held in check by virtue of the fact that it could discuss only the measures brought before it by the council. The council was recruited from the four tribes, one hundred from each. An important innovation was Solon's creation of the *heliaea.* These were courts to which men over thirty years of age from all four property classes were eligible. Their functions were to receive appeals from the judicial decisions of the archons, thus permitting the people themselves to be the court of last resort and, if necessary, to try retiring magistrates for misconduct in office.

Peisistratus. The landed nobility, roughly the Party of the Plain as it is sometimes called, did not like Solon's reform. There was a counterpoise, however, centered in the men of the coast—the city craftsmen and others. These were the newer citizens who had recently come to Athens and were satisfied with their lot. The decision in factional strife was to lie largely with the men beyond the hills, disaffected nobles and turbulent shepherds, who had expected land as well as freedom from Solon. The leadership of these malcontents fell in time to Peisistratus, a distant relative of Solon, a soldier, smooth talking, diplomatic, and politically devious. Persuading the assembly to vote him a personal guard on the ground that his life was in danger, he seized the Acropolis in 560 B.C. and, though he was twice sent into exile and thus became tyrant *three* times, he finally established himself as tyrant with the aid of mercenaries (540-539).

The Tyrant's Policy. Peisistratus was a brilliant political "boss." At home he enforced the existing laws and constitution, permitting even potential enemies like the Alcmeonids to be elected to the chief offices. Partly to keep people safely on their farms, he sent judges on circuit about the countryside. A subterranean aqueduct, a network of roads through Attica, the extensive building of temples, the enlargement of religious festivals—such as the City Dionysia (the cradle of Greek drama) and the great Panathenaic festival—and the patronage of poets and artists all made him popular and nurtured much of the civilization of archaic Greece. These benefits attached the masses to Peisistratus. Many of the nobles liked the social attractions of his court, but those aristocrats who were too independent were forced into exile. Their estates were divided among the poor, who also received seed and work animals for stocking their farms, and so the land problem of Attica was solved. At the same time Peisistratus developed Solon's ideas on industry and commerce; more Attic wine and oil than ever before were now shipped to Etruria, Egypt, Asia Minor, and the Black Sea. In brief, Peisistratus did much to make Athens an influential city-state.

End of the Tyranny. When Peisistratus died of old age in 527 B.C., his sons Hippias and Hipparchus continued his policy, but in 514 B.C. two nobles, Harmodius and Aristogeiton, acting on personal motives, assassinated Hipparchus. Hippias, growing suspicious and harsh, then became a tyrant in the unfavorable sense of the word. The Alcmeonidae, once again in exile, allegedly bribed the Delphic Oracle to convince the Spartans to intervene in Attica. In any case, the Spartan king, Cleomenes, drove Hippias into exile. Thus the tyranny of the Peisistratidae came to an end in 510 B.C.

DEMOCRACY

Aristocratic Reaction and Cleisthenes.   The downfall of Hippias was a victory for the exiled nobles, who on their return hoped to secure political control and repossession of their estates. Under the leadership of Isagoras they revised the citizen lists and eliminated many individuals whose ancestors had been enrolled by Solon and Peisistratus. Thereupon the Alcmeonid Cleisthenes, grandson of Cleisthenes, tyrant of Sicyon, rallied the disfranchised masses and forced Isagoras into exile (508 B.C.).

The Tribes.   The great noble Cleisthenes was to prove himself a statesman and democrat. The all-important task of bringing harmony to the state demanded the abolition of the power (though not necessarily the existence) of certain associations, religious and otherwise, such as the phratry and the clan. It was also necessary to reduce the potential threat of the nobles and to permit the enrollment of those recently disfranchised as the equals of citizens of pure Athenian descent. Determined to dissociate kinship and religion from citizenship, Cleisthenes abolished the four old Ionian tribes (except for ceremonial purposes) in favor of ten new ones. He then made residence in a deme the basis of membership in a tribe. Henceforth the demes—townships of Attica and sections of Athens itself—were the units of local self-government. Cleisthenes then constituted the ten new tribes in the following manner. He grouped the demes in "thirds" (*trittyes*); while the number of demes in a *trittys* varied, three *trittyes* formed a tribe, giving a total of thirty *trittyes*. The *trittyes* of a tribe did not come from the same area, but one *trittys*, with its various demes, represented the people of the coast, another the interior, and still another the city.

This is the first known instance of gerrymandering and was designed to make each tribe a cross section of the population; the effect of Cleisthenes' tribal arrangement with its emphasis on mere residence was to prevent any element, such as the nobles, from gaining control of the government. But the fact that the voting in the assembly, on the basis of "one man one vote," took place at Athens made it possible for the city *trittys* to influence a tribe's vote; because the city *trittys* was more closely knit in sentiment than the two other *trittyes*, composed as they were of rich and poor farmers. Whether this favoring of the urban electorate was due to accident or design we do not know.

The Council and Assembly.   A new Council of Five Hundred (*boule*), with fifty members chosen annually by lot from each of the ten tribes, was substituted for Solon's Council of Four Hundred. Since a tribe's fifty members were distributed among the demes according to the size of the population, the scheme at once recognized the principle of proportional representation. The council met in the Council House, or *Bouleuterion,* and, as the deliberative and governing body in the state, was responsible for financial and foreign affairs and the preparation of the business that was to come before the assembly (*ecclesia*). The assembly met once every ten days on the Pnyx and passed decrees. To facilitate its work, the council was divided into ten committees, or prytanies, each consisting of a tribe's fifty members. Each committee was in charge of affairs for thirty-five or thirty-six days; thus a prytany came also to be a measure of time. The archons remained the executive officials, but when the army was reorganized in 501 B.C., a board of ten generals (*strategoi*) was formed. During the crisis of the Persian Wars this became the most powerful body at Athens.

The ancient tradition holds that Cleisthenes devised a means of preventing the return of tyranny. This was the curious practice of ostracism, so-called since the voting was done on *ostraka* or potsherds. The assembly yearly decided if they wanted to hold an ostracism; if so, in plenary session of six thousand, they voted a man whom they considered dangerous into exile for ten years, after which time he might return with full citizenship rights restored. Ostracism was first used much later than Cleisthenes, in 487 B.C., and it is difficult to explain the delay of twenty years in its first use if it was truly Cleisthenes' institution.

Athens was now a democracy. The property qualifications for magistrates probably did not debar large numbers from office, in view of the wider distribution of wealth. Nevertheless there remained real conservative checks, such as the absence of pay for public service, which kept the poor from participation in assembly and courts. At the same time, the energizing of the political and patriotic spirit of the people—in the demes, in the Council of Five Hundred, in the assembly, and in the courts—produced prodigious military, artistic, and intellectual activities. To some of these we must now turn.

10

The Civilization of Archaic Greece

RELIGION

To the civilization of archaic Greece—those centuries of exuberant growth from the end of the Middle Age to the conclusion of the Persian Wars (ca. 750–479 B.C.)—the entire Greek world contributed. It was perhaps due to Homer, more than to anyone else, that Greek religion became refined and received a definite stamp. Under his inspiration the process was carried on by Ionic poets of the eighth and seventh centuries, who composed various poems known as the Epic Cycle. The gods of long ago had lived on earth with mortals, but the epic brought them to the sky, to the peaks of Mount Olympus, where they lived under the presidency of Zeus.

The Gods. There were many gods. Zeus was the least primitive of them all and the most godlike. His wife-sister was Hera. Athena and Artemis were Minoan in origin; Apollo came from Asia but developed nevertheless into the great symbol of Hellenism, the champion of mankind; Poseidon had been a mighty god of the earth, but changed to a lesser god, concerned with the crafts of the sea. Similarly the other gods acquired special functions: Ares was the god of war, Aphrodite the goddess of love, and Hermes the messenger of the gods, and so on. Every state had its own special guardian deities, and the Athena or Zeus of a given state was a personal being distinct from every other Athena or Zeus.

Festivals. To promote the happiness of the gods, festivals were regularly held, generally in the city-state. For unknown reasons a few of these festivals became Panhellenic, such as those at Delphi, on the Corinthian Isthmus, at Nemea, and at Olympia, in honor of Apollo, Poseidon, Nemean Zeus, and Olympian Zeus, respectively. The Greek love of athletics was probably inherited from Minoan days. Eventually the most popular events at the Olympic Games were the foot race, wrestling, and the pentathlon, which comprised running, wrestling, leaping, spear hurling, and discus throwing. In addition to advancing physical excellence and an appreciation of music and poetry, the national festivals were held under a sacred truce, when states ceased war, merchants gathered to sell their wares, and the entire Greek world exchanged ideas. Thus was generated a spirit of ethnic unity, and the Greeks

133

came to see that they were different from other peoples—"barbarians," as Greeks called those who spoke languages other than Greek.

In addition to festivals honoring Panhellenic gods, there were also many cults and festivals celebrating local heros of individual city-states, like the founders (oecists) of colonies.

The most famous of local festivals was the Panathenaea at Athens, which, after the reforms of Peisistratus, was given with special magnificence every fourth year as the Greater Panathenaea. Prisoners were set free; slaves were permitted to feast with their masters; there were races, war dances in armor, athletic competitions, and a grand procession. The procession, which was later commemorated on the frieze of the Parthenon, consisted of all the free population. Peisistratus also added to the Panathenaea the recitation of Homer's poems. This immediately bore fruit by introducing epic subjects into the art of painting and by giving an epic content to infant drama.

Oracles. Hero worship, which began with the cult of dead chieftains and was extended to ordinary mortals till every association had its real or fictitious ancestor, spread rapidly in post-Homeric Greece. As the gods became universalized, the heroes remained local. The life of the Greeks, obviously, was permeated with religion, and it was only natural that they should seek means of communicating with the gods, either through the flight of birds or the vitals of a sacrificed animal or an oracle. The most venerable oracle was that of Zeus at Dodona. Favoring conditions brought to preeminence the oracle of Apollo at Delphi, where his prophetess, the Pythia, sat on a tripod in the shrine and received her answers from the god. Often unintelligible, her mutterings were interpreted to the inquirer by priests. An occasional function of the oracle was to reveal the future, and such responses were couched in ambiguous terms so as to be surely right. Delphi's great authority really derived from its wise advice on the moral or religious conduct of individuals and states.

LITERATURE

Elegiac Poetry. The old epic verse of calm, stately meter—the dactylic hexameter—proved inadequate. It yielded to new and varied measures, which would better exhibit the play of individual or communal thought and emotion that was characteristic of the new era. The elegiac pentameter, whose spirit may be either meditative or emotional, was the first variation from the epic verse. Accompanied by the pipe, it lent itself to the expression of political and social thought, and to erotic, religious, and martial themes. The first great master of the elegy was Callinus of Ephesus, who in the middle of the seventh century roused his countrymen to battle, inspiring patriotic ideals and martial spirits. A greater personal intensity distinguishes the poetry of Archilochus (ca. 670), a native of Paros who became a wanderer over sea and land. In addition to composing elegies, he was the first master of the iambic, a measure adapted to the energetic utterance of the range of human passions, from love to sarcasm and hate. Perhaps the greatest of the elegists was Mimnermus of Colophon, who loved a flute girl, Nanno, and addressed to her many poems on love or past lovers. The music and spirit of Mimnermus had a considerable influence on the elegiac movement of Alexandria and its Roman imitators.

Lyric Poetry. The true discoverers of individualism and skepticism were the great lyric poets of Aeolis in the sixth century. Reflecting the general feeling about the gods and human dependence on them, they give us an invaluable insight into the life and character of their times. One of these writers of personal lyrics was Alcaeus. Another was a brilliant woman, Sappho, who became the head of a school of girls at Mytilene on the island of Lesbos, a literary circle, or guild, sacred to Aphrodite. Music, dancing, and the technique of poetry were studied. Between Sappho and her pupils there was the warmest attachment, both intellectual and erotic. The chief interest of Sappho, which was expressed with intense feeling in melodious verse, was in her girls, their sorrows, joys, loves, and marriages. There is at the same time a delicate appreciation of natural beauty in the night, the sea, flowery fields, cool streams, and singing birds.

Drama. In Greece there was no real distinction between society and state. The citizens were mostly known to one another, and the reunions of kinsmen, neighbors, phratries, and entire communities in festivals were not only social but also religious and civic functions. These circumstances explain the existence of a form of poetry—choral lyrics or odes, with song and dance—that was religious, social, and civic. This kind of poetry was expected to express the feelings of both the writer and the whole community. One form of ode contained the germ of the drama.

The origin of the drama is obscure, but it may have developed from a ritual when people celebrated the birth, marriage, death, and rebirth of the god, Dionysus. He was a great vegetation spirit and the happy god of wine. Hence, as the wild strain sung to Dionysus was transformed by poetic art into a choral ode, there arose comedy, which dealt with the marriage ritual, and tragedy, which dealt with the death ritual of the god. The singing was interspersed with recitation, which gradually developed into dialogue in the hands of poets, such as Arion, who worked at Corinth in the days of Periander, and Thespis, who graced the court of Peisistratus. The tyrants fostered the growth of the drama, since it was through the encouragement of popular cults, as distinguished from those monopolized by the nobility, that they tried to win a reputation. Dramatic festivals were held in various parts of Greece; for example, in December the villages of Attica celebrated the Rural Dionysia, in which a chorus of men, in rustic attire, sang in honor of Dionysus an unpolished but joyous song, the dithyramb; in January there was a festival in Athens itself, the Lenaea, and another, the City Dionysia, in March. For a long time the drama continued to be crude and immature, and even at the close of the archaic period it was essentially a cantata in which the singing was occasionally interrupted by dialogue.

The Eleusinian Mysteries. The Athenians did not hesitate to join the worship of Dionysus with that of Demeter and her daughter, Persephone. Once a year the devotees of these goddesses, gathering at Athens, moved in procession along the Sacred Way to Eleusis, where, in the Hall of the Mysteries, or Telesterion, the initiated performed sacred rites that none dared disclose. The Eleusinian mysteries seem to have consisted chiefly of a "passion play" representing the sorrows of Demeter, when her daughter was carried off by Hades, and the joy of recovering her. In archaic Greece the ceremony, which once referred to the death of vegetation in winter and its rebirth in spring, came to signify death and the resurrection of the soul to eternal happiness. Thus the joys of Elysium, in Homer's conception available to the favored few, were democratized by the progress of Athens toward popular liberty and equality.

Orphism.   During the sixth century an effort was made to transform the worship of Dionysus, much of which was orgiastic, into a theology. According to myth, Zeus wanted to transfer his power to Dionysus, who was devoured by Titans, only to be restored whole by Athena. The Titans were then burned to ashes, out of which mortals were formed. The leaders of the new movement looked back for their master to Orpheus, a legendary Thracian singer and poet, to whose name eventually everything mystical was attached. The essential belief was that the soul suffered the punishment of sin, committed in a previous existence, and that the body was an enclosure, or prison, in which the soul was incarcerated. By purity of living and the practice of rituals the initiated were able to cleanse themselves from sin and secure eternal happiness and even to redeem the souls of the dead from punishment in Tartarus. In spite of the zealous work of missionaries, however, no state accepted Orphism as part of the public worship.

Hesiod.   The early Greek believed that the gods were the causes of all things in nature and the arbiters of human destiny. With the dawning consciousness of moral and physical unity and order, the poets devised a system, or cosmogony, in which all existing things might have a due part. They explained the multitude of deities, as of humans, and even the plurality of all natural objects, by the one process of birth. Hesiod, the seventh-century Boeotian poet whose *Works and Days* bemoaned contemporary life, was the earliest cosmogony, of which his *Theogony* is the surviving example. He assumed the creation, he did not say how, of Chaos, then Earth. From Chaos sprang Erebos and black Night; and from Night, in turn, sprang bright Ether and Day. Earth gave birth to Heaven, and from them was born Cronos of crooked counsels. When Zeus, the son of Cronos, grew to manhood in the island of Crete, he conquered the Titans and other monstrous beings, and himself reigned supreme. In this way, the poet thought, came unity, system, and order from chaos.

The Ionian Scientists.   The inquiring spirit of the Ionian Greeks could not be satisfied with such reasoning nor even with the quickening influences from the Orient. The organized priesthoods of Egypt and Babylonia had cultivated a study of arithmetic, geometry, and astronomy and the elements of architecture and civil engineering. Their knowledge consisted of facts ascertained by experience and arbitrarily classified, so that it lacked the elements of reason and demonstration and was far from science. The contribution of the Greek mind, imaginative and untrammeled by religious or other convention, was to pierce beneath the fact to the underlying cause and thus to create real science. The first step in this process, taken by Thales of Miletus early in the sixth century B.C., makes him the founder of science.

Thales.   Thales' fame rests not on any individual scientific discovery (his foretelling of the sun's eclipse on May 28, 585 B.C. may be apocryphal) but on his new conception of cause, which he sought in nature rather than among the gods. Wrong though he was in choosing one material substance, water, as his first principle, yet in displacing the gods with natural causation, he took the all-important step from mythology and theology to science and philosophy. This change has proved the most momentous revolution in the intellectual history of humankind.

Anaximander. Thales' pupil, Anaximander, who is famous as having made the first map of the earth, published a scientific treatise, which is probably the earliest prose work in Greek. He chose as his fundamental principle the "unlimited," evidently a boundless reservoir from which all things come and to which everything returns, a mechanical process for explaining the formation and ultimate destruction of the existing world.

Pythagoras. A new and deeper meaning was given to philosophy by Pythagoras of Samos, who in 522 B.C. migrated to Croton in Italy. Learned in the mathematics of the Ionian school, he sought in numbers the primary cause of all things, whether musical harmonies, stellar movements, the nature of the gods, or even abstract ideas. The exactness he gave to science was marred by his attaching mystical powers to numbers. In fact, Pythagoras is distinguished as a mystic and a moral reformer even more than for his contribution to science. His chief aim seems to have been a life of moral purity, to which philosophy, religion, and mystic initiations were merely contributory. His school was a secret association, with adherents in many of the cities of southern Italy, and as these societies took a political turn, an attempt was made to manage affairs according to their ethical standard.

Xenophanes. A further advance in these general philosophic and ethical directions was made by Xenophanes of Colophon (ca. 572–480 B.C.), who migrated to Elea in Italy, where he founded the so-called Eleatic school. He indignantly assailed the Homeric conception of the gods as beings of human form, who lied and stole and committed such other sins as would shame the human race. He considered beings of this kind the creation of human fancy. The real God, Xenophanes maintained, was One, like mortals in neither form nor thought, but eternal, unchangeable, and spiritual. This seems to have been an enunciation of a pure monotheism. It is clear, too, that Xenophanes' interest centered in moral improvement. It was the duty of sensible men, when they gathered at banquets, for example, to pray God to give them power to do justice. His God therefore was a moral force; and Xenophanes was as much a theologian and a moral reformer as a philosopher.

Heracleitus. On the other hand, with Heracleitus of Ephesus (ca. 500 B.C.), philosophy began to concern itself with the flux, motion, change, and life of nature. Not Being, he asserted, but Becoming was the fundamental essence of things. Meditation on this subject led him to imagine a world-ruling reason (*logos*), which produced the ever-changing phenomena of the universe. This controlling principle could be apprehended only by a few sages like himself, who also possessed a *logos* similar in kind to that of the universe, whereas the masses were doomed to eternal ignorance and folly. His teaching gave pronounced encouragement to mysticism.

Moral Progress. From this intellectual progress arose a better conception of virtue (*arete*), which required not so much physical perfection as moral excellence. This morality demanded *sophrosyne* (self-restraint), an important word in the

Greek vocabulary, and one involving the most binding of Hellenic precepts. Moral progress showed itself in a greater humanity, in the development of law codes, in the treatment of prisoners of war, in the practice of defining interstate relations by treaties, and in the submission of disputes to arbitration.

History.   The Greek mind, which in time produced the scientific point of view toward all things connected with the world and humanity, led also to the birth of historical thought. Prose writers known as logographers interested themselves in the present and in human affairs. The greatest of them, Hecataeus of Miletus (ca. 500 B.C.), set the stage for Herodotus, founder of the art of history. Hecataeus applied in his *Genealogies* a free, inquiring mind, unwilling to give any greater weight to Greek tradition, simply because he was a Greek, than to that of another race. An awakening consciousness of the distinction between myth and fact is shown by his own words: "I write what I believe to be true, for the various stories of the Greeks are, in my opinion, ridiculous."

ART

Pots.   The fact that the entire Greek world, east and west, contributed to the development of archaic Greek civilization becomes even more obvious when we turn from literature to art, and particularly to the pottery, which is found in large quantities at every site and has been studied in detail. The pots reveal the best in archaic art, for artists had not yet devoted themselves exclusively to the major arts of architecture and sculpture and did not hesitate to decorate objects that were intended for everyday use.

The Orientalizing Style.   The wonderful development of pots from the end of the eighth century proceeded hand in hand with the growth of Greek culture as a whole. Colonization, commerce, and the penetration of new ideas from the East stimulated progress. The old geometric style, with its elaborate surface decoration, then yielded to strong Oriental influence: lotus flowers, processions of winged lions and other animals, sphinxes, griffins, and contrasting colors. A combination of color and design was achieved in a delightful decorative effect. Exuberance is what strikes us, rather than narrative, discipline, or formalism. The pots from Rhodes and Corinth, two important centers of the new ware, show gorgons, mythological tales, and human figures that move and have volume. (Contrast p. 115.)

The Black-Figured Style.   In the course of the seventh century the practice of painting figures in black arose, the natural color of the clay forming the background. This was the so-called black-figured style, in which the figures of Theseus and the Minotaur were especially popular. The emphasis was now on narrative, the exuberant was being disciplined by the formal, and a truly national style, which had absorbed the foreign influences, was emerging. Put briefly, the technique of the famous black-figured style was as follows. After the vase had been shaped on the wheel and had been allowed to dry, the surface was polished in preparation for the decoration. The figure was first drawn in black outline and then filled in with a black varnish, thus presenting a black silhouette against the red background, which

FIGURE 26. Orientalizing
Corinthian wine jug depicting
real and imaginary animals,
625 B.C. Height: 12 inches.

The Granger Collection

in reality was merely the natural color of the clay slightly tinted by a transparent
wash. Other colors—white, purple, red, brown—might be added to the figure; the
inner lines could be marked by incision, and so too could the outlines of figures
where they crossed one another. The firing in the oven added a luster to the black
glaze.

The Red-Figured Style.   About 530 B.C. a new style of vase painting became
popular and held sway throughout the fifth century. The red-figured style, as it is
called, shows the figures in the color of the clay, and the background was painted
black. Archaic exuberance was combined with a discipline and vigor that created a
simple air. The artist was now able to draw the human form more skillfully, and
though myths were still popular, his chief interest lay in subjects from everyday
life. Some red-figured ceramic artists, like Euphronius, Euthydimes, and others
were painters of real genius. The red-figured technique, which enabled the decora-
tor to draw the details of figures with greater ease, exhibits some of the finest free-
hand drawing in the history of art. In his work, the painter first sketched the figure
with a dull-pointed instrument on the clay. He then painted *around* this outline and
thus obtained a red silhouette, since, as in the case of the black-figured style, the
vase had already received a transparent wash. The details of muscles and drapery

FIGURE 27. Warriors arming. Detail from an Attic red figured calyx, krater, c. 515 B.C.

were drawn in relief lines and wash lines, and the whole background was painted with a black varnish. Finally, the pot was fired.

Architecture.   During the archaic period, a preparation was made in architecture for the triumphs of the fifth century. The typical Greek building was the temple, whose floor plan resembled the Mycenaean megaron. In time, the side walls of the main room, or *cella,* projected to the front and rear, forming vestibules known as the *pronaos* and the *opisthodomus;* between the projecting walls (*antae*) were placed columns to carry the superstructure. Such a temple is accordingly called a temple *in antis.* A temple with columns in front is known as *prostyle.* The greatest temples, which, of course, were evolved after long experimentation, had columns in front of the *pronaos* and the *opisthodomus* and along the sides. The covered walk around the temple between columns and cella was known as the *peristyle,* and the temple itself was called *peripteral;* the external columns often numbered 6 by 13.

The Architectural Orders.   Eventually two orders[1] were evolved for the super-structure: the majestic Doric, which grew up in old Greece and the West, and the graceful Ionic, which developed in Ionia. Ultimately temples of the two orders were found side by side, especially in Athens, where all ideas were at home. The two orders developed from construction in wood, with Mycenaean and Egyptian influences, and a glance at the diagram (p. 142) will show how different are their details. Each order has the column, crowned by a capital, and an entablature: first the

[1] The Corinthian order, except for its acanthus capital, is substantially the same as the Ionic.

architrave course, then the frieze course, and finally the horizontal cornice, and roof.

Architectural Refinements.   Through the genius of the architects, an elasticity, as well as a perfection of proportions, was breathed into this architecture, which was simply post-and-lintel construction; for example, the platform upon which the temple rose was curved and crowned—originally perhaps to get rid of rainwater—in order to do away with an inevitable impression of sagging. The column itself leaned a little inward, so that the long row would not appear rigid, and swelled (*entasis*) to create the illusion that the building was not top-heavy.

Every city-state had temples. Enough is preserved of the temple of Hera at Samos and that of Artemis at Ephesus to justify the Ionian reputation for size and magnificence. The early sixth-century temple to Hera at Olympia illuminates the development of the Doric order. The best-preserved Doric temples are not in Greece itself, but in the West, at Acragas, Selinus, Syracuse, and Paestum, reminders of the widespread culture of the ancient Greeks. Temples stood in an open sanctuary, or *temenos,* facing the east generally, and except for lamps, the sole illumination came from the door at the east end of the cella. Opposite, at the far end of the cella, stood the cult statue of the deity to whom the temple was dedicated.

Sculpture.   Although statues were frequently carved without any reference to a building, sculpture was in many ways a handmaiden of architecture. The earlier examples show strong Egyptian and Mesopotamian influence. While the willingness of the Greeks to borrow ideas from any quarter redounds to their credit, these influences were quickly absorbed. Even where they are obvious, as in the stance of the early male figures,[2] they touch the surface only, and the great qualities are essentially Greek.

The consuming interest of the early sculptor was humanity, not mere men and women. That is to say, he portrayed the generic and the typical rather than the particular and the unique. It delighted him to paint his statues and stylize their features. Because of his inability to carve the figures according to nature, the early sculptor resorted to a certain decorativeness, which is the chief characteristic of the art; there is also a grand aloofness, an otherworldly quality, as befitted statues of gods. Since, however, the Greek believed also in reason, the sculpture became increasingly realistic with the progress of observation and sculptural technique.

Technique.   If Greek artists made any large statues before 650 B.C., they were of wood and have long since perished. We know that they later worked in limestone and marble, terra-cotta and bronze. Bronze became the most popular material after the discovery, in the late sixth century, of how to cast large figures, though the melting pot has claimed most of them. Rough sketches and living models served the sculptor, and the worker in stone had many tools—not unlike modern ones—at hand. He first blocked out his statue with iron chisels and abrasives, and as the work progressed, he called on pointed and dentated chisels, the claw chisel, and the gouge. A straight chisel and drill were used for folds of drapery and locks of hair,

---

[2] These standing male figures, generally nude, are called *kouroi* (*kouros,* "youth"), the draped female figures *korai* (*kore,* "maiden").

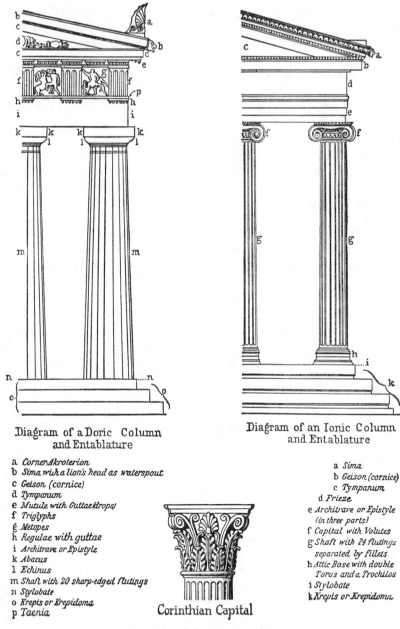

Diagram of a Doric Column
and Entablature

Diagram of an Ionic Column
and Entablature

a Corner-Akroterion
b Sima with a lion's head as waterspout
c Geison (cornice)
d Tympanum
e Mutule with Guttae (drops)
f Triglyphs
g Metopes
h Regulae with guttae
i Architrave or Epistyle
k Abacus
l Echinus
m Shaft with 20 sharp-edged flutings
n Stylobate
o Krepis or Krepidoma
p Taenia

a Sima
b Geison (cornice)
c Tympanum
d Frieze
e Architrave or Epistyle
   (in three parts)
f Capital with Volutes
g Shaft with 24 flutings
   separated by fillets
h Attic Base with double
   Torus and a Trochilos
i Stylobate
k Krepis or Krepidoma

Corinthian Capital

The orders of Greek architecture.

and at the end the statue's surface was smoothed with soft stones and emery, but
the surface remained relatively rough and was never polished.

Early Kouroi. The earliest statues of Kouroi illustrate the decorativeness and
simplicity of archaic Greek sculpture (see p. 144). The broad shoulders, tapering
waist, and advanced left leg remind us of Egypt. The formalized treatment of the

FIGURE 28. Marble Hera of
Samos in Archaic style c.
550 B.C.

hair, the broad sweep of the eyebrows, the arched upper eyelid, the decorative rendering of the ears, which are set too far back, and the high cheekbones are characteristic of the period, as is the frontal pose. A magnificent *kouros* from Paros (ca. 550 B.C.) shows that exact faithfulness to nature is artistically irrelevant, and that the artist may convey his message through simplicity and vigor. The sweep of collarbones and kneecaps, the diamond-shaped abdomen, and the gouges that serve for shoulder blades—these decorative touches add a unique quality. They heighten its charm and tone down its deviations from nature. This is not academic art, but a vital, national style. The similarity of such statues derives from a common background, for artists traveled about, especially to tyrants' courts.

Sculptural Progress. Decade by decade, the rendering of the human form improved. Attic sculpture continued to resemble the Peloponnesian, with its Dorian

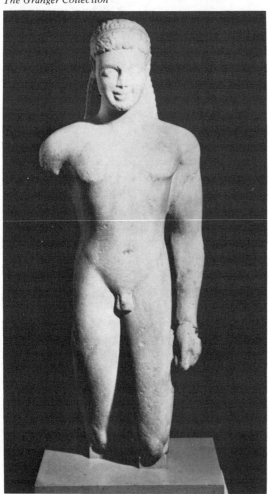

FIGURE 29. Archaic Greek marble Kouros from Paros. Mid-6th century B.C.

emphasis on the physical, until about 550 B.C., when the effect of Solon's invitation to foreign artists, especially Ionians, to settle in Athens began to take effect.
Ionian sculpture stressed the magnificent and emphasized details such as hair and
drapery. In particular, the women wear the diagonal himation, which is asymmetri-
cal and presents complex areas, while beneath it is the thin long-sleeved linen chiton, whose ruffled surfaces invite decorative stylization. Athenian women were
slow to give up the Doric *peplos,* but the influx of Ionian artists, combined with the
splendor of Peisistratus' court, introduced a new and sophisticated mode in art as in
life itself.

Great Attic art resulted in part from the happy union at Athens of Peloponnesian
and Ionian influences. The task of combining these influences with the early sixth-
century emphasis on simplicity was facilitated by political developments, for the
establishment of democracy permitted the Athenians to express themselves as they
genuinely felt. We can see this, as we come into the fifth century, in the magnificent Euthydikos *kore,* strong, simple, restrained, and vital. The wavy lines of the
hair, the horizontal eyes, the sculpturesque face, and the truly three-dimensional
body hold out to us the promise of the great works that have made the fifth century famous.

The achievements of archaic Greece in literature and art were quickly leading to
an even greater era, at the very time when the danger of Oriental conquest, which
might have stifled further development, presented itself. A Greek victory, on the
other hand, would have a tremendous effect on the country. For some years the
decision remained in the balance.

11

The Persian Empire

EUROPE AND ASIA

Scattered as they were around the Mediterranean and Black seas, the Greeks were in constant touch with other peoples. This contact greatly stimulated their development, and it also led to many quarrels and wars. A real conflict was inevitable, however, as soon as the expansion of a first-rate power brought it actively within the orbit of the Greeks. In the west, Etruria was a potential danger, but it was too far north in Italy to be a serious one. Carthage, on the other hand, was disputing Sicily with the Greeks. The main struggle was destined to occur in the east, the home of older and more powerful empires.

Characteristically, the growth of Ionian culture was accompanied by continued wars among the states that produced this versatile life and by fiercer factional struggles within the individual cities. In some states aristocracy survived; in others democracy gained the upper hand; but in general, governments were giving way, one after another, to tyranny. Civil discord and interstate warfare rendered the Asiatic Greeks unfit to defend themselves against foreign attack.

The need for united action increased with the growth of Lydia in the interior of Asia Minor to an aggressive power under King Gyges (ca. 660 B.C.). It was probably in resistance to this aggression that twelve cities of Ionia joined in a league, centered at the Panionion, a shrine of Poseidon on the promontory of Mycale. The Aeolians and Dorians of Asia Minor formed similar leagues, but the idea of uniting the Asiatic Greeks under a single government seems to have occurred to no one. On critical occasions the deputies of the allied Ionian states met at the Panionion to deliberate on the common welfare; but the central government possessed no means of enforcing harmonious or efficient action.

Under these circumstances the Lydian conquest of the Asiatic Greeks was commenced by Gyges and completed by Croesus (ca. 560-546 B.C.). Miletus alone, which had taken no part in the resistance, remained an ally under treaty. These events were quickly followed by Cyrus' overthrow of the Medes and by his defeat of Croesus. Lydia then became a part of the Persian Empire (546 B.C.).

The Aeolians and Ionians were loth to exchange Croesus, a benevolent Hellenized king, for the new Persian conqueror, and they now sought from him the same terms of subjection as they had received from Croesus. When Cyrus refused, the Greeks began to wall their towns; and calling a council at the Panionion, the Ionians resolved to ask the aid of Sparta, the strongest power in Greece, but the Lacedaemonians would not consider so distant an enterprise. It is said, however, that they sent an embassy to warn Cyrus not to harm any Greek city. The Persian king heard the message with contempt and ordered his lieutenant, Harpagus, to attack Ionia. Unwilling to submit, the Phocaeans sailed away to found a colony in Corsica, and the people of Teos abandoned their city and founded Abdera in Thrace. The rest of the Ionians, with the exception of the Milesians, who had allied themselves with Cyrus, submitted; most of the neighboring islands followed their example. Meanwhile, Cyrus had overthrown the Chaldaean Empire and captured its capital, Babylon (539 B.C.). This cardinal event in the history of the ancient Near East established a mighty empire throughout Asia.

Our chief source of the ensuing Persian Wars, as they are called, is the famous *History* of Herodotus. Herodotus was a native of Halicarnassus in Asia Minor; he was perhaps four years old at the time of the battle of Salamis. Later on, at Athens, he wrote of the stirring events of his youth. His philosophy of history stressed the divine working of Nemesis (Retribution) and the transitory nature of human fortunes. In his work, as in that of Sophocles and other writers, we catch the Greek admiration for *arete,* the specific and proper excellence of a genius. In his famous account of a conversation between Solon and Croesus, Herodotus tried to make the reader understand at the very outset the nature of the contestants in the forthcoming world struggle. The fundamental difference of ideals between East and West is heightened by Herodotus' choice of the Hellenized Lydian king as the exponent of non-Greek ways. During a visit to Croesus, late in life, Solon was shown the royal treasures. Croesus then asked him who, in his opinion, was the happiest of mortals, for he had no doubt that Solon would name him. When Solon mentioned first one person and then another, Croesus angrily protested, and Solon replied:

"For yourself, Croesus, I see that you are wonderfully rich, and the lord of many nations; but with respect to your question, I have no answer to give, until I hear that you have closed your life happily. For assuredly he who possesses great store of riches is no nearer happiness than he who has what suffices for his daily needs, unless it happens that luck attend upon him, and so he continue in the enjoyment of all his good things to the end of life. For many of the wealthiest men have been unfavored of fortune, and many whose means were moderate, have had excellent luck. Men of the former class excel those of the latter but in two respects; these last excel the former in many. The wealthy man is better able to content his desires, and to bear up against a sudden buffet of calamity. The other has less ability to withstand these evils (from which, however, his good luck keeps him clear), but he enjoys all these following blessings: he is whole of limb, a stranger to disease, free from misfortune, happy in his children, and comely to look upon. If, in addition to all this, he end his life well, he is of truth the man of whom you are in search, the man who may rightly be termed happy. Call him, however, until he die, not happy but fortunate. Scarcely, indeed, can any man unite all these advantages: as there is no country which contains within it all that it needs, but each, while it possesses some things, lacks others, and the best country is that which contains the most; so no single human being is complete in every respect—something is always lacking. He

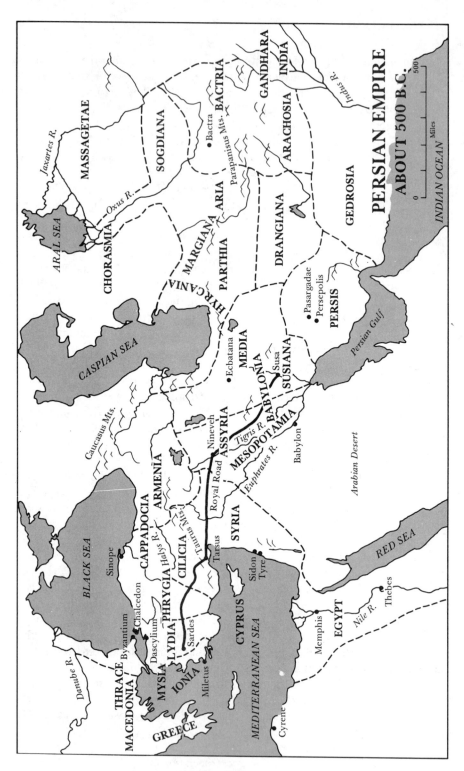

PERSIAN EMPIRE
ABOUT 500 B.C.

MASSAGETAE

Jaxartes R.

ARAL SEA

CHORASMIA

SOGDIANA

Oxus R.

• Bactra BACTRIA GANDHARA INDIA

Parapanisus Mts. ARACHOSIA

MARGIANA ARIA

Indus R.

HYRCANIA PARTHIA DRANGIANA GEDROSIA

CASPIAN SEA

• Pasargadae
• Persepolis PERSIS

Persian Gulf

INDIAN OCEAN

Caucasus Mts.

• Ecbatana MEDIA BABYLONIA SUSIANA
• Susa

ARMENIA Nineveh ASSYRIA
Tigris R. MESOPOTAMIA • Babylon

CAPPADOCIA *Royal Road* SYRIA *Euphrates R.*

Arabian Desert

Sinope *Halys R.* *Taurus Mts.* Tarsus

BLACK SEA PHRYGIA CILICIA

THRACE Byzantium Chalcedon LYDIA Sardes CYPRUS Sidon Tyre RED SEA

MACEDONIA MYSIA Dascylium IONIA Miletus MEDITERRANEAN SEA EGYPT Memphis *Nile R.* Thebes

GREECE Cyrene

Miles
0   500

148

who unites the greatest number of advantages, and retaining them to the day of his death, then dies peaceably, that man alone, sire, is, in my judgment, entitled to bear the name of "happy." But in every matter it behooves us to mark well the end; for oftentimes God gives men a gleam of happiness, and then plunges them into ruin.

"Such was the speech which Solon addressed to Croesus, a speech which brought him neither largess nor honor. The king saw him depart with much indifference, since he thought that a man must be an arrant fool who made no account of present good, but bade men always wait and mark the end." [1]

Another Greek, the poet Aeschylus, who fought at both Marathon and Salamis, was also able to catch the fundamental difference between Oriental and Occidental. In the *Persians,* which has a valuable eye-witness account of the battle of Salamis, the Persian queen asks a question: "What is this Athens, of which all men speak?" But perhaps the answer was best suggested by the ancient playwright himself when he set the quality of Athens in the democratic spirit of her people, and let a Persian give his queen the incomprehensible response, "They bow to no man and are no man's slaves."

THE REIGN OF DARIUS I (522–486 B.C.)

Cambyses. When Cyrus the Great—famous conqueror of Medes, Lydians, Asiatic Greeks, and Chaldaeans—died in 529 B.C., his son and successor, Cambyses (529–522 B.C.), inherited an empire that stretched from the Hellespont to the frontiers of India. Egypt alone was missing from the states that might round out the boundaries of the empire. In 526–525 B.C. Cambyses subjugated Egypt. Misfortune, however, befell his other ambitions. His Phoenician sailors refused to follow him in an attack on Tyre's colony of Carthage; an army was destroyed by a sandstorm as it crossed the Libyan desert to the oasis of Ammon (cf. map, front endpaper); and an attempt to conquer Ethiopia failed.

Darius. The conquest of Egypt was a solid achievement. Cambyses was then called home by the revolt of a Median pretender, who asserted that he was Smerdis, the brother whom Cambyses had secretly murdered on his accession. On the way back to Persis, Cambyses, for some unknown reason, committed suicide. The Median pretender did not last long, and his place was taken by Darius, the son of Hystaspes, a high Persian official. Darius belonged to a collateral line of the royal Achaemenid family and was forced to spend several years putting down revolts. His famous cuneiform inscription proudly records his trials and achievements.

Government. The chief task facing a Persian monarch at this time was to consolidate the vast empire that had been gained so rapidly. Fortunately Persia possessed in Darius I (522–486 B.C.) one of the great organizers and administrators of history. Following and developing the Assyrian imperial system, Darius divided the empire—except for the homeland of Persis—into more than twenty satrapies or

---

[1] Herodotus, I, 32-33. Translated by G. Rawlinson.

provinces. Each satrapy was under a satrap, or governor, who belonged to either the royal family or the nobility. The satrap was appointed by the king and held office at his pleasure, often for a long term; sometimes satrapies were hereditary. According to the Persian scheme, military and civil functions were divided, so that the satrap was the civil head of his satrapy; in case of real danger, however, he had some military authority. Among his chief duties was the collection of tribute and taxes. In general, the western satrapies, which were accustomed to coinage, made their annual payments in money, whereas the payments of the eastern ones were made in kind. Persis was not taxed, but together with Media it supplied some of the finest imperial troops: two thousand nobles, who constituted the royal bodyguard, the Ten Thousand Immortals, famous bowmen. All the subject peoples were required to furnish troops for the imperial army; they were armed in their national fashion and fought according to their own ways. The Phoenicians, the Egyptians, and the Asiatic Greeks made up the navy.

The satraps, particularly those far distant, were in effect princelings; often jealous of one another, they could contrive to wage war beyond the confines of the empire and might at any time declare their independence of the central government. As a check on them, therefore, the king appointed a secretary, responsible to himself alone, with the duty of sending periodically confidential reports on the satraps. Another check was provided by the satrapal military commanders, who were independent of the satraps. In command of the garrisons in the chief towns, the military commander embodied the armed authority of the king. Darius developed yet another means of controlling his officials. From Susa, the former capital of Elam and now his administrative capital, the famous Royal Road ran a distance of almost fifteen hundred miles to Sardis in Lydia. Other excellent roads connected the remotest satrapies and cities of Darius' empire. The roads made possible fast communication, with relays of mounted messengers available at short intervals for the forwarding of official letters. A chief duty of the postal inspectors was a report to the king about his officials. Finally, the "King's Eye," a near relative of the sovereign and invested with great dignity and military power, traveled throughout the empire and noted the efficiency and loyalty of the officials. (Cf. map, p. 148.)

It was the genius of Darius to be very tolerant of the various peoples within his state; doubtless this royal attitude was one of the main reasons for the empire's survival until Alexander the Great. As a rule, local self-government was permitted. For example, the satrap of Lydia, residing at Sardis, governed the coastal Greeks by means of tyrants. The Greeks chafed under the arrangement, but at least they were under the direct rule of fellow Greeks, and, moreover, the system of tyranny antedated the Persian conquest. Persian tolerance extended to national customs and religions. This is not to suggest that Darius was not an absolute monarch. With the high-sounding title of "The Great King, King of Kings," he was a hereditary sovereign, surrounded by a complex bureaucracy and a court ceremonial that included *proskynesis* (prostration) in his presence. His power was checked by a large council of nobles, whom he consulted concerning policy. In routine matters he was aided by seven councilors; appeals direct to the king were possible for any subject.

Prosperity.   Despite tribute and taxes, the support of the army, and forced labor on public projects, the Persian Empire brought great prosperity and relative peace to a large area of the world. To promote trade, Darius reopened the old canal connecting the Nile and the Red Sea and caused the water route between India and Egypt to be explored. The empire's economy was further stimulated by uniform weights and measures, and very especially by Darius' creation of a system of coinage. The gold coin, which the king alone might strike, was known as the *daric.* The satraps were allowed to strike silver and bronze coins at a gold and silver ratio of value of approximately thirteen to one. The Persians never minted enough money to satisfy demand, and vast hoards of gold and silver were collected in the royal storehouses.

Art.   The Persians were a hardy race, who were long able to maintain their simple habits. Herodotus tells us that they educated their children "in three things

FIGURE 30. Glazed brick relief panel from the Palace of Darius at Susa showing a Persian "immortal," c. 500 B.C.

only: in riding, in shooting, and in speaking the truth." Their arts were extensively borrowed from others, from the Assyrians, the Babylonians, the Egyptians, and even the Greeks. From the Babylonians they borrowed the terrace, which was the chief feature of their architecture. With an abundance of fine limestone in their country, they often used it in their buildings, and they showed their independence of Babylon by employing the stone column as a second great feature of their architecture. In contrast with the Egyptian, Persian columns were tall and graceful, doubtless owing to Greek influence. They were placed farther apart than in Egyptian temples, thus giving the Persian building a lighter and more airy effect. For the foundation of his palace at Persepolis (ultimately fired by Alexander the Great), Darius erected a terrace of stone, mounted by beautifully sculptured stairways. On one part of the terrace stood his dwelling, a large hall with a porch in front and rooms at the rear and on the sides. Nearby was the pillared audience hall for state and festive occasions. Colored glazed tiles decorated the palace at Persepolis. Among the reliefs are lions, bulls, and monsters reminiscent of Assyria, though better proportioned and more natural. Some reliefs show the king fighting with lions, others represent courtly pleasures and religious formalities.

Religion. The Persian masses long remained polytheistic and worshiped the powers of nature. A professional priesthood, known as *magi,* ministered to their needs (whence our word *magic*). One of its functions was to win the gods and expel evil spirits by charms. During the course of the sixth century there arose in Media a great religious leader, Zoroaster, who preached a militant, ethical religion. Zoroaster taught the existence of one supreme God, Ahura Mazda, creator of heaven, earth, and humankind, and his earthly agent, Mithra, conceived of as a soldierly young man. Ahura Mazda was wise and holy; he honored truth and bravery. As the god of light, he warred continuously against the forces of darkness and evil. These were led by Ahriman, the counterpart of the Christian devil. Those who supported Ahura Mazda gained a happy immortality, whereas the wicked fell into the pit of the demons. Occasionally Ahura Mazda was represented by symbols and images, but more generally he was worshiped on hilltops with fire, prayers, and drink offerings. The magi were happy to serve the new cult, especially after Darius personally accepted it. During the third century A.D. there was a great resurgence of Zoroastrianism under a new Persian dynasty, the Sassanids. However, their collection of sacred hymns and prayers, known as the *Avesta,* contains little that can be traced to Zoroaster himself.

Imperial Expansion. During his long reign Darius extended his empire to win more defensible frontiers. Eastward he conquered as far as the Indus River and perhaps beyond. Westward the problem was somewhat different, and he had to decide on his policy toward the Greeks of the mainland. Absorption was a tempting answer, for he knew that like the Asiatic Greeks, they were good fighters and mariners. Before he could think of an invasion of Greece, however, it was necessary to make certain that his line of communications would not be attacked on the flank by the Scythians, who even now were raiding his realm. Apparently Darius conceived the idea of attacking the new Scythian Empire, which had been established on the north of the Black Sea, in the rear, from the European side. Darius led a large army in 513 B.C. across the Bosporus on a bridge of boats and thence marched away to the Danube. This he crossed on a similar bridge made from the fleets of the Ionian tyrants who were supporting him. As the Scythians would not meet Darius in open battle but harassed his army interminably, and as provisions and water were insufficient, their conquest proved impossible. Forced to retreat into Asia with considerable loss, Darius had, however, made his might known in that part of the world. Of greater consequence, through his lieutenant Megabazus, Thrace, from the Propontis to the Strymon River, together with the islands of Lemnos and Imbros, became a Persian province.

The Athenians, probably more than anyone else, realized the approaching danger, for they had lost Sigeum and the Thracian Chersonese to Persia. They knew, too, that their exiled tyrant, Hippias, now at Sigeum but hoping to be restored through Persian aid, was doing his utmost to persuade Artaphrenes, the satrap of Sardis, to attack Athens. To counteract the influence of Hippias, the Athenians sent an embassy to Artaphrenes, but the Persian abruptly ordered them to take Hippias back if they wished to escape ruin. Thereupon the Athenians, who rejected the proposal, rightly felt that a state of war was threatening between them and Persia.

12

The Persian Wars

THE IONIAN REVOLT (499–493 B.C.)

The Ionian Greeks Revolt. Darius was unable to follow up his victories in Thrace immediately, because the Ionian Greeks chose this moment to revolt. Herodotus, who is our chief source here, fails to make clear the cause of the Ionian revolt, but it is clear that the Greeks of Asia Minor were discontented under Persian rule. Their formerly great prosperity was declining, and they chafed under the system of tyrants that the Persians had imposed. This must have been a particularly sore point, for after the suppression of the revolt, Darius permitted democratic government in most states. The immediate cause of the revolt lay in the ambition of Aristagoras, tyrant of Miletus, who hoped to add the island of Naxos to his rule and, needing help, suggested to Artaphrenes, the Persian satrap, that here would be a good way to advance gradually on Greece. The enterprise failed, and the tyrant, to escape inevitable punishment, and realizing that the Greeks were ready to strike for liberty, decided on revolt (499 B.C.).

Aid from Athens. Abdicating his tyranny and accepting a constitutional office, Aristagoras proceeded to overthrow the despots in the remaining Ionian cities, so that now all Ionia was free and committed to rebellion. Aristagoras then went to Sparta to ask for an alliance, but the Lacedaemonians, as usual, could not think of so distant an expedition. Thereupon he went to Athens, where the threats of Artaphrenes and Hippias, and the loss of territory, had produced conditions more favorable to his cause. The Athenians resolved to send twenty ships, which were reinforced by five from Eretria. The crews of these vessels joined the Ionians in an attack on Sardis, hoping that a victory at this vital point might decide the issue. They burned the city but, failing to take the citadel, were forced to retreat; on their way to the coast they were overtaken and defeated by the Persians at Ephesus. The Athenians then returned home and declined further participation in the war.

Destruction of Miletus. The burning of Sardis, at least, encouraged the revolt, which rapidly spread to all western Asia Minor, Thrace, and Cyprus. At the same time it roused Darius to extraordinary efforts. A decisive battle was fought in 494 B.C. off Lade, near Miletus, between the Greek and Phoenician fleets, 353 ships against 600 according to Herodotus, who exaggerated the size of the enemy's fleet. The Greeks might easily have won but for the treachery of the Samians, who at a critical moment deserted. The result was disaster. Miletus, now besieged by land and sea, was captured and sacked, and most of the surviving population was transplanted, in Asiatic style, to the mouth of the Tigris. By 493 B.C. the entire rebellion was suppressed, and Darius, by his generally lenient treatment of the Greeks, proved himself a wise ruler.

Themistocles Archon. The results of the revolt were threefold: the Ionian enlightenment was forever ended; Darius had a *casus belli* against Athens; and the Persian conquests in Thrace had to be rewon. These events were extremely significant. For centuries the Ionians had been standard bearers of Western civilization. Miletus, the home of commerce and industry and of the fine arts, of poetry and science, the most brilliant city in Hellas, was blotted out of existence. The effect on Athens was electric. When the poet Phrynichus produced his play, *The Capture of Miletus,* in 493 B.C., the Athenians were so overcome that they fined him a thousand drachmas for reminding them of their own misfortunes. The poet had made them see vividly the horrors that attended the Persian triumph over a city of kindred blood, and that surely impended over themselves. In this mood they elected to the archonship for 493–492 B.C. an uncompromising advocate of war for the defense of the state, a man of great energy and mental resources, Themistocles. Even at this early date Themistocles seems to have understood the weak point in any effort of Persia to conquer Greece. The country was too barren to support an invading army, which consequently would be dependent on a fleet for its provisioning. It seemed obviously necessary to Themistocles to build a fleet large enough to gain the supremacy of the sea. Thus Greece would be saved and his own city raised to preeminence. During his year of office he improved the three natural harbors of Piraeus, which would serve not only the new fleet but the merchant ships that till now had been content with the open roadstead of Phaleron.

Trial of Miltiades. The rise of Themistocles, a *novus homo*, illustrates the progressive democratization of Athens. His support came largely from the city classes, the very element that had supported the Alcmeonid Cleisthenes. The alignment of the political parties at Athens at this time is not wholly clear, but it is commonly assumed that the Alcmeonidae, opposing Themistocles, were necessarily pro-Persian, even though this policy would drive them into the arms of their enemy Hippias. We can understand the factional struggles better if we imagine the Alcmeonidae and Themistocles as appealing for support to the same body of voters, the city masses. The issue was brought to a head by the sudden return to Athens of Miltiades, nephew of the settler in the Thracian Chersonese. Miltiades was thoroughly familiar with the Persians and their military tactics, for he had served under Darius on the Scythian expedition; later he had won Persia's enmity by joining the Ionian revolt. Now, in Athens, this leader of the Philaid clan could not be expected to cooperate with the Alcmeonidae. Indeed, these rivals might be crushed by an alliance between Themistocles, with his popular appeal, and Miltiades, who combined with a distinguished name a useful knowledge of Persia. To prevent defeat, the Alcmeonidae brought Miltiades to trial on a charge of tyranny in the Chersonese. He was acquitted and elected general for the next year. The Athenians had chosen the radicalism of Themistocles and the special knowledge of Miltiades. Miltiades, for his part, abandoned the naval program of Themistocles and devoted the state's whole attention to the heavy infantry. The Ionian revolt, then, had given the

Athenians time to get their bearings, and none too soon, for the Persians were already on the march.

Mount Athos. With the crushing of the revolt, it was clearly Darius' duty to restore his authority in Thrace, a plan that might be extended to Greece proper. Accordingly, in 492 B.C. he sent his son-in-law Mardonius across the Hellespont at the head of a large army and fleet. Thrace, Thasos, and Macedon were conquered, but the fleet was shattered in an attempt to round Mount Athos. As a consequence Mardonius returned home, though he had accomplished his primary purpose. The next step was to punish Athens and Eretria for their share in the Ionian revolt. Darius began at once to gather his ships and at the same time sent heralds among the Greek states to demand "earth and water." Though his designs may have been limited to Athens and Eretria, it was essential to prevent those cities from gaining allies. Hopeless of resistance, the islanders yielded; and many on the mainland acted likewise. Among the more independent states that thus "Medized" were the Thessalian cities, Thebes—doubtless irritated by the aggressions of Athens—and Argos, Sparta's enemy. Aegina was hostile to Athens at the moment, but the rest of the Peloponnesian League, directed by King Cleomenes, declined to Medize. As usual, the Greek states were divided, but the two strongest, Sparta and Athens, maintained a consistent policy toward Persia. Sparta probably found it easier to cooperate with Athens with Themistocles at the helm instead of her old enemies, the Alcmeonidae, a fact that, no doubt, had been appreciated at Athens itself. The Athenians exerted themselves to the utmost to prepare for impending invasion, and, as we have seen, elected Miltiades to the board of generals.

MARATHON (490 B.C.)

In the summer of 490 B.C. an Asiatic fleet, conveying a force of infantry and cavalry, moved westward across the Aegean Sea. It was commanded by Datis, a Mede, and Artaphernes, son of the satrap of Sardis and nephew of Darius. Most of the islanders along their route submitted. The immediate object was to subdue Eretria and Athens. After a siege of six days, Eretria was betrayed by traitors, the city was sacked, and the population was taken captive. From Eretria the Persians, under the guidance of the aged Hippias, crossed over to Marathon, on the coast northeast of Athens, where they hoped for support from partisans. The Athenians, who had been unwilling to send a force to Eretria and thus expose their own city, prepared to take up their position in a narrow valley (Vrana) facing the Persians in the plain by the shore, whence deployment would be easy and, should the Persians take the road to Athens, an attack could be made on their flank.

A runner was sent to Sparta for help, but the Spartans, then celebrating a religious festival, declined to come until the next full moon. The Athenians thus went into battle at Marathon aided only by a contingent from tiny Plataea, just across the border in Boeotia. There were about ten thousand Athenians under Miltiades engaged in this battle, the Persian force being possibly three times as large. More than a week after the Persians landed at Marathon, the Athenian army attacked them on the run. Herodotus described the ensuing events as follows:

"The Athenians, for their part, were drawn up at Marathon in order of battle in a sacred precinct belonging to Heracles, when they were joined by the Plataeans, who came in full force to their aid. The Athenian generals were divided in their opinions; and some advised not to risk a battle, because they were too few to engage such a host as that of the Medes, while others were for fighting at once; and among these last was Miltiades. He therefore, seeing that opinions were thus divided, and that the less worthy counsel appeared likely to prevail, resolved to go to the polemarch, and have a conference with him. For the man on whom the lot fell to be polemarch at Athens was entitled to give his vote with the ten generals, since anciently the Athenians allowed him an equal right of voting with them. The polemarch at this juncture was Callimachus of Aphidnae; to him therefore Miltiades went, and spoke with him.

"Miltiades by his words gained Callimachus; and the addition of the polemarch's vote caused the decision to be in favor of fighting. Hereupon all those generals who had been desirous of hazarding a battle, when their turn came to command the army, gave up their right to Miltiades. He, however, though he accepted their offers, nevertheless waited, and would not fight, until his own day of command arrived in due course.

"Then at length, when his own turn was come, the Athenian battle was set in array, and this was the order of it. Callimachus the polemarch led the right wing, for it was at that time a rule with the Athenians to give the right wing to the polemarch. After this followed the tribes, according as they were numbered, in an un-

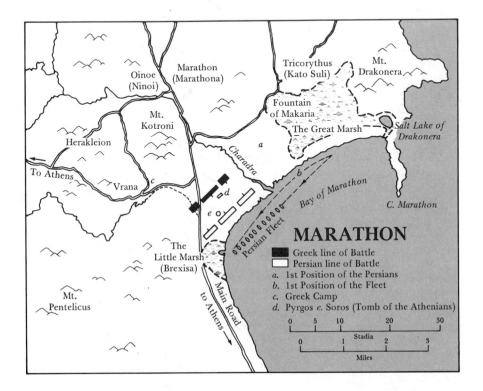

broken line; while last of all came the Plataeans, forming the left wing. And ever since that day it has been a custom with the Athenians, in the sacrifices and assemblies held each fifth year at Athens, for the Athenian herald to implore the blessing of the gods on the Plataeans conjointly with the Athenians. Now, as they marshalled the host upon the field of Marathon, in order that the Athenian front might be of equal length with the Median, the ranks of the center were diminished, and it became the weakest part of the line, while the wings were both made strong with a depth of many ranks.

"So when the battle was set in array, and the victims showed themselves favorable, instantly the Athenians, so soon as they were let go, charged the barbarians at a run. Now the distance between the two armies was little short of a mile. The Persians, therefore, when they saw the Greeks coming on at speed, made ready to receive them, although it seemed to them that the Athenians were bereft of their senses, and bent upon their own destruction; for they saw a mere handful of men coming on at a run without either horsemen or archers. Such was the opinion of the barbarians; but the Athenians in close array fell upon them, and fought in a manner worthy of being recorded. They were the first of the Greeks, so far as I know, who introduced the custom of charging the enemy at a run, and they were likewise the first who dared to look upon the Median garb, and to face men clad in that fashion. Until this time the very name of the Medes had been a terror to the Greeks to hear.

"The two armies fought together on the plain of Marathon for a length of time; and in the mid battle, where the Persians themselves and the Sacae had their place, the barbarians were victorious, and broke and pursued the Greeks into the inner country; but on the two wings the Athenians and the Plataeans defeated the enemy. Having so done, they suffered the routed barbarians to fly at their ease, and joining the two wings in one, fell upon those who had broken their own center, and fought and conquered them. These likewise fled, and now the Athenians hung upon the runaways and cut them down, chasing them all the way to the shore, on reaching which they laid hold of the ships and called aloud for fire.

"It was in the struggle here that Callimachus the polemarch, after greatly distinguishing himself, lost his life; Stesilaüs too, the son of Thrasilaüs, one of the generals, was slain; and Cynaegirus,[1] the son of Euphorion, having seized on a vessel of the enemy's by the ornament at the stern, had his hand cut off by the blow of an axe, and so perished; as likewise did many other Athenians of note and name.

"Nevertheless the Athenians secured in this way seven of the vessels; while with the remainder the barbarians pushed off, and taking aboard their Eretrian prisoners from the island where they had left them, doubled Cape Sunium, hoping to reach Athens before the return of the Athenians. The Alcmaeonidae were accused by their countrymen of suggesting this course to them; they had, it was said, an understanding of the Persians, and made a signal to them, by raising a shield, after they were embarked in their ships.

"The Persians accordingly sailed round Sunium. But the Athenians with all pos-

---

[1] Brother of the poet Aeschylus; he and Callimachus and 190 other Athenians were buried on the battlefield, which is still marked by a great mound.

sible speed marched away to the defense of their city, and succeeded in reaching Athens before the appearance of the barbarians: and as their camp at Marathon had been pitched in a precinct of Heracles, so now they encamped in another precinct of the same god at Cynosarges. The barbarian fleet arrived, and lay to off Phaleron, which was at that time the harbor of Athens; but after resting awhile upon their oars, they departed and sailed away to Asia.

"There fell in this battle of Marathon, on the side of the barbarians, about 6,400 men; on that of the Athenians, 192. Such was the number of the slain on the one side and the other. A strange prodigy likewise happened at this fight. Epizelus, the son of Cuphagoras, an Athenian, was in the thick of the fray, and behaving himself as a brave man should, when suddenly he was stricken with blindness, without blow of sword or dart; and this blindness continued thenceforth during the whole of his after life. The following is the account which he himself, as I have heard, gave of the matter: he said that a gigantic warrior, with a huge beard, which shaded all his shield, stood over against him; but the ghostly semblance passed him by, and slew the man at his side. Such, as I understand, was the tale which Epizelus told.

"After the full of the moon 2,000 Lacedaemonians came to Athens. So eager had they been to arrive in time, that they took but three days to reach Attica from Sparta. They came, however, too late for the battle; yet, as they had a longing to behold the Medes, they continued their march to Marathon, and there viewed the slain. Then, after giving the Athenians all praise for their achievement, they departed and returned home."[2]

The moral effect of the victory was stupendous, since it was now demonstrated that the Greek warrior could be superior to the Persian. The westward advance of the Asiatic empire was halted, and the Greeks were inspired with a hope of staying free. To the Athenians, who almost single-handed had beaten a power thought to be irresistible, this victory served as an incentive to heroism. The glory of the Marathonian warriors never faded.

The Parian Expedition. The next year, 489 B.C., Miltiades, now the most popular man in Athens, persuaded the people to give him a fleet of seventy ships, saying he would lead his countrymen to a place where they could enrich themselves, but not explicitly letting them know his purpose. With this armament he sailed against the Parians, on whom he levied a fine of one hundred talents for having joined the enemy in attacking Athens. On their refusal to pay, he besieged the island, but failed to capture it and returned home wounded. In their disappointment and anger, the Athenians tried Miltiades before the assembly on the charge of having deceived the people. He was found guilty of the charge, but the assembly, reminded by friends who pleaded his cause that his previous services to the state had been estimable, chose instead of the death penalty to fine him fifty talents. The condemned man died of his wound, and the fine was paid by his son Cimon.

Political Strife at Athens. Miltiades had embarked on a policy of conquering the Medizing islanders in order to create a bulwark against the next Persian invasion.

---

[2] Herodotus, VI, 105-120. The translations here and elsewhere are those of G. Rawlinson, with a few slight changes and much abbreviated.

His failure gave his enemies their opportunity to strike at him, and so, indirectly, at Themistocles as well. The prosecutor was an Alcmeonid by marriage, Xanthippus, husband of Cleisthenes' niece, Agariste, and father of Pericles. The ensuing conviction of Miltiades was a great victory for the opposition, and shortly afterward a member of the Alcmeonid party, Aristeides, was elected to the archonship.

But Themistocles struck back. A man of restless energy, a statesman of great vision, he would tolerate no rivals. In rapid succession his opponents were now ostracized—first Hipparchus, leader of the Peisistratid party, then the Alcmeonids, Megacles, Xanthippus, and finally in 482, Aristeides. Themistocles, however, yearned for more than this; he must have power himself, a difficult matter, since re-election to the archonship was not allowed. At about this same time, an important change was made in the Athenian constitution, although its relation to Themistocles and to contemporary factional politics is obscure. In 487-486 B.C. the archonship was thrown open to lot. There was nothing startling in the proposal, for sortition was a common practice, and the people were abolishing, in effect, an office so long associated with aristocracy. Henceforth the archonship was not a source of political power, no matter who held it. The board of ten generals now became the new executive body. One general was elected from each of the ten tribes, and later, under Pericles, it became possible for one of the tribes to elect two generals in any given year. The generals were the chief officials of the state, military functions being only part of their duties, and repeated reelection was possible. Themistocles' victory meant the abandonment of an army policy and the creation of a large navy for the war with Persia. A particularly rich vein in the silver mines at Laurium had recently been tapped, and Themistocles urged that the surplus in the treasury be used for the construction of two hundred ships.

THERMOPYLAE (480 B.C.)

Xerxes. The battle of Marathon shook the military prestige of the Great King and encouraged rebellion within the empire. The conquest of Greece became, consequently, even more than ever a question of practical necessity. Preparations for a new invasion, however, were suspended by the revolt of Egypt and the death of Darius in 486 B.C. After the reconquest of Egypt, Xerxes, Darius' son and successor, devoted himself to gathering the whole available strength of the empire to overwhelm Greece by force of numbers. As Mardonius' route of 492 B.C. was to be followed, engineers and workmen soon bridged the Hellespont with boats and cut a canal through the isthmus of Mount Athos. Great depots of provisions were established along the projected route. With his host Xerxes spent the winter of 481-480 B.C. at Sardis waiting to set out early the next spring.

Activity in Greece. Thus far, outside of Athens, the disunited Greeks had made no preparation to resist. The heralds of Xerxes, as they passed throughout Greece during the winter preceding the invasion, found many states ready to purchase safety by the gift of earth and water and "Medize." The patriot cause could place no reliance on Thessaly, Thebes, or Argos, or on the less progressive states of the center and west of the peninsula, or on the widely scattered islands. Gelon, tyrant of Syracuse, might have given powerful aid but had to face a Carthaginian attack. The brunt was to be borne by the Peloponnesian League, Athens, and a few small communities on the peninsula and the neighboring islands; even here the prevailing sentiment was close to despair. A feeling of common nationality was nevertheless apparent.

Under these circumstances a congress of deputies from the loyal states was held at Corinth in 481 B.C. to discuss defense. The call had been issued by Sparta but at the suggestion of Athens, undoubtedly on the motion of Themistocles. Various states, including Athens and Aegina, were reconciled. Envoys were sent to unrepresented Greek states to invite their active support, a barren hope. Spies, sent to Xerxes' camp, were captured, shown everything, and dismissed in the expectation that their report of his immense army would induce the Greeks to yield without resistance. The congress of deputies conferred the chief command, by sea as well as by land, on Sparta, to whose leadership most of the states had long been accustomed. There can be no doubt that the proceedings were directed by Themistocles and that his determination to fight out the issue on the sea was accepted by all concerned. The strategy was to try to inflict a decisive defeat on the Persian fleet, for this would automatically cause the army, which needed the fleet for its support, to

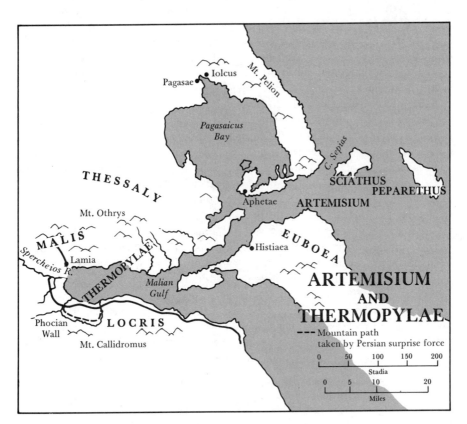

retire, as in 492 B.C. Meanwhile, the Greek army was to take up its position as far north as feasible, in order to protect as much of the country as possible, and also because all states north of that point would of necessity be pro-Persian. For this reason the Spartan suggestion that the stand be made at the isthmus was refused. In the north, the Vale of Tempe, giving access to Thessaly, was impossible, on account of other passes in the neighborhood. This left Thermopylae, the key to central Greece. (See map, p. 161.)

Xerxes, with his vast host,[3] entered Thessaly unopposed in 480 B.C., whereupon the states of this district under the lead of Medizing oligarchs passed over to his side. In accordance with the plan of Themistocles, who was now general at Athens, the Greek navy of three hundred ships took up its station at Artemisium, off northern Euboea, to meet the Persian fleet, while a force of several thousand Greeks, under Leonidas, king of Sparta, occupied the pass of Thermopylae to check the enemy until a decisive battle at sea had been fought. (See map, p. 161.)

"King Xerxes [says Herodotus] pitched his camp in the region of Malis called Trachinia, while on their side the Greeks occupied the straits. These straits the Greeks in general call Thermopylae (the Hot Gates); but the natives and those who dwell in the neighborhood, call them Pylae (the Gates). Here then the two armies took their stand; the one master of all the region lying north of Trachis, the other of the country extending southward of that place to the verge of the continent.

"The Greeks who at this spot awaited the coming of Xerxes were the following: From Sparta, 300 men-at-arms; from Arcadia, 1,000 Tegeans and Mantineans, 500 of each people; 120 Orchomenians, from the Arcadian Orchomenus; and 1,000 from other cities; from Corinth, 400 men; from Phlius, 200; and from Mycenae, eighty. Such was the number from the Peloponnesus. There were also present, from Boeotia, 700 Thespians and 400 Thebans.

"Besides these troops, the Locrians of Opus and the Phocians had obeyed the call of their countrymen, and sent, the former all the force they had, the latter 1,000 men. For envoys had gone from the Greeks at Thermopylae among the Locrians and Phocians, to call on them for assistance, and to say, 'They were themselves but the vanguard of the host, sent to precede the main body, which might every day be expected to follow them. The sea was in good keeping, watched by the Athenians, the Aeginetans, and the rest of the fleet. There was no cause why they should fear; for after all the invader was not a god but a man; and there never had been, and never would be, a man who was not liable to misfortunes from the very day of his birth, and those misfortunes greater in proportion to his own greatness. The assailant therefore, being only a mortal, must needs fall from his glory.' Thus urged, the Locrians and the Phocians had come with their troops to Trachis.

"The various nations had each captains of their own under whom they served; but the one to whom all especially looked up, and who had the command of the entire force, was the Lacedaemonian king, Leonidas. He had now come to Thermopylae, accompanied by the 300 men which the law assigned him, whom he had him-

[3] The numbers given by Herodotus, amounting to more than five millions, including noncombatants, and 1,207 warships, are an enormous exaggeration. A reasonable estimate would be 150,000–200,000 combatants and 700 warships.

self chosen from among the citizens, and who were all of them fathers with sons living.

"The force with Leonidas was sent forward by the Spartans in advance of their main body, that the sight of them might encourage the allies to fight, and hinder them from going over to the Medes, as it was likely they might have done had they seen that Sparta was backward. They intended presently, when they had celebrated the Carneian festival, which was what now kept them at home, to leave a garrison in Sparta, and hasten in full force to join the army. The rest of the allies also intended to act similarly; for it happened that the Olympic festival fell exactly at this same period. None of them looked to see the contest at Thermopylae decided so speedily; wherefore they were content to send forward a mere advanced guard. Such accordingly were the intentions of the allies.

"The Greek forces at Thermopylae, when the Persian army drew near to the entrance of the pass, were seized with fear, and a council was held to consider about a retreat. It was the wish of the Peloponnesians generally that the army should fall back upon the Peloponnesus, and there guard the Isthmus. But Leonidas, who saw with what indignation the Phocians and Locrians heard of this plan, gave his voice for remaining where they were, while they sent envoys to the several cities to ask for help, since they were too few to make a stand against an army like that of the Medes.

"While this debate was going on, Xerxes sent a mounted spy to observe the Greeks, and note how many they were, and see what they were doing. He had heard, before he came out of Thessaly, that a few men were assembled at this place, and that at their head were certain Lacedaemonians, under Leonidas, a descendant of Heracles. The horseman rode up to the camp, and looked about him, but did not see the whole army; for such as were on the further side of the wall (which had been rebuilt and was now carefully guarded) it was not possible for him to behold; but he observed those on the outside, who were encamped in front of the rampart. It chanced at this time the Lacedaemonians held the outer guard, and were seen by the spy, some of them engaged in gymnastic exercises, others combing their long hair. At this the spy greatly marveled, but he counted their number, and when he had taken accurate note of everything, he rode back quietly; for no one pursued after him, nor paid any heed to his visit. So he returned, and told Xerxes all that he had seen.

"Four whole days Xerxes suffered to go by, expecting that the Greeks would run away. When, however, he found on the fifth that they were not gone, thinking that their firm stand was mere impudence and recklessness, he grew wroth, and sent against them the Medes and Cissians, with orders to take them alive and bring them into his presence. Then the Medes rushed forward and charged the Greeks, but fell in vast numbers: others however took the places of the slain, and would not be beaten off, though they suffered terrible losses. In this way it became clear to all, and especially to the king, that though he had plenty of combatants, he had but very few warriors. The struggle, however, continued during the whole day.

"Then the Medes, having met so rough a reception, withdrew from the fight; and their place was taken by the band of Persians under Hydarnes, whom the king called his Immortals: they, it was thought, would soon finish the business. But when they joined battle with the Greeks, it was with no better success than the Median detachment—things went much as before—the two armies fighting in a narrow space, and the barbarians using shorter spears than the Greeks, and having no advantage from their numbers. The Lacedaemonians fought in a way worthy of note, and showed themselves far more skillful in fight than their adversaries, often turning their backs, and making as though they were all flying away, on which the barbarians would rush after them with much noise and shouting, when the Spartans at their approach would wheel round and face their pursuers, in this way destroying vast numbers of the enemy. Some Spartans likewise fell in these encounters, but only a very few. At last the Persians, finding that all their efforts to gain the pass availed nothing, and that, whether they attacked by division or in any other way, it was to no purpose, withdrew to their own quarters.

"During these assaults, it is said that Xerxes, who was watching the battle, thrice leaped from the throne on which he sat, in terror for his army.

"Next day the combat was renewed, but with no better success on the part of the barbarians. The Greeks were so few that the barbarians hoped to find them disabled, by reason of their wounds, from offering any further resistance; and so they once more attacked them. But the Greeks were drawn up in detachments according to their cities, and bore the brunt of the battle in turns, all except the Phocians, who had been stationed on the mountain to guard the pathway. So when the Persians found no difference between that day and the preceding, they again retired to their quarters.

"Now, as the king was confused, and knew not how he should deal with the emergency, Ephialtes, the son of Eurydemus, a man of Malis, came to him and was admitted to a conference. Stirred by the hope of receiving a rich reward at the king's hands, he had come to tell him of the pathway which led across the mountain to Thermopylae; by which disclosure he brought destruction on the band of Greeks who had there withstood the barbarians.

"The Persians took this path about the time of the lighting of the lamps, and, crossing the Asopus, continued their march through the whole of the night, having the mountains of Oeta on their right hand, and on their left those of Trachis. At dawn of the day they found themselves close to the summit. Now the hill was guarded, as I have already said, by 1,000 Phocian men-at-arms, who were placed there to defend the pathway, and at the same time to secure their own country. They had been given the guard of the mountain path, while the other Greeks defended the pass below, because they had volunteered for the service, and had pledged themselves to Leonidas to maintain the post faithfully.

"The ascent of the Persians became known to the Phocians in the following manner: During all the time that they were making their way up, the Greeks remained unconscious of it, inasmuch as the whole mountain was covered with groves of oak; but it happened that the air was very still, and the leaves which the Persians stirred with their feet made, as it was likely they would, a loud rustling, whereupon the Phocians jumped up and flew to seize their arms. In a moment the barbarians came in sight, and, perceiving men arming themselves, were greatly amazed; for they had fallen in with an enemy when they expected no opposition. Hydarnes, alarmed at the sight, and fearing lest the Phocians might be Lacedaemonians, inquired of Ephialtes to what nation these troops belonged. Ephialtes told him the exact truth, whereupon he arrayed his Persians for battle. The Phocians, galled by the showers of arrows to which they were exposed, and imagining themselves the special object of the Persian attack, fled hastily to the crest of the mountain, and there made ready to meet death; but while their mistake continued, the Persians, with Ephialtes and Hydarnes, not thinking it worth their while to delay on account of the Phocians, passed on and descended the mountain with all possible speed.

"The Greeks at Thermopylae received the first warning of the destruction which the dawn would bring on them from the seer Megistias, who read their fate in the victims as he was sacrificing. After this deserters came in, and brought the news that the Persians were marching round by the hills: it was still night when these men arrived. Last of all, the scouts came running down from the heights, and brought in the same accounts, when the day was just beginning to break. Then the Greeks held a council to consider what they should do, and here opinions were divided: some were strong against quitting their post, while others contended to the contrary. So when the council had broken up, parts of the troops departed and went their ways homeward to their several states; part however resolved to remain, and to stand by Leonidas to the last.

"It is said that Leonidas himself sent away the troops who departed, because he tendered their safety, but thought it unseemly that either he or his Spartans should quit the post which they had been especially sent to guard. For my own part, I incline to think that Leonidas gave the order, because he perceived the allies to be out of heart and unwilling to encounter the danger to which his own mind was made up. He therefore commanded them to retreat, but said that he himself could not draw back with honor; knowing that, if he stayed, glory awaited him, and that Sparta in that case would not lose her prosperity. For when the Spartans, at the very beginning of the war, sent to consult the oracle concerning it, the answer which they received from the priestess was 'that either Sparta must be overthrown by the barbarians, or one of her kings must perish.' The prophecy was delivered in hexameter verse, and ran thus:

> O ye men who dwell in the streets of broad Lacedaemon!
> Either your glorious town shall be sacked by the children of Perseus
> Or, in exchange, must all through the whole Laconian country
> Mourn for the loss of a king, descendant of great Heracles.
> He cannot be withstood by the courage of bulls nor of lions,
> Strive as they may; he is mighty as Zeus; there is nought that shall stay him,
> Till he have got for his prey your king, or your glorious city.

The remembrance of this answer, I think, and the wish to secure the whole glory for the Spartans, caused Leonidas to send the allies away. This is more likely than that they quarreled with him, and took their departure in such unruly fashion.

"So the allies, when Leonidas ordered them to retire, obeyed him and forthwith departed. Only the Thespians and the Thebans remained with the Spartans; and of these the Thebans were kept back by Leonidas as hostages, very much against their will. The Thespians, on the contrary, stayed entirely of their own accord, refusing to retreat, and declaring that they would not forsake Leonidas and his followers. So they abode with the Spartans, and died with them. Their leader was Demophilus, the son of Diadromes.

"At sunrise Xerxes made libations, after which he waited until the time when the market place is wont to fill, and then began his advance. Ephialtes had instructed him thus, as the descent of the mountain is much quicker, and the distance much shorter, than the way round the hills, and the ascent. So the barbarians under Xerxes began to draw nigh; and the Greeks under Leonidas, as they now went forth determined to die, advanced much further than on previous days, until they reached the more open portion of the pass. Hitherto they had held their station within the wall, and from this had gone forth to fight at the point where the pass was the narrowest. Now they joined battle beyond the defile, and carried slaughter among the barbarians, who fell in heaps. Behind them the captains of the squadrons, armed with whips, urged their men forward with continual blows. Many were thrust into the sea, and there perished; a still greater number were trampled to death by their own soldiers; no one heeded the dying. For the Greeks, reckless of their own safety and desperate, since they knew that, as the mountain had been crossed, their destruction was nigh at hand, exerted themselves with the most furious valor against the barbarians.

"By this time the spears of the greater number were all shivered, and with their swords they hewed down the ranks of the Persians; and here, as they strove, Leonidas fell fighting bravely, together with many other famous Spartans, whose names I have taken care to learn on account of their great worthiness, as indeed I have those of all the 300. There fell too at the same time very many famous Persians: among them, two sons of Darius.

"Thus two brothers of Xerxes here fought and fell. And now there arose a fierce struggle between the Persians and the Lacedaemonians over the body of Leonidas, in which the Greeks four times drove back the enemy, and at last by their great bravery succeeded in bearing off the body. This combat was scarcely ended when the Persians with Ephialtes approached; and the Greeks, informed that they drew nigh, made a change in the manner of their fighting. Drawing back into the narrowest part of the pass, and retreating even behind the cross wall, they posted themselves upon a hillock, where they stood all drawn up together in one close body, except only the Thebans. The hillock whereof I speak is at the entrance of the straits, where the stone lion stands which was set up in honor of Leonidas. Here they defended themselves to the last, such as still had swords using them, and the others resisting with their hands and teeth; till the barbarians, who in part had pulled down the wall and attacked them in front, in part had gone round and now encircled them upon every side, overwhelmed and buried the remnant left beneath showers of missile weapons.

"Thus nobly did the whole body of Lacedaemonians and Thespians behave, but nevertheless one man is said to have distinguished himself above all the rest, to wit, Dieneces the Spartan. A speech, which he made before the Greeks engaged the

Medes, remains on record. One of the Trachinians told him, 'Such was the number of barbarians, that when they shot forth their arrows the sun would be darkened by their multitude.' Dieneces, not at all frightened at these words, but making light of the Median numbers, answered, 'Our Trachinian friend brings us excellent tidings. If the Medes darken the sun, we shall have our fight in the shade.' Other sayings too of a like nature are said to have been left on record by this same person.

"The slain were buried where they fell; and in their honor, nor less in honor of those who died before Leonidas sent the allies away, an inscription was set up, which said

> Here did four thousand men from Pelops' land
> Against three hundred myriads bravely stand.

"This was in honor of all. Another was for the Spartans alone:

> Tell them in Lakëdaimon, passer-by,
> That here obedient to their word we lie.[4]"

Meanwhile the Greeks at Artemisium were encouraged by their successful engagements with the enemy, and by the damaging of the Persian fleet in a storm. When, however, they learned that Xerxes had forced the pass at Thermopylae, they had to withdraw, though they had fought no decisive battle. The result of these engagements by sea and land was victory to the Persians, and a waning of Greek hopes that under more favorable conditions the struggle might yet be successful.

SALAMIS (480 B.C.)

Xerxes now advanced through Boeotia toward Athens, and the states of central Greece all Medized. As the Greek fleet was retiring to Salamis, Themistocles returned to his city, to find it full of gloom. The Delphic Apollo had said that they should place their confidence in the "wooden wall," which some thought referred to the palisade around the Acropolis, where they accordingly took refuge. Themistocles, however, declared that it meant the fleet and persuaded most of the Athenians to abandon their homes for Salamis, Aegina, and Troezen. According to Herodotus, the decision to evacuate Athens was made in a panicky mood *after* Thermopylae and Artemisium. In 1959, however, an inscription was discovered at Troezen that gives a very different picture. This so-called Themistocles Decree purports to be the very decree of the Athenian assembly passed at Themistocles' behest ordering the abandonment of the city and projecting a naval battle at Salamis, but well *before* Thermopylae and Artemisium. If authentic (and there are many modern historians who doubt its authenticity), this part of the war strategy was planned far ahead in calm deliberation of the worst eventualities, and not after the fact of failure to check the Persians in central Greece. In any case, the removal of the population and personal property was supervised by the council of Areopagus, directed by

---

[4] Various hands, *The Oxford Book of Greek Verse in Translation.*

Themistocles and his associates. The Greek fleet halted in the bay of Salamis to cover the Athenian retreat, with the intention, too, of making there a further stand against the enemy. The place was well chosen, for the enemy would be compelled to fight in the strait, where superior numbers would not count. Further retreat would in fact be almost equivalent to abandoning the cause, for it would leave the enemy free to land troops on the coast of the Peloponnesus in the rear of the isthmian line of defense then being prepared by the Spartans.

Xerxes laid waste the country as he advanced to Athens. From the island of Salamis, the Athenians viewed their city in flames, and scouts reported the Persian fleet at anchor in the bay of Phaleron. These circumstances tended for the moment to depress morale and to suggest to the admirals the wisdom of retiring to the isthmus, where they could cooperate with the land forces. Themistocles, however, strongly urged Eurybiades, the Spartan commander in chief, to remain, and even threatened in case of retreat to use his ships in conveying the Athenians to a new home in Italy. While thus pleading with the admirals, Themistocles secretly dispatched a slave to Xerxes, (who was encamped on the shore), falsely informed him that the Greeks, panic-stricken, were about to sail away, and urged him to cut off their retreat at once.

Xerxes fell into the trap and dispatched many of his ships to blockade the rear of the Straits of Salamis, where the Athenian fleet was stationed and where Themistocles wanted to do battle. The deployment of this part of the Persian contingent reduced their numerical superiority, since it did not participate in the ensuing engagement. The Greeks won the Battle of Salamis, decisive for the war, because they were able largely to neutralize the advantage of numbers enjoyed by the Persians, by fighting in a narrow channel where the Persians' maneuverability was decisively reduced.

Too thoroughly crippled to renew the fight, the Persian fleet retired to Asia. Thereupon Themistocles urged the Greeks to sail at once to the Hellespont and by destroying the bridge, cut Xerxes off from his base of supplies. The advice was sound and, if taken, would probably have ended the war; but to the other Greeks the idea seemed too daring, and the war continued another year. Xerxes himself returned to Asia, leaving Mardonius with most of the army to spend the winter in Thessaly. Mardonius' plan was to make peace with Athens and then, freed from the threat of the Athenian fleet, to crush Sparta at a blow. He sent Alexander, king of Macedonia, as his emissary, but Athens refused to desert the allied cause. There were doubts, however, and an apparent desire to hedge. Under a general amnesty decreed the year before, the exiles had returned to the city. Among them were Themistocles' opponents Xanthippus and Aristeides; the former was now placed in charge of the Athenian navy, and the latter was given command of the army.

PLATAEA AND MYCALE (479 B.C.)

It became clear to Sparta that speed was essential if Athens was to be kept in line. Once again Attica was ravaged by the enemy. The Spartans therefore abandoned their insistence that the stand should be made at the isthmus and marched north

(479 B.C.). At Plataea, just across Mount Cithaeron in Boeotia, the allied Greek army gathered under command of the Spartan Pausanias, who was the regent for the young son of Leonidas. The Greeks numbered nearly 100,000 men, only slightly less than the Persian force. For almost two weeks there were maneuvers and countermaneuvers, until at last Mardonius saw his opportunity to attack the Greeks while they were in the midst of deploying. The main attack was directed against the Peloponnesians, who patiently waited under the shower of arrows from the enemy's horsemen. But when the main body of Persians had drawn up within bowshot behind their fence of wicker shields, the order to charge was given, and the heavy Peloponnesian infantry dashed at a run upon the enemy's line. Mardonius and those about him fell. The result was decisive. The remnant of the Persian army under Artabazus hurriedly retreated to Asia. The Greek allies then besieged Thebes, and upon its fall the Boeotian League was disbanded.

The Greek ships, meanwhile, had been at Delos, keeping an eye out for the Persian fleet. Assured of help from Chios and Samos, they crossed over to the Asia Minor coast and landed at Mycale, where the Persians held a fort. During the battle that followed, the Asiatic Greeks in the Persian force deserted, the Persian army was destroyed, and the warships were burned. This victory, according to legend fought on the same day as Plataea (late August 479 B.C.), pointed the way to the liberation of Asiatic Greece. Sestos, on the Hellespont, was now besieged, but as the siege promised to be a lengthy undertaking, the Peloponnesians, under King Leotychidas of Sparta, returned home. The Athenians remained. The essential difference between Athens and Sparta was here revealed, and inevitably it led to rivalry and conflict.

THE CARTHAGINIAN INVASION OF SICILY

Carthage.   During these momentous events, a life-and-death struggle took place in the west between the Sicilian Greeks and Carthage. Carthage, the famous Phoenician colony, was the head of a wealthy empire that extended along the North African coast from Cyrenaica to the Atlantic; it included settlements in Sicily, Sardinia, and Spain. By the middle of the sixth century Carthage had begun to make treaties with coast towns of Etruria for the regulation of trade and the defense of their common interests against the Greeks. Although the Greeks of Massilia maintained their independence, an allied fleet of Carthaginians and Etruscans defeated the Phocaean colonists in a naval battle at Alalia (535 B.C.) and drove the Greeks from Corsica. (See the map, p. 118.)

The Battle of Himera (480 B.C.).   Fortunately for the cause of western Hellenism, the Greeks of Sicily during the fifth century tended toward political unification, under the leadership of Gelon, a young cavalry officer of remarkable genius in war and statecraft. Tyrant of Gela, Gelon also made himself master of Syracuse and took up his residence in this, the richest and most powerful city of Sicily. These developments thoroughly alarmed the Carthaginians, who resolved upon attack. In 480 B.C., doubtless in collusion with Persia, a Carthaginian army, consisting of many mercenaries and under the command of Hamilcar, advanced on Sicily. A fierce battle was fought before Himera, the Carthaginian army was routed, much of the fleet went up in flames, and vast spoils and countless prisoners were taken. To save her Sicilian colonies, which in reality were trading posts, Carthage bought peace with a heavy war indemnity.

In East and West, Hellenism had won, and the Greeks were free to work out their destiny. Persia henceforth was on the defensive, and not for seventy years did Carthage dare attack again. The success of Gelon in defeating Carthage added to the prestige and power of Syracuse, which, under him and his brother Hiero, became the head of a Sicilian union. But the spirit of liberty and equality, which was alive in the minds of older Hellas, lived, too, among the western Greeks. By the middle of the fifth century, democratic waves swept over Sicily and Italy and converted tyrannies and aristocracies into more popular forms of government.

13

The Athenian Empire

THE DELIAN LEAGUE

The victories of Plataea and Mycale threw down a challenge to the Greeks to clear the Persians from the Aegean world, and naturally it was expected that Sparta, by virtue of her chief command at the decisive battles, would take the lead. This indeed she did, and in 478 B.C. an allied fleet under Pausanias sailed for Cyprus, where the Greek cities were freed; soon thereafter Byzantium was captured and the grain route to the Black Sea opened. Pausanias now began to assume the airs and habits of an Oriental despot, and the Spartans, feeling that they never should have engaged in so distant an enterprise in the first place, recalled Pausanias and settled down to their familiar Peloponnesian isolation.

The people of Athens by their character and outlook on life, regarded the new opportunity with enthusiasm, for they, and many others, considered the Athenian fleet, and the strategy back of it, as the real saviors of Greece. It was proper, so they thought, that they should free the Ionians, who after all were their kinsmen. Athenian success in this undertaking, combined with the expulsion of the Persians from Sestos and Thrace, foretold the eclipse of Sparta and the emergence of Athens as the center of the civilized world, greater than Ionia in its prime. Even within Greece itself Athens was strong enough to oppose Sparta, for apparently Sparta had asked, or perhaps commanded, her not to rebuild her walls, but to join with Sparta in razing the fortifications of all Greek cities outside the Peloponnesus. This proposal would have been fatal to Athens. To give his city precious time, Themistocles went to Sparta as an envoy, and there, first by delays and then by deliberate falsehoods, he concealed the truth while the Athenians feverishly rebuilt their walls. Not long afterward he persuaded his fellow citizens to build dockyards at Piraeus and surround the whole promontory with a massive wall, pointing out that, in case of trouble, they should go there to live, since their command of the sea would save them from starvation.

Alliance Against Persia. The bold imagination of Athens could not content itself with mere victories over Persia, for no one could yet be certain that there would not be another invasion. In the year 477 B.C., accordingly, representatives from the islands and the coast of Asia Minor joined with Athens in an offensive and defensive alliance against Persia. Casting masses of iron into the sea, they swore to remain faithful to their obligations till the metal should rise and float on the surface. They chose the island of Delos, sacred to all Ionians, and its temple of Apollo as the meeting place and treasury of the new confederacy. Nothing was said about possible withdrawal from the alliance, and the individual states were bound by treaty to Athens, which from the very beginning was the dominant partner. Athens swore to respect the consitutions of the members, to allow them representation in the central synod, and, in return for an annual payment, to protect them. The larger states, such as Lesbos, Chios, Samos, Naxos, and Thasos, preferred to make this payment in ships, whereas the smaller communities found it easier to contribute money. An Athenian, Aristeides, known as "the Just," was appointed to carry out the first assessment; while the figure is now uncertain, the tribute (*phoros*) a little later, when the Delian League was larger, stood at 460 talents. (A single talent would provide the daily wage of twelve thousand Athenian jurors or laborers.)

Cimon. If the statesmanship of Themistocles laid the foundation of this confederacy, the work of expanding it fell chiefly to Cimon, the son of Miltiades. By his marriage to the granddaughter of Megacles he had allied himself with the Alcmeonidae, while his sister was married to Callias, the wealthiest man in Athens. Winning brilliant victories between 476 and 462 B.C., Cimon raised Athens to the heights of power and secured the political eclipse of Themistocles. It seems one of the tragedies of history, albeit eminently Greek, that the great patriot should have become a victim of party politics and died in Asia Minor in the employ of the Persians.

Imperialism. Cimon believed in cooperation with Sparta, but he was sensitive enough to democratic sentiment to recognize the popularity of the Delian League. Between warring on Persians and pirates, he found time to add to the might of Athens by founding cleruchies, as the distinctive Athenian colonies were called. Unlike an ordinary colony, which became an independent state, the people of a cleruchy remained Athenian citizens; it was like a bit of Athens planted in foreign soil. When Cimon forced Carystus, a state of southern Euboea, into the Delian League, some Greeks began to resist Athenian aggrandizement, and in 468 B.C. Naxos announced its intention to withdraw. Athens promptly met this threat to her leadership by crushing the Naxians. Adopting a policy that was to be characteristic and of more benefit to Athens than others, she compelled them to adopt a democratic constitution and to contribute sums of money rather than ships to the treasury.

Cimon's greatest victory was gained in the year 466 B.C. at the mouth of the Eurymedon River in Asia Minor, where he destroyed a strong Phoenician fleet, a fact that made it clear to the world that all danger from Persia had ceased. The neighboring people of Caria and Lycia were joined to the league. Continuing his career of welding the maritime confederacy into an empire, Cimon forcibly added the Thracian Chersonese and then proceeded to the Strymon River. Here, at a place known as the Nine Ways, Cimon tried to settle ten thousand colonists, but they were badly beaten by the Thracians, and the venture had to be abandoned for some years. Later on, the place was colonized as Amphipolis. It was a site of great strategic value, the only spot where the Strymon could be bridged, commanding at once the route to the Bosporus and the road to the mines of Mount Pangaeus.

The obviously complete defeat of Persia brought to the fore the question whether contributions for military and naval expenses were to end with the establishment of peace in Asia or whether Athens, on the plea of eternal vigilance, could maintain the Delian League by force. The answer was soon given when revolting Thasos (465–463) met the fate of Naxos. The leading statesmen of Athens all agreed to support the confederacy, since it made Athens influential throughout the Greek world, an undoubted equal to Sparta, and since it gave thousands of the poorest Athenians perennial employment as rowers in the fleet. In domestic politics, however, there was a sharp line of cleavage. Because Sparta was secretly encouraging rebellion within the Delian League and stood forth as the champion of particularism, of the complete independence of city-states, those Athenians who favored further democratization of the constitution believed that Athens should break away from Sparta in order to make the most of her opportunity in world politics unhampered. Conservatives, however, had a natural affinity for Sparta and, though they dared not give up the Delian League, feared the consequences if Sparta were added to Persia as an enemy. Cimon's downfall was intimately connected with his support of Sparta.

The Messenian Revolt. The situation at Sparta was disturbed by unrest within the Peloponnesian League, and then in 464 B.C. an earthquake there leveled most of the houses and killed thousands of the inhabitants. The helots took this moment to revolt and, seizing Mount Ithome, inaugurated the so-called Third Messenian War. They defended themselves so stoutly that Sparta had to appeal for aid to its allies, including Athens. The democratic faction, led by Ephialtes with the aid of Pericles, a young noble just beginning his public career, believed that the request should be declined. Cimon's faction won the day, however, and marched to the relief of Sparta with a force of hoplites (462 B.C.). For some reason not now wholly clear, the Spartans dismissed Cimon and his troops soon after their arrival.

Cimon and Ephialtes. This insult thoroughly discredited the pro-Spartan faction in the assembly and brought to the front Ephialtes and the democratic group, which was determined to change foreign and domestic policy. The first fruits of the new policy were the ostracism of Cimon (461 B.C.) and a reform of the council of the Areopagus, whose members held office for life and were associated in the public mind with aristocracy.[1] The reform left to the Areopagus all jurisdiction in matters of homicide but divided its other powers as a kind of supreme court—"the guardianship of the laws," as they were vaguely defined—among the Council of Five Hundred, the assembly, and the *heliaea.* Ephialtes, however, was soon murdered by a member of one of the oligarchical clubs, and his place as leader of the democratic faction was taken by Pericles.

THE GREEK WORLD AFTER PLATAEA

Economic Life. The Greek world, which Athens came to dominate, was united by trade and commerce no less than by the exchange of ideas. Its economic basis,

---

[1] The council, however, must have been full of mediocrities, for it consisted of ex-archons who, since Themistocles' reform, had been chosen by lot.

however, was agriculture, and concerning this the Greeks knew surprisingly little. Even in the fifth century the advantage of rotating crops was only slowly recognized, and half the land was allowed to lie fallow in alternate years; the farms were small, the plough was simple, and the use of manure was restricted by the lack of animals. The farmer, nevertheless, took pride in being engaged in an ancient profession, in which only citizens were allowed to own land, and he worked his field himself, aided perhaps by a few slaves. Certain areas naturally lent themselves better to the cultivation of specific crops; for example, Sicily, Egypt, Cyprus, Euboea, and southern Russia were the chief grain-growing districts; wine and oil were prized products of Attica and the Aegean islands; the uplands of Asia Minor were famous for their woolens; flax came from the Black Sea regions, dried fish from the Bosporus; and as more and more land was put under the plough, timber had to be imported, for warships and buildings, from the Black Sea, Thrace, and Magna Graecia.

The chief industrial centers were Athens, with its famous potteries; Corinth, Sicyon, Argos, and Chalcis, which were noted for their metalwork; and Miletus and Samos, for their furniture and textiles. Marble came from the quarries of Pentelicus and Paros, silver from Laurium and Mount Pangaeus, gold from Mount Pangaeus and Thasos, iron from Laconia and the Black Sea, copper from Cyprus, and tin from southern Gaul and Spain. The Orient produced a variety of luxury wares.

It was left to private initiative to arrange for export, since Greek states rarely had a commercial policy. The exchange of goods—the products of small shops, where specialization, in our sense, was unknown—was facilitated by the widespread use of coinage. The many different issues and weights must have been confusing, but in practice it was the money of the great commercial states that circulated widely, such as the "owls" of Athens, whose coinage the empire was compelled to adopt. On account of the rough nature of Greece and the poor roads, most traffic was by sea, in boats of about 250 tons. These were propelled by oars and sail and could cover more than 125 nautical miles in a day. The sea was cleared of pirates by Athenian triremes, but commerce was constantly disturbed by warfare, which remained nevertheless a very inexact science conducted by citizen armies, who as a rule were willing to fight only in the summer.

Literature.   During this period, when the Delian League was being transformed into an empire, Athens won the leadership of the intellectual world. In the hands of Aeschylus of Eleusis (ca. 525-456 B.C.), for example, the drama became a new and great art.

Aeschylus was an aristocrat, a warrior, and a great poet. He was a boy when tyrants ruled Athens, and a man at Salamis, where he fought for an Athens whose constitution became democratic but whose ruling spirits were still nobles. Toward the end of his life, he saw and remarked the introduction into judicial procedure of the secret ballot, characteristic instrument of a full democracy. Like his fellow citizens, he was fully and vitally committed to the affairs of Athens. During all of what we know of his artistic life, he wrestled with the sublimely difficult questions of human and divine justice. He asked himself why the innocent suffer and how the term of that suffering is fixed. His answers—at times grim, even despairing, at times informed with distant hope—were elaborated in his own ornate, potent, and massive vocabulary throughout the terrifying spectacles that he created in honor of Diony-sus at Athens.

His are the earliest Greek tragedies that have been preserved. We have seven complete plays and excerpts from many others. The origins of this form of drama are obscure, but the *Suppliants,* although not his earliest play, shows the primitive scheme. The suppliant maidens themselves, who form a chorus or troop of dancers, make up the central character of the play, and their songs, dances, and prayers the action.

In *Prometheus Bound,* he created a symbol of intellectual man that endures today. Only this one of the three plays that formed the trilogy is preserved, and so the nature of Zeus, paradoxical when viewed against the essentially just deity of Aeschylus' other work, is hard to assess. What we have is a Titan nailed to a rock at the end of the world, paying for his effrontery; he had brought fire to man, when Zeus had not permitted it.

Two brothers destroy each other at the end of *Seven Against Thebes* in expiation of an offense their father committed against a god. Aeschylus and others before and after him believed that children were punished for their parents' crime. The original crime, for which the perpetrator himself could also be punished, seemed to be at once a part of the offspring's allotted portion in life—not even a god could change it—and yet the offspring themselves also bore some responsibility. Demonic forces were thought to be at work, as well. The *Persians,* in which a historical event is exalted to a mythic plane, shows Xerxes undone by his own excess, but demons have somehow driven him. Distant hope lights the end of Aeschylus' great master-piece, the *Oresteia.* Orestes, innocent, must execute his mother, for she murdered his father (who was himself guilty). Orestes does what he must do and is subsequently tortured by Furies, but he is finally exonerated in a judicial trial whose outcome the goddess Athena directs. This hope of eventual exoneration, however, must have weighed little in the balance in a world where knowledge came from suffering, and the gods, who one hoped were just, remained inscrutable.

Simonides of Ceos, Bacchylides of Ceos, and Pindar were lyric poets who lived, like Aeschylus, when aristocracies and tyrannies flourished in Greece, when democracy was established at Athens, and when the Persians were turned back from Greece. Simonides spent some time at Athens when Hipparchus was tyrant there, but he was above all a world traveler. Although an Ionian, he wrote some of his poems in Doric Greek. From one dithyramb, we have a few precious lines in which Danae quiets her infant son, Perseus, but not much more of his lyric poetry. There are also a number of epigrams that antiquity knew as his. Bacchylides, nephew of Simonides, was exiled from Ceos, lived in the Peloponnese, and visited Hiero's court. Some of his admirable poems were restored to the world by the discovery of a papyrus in Egypt. Pindar (ca. 522–441 B.C.) was a Boeotian noble who glorified his class by his choral songs in honor of victors at the national games. The Pindaric glitter, however, reflects the glory of earth and of the gods who live no higher than Olympus, whereas the words of Aeschylus spring from a loftier spiritual and moral inspiration. Pindar, nevertheless, is one of the greatest Greek poets. His Olympic odes are the best statement of those aristocratic ideals of *arete,* typical of the archaic period, but rapidly waning as the fifth century B.C. progressed.

Art. The emphasis of these decades between 480 and 450 B.C.—the so-called transitional period between the end of the Persian Wars and the firm establishment of the Athenian Empire—was on balance. This can be seen as clearly in art as in literature. The most beautiful building erected during this time was the temple of Zeus (ca. 460 B.C.) in the Altis, or sanctuary, at Olympia. The grand pedimental sculptures are almost exact in their portrayal of the human form, strong, virile figures with varying emotions freely expressed or suggested. They have a quiet simplicity and restraint that make even the mortals appear superhuman. The western pediment has the conventional scene of violence, but it is no ordinary violence,

The Granger Collection

FIGURE 31. The Charioteer of Delphi in bronze, 474 B.C.

FIGURE 32. The Discobolus
(discus thrower): Roman marble
copy of the lost bronze by
Myron of about 450 B.C.

The Granger Collection

for the tremendous struggle between Lapiths and Centaurs symbolizes the never-ending conflict between civilization and barbarism. In the center, undisturbed by the confusion around him, stands Apollo, the great god of youth and Hellenism, looking along his extended right arm and leaving us in no doubt as to the outcome.

The only statue from ancient Greece that can compare with the Olympia Apollo in profound Aeschylean grandeur is the large bronze Zeus found by fishermen in 1927 in the sea near Cape Artemisium off Euboea. Here is depicted the father of gods and mortals in all his simple, yet mighty majesty. There is a wonderful balance to the figure as he hurls the thunderbolt. In the bronze charioteer from Delphi, and more particularly in Myron's discus thrower, we notice that the faces are often idealized and have a quiet expression that contrasts with their bodily action. The old archaic stiffness with its frontal pose has disappeared, and the figures are at once simpler and more massive.

THE ATHENIAN DEMOCRATIC CONSTITUTION

No great contemporary historian has left a detailed history of the momentous half century between 478 and 431 B.C. (the so-called *Pentecontaetia*), for Herodotus concluded his *History* with the Persian Wars, Thucydides' chief interest was in the Peloponnesian War, and later writers, such as Ephorus, have survived only in fragments. This means that the historian of the period is confronted with some challenging chronological problems. It is a period of peculiar fascination and value, because, in addition to the transformation of the Delian League into a maritime empire, we have the growth of an Athenian land empire and a concomitant democratization of the constitution. Athens had not the strength to maintain her land empire for long. By the end of the century the maritime empire had also disappeared, but the constitution endured until late in the fourth century B.C. Meanwhile the enthusiasm, taste, and ability of the Athenians produced masterpieces in art and literature; their city became "the teacher of Greece," the meeting place of most of the leading minds of the time; and later their Greek, with some changes, became the "common tongue" of the Eastern world. By the suppression of piracy and the elimination of the Persian danger, as well as by the promotion of commerce and prosperity, their empire could be claimed to benefit Greece and seemed to promise future security and stability. There is no doubt, however, about a corresponding loss of life and liberty and about the steady interference in the affairs of sovereign states; a task of the historian, therefore, is properly to evaluate and weigh the successes and failures of Periclean imperialism.

Pericles.   It was Pericles (490–429), of course, who brought Athens to a summit of civilization never before reached by the human race and who expressed in his own personality the highest ideals of his age. He inherited the inspiring traditions of two illustrious families, those of his father, Xanthippus, who had been an admiral at the battle of Mycale, and of his mother, Agariste, a niece of Cleisthenes, the great Alcmeonid reformer. The thrilling events of his childhood and youth attending the struggle for freedom and the founding of empire were in Pericles transmuted into force and nobility of character directed to the political and intellectual elevation of his country. The friend and associate of artists and thinkers throughout his life, Pericles had been instructed in music by Damonides, who became a political adviser, and in philosophy by Anaxagoras of Clazomenae, who freed his mind from superstition by directing it to a search for natural causes. Character and education combined to give weight to his words and majesty to his person, and his obviously deep earnestness won the confidence of the people in his patriotism, wisdom, and incorruptibility. Except for two years following Cimon's return from exile, Pericles, as an annually elected general (twice before 450 and almost continually thereafter, until his death in 429 B.C.), was virtually master of Athens. He was not, however, a distinguished military commander, and his foreign policy was frequently unsuccessful, sometimes even disastrous (p. 181).[2]

---

[2] A kinswoman, Telesippe by name, became Pericles' wife, but as they could not live happily together, he found her another husband at her request and afterward was himself attracted to Aspasia, a highly accomplished woman from Miletus. As Athenian women had merely a domestic education and were now kept more strictly at home, a class of non-Athenian women, termed *hetaerae,* or "companions," better educated and more attractive, usurped their place in the society of men. It may be added that divorce at Athens was easy for a man, more difficult for a woman, and that parents not only had the power to name their sons (the eldest being named generally after his grandfather) but could also delete their names from the register and disin-

Classes of Society.   It was the possession of an empire, and the concentration of its control in the city masses of Piraeus and Athens, that determined the character of the Athenian constitution. The metics (resident aliens) and slaves possessed no political rights, but within the citizen body the old issue of the few against the many persisted, and in the new democratic world many of the old nobility, the eupatrids, found themselves totally out of place. One of their number, usually now called the Old Oligarch, has left us a political treatise whose words reveal the existence of a class of men, strong in wealth, social standing, and intelligence, who were watching their opportunity to usurp the government and rule the populace. Under Pericles they could not prosper and were confined to indirect attacks on the leading statesmen, but well before the end of the century Athens was to see their mode of rule.

Notwithstanding such people, the commons cherished profound respect for the nobility, and it was chiefly the eupatrids, not men from the masses, who developed and gave form to the constitution, which was unwritten and authoritative. The nobility were a small minority of the population, but their sympathies were largely shared by the *zeugitae,* the freeholders of little farms, conservative middle-class citizens who were opposed to forces that made powerfully for innovation. The "poor," whom the Old Oligarch so despised, were in general self-sustaining—the smallest land proprietors, shepherds, shopkeepers, artisans, laborers, and sailors; in short, the lowest class in the Solonian census (the *thetes*). The growing complexity of economic conditions, created by the development of commerce and industry and making greater and greater demands on intelligence, produced an increasing number of persons who were incompetent to earn a living for themselves. Under an aristocracy they would have died of want or fallen into slavery, and the task of the broader and more humane democracy was to lift them to a place of respectable citizenship. This it did through colonization, through military and civil service, and through public works. A large state income, however, was necessary for all this. The masses, taking apparently the easy road, decided to maintain and organize the empire for their own benefit. Since that empire was dependent on the navy, and the navy on the poorest citizens, who acted as rowers, the *thetes* exerted special influence on the development of the constitution.

Assembly and Council.   The sovereignty of the people was vested in the popular assembly (*ecclesia*),[3] which met forty times a year, passed the laws, and decided matters concerning foreign policy, war, food, and a multitude of details. Any person could debate in the assembly, but, since it could not initiate a measure, a resolution (*probouleuma*) was brought before it by the Council of Five Hundred (*boule*). The members of the council were chosen by lot from citizens over thirty years of age, were paid a drachma a day, and acted as the presiding officers of the

herit them, though the sons would not lose their political status. Athenian women, although often both respected and loved as daughters, mothers, and wives, had no legal status of their own and were regarded essentially as wards of their fathers, husbands, or nearest surviving male relatives, depending on circumstance. The sexual "double standard" was accepted.

[3] The assembly embraced all male citizens over eighteen years of age, but men of nineteen and twenty were generally absent on military training.

assembly. The council examined the fitness of candidates for office, arranged for their election or sortition, kept strict watch over the magistrates, and attended to many other matters, such as the construction of public buildings and triremes and other ships of war, and prosecuted before the assembly cases of treason (*eisangelia*). Far from giving rein to license, Athenian democracy in the lifetime of Pericles sternly enforced the discipline to which the people had grown accustomed under aristocratic rule. But the theory that, under the laws, the people themselves were sovereign could not be put into strict practice, for the actual administration had to be entrusted to the council, and through it to the prytanies, the ten smaller groups (fifty from each tribe) who served, each of them, as a committee of the council for thirty-five or thirty-six days.

The Heliaea. The council, through its prytanies, was in continuous session and, since it formulated the measures to be considered by the people, served as a brake on the assembly, as did the *heliaea* (popular court). Athens outstripped other Greek states in the conception of its duties and powers in criminal law, but public administration of justice was comparatively undeveloped, for much was left to private initiative; each person had to plead his own case, although some had recourse to professional speech-writers. The court was a panel drawn from the 6,000 jurors (dicasts, 600 chosen annually by lot from each tribe)—it might be a panel of 501, 1001, or 1501, a large enough number, it was hoped, to prevent both bribery and intimidation—and it served as judge and jury. A number of panels might sit on the same day, and the judgment of each was final. There was no appeal, for by a legal fiction, the panel was the city, and so once a citizen had appeared before it, he had already appealed to the ultimate tribunal. Also, every heliastic decision was a fresh restatement of the general sense of right, which the Athenians considered superior to case law and precedent. With the growth of her empire, Athens gradually obtained jurisdiction over the allies in important cases. While this was another factor in the political education of the Athenian citizens, their delays and democratic bias made many states wonder if they were not paying a high price for the suppression of piracy and Persia.

In the year 451–450 B.C. Pericles carried a measure for the payment of jurors, at the rate of two obols a day. This act further democratized the consitution since it enabled the poorest to attend regularly. The jurors, whom Aristophanes characterized in his burlesque of the system as old men, may have had pay in lieu of an old-age pension, a very democratic idea. Pericles' other measure of this year, that limiting the franchise to those who could show citizenship on both sides of the family, narrowed the benefits of empire to a more restricted group. In this virtual democracy, the chief safeguard to the constitution was the *graphe paranomon,* an indictment for bringing before the assembly measures in conflict with the laws.

Magistrates. The number of officials at Athens was very large, and since all the magistrates were paid, excepting the military officers, there must have been twenty thousand people on the pay roll, when we consider jurors, soldiers, and sailors. The empire made this possible, and payment simply meant that every Athenian male had the opportunity of sharing in the actual government of his state. The highest magistrates were the ten generals, who were elected annually, reelection being allowed; in addition to commanding the army and navy, they embraced most of the functions falling in a modern state to the ministry or cabinet. An Athenian, accordingly, who undertook to guide the policy of his state had to bear a heavier weight of responsibility than has been necessary in any less democratic form of government, for the assembly could not be expected to have the same acquaintance with the details of policy that might be presupposed in a select body of men, such, for instance, as the Roman Senate or a modern parliament. The democracy had to place greater trust in its advisers, although the right of debate in the assembly on occasion permitted a demagogue to impose upon a magistrate a policy in which he had no confidence.

THE LAND EMPIRE

Cimon's dismissal from Mount Ithome, his subsequent ostracism, and the triumph of the anti-Spartan democratic party of Ephialtes and Pericles meant that Athens was now committed to the possibility of simultaneous war on land and sea. When an Athenian embassy under Callias sought peace with Persia and returned unsuccessful, Athens decided that at any rate Persia would not dare to attack her fleet. She then resolved to weaken the Peloponnesian League by an indirect blow at Corinth, its second most powerful member.

Athenian Aggression. This she did in 460 B.C. by accepting the plea of Megara for aid against Corinth. The alliance with Megara gave Athens control of the mountain passes leading to the isthmus and of a convenient harbor, Pegae on the Corinthian Gulf, from which to trade with the West. Moreover, when the rebellious helots on Mount Ithome surrendered a few years later, with the privilege of withdrawing from the Peloponnesus, Athens settled them at Naupactus, a Gibraltar near the entrance of the Corinthian Gulf (map, p. 98). It was becoming abundantly clear that Athens intended to gain the same control over this water that she exercised in the Saronic Gulf and the Aegean Sea, in fact, that she was interfering in a Corinthian sphere of interest. It is little wonder, as the historian Thucydides remarked, that the Corinthians now conceived an "extreme hatred" for Athens.

The resources of Athens were matched by her vitality. Although she had a large fleet before Egypt and Cyprus, she was able to lay siege to and conquer Aegina. After a preliminary reverse in Boeotia (where Sparta was trying to erect a counterweight to Athens), Myronides, the Athenian general, conquered all Boeotia except Thebes. Locris was forced into the league; Phocis became an ally; Troezen, on the opposite Peloponnesian coast, and Achaea cast their lot with Athens. At the same time the Athenians completed their long walls, which connected the city with Piraeus, four and a half miles distant, and ensured that they could never be effectively besieged as long as their fleet held the sea.

Height of the Land Empire. The height of Athenian power on land was reached in 456 B.C. The imperial ambition of Pericles seemed to be justified, for in a period of five years Athens had built up a continental federation that included parts of the Peloponnesus and the entire territory from the isthmus to Thermopylae and embracing intermittently the Thessalians. Here was a threat to the Peloponnesian League. Could Athens hope to maintain both her land and sea empires? As if the control of the Saronic Gulf, through her possession of Megara, Aegina, and Troezen, were not enough, she now became, thanks to Pegae, Achaea, and Naupactus, a power on the western seas as well. Could Athens with impunity so threaten the Peloponnesians by opposing to them a mightier empire than their own? And, above all, could she fight Persia at the same time? Even if she had the money, did she possess the manpower?

Callias' Embassy to Susa.   Maneuvers of the Persian navy off Phoenicia, which resulted ultimately in a devastating attack on the Athenian fleet before Egypt, led Pericles to fear that in reality the Persians might be planning a descent on the Aegean. In 454 B.C., therefore, he transferred the treasury of the league from Delos to Athens for safekeeping. The next years were disturbed by Cimon's return from exile (451 B.C.) and party strife, during which Cimon won temporary control of foreign policy at Athens. Making peace with Sparta, he set sail with two hundred ships for Cyprus, where his troops won a brilliant victory that raised Athenian prestige in the eastern Mediterranean, though he himself was killed. His death left Pericles stronger at Athens, and recognizing the limitations on the capacity of his city and the futility of war with Persia, he apparently sent an embassy under Callias to Susa to make peace, although the historical reality of the embassy is debatable. Artaxerxes, who had succeeded Xerxes, refused to acknowledge formally the cession of his former Greek provinces in Asia Minor, but he did consent to leave them undisturbed within Athens' Empire. Athens, on her part, agreed to cease attacks upon his possessions.

From Delian League to Empire.   The Peace of Callias, as it is called, meant that the war with Persia was finally finished, and consequently very little tribute came into the treasury of the Delian League for that year (449 B.C.). During the spring, however, Pericles suggested that the end of the war be celebrated by a Panhellenic congress at Athens to discuss the rebuilding of temples destroyed during the Persian invasion. It was a shrewd idea calculated to win for Athens the implied moral leadership of the Greek world and was certain of refusal by the Peloponnesian states. Pericles then proposed to the Athenians that they should rebuild their own temples and pay for them with the allied money. These funds were in the care of the goddess Athena, whose treasurers could use the funds as they saw fit. The idea was popular, and in this momentous year of 449 B.C. the Athenians decided to charge tribute once more (beginning with 448-447 B.C.), an act that marks the formal change of the Delian League into the Athenian Empire. As Plutarch remarked, Pericles now set about adorning Athens like a vain woman, draping around her neck precious stones and statues and temples and teaching the people that, as long as they protected the allies, they did not need to give them any reckoning.

Collapse of the Land Empire.   The very next years, however, witnessed a general revolt in Greece against Athens. The Theban oligarchs won back Boeotia; Locris and Phocis deserted their alliance; Megara returned to the Peloponnesian League; Pleistoanax, the Spartan king, invaded Attica; and even Euboea attempted rebellion. In fact, the Athenian land empire collapsed almost overnight (446 B.C.).

THE THIRTY YEARS' PEACE

Pericles saw the exhaustion of the state, and in 445 B.C. he agreed with the Peloponnesians to a Thirty Years' Peace. Athens surrendered her entire land empire, including Megara's harbor (Nisaea), Pegae, Troezen, and Achaea, and retained only Plataea, Aegina, and Naupactus. The peace treaty practically reduced her to the territory she had held on the mainland in 461 B.C., when Pericles had succeeded to Ephialtes' leadership. Sparta, on her part, acknowledged Athens' maritime empire, and neither party was to interfere with the allies of the other. Thus ended the conflict that is sometimes referred to as the First Peloponnesian War. Pericles had had the wisdom to act just in time to save the Athenian Empire in the Aegean, but the peace terms he got from Sparta can only be described as destroying his dreams of a land empire.

Advantages of Empire.   By drawing on imperial tribute, Pericles was able to continue his building program for the Athenian Acropolis, which included erecting the Parthenon; building an Odeon, or music hall, on its southern side; and carrying on the construction of a new Hall of Mysteries at Eleusis. The dockyards of Piraeus were substantially enlarged, and Hippodamus, a philosopher and practical scientist of Miletus, was engaged to lay out anew the harbor town, with broad, straight avenues crossing each other at right angles. All this imperial activity, which was thrown into relief by the fact that the synod of the old league no longer met and its officials (the *Hellenotamiae*) were Athenian magistrates, roused the conservatives to action. Their leader, Thucydides, the son of Melesias, charged that Pericles was a traitorous tyrant, in very truth another Peisistratus.

The Tribute Districts.   The ostracism of this Thucydides in 443 B.C. left Pericles without opposition. In order to bring more system into the administration of the empire, it was divided, for purposes of quadrennial assessment, into five tribute districts—Ionia, the Hellespont, the Thracian district, Caria, and the islands—but in 438 B.C., Caria was merged with Ionia. These four districts remained until the last assessment in Athens in 410 B.C. It should be emphasized, because it illustrates so well the Greek ideal of the citizen as man of action, that the person Pericles saw fit to appoint as chief treasurer for the reorganization of the empire in 443 B.C. was the poet Sophocles, who produced his *Antigone* the following year and two years later was general at Samos.[4]

The Allied States.   Athens brought peace and prosperity to her empire, but they were regarded as mixed blessings because of the steady encroachment of the Attic language and laws, monetary standards, and cleruchies. All this pointed to the ultimate consolidation of the empire, yet no ally demanded citizenship in Athens, and had it been offered, few would have accepted. The fundamental defect in the Athenian imperial system was that the allies were given no hope of acquiring representa-

---

[4] After its revolt was put down (439 B.C.), Samos received the punishment formerly meted out to Naxos and Thasos.

tion in the central government and were convinced that Athens was bent on forever maintaining her place, not as president, but as master.

Athenian Power East and West. Perhaps with the hope of weakening Dorian Syracuse, and certainly with the idea of creating a strategic base in the west, Pericles established a colony in 443 B.C., made up of Athenians and other Greeks, at Thurii, a fertile spot in southern Italy. In 437 B.C. he set out on a voyage around the Black Sea, with the intention of impressing barbarian tribes in the area with a sense of the far-reaching strength of the Athenian navy. This same year a colony was planted at Amphipolis, the Strymon crossing that controlled the approaches to the mines of Mount Pangaeus and, moreover, could watch the growing Macedonian and Thracian kingdoms; and in the northwest, the Athenian admiral, Phormio, was busy weakening the prestige of Corinth. East and West the might of Athens was respected and feared, but in spite of Pericles' own unassailable position, the ever fickle people exiled his instructors, Damonides and Anaxagoras, on charges of impiety, and even the great sculptor Phidias, on the charge of embezzling gold and ivory intended for the statue of Athena in the Parthenon.

The "Grievances." It appears that in general Athenian subjects abroad, of whatever class and political outlook, disliked the empire as an instrument of tyranny, even though it might bring them economic and other advantages. This attitude toward Athens underscores the most important priority of the Greek value system: the sovereign independence of every city-state to determine its own destiny. The Athenian Empire was disliked just as much by the Peloponnesian League, especially by Corinth, Athens' neighbor, because of Pericles' recent aggression by land. If Corinth was to persuade Sparta to lead the Peloponnesian League to war, an overt act had to be committed, or, as Thucydides expressed it, a "grievance" had to be found. Sparta, however, refused to stir even when Athens violated the Thirty Years' Peace at the sea battle of Sybota by preventing the Corinthians from taking vengeance on their unfilial colony, Corcyra. Then, a second "grievance" came from the north. Potidaea, a member of the Athenian Empire though a colony of Corinth, chafed under her recently increased tribute and the presence of nearby Amphipolis. Urged on by Perdiccas, the ambitious king of Macedon, Potidaea revolted in 432 B.C. Athens dispatched forces to besiege the city, and Corinth replied with aid. Pericles, to bring matters to a head and perhaps, too, to obtain again a western outlet in the Megarid, strategically located between Corinth and Athens, issued his famous decree that excluded Megara from the harbors and markets of the empire and meant her ruin, as well as possible occupation by Athens at Corinth's very doorstep. Pericles, using all his diplomatic skill, offered to arbitrate as the Peloponnesian League, goaded by Corinth, prepared for war. Thus the winter dragged on, when suddenly, in March 431 B.C., Thebes set the Greek world afire by claiming Plataea, Athens' ally, as a member of the Boeotian League and laid siege to the city. The Thirty Years' Peace had not run half its course.

14

The Peloponnesian War (431–404 B.C.)

THE CAUSES OF THE PANHELLENIC CONFLICT

Our chief source of the terrible and tragic war between Athens and Sparta is the *History* of Thucydides.[1] An impartial writer, with the ability to penetrate beneath the surface, Thucydides also had the genius to reduce the actualities of life to their generic and hence their lasting patterns. Small though his world may have been, he was able to expose the forces that move political beings. Some of these forces, he believed, sprang from chance or fate. It is because of Thucydides' great powers that the Peloponnesian War assumes the qualities of a universal conflict of eternal significance. He fought in the war and, after an unsuccessful campaign in 424 B.C., was exiled from Athens for the duration, since he feared reprisals from his fickle compatriots. He thus had an opportunity to view the conflict from the vantage point of participants in it other than Athens, which presumably contributed to the balance and objectivity of his narrative. In any case, he returned home in 404 B.C.

Thucydides opened his *History of the Peloponnesian War* with these words:

"Thucydides, an Athenian, wrote the history of the war in which the Peloponnesians and the Athenians fought against one another. He began to write when they first took up arms, believing that it would be great and memorable above any previous war. For he argued that both states were then at the full height of their military power, and he saw the rest of the Hellenes either siding or intending to side with one or other of them. No movement ever stirred Hellas more deeply than this; it was shared by many of the barbarians, and might be said even to affect the world at large. The character of the events, which preceded, whether immediately or in more remote antiquity, owing to the lapse of time cannot be made out with certainty. But, judging from the evidence which I am able to trust after most careful enquiry, I should imagine that former ages were not great either in their wars or in anything else. And, though men will always judge any war in which they are actually fighting to be the greatest at the time, but, after it is all over, revert to their admiration of

---

[1] Thucydides, the son of Olorus, took part in the Peloponnesian War; see pp. 224 ff. for a fuller discussion. Thucydides' *History* ends during 411 B.C.; for the remainder of the war we are dependent on Xenophon's *Hellenica*. Also useful are Diodorus (who drew from Ephorus), various *Lives* of Plutarch, the comedies of Aristophanes, the tragedies of Sophocles and Euripides, Aristotle's *Constitution of Athens*, the Oxyrhynchus *Hellenica*, and inscriptions.

some other which has preceded, still the Peloponnesian, if estimated by the actual facts, will certainly prove to have been the greatest ever known.

"As to the speeches which were made either before or during the war, it was hard for me, and for others who reported them to me, to recollect the exact words. I have therefore put into the mouth of each speaker the sentiments proper to the occasion, expressed as I thought he would be likely to express them, while at the same time I endeavored, as nearly as I could, to give the general purport of what was actually said. Of the events of the war I have not ventured to speak from any chance information, nor according to any notion of my own; I have described nothing but what I either saw myself, or learned from others of whom I made the most careful and particular inquiry. The task was a laborious one, because eyewitnesses of the same occurrences gave different accounts of them, as they remembered or were interested in the actions of one side or the other. And very likely the strictly historical character of my narrative may be disappointing to the ear. But if he who desires to have before his eyes a true picture of the events which have happened, and of the like events which may be expected to happen hereafter in the order of human things, shall pronounce what I have written to be useful, then I shall be satisfied. My history is an everlasting possession, not a prize composition which is heard and forgotten.

"The greatest achievement of former times was the Persian War; yet even this was speedily decided in two battles by sea and two by land. But the Peloponnesian War was a protracted struggle, and attended by calamities such as Hellas had never known within a like period of time. Never were so many cities captured and depopulated—some by barbarians, others by Hellenes themselves fighting against one another; and several of them after their capture were repeopled by strangers. Never were exile and slaughter more frequent, whether in war or brought about by civil strife. And rumors, of which the like had often been current before, but rarely verified by fact, now appeared to be well grounded. There were earthquakes unparalleled in their extent and fury, and eclipses of the sun more numerous than are recorded to have happened in any former age; there were also in some places great droughts causing famines, and lastly the plague which did immense harm and destroyed numbers of the people. All these calamities fell upon Hellas simultaneously with the war, which began when the Athenians and Peloponnesians violated the thirty years' truce concluded by them after the recapture of Euboea. Why they broke it and what were the grounds of quarrel I will first set forth, that in time to come no man may be at a loss to know what was the origin of this great war. The real though unavowed cause I believe to have been the growth of Athenian power, which terrified the Lacedaemonians and forced them into war; but the reasons publicly alleged on either side were as follows." [2]

Thucydides made it clear that the ancient naval democracy, guided by one man, pursued revolutionary policies that so terrified other Greeks that war became inevitable. This was emphasized by the Corinthian envoys at Sparta before the outbreak of the hostilities, when they said: "The Athenians are innovators, equally quick in the conception and in the execution of every new plan; you, on the other hand, are conservative, careful only to keep what you have." With remarkable candor the

---

[2] The translations in this chapter are those of B. Jowett. Thucydides, I, 1; 21–23.

Athenian envoys remarked: "An empire was offered to us: can you wonder that, acting as human nature always will, we accepted it and refused to give it up again, constrained by three all-powerful motives, ambition, fear, interest. We are not the first who have aspired to rule; the world has ever held that the weaker must be kept down by the stronger. And we think that we are worthy of power; and there was a time when you thought so too; but now, when you mean self-interest, you resort to talk about justice. Did justice ever deter anyone from taking by force whatever he could?"

The point about Athenian aggressions in the preceding half century was that they had been aimed at many different quarters. Was there a limit to Athenian ambition, or must all states eventually bow before it? The Athenian claim to leadership was generally considered incompatible with the liberties of individual states and with the long-established policy of Sparta. The Athenians, however, asserted that their hegemony had been forced upon them by Sparta's unwillingness to continue the war with Persia, that circumstances not under their control had converted the Delian League into an empire, and that, though they had been compelled thus to usurp authority, they had made good their right to it by an unparalleled justice and a moderation. Against this claim their enemies, particularly the Corinthians, charged Athens with the enslavement of her allies and with the design of reducing other Hellenes to servitude, and they called on Sparta to take the lead in putting down the tyrant. The Spartans, despite their own constitution, considered themselves champions of the principle of city sovereignty, and they were so regarded by their allies. Fear of Athens and the universal Greek love of liberty were certainly contributing factors to the Peloponnesian War. Here, then, was a variety of ideas and factors that so charged the atmosphere of Greece with suspicion and hatred that any incident might force Sparta to lead the Peloponnesians against her rival. Even so, Greece might have survived the Megarian decree and the incidents at Corcyra and Potidaea, but the Theban attack on Plataea showed that it was futile to hope for peace any longer.

THE ARCHIDAMIAN WAR (431–421 B.C.)

The Strategy. Pericles, now a man of sixty, not only was reconciled to war but was convinced that it was better that it should come while he was still in the prime of life and Athens in excellent military condition. Hence he persuaded his countrymen to oppose every concession to the Peloponnesians. Knowing better than any contemporary the resources of Athens and her enemy, Pericles had ground for confidence. Arrayed against his state were the forces of nearly all the Peloponnesians, consisting of 24,000 hoplites and many light-armed troops; of the Boeotian confederacy under Theban leadership, with 10,000 hoplites and 1,000 cavalry; and of lesser allies in the center and west of the peninsula. Obviously the strategy of the Peloponnesians was to invade and devastate Attica, hoping that the Athenians would be provoked into making a sally from their walls.

The Athenian army consisted of 1,200 cavalry and 13,000 hoplites, as well as another 16,000 hoplites to defend the long walls and the frontier forts, while others were absent at the siege of Potidaea. The strategy of Pericles consisted of bringing the entire population of the country, with their movable goods, into the city, although this meant devastation of the fields. The enemy would not remain long in the country, because most of the Peloponnesians were small farmers, who personally tilled their lands, and because they had to bring their food supplies with them. The Spartans, of course, were uneasy leaving their helots unattended for any length of time, and however much they might destroy real estate, they could accomplish nothing against the fortifications of Athens and Piraeus. The Athenian fleet, manned by the *thetes* and allies, commanded the sea and ensured the steady arrival at Athens of food supplies. In addition, the fleet attacked the coasts of the Peloponnesus and cut off its commerce; thus, while partially compensating the Athenians for damage to their fields, Pericles would gradually force the enemy to a more favorable peace than that of 445 B.C. Against the almost total lack of public funds among the enemy could be reckoned 6,000 talents stored in the treasuries on the Acropolis and an annual income from the tribute and other sources amounting to about 1,000 talents. The Peloponnesians tried to borrow from the treasuries of Delphi and Olympia to enlarge their fleet, but they were unsuccessful.

In the spring of 431 B.C. the enemy entered Attica, under the able Spartan king, Archidamus, after whom the first ten years of the Peloponnesian War were named. The orchards and the grain in the fields were cut down. Pericles' calculating plan of removing the population into the city strained Athenian nature excessively. The people were both reluctant to leave their homes and eager to fight the enemy. Gathering on the streets, they complained bitterly of their plight and laid the whole blame of the war and their losses on Pericles. This first tragic year of war was nothing compared with the years ahead. Two decades later, while the war still had several years to run, we can catch the pathos of it all in the *Lysistrata* of Aristophanes, for in spite of the buffoonery of the comic poet, we see the ruin of family life at Athens: two generations of men were swept away, leaving the women desolate, robbed of husbands, lovers, and children.

The Funeral Oration. Pericles maintained his policy at home in spite of the grumblings and sent a fleet to ravage the Peloponnesian coast. In autumn he persuaded the people to decree a reserve of one thousand talents, to be used only in case of an attack by sea, and to keep one hundred triremes always at home to defend Piraeus. After the campaign the remains of those who had fallen in battle during the summer were solemnly conveyed to the cemetery in Cerameicus—a beautiful spot outside the walls—and interred amid the lamentations of their kin, citizens and metics, women and men. An empty bed, covered with a sheet, honored those whose bodies had not been recovered. After the burial Pericles addressed the people in a Funeral Oration, one of the most precious documents in history. The Funeral Oration is much more than a defense of his own policy or a mere eulogy of Athens. It is a description of the ideal of Pericles in his best moments and an analysis of the strength of ancient democracy. The Funeral Oration lets us see the value of majority rule and free public debate. Above all, it makes clear a fundamental trust in human nature and a belief in progress.

"Our constitution is called a democracy [Thucydides reports Pericles as saying] for the administration is in the hands of the many and not of the few. But while the law secures equal justice to all alike in their private disputes, the claim of excellence is also recognized; and when a citizen is in any way distinguished, he is preferred to the public service, not as a matter of privilege, but as the reward of merit. Neither is poverty a bar, but a man may benefit his country whatever be the obscurity of his condition. There is no exclusiveness in our public life, and in our private intercourse we are not suspicious of one another, nor angry with our neighbor if he does what he likes; we do not put on sour looks at him which, though harmless, are not pleasant. While we are thus unconstrained in our private intercourse, a spirit of reverence pervades our public acts; we are prevented from doing wrong by respect for authority and for the laws, having an especial regard to those which are ordained for the protection of the injured as well as to those unwritten laws which bring upon the transgressor of them the reprobation of the general sentiment.

"And we have not forgotten to provide for our weary spirits many relaxations from toil; we have regular games and sacrifices throughout the year; at home the style of our life is refined; and the delight which we daily feel in all these things helps to banish melancholy. Because of the greatness of our city the fruits of the whole earth flow in upon us; so that we enjoy the goods of other countries as freely as of our own.

"We are lovers of the beautiful, yet simple in our tastes, and we cultivate the mind without loss of manliness. Wealth we employ, not for talk and ostentation, but when there is a real use for it. To avow poverty with us is no disgrace; the true disgrace is in doing nothing to avoid it. An Athenian citizen does not neglect the state because he takes care of his own household; and even those of us who are engaged in business have a very fair idea of politics. We alone regard a man who takes no interest in public affairs, not as a harmless, but as a useless character; and if few of us are originators, we are all sound judges of a policy. The great impediment to action is, in our opinion, not discussion, but the want of that knowledge which is gained by discussion preparatory to action. For we have a peculiar power of thinking before we act and of acting too, whereas other men are courageous from ignorance but hesitate upon reflection. And they are surely to be esteemed the bravest spirits who, having the clearest sense both of the pains and pleasures of life, do not on that account shrink from danger. In doing good, again, we are unlike others; we make our friends by conferring, not by receiving favors. To sum up: I say that Athens is the school of Hellas, and that the individual Athenian in his own person seems to have the power of adapting himself to the most varied forms of action with the utmost versatility and grace.

"I have paid the required tribute, in obedience to the law, making use of such fitting words as I had. The tribute of deeds has been paid in part; for the dead have been honorably interred, and it remains only that their children should be maintained at the public charge until they are grown up: this is the solid prize with which, as with a garland, Athens crowns her sons living and dead, after a struggle like theirs. For where the rewards of virtue are greatest, there the noblest citizens are enlisted in the service of the state. And now, when you have duly lamented, every one his own dead, you may depart."[3]

The Plague. In the second year of the war there was the usual invasion of Attica

---

[3] Thucydides, II, 37-46.

by the Peloponnesians and Athenian attacks on the Peloponnesian coast. These operations were as a rule repeated during the early period of the war. The season had not far advanced, however, before a terrible plague (perhaps smallpox), beginning in the East, reached Piraeus and swept into Athens.

"As to the plague's probable origin [says Thucydides] or the causes which might or could have produced such a disturbance of nature, every man, whether physician or not, will give his own opinion. But I shall describe its actual course, and the symptoms by which any one who knows them beforehand may recognize the disorder should it ever reappear. For I was myself attacked, and witnessed the sufferings of others.

"The season was admitted to have been remarkably free from ordinary sickness; and if anybody was already ill of any other disease, it was absorbed in this. Many who were in perfect health, all in a moment, and without any apparent reason, were seized with violent heats in the head and with redness and inflammation of the eyes. Internally the throat and the tongue were quickly suffused with blood, and the breath became unnatural and fetid. There followed sneezing and hoarseness; in a short time the disorder, accompanied by a violent cough, reached the chest; then fastening lower down, it would move the stomach and bring on all the vomits of bile to which physicians have ever given names; and they were very distressing. An ineffectual retching producing violent convulsions attacked most of the sufferers; some as soon as the previous symptoms had abated, others not until long afterwards. The body externally was not so very hot to the touch, nor yet pale; it was of a livid color inclining to red, and breaking out in pustules and ulcers. But the internal fever was intense; the sufferers could not bear to have on them even the finest linen garment; they insisted on being naked, and there was nothing which they longed for more eagerly than to throw themselves into cold water. And many of those who had no one to look after them actually plunged into the cisterns, for they were tormented by unceasing thirst, which was not in the least assuaged whether they drank little or much. They could not sleep; a restlessness which was intolerable never left them. While the disease was at its height the body, instead of wasting away, held out amid these sufferings in a marvelous manner, and either they died on the seventh or ninth day, not of weakness, for their strength was not exhausted, but of internal fever, which was the end of most; or, if they survived, then the disease descended into the bowels and there produced violent ulceration; severe diarrhoea at the same time set in, and at a later stage caused exhaustion, which finally with a few exceptions carried them off. For the disorder which had originally settled in the head passed gradually through the whole body, and, if a person got over the worst, would often seize the extremities and leave its mark, attacking the genitals and the fingers and the toes; and some escaped with the loss of these, some with the loss of their eyes. Some again had no sooner recovered than they were seized with a forgetfulness of all things and knew neither themselves nor their friends.

"The crowding of the people out of the country aggravated the misery; and the newly arrived suffered most. For, having no houses of their own, but inhabiting in the height of summer stifling huts, the mortality among them was dreadful, and they perished in wild disorder. The dead lay as they had died, one upon another, while others hardly alive wallowed in the streets and crawled about every fountain craving for water. The temples in which they lodged were full of the corpses of those who died in them; for the violence of the calamity was such that men, not knowing where to turn, grew reckless of all law, human and divine. The customs which had hitherto been observed at funerals were universally violated, and they buried their dead each one as best he could. Many, having no proper appliances, because the deaths in their household had been so frequent, made no scruple of using the burial place of others. When one man had raised a funeral pile, others would come, and throwing on their dead first, set fire to it; or when some other corpse was already burning, before they could be stopped would throw their own dead upon it and depart.

"There were other and worse forms of lawlessness which the plague introduced at Athens. Men who had hitherto concealed their indulgence in pleasure now grew bolder. For, seeing the sudden change, how the rich died in a moment, and those who had nothing immediately inherited their property, they reflected that life and riches were alike transitory, and they resolved to enjoy themselves while they could, and to think only of pleasure. Who would be willing to sacrifice himself to the law of honor when he knew not whether he would ever live to be held in honor? The pleasure of the moment and any sort of thing which conduced to it took the place both of honor and of expediency. No fear of God or law of man deterred a criminal. Those who saw all perishing alike, thought that the worship or neglect of the gods made no difference. For offenses against human law no punishment was to be feared; no one would live long enough to be called to account. Already a far heavier sentence had been passed and was hanging over a man's head; before that fell, why should he not take a little pleasure?"[4]

Perhaps a third of the population was swept away by the plague. The discouragement was profound because at the beginning of the war the Delphic Apollo had promised aid to the foe; and the people now attributed the plague to his enmity. Humbly the Athenians sought peace of Sparta; but, repulsed, they turned against Pericles as the author of their woes. In spite of all he could say in defense of his policy, they suspended him from office and fined him. Having thus satisfied their resentment, they then reelected him general. In 429 B.C., however, Pericles himself fell a victim of the plague. Thus died the only man who stood sufficiently high above all individuals and parties to command universal respect. Pericles' successors were not demagogues so much as unsuccessful heirs to Periclean policy. The leadership of the government now passed to men of the commercial class, statesmen such as Cleon, who owned a tanning factory, and whose leadership was less Olympian than Pericles'. In her war with the Peloponnesus, Athens lost, through the death of Pericles, centralization of leadership and continuity of policy.

The war, with its many expeditions, small defeats, and victories, grievously afflicted the Athenians. No land could be tilled beyond the neighborhood of Athens and Piraeus; the work in the mines of Laurium nearly ceased; despite Athenian

---

[4] Thucydides, II, 48–53.

naval supremacy, commerce was hampered by pirates and by the enemy's fleet. Athens operated at a deficit. For a time it was met by loans from the funds of Athena and of other gods. Attitudes toward the war differed among various classes. Merchants and mechanics expected to suffer little from it and might hope to extend their business through conquests, while the poor found a livelihood in naval service or looked to the enlargement of the empire for increased tribute and a lengthened payroll. The intellectuals, however, longed for peace.

Mytilene. Despite plague and hardship, the advantage lay with Athens in the first years of the war. Potidaea finally fell in 430 B.C., but the siege cost Athens two thousand talents and she was unable to follow up her success in the Chalcidice. Similarly, in the northwest, the admiral Phormio won naval victories and damaged Corinthian trade, but no permanent gain resulted. The Peloponnesian army avoided Attica in 429 B.C., because of the plague, and after a siege of two years took Plataea. The Peloponnesians hoped for aid from Persia and Sicily, but in vain. In 428 B.C., however, news arrived that Mytilene and other towns of Lesbos had revolted. In the face of this new peril and the huge cost of sieges, the Athenians for the first time resorted to a property tax (*eisphora*), which yielded two hundred talents. The following year Mytilene fell, and the Athenians, wishing to terrorize their disaffected allies, voted to kill all the men of Mytilene and to enslave the women and children. Cleon advocated this policy of terrorism. The next day the Athenians met again to reconsider their cruel sentence. Cleon urged them not to repent: "I still maintain that you should abide by your former decision, and not be misled either by pity, or by the charm of words, or by a too forgiving temper. There are no three things more prejudicial to your power." The arguments against Cleon prevailed because of an appeal not to pity, kindness, or justice, but simply to Athens' self-interest. The punishment of death was limited to the Mytileneans most guilty, but the lands of the rebels were confiscated and divided among Athenian colonists.

Revolution at Corcyra. Despite his admiration of Pericles—despite the fact that both men saw in power the basis of civilization—Thucydides tells us that the real cause of the Peloponnesian War was the Spartans' and their allies' fear of Athens' power. Periclean imperialism produced the war. It is possible to agree further with Thucydides when he says that war produces violence, and violence political chaos. This he brings out with a vivid psychological insight when, in his description of revolution at Corcyra (427 B.C.), he analyzes the effect of war on human character: "Revolution brought upon the cities of Hellas many terrible calamities, such as have been and always will be while human nature remains the same, but which are more or less aggravated and differ in character with every new combination of circumstances. In peace and prosperity both states and individuals are actuated by higher motives, because they do not fall under the dominion of imperious necessities; but war which takes away the comfortable provision of daily life is a hard master, and tends to assimilate men's characters to their conditions.

"When troubles had once begun in the cities, those who followed carried the revolutionary spirit further and further, and determined to outdo the report of all who had preceded them by the ingenuity of their enterprises and the atrocity of their revenges. The meaning of words had no longer the same relation to things, but was changed by them as they thought proper The lover of violence, moreover, was always trusted, and his opponent suspected. The tie of party was stronger than the tie of blood, because a partisan was more ready to dare without asking why. The seal of good faith was not divine law, but fellowship in crime. Revenge was dearer than self-preservation.

"The cause of all these evils was the love of power, originating in avarice and ambition, and the party spirit which is engendered by them when men are fairly embarked in a contest. For the leaders on either side used specious names, the one party professing to uphold the constitutional equality of the many, the other the wisdom of an aristocracy, while they made the public interests, to which in name they were devoted, in reality their prize. Thus revolution gave birth to every form of wickedness in Hellas. The simplicity which is so large an element in a noble nature was laughed to scorn and disappeared. An attitude of perfidious antagonism everywhere prevailed. Each man was strong only in the conviction that nothing was secure; he must look to his own safety, and could not afford to trust others. Inferior intellects generally succeeded best."[5]

Pylos and Sphacteria. During the early years of the war Athens sent aid to her friends in Sicily, to Segesta, Rhegium, and Leontini, the purpose of which was to check the power of Syracuse and possibly to prevent the export of grain to the Peloponnesus. The expeditions, however, were ineffective, for the Sicilians ironed out their differences in a conference at Gela. In May 425 B.C. an Athenian fleet, which was supposed to aid Corcyra, was driven by a storm into the harbor of Pylos on the southwestern coast of the Peloponnesus. Demosthenes, a leader of the expedition, had hoped to halt here in any case, for it was an excellent spot from which to raid the Peloponnesian coast. The generals, Eurymedon and Sophocles, at storm's end, proceeded on their journey, leaving Demosthenes with five triremes to fortify the peninsula of Pylos.

Alarmed by the news that an Athenian contingent was established in the southwestern Peloponnesus, the Spartan government ordered its army home from Attica and told Brasidas, its extraordinarily able general at Corcyra, to return with the fleet. On his arrival at Pylos, attacks were launched, but Demosthenes held and Brasidas was wounded. The Spartans then landed 420 hoplites, with their helots, on the island of Sphacteria, which was separated from Pylos by a narrow strait, and prepared to blockade the Athenians by sea. At this point Eurymedon and Sophocles returned and in a surprise attack overwhelmed the Spartan fleet.

The Peloponnesians on Sphacteria were now besieged, and the Spartan government was so disturbed by their predicament that a truce was negotiated and envoys were dispatched to Athens to offer not only peace but alliance. Cleon destroyed all hope of a truly great Hellenic peace by demanding Nisaea and Pegae, Troezen and Achaea, which Athens, twenty years earlier, in the days of Pericles, had been too weak to hold. So the war continued.

Demosthenes could not take Sphacteria, and by August Cleon was demanding in the assembly that reinforcements be sent. Nicias, the commander in chief, told Cleon that he might have his own powers as general, if he were so sure of himself; and Cleon, his bluff called, went off with overwhelming forces, saying that he

---

[5] Thucydides, III, 82–83.

would be victorious in twenty days. He relied, not without reason, on the generalship of Demosthenes. A surprise dawn attack on the island was successful, the Spartans were driven behind some prehistoric walls, and then Cleon, realizing the value of capturing the enemy alive, offered quarter. The Spartans—their commander and 127 hoplites dead, no succor in sight, and being in dire straits—asked their comrades on the mainland for advice and, when they were told to consult their own safety, surrendered. This act astonished the Greek world. Cleon returned to Athens with his prisoners.

Cleon now stood without a rival at Athens, and in the flush of victory a reassessment of the empire's tribute was carried through in 425 B.C. The new assessment stood at more than 1,460 talents, over three times the original assessment of Aristeides. The Athenians could now prosecute the war with greater energy and raise the daily pay of the jurors from two obols to three. In vain the conservatives stood against Cleon. He was elected general in the spring of 424 B.C. and became more popular and dominant than ever.

Death of Cleon and Brasidas.   It was unfortunate for Athens that Brasidas, Sparta's ablest general, now found the weak point in the Athenian Empire—the only part assailable by a land army—Chalcidice and its Thracian neighborhood. With a small force he moved northward and, appearing before Amphipolis, persuaded that important city to revolt. These reverses induced the Athenian majority again to think of peace (423 B.C.). A truce of one year was followed by a renewal of the war, and then in a battle before Amphipolis both Brasidas and Cleon, the chief obstacles to peace, were killed.

Peace (421 B.C.).   Both sides were disappointed with the war. The Peloponnesians had hoped to bring Athens to speedy terms by invading her territory but had accomplished nothing in this direction, and they now saw their coast ravaged, their commerce cut off, and slaves and helots incited to desertion or rebellion by permanent Athenian garrisons on their border. Furthermore their triremes as well as their merchant ships were swept from the seas. Athens, too, could balance her gains by as heavy losses in life and money; the reserves in the Acropolis were nearly exhausted; the main sources of prosperity had been choked by invasions; and the temper of the allies under their tribute was ominous. Under these circumstances the peace party, which had always been strong, gained a majority in the assembly. Their leader was Nicias, a man of wealth and respectable family. In the spring of 421 B.C. he negotiated the peace that bears his name. The Spartan king, Pleistoanax, was equally anxious for peace. The Peace of Nicias, according to the agreement, was to endure for fifty years, and in a general way it provided for the exchange of prisoners and captured cities.

THE PEACE OF NICIAS

Although the terms of peace were kept by neither side, the Lacedaemonians and the Athenians refrained from invading each other's territory for almost seven years. To many Athenians peace came as a boundless joy. Euripides, in the *Suppliants,* prayed that war might never come again. The Agora overflowed with happy life, as provisions grew more plentiful and prices dropped. The *Peace* of Aristophanes, presented at the City Dionysia of 421 B.C., represented the rural party as even more delighted with conditions.

The Rise of Alcibiades.   The outstanding feature of Athenian foreign policy in the next years was the dominating influence of Alcibiades, the nephew and ward of Pericles. Handsome, brilliant, vain, and daring, this young man had been indulged by his family and fellow citizens. Educated by Sophists, he recognized no principle but self-seeking, and he recklessly disregarded law and custom. Combining the arts of the demagogue with his own personal fascination, he won the generalship in 420 B.C. and at once began to rehabilitate the war party to advance his own interest.

Choosing a moment that was unfavorable to Alcibiades, Nicias, who had consistently stood for peace, decided to overthrow him by a vote of ostracism. There was, however, a third party to the political struggle, Hyperbolus, the lampmaker, who with no knowledge of military affairs had risen to the leadership of those Athenians who looked to war for gain. Trained in oratory and successor to Cleon, though evidently inferior in ability, Hyperbolus dreamed of conquering Sicily and even of assailing Carthage. Alcibiades suggested to Nicias the advisability of joining forces to rid themselves of a common rival. The result was the ostracism of Hyperbolus in 417 B.C. It was the last time that ostracism was used at Athens, for *graphe paranomon* was regarded as a sufficient safeguard for the state and a satisfactory weapon for assailing opponents. Hyperbolus' ostracism increased the importance of Alcibiades, whose war policy continually grew more popular.

Melos.   Under Alcibiades' influence the Athenians sent an expedition against the little island of Melos, a Dorian colony. In the famous Melian Dialogue, Thucydides, seemingly without passion, laid bare the soul of a despot nation, his own. Chillingly, he observed that it was part of the natural order of things that stronger powers should dominate weak ones, and that the Athenians used this argument to make the Melians surrender.

The triumphant rise of Alcibiades meant a resumption of the policy of conquest, and led to Athenian intervention in Sicily. In 416 B.C. Segesta, a Sicilian ally, asked Athens for protection against Selinus and promised to pay the expenses of an expedition. This was a pretext for an invasion of Sicily. Nicias strenuously opposed the undertaking. His contention was that Athens needed all her strength to restore and maintain her empire and to defend herself against Thebes and the Peloponnesus. Furthermore, he said, even if Sicily could be conquered, it would be impossible to hold the island. Alcibiades, of course, urged war, hoping that it would yield him the mastery of Athens. As a last resort, Nicias tried to dissuade the Athenians by magnifying the size of an expedition needed to conquer Sicily, but the Athenians replied by granting all that he asked.

THE SICILIAN EXPEDITION

The Start.   All the financial reserves of Athens were devoted to the expedition. The fleet consisted of 134 triremes, with 130 supply boats. Over 5,000 hoplites, 1,300 light-armed troops, and 30 cavalry comprised the army. Counting the crews, at least 27,000 men made up this armada. The Athenians placed three generals in charge: Alcibiades, Nicias, and one Lamachus. Shortly before the departure the Athenians were horrified one morning in 415 to find that the Hermae—stone busts— in front of their doors had been mutilated. The people were terrorized in the belief that a band of conspirators had attempted to deprive the city of her divine protectors. In a panic the citizens assembled on the Pnyx and voted immunity and rewards to anyone who gave information against the perpetrators. No one came forward, but it was revealed that certain persons, among them Alcibiades, had once profaned the Eleusinian mysteries by parodying them at drinking parties in the presence of the uninitiated. Democratic politicians, opposed to Alcibiades, schemed to prosecute him for the sacrilege, and he demanded an immediate trial. But, appreciating his popularity with the voters, they delayed.

Nothing was to be allowed to interfere with the expedition. "All alike," says Thucydides, "were seized with a passionate desire to sail, the elder among them convinced that they would achieve the conquest of Sicily; the youth were longing to see with their own eyes the marvels of a distant land; the main body of the troops expected to receive present pay, and to conquer a country which would be an inexhaustible mine of pay for the future."

Thucydides paints the picture of the expedition as it was ready to sail in midsummer of 415 B.C.: "Early in the morning of the day appointed for their departure, the Athenians and such of their allies as had already joined them went down to Piraeus and began to man the ships. The entire population of Athens accompanied them, citizens and strangers alike. The citizens came to take farewell, one of an acquaintance, another of a kinsman, another of a son; the crowd as they passed along were full of hope and full of tears; hope of conquering Sicily, tears because they doubted whether they would ever see their friends again, when they thought of the long voyage on which they were sending them. At the moment of parting the danger was nearer; and terrors which had never occurred to them when they were voting the expedition now entered into their souls. Nevertheless their spirits revived at the sight of the armament in all its strength and of the abundant provision which they had made.

"No armament so magnificent or so costly had ever been sent out by any single Hellenic power. On the fleet the greatest pains and expense had been lavished by the captains and the state. Men were quite amazed at the boldness of the scheme and the magnificence of the spectacle, which were everywhere spoken of, no less than at the great disproportion of the force when compared with that of the enemy against whom it was intended. Never had a greater expedition been sent to a foreign land; never was there an enterprise in which the hope of future success seemed to be better justified by actual power.

"When the ships were manned and everything required for the voyage had been placed on board, silence was proclaimed by the sound of the trumpet, and all with one voice before setting sail offered up the customary prayers; these were recited, not in each ship, but by a single herald, the whole fleet accompanying him. On every deck both officers and men, mingling wine in bowls, made libations from vessels of gold and silver. The multitude of citizens and other well-wishers who were looking on from the land joined in the prayer. The crews raised the paean, and when the libations were completed, put to sea. After sailing out for some distance in single file, the ships raced with one another as far as Aegina."[6]

After the fleet had departed, the Athenians decided to vote an indictment for sacrilege against Alcibiades. The state trireme was ordered to Sicily to bring him back. On the homeward voyage Alcibiades jumped ship, made his escape to the Peloponnesus, and finally took up his residence at Sparta. There his counsels proved disastrous to his country's welfare.

Syracuse. In Sicily, the Athenian commanders, disagreeing as to plan, frittered away several months, wasting their resources, discouraging their own men, and earning the contempt of the Sicilian Greeks. The following year, 414 B.C., they besieged Syracuse (see map, p. 118). A strategic fort and a commanding plateau were captured, but Lamachus was killed. This left Nicias, who had opposed the expedition from the beginning, in sole command. The Syracusans were further encouraged by the arrival of an able Spartan officer, Gylippus, with reinforcements. Nicias proved incompetent. When autumn came, the besiegers were in a wretched plight; and Nicias, having made no appreciable headway, would gladly have abandoned the siege but dared not face the Athenian assembly. When, however, the Athenians received his report, which detailed the condition of the army and asked that it be recalled or reinforced, they voted heavy reinforcements. Eurymedon was sent off at once with a small force, and the next spring Demosthenes arrived with an armada of fifteen thousand men. The persistence of the Athenians and their vitality in mustering all available resources were extraordinary. The new fleet had been prepared in the midst of grave dangers at home, for in the spring of 413 B.C. the Peloponnesians, under King Agis, and the Boeotians resumed the war and invaded Attica. On the suggestion of Alcibiades they established a permanent garrison at Decelea in northern Attica, not far from Athens. As a result, the Athenians were forced to give up the country and to withdraw permanently into the city. Thousands of slaves deserted to the enemy, and industry and commerce shrank.

When Demosthenes arrived at Syracuse in 413 B.C., he found the besiegers in a miserable condition. They had lost a naval battle in the harbor, and this failure, together with sickness and privation, had demoralized them. The only hope was in immediate success. The strenuous offensive of Demosthenes, however, utterly failed, and when he proposed to embark the army and sail away, an eclipse of the moon caused the superstitious Nicias to urge delay. The Syracusans then blocked the mouth of the harbor. Nothing remained for the Athenian fleet but to try to force its way into the open sea. The description of the ensuing sea battle, the retreat by land, and the annihilation of practically all the forty-five thousand Athenians and their allies, who had sailed in two great fleets against Syracuse with such high hopes, gains in the pages of Thucydides the power of a great tragedy:

"When Gylippus and the other Syracusan generals had, like Nicias, encouraged their troops, perceiving the Athenians to be manning their ships, they presently did the same. Nicias, overwhelmed by the situation, and seeing how great and how near

---

[6] Thucydides, VI, 30-32.

the peril was (for the ships were on the very point of rowing out), feeling too, as men do on the eve of a great struggle, that all which he had done was nothing, and that he had not said half enough, again addressed the captains, and calling each of them by his father's name, and his own name, and the name of his tribe, he entreated those who had made any reputation for themselves not to be false to it, and those whose ancestors were eminent not to tarnish their hereditary fame. He reminded them that they were the inhabitants of the freest country in the world, and how in Athens there was no interference with the daily life of any man. He spoke to them of their wives and children and their fathers' Gods, as men will at such a time; for then they do not care whether their commonplace phrases seem to be out of date or not, but loudly reiterate the old appeals, believing that they may be of some service at the awful moment. When he thought that he had exorted them, not enough, but as much as the scanty time allowed, he retired, and led the land forces to the shore, extending the line as far as he could, so that they might be of the greatest use in encouraging the combatants on board ship. Demosthenes, Menander, and Euthydemus, who had gone on board the Athenian fleet to take the command, now quitted their own station, and proceeded straight to the closed mouth of the harbor, intending to force their way to the open sea where a passage was still left.

"The Syracusans and their allies had already put out with nearly the same number of ships as before. A detachment of them guarded the entrance of the harbor; the remainder were disposed all round it in such a manner that they might fall on the Athenians from every side at once, and that their land forces might at the same time be able to cooperate wherever the ships retreated to the shore. Sicanus and Agatharchus commanded the Syracusan fleet, each of them a wing; Pythen and the Corinthians occupied the center. When the Athenians approached the closed mouth of the harbor the violence of their onset overpowered the ships which were stationed there; they then attempted to loosen the fastenings. Whereupon from all sides the Syracusans and their allies came bearing down upon them, and the conflict was no longer confined to the entrance, but extended throughout the harbor. No previous engagement had been so fierce and obstinate. Great was the eagerness with which the rowers on both sides rushed upon their enemies whenever the word of command was given; and keen was the contest between the pilots as they maneuvered one against another. The marines too were full of anxiety that, when ship struck ship, the service on deck should not fall short of the rest; every one in the place assigned to him was eager to be foremost among his fellows. Many vessels meeting—and never did so many fight in so small a space, for the two fleets together amounted to nearly 200—they were seldom able to strike in the regular manner, because they had no opportunity of first retiring or breaking the line; they generally fouled one another as ship dashed against ship in the hurry of flight or pursuit. All the time that another vessel was bearing down, the men on deck poured showers of javelins and arrows and stones upon the enemy; and when the two closed, the marines fought hand to hand, and endeavored to board. In many places, owing to the want of room, they who had struck another found that they were struck themselves; often two or even more vessels were unavoidably entangled about one, and the pilots had to make plans of attack and defense, not against one adversary only, but against several coming from different sides. The crash of so many ships dashing against one another took away the wits of the sailors, and made it impossible to hear the boatswains, whose voices in both fleets rose high, as they gave directions to the rowers, or cheered them on in the excitement of the struggle. On the Athenian side they were shouting to their men that they must force a passage and seize the opportunity now or never of returning in safety to their native land. To the Syracusans and their allies was represented the glory of preventing the escape of their enemies, and of a victory by which every man would exalt the honor of his own city. The commanders too, when they saw any ship backing water without necessity, would call the captain by his name, and ask, of the Athenians, whether they were retreating because they expected to be more at home upon the land of their bitterest foes than upon the sea which had been their own so long; on the Syracusan side, whether, when they knew perfectly well that the Athenians were only eager to find some means of flight, they would themselves fly from the fugitives.

"While the naval engagement hung in the balance the two armies on shore had great trial and conflict of soul. The Sicilian soldier was animated by the hope of increasing the glory which he had already won, while the invader was tormented by the fear that his fortunes might sink lower still. The last chance of the Athenians lay in their ships, and their anxiety was dreadful. The fortune of the battle varied; and it was not possible that the spectators on the shore should all receive the same impression of it. Being quite close and having different points of view, they would some of them see their own ships victorious; their courage would then revive, and they would earnestly call upon the Gods not to take from them their hope of deliverance. But others, who saw their ships worsted, cried and shrieked aloud, and were by the sight alone more utterly unnerved than the defeated combatants themselves. Others again, who had fixed their gaze on some part of the struggle which was undecided, were in a state of excitement still more terrible; they kept swaying their bodies to and fro in an agony of hope and fear as the stubborn conflict went on and on; for at every instant they were all but saved or all but lost. And while the strife hung in the balance you might hear in the Athenian army at once lamentation, shouting, cries of victory or defeat, and all the various sounds which are wrung from a great host in extremity of danger. Not less agonizing were the feelings of those on board. At length the Syracusans and their allies, after a protracted struggle, put the Athenians to flight, and triumphantly bearing down upon them, and encouraging one another with loud cries and exhortations, drove them to land. Then that part of the navy which had not been taken in the deep water fell back in confusion to the shore, and the crews rushed out of the ships into the camp. And the land forces, no longer now divided in feeling, but uttering one universal groan of intolerable anguish, ran some of them to save the ships, others to defend what remained of the wall; but the greater number began to look to themselves and to their own safety. Never had there been a greater panic in an Athenian army than at that moment. They now suffered what they had done to others at Pylos. For at Pylos the Lacedaemonians, when they saw their ships destroyed, knew that their friends who had crossed over into the island of Sphacteria were lost with them. And so now the Athenians, after the rout of their fleet, knew that they had no hope of saving themselves by land unless events took some extraordinary turn.

"Thus, after a fierce battle and a great destruction of ships and men on both sides, the Syracusans and their allies gained the victory. They gathered up the wrecks and bodies of the dead, and sailing back to the city, erected a trophy. The Athenians, overwhelmed by their misery, never so much as thought of recovering their wrecks or of asking leave to collect their dead. Their intention was to retreat that very night.

"Hermocrates the Syracusan suspected their intention, and dreading what might happen if their vast army, retreating by land and settling somewhere in Sicily, should choose to renew the war, contrived the following plan: when it was growing dark he sent certain of his own acquaintances, accompanied by a few horsemen, to the Athenian camp. They rode up within earshot, and pretending to be friends (there were known to be men in the city who gave information to Nicias of what went on) called to some of the soldiers, and bade them tell him not to withdraw his army during the night, for the Syracusans were guarding the roads; he should make preparation at leisure and retire by day. Having delivered their message they departed, and those who had heard them informed the Athenian generals.

"On receiving this message, which they supposed to be genuine, they remained during the night. And having once given up the intention of starting immediately, they decided to remain during the next day, that the soldiers might, as well as they could, put together their baggage in the most convenient form, and depart, taking with them the bare necessaries of life, but nothing else.

"Meanwhile the Syracusans and Gylippus, going forth before them with their land forces, blocked the roads in the country by which the Athenians were likely to pass, guarded the fords of the rivers and streams, and posted themselves at the best points for receiving and stopping them. Their sailors rowed up to the beach and dragged away the Athenian ships. The Athenians themselves burnt a few of them, as they had intended, but the rest the Syracusans towed away, unmolested and at their leisure, from the places where they had severally run aground, and conveyed them to the city.

"On the third day after the sea fight, when Nicias and Demosthenes thought that their preparations were complete, the army began to move. They were in a dreadful condition; not only was there the great fact that they had lost their whole fleet, and instead of their expected triumph had brought the utmost peril upon Athens as well as upon themselves, but also the sights which presented themselves as they quitted the camp were painful to every eye and mind. The dead were unburied, and when any one saw the body of a friend lying on the ground he was smitten with sorrow and dread, while the sick or wounded who still survived but had to be left were even a greater trial to the living, and more to be pitied than those who were gone. Their prayers and lamentations drove their companions to distraction; they would beg that they might be taken with them, and call by name any friend or relation whom they saw passing; they would hang upon their departing comrades and follow as far as they could, and when their limbs and strength failed them and they dropped behind many were the imprecations and cries which they uttered. So that the whole army was in tears, and such was their despair that they could hardly make up their minds to stir, although they were leaving an enemy's country, having suffered calamities too great for tears already, and dreading miseries yet greater in the unknown future. There was also a general feeling of shame and self-reproach—indeed they seemed, not like an army, but like the fugitive population of a city captured after a siege; and of a great city too. For the whole multitude who were marching together numbered not less than 40,000. Each of them took with him anything he could carry which was likely to be of use. Even the heavy-armed and cavalry, contrary to their practice when under arms, conveyed about their persons their own food, some because they had no attendants, others because they could not trust them; for they had long been deserting, and most of them had gone off all at once. Nor was the food which they carried sufficient; for the supplies of the camp had failed. Their disgrace and the universality of the misery, although there might be some consolation in the very community of suffering, was nevertheless at that moment hard to bear, especially when they remembered from what pomp and splendor they had fallen into their present low estate. Never had an Hellenic army experienced such a reverse. They had come intending to enslave others, and they were going away in fear that they would be themselves enslaved. Instead of the prayers and hymns with which they had put to sea, they were now departing amid appeals to heaven of another sort. They were no longer sailors but landsmen, depending, not upon their fleet, but upon their infantry. Yet in face of the great danger which still threatened them all these things appeared endurable."

The long retreat across land ended in the death of many Athenians and their allies and in the capture of the remainder. Nicias and Demosthenes were executed; the others were thrown into the quarries of Syracuse, where most of them died, the remainder being enslaved (September 413 B.C.).

"Those who were imprisoned in the quarries [continues Thucydides] were at the beginning of their captivity harshly treated by the Syracusans. There were great numbers of them, and they were crowded in a deep and narrow place. At first the sun by day was still scorching and suffocating, for they had no roof over their heads, while the autumn nights were cold, and the extremes of temperature engendered violent disorders. Being cramped for room they had to do everything on the same spot. The corpses of those who died from their wounds, exposure to the weather, and the like, lay heaped one upon another. The smells were intolerable; and they were at the same time afflicted by hunger and thirst. During eight months they were allowed only about half a pint of water and a pint of food a day. Every kind of misery which could befall man in such a place befell them. This was the condition of all the captives for about ten weeks. At length the Syracusans sold them, with the exception of the Athenians and of any Sicilian or Italian Greeks who had sided with them in the war. The whole number of the public prisoners is not accurately known, but they were not less than 7,000.

"Of all the Hellenic actions which took place in this war, or indeed of all Hellenic actions which are on record, this was the greatest—the most glorious to the victors, the most ruinous to the vanquished; for they were utterly and at all points defeated, and their sufferings were prodigious. Fleet and army perished from the face of the earth; nothing was saved, and of the many who went forth few returned home.

"Thus ended the Sicilian expedition." [7]

OLIGARCHICAL REVOLUTION IN ATHENS

When the Athenians at home comprehended the extent of the disaster that had befallen them, they vented their rage on the orators and soothsayers who had persuaded them to the expedition. But soon their elastic spirits rose, and they determined to persist at all odds. To increase their revenue without seeming to add new burdens to their allies, they had replaced the tribute in 414 B.C. by a 5 per cent tax on all imports and exports throughout the Empire. The new system was effective, though the tribute was revived in 410 B.C.

Greeks now flocked to the Spartan side in the hope of defeating the common foe. The Persian king, on condition of recovering the Greek cities of Asia Minor, gave money and promised the aid of a Phoenician fleet. Athens' maritime subjects began to revolt, and the victorious navy of Syracuse appeared in Aegean waters. The persistence of the Athenians, stripped of resources, against these overwhelming odds during a period of eight more years is evidence of an indomitable will.

The Four Hundred. The Sicilian disaster had a serious effect on Athenian politics. There had always been a strong minority opposed to popular government, and it now found its leadership within an oligarchic group of officers encamped in Samos. Alcibiades, who had fallen out with the Spartan king Agis, and had gone over to the Persians, saw his chance of returning to Athens. He told the officers that Tissaphernes, the satrap of Sardis, would transfer his support from Sparta to Athens, if the Athenians set up an oligarchy. With this news, the oligarchs went to Athens and actively lobbied for a change in existing democratic institutions. The assembly, disheartened by events in Samos and without proper leadership, permitted the creation in 411 B.C. of a Council of Four Hundred. It was regarded as a provisional form of government, which would yield in time to a group of the five thousand wealthiest citizens. This oligarchic constitution, which was to prove abortive, was the result of a general reaction against radical democracy, discredited by its evident failure to wage the war successfully. Furthermore supporters of the Council of Four Hundred alleged that they were merely restoring the "ancestral constitution" as it had existed under Solon.

Democracy Restored. The next year (410 B.C.), however, the Athenians restored their democracy. Alcibiades, a democrat once more, was home again and ready to devote his talents to repairing his country's fortunes. He promptly wiped out an entire enemy fleet at Cyzicus. The Spartans now offered peace on the basis of the status quo, but the Athenians, swayed by a new leader, Cleophon the lyremaker, rejected the terms. He had a sharp eye for finance and began to build up the state's depleted reserves. In 409 B.C. he started the conversion of temple properties

[7] Thucydides, VI, 30-32.

into money, and two obols were distributed daily to the most needy within the city.

In 408 B.C. Darius II, who was dissatisfied with his governors in Asia Minor, sent his younger son, Cyrus, to Sardis as satrap. Cyrus was given large powers to aid the Peloponnesians and end the war. In the same year Lysander emerged as the most important Spartan leader. An able commander and a crafty manager of men, he aimed at becoming a Spartan king. To reach his political goal, he needed military renown and a devoted army. Cyrus readily fell under his influence. Athenian defeats the following year destroyed the ascendancy of Alcibiades. He retired to estates he owned on the Hellespont and Propontis, from which he reviewed the further operations of the war. The Persians executed him later on.

THE FALL OF ATHENS

Both sides tried energetically to decide the struggle in one more campaign. One hundred and fifty Athenian triremes met and defeated a Spartan navy near the islands of Arginusae, between Lesbos and the coast of Asia Minor (406 B.C.). Seventy vessels of the Peloponnesians with their crews, amounting to fourteen thousand men and including their commander, were lost. The Athenians lost twenty-five ships, but because of a sudden storm, it proved impossible to rescue some two thousand sailors. Outraged at this, the assembly deposed the commanders and brought to trial the six who dared to return. In violation of the consititution, they condemned the accused to death as a group. Among these victims of popular fury was Pericles' son.

Battle of Aegospotami. By 406 B.C. financial strain in Athens was so great that temple properties were melted down, gold coins were issued for the first time, and bronze coins were plated with silver. Yet the Athenians still refused offers of peace. Consequently, the Spartans sent Lysander to the eastern Aegean to cut the Athenian life line. The Athenians dispatched against him their last possible fleet manned with their last available crews (405 B.C.). Stationed on the European side of the Hellespont at the mouth of the Aegospotami River, this fleet was taken by surprise while the crews were searching for provisions on shore. The Athenians were massacred. Conon, one of the generals, escaped to Cyprus with eight ships, having sent the state trireme to Piraeus to announce the defeat (404 B.C.). The Athenian Xenophon has left a memorable description of its arrival and the last days of imperial Athens:

"It was night when the *Paralus* reached Athens with her evil tidings, on receipt of which a bitter wail of woe broke forth. From Piraeus, following the line of the Long Walls up to the heart of the city, it swept and swelled, as each man to his neighbor passed on the news. On that night no man slept. There was mourning and sorrow for those that were lost, but the lamentation for the dead was merged in even deeper sorrow for themselves, as they pictured the evils they were about to suffer, the like of which they had themselves inflicted upon the men of Melos, who were colonists of the Lacedaemonians, when they mastered them by siege. Or on the men of Histiaea; on Scione and Torone; on the Aeginetans, and many another

Hellenic city. On the following day the public assembly met, and, after debate, it was resolved to block up all the harbors save one, to put the walls in a state of defense, to post guards at various points, and to make all other necessary preparation for a siege. Such were the concerns of the men of Athens.

"In obedience to a general order of Pausanias, the Spartan king, a levy in force of the Lacedaemonians and all the rest of the Peloponnesus, except the Argives, was set in motion for a campaign. As soon as the several contingents had arrived, the king put himself at their head and marched against Athens, encamping in the Academy, as it is called. Lysander now anchored at Piraeus with 150 ships, and established a strict blockade against all merchant ships entering that harbor.

"The Athenians, finding themselves besieged by land and sea, did not know what to do. Without ships, without allies, without provisions, the belief gained hold upon them that there was no way of escape. They must now, in their turn, suffer what they had themselves inflicted upon others; not in retaliation, indeed, for ills received, but out of sheer insolence, overriding the citizens of petty states, and for no better reason that these were allies of the very men now at their gates. In this frame of mind they enfranchised those who at any time had lost their civil rights, and schooled themselves to endurance; and, although many were dying of starvation, they refused to negotiate for peace. But when the stock of grain was absolutely insufficient, they sent an embassy to Agis, the other Spartan king, proposing to become allies of the Lacedaemonians on the sole condition of keeping their fortification walls and Piraeus; and to draw up articles of treaty on these terms. Agis bade them betake themselves to Lacedaemon, seeing that he had no authority to act himself. With this answer the ambassadors returned to Athens, and were forthwith sent on to Lacedaemon. On reaching Sellasia, a town in Laconian territory, they waited till they got their answer from the ephors, who, having learnt their terms (which were identical with those already proposed to Agis), bade them instantly to be gone, and, if they really desired peace, to come with other proposals, the fruit of happier reflection. Thus the ambassadors returned home, and reported the result of their embassy, whereupon despondency fell upon all. It was a painful reflection that in the end they would be sold into slavery; and meanwhile, pending the return of a second embassy, many must needs fall victims of starvation. The razing of their fortifications was not a solution which any one cared to recommend. Things having reached this pass, Theramenes made a proposal in the public assembly as follows: If they chose to send him as an ambassador to Lysander, he would go and find out why the Lacedaemonians were so unyielding about the walls; whether it was they really intended to enslave the city, or merely that they wanted a guarantee of good faith. Dispatched accordingly, he lingered on with Lysander for three whole months and more, watching for the time when the Athenians, at the last pinch of starvation, would be willing to accede to any terms that might be offered. At last, in the fourth month, he returned and reported to the public assembly that Lysander had detained him all this while, and had ended by bidding him betake himself to Lacedaemon, since he had no authority to answer these questions, which must be addressed directly to the ephors. After this Theramenes was chosen with nine others to go to Lacedaemon as ambassadors with full powers.

"Theramenes and his companions presently reached Sellasia, and being here questioned as to the reason of their visit, replied that they had full powers to treat of peace. After which the ephors ordered them to be summoned to their presence. On their arrival a general assembly was convened, in which the Corinthians and Thebans more particularly, though their views were shared by many other Hellenes also, urged the meeting not to come to terms with the Athenians."[8]

Sparta's allies suggested that Athens be totally destroyed, so bitter were their feelings; Sparta advocated less draconian terms, citing Athens' past services to Greek civilization during the Persian Wars. More cogent, if unspoken, was Sparta's fear that the destruction of Athens might create a power vacuum and destabilize the political situation throughout Greece. Therefore Theramenes, the Athenian negotiator, was given peace on the following terms: Athens was to destroy her forts and walls, reduce her navy to twelve ships, and become a Spartan dependency. The peace was to be enforced by a Spartan garrison supported by Athenian quislings known as the Thirty Tyrants.

In September 404 B.C., the Thirty Tyrants began their rule at Athens. This board was instituted under intimidation from Lysander, ostensibly to draw up a new constitution for Athens, but in reality to govern absolutely in Sparta's interest. One of the leaders was Critias, a eupatrid poet and rhetorician, in politics a heartless, calculating schemer. His colleague was the shifty Theramenes, who managed to emerge triumphant from every difficulty through which he passed.

Beginning moderately, the rule of the Thirty Tyrants rapidly degenerated into despotism. Supported by their Spartan *harmost* (garrison commander), they proceeded to condemn and put to death their enemies, mainly democrats. Executions were always accompanied by confiscations of property. Still needing funds for the payment of the garrison, they next proceeded against wealthy oligarchs and metics. There were wholesale banishments. Many fled for their lives, so that the surrounding states were full of fugitives. More violent grew the reign of terror, till the dead numbered fifteen hundred in eight months. Even Theramenes was compelled to drink the hemlock.

Despite orders from Sparta, the neighbors of Athens received the exiles sympathetically. From Thebes, Thrasybulus, one of these refugees, led a small band of Athenians across the border to seize Phyle, a fortress on Mount Parnes. Thence, after increasing his force to a thousand, he occupied Piraeus. This was a bold stroke, and the port welcomed him and reinforced his army. In the streets of Piraeus the patriots battled with an army of the Thirty Tyrants, defeated it, and killed Critias (403 B.C.). Soon afterward the democracy was restored.

The war was a catastrophe for all the Greeks. It revealed the basic weakness of the city-state system, the inability of Hellenes to get along with one another, which was their undoing. The war initiated a period of instability in the next century, which continued to drain away their political energies even while they continued to be culturally productive.

[8] Xenophon, *Hellenica*, II, 2.

15

The Periclean Age

SOCIAL AND ECONOMIC LIFE

The culture of the Periclean Age rested on belief in the totalitarian perfection of the state, to whose good the citizens were to subordinate their individual interests and devote their lives alike in war and peace. The ability of the Athenians, combined with the attraction their city held for others, realized Pericles' ambition that Athens should be the center of Hellas, at once the strongest and most beautiful city in the Greek world.

The manufactures and commerce of the imperialist democracy spread far and wide. In the busy city and its port labored citizens, metics (resident aliens), and slaves, while farmers cultivated the olive, the vine, the wheat fields, and kitchen gardens. Marble quarries on Mount Pentelicus, silver mines at Laurium, and clay fields of the Attic plain added to the natural wealth; imperial tribute helped pay for public buildings, provided jobs for stone masons and other laborers, and, through payment for public service, helped give the ordinary citizen enough leisure to participate in government.

Daily Life. Quite naturally the Athenian's chief concern was to provide for himself and his family. He lived just above subsistence level and existed on what has been called the golden mean of poverty. His diet consisted of greens, bread, cheese, and olives, and though they were considered delicacies, fish and pork were eaten more often than other varieties of meat. The house itself was unpretentious, an adobe structure one or two stories in height, its blank exterior facing the narrow, crooked street; life centered on the courtyard within. Burglary was a simple act effectuated by digging a hole in the wall. Stone floors were uncommon. Athenian families even in the city frequently shared their houses with chickens and goats. Sanitary facilities were less than primitive.

The simple abode was merely a place to store possessions and to sleep, for the warm climate and democratic spirit invited outdoor life. The ordinary male citizen, on a day when work did not call, rose early, dressed in his short woolen chiton, had a glass of wine, and then, attended perhaps by a slave or two, walked to that part of the marketplace in the center of town where he wished to shop—to the section devoted perhaps to clothing, metalwork, fish, or oil. Water clocks and sundials told the time, barbershops provided the gossip, and eventually he returned home for lunch with his family. Unlike the Roman, the Athenian enjoyed neither a large meal nor a long siesta. The afternoon, if it was an off day and affairs of government were not pressing, he might spend at a gymnasium, where he wrestled, boxed, ran, or played games, and he might also listen to his fellow men as they discussed some matter of moment with a sophist. The evening would be spent quietly at home, unless guests had been invited to dinner. In that event the men reclined on couches and reached for food on the tables in front of them; at the end of the meal the diners elected the king of the symposium, whose functions were to decide how much water should be mixed with the wine and to choose the topic of conversation. It will be observed that women played but a small part in public life and were relegated to the home. Women of good families rarely appeared unescorted on the streets, though they were expected to attend funerals, weddings, and the presentations of the tragic dramas and had their own public festival, the Thesmophoria.

Since the ancient Greeks took no census, it is impossible to state the population of Hellas or of various sections of it, but reasonable estimates have been made for Athens: 150,000 citizens, 35,000 metics, and 80,000 slaves (men, women, and children in each case) would be the minimum. Extremes of wealth were not as great nor as obvious as in a modern state. The state demanded of each citizen his best and in return gave him ample opportunity to satisfy his ambition. The many festivals gave the people the opportunity to gather in holiday mood; here, as elsewhere, complete freedom of speech was enjoyed, and the Athenians tolerated all sorts of criticism until finally, at the end of the fifth century, with the crises and disillusionment produced by the Peloponnesian War, comic license was restrained.

Slavery unquestionably contributed to the leisure of the citizen and made it possible for him to give himself to the affairs of state, but it supplemented, rather than replaced, free labor in Athens. A man might own a half dozen slaves, who were non-Greeks, and together, in house, shop, or farm, the master and slave worked. The slave could hope for ultimate freedom.[1] Business at Athens was largely in the hands of the metics, mostly because of the citizens' traditional concern with land, politics, and wars. Problems of government and empire challenged intellect and nourished pride; traffic at Piraeus and a democratic constitution made the citizens increasingly cosmopolitan and diverse.

The Agora.   Much of Athenian life centered in the marketplace, or Agora, a large public square north of the Acropolis. The site of shops, temples, and buildings of state, it has been excavated by the American School of Classical Studies at Athens. The Agora was dominated on the west by the hill of Colonus Agoraeus, where the metalworkers congregated, and on its top was placed, appropriately, the great Doric temple of Hephaestus, built soon after 450 B.C. Further to the west lay the potters' quarter, or Cerameicus, from which the Sacred Way led through the Dipylon, or double gate in the city wall, past the cemetery to Eleusis. East of the temple of Hephaestus, and on lower ground, lay some of the chief buildings of the Agora. In Pericles' time, a meeting place for the Council of Five Hundred (Bouleuterion) stood on the west side of the Agora, where later other impressive structures

---

[1] In addition to these apprentice slaves, however, there were also chattel slaves, who were worked like animals in the ancient quarries and mines.

The Granger Collection

FIGURE 33. Present-day appearance of the Agora, showing the restored Stoa of Attalus to the right.

were to rise and form an administrative complex. By about 350 B.C., a visitor who entered the marketplace at its southwestern corner and walked north would pass first a circular building (Tholos) where members of the daily committee of the council (Prytany) were lodged, next a new Bouleuterion, which included the Metroon, sanctuary of the Mother of the Gods and state archive, next a temple of Apollo, then a small temple, and finally the Stoa of Zeus or Royal Stoa. This was a large covered colonnade with projecting wings. Richly adorned, it served the deliberations of the polemarch, and at times those of the council of the Areopagus. Socrates first heard there the formal charge of impiety that was to end in his death.

Toward the middle of the second century B.C., Attalus, king of Pergamon, closed off much of the east side of the Agora with an opulent stoa, which has now been restored in every detail. It illustrates vividly how Hellenistic princes, in the days after Alexander, loved to embellish the cultural capital of the world. The Roman Sulla destroyed some of Athens in 86 B.C., but the city was never sacked until the disastrous raid of the Herulians, barbarians from the north, in 267 A.D.

The Theater. Fairly early in the fifth century, a theater of Dionysus was built low on the south slope of the Acropolis. Originally just a space enclosed partly by wooden bleachers, it was augmented in Pericles' time. We can perhaps imagine an outdoor theater seating fourteen thousand spectators, the hillside auditorium lined with stone seats and aisles and looking down on the dancing floor (orchestra), where the action took place. In the middle of the orchestra was the *thymele*, an altar dedicated to Dionysus, beside which sat the musicians, for there was much singing in a Greek play. Beyond the orchestra lay the *skene* (scene building), a long building for properties, from which the actors emerged, and in front of it, connected by a high roof, was the *proscenium*—a line of columns almost tangent with the orchestra—which served as a background for chorus and actors. At either end of the *proscenium* was a projection forward (*parascenium*), and between it and the auditorium was the entrance passage (*parodus*) for chorus and audience.

At the time of the City Dionysia,[2] the people of Athens, together with many foreigners, gathered to witness the best plays of the year, produced in a religious atmosphere and supported by the best amateur talent of the state. It was a critical audience, educated as it had been by a succession of great dramatists. A procession normally occupied the first day of the festival; on the second day ten dithyrambic choruses of fifty each competed; and on the third, five comic poets each produced a play. The last three days were given over to the tragic poets, each of whom presented a tetralogy, that is, a trilogy, or group of three plays, often, though not always, on the same general theme, followed by a mock-heroic piece known as a satyr play. When it was over, the judges, who sat in the front row with the priest of Dionysus and other officials, rendered their verdict, and the names of the winning dramatist, his plays, and the protagonist were carved on stone. The fortunate *choregos,* or "angel" of the production, was allowed to commemorate his service by building at his own expense a small monument beside the Street of Tripods, which wound around the eastern end of the Acropolis to the theater.

Pericles' Odeon stood just east of the Theater of Dionysus. The area west of the Theater and Odeon (still on the south slope of the Acropolis) was further developed when a sanctuary of Asclepius, god of healing, was established there. In Hellenistic times, Eumenes II of Pergamon built a long stoa, and in the second century after Christ, Herodes Atticus built his splendid Odeon.

ART

The Parthenon.   The most beautiful buildings of Athens, and of all Greece, were located on the Acropolis. Begun in 447 B.C., the Parthenon was dedicated during the Panathenaic festival of 438 B.C. to Athena Parthenos, patroness of arts and labors, the protecting deity and symbol of the state. The architects were Ictinus and Callicrates, the chief sculptor Phidias. Built of Pentelic marble throughout (except for the timber roof and the doors), the temple was Doric peripteral, with 8 by 17

---

[2] Long in advance of the City Dionysia—the March–April festival in celebration of spring and Dionysus, the god of fertility and patron of the theater—authors submitted their manuscripts to a committee, which selected three tragedians and five comic poets to compete. (The Lenaean festival in January was given over principally to comedy.) To each author was assigned a *choregos,* a wealthy citizen who assumed the financial burden (liturgy) of supplying and training the chorus. Since it would have been unfair for an author to obtain the three best actors, the chief actor (protagonist) was also assigned. On account of his weak voice, Sophocles broke with the rule that the dramatist should be the protagonist, and it was he who introduced simple scenery (painted panels set between the columns of the proscenium). In the days of Sophocles the chorus numbered fifteen and the actors three, though an actor might take more than one part.

FIGURE 34. The Acropolis from the south-west, Athens.

columns, and measured approximately 100 by 230 feet. There were two cellas, a small one, that was used as a treasury and, to the east, the main room.

Through the genius of Ictinus, the Parthenon achieved a noble majesty, to which the proportions and the delicate refinements, the curves and deviations from the normal, contributed. Its charm was greatly enhanced by the sculpture. Within the main room stood Phidias' colossal chryselephantine statue of Athena, long since lost. On the outside of the building the carved metopes showed scenes of strife, grand compositions in themselves, while an unusual feature was the continuous Ionic frieze that ran around the outside of the cella, at the top. This famous frieze, an outburst of civic pride and religious feeling, commemorates the Panathenaic procession, when the best blood of Athens, young and old, youths and maidens, brought a new robe or *peplos* for the old wooden statue of Athena on the Acropolis.

For five years after the dedication, the sculptors worked on figures in the round, which were to go in the pediments. To the west was depicted the momentous struggle between Athena and Poseidon for the lordship of Attica, and to the east, the birth of Athena, an event of significance for Athens and the world.

The Other Buildings of the Acropolis. No sooner had the Parthenon been dedi-

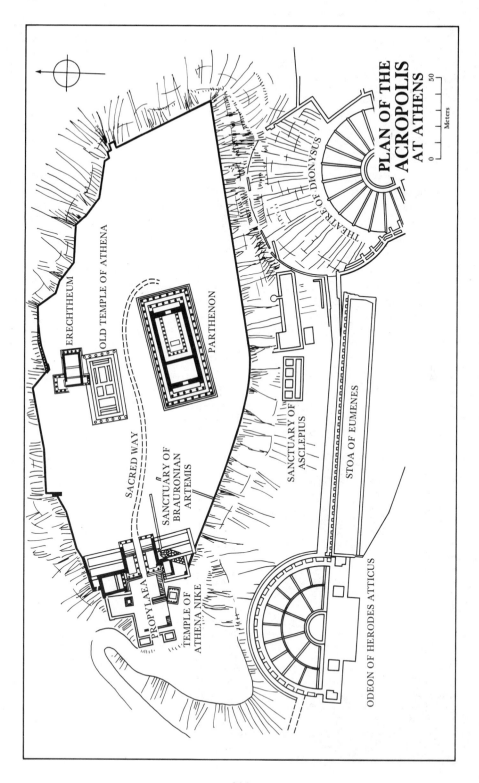

ERECHTHEUM

OLD TEMPLE OF ATHENA

PARTHENON

SACRED WAY

SANCTUARY OF BRAURONIAN ARTEMIS

PROPYLAEA

TEMPLE OF ATHENA NIKE

SANCTUARY OF ASCLEPIUS

STOA OF EUMENES

THEATRE OF DIONYSUS

ODEON OF HERODES ATTICUS

PLAN OF THE ACROPOLIS AT ATHENS

0   50

Meters

cated than Pericles inaugurated the construction of a new and finer gateway to the Acropolis—at its western end, where the only entrance was possible—the great Propylaea, built from the designs of Mnesicles between 437 and 423 B.C. The outbreak of the Peloponnesian War curtailed its original plan somewhat, but in 423 B.C. the Athenians went ahead with a graceful little Ionic temple, that of Athena Nike (Victory), on the bastion before the Propylaea. About the same time a marble parapet, carved with Victories, was placed along the edge of the bastion. The Peace of Nicias (421 B.C.) enabled the Athenians to commence the Erechtheum—sacred to the guardian of the city, Athena Polias, to Erechtheus, the ancestral god of Attica, and to Poseidon—but work on it was soon abandoned and not begun again until 409 B.C. The Erechtheum is easily the most elaborate building on the Acropolis, graceful and delicate, rich with honeysuckle and other ornamentation that blend with the Ionic order. Built of Pentelic marble, it had a frieze of black Eleusinian limestone, against which were pinned white marble sculptures. The opposition of priests of other sanctuaries to encroachment on their land probably accounts for the unusual shape of the Erechtheum, but it was possible to include two porches,

The Granger Collection

FIGURE 35. The Temple of Athena Nike (Wingless Victory) on the Acropolis.

FIGURE 36. Centaur and
Lapith. South metope of
the Parthenon, c. 445 B.C.

The Granger Collection

the caryatid porch on the south, where stately maidens support the roof, and an
even more beautiful one to the north, with an elaborately carved doorway.

Other Works. Foreign artists were naturally attracted to Athens, just as Athenians received important commissions elsewhere. Ictinus, for example, designed the
temple of Apollo Epicurius at Bassae, in the wild uplands of Arcadia. But despite
this era of widespread activity in architecture and monumental sculpture—witness
the Argive Polycleitus, who was much interested in anatomy—it is perhaps the simple tombstones (*stelae*) from the Athenian Ceramicus, made as they were by unknown sculptors, that impress us with artistic genius. The gems and coins also have
an exquisite beauty, but all traces of the work of Polygnotus and other painters
have vanished.

LITERATURE

The literature of the Periclean Age rested on belief in the all-comprehensive perfection of the state; it rested also on tradition purified by an expanding intelligence
and humanism—belief in the power, wisdom, and goodness of the gods, in the superiority of the fathers, in the beneficence of the heroes of old. Into this culture
had been implanted the germ of individualism. Poets and sophists took the lead in
questioning the problems of life and the old answers to them, and during the second half of the fifth century the new progressive tendencies struggled with the old
conservatism in an intellectual conflict. Thus the poet, while continuing to deal
with larger forces, did not treat them in the usual Olympian sense.

Religion. Human love of symbolism and hope of future life went far to break the supremacy of traditional faith. Many people found the Olympian gods too cold and turned from them to mystery religions and deities brought in by foreigners. These were the exciting mysteries from Samothrace, the worship of Cybele, the Great Mother from Phrygia, and of Aphrodite's companion, Adonis, from Cyprus. They all had their priests and curious rites, emotional and noisy, or secret and mystical, and all alike appealed to individuals in contrast with the recognized civic cults. Scorned by the educated and the conservative, such innovations tended to loosen the hold on the community of its hereditary gods. A far more active solvent, however, was rationalism. Euripides, for example, though he treated with forbearance the myths that formed the tragic poet's stock in trade and the background of his country's history, gives us to understand that many supernatural powers, traditionally assumed, have no real existence. He lays the responsibility for conduct on the individual and assures us that the Furies that goad Orestes are but the creations of an excited mind. The great comic poet Aristophanes, in other ways conservative, ridicules the gods and their weaknesses. The drama, then, spread advanced ideas over a large audience.

Education.   The Athenian needed the teaching and the inspiration of his great poets, for to meet the various requirements of citizenship in this democracy, where life was civic duty, a man had to be well educated, not in books but in public affairs. The real school for most Athenians was thus the theater, the assembly, and even the streets. Athenians began their training on a small scale in the deme, where local matters were discussed in town meeting, and where local offices gave some practice in communal management. Further experience might be gained in one or

FIGURE 37. Greek coin, obverse and reverse, c. 440 B.C. left: Athena with an olive diadem on her helmet; right: Owl and olive sprig.

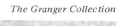
The Granger Collection

FIGURE 38. Pericles. Athenian statesman who died 429 B.C. Marble herm is a
copy from an original of the mid 5th century B.C.

The Granger Collection

more of the many administrative offices of the state and the empire, and in the
assembly and the law courts. This practical instruction was narrow. A broader,
more idealistic education the Athenian received from the choral songs at festivals
and particularly from the drama presented in the theater. During the year more
than sixty days were given to festivals, including dramatic exhibitions and the holidays of the demes. Every year, moreover, from one to two thousand boys and men
appeared before the public in choruses for the dramatic and other exhibitions that
required them. These choral services, as well as others, were generally rotated
among the qualified citizens, thus giving all, or nearly all, a training in music and a
close contact with literature. This training accounts for the high level of taste in
Athenian audiences, most of them being ex-choristers, trained in poetry, and able
to distinguish good poetry from bad.

   Sophocles.   While it is true that the poets were the teachers of Athens, they had
no sense of mission. Certainly Sophocles (496–406 B.C.) did not regard himself as
a teacher, nor was he a religious skeptic, like Euripides; he simply presented the
better side of the gods as normal. The real concern of Sophocles was the human

fortunes of his characters. This concern inevitably grew out of his background, for as a man of wealth and education, he served the state in various capacities and mingled with all classes of people. As a poet, he was chiefly interested in what effect life has upon character and soul. The old legends were his vehicle, and his plays, which combine an exceptional harmony of beauty and reason and are almost perfect from the point of view of dramatic technique, show him to be not only a great artist but the most human of Greek tragedians. It has been said of him that he portrayed people not as they were but as they ought to be.

Sophocles composed about 120 plays, but only 7 survive entire. Of these, *Oedipus the King* is probably the greatest. The house of Cadmus, founder of Thebes, is doomed to misfortune because it has offended the gods. Oedipus, heir to the power and the woes of this stock, is driven unwittingly to the commission of dreadful sin, for he fulfills the prophecy that he will murder his father and marry his mother. He suffers unspeakable agony of mind and blinds himself, and his wife-mother, Jocasta, commits suicide. In Sophocles' earlier play, *Antigone,* Oedipus' daughter Antigone dies in defense of a higher, unwritten law, which a contemporary statute has contradicted. Her death is a result of the old curse only in the larger context of the legend that Sophocles used. Because of that curse, her two brothers killed each other, and from the death of one arose the question she had to answer. The time of the dramatic action of *Oedipus at Colonus,* Sophocles' last play, falls between the events of *Oedipus the King* and *Antigone.* It seems a kind of summing up. Blind Oedipus comes to Attica, with Antigone as his guide, and stops at Colonus, and we learn of his sufferings and wanderings. At the end of-the play, he is translated to another plane of being. He has become sacred, and Attica will be the safer for his influence.

Euripides.   The great exponent of the new spirit of individualism and the new humanism was the poet Euripides (480–406 B.C.). His life was contemporary with the manhood of Sophocles; his activity, beginning with the age of Pericles, terminated shortly before the end of the Peloponnesian War; and yet an age seems to separate him from Sophocles. In the older poet beat the heart of Hellenism; his younger contemporary was distinctly the first of the moderns, profoundly influenced by sophistry, the intellectual "new wave" of the century. It was characteristic of Euripides that he held aloof from public life to apply his energy to the composition of plays—through no disparagement of politics, but in the consciousness that his own mission was superior to any civic achievement of the individual. The apostle of humanism, he issued his dramas as epistles to humankind. His message was a moral and spiritual interpretation of the utterance of Protagoras: man is the measure of all things. The keen intellect and the sensitive conscience, developed by civilization, are presented with all the artistic allurements of dramatic genius as the standards for judging truth and right on earth and in heaven. Casting off from traditional moorings, he piloted humankind over surging seas of thought and emotion, but his ship reached no harbor, and his plays were extremely controversial. The poet of the submerged majority of humanity descended to the level of common folk, to sympathize with beggars and cripples, with women and slaves.

Skeptic and realist, Euripides wrote some magical and brilliant verse; he wrote not only violent invective but tender pathos as well. *Medea,* one of the eighteen plays that have survived from the original total of approximately ninety-two, is high tragedy, the story of a woman who is abandoned by the man she loves and for whom she has surrendered everything. Medea helped Jason, against tremendous odds, to obtain the golden fleece and then fled with him from her native country. At Corinth Jason finds that he can marry the daughter of the king and dismisses Medea. Her love is turned to violent hatred and she murders their children. Euripides gave us in Jason the picture of an egotist and a scoundrel; in Medea, a woman who is heartbroken through tragedy, but who, having the power to do as she wishes, reacts without the restraints that civilization imposes. There is no solution of the problem, and at the end Medea flees to Athens in a magic chariot drawn by winged dragons.

Aristophanes. Boisterous comedy, rather than tragedy, constitutes the medium by which a poet can impress some kinds of views on his audience. Aristophanes (ca. 445-385 B.C.), the brilliant poet of Old Comedy, was before everything else a comedian. He did not hesitate to ridicule his enemies and to advance the interests of his own conservative class, although the relevance of his plays to contemporary politics is frequently unclear. A large number of Aristophanes' plays are full of fierce attacks on prominent persons, cruel caricatures, although they contain delicious humor and a high quality of true lyric genius. There is much bawdiness as well, which is to be explained partly by the origin of comedy in a fertility rite, partly by the fact that Greeks had no conception of sex as sinful, and also by the truth that perhaps there was nothing Aristophanes loved more. A special object of his hatred was Cleon, but the *Knights* failed to crush the demagogue, if that, in fact, was Aristophanes' intention. It was different with the *Clouds,* for this made a lasting impression on the Athenians and may have contributed eventually to the death of Socrates. As a conservative of the old school, Aristophanes disliked the "new thought" of sophistry, and in the *Clouds,* he tried to discredit it by attacking the leading intellectual of the day, Socrates. In the *Frogs,* he attacked Euripides, and he opposed the Peloponnesian War in plays like the *Peace* and *Lysistrata.* It speaks well for Athenian tolerance and willingness to hear all points of view that complete freedom of speech was allowed, but finally in the fourth century, with disillusionment and a new day, comedy forsook politics for social life. This change of subject marks the transformation from Old to Middle Comedy, which was tamer and more realistic and attempted, in quiet humor or good-natured satire, to set forth the manners and morals of the age, to picture scenes and characters from real life.

Science. The scientific spirit of the Periclean Age was by no means limited to the dramatic poets, or to Athens itself, for ever since the intellectual awakening in sixth-century Ionia it had spread through Hellas, to incite in some few individuals a love of collecting facts and of systematizing them on a rational basis. Literary products served useful as well as theoretical purposes. Works on sculpture and architecture, music and literary criticism were handbooks for learners of the respective arts. From the time of Pythagoras, advances were made in arithmetic, geometry, and astronomy. His followers taught the rotundity of earth, sun, and moon. A more careful study of the heavens enabled the astronomer Meton of Athens to devise a nineteen-year cycle for bringing the lunar and solar year into harmony. In this system the solar year was estimated at 365 $\frac{5}{19}$ days, about a half-hour short of our modern calculations.

Medicine. From the time of Pythagoras, too, notable progress was made in medicine. Although cities were backward in general sanitation, they supported physicians who treated citizens free of charge. While the masses still believed in expelling diseases by charms and prayer, or by visits to the shrines like those of Asclepius, the medical profession of the Periclean Age had eliminated magic and much superstition from theory and practice, and it stood more on the solid ground of scientific observation and experiment. Hippocrates of Cos (ca. 460-377 B.C.) was the most noted physician of the ancient world. In his family the profession had been hereditary, as was generally true of trades or other fields of technical skill. Although medical knowledge had accumulated at the temples of Asclepius, where the sick and the maimed sought divine healing, it is significant of the scientific spirit of Hippocrates that in his writings he never prescribed a visit to such a shrine. "Every illness," he declared, "has a natural cause; and without natural causes, nothing ever happens." He stressed hygiene, and especially diet, but he was ready to use drugs or, when necessary, cutting and cauterizing. He repelled all assaults of sophists and speculative philosophers, and while maintaining and expanding the scientific method of his predecessors, he upheld for his profession the noblest ideals of devotion to duty and right. Physicians today subscribe to the Hippocratic Oath.

Philosophy. Not only were special branches of knowledge being cultivated, but great progress was taking place in the philosophic attitude toward the world as a whole and its problems, although Greeks in general and Athenians in particular regarded philosophers with some suspicion, since they found their ideas unsettling. In spite of the repudiation of Being by Heraclitus and his insistence on Becoming as reality, the successors of Xenophanes the Eleatic continued more strongly than ever to deny motion and change and to claim for Being alone a real existence. An attempt was made by Empedocles of Acragas (ca. 495-430 B.C.) to harmonize these views. With the Eleatics he denied absolute origin and decay; but unlike them, he believed in the plurality of Being; there were, he asserted, four elements—earth, water, air, and fire—of which all things were composed. The forces that combined and separated them were Love and Hate, the poetic antecedents of attraction and repulsion. In this way he was able to use both Being and Becoming in his theory of the formation of the world. He paid less attention to the character of his elements than to the processes of nature. In accounting for plant and animal forms, he enunciated a principle crudely anticipative of the "survival of the fittest."

Every new philosopher, after learning what his predecessors had to teach, attempted to correct the faults of their suppositions or methods with a view to approaching nearer the truth. Thus it was that Leucippus, a younger contemporary of Empedocles, began working out the problem of that thinker in a more scientific way. Seeing no reason for Being to be limited to precisely four elements, he assumed instead its division into an indefinite number of minute indivisible particles, termed *atoms.* By the side of Being, which he interpreted as matter, he assumed the existence of Void—empty space—in which the atoms moved; in place of the mythical Love and Hate he substituted Gravitation, a strictly physical force. With Being, Void, and Gravitation, he explained Creation, the processes of nature, and even feeling and thought in a purely mechanical way. The atomic theory, which was developed into a system by Leucippus' famous pupil Democritus in the fourth century, was generally denounced by the ancients as materialistic, hence as ethically demoralizing.

More influential was Anaxagoras of Clazomenae (ca. 500–428 B.C.), the teacher of Pericles. His lasting contribution to philosophy was to substitute for gravitation an infinite and omniscient Intelligence, which ordered all things. He did not consciously think of it as a person or as a deity but regarded it merely as a directing force. If not immaterial, it was at least a substance unmixed and in quality unique. The religious and ethical consequences of his theory, however, were left mainly to future thinkers to work out. The Athenians burned his books and banished him from their city for impiety.

The influence of these philosophers, or scientists, was limited to narrow circles. To the public the thinker seemed an odd, unnatural being, who in his search for the undiscoverable and the unpractical neglected everything that the Greek held dear—a subject for ridicule in comedy or for prosecution on the charge of atheism, of having substituted whirligig for Zeus. Those who, braving public opinion, became acquainted with the various systems of thought were generally struck by their contradictions, the uncertain foundations on which they rested, and their utter uselessness in life. Thus far, in fact, Hellenic thinkers, while discovering the most fundamental principles of science and philosophy, had pursued the faulty method of generalization on the basis of too few facts. Little more could be accomplished without a careful and extensive study of nature, and the scientific instruments were lacking for such a study.

The Sophists. Meanwhile, with the rise of democracy, involving the theory of human equality, a demand was created for a technical education that would fit any man who wished for public life; statesmanship, once based on inborn gifts of birth, speech, and political wisdom, had to be democratized. This demand could not be met by the philosophers and therefore called into being the art of rhetoric, whose aim was to equip any man, however humble in his talent, for public speaking. Shortly after the establishment of democracy in Syracuse (466 B.C.), Corax of that city developed the first method of juridicial oratory. Rhetoric, however, concerned itself only with the communication of thought and the persuasion to belief or action; it had to be supplemented by a working knowledge of government and society. Hence arose a class of men who professed to teach not only rhetoric but all knowledge essential to the statesman. Such instructors in wisdom were termed *Sophists.* They traveled from city to city, giving exhibitions of their knowledge and of their skill in argument, and imparting instruction to all who desired it and who were able to pay the required fee. The rise of sophistry marks one of the crucial turning points in Western intellectual history, since the central role of rhetoric and argumentation marked a new moment in education.

The earliest of this class, and by far the most eminent, was Protagoras of Abdera (ca. 485–410 B.C.). The speculations of philosophers had led many to doubt the possibility of knowledge. Abandoning all hope of discovering the one true essence of the universe, Protagoras boldly declared that "Man is the measure of all things." In two respects this declaration opened a new era. First, it directed attention to the mind and its relation to the outside world and thus paved the way to mental philosophy, or psychology. Second, by shifting the center of attention from the world to human beings it gave, along with many cooperating forces, a tremendous impetus to the growth of individualism. Protagoras also had a theory to offer as to the basis of society and the state. The desire of self-preservation gathered humankind into cities, but fearing that people might destroy one another, Zeus sent Hermes to them all, bearing reverence and justice as the ordering principles of cities and the bonds of friendship and conciliation. Here was the beginning of a line of thought that led to the creation of sociology and political science.

Prodicus of Ceos, Hippias of Elis, and other Sophists borrowed from Protagoras his theory of knowledge and, with varying motive and ability, pursued the same methods. All laid stress on the distinction between Nature, whose laws, observed by all nations, were morally binding, and convention—man-made customs and statutes, for which they had no reverence. The effect of this principle was to dissolve tradition, including religion and moral usages. In their view the past was an age of ignorance and superstition; the present alone was worthy of consideration. The same principle tended to break down equally the barriers of social class and the boundaries of states. Though solvents of the established political, social, and religious order, the Sophists were preparing the way to a worldwide humanism. It is significant that one of the greater Sophists, the Sicilian Gorgias of Leontini (ca. 483–376 B.C.), seeing perhaps dimly the need of a universal language of culture, adopted for that purpose the Attic dialect. He is alleged to have stated that "Nothing exists, and if anything did, we could not know about it." His *Encomium of Helen* was very influential because of its extremely sophistic, antithetical style.

Sophists without character or earnest purpose, however, pushed to ridiculous extremes the doctrine of Protagoras and asserted that everything was precisely as it appeared to each individual. No affirmation could be false because it was impossible to state what did not exist. If a thing was true, the opposite was equally true. Thus arose a class of disputants whose sole purpose was to confute their adversaries by quibbling with words, by fallacies of logic, and by sheer effrontery of manner. The effect was to fill the right-minded with disgust at sophistry. It is not surprising, therefore, that as an escape from hopeless skepticism a reaction should arise toward religious and philosophic faith. Here and there through the plays of Euripides there may be found, along with penetrating psychological studies, expressions of faith; and in his *Bacchae,* composed shortly before his death, the aged poet contemplated the implacable vengence of gods who are denied their due, as he had done in his earlier works.

Socrates. A contemporary of Euripides, and a kindred spirit, was Socrates the philosopher (ca. 470–399 B.C.), whom the masses wrongly regarded as a sophist. He was relatively poor; his estate barely enabled him to serve as a hoplite; and in youth he had trained as a sculptor in his father's shop. He had little schooling, and his moderate acquaintance with existing philosophers was only gained incidentally.

From early life he neglected his worldly affairs in order to devote himself to thought. Forsaking a trade that could have afforded him only a meager sustenance, he devoted his entire life to the pursuit of truth. In this vocation he was encouraged by an oracle of Apollo, which declared him to be the wisest of men.

Through his whole life Socrates accepted and faithfully practiced the religion of the state, and he was often seen sacrificing at the public altars. His ideas of the gods, however, were enlightened. Socrates held that the gods were present everywhere and knew all things. A divinity or inner voice (*daimonion*), accompanying him through life, gave him warnings, which he always heeded.

The Granger Collection

FIGURE 39. Socrates. This Roman marble statuette is a copy of a lost Greek original of the fourth century B.C.

Although Socrates' religious views are highly debatable, his apparent belief in the greatness and the wisdom of the gods was strengthened by the argument of design. The world is made for humankind, and every part of a human being is admirably adapted to a good purpose. Existing things must, therefore, be the handiwork of a wise artificer, full of love for all things living. As humans are superior to animals, the deity has taken special thought for them. This god is pleased with those things in us that lead most to our well-being. Socrates drew, too, from experience that the wisest and most enduring of human institutions are the most god-fearing, and that in the individual, the riper his age and judgment, the deeper his religion. It was necessary for Socrates to make his sacrifices correspond with his small means, but he believed that the joy of the gods was great in proportion to the holiness of the worshiper; and in the conviction that they well knew his own interest, he used to pray simply, "Give me what is best for me."

Socrates was not the mere prosaic teacher of Xenophon's memoirs; in addition to an ample fund of common sense, he had within him humor, imagination, intellectual power, and a love of truth so burning as to become ecstatic. With such qualities he fascinated his young companions, and some of them, especially Plato, he awakened to a life of intense mental productivity. Indeed, Plato's subsequent works are our main sources for Socrates' doctrine, although it is difficult to separate in them the ultimately Socratic ideas from Plato's own development and modification of them. With Socrates true knowledge was not simply the source but the substance of virtue; and he preferably sought the kind of truth that should determine human conduct—for example, "What is piety and what impiety? What is the beautiful and what the ugly? What is the noble and what the base? What are meant by just and unjust? What by sobriety and madness? What by courage and cowardice? What is a state and what a statesman? What is a rule over men and what a ruling character?" and other similar problems.

The Socratic method of research was through conversation with one's fellows. It was easy for him to prove his opponent ignorant of the topic under discussion, as he was the most formidable reasoner of his age. Having thus cleared the ground, he proceeded by induction to establish precise definitions of general terms. "There are two things," declared Aristotle, "that one would rightly attribute to Socrates: inductive reasoning and universal definition. In fact these two things are the very foundation of knowledge." It was thus that, while professing ignorance on all subjects, he built up a body of ethical science that might serve as a guide to himself and to others. In assuming man to be the measure of all things, he stood on sophistic ground; but he made a vast advance in pointing to the reason, rather than the senses, as the universal and eternal human element, the infallible criterion of truth, therefore, in the realm of conduct of nature. As intellectual education, however, merely increased a person's power for evil, he was careful first of all to instruct his associates in self-control and to inspire them with a wise spirit in their relations with the gods. Wisdom and justice we should seek not only because of their use to us but also because they are pleasing to the gods. His teachings were as religious as they were philosophic.

Throughout his life Socrates gave evidence of loyalty and love for his fellow citizens and his country. Living frugally, he charged no fee for instruction but lavished the wealth of his spirit on rich and poor alike. Many were his exhortations to brothers to love one another, to children to respect and obey their parents, and to citizens to be true to their country. As a soldier, he performed his duties faithfully. As chairman of the assembly, when the generals were tried illegally after Arginusae, he fearlessly adhered to law against the popular clamor for injustice. It is true that he criticized the use of the lot for the appointment of officials on the ground that it brought incompetent men into public service. Rather than give his time to the holding of offices, he chose as a higher duty the task of instruction. No matter how noble his motives, Socrates was unpopular because he was associated in the public mind with sophists and because many of his disciples were antidemocratic. His condemnation to death on the ground that he was a corrupting influence on the young and had introduced new deities is understandable.

Herodotus. The desire for serviceable knowledge, the interest of mankind, and the absorption in the present that characterized the intellectual movement of the Periclean Age found notable expression in history. The spirit of scientific inquiry naturally involved an eagerness to know the past of the human race; and this desire created history. The first historian was Herodotus (ca. 484–425 B.C.). We cannot say definitely how great an advance he made beyond Hecataeus, his most distinguished predecessor, although we know that he borrowed extensively from him. Born in the period of the conflict with Persia, Herodotus lived through the earlier years of the Peloponnesian War. His native city was Halicarnassus, in Asia Minor. He spent much of his life at Athens and traveled to Egypt, into Asia as far as Susa, to the countries about the Black Sea, to Italy—in brief, to most of the known world. Everywhere he gathered material that found its way into his work. His sources, accordingly, are of uneven value, but where he trusted his own observations, Herodotus is, on the whole, reliable.

As the genealogists were the literary heirs of Hesiod, Herodotus was a son of Homer, and his *History* might well be termed a great prose epic, influenced by his friend Sophocles and contemporary drama. A brief preface explains the object of his work: "This is a presentation of the *Inquiries–Historiae–of Herodotus of Halicarnassus* to the end that time may not obliterate the great and marvelous deeds of Hellenes and barbarians, and especially that they may not forget the causes for which they waged war with one another." In his search for causes he narrated from earliest times the notable achievements of all peoples involved in the Persian Wars, and thus his book may be described as a universal history. He used the Persian Wars as the unifying element of his work, and though he was ignorant of strategy and tactics, his *Inquiries* remain our chief source for the conflict. A fair-minded historian and a friend of Pericles, Herodotus described the glorious deeds of Athens, for it was Athens that had saved Greece.

Herodotus was the first to apply the word *history,* in its original sense of inquiry, to this field of literature. It aptly describes his method of gathering information by personal inquiry of those who were supposed to know. The main advance made by him was his interest in and treatment of causation in history. Often unsatisfied with an individual source, he pursued his investigation among various authorities, thus introducing the comparative method of research. We find him expressing doubt as to what he has heard, comparing the more with the less credible, or reasoning about the reliability of his source. Although his work abounds in myths and fictions—for no one loved a good story more than Herodotus—and though he was often at the mercy of untrustworthy informants, he was far from credulous. Even the fictitious tales are of value for illustrating the thought and life of the age.

Another great quality of Herodotus was his broad-mindedness, to which his cosmopolitan birthplace, on the borderland between Hellas and the Persian Empire, and his extensive travels contributed. He could understand that many foreign customs were at least as good as the Hellenic, that there were great and admirable characters among the barbarians, and that monarchy as well as democracy had its good features. A comparison of Egyptian with Hellenic tradition taught him the emptiness of the claim of certain Greeks to near descent from a god. His comparative study of religion convinced him that his compatriots entertained many false notions as to their own gods and the beginnings of the human race. Regarding the existence of the gods, however, and their providential dealings with mortals, he betrayed no skepticism. With other enlightened people of his age, he believed in a divine providence, who ruled the world and in a kindly spirit watches over humans, revealing his will through omens, dreams, and oracles. Like Aeschylus he seems to have believed that the downfall of the great—for example, of Xerxes—was in punishment for insolence (*hubris*), which unusual prosperity often induces.

In religion, therefore, though casting off much that was extraneous, Herodotus held firmly to the enlightened orthodoxy of the time. From the point of view of strict historical science, while advancing beyond Hecataeus, he was still crude and imperfect, whereas his broad sympathy and kindly interest in everything human, his high religious and moral principles, his inexhaustible fund of anecdotes illustrative of customs and character, his charming style, and his genial personality have entitled him to his place as the "father of history," as Cicero called him, and have given his literary production a universal and eternal interest.

Thucydides.   The greatest ancient historian, and in some respects still without a rival, was the Athenian Thucydides (ca. 471–399 B.C.), son of Olorus. Thucydides resembled the men of the Periclean Age, not only in intensity and power of thought and style, but also in the fact that he was a man of action, as well as of words, a general in the Peloponnesian War, who could therefore season his writings with practical experience. His slowness in coming to the protection of Amphipolis led to his exile in 424 B.C. At the outbreak of the war, forseeing that it would be memorable, he had begun to collect material for a history of it; and during the twenty years of his exile he traveled about, visiting the scenes of military operations and ascertaining facts from eyewitnesses. Doubtless he kept a record of events, which he corrected and expanded with the acquisition of new and more precise information. At the close of the war he undertook a final recomposition of his work, which described the great conflict between Athens and Sparta, although the first book contains a valuable sketch of the earlier years of Greece. The *History* comes to an end in the course of 411 B.C., doubtless cut short by Thucydides' death.

Thucydides carefully examined his evidence, distinguished between primary and secondary sources, and was impartial. Though he loved Athens, he did not hesitate to criticize her. Like Pericles he appreciated magnificence and display, and like Pericles he was an imperialist. He believed that it was natural for a state to expand, since the state represented power, and war, he felt, was only an expression of the state's growth. The Peloponnesian War, Thucydides believed, was the most important event in the entire history of Greece—indeed, he was convinced that, compared with the present, the past in general was insignificant. In studying the war, he was interested in the causes underlying the political actions of states. With Thucydides the forces that made history were the statesmen, who consciously operated to effect a given purpose, secondarily the people in their assembly, moved by capricious feeling to a wise or foolish resolution. The ideal republic was one like Athens in the age of Pericles, in which the best and wisest citizen was able to control the rest, but, he recognized, chance could also affect the course of events.

The *History* is a literary masterpiece, influenced by the dramatists and especially the Sophists. The speeches, which occupy a large part of the work, are, so to speak, its soul. Usually they are given in pairs, representing the opposing views of a situation or a question for decision before an assembly. The language of the speeches is Thucydides'; the ideas, so far as one can ascertain, are the orators', though even here, as the actual speeches were unwritten, the historian exercised large discretion in including what he considered appropriate to the occasion. Generally, therefore, the speeches embody the historian's understanding of the situation that they present.

Notwithstanding certain differences between ancient and modern conceptions of history, we may still look to Thucydides as a master. In his own personal reserve; in the determination with which he pursued his aim, rejecting every extraneous matter; in the relentless analysis that lays bare the souls of individuals, of factions, of communities; in the fairness and mental placidity with which he treated personal enemies and opposing parties, in intellectual depth, keenness, and grasp—all of these, we may safely say that he has thus far had no equal.

Greece in the fifth century produced a galaxy of brilliant men, many of whom were Athenians or chose to live in Athens. It was a crowded, complex century. While admiring the Parthenon and the Sophoclean drama, we recognize that they are so essentially Hellenic as to defy imitation, whereas the sculpture of the Nike parapet, the plays of Euripides, and the reasoning of Socrates, however high their excellence, have an appreciable kinship with modern civilization. Needless to say, neither private nor public life was faultless. The blemishes of the civilization show themselves, for example, in the cramping of the lives of the women, in the existence of slavery, in the narrowness and exclusiveness of Athenian interests, as opposed to those of metics, allies, Hellenes, and the world. A part of this narrowness—at once the strength and the weakness of ancient Greece—was the self-sufficiency, the particularism, of each independent city-state. The morality of Hellas was essentially civic. The fundamental motive to right conduct, as Pericles himself asserted, was the good of the state. The patriotic devotion required was too intense to be lasting. Not long after Pericles the gradual disintegration of the city-states resulted in depriving citizens of their moral basis and compelled them to fight out anew the whole battle of conduct on other, very different ground.

16

The Era of Hegemonies and Persia (404–336 B.C.)

INTRODUCTION

The end of the fifth century B.C. was probably the most important turning point in the history of the Greek world. Political and military events revealed the instability of the city-state, upset the balance of power, and helped modify the nature of Hellenic civilization. To some extent, instability was a legacy of the Peloponnesian War, which had made clear the basic weaknesses inherent in the city-state system. Even in peacetime, the city-states were never noted for their cooperation, and the war did much to accentuate already strong cleavages and to engender new animosities. Conflict between city-states was complicated by civil war within them, the Peloponnesian War having also in many places intensified traditional competition for control of government by democratic and oligarchic factions, which sometimes relied on foreign help to overthrow their rivals. In some cities, civil war was encouraged by economic depression, which led to an increasing disparity in living standards between rich and poor and to a growth in antagonism between the classes.

The period is sometimes called the Era of Hegemonies, since leading powers, notably Sparta and Thebes, attempted to fill the power vacuum created by the collapse of the Athenian Empire and to dominate Greece. There were other political developments, no less important, like the surprising revival of Athenian power, but especially interference by Persia in Greek affairs. Indeed, if there is any obviously centralizing theme during the period it is the frequent ability of the Persian government to manipulate quarreling Greek states and to play them off against one another. As during the final phase of the Peloponnesian War, so during the first decades of the fourth century, Persian gold was often the determining factor in Greek affairs, and Persian diplomacy successfully stirred up troubled waters and kept the Greeks weakened through division. Frequent and prolonged warfare was the result of such conditions, as shifting coalitions of city-states resisted domination by strong powers in their midst. Ultimately Macedonia, under the leadership of a clever king, profited by divisions among and within the city-states to impose its will on all of them, and the colonial cities of Magna Graecia and Sicily similarly faced absorption by barbarian powers on the fringes of their world. Thoughtful Greeks realized that Hellenism was in a state of self-induced crisis and attempted to dis-

226

cover theoretical and practical solutions to their difficulties, but they could not arrest the decline of the city-state system.

ECONOMY AND SOCIETY

It is difficult to generalize about the state of the Greek economy in the fourth century B.C. Conditions varied rather widely from place to place, and surviving evidence on the subject is very distorted, because most of it pertains to Athens, which in many ways was an exceptional case. Although it seems unlikely that Greece was collectively poorer than in the fifth century, it appears that the distribution of wealth was increasingly inequitable and that this development and certain other factors contributed to a growing economic crisis.

Agriculture. Certainly agriculture continued to be the livelihood of the overwhelming majority of Greeks. The Peloponnesian War and subsequent conflicts reduced farm production in those parts where fighting was frequent, particularly devastating vineyards and orchards, which required many years to recover. However, it seems that the depressing effects of war on agriculture were more than counterbalanced in many areas by greater efficiency, as large estates producing cash crops replaced subsistence farmers. Although there was no notable increase in the use of slave labor, the concentration of property in fewer hands tended to make inefficient peasant proprietors economically redundant, and these drifted to the cities. The ability of cities to absorb them was limited, despite a growing specialization of industry leading more frequently than in the fifth century to primitive factories, and migrants to cities tended to become an unemployed or underemployed proletariat.

Commerce. These developments were taking place just as Greek commerce was experiencing difficulties caused by political instability, by a resurgence of piracy on the high seas, and especially by the tendency of ancient industry to export itself. Markets for traditional Greek exports like wine, olive oil, pottery, textiles, jewelry, and metalware in the Persian Empire, Thrace and the Black Sea coasts, the Adriatic, Italy, and Sicily markedly declined in the fourth century. Emancipation from reliance on imports from Greece grew as these areas developed their own agriculture and industry, sometimes creating local imitations of Greek products that were preferable because they were cheaper. In any case, the Aegean world experienced an increasingly unfavorable balance of trade with other parts of the Mediterranean basin, which was covered by larger exports abroad of specie.

The ranks of unemployed created by the spread of large estates and the contraction of overseas commerce were also swelled by thousands of political exiles, victims of civil war. Perhaps the clearest sign of economic malaise was the appearance in many areas, especially in the Peloponnese, of a large, pauperized, floating class of such people. Many of them eventually found employment by Persian and even city-state governments in mercenary armies, one of the new phenomena of the age, the increasing specialization of warfare having made professional fighters more desirable than citizen militia.

Under the circumstances, the ever-present problem of overpopulation became more acute in the fourth century, even though some city-states had fewer people following the Peloponnesian War. A drop of one quarter in the number of citizens to about 112,000 at Athens probably reflects manpower losses in the war and a nearly matching contraction in the economy following the collapse of her empire. The decline in the citizen population of Sparta, already noticeable in the fifth century, accelerated in the fourth. This decline was not due primarily to losses in war but rather to the widespread Spartan practice of limiting families to only one son. Spartans tried to avoid division of patrimony among several heirs, each of whom might receive a share of land with insufficient income to maintain their payments to the military mess, in which case they would sink to the status of inferiors. When family lines died out, land often passed to already propertied legatees, frequently heiresses, so that landholding, and the number of peers, was increasingly restricted, some 40 per cent of Spartan real estate in the fourth century coming under the control of women.

Athens. Overcoming initially severe economic dislocation immediately after the Peloponnesian War, within a generation Athens had revived to become one of the most stable and prosperous city-states in the fourth century. Although there were important, if subtle, changes in her government and society, her political institutions continued to function rather efficiently, and Athenians, with some notable exceptions, respected freedom of speech and equality before the law. The loss of the empire was a crippling but not a mortal blow to the Athenian economy, although it eliminated an important source of income to subsidize the navy, public works, and payments for government service, all of which suffered from financial retrenchment. To a certain extent, the burden of running the city was shifted to the wealthy citizens in the form of heavier liturgies, but even they could not maintain public services at fifth-century levels. Although the Piraeus was no longer the economic focal point of an empire, it benefited from the continuation of prewar trading patterns. Its share of Greek commerce tended to diminish in relation to that of other cities like Corinth and Rhodes, but well into the fourth century it remained a busy port and entrepôt, exporting Athenian oil, pottery, and specie in return for imports of essential foodstuffs, mainly grain and fish.

Athenian stability was attributable largely to her social structure, which survived the war with remarkably few changes from the Periclean period, except for a decrease in population. There was, perhaps, a greater concentration of wealth than previously in the first families, which numbered some three hundred, but even the fortunes of these wealthy were still relatively modest. At the very bottom of the scale were the proletariat and the casual laborers, but they were of insignificant numbers. The vast majority of the population, as before, were a middle class of farmers and shopkeepers, among whom the ownership of property, especially real estate, was widespread.

Although the contrary is sometimes alleged, fourth-century Athenians were not necessarily less patriotic than their ancestors of the fifth, but attitudes toward their state were necessarily affected by changed financial circumstances. The Periclean principle of pay for government service found its logical extension to the assembly, where participating citizenry received a drachma or more a day as compensation for taking time off from their work. This amount compares with the two obols a day paid to jurymen in the fifth century and is a measure of the inflation prevailing at Athens in the fourth. Poorer Athenians did not attend in great numbers, however, because their participation in legislation seemed pointless when the laws they passed were successfully challenged so frequently in the courts. Wealthy, and hence conservative, citizens tended to dominate the other branches of government, especially the juries, where the real issues were decided. Critics of fourth-century Athens sometimes single out the so-called Theoric Fund as indicative of growing Athenian frivolity. Fed by the normal peacetime surplus of government income over expenditure, the Theoric Fund distributed pin money to all citizens, rich and poor, on the occasion of festivals, which provided a financial margin permitting the poor to leave their work and attend the celebrations. The total payments were, it seems, a very small part of the Athenian budget and are no more or less open to criticism than regular welfare expenditures of the Periclean period.

Frequent Athenian complaints concerning heavy taxation are perhaps best interpreted as evidence of an inequitable system of levies rather than of unwillingness to shoulder a reasonable burden to support the state. The main tax on capital, the *eisphora,* was collected from only six thousand of the twenty-one thousand adult male citizens, but these included even men of rather limited means. The rate corresponded to an annual income tax of over 10 per cent, which the poorer taxpayers found unfairly high, especially as the levy on greater wealth was not graduated. Athenian citizens of the fourth century are frequently censured as cowards for their evident reluctance to serve as hoplites or as rowers in the navy. They preferred, it is true, to entrust their wars to mercenary armies, whose payment was made difficult by the financial straits of the government. Nevertheless, on important occasions, thousands of Athenians served in their army and navy in the best Periclean tradition, although hoplites and thetes—respectively, the middle and poorer classes— obeyed the draft reluctantly. Payments for military or naval service by citizens were drastically reduced in the fourth century and sometimes eliminated altogether, so that prolonged campaigns, which pauperized soldiers and sailors and their families, were understandably unpopular.

The Hegemony of Sparta. As head of the Peloponnesian League and master of the former Athenian Empire and of Athens herself, Sparta was in 404 B.C. by far the most powerful state in Greece. Despite her leading position, she was far more unsuited to ruling an empire even than Athens, notwithstanding the sometimes adroit maneuvers of Lysander, the Spartan general. Spartan difficulties arose from the unpopularity she earned abroad by her inability to deal with free men. She ineptly squandered the capital of goodwill she had earned by liberating Athenian subject states, on which she imposed tyrannical government by Committees of Ten called *decarachies,* pro-Spartan collaborators often supported locally by Spartan military commanders and harmosts and their garrisons. She also taxed the subject states heavily at an annual rate of one thousand talents to build and maintain her navy. Her treatment of long-standing allies in the Peloponnesian League was just as clumsy, and she managed to alienate them by interfering in their internal affairs and by imposing on them pro-Laconian oligarchies. Having just concluded a war to preserve their freedom from the imperialism of Athens, members of Sparta's own league were not about to accept Spartan infringement on their autonomy.

The first break in the Spartan system came at Athens in 403 B.C., with the overthrow of Critias and the Thirty Tyrants, the expulsion of the Spartan garrison from Attica, and the restoration of democracy. Sparta was prevented from supporting its Athenian puppets or from retaliating with full force, dissension having arisen between Lysander and King Pausanias. She merely constrained Athens to remain a Spartan ally, but ungarrisoned, and to enforce an amnesty protecting those members of the Thirty who had survived the counterrevolution.

Anabasis. Upon claiming from Athens leadership of the Greek world, Sparta also inherited the responsibility of protecting the Greeks against Persia, but during the Peloponnesian War she had actually sold out the Ionian cities to the Persians in return for money to build a navy. Circumstances soon permitted a change in policy, although for a time the Spartan government remained pro-Persian at the expense of the Asia Minor Greeks. In 401 the Persian prince Cyrus the Younger, contending for the throne with his brother Artaxerxes II, recruited an army of over ten thousand Greek mercenaries and won official Spartan support. Armies of the two rivals met in battle near Babylon, where Cyrus was killed and the Greek mercenaries, although undefeated, lost their officers. They elected two new commanders, one a Spartan, the other the Athenian Xenophon, who led their troops out of the Persian Empire from the Tigris River to the Black Sea, and eventually to the Aegean, in an *anabasis* or "march up-country," immortalized in Xenophon's book. The expedition revealed the internal weaknesses of the Persian Empire as it did the military potential of Greek soldiers, despite the difficulties of city-state governments. Sparta took advantage of that weakness by hiring some of the ten thousand to drive the Persians out of the Asian Greek cities, which they accomplished by 397.

Corinthian War and Its Aftermath. By then Sparta had almost totally lost the goodwill of her former allies in the Peloponnesian League, and her reputation was not enhanced among them when she tried to discipline the Boeotians in 396 for waging war on their own against Phocis, Lysander perishing in the attempt. Thereafter a diplomatic revolution took place in which Sparta's ex-allies, Thebes and Corinth, admitted into a widespread anti-Spartan coalition their own ancient enemies, Athens and Argos, along with other states. The Athenian government sanctioned the alliance with some reluctance, since breaking their peace treaty with Sparta would mean more war and an increase in the already heavy taxes and liturgies borne by the wealthy. It was advantageous for Athens to join the coalition, however, because it made possible her reemergence as a ranking power. This took place during the ensuing Corinthian War (395–387), waged by the coalition against Sparta, a conflict in which Persia freely meddled. At first, the Persian government commissioned Conon, an Athenian admiral serving the Great King since the end of the Peloponnesian War, to take an active part in the hostilities against Sparta. Conon returned to Athens in 395 with his largely Greek fleet and rebuilt her fortifications and long walls.

The Corinthian War dragged on with victories and defeats almost evenly matched on either side, Persia ultimately encouraging the Greeks to bleed themselves white by secretly subsidizing *both* the Spartans and their enemies. At length, all the belligerents were so exhausted that they agreed to submit their differences to the arbitration of the Persian king. The resulting Peace of Antalcidas (387), so-called from the Spartan admiral who negotiated its terms with the Great King, enabled Persia to gain by diplomacy what she had failed to accomplish by war. The peace made her the real arbiter of international city-state affairs and even of internal Greek politics. Persia received back the Greek cities of western Asia Minor, but Artaxerxes II was also careful to perpetuate division and weakness among the Greeks on the other side of the Aegean. Empire building by any *polis* was forbidden, every city-state was to be sovereign, and combinations or leagues of states, such as that of Athens and her newly found allies, were prohibited. Sparta determined to use the peace to her own advantage by claiming to be the enforcement agent on behalf of Persia, keeping her own league, whose members she claimed were autonomous, while fighting against alliances of her enemies. The peace was denounced by some powers like Athens and Thebes, which harbored imperialistic intentions of their own. Athenian orators in particular decried the Spartan abandonment of the Asia Minor Greeks and derisively compared Spartan acquiescence to Persian terms with the Athenian actions on behalf of the Ionians in the early phases of the Delian Confederacy a century before. As a matter of fact, the abandonment of Asia Minor evoked only mild protest elsewhere in Greece, and on balance, the treaty was popular, especially among the smaller city-states, because it enunciated the principle of autonomy—a traditional political ideal—and of peace.

Persian hopes that the peace would perpetuate instability in the Greek world were soon realized. Sparta fomented new trouble, extending her own sway in the guise of enforcing it, in particular against Olynthus, head of the Chalcidicean League, and Thebes, capital of the Boeotian Confederacy. Farther to the north, Jason of Pherae, the talented tyrant of Thessaly, successfully withstood spreading Spartan hegemony, making his state a factor to be reckoned with in Greek politics until his own assassination in 370. Aided by civil war, the Spartans installed garrisons at Thebes and at Corinth and other places. Their exploitation of the king's peace made them as powerful as they had been right after the Peloponnesian War, but once again their own ineptness in treating subject states caused a swift deterioration of their hegemony. Sparta lost control of Boeotia in 379 when exiles from Thebes returned to their city, assassinated their quisling rulers, and expelled the Spartan garrison. Even more momentous was the creation in 378–377 of a second Athenian Naval League, which many maritime cities and even Thebes joined as an anti-Spartan coalition. Having denounced the king's peace only a few years before, Athenian leaders rather hypocritically announced that the purpose of their league was proper enforcement of that very agreement, as it was directed against Spartan imperialism. Because many of its members were former subject states of the Athenian empire, they insisted that the league charter not repeat the weaknesses of the Delian Confederacy.

The charter of the Second Naval League indicated that membership in it was not to be perpetual, and it specifically guaranteed the autonomy of its constituents. It also prohibited the levying of tribute (for which voluntary contributions were substituted), the acquisition by Athens of property in allied cities, and their garrisoning. The Spartans countered with a reorganization of the Peloponnesian League, so as to apportion military levies more systematically among its allies. Yet another war broke out, which dragged on for six years with inconclusive results like those of the Corinthian War. Athens eventually favored peace because she was financially exhausted and increasingly suspicious of her Theban allies, who were showing disturbing ambitions of their own in Phocis and central Greece. At the suggestion of the Persian king, no less interested in peace because it would make available to him more Greek mercenaries, a Panhellenic conference was called in 371, including representatives from Sicily and Macedonia.

THEBAN HEGEMONY

Peace was made on terms once again guaranteeing city-state autonomy, except that Sparta refused to recognize the right of Thebes to sign the treaty on behalf of the entire Boeotian Confederacy, and fighting was resumed between these two powers, the Spartan King, Cleombrotus, invading Boeotia that same year. He was confronted by a reorganized Theban army led by the general Epaminondas, who had carefully analyzed Spartan tactics, which, he assumed, the conservative Laconians were not likely to change. The Spartans traditionally relied on a phalanx of heavy infantry, organized in a long, straight line usually four men deep, each of whom was armed with a spear. Their tactics were simple: a push against the enemy line relying heavily on individual courage and skill. Epaminondas rearranged his own tactics accordingly. He, too, used a line of heavy infantry, except that he concentrated his strength in an overwhelming column on his left flank, fifty ranks deep.

Leuctra. The two armies met at Leuctra, where Epaminondas rolled up the Spartan right wing, killing four hundred Spartans (one-third of their military manpower) and their king. This defeat was stunning enough, because it was the first one Sparta had suffered on a battlefield since Thermopylae, and destroyed the legend of their invincibility. In about 370 B.C., with Theban encouragement, Sparta's neighbors in Arcadia seized on her weakness to found the city of Megalopolis in the heart of the Peloponnese as head of an anti-Spartan League. Epaminondas' invasion of Laconia itself followed the next year. Epaminondas freed Messenia and its helots, an action that—by reducing the number of Spartan peers, since it deprived some of them of their estates—had serious economic consequences. Leuctra and its aftermath thus meant a serious decline in Spartan power and severely crippled her ability to sustain a leading role in international affairs.

Mantinea. Under the leadership of Epaminondas, who was a general rather than a great statesman, the Theban government embarked on an unimaginative but predictable foreign policy simply designed to replace Spartan power with their own. With Thebes already being dominant in central and southern Greece, Epaminondas extended Theban influence northward to Thessaly and even Macedonia, realizing a hegemony in the period 371-362. As early as the Battle of Leuctra, the Athenians viewed Theban success with misgivings, and as the Thebans proved to be as high-handed as the Spartans, they alienated their former allies, who made common cause even with recent enemies to confront the new menace to their autonomy. Ulti-mately a broadly-based anti-Theban coalition was formed under Athens and Sparta, which Epaminondas attempted to destroy by invading the Peloponnese in 362. He met his opponents at the Battle of Mantinea, which the Thebans won but were unable to exploit, because Epaminondas was killed in it and no Theban succeeded him who had sufficient talent to maintain the leadership of Greece. The political situation in Greece, accordingly, remained very unstable.

THE WESTERN GREEKS

The political decline of Greek city-states in Italy was caused by the expansion of warlike Samnites, Italic tribes inhabiting the mountainous south-central area of the peninsula. Driven by overpopulation, they periodically encouraged their young men to raid or emigrate into coastal areas settled by Greeks and Etruscans. The first Greek city to fall to them was Cumae (ca. 420 B.C.), a pioneer Hellenic settlement in the West. The pressure of the Samnites on Magna Graecia increased during the fourth century, until other cities turned to Rome for protection. Naples made a formal alliance with Rome in 326, after which Roman influence in Greek Italy spread quickly.

Dionysius.   On Sicily the Greeks were threatened by Carthage, an enemy no less mortal for being civilized, but held at bay for a time by the power of Syracuse. The defeat of the Athenian armada in 413 was followed in Syracuse by democratic government, which for some years failed to resist energetically Punic encroachment on the island. Under the leadership of their general, Hannibal, Punic forces captured Selinus and Himera on the northern coast in 409, Syracusan aid proving ineffective. Although organizing a broader resistance of Greek cities three years later, Syracuse could not prevent the fall to Carthage of Acragas after a protracted siege. Capitaliz-ing on the subsequent popular discontent with the repeated failure of the war ef-fort, a former government clerk and soldier of fortune, Dionysius, discredited the executive board of generals before the Syracusan assembly. He convinced the citi-zenry to unite under his leadership, and in 405 they voted him autocratic powers, sole command of the mercenary army, and a personal bodyguard. Dionysius wielded his authority as tyrant of Syracuse from then until his death in 367.

Dionysius was an intriguing, contradictory character, a champion of Greek civili-zation who nevertheless contributed to its demise in the West. After initial reverses, he succeeded by 392 in driving Carthage from most of Sicily, except its western tip. During his long reign he established an empire, including other Greek cities in Sicily and Italy as a kind of bulwark against future Carthaginian aggression. His imperial-ism was a mixed blessing for the cause of Hellenism, however, because he imposed political stability at a tremendous cost to Greek manpower, finances, and freedom.

He ruthlessly crushed every vestige of self-government in the Greek cities he absorbed, throttling opposition by transplanting populations that showed the slightest aspirations to independence or oppressing them by the use of mercenaries, including barbarian forces. Depriving these cities of their means of self-defense, he made them utterly dependent on himself, so that when he was succeeded by a weakling son, Dionysius II, his empire collapsed and Sicily once again was plunged into turmoil.

THE RISE OF MACEDONIA

The course of Greek history was altered in the second half of the fourth century by the rise of dominance over the Hellenic world by Macedonia, a state to the north of Old Greece, which until then had played only a peripheral role in history. Ancient Greeks disagreed on the question of accepting the Macedonians as true Hellenes, and differences on the same subject have persisted until modern times, perhaps without good reason. Greeks then were willing enough to acknowledge that the language and institutions of Macedonia were closely related to those of the Hellenes, but they distinguished the Macedonian masses, whom they regarded as barbarians, from their nobility and royalty. The latter were alleged to be Greek by virtue of the direct descent they claimed from Homeric heroes. Greek public opinion recognized them as such, since they were admitted to participation in the Olympic games, the most Hellenic of institutions. Modern research suggests that the Macedonian language was identical grammatically with Greek, of which it was apparently a largely unwritten dialect or *patois* that gradually disappeared under more direct civilizing influences from the south. The fact that the kingdom was ethnically heterogeneous and contained Thracian and Illyrian elements is essentially irrelevant to its "Greekness," because the Greeks to the south themselves were the product of an ancient and complicated genetic mixture, and the term *Hellene* in any case is best understood as cultural, not ethnic.

Early Macedonia.   The Macedonians of the early fourth century seem to be accurately described as Greeks in an arrested state of development. Greeks living in city-states observed that Macedonian institutions, primitive and patriarchal, were like those typical of the rest of Greece at the time of the Dorian invasions many centuries before. Macedonia had not evolved beyond that early stage to create city-states, however, and had remained a monarchy reminiscent of the type known to Homer. Regal authority was generally, but not always, hereditary in the same family and was scarcely absolute, as the landed Macedonian nobles regarded themselves in a certain sense as kings and were always ready as a class to reduce the reigning monarch to a mere first among equals or, as individuals, to usurp his throne. The exercise of power accordingly varied with the character of each ruler, although fundamentally his position made him chief warlord, judge, and priest of his people. The power of the nobility was derived from their ownership of estates and their possession of horses, which they used to dominate the army, whose principal offensive force was the cavalry. Political power was realized by their membership in the council of elders, which nominated new kings and, according to custom, advised them before any important undertaking. As in other primitive Greek states, the commoners—arms-bearing males serving as loosely organized foot soldiers in support of the gentry—were mustered in assembly to give formal assent to decisions of king and council and to approve the nomination of new kings.

Early in the fourth century Macedonia was a sleeping giant, a state many times larger in territory and in population than any *polis*. Her natural resources varied from broad, fertile valleys to extensive forests, which supported a hardy, vigorous, martial population of peasants and shepherds, still subject to a citizen draft in an era when city-state Greeks were relying increasingly on mercenary troops. Some notion of Macedonian character and the cultural state of their country was a requirement that male citizens kill a wild boar single-handedly before they could drink with their peers; Macedonia could field tens of thousands of such men as troops.

Greek culture penetrated only slowly into Macedonia in the latter fifth and early fourth centuries, largely because the kingdom remained commercially primitive and self-sufficient, cut off from direct contact with that most important civilizing avenue, the sea. Greek colonies occupying the northern Aegean seaboard were the intermediaries transmitting Hellenism to Macedonia, which, even before 400 B.C., maintained formal relations and alliances with city-states such as Athens. At the end of the fifth century one Grecophile king, Archelaus, had even exposed his court to Greek drama by inviting the poet Euripides to spend his declining days at Pella, his capital, but for two generations thereafter even the Macedonian nobility had only a smattering of Hellenic culture. A situation more favorable to Hellenization was created early in the fourth century by the energetic king Amyntas III (390–369), who firmly established his own dynasty, but the condition of Macedonia was utterly transformed by Philip II, one of his younger sons, who came to the throne at the age of twenty-three in 359 by usurping power from his own reigning nephew, over whom he had been regent.

Philip II Amyntas.　As a youth, Philip spent the years 367–364 as a hostage in Thebes, where he belonged to the circle of Epaminondas. As a result, he was exposed at first hand to the intracicies of city-state diplomacy and was able to observe the new military reforms that made Thebes, for a season, the dominant city. Once king, Philip single-mindedly aimed at making Macedonia, and therefore his dynasty, the most powerful force in Greece. In spite of his years in Thebes, he had little formal education, although he respected Greek culture sufficiently to summon Aristotle to his court later in his reign to tutor his young son, Alexander. He was very much the Macedonians' ideal as a ruler and won their devotion by revealing himself to be an excellent general, a courageous warrior, and a drinker and womanizer of heroic proportions. One of the most remarkable persons of antiquity, Philip was eclipsed only by his even more extraordinary son, Alexander, as the greatest man of action the Greek world ever produced. Absolutely unscrupulous in gaining his ends, Philip was a Machiavellian politician who had little respect for his own promises and agreements; exploited the weakness of his enemies by using force, intrigues, and bribery; and on occasion exercised his considerable personal charm to win over his opponents by persuasion.

Philip's Reforms.　Once on the throne, Philip consolidated his position by killing or exiling rival pretenders and then unified his kingdom by subduing the Illyrians and the Thracians. As preparation for the eventual territorial expansion of Macedonia, he reorganized the prevailing military system, the inspiration for his reforms probably deriving from Epaminondas, although they were basically a realization of Philip's own military genius. The cavalry remained the main offensive weapon, but he enhanced the relative importance of the infantry, cannily developing a potential manpower pool of perhaps half a million men as a kind of military and political counterpoise to his rivals among the aristocracy. He organized his infantry on the Theban model, except that under his direction the Macedonian phalanx was an even more flexible instrument of warfare. He gave his infantry the opportunity of striking first by rearming them with spears called *sarissae*, which were longer than those commonly used by city-state armies. He so arranged his lines that they could be detached, shortened, or otherwise maneuvered without losing their cohesion. The phalanx of heavy infantry was the core of the battle line, designed to hold the enemy while the cavalry, linked to the phalanx by light infantry and massed at the wings, went over to the offensive. Both infantry and cavalry were styled loosely as the king's "companions," but elite cavalrymen were attached to his person, functioned as a bodyguard, and earned the designation "companions" in a very special sense. This organization, as well as that of the Royal Pages, noble cadets trained by the court to be officers, were effective means of indoctrinating the aristocracy with a loyalty to the crown, which, although still precarious, was yet greater than that enjoyed by any previous king.

This reorganized army had great *esprit*, not only because the Macedonians admired a warlike style but also because Philip cleverly used a sophisticated system of rewards and punishments to spur on his soldiers. Philip was also the first continental European militarist to organize a corps of engineers to produce siege artillery and engines of war. He may have learned of such innovations from Dionysius I of Syracuse, who seems to have invented them, although Philip's use of mobile towers, portable bridges of boats, and catapults that shot bundles of arrows, was more extensive than the Sicilian's. The result of all his reforms was the first large national army in Western history, an elastic, well-rounded, well-coordinated force loyal to its commander and superior to that of any *polis*. Philip used his army to the greatest advantage in strategy and tactics that were brilliantly innovative and caught his enemies off guard. Aside from his feints and false retreats on the battlefield, city-state Greeks thought it rather unfair of him to fight all year round, not just during the traditional campaigning season in good weather. He is also said to have been the first general to make a habit of pursuing a defeated enemy, so that they could not re-form and fight again after a lost battle.

Philip's Aggression (357–346 B.C.). Philip lacked two things to support his new military machine and aggrandize his realm: money and an outlet to the sea. It seemed to him that he could attain both ends by capturing the port of Amphipolis on the Strymon River and its hinterland, which included the rich gold and silver mines of Thrace, and in so doing he revealed his considerable diplomatic talents. Amphipolis was a breakaway Athenian colony, which he promised to capture on Athens' behalf and then restore to her, the Athenian government pledging in return to cede Pydna, an unimportant town on the Macedonian border. Having thus neutralized Athens during his military operations, Philip took Amphipolis but kept it, at one stroke acquiring a yearly income of one thousand talents from Thracian mines to maintain his army, build a navy, and bribe foreign ambassadors and their governments. He was also for the first time in history able to place his kingdom firmly on a money economy with a splendid coinage, which was particularly advantageous to use because it was so flexible. It was bimetallic, both gold and silver. Athens had traditionally minted only silver, and Persia, although using both metals, had never coined enough for her domestic and foreign needs.

Macedonian Imperialism.   The conquest of Amphipolis was only the first step in a series of aggressive moves that made Philip, in two stages and after twenty years, the master of Greece. He was considerably aided by strife both between and within city-states: even though some *poleis* were aware that he threatened them, there was no concerted or united effort to stop his expansion until it was too late. He particularly distinguished himself in immobilizing possible opposition by giving a new twist to internal city-state disputes, using his agents in many cities to win factional support, usually of oligarchs, either by the adroit expenditure of Macedonian money or by promising to back conservative forces in opposing social revolution.

Conditions at Athens, better known than in other cities, illustrate the difficulties the Greeks had in coping with Philip. Athens was a natural leader of resistance against him because of her sea power, yet her policy wavered and was weakened by domestic political divisions. She was distracted by other problems at crucial periods and pursued at times an imperialistic policy of her own, despite its failure perhaps no less Machiavellian than Philip's. Her one consistent interest was maintenance of her lifeline north to the Dardanelles and into the Black Sea, which explains Athenian concern for control over sites in the north Aegean basin. Despite its importance, Athens did not at first fight energetically to keep some sort of control over the area, and for eleven years after the fall of Amphipolis Athenian relations with Macedonia fluctuated between armed truce and undeclared war. In the earliest stages of Philip's aggression, when stopping him would have been easiest, Athenian forces were distracted by the so-called Social War (357–355) with the allies of the Second Naval League. Despite assurances to the contrary, Athens tried to convert this league, like the first, into a naval empire subject to her will. She callously contravened the league charter by preventing states from seceding after Sparta ceased to menace them in 371, by installing cleruchies at Samos and Potidaea, and by permitting her mercenaries to extort tribute. Aided and abetted by Mausolus, tyrant of Caria in southwestern Asia Minor, league cities revolted, many successfully asserting their freedom from Athenian control.

At home Athens suffered from marked factional divisions, which, although not producing civil war, led to frequently bitter disagreements among her statesmen, who might under other circumstances have closed ranks against Philip. At one extreme, there were militant imperialists led by the orators Aristophon and Chares, although their party was discredited by the Social War. More influential thereafter was the moderate and cautious group headed by Eubulus, manager of the Theoric Fund, who believed in conserving Athenian resources and in relying on peaceful development rather than in indulging in any foreign adventures. Advantageous to Philip's cause were the ideas of a faction led by Aeschines, who flirted with treason by holding that opposition to Philip was futile and that Athenian independence and prosperity could best be served by cooperation or alliance with him.

At the latest, after 346, the pro-Macedonian group received important support from the intellectual community when Isocrates, the leading educator in Greece, publicly called Philip a new Hercules who would remedy the ills of Hellas. Isocrates thought that Philip was the ideal man to induce Greeks to abandon domestic animosities and to lead them, as independent states, in a crusade against Persia, thus diverting their bellicose energies against a foreign enemy and solving economic problems by opening up parts of the Persian Empire to colonizing by the surplus Greek population.

Opposition against Philip was slow to find a spokesman, and it was only in 351 that the role was filled by Demosthenes, the great Athenian statesman of the century, whose factional affiliations evolved from imperialistic to pacifist in the sense represented by Eubulus, before he realized the danger in Macedonia. As a brilliantly articulate opponent to Philip, Demosthenes exhorted the Athenians to acknowledge and confront the threat to their freedom.

Philip Penetrates Greece.   Beginning with Amphipolis in 357, the initial thrust of Philip's expansion was aimed at cities along the southern Thracian coast, where he advanced until 351, when he attacked Olynthus. It was this aggression that first aroused Demosthenes' alarm, although he could not galvanize sufficient resistance at Athens to prevent the fall of the city in 348. In the same period Philip was extending his influence southward, into Greece proper. The excuse for his intervention was provided by a quarrel over control of the sanctuary at Delphi, important because its treasury could be used by an occupying power to maintain a mercenary army and so threaten other states. Delphi was seized in 357 by Phocis in defiance of the rest of the amphictyony under the leadership of Thebes, which proclaimed a sacred war. The Phocians held the amphictyony at bay and threatened to expand northward into Thessaly, which appealed to Philip for protection in 353. He drove the Phocians out of Thessaly but was thwarted when southern Greek states in an uncharacteristic moment of unity refused to let him march through Thermopylae and invade Phocis proper in 352. He was by then firmly established south of Mount Olympus, however, and Thessaly insensibly slipped into his sphere of influence.

For reasons similar to those causing the first, a second sacred war broke out in 348 between the Phocians and the amphictyony, which worsened when the Phocians overran Boeotia, Thebes calling on Philip for help. Defeating the Phocians, he was rewarded in 346 with two votes on the amphictyonic council, Macedonia being finally recognized as a Greek state among Greeks and Philip becoming the center of further intrigues.

Philip's Aggression (346-336 B.C.).   The failure of Athens to oust Philip from coastal Thrace or to mobilize all Greeks in a united front against him created an atmosphere conducive to peace, especially as Philip wished to consolidate his gains and desired as yet no more serious confrontation with Athens because he still lacked sea power. Peace was arranged in 346 by ten Athenian ambassadors including Aeschines and Demosthenes, who acknowledged himself momentarily thwarted. The peace terms guaranteed the *status quo*, which meant that they left Philip as the most powerful force. His army had proved to be far better than the mercenary forces of the *poleis*, and his highly personal control of Macedonia far more effective a force than the weak, divided, and spasmodic attempts of Athens to resist him. In the same year he was elected archon, permanent warlord or commander in chief of the Thessalian cities, which became thereby not an integral part of Macedonia but an appendage of the Macedonian crown. Militarily Thessaly was very important to Philip because it gave him control over the best supply of horses in Greece.

Chaeronea. The following years were filled with diplomatic intrigues in which Philip attempted to isolate Athens from potential allies, while Demosthenes tried to forge some sort of anti-Macedonian coalition among Athens, Thebes, and other cities. Nominal peace was kept for three years as Philip extended his sway over Epirus, but then, in 343, he again turned his attention toward the seacoasts to the east and attempted the conquest of Cardia, an Athenian dependency in the Thracian Chersonese, and of Perinthus and Byzantium, important links in the Athenian lifeline. Athens reacted with uncharacteristic vigor in a war (342–340) and thwarted Philip's designs by sending north strong naval reenforcements. Even as late as 340, however, Demosthenes could arouse little enthusiasm for an anti-Macedonian coalition, and in 339 Philip intrigued to exploit to advantage the continued instability within the Delphic League. The amphictyonic council, which by then he dominated, voted to have him lead a war against the Locrians, who had trespassed on temple property. The Athenian government declined to permit Philip to use the council for his further aggrandizement without a fight and at the last moment convinced Thebes to join in leading a resistance against his advance into Greece.

In the spring of 338 the Macedonian king came south and met his enemies in Boeotia, where he almost annihilated the Thebans and thoroughly routed the Athenians in a battle at Chaeronea, which was the beginning of the end of city-state liberty; thereafter the Greek world was dominated by large states, starting with Macedonia. In his organization of Greece in 338–337, Philip intended to make sure that city-states would be properly mobilized to support him, which meant among other things an end to interstate and civil wars. All city-states except Sparta were forced to acknowledge his hegemony by treaty, Sparta's aloofness only tolerated at the price of eventual territorial limitations.

The Corinthian League. The nature of the city-states' agreements with Philip is imperfectly known, although they were generally designed to accommodate rather than to antagonize Greek public opinion. There was no need to change most existing governments, the vast majority already being favorable to him as the result of his cultivation of friendly factions before 338 and of pro-Macedonian revolutions after the Battle of Chaeronea. Only in Thebes did he purge the opposition to leave a sympathetic oligarchy in control. Requiring Athenian naval support, he simply demanded that Athens follow his foreign policy, and he did not even punish Demosthenes. His generally mild treatment of leading city-states was tempered, however, by a realistic appraisal of their future conduct, and he stationed garrisons at strategic sites. He weakened three possible leaders of anti-Macedonian resistance by depriving Thebes of its headship of the Delphic amphictyony, Athens of its allies, and Sparta of territory, which he ceded to Messenia. Otherwise, at least formally, he recognized groupings of city-states like the Boeotian, Arcadian, Phocian, Euboean, and Achaean leagues, as it was easier for him to deal with a small number of fairly large units than with numerous individual *poleis.*

After these preliminary arrangements, he convened in 337 a conference at Corinth of all Greece except Thessaly, which already had its own peculiar relationship to the Macedonian crown, and Sparta, which declined to come. The conference provided him with the means for organizing Greece in support of his own ambition: the constitution of a league, called simply "The Greeks." To maintain the illusion that Greeks were not being coerced, the league was certified as a union of city-states, or groups of them, in the person of Philip as the *hegemon,* or warlord, Macedonia being excluded from membership. The autonomy and protection of each member state was pledged and war between or civil war within them forbidden. Existing constitutions were guaranteed, which provision sanctioned a constitutional situation generally favorable to Philip. The seas were proclaimed open, and no further Macedonian garrisons were to be established. The problem of exiles, a pressing one as a result of the frequent civil wars, was solved by a clause permitting their return and compensation if their property had been confiscated.

In any case, existing property rights were guaranteed. The member states pledged themselves to support Philip with troops and money on demand and in proportion to their resources. An official organ of the league was established in a council or *synedrion* of representatives presided over by Philip and elected by constituent cities or leagues in numbers proportionate to the size of the military units they supplied. The *synedrion* was empowered to regulate disputes between states and could intervene if any of them confiscated property or condemned citizens to death or exile contrary to local law.

The league was an important institution, but it was a military alliance designed to support Philip rather than a true federal organization, because it did not provide for common laws, citizenship, or coinage. Its true purpose was revealed in the first meeting of the *synedrion* at Corinth, which heard and acquiesced in Philip's plans for a projected invasion of the Persian Empire and authorized the draft of troops to prosecute the war. His motives for attacking Persia are not clear, as he left no statement about his objectives. It is even unknown to what extent, if at all, he was influenced by Isocrates' suggestion that Panhellenic colonization of Asia Minor was the solution to Greek wars caused by overpopulation, although he may more narrowly have conceived of purely Macedonian settlements of that type. Perhaps he anticipated forestalling a Persian threat to control of the Dardanelles or more general Persian interference in his hegemony over Greece. In any case, he surely did not contemplate conquest of the whole empire, and he restricted his immediate ambitions to liberating the Greeks of western Asia Minor. In 336 he threw a bridgehead of ten thousand men across the Hellespont under Parmenio, his chief of staff, and was preparing to leave for the campaign when he was assassinated at Pella under mysterious circumstances.

17

The Civilization of the Fourth Century B.C.

INTRODUCTION

Despite defeat in the Peloponnesian War, Athens remained the leading cultural center in the fourth century, the creativity in particular of her philosophers inventively meeting the challenges of interpreting a new world in many respects different from that of the fifth century. Cultural change at Athens and elsewhere was primarily a result of the Sophists, who for the first time created standards of civilization distinct from community traditions and folklore. The Sophists tended to replace values commonly accepted as desirable, like austerity, physical prowess, and conventional patriotism, with an idea of education redefined on the basis of book learning, stressing rhetoric, argumentation, a challenge to traditional religion and morality, and an attack on superstition and magic. The new education could be learned only through professional instruction, and only a few upper-class Greeks could afford the high fees demanded by the Sophists for their lectures or spend the time required for formal education. City-state leaders were most interested in a command of dialectic and rhetoric, those aspects of the new education especially suitable for advancing their own political careers. Study of these subjects also subtly molded their characters, because the Sophists teaching them often had highly individualized ideas of virtue, suggested that ends justified means, and believed that true morality existed in expedient or useful acts.

Popular Culture. While the upper classes looked to professional teachers for personal values, the mass of the citizenry continued to be intitiated into Greek culture through ancient folk institutions like the political assemblies, the courts, and the theaters. Excluded from sophistic education, they increasingly lacked exposure to the most dynamic and creative forces of Hellenic civilization, which had moved to the studies, libraries, and lecture halls of the wealthy. The effect of the Sophists on poetry is clearly seen in the speedy decline in quality of Athenian drama after Euripides. Training by Sophists predisposed the most creative literary minds to prefer prose over poetry as their medium of expression, so that the most characteristic and outstanding literary works of the fourth century were in prose. Although poetic tragedies were still written, they lacked the spontaneity of the

241

great fifth-century dramas. The delicate interplay between the patriotic or religious inspiration of playwrights and the ingenuous involvement of citizens in what had been the emotionally moving experience of a genuine folk art lost relevance in a much more personal and specialized world, where ancient religious and political ideals were often less immediate. Even the writing of comedy was affected by the tastes of the newly emerging upper class of the genteel and well read, and the last plays of Aristophanes (died 385 B.C.) reflect the taste of such audiences for works that were less earthy and ribald, more sedate and introspective, than had been the case in the heyday of the Old Comedy.

Ethics.   By challenging traditional morality through its relativism and pluralism, sophistry spawned the philosophy of ethics, which for the first time branched completely away from natural science. The first and surely greatest ethical philosopher, as we have seen, was Socrates, an outstanding specimen of the human race, one of the most important figures in the intellectual history of classical antiquity, and a significant molder of the Western outlook. His impact on the continued development of Greek thought in the fourth century was tremendous, even though only a small minority of his friends and associates turned out to be philosophers themselves. However, as Socrates had posed basic questions concerning the proper ideals of state and society just as city-states throughout the entire Greek world were in political difficulties, the more talented or sensitive among his disciples further developed his quest for *arete* by stressing certain aspects of his thought.

CYRENAICS AND CYNICS

One disciple, Aristippus of Cyrene (ca. 435-356), chose to emphasize that aspect of Socratic doctrine identifying virtue with happiness. He and his followers, known as the Cyrenaic School, discarded preference for intellectual pleasures. Even when indulging themselves in physical luxuries, however, the Cyrenaics acknowledged that the wise and virtuous person should use prudent self-control as a hedonist, because immediate pleasures might well yield an overcompensating degree of later pain. The Cyrenaics held that the law and customs of the community should be respected only insofar as they gave pleasure to the citizenry, because, by definition, the virtuous person would abstain from what was unjust in the pursuit of pleasure.

Socrates made a rather different impression on another follower, Antisthenes (ca. 440-365). Like the Cyrenaics, Antisthenes rejected the purely rational or spiritual side of Socratic teaching, but he pursued the ideal of self-sufficiency, which he interpreted to mean rejection by the truly wise of any accommodation with imperfection and evil in the world. Preaching against the hypocritical conventions of civilized communities masquerading as virtuous laws, he was unique in directing his exhortations to the poor and humble. The name of his philosophy, *Cynicism,* derives from the Greek word for dog (*cyon*), which to contemporaries aptly described the way of living of the "Cynics." Cynicism was really a mode of life rather than a system of thought, and Antisthenes lived up to the Socratic dictum of living simply and naturally. An exaggerated individualist, he preached the universality of all humankind in the sense that one was a cosmopolite, a citizen of the universe and not of any particular *polis.*

PLATO

Socratic doctrine was most notably transcended and expanded by the Athenian nobleman Plato (429–347), perhaps the most creative—and certainly the most influential—mind in intellectual history. An artistic, intuitive personality, Plato, had he been born a century earlier, would probably have been a poet or a statesman. His pursuit of philosophy, not government, reflects the impact of Socrates on his life and his disillusionment with Athens after his master's death. His choice of prose as a medium of expression was characteristic of the aesthetic tastes of his own generation, even though he gave it a grace and a clarity bordering on the poetic and therefore compatible with the essential nature of his thought.

Virtue. It appears that Plato built on Socrates' idea of virtue or *arete,* as having a political purpose and concluded that the obvious problems of society in his day could never be solved until philosophers became rulers or vice versa. To propagate his theories of truth, virtue, and government, he founded in 387, and later endowed, a formal school in a house called the Academy, because it was located adjacent to a garden sacred to the hero Academus in a northwestern suburb of Athens. During the more than nine hundred years of its existence, which even outlasted antiquity, the Academy stood as a symbol for much of what was original in Greek thought.

Plato went beyond the limited, if striking, Socratic realization of virtue as something knowable or teachable and developed what was a medical theory of images or ideas, a concept of one fundamental characteristic shared by many individual cases. For Plato, virtue was an idea whose essence was knowledge and whose observable characteristics were courage, prudence, piety, and justice. Like Socrates, he opposed the moral relativism of the Sophists, and even though they all had something in common in the use of dialectic, he at first rejected their assumption that the adroit use of words was very important to the discovery of the truth. This was so because, although words might describe individual cases in arriving at the idea of *arete,* the idea itself was indescribable because it was pure reason.

Platonists found the models closest to his so-called Theory of Forms (ideas) not in rhetoric but in mathematics. They would claim that in studying a diagram or a formula and suddenly arriving at the concept of a theorem, one realizes its validity not from empirical observation of lines and numbers, which merely help the process along, but from insight within one's mind. Thus knowledge of the truth of the Pythagorean theorem was always within the brain, simply to be realized by the study of a formula on paper. The idea of the Good is similarly innate; remembered ultimately from a previous existence, it has to be evoked by the observation of imperfectly good people in one's experience. It seemed to Plato that the peculiar genius of Socrates was his realization of that fact, his ability to draw insight out of his pupils rather than to teach by giving them information like the Sophists.

The Republic.   After the early *Dialogues* in which Socrates was the chief protag-onist, Plato's theories found further expression (ca. 380–370) in a most influential work, the *Republic.* Even if his ultimate interest was making individuals virtuous, he believed that they could not attain *arete* unless the state assumed the responsi-bility for educating the citizenry in the four cardinal virtues. Like most other Greek ethical philosophers, he assumed as a matter of course that an ideal state would take the form of a *polis.* The only one in Greece that presumed to educate its citizens was Sparta, and because Plato thought that Spartan virtues approximated the cardinal ones, Sparta's system of government became the superficial model for the utopia he described.

Plato's city-state was supposed to promote unity, not the accumulation of wealth or power. Its citizens would need no written laws because they would be trained to obey the unwritten, conceptual Law of *Arete.* One premise conditioning his social thought was the fact that people differed·by nature and ability, so that the *Repub-lic* was based on three classes: workers, guards, and leaders, each with a particular and suitable education. They were not castes, and the Platonic *Republic* left room for mobility. Because families were by definition self-centered organisms, possibly detrimental to social unity and the stability of the larger community, he abolished them and decreed the common sharing of women and children for the guardian class. His second premise was that revolution and war were economic in origin and were caused by greed. To avoid such disturbing movements, he decided that the ideal city-state should be as isolated and as economically primitive as possible.

His educational curriculum for training the class of leaders to practice virtue was very conservative. The traditional arts of gymnastics, music, and poetry formed its core, with a special emphasis on models or examples of the four cardinal virtues. Anything incompatible with these standards was to be excised from the training, and even those parts of Homer, the most revered author in the Greek repertory, not conducive to the inspiration of courage, prudence, piety, and justice were to be censored. This primary education of leaders was followed in their maturity by exposure to dialectic, postponed until after childhood so as not to be misused by young and impressionable minds, which might question commonly accepted com-munity mores. The man excelling in dialectic, called upon to rule the state as king, would assume leadership because he recognized it as his duty. Plato thought that knowledge of dialectic was absolutely necessary for the ideal ruler because only a dialectician could apprehend and cope with reality. In the last analysis, poetry was not very necessary in the ruler's training because it was directed at the cultivation not of reason but of emotion and passion, which were irrational. Thus, in the last analysis, he thought that even the revered Homer had no really essential place in his ideal state. Plato was very interested in putting his theories into practice and made several trips to Syracuse to convince the tyrants Dionysius I and II to assume the role of philosopher-king, but he was disappointed in this hope.

The Laws.   As he grew older, Plato modified rather considerably the theories expressed in his early dialogues and in the *Republic.* He even further poeticized and made more transcendental his idea of goodness by identifying it, like Anaxagoras and Socrates, with a creating and intelligent god, the measure of all things. He gradually came to appreciate rhetoric, which, at its best, was clear and logical, a suitable means to express the truth because it was beautiful.

Perhaps as a result of his failure to realize his utopian republic, he revised his plans for the ideal state (ca. 370–350), the result being a long book, the *Laws,* which was published posthumously. In it, he expressed his conception of the pre-history of the human race as peaceful, moral, and simple, with no need for law-givers. His own age had obviously fallen far from this primitive ideal, and the belief that a republic could get along without written laws was a naive mistake. In the *Laws,* therefore, he set down practical regulations for every detail of life. Although he still believed that thinking men should rule the ignorant, he decided that mon-archy, after all, was not the ideal form of government. He tended to agree with some other political scientists, like the educator Isocrates, that the city-state should be provided with a constitution having mixed monarchic, aristocratic, and demo-cratic elements, with aristocracy predominating. Once again, he thought he saw in Sparta the closest model to the preferred constitution.

ARISTOTLE

Plato's most brilliant pupil and critic, Aristotle (384–322 B.C.), was the son of the court physician to the king of Macedonia and was initially destined to follow his father's profession. He went to Athens at the age of seventeen, however, and first attended the school of Isocrates before falling under Plato's spell when the latter returned to Athens from the court of Dionysius II (ca. 366). Aristotle re-mained affiliated with the Academy for twenty years, until Plato's death in 347. Thereafter he was called to Pella (ca. 343) by Philip II to be tutor to the young Alexander, in which capacity he remained in Macedonia for three years. He then returned to Athens, where, in 335, he opened his own school, the Lyceum, so called from the nearby garden of Lycus. His students, called Peripatetics because of their master's habit of walking about while lecturing, soon rivaled those of the Academy and produced some of the most characteristic thinkers of the Greek world.

Aristotle's genius was very different from Plato's because his instincts were those not of an inspired artist but of a down-to-earth pedagogue, scholar, and scientist. His interests were much broader, if less profound, than Plato's, and his development of a certain competence in so many different fields foreshadowed the encyclopedic intellectual interests of the following, Hellenistic period of Greek history. Aris-totle's contributions to the conception of history, biology, and botany are perhaps best understood in relation to that period, and discussion of his contributions at this point will be restricted to his interest in epistemology, ethics, and politics.

Empiricism. Plato's theory of ideas seemed to Aristotle to be too distant from the physical world and to underrate the importance of empiricism. Aristotle sought to bridge the gap between general concepts and empirically measurable phenomena so that they could describe each other. In so doing, he invented the syllogism, the deduction of a judgment from two other judgments. The act of deduction was an inference, the thought process relating the two original judgments, one of which had to be properly subordinated to the other for the syllogism to work logically. The syllogism is an essential clue to the workings of Aristotle's mind, which was at its best when gathering observed data and then classifying them according to types. Aristotle disagreed with Plato's emphasis on ideas at the apparent expense of underrating the significance of their realization in physical, empirically measurable individuals. He therefore conceived of the existence of something not in an idea but in the observable unfolding of nature in the physical universe. Building on the Socratic and Platonic notion of humans as rational, he concluded that virtue was a state of mind through which humans realized their essence by acting reasonably. Rational behavior itself would give people insights into what was right and proper and suggested a suitably Socratic exercise of self-control over the strongest impulses and emotions.

Like Plato, Aristotle wanted to solve contemporary city-state problems, but his very different approach to political science characterized his method of dealing with data and also revealed some of the limitations inherent in his system. An inference in an Aristotelian syllogism depended on the collection and observation of facts to form the first two premises. Aristotle was ethnocentric enough to convince himself that the city-state was the only really suitable form of government because it offered the greatest opportunity for rational self-development of individuals. He therefore arrived at the first premise of a syllogism in his famous judgment that "Man, by nature, is a political animal," that is, that he was destined to live in a *polis*. But city-states themselves differed in stability, so that Aristotle had to decide the kind of city-state constitution most suitable to man's ethical development. He assigned his students the collection of data on the constitutions of as many *poleis* as possible to determine which tended to be the stablest periods of their development because he thought that the laws of organic nature applied to constitutional history, certain phases of which would be the most flourishing. In the case of Athens he concluded that the most desirable state came under Cleisthenes, when the propertied classes balanced and restrained the democratic elements, and he implied that to reattain greatness, fourth-century Athens should return to the constitution of the sixth century B.C.

XENOPHON

Men having intellectual interests like those of Plato and Aristotle were very unusual even in Greek society, and a personality more nearly typifying the normal, upper-class viewpoint was Xenophon (434–ca. 354). Talented but uncomplicated, Xenophon was associated with the Socratic circle as a young man, although he was not at all interested in philosophy. An opponent of democracy, he was banished from Athens, became a soldier of fortune serving Cyrus the Younger in 401 with the ten thousand mercenaries, and, after leading them out of Persia, settled down to live for almost fifty years near Laconia on an estate given him by the Spartan government. He returned to Athens shortly before his death.

Xenophon was a prolific writer, a journalist by instinct, and his literary output ranged over many topics. He wrote a *Panhellenic History* covering the years 411–362, conceiving of it as a sequel to Thucydides. Although important as a source for the period, it lacks the analytical quality of its model. His most famous work was the *Anabasis,* describing the march of the ten thousand out of Persia, an influential account of Hellenic military courage because it suggests that Persia was a giant with clay feet ready to fall before the first Greek conqueror. He wrote two books that expressed his interest in outstanding personalities and did much to contribute to the development of biography as a separate literary genre: *Memoirs* of Socrates, whom he portrayed as a commonplace old codger rather than a sublime thinker, and the *Cyropaideia,* a romanticized life of the young Cyrus the Great, in which he indicated his admiration of the simplicity inherent in the training of hard-riding, straight-shooting Persian nobles. The *Cyropaideia* also pointed the way toward an increasing cosmopolitanism of the Greeks, Xenophon's belief in the superiority of Greek culture obviously having been tempered by a recognition that admirable qualities could also be found even among barbarians.

In his own way, Xenophon was no less interested than Socrates and Plato in educating Athenians, although he thought more simply than they in terms of restoring Athenian power. To that end, he suggested a program of state-sponsored education based on Persian and Spartan models, and his interest in Sparta as a second state worthy of emulation found expression in his *Constitution of the Lacedaemonians,* which unfortunately provides few penetrating insights into Spartan history. His notion of ideal education, which was simple and unintellectual, is also implicit in the *Oeconomicus,* in which he praised the old-fashioned value of country living to a gentleman farmer like himself, and in the *Cynogeticus,* in which he suggested that hunting was desirable training in physical fitness, endurance, and self-control.

ISOCRATES

Neither ethical philosophers nor old-school gentlemen like Xenophon influenced as many educated people in the fourth century B.C. as Isocrates (436–338), one of the outstanding professional teachers of antiquity. The first native Athenian exponent of rhetoric and a pupil of the famous Sophists Gorgias and Protagoras, Isocrates preferred to call himself a "philosopher," understanding by that term a man of broad intellectual cultivation or *paideia,* and he had no patience with Sophists who were morally irresponsible. Ethnocentric in the traditional sense of believing that the essence of Hellenism was *paideia,* he reflected on an educated level the cosmopolitanism of Xenophon by stating that some foreigners might be receptive to *paideia,* and some Greeks not.

Rhetoric. Because he was a poor forensic orator and could not hope to be a successful politician, Isocrates capitalized on his theoretical knowledge of rhetoric by opening a school at Athens in about 390 B.C. Through his pupils and his own published works, he attempted to affect contemporary politics, and with some success. Even more important was his foundation of that kind of humanistic education emphasizing the development and use of attractive prose style, which dominated the Western educational tradition until the end of antiquity and from the Renaissance until the twentieth century A.D., when it has been gradually displaced by greater emphasis on the social, physical, and natural sciences.

Isocrates conceived of rhetoric as being much more than training in artistic written or oral expression. It was a practical tool for leaders, who were to use it to improve Greece, because he fervently believed that the power of expression was the civilizing power of persuasion and explanation, the only faculty separating humankind from inarticulate beasts. Unlike the Sophists, however, Isocrates thought that the true orator should have positive values and a firm belief in what was the proper form of society and government. He disagreed with Socrates and did not think that ultimate values could be proved dialectically. For this reason, he was often impatient with and hostile to the Socratics, particularly Plato, because they seemed to raise false hopes of attaining provable knowledge of virtue and led to cloistered, utopian theories, whereas he, Isocrates, wanted practical solutions to contemporary political problems. He was sufficiently sophistic to hold that ideals were ultimately matters of opinion rather than knowledge, common sense rather than proof, so that the social and political standards he advocated were those held widely by upper-class men like himself.

Foreign Policy. Isocrates aimed to make the Greeks not ethically perfect but as prosperous and powerful as possible by uniting them and ending class struggles and by diverting warlike energies and superfluous population into a war against Persia. He expressed his views in a series of open letters to the Greek world and its leaders, beginning with the *Panegyricus* (380), in which he encouraged Athens and Sparta to abandon their old animosity in the cause of Panhellenic unity. The Battle of Leuctra and the collapse of the Second Naval League, however, caused him to reexamine his assumptions that either state was a potential leader and produced his searching analysis of the Athenian constitution in the *Areopagiticus* (355) to discover what went wrong. Although his analysis did not correspond to the facts, like Aristotle at a later date he convinced himself that the government was weakened by rule of an uncultivated mob over an educated minority, and he advocated a return to the constitution of Solon or Cleisthenes, when, it seemed, the "better" (propertied) citizens prevailed. In his essay *On Peace* of the same year, he took a position close to that of Eubulus, manager of the Theoric Fund, by advocating financial consolidation, abolition of domestic poverty, and abandonment forever of Athenian imperialism in Greece.

Government. Approving of moderate oligarchy at Athens, Isocrates was always interested in monarchy on a theoretical level. His conception of it is illustrated by the instructions he drew up for the education of Nicocles, king of Cyprus, which contrast with Plato's ideal curriculum for rulers. Isocrates' exhortation that the king use self-control and philanthropy was commonplace enough, as was his emphasis on study of the poets like Homer and Hesiod, dialectic being given no necessary role. His inclusion of history was a new feature, and he was the first to apply it as a tool for statesmen, adapting Thucydides' suggestion that history might have practical value. Isocrates himself was influential in determining the canons of historiography for the rest of antiquity. Interested primarily in the sophistic, psychological, and stylistic aspects of Thucydidean history, he eschewed its real essence, which was detached and scientific. Because history was to be a tool for politicians, he conceived of it as moralistic, a matter of praising or blaming statesmen, and rhetorical, as he held that objectivity should always yield to a dramatic or moving style. His concept of what history should be became the norm observed by succeeding historians, like Ephorus of Cyme, who wrote the standard reference work of Greek history to 356 B.C.; Theopompus, who portrayed Greece in the age of Philip II; and the Atthidographer Androtion.

Isocrates' disillusionment with the ability of Sparta and Athens to unify Greece and his interest in the training of princes led him to write open letters to strong men to convince them to organize the Panhellenic crusade against the Persians. Jason, tyrant of Pherae in Thessaly; Dionysius I of Syracuse; and Archidamus III of Sparta—all declined to be persuaded by Isocrates' blandishments, and at last (346) he turned to Philip II of Macedonia. Encouraging Philip to use diplomacy to persuade the leading powers—Sparta, Thebes, Argos, and Athens—to cooperate, Isocrates believed that the remaining states would also follow his lead in a Persian war. Philip, he argued, would gain fame and goodwill and would be honored "as a god" by his Greek followers. There is no indication that Philip ever read, or was affected by, this letter. In any case, subsequent events did not evolve as Isocrates intended, and the ancient educator lived to witness the death throes of a free Greece in the very year of the Battle of Chaeronea, when Philip imposed unity by using the mailed fist and not peaceful persuasion.

DEMOSTHENES

Predictably, the study of rhetoric produced a series of famous orators, starting with the metic Lysias at the beginning of the century and culminating in Demosthenes (384-322), a brilliant combination of orator and statesman and one of the most famous Athenians of any epoch. Unlike other political scientists of his day, he was an active politician, very flexible in his views on government and society, at the last stage of his career even a democrat. The son of a wealthy factory owner, he had to fight in court on reaching his majority to claim his inheritance from greedy relatives and guardians, and the speeches he made on his own behalf made him the first person in Western history whose youth can be reconstructed in some detail. Success at law, of course, meant command of rhetoric, and he studied with Isocrates' chief rival, Isaeus, although his own prose displays Isocratean and even Thucydidean turns of phrase. At first embarrassed and inhibited before an audience, he earned his living as a speech writer for others, in which capacity he mustered the commonly accepted technique of describing the pleaders' own character, which, rather than the point of the suit, was the main element in swaying Athenian jurymen.

Orations. Demosthenes was a member of that generation of Athenians drawn into politics during the rise of the Second Naval League, and at first, he was an enthusiastic supporter of its conversion into an instrument of Athenian imperialism.

FIGURE 40. Demosthenes, Athenian orator and statesman, 384–322 B.C.

The Granger Collection

Thereafter his political career, as evidenced in his speeches, shows a certain evolution, although his main interest was always foreign policy. Following the Social War, he seems to have taken a stand close to that of Isocrates and Eubulus, and in his speech of 354 *On the Symmories,* he supported peace abroad and financial retrenchment at home, which would have spared the rich from excessive taxation. Influenced by Thucydides' notions of the balance of power, he moved away from Eubulus' isolationism, and in the oration *For the Megalopolitans* (352), he conceived of Athens as a third force counteracting the power of Thebes and Sparta.

This stand was followed rather quickly by the realization that Philip was a real danger to Athens and to all of Greece, and in 351 Demosthenes delivered the first of three *Philippic Orations,* in which, perhaps anachronistically, he assumed the role of a great democratic leader in the Periclean tradition. Believing that the Athenians could face the danger if they only understood it, he appealed directly to the electorate to inform them of the Macedonian threat, thus interpreting the role of the orator as an educator. He believed as passionately as Socrates, Plato, Aristotle, Xenophon, and Isocrates that the city-state was a viable institution. If his Athenian patriotism seems narrowly nationalistic in the light of the vast expansions of political horizons soon to be effected by Macedonian power, Demosthenes cannot be faulted for calling on the Athenians to defend their liberty, as they themselves understood the term.

ART AND ARCHITECTURE

The profound changes in cultural outlook appearing in belles-lettres and ethical philosophy toward the end of the fifth century B.C. were also apparent in the development of the plastic arts. Although the fourth century is sometimes interpreted as a concluding phase of the "classical" age, it seems more fitting to regard it as the formative period of aesthetic genres and outlooks that characterized the concluding, Hellenistic phase of Greek civilization.

Sculpture.   Surviving specimens of the work of fourth-century sculptors and the reputations they enjoyed in antiquity indicate stylistic shifts that reflected in works of bronze and marble the impact of sophistry on literature. Beauty and grace replaced nobility and grandeur as primary artistic canons. Fourth-century works of art display a maturity and a richness that contrast with the more vigorous, slightly abstract, and rather distant feeling imparted by the more "classical" works of the fifth century. Artists for the first time were interested in portraying individuals as distinct personalities, and this humanizing of types was most clearly expressed in the first portrait statues and in the interpretation of the gods as ordinary mortals. Interest in the psychological element is especially noticeable in the rendering of mythological genres, which no longer attempted to inspire pious awe, as had been the case in the fifth century, but to depict essentially human feelings, sometimes dramatically. Until the reign of Alexander the Great, relatively more goddesses and fewer gods were portrayed, probably because of the increasing popularity of the worship of Demeter, Persephone, and Aphrodite. Divinities were no longer depicted as having superhuman dignity, and for the first time since very primitive days, the motive of the nude goddess was accepted.

Among the outstanding artists whose work set trends was Praxiteles of Athens (fl. 375-330). In portraying gods and goddesses, he wanted to reveal what was sensitive, the emotion of mood rather than passion, in which he foreshadowed certain Hellenistic preferences. His most famous statue was the nude Aphrodite of Cnidus, whose soft, rather flabby lines resemble those of other fourth-century works. Praxiteles' portrayal of gods is very interesting. His Apollo the Lizard Slayer, for example, depicts not a transcendental force but a simple youth, and an unenlightened observer would never recognize in him the presence of divinity. The famous Apollo Belvedere (ca. 350) by another sculptor, Leochares, reveals divine authority not in the manner of the fifth century with manly, athletic stance, but emotionally and theatrically. A similar contrast of types appears between the Ludovisi Hermes of that same century, especially striking because of its concentration of energy, and the Hermes of Praxiteles. Quite possibly an original work of the Greek master and not a Roman copy, Praxiteles' interpretation of the god, as he dangles a bunch of grapes before the baby Dionysus, is light, playful, relaxed, and even dreamy. The treatment of the god's body is not that of a lean, fifth-century athlete; it is fleshy and even faintly effeminate. Praxiteles is noted for the special effect he created by shifting the weight of his statues so as to thrust a hip outward and produce a rather pleasing S-shaped curve.

Skopas of Paros (fl. ca. 350), along with Praxiteles, was very important as a stylistic innovator influencing later Hellenistic artists. Nothing certainly attributable to his studio survives, although he is said to have collaborated with other sculptors in decorating with statuary the Mausoleum of Halicarnassus, the Temple of Athena Alea at Tegea, and perhaps the reconstructed Temple of Artemis at Ephesus. Unlike Praxiteles, he is supposed to have excelled at portraying passion, especially anger and violence, which he may have expressed by suitable handling of face and body postures. Some heads from the Temple at Tegea, possibly his work, render forceful emotion through deep-set eyes and a striking impressionistic ridge of flesh just above the eyebrows.

A rather different artistic genius was Lysippus of Sicyon, one of the most prolific sculptors of antiquity, who allegedly produced fifteen hundred statues of gods and athletes, as well as portraits. His very long life almost spanned the fourth century, during which his style apparently underwent considerable evolution. His longevity combined with his originally conservative artistic tastes to give him a significance rather different from that of Praxiteles and Skopas, because he was more distinctly a transitional figure from classical to Hellenistic styles. He is said to have preferred neither idealism nor naturalism and to have quipped that while other sculptors portrayed men as they were, he preferred to depict them as they appeared to be. He abandoned canonical proportions in portraying the nude male, making the head smaller and the body slimmer and less muscular, thus increasing apparent height. He was the official sculptor to Alexander the Great from the latter's boyhood, rendering the adult king in a heroic manner blending both human and divine qualities.

Painting.   On the Greek mainland few vases were decorated after about 400 B.C., although the tradition of ceramic painting was maintained by the colonial Greeks of south Italy. According to tradition, however, the greatest painter in all of antiquity, Apelles, worked during the period. Official painter to the Macedonian court, he was famous for his portraits of Philip II, and especially of Alexander the Great, and for an allegorical composition entitled "Aphrodite Rising from the Waves." He apparently invented the chiaroscuro technique, used line and color naturalistically, and successfully mastered problems of perspective so as to impart to his works a feeling of depth.

FIGURE 41. The Palaestra at Olympia, site of the Olympic Games of antiquity.

The Granger Collection

Architecture. In the field of architecture the fourth century B.C. was a transitional phase between classicism and the Hellenistic period. It witnessed a notable diversification of building types, a decline in the relative importance of temple architecture, and a corresponding rise in secular architecture. The evolution of the theater reached its most developed form at Epidaurus, a well-engineered structure noted for its permanent *skene* and the large ramps leading to the stage from each side. By the end of the century the form of gymnasia, which had developed out of open-air athletic training grounds in public parks, had been standardized as wide interior peristyles surrounded by porticoes and rooms for exercise, lectures, and entertainment. Domestic house architecture gradually moved toward the so-called peristyle plan and so became much more livable than austere classical dwellings.

Two monuments in particular pointed toward future, Hellenistic trends: the Temple of Artemis at Ephesus and the Mausoleum at Halicarnassus, both dating from mid-century and both regarded by the ancients as among the Seven Wonders of the World. The former illustrates the tendency to increase temple size to overpowering proportions. It rested not on a simple stylobate but on a gigantic stepped podium, where two rows of monumental columns, mounted on double bases, led to the cella, which was entered through a large portico. The Mausoleum, tomb of Mausolus, the puppet ruling Caria for the Persians, inaugurated a new kind of sepulchral architecture popular in the Hellenistic period. The richness and extravagance of its decoration also pointed toward an increasingly ornate character in building. The decorative element in fourth-century architecture was sometimes expressed in the mixing of Doric and Ionic orders, the further development of the Corinthian style, and a general elongation of columns. A certain sterility was apparent in merely giving greater refinement to preexisting techniques, which were replaced by new conceptions only in the century after Alexander the Great.

18

Alexander the Great

SOURCE PROBLEMS

Greece and the Near East were transformed by Alexander the Great, the extraordinary son of Philip II Amyntas. Our knowledge of Alexander's career and personality scarcely matches their interest, as his life must be reconstructed almost exclusively from literary sources of limited value. The historical traditions about him that survive from antiquity are contradictory, so that he may be seen either as a heroic embodiment of idealistic Hellenism or as a half-barbarian adventurer. Many of his associates and contemporaries described his conquests and other exploits, but none of these works has survived except in fragments excerpted by later writers. Contemporary accounts apparently varied widely in their purpose and credibility and, with one possible exception, did not seriously study his character. Most of his associates preferred to write memoirs about him without attempting a comprehensive account of all aspects of his life, and the works of others, having no claim to history, mixed truth and fantasy, with the result that they transmitted much gossip and propaganda. Political prejudice colored most of this lost literature, because Alexander generated partisan animosities even more violent than those felt for his father.

Modern historians recognize several traditions in the ancient literature concerning Alexander: one that was relatively disinterested, another deriving from court historians and propagandists, and a third overtly hostile to him. The first depends ultimately on the lost works of three men closely associated with the expedition against Persia: the general Ptolemy Lagos, the engineer Aristobulus, and the admiral Nearchus. These works were consulted by a Greek author, Arrian, who wrote an *Anabasis* of Alexander in about A.D. 125, which survives as the most trustworthy source for the king's campaigns.

The second or "vulgate" tradition derives from lost accounts like those of Aristotle's cousin, Callisthenes, the expedition's official historian, who portrayed Alexander heroically; the chamberlain Chares, who wrote piquant anecdotes of his court life; and especially the Sophist Cleitarchus, whose very rhetorical biography of the king improved on facts for the sake of effect. Such a book was the prototype of the Alexander Romance, a fantastic genre of folktales about the king that arose in the Near East during the early Middle Ages and survived to modern times.

The tradition hostile to Alexander prevailed among Greek intelligentsia and in Rome until the time of Arrian. It arose in Athenian philosophical schools, especially the Lyceum, which the king alienated by his eventual execution of Callis-thenes, who became for the Peripatetics a tyrant's martyr. Tendentious traditions, both idealizing and hostile, affected even Arrian's book, although their influence is much greater on other surviving accounts of Alexander, which are therefore less reliable sources for his life. These latter are all products of Greek and Roman authors writing, like Arrian, under the Roman Empire, hence many centuries after their subject. The most famous of them is the Greek biographer Plutarch (ca. A.D. 100), who was interested in relating anecdotes from the king's life that might give his readers instruction in morality. Plutarch's ability to weigh sources and inter-pret evidence critically was limited, so that his *Life* of Alexander often mixes fact with fancy.

Granted the sketchy, confusing, and generally unsatisfactory state of the sources concerning the personality and motivations of this extraordinary man, it is no wonder that modern historians have disagreed widely concerning his mission and achievements. An earlier generation of twentieth-century scholars tended to see Alexander as a romantic idealist, a kind of apostle of Hellenism to the Near East. But every generation tends to reinterpret the past in terms of its own historical experience, and it is therefore understandable that a current influential school of historians has revised the earlier interpretation of him along more "realistic" (their critics would say "cynical") lines. The revisionists see Alexander as a cold-blooded, even ruthless, autocrat not unlike twentieth-century dictators, and it is this inter-pretation that has most affected the pages that follow.

ALEXANDER'S YOUTH

Alexander was born in 356 B.C. of the marriage between a tempestuous Epirote princess, Olympias, his filial attachment to whom was perhaps unnaturally close, and Philip II. It is difficult to discover the truth behind the anecdotes, deriving from Chares and known to Plutarch, concerning his childhood because they may have been invented after the fact to suggest early signs of precocity. The relative extent to which his heredity from two passionate parents and his environment at the rough-and-ready, semibarbaric Macedonian court contributed to development of his character is naturally unknown. As an adult he was violent and impression-able, recklessly brave yet a careful planner, persistent and generous, but also cun-ning and ruthless. As an adolescent he at least seems to have convinced his father that he was a natural leader because the king made him regent of Macedonia when he was abroad fighting in 340 and gave him command of the left wing at Chaeronea in 338.

Education. It is difficult to establish the influence of formal education on Alexander's development. He had many teachers, including his mother's relative Leonidas, and then for two years beginning in 343 B.C. Aristotle, who was sum-moned to Pella and remained there until after Alexander ascended the throne. What Aristotle taught the prince and what the boy was prone to learn are unknown. There is no reason to believe that the philosopher established any kind of moral

FIGURE 42. Bust of Alexander the Great, 356–323 B.C.

The Granger Collection

ascendancy over his young charge or that he inspired him with idealistic or sentimental phil-Hellenic feelings. Certainly Aristotle's concept of the city-state as the ideal form of government made no discernible impression on Alexander's political outlook, nor did the philosopher's advice, given him shortly after his accession, to treat barbarians as slaves and animals change his pragmatic way of dealing with people once he was king. Aristotle was perhaps more successful in making his pupil appreciative of Greek literature, particularly Homer, and interested in investigating exotic flora and fauna. Such pursuits did not necessarily indicate, however, a very Hellenized person because Alexander the Great's Greek culture was, so far as we know, not very different from that of certain satraps and dynasts serving Persia in Asia Minor, who were little more than superficial "culture-Greeks."

Family Feuds. Philip II's reforms had the effect of converting noble rivalries into cabals at his court, and he exacerbated the situation by divorcing Olympias and marrying the noblewoman Cleopatra in 337 B.C. Alexander's former admiration of his father turned to repugnance. Philip and his son were estranged because although a Macedonian prince normally expected his father to have casual *amours,* formal marriage to another woman might potentially threaten his own succession. Both Alexander and his mother were forced to leave Pella, she for her native Epirus, he for Illyria, although he was permitted to return after a superficial reconciliation was arranged with Philip. Alexander's position was nevertheless insecure, and neither he nor others in a position to know apparently rated his chances of gaining the throne very highly, the faction of one Attalus, Cleopatra's uncle, having gained ascendancy at court. Some courtiers even believed that Alexander engineered his father's assassination in 336, although this was probably malicious gossip. In any case, he was presented to the army, which acclaimed him king. He promptly charged Attalus and his supporters with the guilt of Philip's death and wiped them out, even their children. Alexander was thus raised to power by a noble clique, which intended, no doubt, to rule through him. The constant political factor behind his subsequent military campaigns was his spectacularly successful assertion of his own independence from their tutelage.

MACEDONIA VERSUS PERSIA

The prestige of Alexander's crown depended on validation of his role as a military leader, and he thus could scarcely avoid committing himself to prosecution of his father's projected Persian War. Like those of Philip II, his initial military ambitions were undoubtedly limited to occupying parts of Asia Minor, and only later did vistas of ever greater conquests gradually unfold before him.

Whereas Parmenio enlarged his bridgehead at the Hellespont in 336–335 by attacking, with some success, the neighboring Greek cities in Asia Minor subject to the Great King, Alexander prudently decided to secure his northern frontiers before leaving for Asia. He campaigned across the Danube in 335, pacifying hostile tribes and making a treaty of mutual nonaggression with Celtic peoples migrating there. During his temporary loss of contact with Macedonia and Greece, a rumor spread that he had been killed in battle. Thebes actually revolted against Macedonian control, but in a lightning strike south from the Danube basin, Alexander crushed the rebellion. He intended to terrorize the rest of Greece by destroying the city utterly, but he avoided the opprobrium that would have attached to so brutal a measure by having the doom of Thebes duly voted by the *synedrion* of Hellenes, an action technically conforming to the league charter. Then, as a studied gesture to win Greek public opinion by advertising his clemency, he intervened to spare the Theban temples and the poet Pindar's house. He was then free to turn his attention to Asia.

Macedonia versus Persia.   The final outcome of a struggle between Macedonia and Persia was by no means predictable in 334 B.C. In some respects the Persian Empire seemed extremely vulnerable. Xenophon's march of the ten thousand suggested that a hostile Greek army under proper leadership could traverse it successfully. The revolt of Egypt (405/4–343 B.C.), only recently ended, was symptomatic of Persia's decentralization; a serious rise in interest rates throughout the Near East, due to heavy borrowing by taxpayers needing ready cash, which was in short supply, had alienated the commercial classes. Discontent with Persian rule was widespread in places like Egypt and Mesopotamia on religious and economic grounds, but it did not crystallize in pro-Macedonian uprisings. Despite her difficulties, Persia was still powerful, her diplomatic intervention in Greece during the fourth century having been backed up by the very real threat of military and naval intervention.

Although ruled after 336 by a mediocre king, Darius III, the empire could mobilize a first-rate army stiffened by a core of crack Iranian cavalry and supported by diverse units drawn from its heterogeneous subjects and by thousands of Greek mercenaries. At full strength it included more than 100,000 men and so outnumbered Alexander's total force by about three to one. The Persians also enjoyed naval superiority in the eastern Mediterranean, their fleet threatening Alexander's lines of communication with the Aegean.

Macedonian power, untested outside the Balkans, was apparently limited by political and other realities. Although royal income from mines was considerable, Philip's expenses had been heavy, and Alexander inherited an empty treasury. He could thus not afford to build a fleet and was forced to rely on Greek naval contingents of questionable loyalty. His army had already proved itself, but, although large by Greek standards, it was puny when compared with the manpower available to Persia. His own control over the Macedonian nobility was questionable, and he had only qualified faith in the effective support and loyalty of the Corinthian League. Despite his possible display of military and administrative talents at a tender age, his own qualities in a prolonged campaign were untried.

He was already beginning to display his genius as a warlord, however, in the Danubian and Theban campaigns during the first year of his monarchy. Thanks to Arrian, his generalship is the best-known facet of his talents. He was famous for speed, tactical flexibility, and resourcefulness in meeting the enemy, and his sieges were noted for their vigorous ferocity. Normally his relatively inflexible phalanx occupied his left, and the right, or offensive, wing was taken up by his cavalry. Alexander rarely left important matters to chance, and although his battles seemed daring, his tactics were never reckless and, whenever possible, were carefully planned in advance. His army actually fought only four pitched battles, and most of his campaigning was of a guerrilla nature, which gave freer play to his inventiveness. He also showed himself to be even more adept a propagandist than his father. He was a master of theatrical gestures designed to cultivate the mystique of his own personality and had an uncanny ability to make other men seem responsible for his own "dirty work." Despite his inheritance of leadership over the Corinthian League, however, and his strident insistence on the coming Persian campaign as a kind of crusade in retaliation for their invasion 150 years before, few educated Greeks believed that the war had any purpose other than to aggrandize the young king and his realm.

His grand strategy in the first years of the war illustrates his foresight. Realizing the vulnerability of his overland supply lines and of his communication with the homeland by sea, he aimed at occupying the seaboard controlled by Persia, thereby neutralizing enemy naval bases and the potential threat to him of their fleet. The correct strategic response of the Persians would have been swift naval action in the Aegean to encourage revolt in Greece, which operations, in fact, they began during the first year of the war. They did not continue this offensive, however, and they met Alexander's invasion thereafter unimaginatively in a series of pitched battles on the land, thus permitting him to exercise his tactical genius.

THE CAMPAIGN AGAINST PERSIA

The Granicus.   Early in 334 B.C. Alexander crossed the Hellespont with almost 34,000 soldiers, some 14,000 of whom were Macedonians, about half the mobilized fighting strength of his kingdom. The other half stayed in Macedonia to support Antipater, whom he left behind as regent and acting *hegemon* of the Corinthian League. The Persian campaign seriously drained Macedonian manpower, Antipater in the following years having to find a minimum of about 28,000 recruits to send the king as replacements for battle and other casualties and, in 331 B.C., to raise the total strength of his army to 47,000 men. At the beginning of the war in 334 B.C., Alexander also used 8,000 Thracians and Illyrians, 7,000 men drafted from the Corinthian League, and 5,000 Greek mercenaries. The league troops were primarily hostages for the good behavior of the city-states. Alexander did not trust their fighting spirit, from the first used them for garrison duty, and demobilized them at the earliest opportunity. Although he employed some hand-picked Greeks as officers, like his aide Eumenes, the greatest commands were held by Macedonian nobles. Parmenio, his powerful chief of staff, was a dominant figure because his sons and adherents occupied sensitive posts.

Alexander dramatized the invasion as a crusade by visiting the site of Troy, where, as a new Achilles, he sacrificed to the shades of his Homeric forebears to remind Greece of that earlier expedition against an Asian power, which, in a sense, he was reenacting. Not far from Troy, at the river Granicus, he fought a battle with the Persian garrison of the western Asia Minor satrapies (334). The outcome was close, and he won only after narrowly escaping death, his life having been saved on the field by his friend "Blackie" Cleitus. As a conciliatory gesture he dedicated his Persian booty to Athena, although the sullen Athenians, like most other Greeks, stubbornly refused to be enthusiastic about a war against people they no longer feared or hated. His enslavement of Greek mercenaries serving Persia, whom he captured at the Granicus, proved to be a mistaken policy because in the future such soldiers tended to resist bitterly. Alexander eventually decided that it was better to enlist them in his own forces or to provide for their orderly demobilization. After Granicus, Alexander dismissed the allied fleet, which he distrusted, and occupied the Greek cities of western Asia Minor, for which "liberation" meant compulsory membership in the Corinthian League and, hence, contributions to the war effort. Alexander was quite ready to treat savagely any Greek city-states in Asia that resisted Macedonian intervention in their affairs, which was evidently more oppressive than Persian domination. He came to realize, however, that he could benefit more in the long run by their goodwill, which he tried to obtain by granting them democratic constitutions. In southwestern Asia Minor he won a claim to Caria through adoption by the local dynast, Queen Ada, whom he helped against a rival supported by Darius III. Thence he turned inland to winter on the high plateau of central Anatolia, where he could find fodder for his horses and provision for his men. There, at Gordium, he is said (according to the best tradition) to have untied a sacred knot, which act allegedly presaged conquest of Asia.

Issus. Despite his notable successes, Alexander by no means achieved dominance over Persia during the first year of fighting, and it would be accurate to say that military honors were at that point rather evenly divided between him and Persia. From the very beginning one Greek leader, Agis III, the shrewd and courageous Spartan king, showed considerable initiative in opposing Macedonia by attempting to activate and coordinate Greek resistance with the Persians, with whom he was in contact. Memnon, a Greek admiral serving Persia, actually struck at Alexander's rear with some success, capturing Mytilene and investing Halicarnassus and Miletus, a strategy that, if pressed, could have been disastrous for the Macedonian. The Persian offensive in the Aegean lapsed with Memnon's death in 333, however, and Agis was forced to delay his projected revolt in Greece because a crucial turning point in the war, favorable to Alexander, occurred in that year.

In the spring of 333 Alexander marched southeast, entering northern Syria through the Cilician Gates, where, for once, his intelligence proved faulty: late in the year, Darius with his entire field army succeeded in occupying the coastal road behind Alexander to the north, near Issus. The Persians accepted battle on a narrow front between sea and hills, where deployment of their best units, cavalry and scythed chariots, was limited by the terrain. At a crucial point in the fighting, Darius abandoned the field, whereupon his forces were immediately routed. Alexander captured the Great King's personal treasure and his female relatives, whom he treated with respect. Certainly by that time he began to entertain seriously the notion of claiming the Persian Empire as his own because he taunted Darius as a usurper, although for the time being he did not pursue his opponent eastward. Instead he followed his original strategy and continued south to occupy the remaining Persian-held seaboard. The naval bases of Phoenicia were, of course, a coveted prize, but despite the fact that, after Issus, Alexander was emerging as the probable winner in this war, the island city of Tyre refused to submit to him. He besieged it for seven months, using all the available military engines built by Aristobulus, which he transported across a specially constructed mole from the mainland to the walls. Tyre would probably have held out, had not Alexander opportunely been aided by the fleets of Cyprus and Sidon. Having taken Tyre, he gave the Phoenician cities, like the Asia Minor Greeks, privileged status by exempting them from satrapal organization and by leaving them internally "free."

Egypt. Thence he marched south and in 332 entered Egypt, where he was hailed as the true pharaoh at Memphis by the Egyptian priesthood, acting as spokesmen for a nation still resenting the harsh punishment imposed on it by the Persians following their recent revolt. Appreciating the delicate situation in that country, for the time being Alexander accommodated his administration to native custom by organizing it under nomarchs rather than satraps and even by employing Egyptians as tax collectors. His stay in Egypt was marked by two especially noteworthy acts. He founded a city that still bears his name, and he undertook a perilous expedition across the Cyrenaic desert to visit a famous oracle. Alexandria grew up on the site of several native villages situated between a lake and the sea near the west branch of the Nile Delta, although it did not become a great city until after Alexander's death. His trip with a few friends to the Sihwah Oasis, site of an oracle of Baal-Ammon identified by the Greeks as Zeus, was no doubt important psychologically for him, although its significance is otherwise debatable. The trip is sometimes cited as the first evidence of Alexander's belief in his own divinity because the oracle-priest apparently greeted him as "son of Ammon," that is, a god. This was, how-ever, the normal nomenclature for an Egyptian pharaoh, which Alexander already was, and the incident is therefore not nearly so significant as the encouragement Alexander gave to Callisthenes, the court historian, who shortly was to advertise him as "son of Zeus." Alexander was a superstitious man, and like many other Greeks, he was interested in the oracle's power to foretell the future. He was im-pressed by the message he received, although he never divulged its contents.

Arbela. In the spring of 331 Alexander left Egypt via Palestine and Damascus and proceeded into Mesopotamia. His second and final encounter with Darius and his field army took place near Arbela, just east of the Tigris River, in October 331. A timely cavalry charge led by Alexander won the battle before Persian mercenaries were able to exploit a breakthrough in his line of infantry. Darius fled in the direc-tion of the Caspian Sea, and Alexander moved a step closer to supplanting him as Great King. Although he honored the priests of Babylon, who regarded him as a liberator, he appointed his first Persian as satrap over them, an indication of his growing desire to win future recognition in Persia itself.

Although proper strategy dictated immediate pursuit of Darius, Alexander turned southeast to spend four crucial months (December 331–March 330) at the Persian capitals, Susa and Persepolis. At Susa he discovered works of art looted in Athens by Xerxes in 480 B.C., which he sent back as another gesture of goodwill. In the basement of the Achaemenid palace he expropriated an immense hoard of coined gold darics amounting to 9,000 talents (270 tons) and 40,000 talents (1,200 tons) of raw silver ingots, whose withdrawal from circulation within the empire had caused a catastrophic shortage of ready money. He apparently minted the silver and, by spending both it and the gold coins, initiated a period of currency inflation that lasted over a century. He moved on to Persepolis, having received alarming news from reinforcements sent from Macedonia by Antipater that a major revolt had broken out in Greece some months before under the leadership of Agis of Sparta. Although Alexander is said to have called it contemptuously "a battle of mice," he seems to have been genuinely worried by it, and with good reason.

Slowness of winter communications prevented him from knowing until much later the fact that Agis was finally crushed by Antipater, who took advantage of the refusal of Athenian leaders like Demosthenes and Lycurgus to permit Sparta to lead Athens, if even in a venture aiming at Greek freedom. Alexander suddenly realized his utter dependence on his army, and to dramatize the fact that he was first and foremost a Macedonian king, despite his increasingly obvious desire to replace Darius, he burned the Persian palace at Persepolis, his arson, it is said, being abetted by drunkenness. Having been apprised of the pacification of Greece, he left Perse-polis in the spring of 330 in pursuit of Darius to the north, who was assassinated by his entourage before Alexander could capture him. He could well afford to honor the dead monarch whom he had ridiculed while living, as esteem for the last Achae-menid would further advance his own ambitions to become the legitimate Great King in the eyes of his Iranian subjects.

THE PERIOD OF CRISIS (330–327 B.C.)

These ambitions had serious military and political consequences. They meant further conquests in the easternmost Persian satrapies, which would entail hard fighting in what today is northern Iran, southern Russia, and Afghanistan. Here Alexander faced not civilized enemies in pitched battles but continuous guerrilla warfare with fiercely independent Iranian tribes, on whom the Persian yoke had rested only lightly. His dismissal of the troops supplied by Thessaly and the Corinthian League in 330 immediately before the march east, and the demobilization and settlement in Bactria of his Greek mercenaries during the guerrilla campaign there, were well-calculated moves. The importance of the Greeks to his plans declined in proportion to his success, and he intended war in the eastern satrapies to be a peculiarly Macedonian adventure, one that would increase his charismatic stature as a leader and leave his men innocent of any ideas except loyalty to him. These intentions provoked antagonism and opposition among his nobles, who were reluctant to see the young king, lately their puppet, free himself from their domination and so become a far more powerful person than a first among Macedonian equals.

The Philotas "Conspiracy." Parmenio, the chief of staff, led the most important noble faction seeking to maintain ascendancy over the king, and a rupture between the two, developing for some time, presumably widened as Alexander's plans to claim the powers of an Achaemenid began to unfold. Parmenio had originally supported the claims of his own father-in-law, Attalus, Alexander's rival for the throne in 336, but had opportunely switched sides at the last moment. At the beginning of the Persian War, Parmenio and his family interposed themselves between Alexander and his troops by monopolizing the most important commands, Parmenio's oldest son, Philotas, leading the Companions, his second son, Nicanor, the heavy infantry. As Alexander gradually felt surer of himself, he began to remove from their commands some of Parmenio's friends, substituting his own creatures, and he even allegedly bribed Parmenio's mistress to spy on her lover. As Alexander left nothing to chance, he used Callisthenes to blacken Parmenio's reputation by publicizing an interpretation of the battles at the Granicus, Issus, and Arbela, implying that Alexander frequently had to rescue him from defeat. This was credible, if untrue, because Parmenio normally commanded the defensive wing and so occasionally found himself in difficulties, but through no fault of his own.

When Alexander departed for Media in pursuit of Darius, he left Parmenio behind at Ecbatana to guard supply lines. Months later, when he had reached the border between eastern Iran and southwestern Afghanistan, Alexander accused Parmenio's son Philotas of treason and tried him before the army, traditionally the highest court in capital cases. There was no proof of guilt, Alexander merely insisting that the army decide between his word and Philotas'. This apparently fictitious accusation was Alexander's crafty first move to consolidate his hold over his troops and eliminate opposition. Philotas was duly found guilty and executed, agents were hastily sent to execute Parmenio, accused of implication in the "plot," and many of his other associates were brought to trial. These latter were replaced by men more directly dependent on the king, like his friends Cleitus and Hephaestion, who jointly commanded the Companion Cavalry. The Parmenio affair, however, poisoned Alexander's relations with his comrades, and when Cleitus bitterly criticized the king's increasing high-handedness at a drunken party in farthest Samarkand (328), an enraged Alexander killed him with his own hand. The Macedonian army, which needed its king, later legitimized the murder.

"Conspiracy" of the Pages.   Cleitus' murder was, it seems, an important event in the development of Alexander's personality; having apparently eliminated all opposition and successfully bound the army to him directly, for the first time he felt liberated from the restraints imposed on his ambitions of being a Persian king. Having previously experimented with Persian dress, he now normally wore an adopted form of attire suitable for a Great King. He married a Bactrian princess, Roxane, instituted a second, Persian court in addition to his Macedonian one, and contemplated reinforcing his army by training thirty thousand young Persians in Macedonian drill. He clearly overestimated his ascendancy over the army and the extent to which his men would accept his Persianizing policies.

They rebuffed him when he tried to orientalize his Macedonian court by introducing the act known as *proskynesis,* ceremonial prostration by Persian subjects before their king, who ennobled this subservient act by raising them to their feet with a kiss. Alexander required the ceremony of his Macedonian officers, who regarded it as undignified, comic, or even blasphemous because it completely destroyed the bluff, hearty relationship that was normal between them and their ruler. His insistence on *proskynesis* also alienated the intellectuals, notably his former friend Callisthenes, who cuttingly refused to go through with it, saying merely that he preferred to lose a kiss. As the king's propagandist, Callisthenes knew exactly how far Alexander would go to develop the mystique of his own power, but Callisthenes had principles and withdrew his support of a ruler who increasingly claimed autocratic powers and their trappings. So widespread was the opposition to *proskynesis* that Alexander was forced to exempt the Macedonians from it. His resentment against Callisthenes grew into fear of him as a threat, and the pattern first realized in the Parmenio affair was repeated early in 327, when Alexander discovered a "conspiracy" among his pages that included Callisthenes, who was duly executed for treason.

THE INDIAN CAMPAIGN AND ITS AFTERMATH

Having subjugated the northern tier of satrapies in very hard fighting that included trying sieges of mountain fastnesses, Alexander might have turned back, as he had virtually reached the easternmost boundaries of the Persian Empire. This was not to be because the king wished to expunge totally the bitter memory of purges, recently revived in the "conspiracy" of the pages, by demonstrating again the utter dependence of the army on him alone. Undaunted by the distances involved, which he probably knew, he envisioned another brilliant campaign to master Nature herself, one beyond the Indus Valley to the Ganges River and eventually the sea. With Hephaestion functioning as his grand vizier, he recrossed the Hindu Kush in the summer of 327 and proceeded eastward to the Indus, his army suffering extreme hardship en route. He filled his depleted ranks by enlisting seven thousand Indian mercenaries, whom he later executed when they refused to fight against their own countrymen. Having reached the Jhelum River, one hundred miles east of the Indus, by June 326, Alexander fought his fourth, and last, pitched battle, with the rajah Porus, who was defeated despite his offensive use of elephants. Alexander left Porus behind as a vassal king and continued eastward until his army refused to go on and mutinied under Coenus, Parmenio's son-in-law, one of the few members of the faction surviving the first purge.

Megalomania. The failure of his grandiose Indian plans apparently shocked Alexander and marked what seems to have been the beginning of a profound deterioration in his character. His power seemed, after all, to be insecure, his leadership was evidently not indispensable, and alliance between his army and a potential rival, like Coenus, was still possible. Fortunately for him, his men restored their allegiance when he turned back from the Ganges watershed, and Coenus soon died, allegedly in action. Alexander confronted renewed threat to his position with greater exercise of power. Once again he intended to prove his indispensability to the army by leading it successfully in other difficult campaigns, the inspiration of a personality, it would seem, no longer merely egocentric but driven by megalomaniacal urges. The descent of the Indus to its mouth, which he reached in the summer of 325, was trying enough, but what followed almost defies rational explanation. Alexander dispatched his admiral, Nearchus, to sail along the Persian Gulf toward Mesopotamia, while he and his army, without naval support or proper supplies, traversed the plateau of Baluchistan, one of the most desolate and extensive wastes in all the Near East, where the army suffered more than ever it had when fighting.

Alexander's reaction against new threats to his power, real and imagined, created greater crises when he emerged from the desert (325–324) and arrived back at Susa. During his long absence in Afghanistan and India, he had been in only tenuous contact with the administration of the western territories, which had been virtually independent of his direction. Because he was so totally occupied in campaigning, he never attempted to give his empire a more centralized government than that provided by the Persians before him. He tended to use the existing administrative system as he found it, but he was statesman enough to be flexible and to adapt it to his peculiar needs by changing it, as in western Asia Minor, in Phoenicia, and (initially, at least) in Egypt. Basically, however, the empire remained divided into satrapies, headed by Macedonians, but also by Persians and Iranians appointed when the king began to seek a rapprochement with Oriental nobility. The Iranian governors were generally loyal, although Persian nobles who had been disappointed in their hopes of satrapies or those with even greater ambitions were restive during his five-year absence, and there had even been some minor rebellions. The suspicions held by the king of his own Macedonian administrators became even more morbid following Coenus' mutiny, and scapegoats had to be found to divert attention from his own responsibility for the mistaken march across Baluchistan.

THE PURGES

The king no longer seems to have believed in anyone, nobles or soldiers, and his suspicions resulted in what seems to have been a superpurge, dwarfing those of Parmenio and Callisthenes and lasting for months. The commonest charge against doomed satraps and generals was maladministration during his absence, which in many cases may have been true, although Alexander would surely have excused officials he trusted implicitly. Significantly enough, the first to be executed was Coenus' brother, Cleander, and his associates, although Cleander himself had arranged Parmenio's assassination some years before. The veil of secrecy surrounding subsequent events is almost impenetrable, but a veritable bloodbath of administrators, both Iranian and Macedonian, took place. Somewhere between one-third and two-thirds of the empire's twenty-two satraps were dismissed and/or executed, and other officials subsequently summoned to Alexander's court were probably saved from death only by his own end.

The purge culminated in the spring of 324, when Alexander, from Susa, dismissed his secretary of the treasury, Harpalus, who functioned at Babylon, charging him with embezzlement. The accusation seemingly masked something more sinister, since Harpalus disobeyed the order to appear at Susa and left Babylon for Italy with some of the royal treasure. Alexander replaced most of his dismissed or executed satraps with nonentities who posed no threat to him, but to neutralize their power utterly, he ordered them all to disband their mercenary armies. Only a very few of his important associates—like the Greek Eumenes, his private secretary; Antigonus, satrap of Phrygia; Ptolemy Lagos, his childhood friend and chief of intelligence; and Hephaestion, the grand vizier—escaped death.

Marriages. Because in India the army had proved as unreliable as its officers, Alexander decided that he must reduce the relative military importance to him of Macedonians by creating a new, ethnically mixed, or nationally rootless, class of soldiery having no common interest except loyalty to him, their creator. While at Susa in the spring of 324, he arranged for a public marriage ceremony in which he took as a second wife Barsine, one of Darius III's daughters. Hephaestion married her sister, and at the king's behest eighty of his principal commanders married other Iranian noblewomen. They apparently did so reluctantly because after Alexander's death many of them divorced their Oriental wives. Simultaneously the king formally sanctioned the common-law connections of ten thousand Greek and Macedonian veterans with native women and summoned from Bactria the thirty thousand Iranian youths who had received Macedonian military indoctrination. Slightly later at Opis on the Tigris, he publicly dismissed many Macedonian troops, an action that was surely intended as a dramatic gesture to advertise the fact that he no longer had to rely on them exclusively and could even do without them. The lesson was not lost on the troops, who realized their dependence on their commander. As Alexander perhaps foresaw, they requested reenlistment in an emotional confrontation with him. They were, after all, his best soldiers, even better for having understood that in future they would be only part of a multi- or supranational army. His gracious consent to their reenlistment was formally symbolized by a reconciliation banquet attended by Macedonians, Greeks, and Persians.

THE UNITY OF MANKIND

The marriage ceremony at Susa and the banquet at Opis have sometimes been cited in the modern literature on Alexander as evidence for the view that he believed in the brotherhood of man, that his empire was to be cemented by a union of various ethnic groups and cultures—Greek, Macedonian, and barbarian—in the interest of harmony among men. Such a view rests on the presupposition that Alexander was an idealist, possibly even a romantic, and it seems rather incompatible with a character that otherwise displayed the traits of a ruthless, hardheaded, yet suspicious opportunist. The theory merits examination and criticism, however, not merely because of its intrinsic interest but also because, when suitably revised, it may help us to understand Alexander's policies in the last years of his life.

The Opis Banquet.   Alexander is quoted by Plutarch as stating that God was the common father of all, Greeks and barbarians, but even if he really made the remark, it does not necessarily imply that all human beings should live in concord or that the various subject peoples of his realm were to share in its government. According to Plutarch, the king went on to qualify his statement by observing that certain "best" men were more peculiarly God's children than the rest, which would be grounds for classifying people hierarchically and for stressing their differences. Actually his statement had been a commonplace in Greek thought since the time of Homer and did not connote a new belief in the physical fatherhood of God over humanity or its essential similarity. Again, it was Plutarch who, at some length, discussed Alexander as the mixer of nations at his wedding feast, sharing his own nuptials with those of his officers and men at Susa. Plutarch described the event, however, in a flight of rhetoric that appears to distort the actual significance of the ceremony because not all the races of the empire were being united by marriage at Susa, but merely Greco-Macedonian men and Persian women. As for the banquet at Opis, no ancient source accorded the event an importance equal to its alleged symbolism of racial brotherhood in the military establishment. It was surely no more than a theatrical gesture calculated to produce a certain psychological effect leading to reconciliation between the king and his Macedonian troops. In the seating arrangements at Opis, Alexander was surrounded by Macedonian officers and courtiers, with whom he shared his drinking cup, and whom he flattered by evidently preferring their company to that of the Persian nobility reclining at segregated tables set apart from his own.

Alexander apparently was exposed to the doctrine held by Aristotle almost until the very end of his life that barbarians were slaves by nature, Greeks their masters. If the king had been an apt pupil, he scarcely would have been prone to believe in the unity of a common humanity. But Alexander was also a practical man, and, quite apart from his probable desire to create a new establishment peculiarly dependent on him alone, he could not have avoided realizing that there were too few Macedonians and Greeks at his disposal to conquer, defend, and administer an empire. His experience with Persians and other Iranians apparently convinced him that they had many admirable administrative and military talents, which were not to be wasted in his new order. The events at Susa and Opis thus suggest not the mixture and equality of all nationalities of his realm but the creation of a new social and military elite by the melding of Greco-Macedonians and Iranians, a new master race to unify the loosely connected empire. From Alexander's viewpoint the idea made sense because it was justified by, and would help reinforce, his claim to the heritage of the Persian Great King.

THE LAST YEAR

Consolidation of this class took place against a background of increasing social tension in Asia and Greece, which was produced by Alexander's order to his satraps to disband their mercenary armies. This last crisis of his reign in some ways was the greatest because it was produced by converging social, military, and political difficulties. No provision had been made for giving mercenary troops subsistence after demobilization, a striking departure from Alexander's habit of settling soldiers in cities or colonies while he was on the march. Most of these ex-mercenaries were Greek, and they tended to gravitate back to their home city-states in Greece, many of which could not absorb them economically. The empire was filled with several tens of thousands of wandering, dissatisfied ex-soldiers, whose numbers were matched by bands of exiles in Greece expelled by the many pro-Macedonian puppet oligarchies in contravention of the charter of the Corinthian League. It soon became obvious that this floating population threatened social and economic stability, and as always when confronted with a crisis, Alexander acted quickly and decisively. In the fall of 324 he ordered the mercenaries and exiles to return to their native cities and the latter to accept them, claiming that the plight of these people was not his fault, which was only technically true.

The Exiles' Decree. The so-called exiles' decree is very interesting from several points of view, not the least of them being its revelation of the king's order of priorities. For him, apparently, the Corinthian League had become by this time an absolute inconvenience, and he did not hesitate to intervene arbitrarily in its affairs by fiat. He evidently envisioned less trouble from the Greek city-states, whose governments he might antagonize by compelling them to reabsorb their political opponents, than from possible social and military revolution in both Greece and Asia caused by wandering bands of desperate men. In a very real sense the decree represented the ultimate failure of Alexander's statesmanship because he had been responsible for the purges, the maintenance of puppet regimes in Greece, and the decision to disband satrapal armies that had led to a dangerous situation. The decree might also have had the effect of politically embarrassing Antipater, the regent, who would be responsible for its enforcement, and Alexander was willing to use it against the old nobleman, his first political friend and mentor. No less than the other Macedonians of Alexander's original following, Antipater disliked the king's orientalizing policies, and relations between monarch and regent were strained. Alexander even went so far as to give a sympathetic hearing to embassies from Greek cities arriving at his court to complain of Antipater's alleged misgovernment.

Deification. The exiles' decree has also been linked in the modern literature concerning Alexander with a request of deification he is said by some ancient sources to have made of the Corinthian League in 324. The very historicity of this event, not to mention its significance, has been hotly debated because the ancient evidence that Alexander requested or received deification is neither clear-cut nor unanimous and because the very sense of his deification, if it in fact took place, is questionable. It might mean no more than the excessive flattery implicit in the official granting by cities of divine titles to famous men, or, more seriously, their actual worship in cult. Educated Greek opinion in such matters was clear. Before Alexander, Greek cities had never deified any living person in the second sense of the term, although it was possible to flatter, or admire excessively, prominent personalities in their lifetimes without actually worshiping them. Anything more than that would have been regarded as blasphemy, even the exaltation above ordinary mortals implied by *proskynesis* having appeared to a person like Callisthenes to be unsuitable.

One opinion justifies belief in Alexander's deification in the sense of actual worship by assuming that as mere *hegemon* of the Corinthian League, he could not legally interfere in the domestic affairs of city-states. Deification would have given him greater authority concerning exiles because the city-states could not very well question the pertinent decree of a divine ruler. This seems rather implausible, however, because Alexander did not trouble excessively about constitutional niceties if he could help it. If he chose, he could have wielded more than enough power to impose his will on the city-states to make them take back exiles or to do anything he wanted. He also stood to lose much more in ill will than he might conceivably have gained politically by deification.

Another, more attractive opinion holds that the city-states controlled by his puppets voted him divine honors, if not cult, but without any request of his. These supporters in many places perhaps anticipated his eventual return home once the Oriental campaigns were over and intended to ingratiate themselves by flattery and to embarrass his opponents by forcing a public issue on his behalf. Most compelling of all, however, is the view that Alexander requested deification in terms of both honors and cult and for psychological, not political, reasons, which were no more important to him than any educated resentment against his blasphemy. Alexander seems for years to have abetted popular belief that he was the "son of Zeus," and the megalomaniacal deterioration that he seemingly experienced after the Indian campaign led him to believe that he actually had supernaturally divine powers. In any case, envoys from Greece apparently arrived at his court shortly before his death wearing garlands, as if they were approaching a god.

The End. Alexander's megalomania accelerated after Hephaestion's death, apparently of acute alcoholism, in the fall of 324, and the last months of his life were occupied with grandiose schemes that seem best explained by assuming his irrationality. He is said, for example, to have simulataneously contemplated a war against Carthage, the circumnavigation of Arabia, the construction of immense monuments and roads, and the transplantation of populations. The ultimate political tragedy of his reign was his complete break with Antipater, the exiles' decree having had an effect rather different from the one intended, because it gave both the city-states and the regent a common grievance. Late in 324 they began to draw together for possible future cooperation against Alexander, and the king decided that Antipater, too, must go. He summoned the regent to appear before him, but Antipater reacted as an administrator confident of the support of an army in Macedonia that knew him and not their own king. Relying also on city-state support, he coolly disobeyed the order, sending instead his son, Cassander, whom Alexander abused. Finally, Alexander dispatched to Macedonia as Antipater's replacement the general Craterus in the spring of 323.

All of these schemes, including Antipater's dismissal, were destined to be abortive because Alexander fell mortally ill at Babylon in June 323 B.C., before they were carried out. The precise nature of his sickness is unknown, although there is a curiously detailed description of his last days, deriving, it seems, from local city records. In any case, he aggravated his condition by continued heavy drinking. When he was obviously dying, he was asked who should succeed him. His alleged answer, "The strongest man," points to the disinterest of an unnaturally egotistical autocrat in a future he could not control. He seems to have recognized as the "strongest" in his entourage Hephaestion's successor as commander of the Companion Cavalry and vizier, Perdiccas, to whom he entrusted his signet ring shortly before expiring. He was not yet thirty-three years of age.

ALEXANDER AND HISTORY

Alexander was above all a conqueror, essentially a *condottiere* in the grand style, like his father. He lived out the average ancient life span, and it seems otiose to speculate excessively on his possible accomplishments had he lived to middle or old age. Certainly the apparently megalomaniacal developments in his personality during the last years of his life do not suggest that he would have enjoyed a productive or successful further career, had he lived.

Despite, or because of, the fact that his real accomplishments were almost exclusively military, he significantly influenced the further development of Western civilization. He became a gigantic figure stimulating the emulation of others, especially in the matter of deifying kings, but even more important, through his agency the geographical dimensions of Hellenism were vastly increased. It seems very improbable, however, that he envisioned himself as the apostle of Greek culture in the Near East, and the belief that he founded many cities as cells for the further spread of Hellenism or for regional economic development is unwarranted. Popular tradition in antiquity knew of seventy "cities" that he founded, but both their number and their civilizing nature are perhaps exaggerated. The only city that he established in that area of the Near East west of the Euphrates, destined to be the heartland of Hellenic culture in the centuries following his death, was Alexandria in Egypt. All the others were east of Mesopotamia, mainly in Bactria, and were settlements of veterans, especially Greek mercenaries, often on the sites of already existing native villages. They perhaps had a certain value as garrison outposts, but, absorbed by their alien surroundings, they rather quickly faded as centers of Hellenism. Subsequently they attained only vague historical importance when a Greek dynasty was established in Bactria. Alexander himself seems not to have been very interested in them, apart from their possible military value.

Probably Alexander's real importance to history lies in the fact that he was the unwitting instrument encouraging penetration into the Near East of Greeks and their institutions on a scale hitherto unprecedented. The Persian Empire, it is true, had for centuries been familiar with Greek artists, businessmen, and soldiers finding employment there, and this cultural osmosis from West to East had tended to increase, especially in the century preceding Alexander. Obviously it would have continued even had there been no Alexander, but this supposition does not detract from the peculiar role he assumed in the process. The Hellenization of the Near East would probably never have been so intense and widespread had it not rested on Greek political control of the area, and this presupposed a conquest such as Alexander's. It remained to be seen, however, whether the unity of his empire could survive his passing. In particular, the future position of Hellenism in the territories he conquered remained uncertain, granted the imponderables surrounding the succession of Perdiccas.

PART IV

THE HELLENISTIC AGE

19

The Hellenistic World

THE BREAKUP OF ALEXANDER'S EMPIRE (323–275 B.C.)

Introduction. The concluding phase of Greek history ushered in by Alexander the Great's conquest of the Near East is traditionally called the Hellenistic period, to distinguish it from the preceding classical, or Hellenic period. The removal of his dominant personality left initiative in the hands of his generals at Babylon and elsewhere, most of them Macedonian nobles, all of them ambitious, talented men eager to wield authority. For two generations thereafter they and their descendants competed for power, and a stable system of states only gradually emerged as Alexander's empire broke up.

The Regency. Assuming a constitutional role as a kind of council of the nobility, the generals at Babylon deliberated the fate of the empire. There was some disagreement on the question of centralizing power. One faction, led by the general Perdiccas, favored a strong regency governing in the interests of the Macedonian royal house. Another group led by Ptolemy Lagos, more thoughtful of their own independence, suggested that sovereignty be vested in an occasional assembly of satraps. Perdiccas prevailed, but the generals' council declined to approve the succession of Alexander's illegitimate half-brother, Philip Arrhidaeus, who was either half-witted or insane. Instead, they proposed to anticipate the birth of a posthumous son to Alexander's wife, Roxane, who was in advanced pregnancy. Assuming the role of the Macedonian citizen assembly, the army almost mutinied against their officers and refused to accept a king who would be half Oriental. When Roxane in fact produced a boy (Alexander IV) in August 323, a compromise was worked out. Philip and Alexander IV were acclaimed joint kings with a regency council consisting of three men governing on their behalf: Perdiccas held chief executive authority, Craterus, Alexander's second in command, the royal treasury, and Antipater viceregal power in Macedonia and Greece.

This division of authority, reflecting jealousies within the high command, weakened the regency and encouraged other generals to assert themselves, especially as the regents confirmed many satraps in their commands and assigned new ones. The very heterogeneity of the empire encouraged dismemberment, although the idea emerged only gradually. Appointments by the regency involved men who were essentially dynasts, ruling rather vaguely-defined territories by virtue of their outstanding personal qualifications as generals and administrators. Among others, they included Lysimachus, satrap of Thrace; Eumenes, the only Greek prominent in Alexander's military suite, who received Cappadocia; Antigonus "One-Eyed," the most formidable of the successors, who governed Phrygia with his young son, Demetrius; Seleucus, named head of the Companion Cavalry, but shortly to be assigned Babylonia as a satrapy; and Ptolemy Lagos, perhaps the cleverest of them all, who always limited his ambition to mastery of only a part of the empire, but that the richest and most easily defended: Egypt.

Many areas of the empire, notably Greece, were restive under the regency, and Perdiccas' position in it was challenged militarily by his colleagues, who suspected that he wanted to usurp all power. After Perdiccas' assassination in 321, Antipater became sole regent, holding the empire together in the interest of the two kings through the great respect the satraps paid him. When he died in 319, the army confirmed the regency of his successor, Polyperchon, but a struggle for power ensued in which Antipater's own son, Cassander, established himself as self-proclaimed "king" of Macedonia in 316. Shortly before, Olympias, mother of Alexander the Great, had had murdered Philip Arrhidaeus, a convenient excuse for her execution by Cassander on charges of treason, although he himself imprisoned Roxane and Alexander IV, suppressing them in 310.

The Successors' Wars. The rise to power of Cassander ended the regency in 316, and for the next thirty-five years the successors fought interminably with each other. A consistent pattern emerged in their wars, however, which gives a kind of unity to the period. Antigonus and/or his son, Demetrius, capitalizing on their interior lines of communication, attempted to rule all the empire, which meant ousting their rivals elsewhere and seizing control of Macedonia, so as to legitimize their government. Predictably, their rivals allied to oppose them.

In 316 Antigonus and Demetrius consolidated control over all Asia Minor upon Eumenes' death and then expelled from Mesopotamia Seleucus, who took refuge with Ptolemy. In the next year a general war broke out involving all the successors. Antigonus solicited support in Greece by promising, if victorious, to treat the city-states as free allies, and in Macedonia by posing as champion of young Alexander, Cassander's prisoner. He was less successful, however, fighting Ptolemy, and his distraction in Europe actually enabled Seleucus to retake Babylon in 312, to reoccupy his Mesopotamian satrapies, and to claim the eastern ones as far as India. Having reached a military deadlock in the Mediterranean, Antigonus and his opponents arranged peace on the basis of the status quo in 311, which merely sanctioned the already advanced state of dismemberment of the empire.

After four years of uneasy truce, Antigonus, then almost eighty, aided by the flamboyant Demetrius, tried a second time to overthrow his rivals and centralize power. Planning first to occupy Greece, then to crush Ptolemy by sea before invading Macedonia, Antigonus almost realized his ambitions. In 307 Demetrius occupied Athens, where he was fulsomely hailed as a liberator from Macedonian oppression, and in the following year he administered a crippling defeat to Ptolemy's navy near Cyprus. Father and son were then acclaimed by their army as kings, in which they were followed by their rivals, who attested sovereignty by minting coins in their own right for the first time. An abortive invasion of Egypt by Antigonus and Demetrius in 305 was followed by the most famous event of the war: the siege by Demetrius of the city of Rhodes, which maintained an entente with Ptolemy and was a potentially important naval base for Egypt. The siege was the greatest such operation of antiquity, and for a year the city held out. Demetrius raised it in 304 when the Rhodians, in effect, promised to be neutral in future wars among the successors. Although he failed to take Rhodes, Demetrius was thereafter known as "The Besieger" for his attempt.

The war dragged on until 301, when Antigonus and Demetrius prepared a massive, and for them hopefully final, attack on Seleucus and Ptolemy. Lysimachus and Cassander mustered armies to support their threatened allies, and the opposing forces met at Ipsus in Phrygia in the greatest battle of Greek antiquity. Close to 100,000 men fought on either side, and several score war elephants were used from a supply of 500 that Seleucus had recently received from the Indian rajah Chandragupta in return for ceding him that part of Alexander's empire in the Indus Valley. Antigonus was defeated at Ipsus and killed, but Demetrius escaped. Rather as a soldier of fortune, he continued to influence events by virtue of his possession of a fleet in the Aegean and of a few naval bases on islands there and in cities of coastal Greece, Asia Minor, and Phoenicia. His power, nevertheless, was much reduced. The Battle of Ipsus guaranteed the breakup of Alexander's empire and reduced the number of important rivals to four kings, who divided Antigonid domains among them. Seleucus added northern Syria and parts of Asia Minor to the core of his domains in Mesopotamia; Ptolemy extended his realm to include Palestine; Lysimachus took western Asia Minor in addition to Thrace; and Cassander was firmly established as ruler of Macedonia until his death in 298.

Despite reduced circumstances, Demetrius reestablished power in Greece and Macedonia by capitalizing on quarrels between Cassander's heirs. He won proclamation as king by the Macedonian army in 294 but was forced to subjugate cities in Greece, which much preferred to be neutral and free, and so he could not consolidate his position. Attacked by Pyrrhus, king of neighboring Epirus, and Lysimachus, who was asserting himself as arbiter of the Aegean, Demetrius lost his kingdom. He was captured in Asia Minor by Seleucus in 285 and was kept in honorable captivity until his death two years later. Lysimachus then attempted to extend his hegemony into western Asia Minor, but Seleucus defeated and killed him in Lydia in 281, thereby acquiring a claim to his European possessions. Landing in Thrace to assert that claim, Seleucus was assassinated in 280 by Ptolemy Ceraunus, a son of Ptolemy I, who intended to carve out an Aegean realm of his own. With the death of Seleucus, the generation of those generals who had fought with Alexander the Great came to an end.

The Celtic Invasion. The already confused situation in the Aegean world was further disturbed in 279 by attack from an unexpected enemy, the Celts, or Gauls. Celtic peoples, faced with overpopulation and pressure from Germanic tribes, had been expanding from their heartland in Bohemia since about 600 B.C. Before 500 they pushed into Gaul and Spain and in the fifth century occupied the Po Valley. In 387 they even briefly occupied Rome (see page 338). The Greeks of Massilia were in early contact with them, and Dionysius I of Syracuse even used Gallic mercenaries, whom he recruited in northern Italy.

During the fourth century Celtic bands appeared for the first time in the lower Danube Valley, and Alexander the Great made a treaty with them in 335 B.C. when he was campaigning in the area, prior to his pacifying southern Greece. Primitive barbarians organized by tribes, they practiced agriculture but preferred to earn their living by plundering their more civilized neighbors, even though their techniques of iron metallurgy for making weapons were poor. Ferocious to the point of foolhardiness, they frequently terrorized their enemies, but they were impatient of discipline, disorganized, incapable of sustained fighting, and innocent of the arts of siegecraft. They kept the peace with Alexander, but the confusion after his death gave them the opportunity to plunder the Balkan Peninsula, where they devastated farms and ruined open villages. After the death of Lysimachus, they reduced Thrace to a wilderness, so that thereafter it never again attained the status of an independent Greek kingdom.

The Celts attacked Greece in three bands, numbering several tens of thousands including camp followers, under their chiefs, Bolgius, Brennus, and Cerethrius. Their invasion had important political consequences in the Aegean area and helped produce an alignment of states that characterized the Greek East for the remainder of the Hellenistic period. Bands under Brennus forced their way into Thessaly, turned the pass at Thermopylae, and penetrated as far as Delphi, where they were beaten back by the Aetolians, who, as the deliverers of Greece, acquired for the first time an international reputation. Ptolemy Ceraunus fell in battle against them while defending Macedonia, which was even more exposed to attack than the peninsula. Bolgius and his tribes ravaged the Macedonian countryside for over two years thereafter, until 276. In the midst of chaos, the able son of Demetrius the Besieger, Antigonus Gonatas, also something of a soldier of fortune, expelled them, winning recognition by the Macedonian army as king and so legitimizing his status against the claims of several pretenders.

The third group of Celts split off from the others and moved eastward along the coast toward the Dardanelles in 278. They were encouraged to cross over to Asia Minor by two native dynasts, Nicomedes of Bithynia and Mithridates of Pontus. These latter foresaw that the confusion caused to Seleucus' son and successor, Antiochus, by the invasion would leave them free to consolidate their own petty kingdoms on the south shore of the Black Sea. Some Ionian cities bought protection from the Gauls, some tried self-defense, others were plundered, until Antiochus beat them soundly in 275. They were given settlements in northern Phrygia, subsequently named Galatia after them, which acted as a kind of buffer state between Seleucid domains and Pontus. Even after the Seleucids paid them tribute to guarantee their pacification, they proved unruly subjects, a constant threat to their more civilized neighbors in western Asia Minor, who increasingly turned for protection to the commanders of the local garrison at Pergamon, a market town in Lydia. The Celtic invasion also had the unforeseen by-product of leading to the tacit renunciation by Antiochus and Antigonus of claims on the other's domains, as they were totally preoccupied with consolidating their own domestic positions. This preoccupation guaranteed that for the future the Antigonids would be an essentially Greek, the Seleucids an Asiatic, power.

THE HELLENISTIC STATE SYSTEM

Introduction. The Hellenistic system of states, attaining virtual completion by 275 B.C., was dominated by the three great kingdoms emerging out of the wars of Alexander's successors, which are conventionally named after the Greco-Macedonian dynasties ruling them. This system ushered in a period of over two thousand years when monarchy of some kind was the most important form of government in the development of Western civilization.

The Antigonid dynasty ruled Macedonia and dominated Greece. The Seleucid dynasty held the coasts and some interior areas of Asia Minor, Syria, and Mesopotamia and parts of Iran. An empire of disparate territories, it had no official name in antiquity, sometimes being called simply Asia, sometimes the kingdom of Syria, the location of the Seleucid capital at Antioch. Egypt was ruled by the Ptolemaic (Lagid) dynasty with power over the Nile Valley and adjacent deserts, Cyrenaica, and, intermittently, Palestine, Phoenicia, Cyprus, certain Aegean islands, and even coastal parts of Asia Minor. Superficially hellenized native dynasties ruled petty kingdoms in Pontus, Cappadocia, and Bithynia along the southern Black Sea coast, and the Celts of Galatia owed only tenuous allegiance to the Seleucids.

Emigration and Cities. Greek rulers in the East realized that they had no broadly based native support for their governments, and so they attempted to staff the bureaucracies they inherited and their military establishments with Greeks and Macedonians. They tried to attract Greek businessmen, civil servants, and soldiers not merely by offering them material inducements to emigrate, like land, but even more by winning an international reputation as rulers genuinely interested in creating an ambience fit for Hellenes. They achieved this in part through propaganda and in part by culturally phil-Hellenic policies, which in notable cases meant the founding of cities. There are no reliable statistics to measure their success in stimulating Greek emigration eastward from the Aegean basin, but it appears to have been on a relatively small scale, even at its height in the latter fourth and third centuries. Old Greece continued to show symptoms of overpopulation, but even before about 200 B.C., when emigration virtually ended, there was a not inconsiderable reverse movement as Greeks, having made their fortunes in the East, returned home to enjoy their wealth in what was for them a more congenial environment.

In any case, scores of cities were founded in the Near East in many areas by Alexander's successors. The act of foundation was merely the grant of a city charter by a king providing for governmental organs traditional to city-states. Such charters sometimes organized a population where none had existed previously, sometimes merely raised in status ancient villages without prior rights of self-government. Such cities need not have been very large, nor were they necessarily dominated by a nucleus of ethnic Greeks. Kings liberally permitted suitably Hellenized Near Easterners, normally native aristocrats, to enjoy urban institutions, and most "Greek"

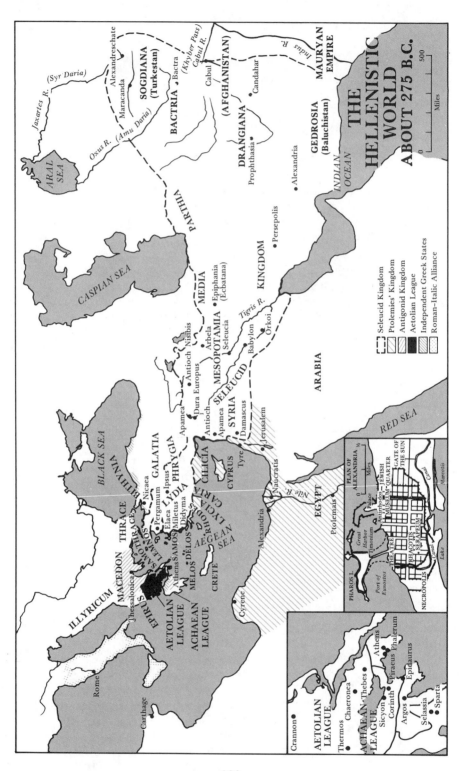

THE HELLENISTIC WORLD ABOUT 275 B.C.

Seleucid Kingdom
Ptolemies' Kingdom
Antigonid Kingdom
Aetolian League
Independent Greek States
Roman-Italic Alliance

MAURYAN EMPIRE

SOGDIANA (Turkestan)

BACTRIA

(AFGHANISTAN)

DRANGIANA

GEDROSIA (Baluchistan)

INDIAN OCEAN

(Syr Daria)

Jaxartes R.

Alexandreschate
Maracanda

Bactra
(Khyber Pass)
Cabul R.
Cabul

Candahar

Oxus R. (Amu Daria)

Prophthasia

Alexandria

ARAL SEA

PARTHIA

MEDIA

Epiphania (Ecbatana)

Persepolis

CASPIAN SEA

Nisibis
Antioch
Arbela
Dura Europus
Seleucia

MESOPOTAMIA

Tigris R.

Babylon
Orkoi

SELEUCID KINGDOM

ARABIA

SYRIA

Apamea
Antioch
Apamea
Damascus

Jerusalem

RED SEA

BITHYNIA

THRACE

GALATIA

Nicaea

Pergamum

PHRYGIA

Ipsus

LYDIA

Elaea
Miletus
Didyma

CILICIA

CARIA

CYPRUS

LYCIA

RHODES

Tyre

Naucratis

Nile R.

Alexandria

EGYPT

Ptolemais

BLACK SEA

SAMOTHRACE

LEMNOS
SAMOS
Athens
DELOS
MELOS

AEGEAN SEA

CRETE

Cyrene

MACEDON

Thessalonica

EPIRUS

ILLYRICUM

AETOLIAN LEAGUE

ACHAEAN LEAGUE

Rome

Carthage

0 500 Miles

PLAN OF ALEXANDRIA

0 ½ Miles

JEWISH QUARTER
MUSEUM
GATE OF THE SUN

Palace
Antirrhodos
Great Harbor
Timonium
THEATRE
RHACOTIS
SERAPEUM
PHAROS I.
Port of Eunostos
NECROPOLIS

Canal
Mareotis
Lake

Crannon

AETOLIAN LEAGUE

Thermos

Chaeronea
Thebes

ACHAEAN LEAGUE

Sicyon
Corinth
Piraeus
Athens
Phalerum

Argos
Selassia
Sparta

Epidaurus

280

cities in the East actually owed their existence to the ambitions of this class, which, often eager to adopt a Greek way of life, petitioned kings for charters. The government of cities was at least formally democratic because the king-founders thus maintained a favorable public image. All citizens as a rule had theoretically equal rights, and the people in assembly, whose agenda was controlled by a probouleutic council, elected their own magistrates. These were generally men of substance so that they had the necessary standing to treat with kings and could be called upon to assume liturgies. The system worked rather well in that class warfare, which had plagued the classical *polis,* subsided for a time, and in that the upper classes had a strong sense of civic obligation, even though this meant that they, and not the assembly, held the initiative in matters of government.

Sovereigns in the Near East carefully maintained the fiction that their cities were independent *poleis,* but normally they were kept under tight political control, enjoyed only a precarious independence even in purely local matters, and were really little more than municipalities. Even in other parts of the Greek world, city-state governments in the classical sense could not compete with the resources of the three great kingdoms, which often had the city-states at their mercy. Perhaps the only city-republic to survive into the Hellenistic era with a degree of freedom permitting it frequently to influence the course of events was Rhodes, but even her liberty was insecure because it depended on a delicate balance of power among the Big Three. Of formerly important *poleis* on mainland Greece, Athens was respected by other powers only as a cultural center, and Sparta was moribund, except in periods when her kings attempted constitutional reform. The city-state was no longer viable except in some larger political context, which was provided in Greece by two federal leagues, the Aetolian and the Achaean. Located, respectively, north and south of the Gulf of Corinth, they occasionally competed with the Big Three as first-ranking powers. The political demise of the city-state was just as evident in the colonial Greek world of the western Mediterranean. Beginning in 326 B.C., Rome gradually absorbed the cities of Magna Graecia, the last of which, Tarentum, fell in 272. On Sicily, Carthage extended her conquests until only Syracuse remained free, and in the far west Massilia (Marseilles) held out as the last important Greek outpost, an ally of Rome.

Warfare.   Although by 275 B.C. the Hellenistic world attained a degree of stabilization unrealized since the death of Alexander, conflicts within it were frequent even thereafter. Not all disputes led to war, and in the Hellenistic era Greek powers more frequently than ever before settled quarrels by arbitration. Arbitration generally involved lesser states, which turned to disinterested cities for help or to some important king whose awards had prestige and could be enforced.

Conflict among important powers, on the other hand, was more usually resolved by war, which meant that the Hellenistic age produced important innovations in military and naval science. The most striking was the widespread use of professional mercenary armies, which were first employed on a large scale during the wars of Alexander's successors. They remained important even after a stable state-system emerged. Macedonia and the two federal leagues created national armies by drafting citizens in emergencies, but their standing armies were mercenaries serving on long-term contracts. Because they were in no sense "national" rulers, the Ptolemies and Seleucids in principle depended on a core of Greco-Macedonian immigrants, although they gradually turned to other sources of supply. In the Aegean basin, aside from Macedonia itself, whose manpower was badly depleted during the successors' wars, Aetolia, Sparta, and Crete provided mercenaries. The most highly valued recruits, especially after 200 B.C., when Greece ceased exporting many fighting men, were Thracians, Galatians, and Jews.

Mercenary armies professionalized warfare and, paradoxically, made it more humane. Mercenaries were valuable, and so it seemed wise not to destroy enemy soldiers but to induce them to surrender and enlist on one's own side. This greater humanity affected even noncombatants, and no city was destroyed by war between Alexander's siege of Tyre and the Roman occupation. Nonmilitary means to victory like propaganda and fomenting of revolution were as frequently used as direct assault on cities. The effectiveness of new siege apparatus was largely negated by countermeasures, and cities spent a disproportionate share of energy and wealth in building walls and stockpiling engines of war and ammunition.

It is generally thought that Alexander the Great revolutionized military tactics by using cavalry rather than infantry as the main offensive arm, and in the third century B.C. the mere demonstration of cavalry strength was sometimes enough to make an army surrender. Until the Seleucid defeat by Rome at the Battle of Magnesia in 190 B.C., elephants were frequently used in connection with cavalry offensives, principally as a screen against opposing cavalry, sometimes also to attack infantry and break fortified positions. They were difficult to control, however, and in any case failed to terrorize experienced troops. Before 300 B.C. the Seleucids monopolized the use of Indian elephants, and other states turned to Africa for their supply. By about 200 B.C. phalanxes of heavy infantry once again replaced cavalry as the principal offensive arm, especially in Macedonian armies, but they were cumbersome because the men were pressed too tightly together and were armed with overly long spears. Their lack of maneuverability and the exposure of their flanks left them vulnerable to the more mobile Roman legionary tactics.

Naval tactics were not revolutionized to the same degree. Only the Ptolemaic dynasty kept a standing navy, and their "control" of the eastern Mediterranean until 246 B.C. meant only that they could send a fleet to any given area faster than it took their rivals to build one. Galleys at no time could blockade ports completely or prevent the passage of armies overseas. Naval engagements involved both ramming and boarding tactics, the latter especially after about 250 B.C. The Rhodians, with the reputation of being the best seamen in the Greek world, were proficient at both. Until an Athenian naval defeat in 322, the typical man-of-war was the trireme, thereafter the quinquereme, which, although light and of shallow draft, was yet a heavier and stronger ship. Propelled by a single row of oars, five men to each one, and covered by a deck, it was not very seaworthy because it was top-heavy, and even in competent hands, it tended to sink in storms. Larger ships and catamarans propelled by various combinations of oars and oarsmen were used. Limitations of ancient nautical engineering, however, restricted their effective size because Greek ships tended to break up if they more than two hundred feet long.

Balance of Power. After 275 B.C., Hellenistic states normally used their military and naval establishments, supplemented by cunning diplomacy, to maintain a balance of power. Although this was often a tortuous process involving shifting alliances, certain basic patterns emerged in the foreign policy of the period. The Antigonids claimed all of Greece as their sphere of interest, but they were resisted by the two federal leagues, which also fought one another, and by the Ptolemies, who subsidized anti-Macedonian factions. The Antigonids were also interested in preventing establishment by either the Ptolemies or the Seleucids of links with the Aegean, essential to the latter as sources of Greek immigrants. The Ptolemies were interested in controlling Phoenicia and Lebanon as a source of naval stores and collided there with the Seleucids, who regarded the area as their own sphere because it was the western terminus of caravan routes to the Middle East. Seleucid foreign policy was further complicated by the tendency of peripheral parts of the empire to break away and by domestic quarrels within the dynasty. All these conflicts weakened the Greek world, and it was so divided by 200 B.C. that it fell easy prey to Rome, drawn into the East by appeals to her for help or arbitration by weaker states threatened by the stronger. After that date, Hellenistic political history merged increasingly with the Roman and is best understood in terms of Roman expansion.

HELLENISTIC GREECE

Macedonia. Demetrius the Besieger had thought of Macedonia primarily as a base to reconquer Asia Minor, the real focus of his attention, but his son and successor, Antigonus Gonatas (276-239), abandoned all such plans when he became king and identified the interests of his dynasty exclusively with those of Macedonia. The circumstances surrounding his rise to power taught him that these interests meant above all defense of his northern frontiers against another invasion like the Celtic incursion, and his successors followed him in this conviction. Antigonus thus defined the historical mission of his dynasty as that of being a northern bulwark, shielding Greece from barbarian attack.

Antigonus consolidated and centralized Macedonia following a period when regal authority had been almost totally destroyed. He reorganized a kingdom that was depopulated after two generations of Macedonian manpower had been drafted to fight for Alexander and his successors and that was bankrupt following exhaustion of gold mines exploited by Philip II and recent Celtic plundering. At home, he confronted claims to independence by Macedonian towns, which had taken advantage of the extinction of the Amyntid dynasty to develop as quasi-autonomous enclaves within the kingdom. Abroad, he had to face the rivalry of Pyrrhus, king of Epirus, who until his death in 272 was backed by the Ptolemies in his claim to the Macedonian throne. Antigonus showed adroit statesmanship, asserting his own identity with the kingdom and reestablishing a monarchy over a nation united essentially by ties of common blood.

Restoring Macedonia's borders, he expropriated all newly annexed territory, which he distributed to farmer-soldiers owing military allegiance directly to him. This centralization of military authority was relatively easy to carry out because the ancient Macedonian aristocracy, traditional opponents of royal power, then counted for little, having been dispersed in Alexander's campaigns and killed off during the successors' wars. Because Macedonia was still essentially a self-sufficient agricultural community little affected by foreign trade, Antigonus was reluctant to use his citizen-militia in prolonged campaigns, for which he relied on mercenary armies. He limited the independence of cities under his rule by appointing military governors to administer them, and a staff of "friends" and advisers managed the state revenue, principally income from mines and forests, which he regarded as his own private property. Doggedly tenacious rather than brilliant, Antigonus was motivated by a strong sense of duty to his people, reflecting, apparently, Stoic training given him in his youth at Athens by Zeno himself, the founder of the school. His cultural phil-Hellenism was probably sincere, and he attracted to his court at Pella a circle of poets, philosophers, and historians.

Having given early priority to internal consolidation, Antigonus pursued with increasing confidence an aggressive foreign policy designed to assert Macedonian political hegemony over Greece. Like his father, he maintained the "fetters of Greece," garrisons at Corinth, Chalcis, Demetrias, and Piraeus, and he came to subsidize pro-Macedonian factions—generally oligarchies, or tyrants—in important cities. Realization of hegemony over Greece meant expulsion of the Ptolemies from their Aegean island bases and breaking their influence on the mainland. Antigonus achieved considerable success in realizing his goals through a series of wars and diplomatic maneuvers that illustrate the complexities of Hellenistic foreign policy. Neutralizing the Aetolian League by acknowledging its control of the Delphic sanctuary, he fought the so-called Chremonidean War (266-262) against Athens and Sparta, which both received Ptolemaic subsidies, and by defeating them, he guaranteed for a time his firm hold on southern Greece. After casting about for allies, he was able with the help of Rhodes to break forever Egyptian domination of the eastern Mediterranean at the Battle of Andros (245) and take over the Ptolemaic league of Aegean islands. His successes, however, provoked reaction by Aratus, leader of Sicyon, who expelled the Macedonian tyrant ruling his city (251), joined it to the Achaean League, and, as its general, liberated Corinth and other cities from Antigonus' control.

At the end of his reign, Antigonus tried to play Aetolians and Achaeans off against one another, but his son and successor, Demetrius II (239-229), had to face the combined resistance of both leagues. His son, Philip V (229-179), nine years old at his accession, was temporarily displaced as king by his able relative and guardian, Antigonus Doson, who usurped regal power for himself in 227 and wielded it until his death in 221. Antigonus Doson vigorously fought the leagues, markedly improved Macedonia's position within Greece, and established a so-called League of Leagues under his leadership. Emerging to maturity, Philip turned out to be a man not unsuited to Macedonia: courageous, even reckless, sometimes cruel and unscrupulous, and an enthusiastic campaigner. He was aided by division among his opponents in the so-called Social War (221-217), when Aetolians and Achaeans had a falling out. For a time much under the influence of Aratus of Sicyon and his oligarchic ideas, Philip joined Achaea against Aetolia, striking at the heart of its territory with calculated ruthlessness, but alienating Macedonians at home by a philo-Achaean policy that seemed to aggrandize Aratus more than it did Philip's own kingdom.

Nevertheless Philip emerged from the war in 217 with great prestige as the dominant force in the Balkans, but then, against the advice of his allies, he went to war with Rome over the question of control over Dalmatia (215-205), having made an entente with Hannibal, who was then invading Italy. Philip and Rome finally made peace on the basis of the status quo, which merely postponed a final reckoning between the two powers. Rome accepted appeals by smaller Greek states, including some of Philip's former allies, to intervene against him in another war (200-196). Philip thus became the historical instrument of Rome's expansion eastward, his defeat reducing Macedonia to a client kingdom, ultimately dissolved when his son and successor, Perseus, failed in a revolt against Roman domination (171-167).

The Federal Leagues.   Federalism was characteristic of the backward fringes of the Greek world where city-state institutions were relatively undeveloped; only two federal states, the Achaean and the Aetolian leagues, played an important political role in the Hellenistic age.

Well into the fourth century B.C. the Aetolians were organized loosely by tribes, which were linked more tightly together as a league only shortly before 300 B.C. Virtually impregnable in rough mountain fastnesses north of the Gulf of Corinth, their villages and cantons were almost all organized around forts. A very martial people, they supplied many mercenaries to other states, and because they lived by banditry and piracy, they were disagreeable neighbors and, at best, allies of very questionable value to more civilized powers. The largest town of the league was Naupactus, but there was, properly speaking, no capital city, although a kind of federal center existed at a temple of Apollo at Thermum, where they kept archives and booty.

About 275, just after winning great prestige by defeating the Celts, the Aetolian League was very democratic, with sovereignty residing in a primary assembly of the citizenry, the arms-bearing males, which met twice a year, before and after the campaigning season. The spring session, the Panaetolica, was held at different towns in turn; the autumn one, the Thermica, was held at Thermum for the purpose of electing officials. On behalf of the league, the assembly legislated, made alliances, accepted new members, decided questions of citizenship, heard ambassadors from foreign powers, declared war, and made peace. It elected military and civil officials like the commander of cavalry, the secretary of the assembly, and the treasurers, and it vested executive power every year in a general, who was both president of the league and commander in chief of its army. Naval operations were left to privateers.

There was also a permanently sitting council, whose members were elected in numbers proportional to the size of the constituent towns and cantons. It functioned as a court of justice and decided pressing matters that could not wait for assembly action. As the league expanded, it conducted foreign policy, although the assembly still decided questions of war and peace. Those citizens attending the assembly or standing for election to the council were unrepresentative of the whole population, as they tended to be well-to-do Aetolians who could afford to take the time to serve. As a result, the league government gradually became oligarchic.

All towns and cantons of the league remained locally autonomous but yielded sovereignty in larger matters to the federal assembly. The league finally expanded beyond Aetolia into Phocis and Boeotia (254-245), stretching across central Greece and even into the western Peloponnesus. In annexing new peoples, it relied on sympolity and isopolity. Sympolity, admission with the right to vote in assembly meetings, was awarded to the cities closest to Aetolia. More distant ones were granted isopolity, potential league enfranchisement, exercised only if their citizens happened to settle where sympolity applied. The Aetolians also insisted on dominating the Delphic amphictyony, although it was not a constituent part of that league.

The organization of the Achaean League was similar to that of the Aetolian, although it differed in significant particulars. The principles of Achaean federalism were historically more influential, having affected politics even in relatively modern times, as when they were studied and adapted by the Founding Fathers of the United States of America. The Achaean League also developed out of the cultural background of a rather backward Greek ethnic group, arising early in the fourth century B.C. as a union of, ultimately, twelve cities just south of the Gulf of Corinth. Unlike the Aetolian League, however, the Achaean League was a federation based exclusively on sympolity with dual citizenship, local and federal.

Sovereignty was vested in an assembly of citizens over thirty and in a council of several thousand representatives proportionately elected. The difference in competence between these two bodies is obscure, although it appears that the assembly elected officials, declared war, and made alliances, whereas the council prepared the assembly's agenda, dealt with foreign policy in general and with military, financial, and judicial affairs, the extension of league citizenship, and so on. New cities entered the league by treaties permitting them to keep their own constitutions and to coin money and raise taxes and citizen militia, although the federal government reserved the right to determine the value of coinage and to initiate taxation and mobilization. The league also maintained a standing army of mercenaries and could try and punish offenders of federal law.

At first, the Achaeans were ruled by two generals annually elected by each city in turn for the league as a whole. Divided executive power seemed dangerous, however, when the league fought wars outside Achaea, and in 255 B.C. the executive was changed to a single general, annually elected by the assembly, with the possibility of successive tenure in alternate years. The league was most powerful after Aratus brought Sicyon into it in 251, and when he dominated it as general every other year in the period 245-215. Aratus was a clever leader, aggrandizing the league by means of a foreign policy that alternately favored or opposed Macedonia and Aetolia, depending on which state was more powerful in southern Greece. After 200 B.C. usually a Roman ally, the league was for a time the most important state in Greece before it revolted against its increasingly dependent status and was disbanded and absorbed by Rome (146).

Athens. Athens was subject to many political and military changes between the death of Alexander and the rise of Roman power in Greece. During the wars of the successors a pawn first of the Macedonian regency and then of Demetrius and Antigonus "One-Eyed," her government oscillated between democracy and oligarchy, depending on whether anti- or pro-Macedonian factions were in control. After the Battle of Ipsus in 301, she proclaimed her neutrality, which was respected for a time because no power was strong enough to coerce her. Demetrius the Besieger, returning briefly to power in Greece and Macedonia, reconquered the city in 294 and established a garrison in Piraeus, which for two generations remained as a symbol of Macedonian hegemony.

In the early years of Antigonus Gonatas' rule, Athens was politically isolated and was treated by the king as the capital of his realm in Greece. Athenian dependence on Egyptian grain for provisioning led to a firm alliance with and subsidies from Ptolemy II, which encouraged the Athenian government to reassert its freedom from Macedonian influence by fighting for it. They lost the ensuing Chremonidean War (266–262), a crucial turning point in Athenian history. Capitulating after a seige, Athens lost its sovereignty, including the right to coin money, and was policed by Macedonian garrisons in rural Attica. The war dealt a serious blow to her commercial and intellectual vigor and left her a decentralized community, playing a merely passive and minor role in Greek affairs.

In 229 Antigonus Doson removed the Macedonian garrison in return for the payment of a large ransom. Possessed of greater freedom of action, the Athenian government in the same year declined the invitation of Aratus of Sicyon to join the Achaean League, her refusal to do so and evident preference of neutrality dramatizing her weakness. For the next generation Athens remained a neutral observer of the many wars in Greece, until a shift in the balance of power in favor of Macedonia seemed to threaten her, and she joined other states in requesting Roman help against Philip V in 200. Thirty years of peace and relative prosperity realized by adroit diplomacy were ended when Philip wantonly ravaged Attica in the same year. In the second century the moderately oligarchic government at Athens maintained steadfast friendship with Rome, and as a client state Athens profited from this relationship, especially after 166, when the Romans made Delos a free port and an Athenian possession.

Sparta. Sparta counted for little in the two generations following Alexander's death. She furnished famous individual mercenary captains to other Hellenistic states and even to Carthage, but depopulation forced her to use mercenaries herself. Her only notable venture into foreign policy before 250 B.C. was the alliance made by her king, Areus, in 266 with Athens and Ptolemy II in the Chremonidean War against Antigonus Gonatas, but Spartan participation was abortive and ended with Areus' defeat and death in 264.

In the second half of the century, however, Spartan history was considerably enlivened by three energetic kings who sought to restore her as a first-class military power. These attempts all involved an ostensible return to ancient "Lycurgan" institutions, although it is doubtful if any Spartan politician then had a very clear idea of what these once had been. The first such leader was young Agis IV (244-241/0), who observed the unhealthy socioeconomic state of his kingdom. Land was held by a very few wealthy aristocrats and the number of Spartiates had sunk to seven hundred, most of them deeply in debt. He decided to abolish debts, to redistribute land, creating thereby forty-five hundred lots for a citizenry swelled by the admission of some perioeci and fifteen thousand lots for remaining perioeci, and to restore the military mess. Most nobles opposed this program, which was rejected by the gerusia and ephors, who arrested, tried, and executed their king as a revolutionary.

Several years later Cleomenes III (237-222), who married Agis' widow, proposed to create four thousand citizen lots and to stifle opposition by abolishing the ephorate and the gerusia. His program might have been effective had he not fallen from power because of his ambitions to replace Aratus of Sicyon as leader of the Achaean League and so make Sparta supreme in the Peloponnesus. This disturbance in the balance of power and the revolutionary overtones of Cleomenes' reform produced an alliance of convenience between Aratus and Antigonus Doson, the Macedonian regent, and led to Cleomenes' defeat and exile.

The most colorful and thoroughgoing revolutionary of the three was King Nabis (206-192), who exiled wealthy nobles and redistributed their land to his mercenaries and Spartan citizens, whose numbers he also strengthened by freeing and enfranchising some slaves. He was a Roman ally in Rome's second war against Philip V of Macedonia, but his exploitation of the propaganda potential in the revolutionary program to extend his power beyond Laconia alarmed Rome and other Greek states, which united to restrict him in 195. After his death, Sparta was absorbed by the Achaean League but was exempted from provincial jurisdiction when the latter was annexed by Rome.

The reforms of Agis, Cleomenes, and Nabis are sometimes described as socialistic because they involved the most extreme kind of social and economic changes known to classical antiquity. Their programs were certainly revolutionary, but they were primarily patriotic in inspiration and intent and were designed to restore Spartan military power rather than to realize doctrinaire notions of egalitarianism. None of the three "Lycurgan" reforms, however, was truly socialistic because they all presupposed a numerous helot population to support the Spartans and thus were predicated on the existence of an inferior and politically deprived class.

Rhodes.   One of the most interesting Hellenistic cities was Rhodes, although its history is badly documented. Incorporated into Alexander's empire in 332, Rhodes regained freedom after his death, successfully resisted siege by Demetrius during the successors' wars, and for a short time kept close ties with the Ptolemies to balance power in the Aegean. When it seemed that the Ptolemies themselves might predominate, however, Rhodes fought Egypt, defeating their navy in 258 and again in 245 as an ally of Antigonus Gonatas. When Macedonia, in turn, threatened to impose an Aegean hegemony, Rhodes participated in the embassy of small Greek states that encouraged Rome to intervene against Philip V in 200. Thereafter she remained a firm client of Rome, under whose auspices she flourished as head of a league of Aegean islands. Rome punished her, however, by establishing Delos as a rival free port in 166, because she had dared to show some independence.

Rhodes owed her remarkable prosperity to her strategic location and to the energy and enterprise of her people. She lay athwart main trade routes, which shifted away from Europe following the eastward expansion of the Greek world, and replaced Piraeus as the greatest entrepôt or port of transshipment for a wide variety of products. She handled wheat, woolens, metals, slaves, and linens shipped south along the old lifeline leading into the Aegean from the Black Sea and on another route along the southern coasts of Asia Minor linking Old Greece with the Levant and Egypt. Enjoying a commercial income several times that of the Athenian Empire at its height, Rhodes became the leading banking center of the Hellenistic age early in the third century B.C. Since freedom of navigation was vital to their prosperity, the Rhodians policed adjacent waters and inherited from Athens the job of suppressing piracy. A by-product of their naval and commercial interests was their sophisticated maritime law, which spelled out the responsibilities and obligations of shipowners and captains to passengers and cargo, for which insurance rates were specified.

The government of Rhodes was vested in a popular assembly, council, and board of magistrates similar to those of most other classical city-states. The assembly had little influence, however, and the executive offices, which acted like a college, were a monopoly of a few aristocratic families. Little is known about Rhodian politics, except that the leading clique showed some enlightenment by providing for poor relief. The navy, staffed by citizens and noted more for its high quality than for its large size, ranked as the senior service, the mercenary army enjoying less prestige. The Rhodians won a unique kind of esteem abroad. When an earthquake destroyed their beautiful city, its harbor, and the Colossus standing at its entrance in 227 B.C., many kings and cities came to their aid in a unique display of Hellenistic solidarity.

HELLENISTIC ASIA

The Seleucid Empire. The Seleucid empire was by far the largest of the Big Three, but its very size was a source of weakness, and it inherited many of the problems of heterogeneity that had plagued the Persian Empire. It naturally fell into three sections with marked cultural, economic, and ethnic differences. To the east were its Iranian satrapies, inhabited by pastoral, Indo-European nomads. Its heartland and center comprised Mesopotamia and Syria, populous, rich, commercial areas inhabited mainly by Semites. Here were located the capital, Antioch-on-the-Orontes, and Seleucia-on-the-Tigris, the empire's largest cities. To the west lay possessions in Asia Minor comprising a seaboard of ancient Greek cities with a rural, only half-hellenized interior. The organization of the kingdom was conditioned by the fact that it was superimposed on territories with such different institutions, principally cities, nations, and tribes. There were two basic parts to it: "free" cities and nations, technically "in alliance" with the sovereign, and the remaining country (*chora*) subject to direct royal administration. The Seleucids founded some fifty-nine cities, chiefly in Syria and northern Mesopotamia, sometimes on virgin sites subtracted for the purpose from royal domain, but more often on preexisting native villages. Cities posed as independent *poleis* and were officially held by the king to be such. They were, however, controlled by royal "recommendations," which were, in fact, obligatory. They might also be recipients of benevolences, as when the king declared them free from taxes or "holy and inviolable," which meant that they enjoyed noncombatant status when he fought his wars.

If the cities were, at least formally, democratic, the rule of tribes was usually aristocratic, being vested in priests, elders, or prominent headmen. In some areas, notably Asia Minor, the Seleucids continued the Persian custom of recognizing dynasts, petty kings governing their principalities as delegates of the Seleucid sovereign. There were also temple states whose legal "lords" were gods; they were not normally at the disposal of the king, except in grave emergency.

Individual rights of private property existed only in areas recognized by the king as being "in alliance" with him, but these were extensive. Properly speaking, the royal domain comprised only a small part of the empire and consisted of property inherited by the dynasty from previous rulers: the Achaemenids, Alexander the Great, and his successors. It tended to diminish, especially as the kings detached territories from it to found new cities or to add to already existing ones. Seleucid hold on remaining crown domain was frequently loose, and tenants, colonists, and natives enjoyed rights of occupation, depending on the payment of rent or the performance of services.

The characteristic institutions of this disparate kingdom were created by its first two monarchs, Seleucus I (312-280) and Antiochus I (280-261). Obviously no national realm, it was united in its various parts in the person of the king, who was living law. Unlike the Macedonian royal house, the Seleucids required no constitutional sanction in acclamation by the army or any other body, and they differed from the Ptolemies by not claiming rule by divine right. There was no state or royal religion demanding allegiance from all loyal subjects, and they never officially used divine or semidivine titles. Technically autonomous Greek cities did, it is true, honor them with complimentary surnames like "Savior" (Soter) or "The God Manifest" (Epiphanes), but not, it seems, at regal behest. Beginning in about 205 B.C., a cult of the Seleucid dynasty developed in some satrapies under the king as grand master, but it bore no relation to the divine honors rendered by the cities and was not compulsory.

The right of the Seleucids to their kingdom was based on military conquest. Once acquired, it was heritable, and in naming his successor, the king simply disposed of his patrimony. Sometimes a son might be associated in rule as his father's lesser colleague, and in the case of succession by a minor, government was entrusted to a guardian, who kept the regalia. The exercise of regal power was very personal, the king being his own military commander in chief, secretary of state, legislator, and supreme court, although he could relegate any of his powers to other men, especially his minister of affairs or vizier (*epi ton pragmaton*), whose competence was not formally delimited.

Although not required to do so, the Seleucids sometimes called on their intimates for advice, and as in other states ruled by an absolute monarch, the court developed into an important institution influencing him. Called in the Macedonian manner "the king's house" or "the king's friends," Seleucid courtiers were ranked according to the degree of their intimacy with their monarch. Little is known about the central institutions of the kingdom, which managed a far-flung and loosely supervised system of satrapies inherited from Alexander the Great. The satraps were the king's governors-general over specific provinces, responsible directly to him, and enjoying both civil and military competence, although sometimes extraordinary commands were created superseding the government of several satrapies.

One of the most important branches of royal government was the treasury, called the *royalty* (*to basilikon*). To it flowed tribute (*phoros*), a kind of perpetual war tax apportioned among various communities and paid in coin or kind, depending on their economic development. Greek fiscal practices, like levying tribute, melde ‹ with the Persian ones of collecting head taxes and poll taxes. Cities were expected to offer the king gold crowns, symbols of victory, on jubilee occasions, and they paid customs duties and taxes on property and sales, among others. The treasury also profited from taxes and rents levied on the use of royal domain, and from extraordinary receipts like booty, confiscations, and expropriations of temple property. These receipts were supposed to cover maintenance of the army and the court, as well as occasional gifts and subsidies to cities and temples.

Except for isolated details, little is known about the methods of tax collection, except that cities managed their own finances and paid taxes to the crown directly. Coinage was minted on the Attic standard in gold for international trade, silver for domestic use, and bronze for small change, although silver was no longer coined after Antiochus II lost the sources of supply in the eastern satrapies. Minting means sovereignty, and the kings normally reserved to themselves the right to coin gold and silver, permitting cities to strike only bronze, which was normally not legal tender outside the place of issue. An index of waning Seleucid authority was the minting by cities, in about 150 B.C., of coins in their own right, without reference to the king.

The army, the kingdom's most strategic and expensive institution, numbered at its height some eighty thousand men, a size that only the Ptolemies could equal. Troops were scattered about in garrisons almost everywhere, their heaviest concentration being in Syria. The nucleus of the permanent, standing army was mercenaries, but in cases of total mobilization, military conscription was applied—at least, in principle—to all sections of the empire, except the cities. In backward areas tribes were expected to furnish contingents on demand, and elsewhere, as in inland Asia Minor, local magnates raised troops on a kind of feudal basis.

There was always a substantial Greco-Macedonian element in the army, composed of the descendants of Alexander's troopers and to a certain extent of subsequent colonists. The degree to which the Seleucids attracted the latter to their kingdom by promising them land in return for service is debatable. There is evidence that they offered Greek immigrants land lots (*kleroi*), but their tenure did not necessarily imply that they were soldiers, as some of them were assigned city territories exempt from military service, like those of Antioch and Dura Europus. Sometimes land tenure was vested in colonies as corporations rather than in individuals, which would also contradict the principle of granting land as a personal reward.

The Seleucids held together their conglomerate empire with difficulty under the best of circumstances because of problems of communication. Their administration was complicated by other factors: interminable and generally inconclusive warfare with the Ptolemies, and occasionally active resistance against them by Near Easterners, the most notable of such instances being the revolt of the Jews in Palestine (166), who resented them as interlopers coming between their quasi-independent temple state and God. Perhaps most important in the eventual decline of the dynasty was the fratricidal warfare within the royal house. Kings had to defend their thrones against their own brothers, wives, and even sons, with the result that only two of the fourteen rulers of the Seleucid dynasty died in the palace rather than on the battlefield. Under such circumstances it was understandable that important peripheral parts of the empire were becoming independent as early as the third century. Attempts of Antiochus III "the Great" (223-187) and Antiochus IV "Epiphanes" (176-164) to recover lost areas were only imperfectly and temporarily successful. Thrown back on its Syrian heartland, the kingdom disintegrated rapidly as the second century progressed.

Pergamon. The first important loss suffered by the Seleucids in the west came in Asia Minor, as commanders in the garrison town of Pergamon gradually established a dynastic state of their own early in the third century B.C. An ancient city with a considerable Greek population, Pergamon was controlled during the successors' wars by a virtually independent dynast, Philetaerus, who gave his allegiance first to Lysimachus of Thrace, then to the Seleucids (ca. 300-263). Probably subsidized by the Ptolemies, his nephew, Eumenes (263-241), broke with the Seleucids, against whom he waged successful war, without, however, proclaiming himself king. That title was taken for the first time in 228 by his cousin and successor, Attalus I (241-197), after he won great prestige in a signal victory over the Gauls, who had taken advantage of Seleucid weakness to plunder western Asia Minor as badly as during their initial invasion. Attalus intended to make his kingdom a peer of the Big Three, and after 200 B.C. he enlisted the help of Rome to realize that ambition. This policy aggrandized the dynasty early in the second century, when the Romans divided up Asia Minor between Pergamon and Rhodes following Rome's defeat of Antiochus the Great (188). As client kings, however, the Attalids were little more than Roman agents having negligible independence of action, and the last of the dynasty, Attalus III (138-133), anticipating the inevitable, willed his kingdom to Rome so that its incorporation into her empire would take place under favorable circumstances.

The Attalids were unusually successful rulers. Their realm was large enough to include important natural resources, which they managed capably, yet small enough to be tightly organized. The dynasty produced a succession of talented, long-ruling kings in a unified royal house, men who capitalized on the weaknesses of possible adversaries in their foreign policy while assiduously developing agriculture, industry, and trade at home.

They resembled the Seleucids in the government and organization of their kingdom, the Ptolemies in its economic exploitation. They were not divine-right monarchs, despite official genealogies linking them to the gods Heracles and Dionysus, divine honors occasionally given them by their subjects, and the existence of a cult of dead kings. Their rule was personal and absolute, but they received advice from a council dominated by their relatives, whose cooperation was remarkable. The capital city had a Greek constitution, but real power was wielded by five *strategoi* appointed by the king. The standing mercenary army, composed mainly of Mysians, was noted for its esprit, and the Pergamene citizenry was subject to draft in emergencies. The dynasty took a personal interest in animal husbandry, especially horse breeding, and in systematic farming. Attalus III even wrote a book on the latter subject, and other Hellenistic authors in the field of scientific agriculture had Pergamene connections. Shepherding was the basis for a flourishing woolens industry centered at Pergamon, which included dyeing, and although the Attalids did not invent it, they popularized the use of parchment to compete with Egyptian papyrus. Some industries, like the production of parchment, woven goods, and pitch, were apparently royal monopolies. The economy of the kingdom was further stimulated by a sound coinage maintained by extensive exploitation of native silver mines.

Bactria and the East. Developments similar to those in Pergamon took place on the eastern fringes of the Seleucid empire, creating a state whose existence is attested to almost solely by its surviving coinage. As early as 302 B.C., Seleucus I ceded his easternmost satrapies to the Indian rajah Chandragupta, and thereafter the dynasty maintained only a tenuous hold beyond the Euphrates, where Greek settlement was very thin, despite Alexander's having founded cities there for some of his veterans.

About 250 B.C. Seleucus II, by marrying off his daughter to the satrap Diodotus, used dynastic means to keep some kind of control over Bactria–Sogdiana (northern Afghanistan), a march state fending off barbarian attack from central Asia. Diodotus revealed his true status and the condition of neighboring Seleucid domains when he expanded his satrapy westward, driving Iranian nomads, the Parni, living near the Caspian Sea, south into the neighboring satrapy of Parthia. They killed the satrap of the region and, taking the name Parthians for themselves, established a neo-Persian kingdom destined to be a crucial factor in subsequent Greek and Roman history. Diodotus' like-named son broke completely with the Seleucid empire by proclaiming himself king of Bactria in about 228, but he was murdered by an ex-satrap from Magnesia in Asia Minor, Euthydemus, a soldier of fortune and an agent of the Seleucid dynasty. Euthydemus himself gained recognition by the Seleucids as an independent king in 208, and his reign and that of his son and successor, Demetrius (ca. 189-167), marked the height of Bactrian independence.

Greek Bactria in the east served the same historical function as Macedonia in the west: a shield protecting more civilized areas from nomadic inroads. The core of Euthydemus' kingdom was fertile, well watered, and commercially strategic, and his dynasty developed trade routes northward to central Asia, whence silk was imported, and eastward to India. Like the Seleucids, the Euthydemids dignified native villages by giving them charters of government, which explains Bactria's ancient reputation as "a land of one thousand cities." Their success as rulers is attributable to several factors. Like the Attalids, they had a strong sense of family loyalty, and when their kingdom expanded, they kept control by appointing subkings, usually their own relatives, over various areas. Lacking a sufficiently numerous class of

Greeks to staff the army and the government, they protected the interests of the native Bactrian nobility, who gave them their loyalty in return.

Demetrius greatly expanded Euthydemid territory when, following the model of Alexander the Great, he invaded India in 183, conquering as far as the middle reaches of the Ganges and the mouth of the Indus. In effecting his conquests, he exploited the religious disunity contributing to the decline of the Mauryan empire by allying with the Buddhists against the Brahmins, winning a reputation among the former as the traditional King of Justice. Returning to Bactria in about 175, he left behind a general, Menander, as subking in India; he became an even more famous Greek ruler in the Indian tradition than Alexander the Great. Relics of his reign survive in a curious bilingual coinage, but the number of Greeks he had at his disposal must have been small.

The Greek position in Bactria and India was shaken when the Seleucid Antiochus IV dispatched his cousin Eucratides to reconquer the East. Eucratides may have been supported by the Greek population in Bactria, possibly alienated from the Euthydemids because of their policies favoring native aristocrats. In any case, Demetrius was killed in 167, and in the next seven years Eucratides disposed of four other Euthydemid kings, although he failed to oust Menander from India before his own death in 159 while fighting an alliance of Parthians with Demetrius' son. The Parthians profited from this warfare among Greeks, rapidly consolidating their hold over Iran, and expanded into Mesopotamia, where they took Babylon from the Seleucids in 141. A much weakened Bactria succumbed to attack by Asiatic nomads called Yueh-chi (ca. 130), who wiped out or dispersed the Greek population. Following the death of Menander (ca. 150), Greek rule in India was broken up into a series of petty kingdoms. These came under attack by Saca nomads sweeping up the Indus Valley beginning in about 120, although the last Greek kinglet did not fall to them until about 30 B.C. Despite the length of their rule, the Greeks scarcely affected Indian civilization, except, perhaps for the idea of representing Buddha as a man and for a certain Hellenistic influence on the sculpture of Gandhara.

HELLENISTIC EGYPT

Introduction. Knowledge of the government, society, and economy of Ptolemaic Egypt is superior to that of other Hellenistic states because of the survival of thousands of papyrus documents, most of them fragments. These documents provide almost unique written evidence—private correspondence, some otherwise lost literary works, but especially official archives—for ancient life unparalleled at any other place or time in antiquity. The historical value of papyrus finds is rather limited, however. Most of them have occurred in the Fayum, a dried-up lake bed on the Nile's left bank not far from the Delta, a fertile, densely populated area in antiquity, and so shed light on only one small part of Egypt. Almost none has survived from areas closer to the Nile or in the Delta, where the water table is high, or from sites continuously inhabited since antiquity, like Alexandria, for which evidence is almost totally lacking. Few papyrus documents date from the early third cen-

COELE

• Damascus

Tyre
Ptolemais (Ake) •
SYRIA
• Gadara

*Syrian
Desert*

• Seleuceia

• Philadelphia (Rabbath–Ammon)

Canopus
Alexandria •
Naucratis •
Sais •
Raphia • Gaza

Rhinocolura

PALESTINE

Bubastis •
Memphis •
Berenice Hormos? •
Pelusium •

N
• Petra

NABATEANS

FAYUM
Caranis •
Arsinoe–Cleopatris •
Heliopolis •

Theadelphia •
Arsinoe •
(Crocodilopolis)
Philadelphia
Philotera?

• Aelana

Oxyrhynchus •
Ptolemais Hormos
Heracleopolis

Hermupolis •

Lycopolis •
Arsinoe? •

• Teima

ARABIA

Myos Hormos

LIHYANITES

• Dedan

Ptolemais •
Tentyra •
Coptos •
Thebes
Latopolis •
Arsinoe? •
Apollinopolis •
Elephantine •
Philae •
Syene
1st cataract

Ampelone •

• Iathrippa

Berenice •

Philometoris? •
2nd cataract
Cleopatra? •

Nile R.

Ptolemais Epitheras •

RED SEA

ETHIOPIA

MINEANS

• Meroe

Karna •

Mariaba •

Berenice the Golden •

SABEANS

KATABANI

HELLENISTIC
EGYPT

Arsinoe? •

0   100   200   300   400

Berenice Epidires •

Miles

tury B.C., the formative period in Ptolemaic history, when institutions took shape that characterized Egypt to the end of the dynasty in 30 B.C. and even, to some extent, under subsequent Roman rule.

Ptolemaic Government. Ptolemy I Soter (305–283), military founder of the dynasty, was an energetic imperialist and established Ptolemaic claims to territories outside the Nile Valley. His son and successor, Ptolemy II Philadelphus (285–246), although pursuing a vigorous foreign policy, was more important for the internal organization he gave his kingdom. The dynasty was most powerful under Ptolemy III Euergetes (246–221), who won considerable territory in the Levant and Asia Minor from the Seleucids, although his naval defeat by Antigonus Gonatas (245) lost him control over the Aegean islands.

Thereafter a decline in military and naval efficiency led to a corresponding decay in the Ptolemaic littoral empire. The number of Greco-Macedonian military immigrants dwindled, and the dynasty relied increasingly on other mercenaries and even on native Egyptians. A Ptolemaic army composed mainly of such mercenary and native contingents was effective enough to win a brilliant victory over the Seleucids in 217 at Raphia in the Gaza Strip, but it also impressed the Egyptians with their own military importance to their foreign dynasty. Once armed, the natives expressed their dissatisfaction with the regime and its heavy taxation in a series of revolts during the second and first centuries B.C. The kingdom, further enfeebled by quarrels and intrigues within the ruling family, became a client state of Rome, which protected.it so long as there were other Hellenistic powers strong enough to threaten the prevailing balance of power. By the first century B.C., Egypt's independence from Rome was only formal, yet the Roman senate refused to sanction its direct annexation, fearing control of its wealth by one of their own dynasts. The last of the Ptolemies, Cleopatra VII, was eliminated in 30 B.C. because of her involvement in what was essentially a civil war between Roman generals for the control of the whole Roman Empire.

Like all Greek dynasties save the Antigonid, the Ptolemies obtained their kingdom by right of conquest. Because of traditions of king worship peculiar to Egypt, they solidified their rule over both Greeks and natives by claiming to be living gods. Their cult, not fully developed until the early third century, found its ultimate Greek precedent in that of Alexander the Great, whose body the first Ptolemy ritually entombed in his own capital, Alexandria. For Greek subjects, Ptolemaic divinity was expressed in such official regal titles as "Savior," "Benefactor," and "Protector." For the large native majority of their subjects, they claimed to be living gods because they posed as pharaohs. Although they sought the support of the Egyptian priesthood through patronage, they won at best grudging acceptance. They never really earned recognition as national kings, and the Egyptians tended to regard them rather hostilely as foreign intruders.

The most important ministers of state at the Ptolemaic court were responsible to their king for military, judicial, and financial administration. Because of the unique economic value of Egypt, the finance minister, called simply "the manager" (*dioicetes*), was very powerful. The Ptolemies inherited from previous rulers, ultimately from pharaonic government itself, a complicated bureaucracy regulating the main branches of administration, which stretched out from the court to regulate some forty nomes and their villages. The Ptolemies further developed this highly complicated form of government, attempting to operate it more efficiently and more pervasively than their predecessors, so as to exploit the Egyptian economy fully and to make their dynasty richer and more powerful.

Egypt was regarded as the king's private estate, with the exception of the three Greek cities (Alexandria, Naucratis, and Ptolemais), which were distinct administrative enclaves standing apart from the country. Unlike the Seleucids, the dynasty founded only one city, Ptolemais, probably because even the merely formal autonomy granted royal cities was incompatible with the highly developed bureaucracy of Egypt. Alexandria grew to have a polyglot population of several hundreds of thousands, including Greeks, Egyptians, and foreigners—in particular, a large Jewish population. The city as a whole was governed by a *strategos* responsible to the king, whereas the Greek community had typical city-state institutions. The Jews, and probably other ethnic groups as well, had corporations of their own. Detailed knowledge of the administration of Alexandria and the other cities is lacking, however.

Although all of the country was owned by the king, only part of it was royal domain in the sense of being tilled by crown peasants and managed directly in the king's interest. Much of it was possessed and enjoyed, on certain terms, by favored corporations and individuals, even though ownership in every case technically resided with the king. There were three such categories of land. Some estates were "set aside" to support temples, whose priests were appointed and controlled, but also conciliated, by the dynasty. The priests managed the peasants and enjoyed the revenue from such estates. There were also "gift lands" (*doreiai*), often with entire villages, which the king granted to his favorites, frequently important bureaucrats, who maintained satellite courts at Alexandria from the rents paid them by their tenants. Gift lands sometimes comprised thousands of acres, like the estate of Apollonius, the finance minister of Ptolemy II, who was perhaps responsible more than any other bureaucrat for the Hellenization of the Egyptian administration and economy. Much of the correspondence of Apollonius' estate manager, Zeno, has survived to show how the Ptolemies sometimes relied on the entrepreneurship of private individuals to reclaim land and stimulate agricultural production.

The third case of tenanted land was that of "cleruchies," smaller lots that were granted extensively to attract soldiers from abroad for settlement. There were always mercenaries paid in coin, soldiers of fortune in the truest sense, but more typically land was the retainer for possibly ninety thousand Greeks, Macedonians, and other soldiers in Egypt in the third century B.C. Perhaps a quarter of the tillable acreage was given to cleruchs, normally in allotments ranging from twenty to forty-five acres, on condition of their providing military service when mobilized. As the state did not strictly enforce its claims to the land or the military service of its tenants after about 200 B.C., they became de facto owners, more gentlemen farmers than soldiers, and the army suffered accordingly.

Ptolemaic Economy. The Ptolemies temporarily succeeded in expanding the Egyptian economy, in the sense that they brought greater energy and organization to its exploitation than had the last Persian rulers. By improvements in drainage and irrigation, largely the work of Greek engineers employed by the crown or by favored entrepreneurs like Apollonius, the area under cultivation increased in the third century and supported new migrants from abroad in addition to the native population. The government received more taxes and services than previously, as the bureaucracy enforcing regulations was enlarged. Although privileged (usually Greek) classes of the population were exempt from the most pressing taxes and services, these were levied in full on Egyptian peasants, whose status was depressed. Peasants tilled even crown land precariously, could be dispossessed at any time, yet could not abandon their plots at will. In addition to paying poll taxes and taxes in kind on agricultural produce, they were forced to do corvee labor on dikes, canals, and roads and sometimes to cultivate additional plots. They had to buy many necessities of life from the government at the king's artificially high monopoly prices, and they always suffered from the casual corruption, extortion, brutality, and red tape of the bureaucracy.

The economy declined after 200 B.C. as the hold of the central government over the administrative apparatus weakened. The peasants took advantage of the situation by revolting or "taking a seat," that is to say, by going on sit-down strikes at temple sanctuaries with the connivance of priests and refusing to return to work until concessions were made. Under such conditions, agriculture was disrupted, land was abandoned and allowed to become waste, irrigation canals fell into disrepair, and the tillable acreage shrank. Nevertheless Egypt even at the end of the dynasty was still the richest Mediterranean country, worth twelve thousand silver talents in taxation.

The Ptolemaic budget was undoubtedly very large by ancient standards. In addition to the usual expenditures for the army and the navy, much money was consumed by diplomacy because the Ptolemies traditionally bought the friendship of states in Old Greece through subsidies. Payments to civil servants, maintenance of cults and clergy, erection of public works, and expenses of a luxurious court consumed their sizable income. Their revenue came from many sources, above all from agriculture. A tax in kind on wheat, Egypt's basic product, was probably the single most important levy. An annual ordinance, determined by the height of the Nile flood and the extent of fertilized land, decreed the wheat acreage to be planted by everybody: royal tenants, temples, holders of gift land, and cleruchs. The tithe of grain requisitioned at harvesttime by royal agents was then transported by donkeys and boats commandeered for the purpose to warehouses at Alexandria to be sold abroad at sizable gain to the Ptolemaic treasury. A similar tax in kind was levied on orchard produce, normally one-sixth of the crop, one-tenth in the case of cleruchs.

The Ptolemies attempted to be economically autarchic and so fostered animal husbandry—the breeding of better strains of farm animals and of horses—to reduce imports from abroad. In the same spirit they tried to domesticate the vine and the olive, traditionally important to Greek life in the Aegean but not to native Egypt. Viticulture was introduced with some success, and because vineyards required the care of specialists, their tenure was made attractive on conditions approximating private ownership with rights of inheritance and alienability. The state taxed one-third to one-half of the grapes produced, an amount characteristic of those branches of the economy not closely administered by the king. The Ptolemies also tried to acclimate olives, but they did not grow well except in the Fayum and the Delta and in any case produced poor oil. Olive oil was a product essential to cooking, lighting, and bathing in antiquity, and the Ptolemies made money by taxing imports of it from Greece and their own overseas dominions at rates upwards of 50 per cent.

The kings' monopoly over the production and sale of domestic substitutes, chiefly sesame and castor oil, illustrates their tight control over the economy. The government ordered farmers to plant a specific acreage in oil-bearing plants and gave them the necessary seed. One quarter of the plants was taken outright as tax, and the remainder had to be sold at a fixed price to state contractors, who stored them in barns approved by the government before the seed was extracted and pressed in state mills. The movement of workers in oil mills was closely circumscribed so as to prevent clandestine manufacture. Like imported olive oil, the finished domestic product was sold at artificially high prices, which netted the government a profit of from 40 per cent to 300 per cent. Similar government monopolies existed on the export abroad of linen and papyrus and on the domestic sale of beer and salt.

Mines and quarries—in principle, in the royal domain—were frequently worked by convict labor. Egyptian mineral wealth was fairly limited. The country was well provided with certain kinds of building stone like granite, porphyry, and basalt and with deposits of semiprecious stones like topaz, and some salt was panned in the Delta. On the southern and eastern borders there were gold mines, largely played out in Hellenistic times, but no silver and little iron. Peasant artisans normally owned no iron instruments, which were instead loaned to them by government officials.

The Ptolemies were interested in foreign trade, channeled mainly through Alexandria, which exported industrial products of weaving and glassblowing and raw materials from the interior, chiefly wheat. The city also became an important place of transshipment for a wide variety of exotic products reaching the Mediterranean world from the Middle and Far East. During the third century, but especially after their hold over caravan cities and other ports in the Levant slipped to the Seleucids, the Ptolemies exploited an alternate route via the Red Sea and the Indian Ocean, using both the old canal between the Gulf of Suez and the Nile as well as newly founded ports on the west coast of the Red Sea, whence goods were shipped overland to the Nile, then down it to Alexandria. Spices, precious stones, and silk thus were funneled through Egypt, enriching both her traders as middlemen and the Ptolemies with their *ad valorem* duties.

20

Hellenistic Civilization

INTRODUCTION

In some respects, Greek political control of the Near East led to striking economic changes, not the least of them being the opportunity for Greeks to exploit much more varied—and in some cases, richer—natural resources than had been available to them in the Aegean world. For the first time they were forced to abandon laissez-faire economic attitudes traditional to the government of the city-states and, as rulers of Egypt and other kingdoms, to come to terms with bureaucracies demanding their active interest in, and even control over, agriculture, trade, and industry. They rose to the challenge and brought to the Near East fresh energy in the production of wealth, so that the Hellenistic period witnessed a notable economic expansion.

ECONOMY AND SOCIETY

That expansion, however, was not uniform or universal, and its benefits were not evenly distributed over the various classes of the population in the Aegean basin or the Near East. It was characterized by a notable inflation of currency in the third century B.C., in which wages lagged behind prices and the lion's share of the new wealth being generated fell to propertied classes, whose standard of living improved markedly. At first, the Aegean basin profited by the export of at least some of its surplus population to the East and of foodstuffs and manufactured products demanded by the new Greek population living there. Well before 200 B.C., however, even this moderate emigration all but stopped. Demand for exports dried up as new Greek states abroad developed their own agriculture and commerce and, in some cases, aimed at economic autarchy. The economic center of gravity in the Greek world moved eastward to new population centers in Asia Minor, Syria, and Egypt. This move benefited Rhodes, Alexandria, and the Levant at the expense of Piraeus and left Corinth, strategically located near an isthmus, as the only significant port on the Greek mainland. The decline of commerce combined with overpopulation to produce poverty and to renew civil strife in many cities of Old Greece in the second century B.C., problems unresolved before the coming of the Romans.

The high degree of social and economic integration characteristic of the classical Aegean world of city-states broke down under Hellenistic conditions, and the situation in the areas of the Near East governed by Greeks was equally unstable. Except to claim their leading place among the governing elite, the Greeks did not disturb the existing social structure, which meant that they sanctioned and even reinforced the millennial traditions of social and economic inequality existing among the natives. Although there were some important exceptions, native aristocracies usually did not resist Greek rule, which left their wealth and property untouched. They even willingly cooperated with their conquerors because it was socially, economically, and politically advantageous for them to do so.

Cities. Despite the widespread development of city life in the Near East after the Greek conquest, the vast proportion of the population—whether small freeholders, tenants, or slaves—remained peasants deriving their sustenance from the land. Nevertheless urbanism had an important impact on all sectors of the economy, including agriculture, although its contribution to sound development was questionable. Political rather than economic motives dominated the founding of cities, and the cities were rarely conceived of as promoting the economic development of the surrounding country, although this development, of course, did happen in places occupying commercially strategic sites. A few old cities like Ephesus and Rhodes grew to be at least as large in the Hellenistic age as fifth-century Athens in her imperial heyday, and the most famous ones—Antioch and Alexandria—each numbered several hundreds of thousands of people, larger than any other places in antiquity before the rise of Rome. The initial expansion of Hellenistic cities was an economic stimulus because much money was spent on their construction and development, but the quality of their economy thereafter was always rather primitive.

Hellenistic cities failed to produce much wealth because, despite notable advances in science, no technological breakthrough occurred that might otherwise have led to an industrial revolution and a numerous class of producers and consumers. Mass-producing industries were exceptional, even in making cheap articles for everyday use. As in classical Athens, the typical factory was a limited operation, an artisan with a few helpers selling the product of their labor over the counter to customers, and both retail and service trades remained similarly fragmented. The small upper class of Greeks and native aristocrats were locally important as consumers far out of proportion to their number because of their wealth, and long-distance trade, mainly in luxuries, also catered primarily to this class.

In the long run, Hellenistic cities created an inequitable economic and social situation, which, inherited eventually by Rome, remained typical for the rest of antiquity. Most businesses, banks, and factories were owned by the upper class, who of course did not personally run them. Upper-class prosperity trickled down to benefit the urban masses only to the extent that they found employment in shops, factories, and other establishments owned by entrepreneurs, but at best, workers lived a haphazard, hand-to-mouth existence and, as a class, were an underemployed proletariat subject to desperate circumstances. The limitations built into the urban economy are illustrated by the fact that upper-class entrepreneurs either spent the profits of their successful professional or commercial ventures on maintaining their urban domestic establishments or invested them in country estates, from which they always derived the bulk of their income. A merchant class divorced from the land and specializing exclusively in trade and commerce scarcely existed.

Because Hellenistic cities were primarily consumers rather than producers of great wealth, they were parasitic on their surrounding hinterland. Trade and industry, dependent primarily on serving rich landlords living in cities, provided almost exclusively for urban needs, and peasants tended to buy their basic necessities only at their local market villages. Although absentee landlords gladly spent money on maintaining and improving their farms, they also spent a disproportionate share of the rents and taxes they collected from their peasants on maintaining their own urban services. Few Hellenistic cities had budgets, although their expenses—such as the maintenance of public works, entertainment, cults, and food subsidies for the poor—were scarcely if ever covered by purely local revenues from market levies, harbor dues, fines, income from endowments, and so on. Although the proportion varied from place to place, probably most municipal expenses were borne by the aristocracy either as liturgies or as philanthropic offerings, often made enthusiastically. The net effect of this situation was that wealth derived from the country tended to sustain cities, which did not provide compensating economic return. The order of priorities was obvious to Hellenistic town fathers, as the urban masses were a highly visible, concentrated, and ever-present pressure group able to voice their grievances at many kinds of public gatherings, ranging from organized political assemblies to tumultuous riots. In times of urban distress caused by famine, city governments did not hesitate to requisition supplies in the country, even if this action reduced the peasants themselves to starvation.

Social Instability.   Despite its top-heavy character, maldistribution of wealth, and widespread poverty, Hellenistic society was never seriously threatened by revolutions that might otherwise have changed the economic structure radically. It is not readily apparent why that structure, although severely strained at times, remained basic to the Mediterranean world without serious alteration until the very end of antiquity. For one thing, it appears that the economically depressed classes were divided and so were incapable of making a common cause. The peasants had little sympathy, for example, with the poor of the great cities, for whose support they were sometimes impoverished, and neither class identified its interests with those of slaves. Perhaps the closest approximation to social revolution came at the end of the Hellenistic period (ca. 140–70 B.C.) in a series of servile uprisings in both the Greek and the Roman worlds. It seems never to have occurred to the free poor and the slaves, however, to unite against the propertied establishment, probably because no one, not even the slaves, questioned as a matter of principle the right of one human being to hold others as chattel.

Other factors also inhibited revolution. Even though philosophers occasionally dreamed of communal utopias and politicians, like the kings of Sparta, advocated revolutionary programs embracing the redistribution of property and the abolition of debts, there was no dogma that would have justified or inspired revolutionaries. None of the leading philosophies preached revolution, not even Stoicism, which, it is true, in some sense held that a basic equality of human beings existed. The educated classes—in modern times, the frequent leaders of social revolution—were not inspired to assume that role in antiquity. They tended to relieve the worst economic and social situations by civic philanthropy and beneficence.

HELLENISTIC CULTURE

A vehicle for the spread of Hellenism to the East was, of course, the emigration of Greeks, which, although essential to the process, was not its most important feature. They were a minority of the population even where they settled rather thickly, as in Egypt, where the native Egyptians are said to have outnumbered them by eight to one. The shortage of female Greeks abroad frequently led to the intermarriage of Greek men with native women and to the production of a hybrid population, but so few were the Greeks that they had little ethnic effect on the population of the Near East as a whole.

Just as important as emigration in the diffusion of Greek culture was its adaptation by native aristocracies and its domestication in Eastern cities. There was, it is true, a certain resistance against Hellenism, which was most successful on the fringes of the Greek world, in Babylonia and Persia, where it was strengthened by an optimistic religious faith and an aggressive political tradition, but which appeared elsewhere also, as among the priestly class in Egypt. Perhaps the most notable case of cultural conflict caused by Hellenization occured in Palestine, where upper-class Jews adopted Greek gymnastic training beginning in 174 B.C. After a long conflict with the Seleucids and within their own community, they established an independent state whose leaders decided that Greek culture was acceptable only so long as its religious content was censored.

Most upper-class Near Easterners, however, found Greek civilization inherently attractive even before Alexander, and that attraction increased appreciably after the conquest, when, in many cases, it seemed that their own cultures had been tried and found wanting. Greek civilization was obviously dynamic. Furthermore it made good sense to accommodate to the ways of the new rulers. Hellenization meant the acceptance of the native upper classes into the governing elite, and so they enthusiastically took Greek names, learned the Greek language, and pursued formal Greek education, although their family and religious customs were sometimes less affected by their Hellenic lifestyles. This process of acculturation was nonetheless extraordinary. Although it affected only a very few natives, they were the very ones on whom the transmission of higher Near Eastern culture depended. Most Oriental languages sank to the level of unwritten patois, although Hebrew survived as a learned language and Aramaic was widely spoken—even by natives using Greek—as a vernacular in the Fertile Crescent. Greek, however, almost always usurped a unique position as a written language of business, law, and government in everyday use by ethnic Greeks and Hellenized natives. Hellenistic Greek, known as *koine,* the "common tongue," was the lingua franca of educated people from the Aegean basin to the Euphrates and even beyond. It was a rather simplified version of the classical Attic and Ionic dialects, which also survived as scholarly or literary languages.

The amenities of life provided by the cities naturally varied widely with their wealth, but they all intended insofar as possible to imitate the original *poleis* of the Aegean world in their architecture, athletic, cultural, and educational institutions. They might boast enlightened town planning, markets, paved streets, baths, theaters, aqueducts, and drainage, sometimes even public doctors, but their police, especially fire, protection was generally inadequate. The largest problem facing them was basic provisioning, as the transportation of foodstuffs from the country-side was both difficult and expensive. Primary education was left to private enter-prise, municipal subsidies in this case being all but nonexistent, which meant that even rudimentary education depended on the ability of families to hire tutors for their sons.

Effectively excluded from primary education, the poor could not hope to enjoy more advanced training, which was provided by the gymnasium, a characteristically Hellenistic institution absolutely essential to the spread of Greek civilization. The first gymnasia were established early in the fourth century; they resembled a high school, in which upper-class adolescent boys, known as *ephebes*, spent anywhere from one to three years studying a curriculum based largely on rhetoric and receiv-ing paramilitary and physical education. As alumni, they were still eligible to enjoy the facilities of the gymnasium, which thus combined the features of a school with those of a men's club. The popularity of the institution spread rapidly, and no Hellenistic city worth the name was without one. Admission to and training in the gymnasia became the surest hallmarks of Hellenism in the Near East for both ethnic Greeks and upper-class natives. They were expensive to maintain, however, and payment of their teachers and supervision of their physical plant were undertaken by a municipal magistrate known as the *gymnasiarch*, a costly liturgy in which he was expected to subsidize the institution liberally.

Hellenistic civilization was inconceivable without cities, but their essential contri-butions to culture were limited. They produced a wide but thin diffusion of Hellen-ism, which was perhaps more notable for its uniformity than originality. They were, of course, important patrons of art and architecture, and the founding and subse-quent embellishment of the cities meant the beginning of a golden age of civic building that lasted until the decline of the Roman Empire. As a rule, they had high standards of education, as the term was then understood, and produced a small class of highly if narrowly trained literati. Wherever there were cities, there were people who appreciated Greek art and read Greek literature, but this very fact illus-trates the limitations and shortcomings of Hellenistic civilization in the Near East.

It had, after all, a clearly mandarin quality because it appealed to only a very small elite and was almost impervious to native influences outside the Aegean basin. Except to a certain extent in the practice of law (in which Greek governments sometimes used Near Eastern practices like writing down contracts), in the forma-tion of *koine*, and in the adoption of eastern religions, the effect of rich and ancient non-Greek cultures on Hellenistic civilization was as negligible as that of India on its British rulers during the last century. Because Hellenistic civilization depended on formal training, the lower classes even of Old Greece were largely alienated from its more sophisticated aspects. Lower-class natives of cities in the Near East might at least be familiar with Greek civic architecture and art by sight, but they were not affected by the real seats of civilization in the gymnasia, had no understanding of Greek drama, and so were involved only very superficially with Hellenistic culture. In the countryside, villages unsubsidized by cities lacked even the barest artistic amenities of Greek life, and the peasants, understanding not even *koine* and almost totally cut off from any contact with urban culture, maintained their own artistic and other folkways, which were destined to prove more vigorous than Greek culture.

Literature. Prose literature was the most characteristic product of Hellenistic civilization, largely because of the influence of the Sophist Isocrates and his school on educational theory and literary interests. Even before about 350 B.C., the dominant themes and characteristic trends of Hellenistic literature had been established, when Isocrates insisted on prose as the medium par excellence of contemporary artistic creativity and on the notion that *paideia,* or initiation into Hellenism, could be got by formal training from books. He virtually canonized the importance of rhetoric and literary form in the curriculums offered in the gymnasia, where successive generations of students exposed to *paideia* learned by heart the classics of their own civilization. These included Homer, the fifth-century tragedians, and the fourth-century orators, which they were trained to appreciate and imitate.

Although very little of the vast output of prose in the Hellenistic period has survived, some estimate of its quality can be made from its very fragmentary remains. Devotion to classics of the past led to a certain antiquarian or even scholarly approach to literature cultivated especially by the Museum at Alexandria. This institution, endowed by the first Ptolemy and dedicated to the Muses, was an important center of research but not a university. The Museum supported scholars in a variety of fields, although literature received more attention than science. Attached to the Museum was a library, which held, it is said, at least one copy of every known Greek work, hundreds of thousands of scrolls. Scholars attached to the Museum— such as Zenodotus (ca. 284), its first head, and Aristarchus of Samothrace (ca. 217–145), the Homeric specialist—created for the first time the art of literary criticism, valuable to a civilization prizing its own classics. On both a philological and a purely subjective basis, they established standard texts and rejected spurious readings and works. A famous by-product of their critical research was the so-called Homeric question, because it seemed to some of them that the *Iliad* and the *Odyssey* could not have been the product of a single artistic genius. They also annotated classics and produced dictionaries as instructional aids to explain standard works to generations whose *koine* had departed rather considerably from the written literary Greek of earlier periods.

Alexandrian literary scholars also prided themselves on being polymaths, men learned in many different fields. Perhaps their most typical representative was Eratosthenes (fl. ca. 240 B.C.), the chief librarian of the Museum, a man of encyclopedic knowledge and, among other things, a leading mathematician. Eratosthenes was an important chronologist and geographer. As a result of his antiquarian research, he canonized the dates (in our time reckoning) of 1184 B.C. for the fall of Troy and of 776 for the first Olympiad and produced a critical history of geographical knowledge from Homer to Alexander the Great, to which he appended a famous map.

Although classes educated by *paideia* might enjoy such scholarship, they normally sought entertainment by reading much lighter contemporary works, so that another characteristic of Hellenistic prose was a wide diversity of genres, ranging from the extremely erudite to the extremely popular. These latter included, above all, handbooks simplifying technical subjects like history, philosophy, and science, which were treated only peripherally in their rhetorically oriented curricula. As part of a much enlarged world, the educated public was interested in myths and romances dealing with sometimes strange and exotic peoples coming for the first time into their orbit, as well as popularized works on geography and exploration, such as the account of one Pytheas of Massilia, who apparently reached by sea the tin mines of Cornwall late in the fourth century.

The diversity of subjects treated by Hellenistic prose, its rhetorical emphasis, and its scholarly and popularizing tendencies are perhaps most clearly illustrated in the genre of history. The influences of Isocrates guaranteed that, with notable exceptions, historical works would be preoccupied with personalities and would be rhetorical, not scientific, in their approach. History so written was concerned not so much with truth as with dramatic literary effect, and in entertainment value it approached the status of historical novels. Such a theatrical approach did not, of course, prevent historians from writing on new themes or from showing off pedantic erudition. One of the most important Hellenistic historians was Hieronymus of Cardia, whose *History of the Successors* covered the period from 323 to 266 B.C. His work, for the first two decades, was preserved by Diodorus of Sicily (ca. 27 B.C.) and shows him to have been a sound writer, chiefly interested in political and military history. The historian most clearly typifying antiquarianism was Timaeus of Taormina (ca. 345–250), who, in writing a history of the western Greek colonies, strove for dramatic or moving emotional effects while cramming his book with academic miscellany. Because Timaeus' work was difficult reading, it was excerpted in the first century B.C. also by Diodorus of Sicily, large portions of whose *Historical Library* survive to illustrate the genre of handbooks designed to popularize and simplify erudition.

By far the greatest of Hellenistic historians was Polybius of Megalopolis in Arcadia, who ranks second only to Thucydides among Greek historians. Polybius came from a prominent family and played an active role in the affairs of the Achaean League. In 167 B.C., after the Third Macedonian War, he was carried off as a hostage to Rome, where he became the friend of Scipio Aemilianus and other important Romans. He soon grew to admire Rome and was inspired with the ambition to tell the moving story of the new world power. His *History* covered the period from 221 to 146 B.C., and of the forty books the first five and various extracts remain. Polybius believed that contemporary politicians could learn much from the past, and he therefore addressed himself to them and not to the general public. As a result, he does not make exciting reading. He often digresses and is verbose; he is unfair to Carthage and allots too much space to the Achaean League. Nevertheless Polybius was a scientific historian who diligently studied his sources and often traveled to various sites to verify his data. Though he lacked detachment, Polybius was industrious, and with his own experience in political affairs, he succeeded to a large degree in writing a critical and immensely valuable account of the Mediterranean world. By Polybius' day, of course, the history of the Hellenistic world had become inextricably mixed with that of Rome.

While helping to mould some typical features of Hellenistic historiography, Aristotle disagreed with the Isocratean school when it came to matters of style. He agreed that history was susceptible to dramatic treatment, although he did not approve of making it theatrical. The collaborative efforts of the Peripatetic school to organize historical research foreshadowed similar projects at the Museum. Aristotle, with his followers, including Theophrastus, also transcended the political orientation of history by giving a historical development to the study of philosophy, medicine, astronomy, and mathematics. Although Aristotle did not write biography, his interest in types of human life led to his interest in outstanding individuals as such and helped develop biography as a separate Hellenistic genre. The Peripatetics became increasingly antiquarian in their collection of facts of all kinds and were limited by Aristotle's own conception of history as a kind of biological development of society from small beginnings to a flourishing phase and then a decline. Nevertheless, although they paid too much attention to trivia and accepted data uncritically, they were, unlike the Isocrateans, at least motivated by a disinterested approach to research.

The decline of the city-state as a closely knit community with clearly defined ideals adversely affected the production of dramatic poetry. At Athens first-rate tragedy did not survive the fifth century because it depended for success on the rather ingenuous involvement of the citizenry in what had been, essentially, a moving religious experience and a kind of folk art. Popular fifth-century dramas were revived frequently during the Hellenistic period, especially those of Euripides, because rhetorically trained audiences preferred his very personal, psychological, even sophistic approach to tragedy over that of the archaic, rather abstract Aeschylus or the placid Sophocles. Aristophanic comedy, depending no less for its popularity on the relevance of city-state life, whose institutions it lampooned, was replaced at Athens and elsewhere by a very different genre called *New Comedy,* whose most famous exponent was Menander of Athens (ca. 342-291). New Comedy was written primarily for audiences formally educated in *paideia,* that is to say, the well-off classes interested not so much in earthy, ribald farce as they were in more refined and sophisticated "situation comedies." As evidenced by several surviving works of Menander, New Comedy was a genteel comedy of manners, a genre in which upper-class Greeks could laugh at amatory intrigues and family problems on the stage that were only exaggerated versions of the ones they experienced in their own lives. The widening cultural gulf between the educated and the uneducated in the Hellenistic world is illustrated by the rise of the mime as entertainment for the masses, who failed to appreciate the subtleties of Menandrian comedy and preferred to experience an art that was more direct, obvious, and lusty.

The rise of formal literary education also conditioned creativity in other types of poetry, which were more intimate and personal than tragedy and comedy because they were written to be read by the educated in their studies rather than to be enjoyed at public performances. The most remarkable such work was produced at Alexandria. Like certain prose genres, it was academic and bookish, its authors showing off their learning with sometimes obscure allusions to the classics, which, they assumed, every educated reader would recognize and savor. Their conception of poetry as a by-product of scholarship is shown by the fact that all the known chief librarians of the Museum were, or claimed to be, poets. They poeticized every conceivable subject, including myths, history, and geography, as well as love stories of mortals and gods, but they generally avoided epic themes.

The poet best exemplifying this academic quality was Callimachus of Cyrene (fl. 250 B.C.), who was patronized by the Ptolemies and rose to become chief librarian. He allegedly wrote eight hundred books of poetry on miscellaneous subjects, but he is best known for his epigrams. Callimachus was also an admirer of Homer but criticized those poets who imitated him excessively. His motto "Big book, big evil" illustrates his belief that bons mots should be short and pointed. More creative, certainly, was the poetry of Theocritus of Syracuse (ca. 315–250), who, read by an oversophisticated, city-bred audience in Alexandria, created a new genre in Greek literature, the idyll. Deriving its ultimate inspiration from the rustic scenes and atmosphere of Homeric hymns, his idylls were pastoral poems evoking with great realism a landscape populated by happy peasants, plowing and reaping, by lovesick shepherds and farm boys, and chaste milkmaids. Worthy artistic creations in their own right, Theocritus' idylls were also important because of their influence on later Roman writers, particularly Vergil.

Philosophy.   Various schools of philosophy, examining problems of epistemology and ethics and deriving ultimately from the many-sided doctrine of Socrates, continued to evolve after the fourth century. As befitted an age when the community-oriented ethical values of city-states had disappeared in a much larger and more loosely organized world, the most creative philosophies tried to adapt to new conditions and to provide appealing ideals of the good life leading to individual peace of mind. The main schools of the fourth century B.C., the Peripatetics and the Academics, stood rather apart from the tendency of philosophy to be concerned with the ethical values of individuals. The Peripatetics were concerned chiefly with historical research, and the Academics, while criticizing other schools, ended up by denying the ultimate certainty of any kind of knowledge. In general, Hellenistic ethical systems otherwise tended to become eclectic and to resemble each other increasingly in their moral tenets.

Epicurus.   The adaptation and transcending of Cyrenaic ethics by one of the most influential moralists of any period, Epicurus, is of great interest. Born at Samos (ca. 341), he led a wandering life and was expelled at one point from Mytilene because of his teaching, after which he never again lectured in a public place. He settled in Athens in 306, remaining there until his death in 271 and instructing his disciples privately in the garden of his own home. Epicurus' was the first missionary philosophy emphasizing social, not political, virtues and preaching belief in friendship, a kind of religion of humanity. An altruistic hedonist, he wished to awaken the world to the good life, which he identified with happiness. To avoid pain he obeyed the motto "Live quietly," which meant that he preached a withdrawal from possible disturbing public affairs, a doctrine not likely to endear him to a world that had traditionally sanctioned political activism by its best citizens. Pleasure, for him, was physical in the sense that it was a definite sensation: it derived, however, from intellectual intercourse with like-minded friends, not from gross physical indulgence.

An important element of his system was the removal of worry caused by fear of divine retribution in this world or of death. To realize that end, he adopted the atomic theories of Leucippus and Democritus and their mechanistic view of the universe. For Epicurus, the gods existed but did not interfere in this world, which was only a chance combination of swirling atoms. Even the soul was material and would decay like the body into its component atoms at death, which was no more dreadful than an eternal sleep. His denial of divine effectiveness seemed unsettling and even subversive to religious traditionalists and made his teachings unpopular with the masses. Although sometimes misinterpreted as an invitation to sensual indulgence, the constructive features of Epicureanism never disappeared from ancient thought and have even influenced important figures of Western civilization in modern times, like John Locke and Thomas Jefferson. Jefferson, for example, agreed with the Epicurean tenet that the least government is the best government and saw to it that the peculiarly Epicurean belief in the basic rights of the human race to life, liberty, and the pursuit of happiness received prominent statement in the American Declaration of Independence.

Cynicism and Stoicism. A very different but no less influential answer to the riddle of the good life developed out of a transformation of the Cynic school. The most famous Cynic, Diogenes of Sinope (died 323), exaggerated the Socratic belief that security and peace of mind lay in living by nature and steeling oneself against any possible unpleasantness. For him, adherence to nature meant apparently the abandonment of commonly accepted law, custom, and convention, which were mere restrictions on perfect liberty. Diogenes won veneration as a kind of Cynic saint because of his forthright exposure of sham and hypocrisy in society. He and other Cynics were also exhibitionists dramatizing their beliefs, basically unconstructive men revolting for the sake of revolt against any accommodation with a very imperfect world.

Their personal boorishness and the lack of intellectual content in their attitude toward life caused one of their more sensitive adherents, Zeno, to break with them and found a school of his own. Born in Cyprus in 336 and probably of Phoenician ancestry, Zeno began teaching in the *Stoa Poikile* or "Painted Porch" (whence the name of his philosophy) of the Athenian Agora in 301 and remained at Athens until his death in about 264. He retained in his philosophy the Cynic idea of the virtues of endurance and self-sufficiency, but he transformed them by constructing on them an elaborate system of thought whose attitude toward the world was basically optimistic.

As developed by Zeno and his follower, Chrysippus (ca. 280–206), Stoicism appropriated the Platonic theories of dualism, which posited a creating, intelligent God and an inanimate world of brute matter. That world was a perfect creation, its development divinely ordained for all time, any imperfections and evil apparent rather than real because of our limited understanding of it. The virtuous man, according to Stoicism, will realize peace of mind by submitting to the Providence governing the world and by living according to nature. The essence of human nature being rational and a spark of the divine intelligence, living naturally meant living by reason. The early Stoic ideal was that of a sage who was tranquil because of his mastery of disturbing passions and because of his adjustment to an unalterable world. Zeno admitted that a Stoic wise man might arise from any race because all men, not merely Greeks, shared the same humanity, as children of God, in their intelligence. He scarcely thought in terms of any real unity of humankind, however, because he rather coldly permitted in his theoretical utopia only a few Stoic sages and excluded the unenlightened mass of humanity, whom he regarded as fools.

During the period of the so-called Middle Stoa, and under Peripatetic influence, this attitude mellowed considerably. In developing a theory of history, the Peripatetics came to believe that not only great but also ordinary people played important roles in life. As adapted to philosophy by the Stoic Panaetius (200–109), this idea suggested that merit be acknowledged not merely in the passionless sage but in all those who, even very imperfectly, lived rationally. This attitude considerably broadened the concept of human brotherhood, even though the Stoics never saw any inconsistency between this idea and the inequalities in ancient society. They rationalized the inferior status of women and the institution of slavery, for example, by regarding them as natural and therefore divinely ordained and just.

Religion.   Religion was one of the very few areas of Hellenistic civilization in which the Greeks were more influenced by the Near East than vice versa. The old Olympian pantheon retained its firmest hold on the population of Old Greece, but when transplanted to a new environment in the Near Eastern Greek kingdoms, it became merely symbolic of community and state life, received veneration mainly within official Greek circles and at festivals, and made very few native converts. Even in Old Greece, however, Near Eastern cults won many followers.

They were widely popular for various reasons. They appealed to individuals rather than to communities, which meant that they seemed to offer protection and peace of mind in a new world far vaster and chancier than that of the city-state. Religion thus fulfilled the same function for the masses as did philosophy for the very highly educated. Some of the cults prescribed ways of life that, if followed, would lead to a happy future or even immortality, and most of them had colorful ceremonies conducted by professional priests, which fulfilled emotional needs unsatisfied by traditional Hellenic ritual. As always, the Greeks were syncretic in their worship and tended to identify new gods with those of their own pantheon who had similar attributes, as in the Egyptian cult of the sun-god Amon, whom they equated with Zeus.

Generally speaking, the Greeks rationalized Near Eastern religion by demanding logical explanations of the traditions and myths behind them. In some cases, they also humanized conceptions of the divinity, and when cults were not "mystery religions" in the sense of having a restricted ritual, they provided initiatory ceremonies. The most famous case was that of Serapis, an anthropomorphized Egyptian bull (Apis), identified with Osiris, a fertility god who bestowed immortality. The Ptolemies patronized the cult of this god, represented iconically as Pluto, along with the cult of Osiris' wife, the goddess Isis, which was very popular among Hellenistic Greeks because of its powers to heal, impart fecundity, foretell the future, and guarantee an afterlife. The Ptolemies hoped that this cult might also link them to their native subjects, who never accepted it and regarded it as an artificial invention rather than as indigenous to their own traditions.

A not dissimilar fertility cult of Cybele, the Great Mother, and her consort Attis (Adonis), famous for its orgiastic ritual, spread from its home in Asia Minor to many parts of the Near East. From Persia came the cult of the Magi, Mithraism, restricted to men and preaching soldierly virtues in the continuing struggle of Mithra, agent of the god of light and goodness (Ahuramazda) against darkness and evil. The Greeks were also very interested in the cult of Yahweh. There were many Judaizers, although they tended to miss the point by identifying Yahweh with Zeus.

In a tolerant polytheistic world, worshipers might, of course, subscribe to the ritual of several cults, the idea of "conversion," naturally, being quite foreign to religions that did not claim the exclusive devotion of their followers or, as it were, a complete renunciation of one's personal past and a new start in life. "Mystery religions" like the worship of Isis and Serapis and Mithraism remained very much rich men's cults because the costs of initiation were high. Poorer worshipers who could not afford initiatory baptism nevertheless might venerate such gods as a special act of devotion, rather like that given in modern times to saints by some Catholic Christians.

Art. Hellenistic sculpture developed organically out of the last classical phase of

FIGURE 43. Women playing Knucklebones. Terracotta, South Italian Greek, c. 300 B.C. This work illustrates the interest of Hellenistic Greek artists in depicting *genre* scenes. Height: 8 inches.

The Granger Collection

German Archeological Institute

FIGURE 44. Hellenistic Boxer, sometimes attributed to Apollonius of Athens, first century B.C. and illustrative of the Hellenistic interest in realism.

the fourth century B.C., which even then was moving away from canonical idealization of subject matter and simplicity of line to naturalism, emotionalism, and specialized effects. Its development after Alexander was an almost exclusively Greek phenomenon, only marginally affected by, or affecting, native Near Eastern styles. Hellenistic sculpture was unified by a very Greek interest in portraying human nature, despite the great diversity of styles and techniques developed over three centuries in workshops spread over the Near East. The basic unity was encouraged by the tendency of artists to move about in search of patronage, which gave a common leavening to regional workshops and schools, like those at Pergamon, Rhodes, and Alexandria, each of which nevertheless kept a distinctive style of its own.

Although a certain development culminating (ca. 230–150) in a rather baroque style is sometimes emphasized, the most striking characteristic of Hellenistic sculpture is the variety of its themes. These included traditional genres like cult statues, but most notably the portrayal of human beings of every conceivable type, appearance, age, and station of life. Portrait sculptures of famous and unknown personal-

FIGURE 45. The Winged Victory
of Samothrace, c. 220-190 B.C. and
generally considered to be one
of the finest examples of the
"baroque" style of the Hellenistic
period.

The Granger Collection

ities, both idealized and realistic, statues of children and even wizened old people, caricatures of dwarfs, representatives of exotic races like Nubians and Gauls—all suggest the virtuosity of Hellenistic sculptors and the range of their interests. These also included a startlingly realistic repertoire of every known emotion, including pathos, pain, serenity, and, for the first time in the Greek artistic tradition, mirth, as they attempted to depict smiles and laughter. A frequently appearing cross-current in many genres is a sense of eroticism, Cupid, Aphrodite, hermaphrodites, nymphs, and satyrs being popular subjects. Important innovations were also made in bas-reliefs, which depicted idyllic rural scenes, indicated an awareness of space and perspective, and had narrative content.

Sculptors frequently showed off their complete command over media by producing tours de force like the very theatrical Altar of the Gods from Pergamon (ca. 190-160), in which a battle between gods and giants was intended to represent allegorically the struggle of the Attalid dynasty, defending civilization against Celtic barbarians. Interest in the Celts was also manifested in other works of the Pergamene school, which reveal the ability of Hellenistic artists to observe human experience searchingly and to portray emotions sensitively. The Dying Gaul is such a piece, in which the artist not unsympathetically transcends a barbarian type to suggest the possibilities of dignity inherent in death for anybody. A very late Hellenistic work, the Laocoön, a product of the Rhodian school (ca. 50 B.C.), although reminiscent in its baroque quality of figures on the Pergamene altar, is also rather academic and facadelike. It stood on the threshold of a new period when Greek art would become both more eclectic and more classicizing.

Ancient critics of art maintained that the best works of painting were created during the fourth and early third centuries B.C. and that the schools of Sicyon, Rhodes, Pergamon, and Alexandria were preeminent. It is difficult to corroborate their impression because scarcely any original works of Hellenistic painting have survived dating from before the first century B.C., and even so, most of them are known only through mosaic versions or Roman and Campanian copies. Painting on easels or walls was intended to decorate private houses, public buildings, and especially theaters; it apparently varied widely in size, from huge scenes depicting major events of history and myth to miniatures.

As in the case of the plastic arts, there seems to have been a real continuity between late classical and Hellenistic painting, which was also characterized by diversity of style and subject matter but most notably by the interest of painters in depicting human beings. Unfortunately, little portraiture has survived, except for mummy paintings in a Greco-Egyptian style, which, although striking, are not purely Hellenistic. More is known about two new Hellenistic genres, landscapes and still life, which predominate in the surviving frescoes at Pompeii and Herculaneum,

FIGURE 46. Laocoön. A product of the Rhodian school ca. 50 B.C. and technically a sculptural tour de force.

either copies of, or works inspired by, Greek originals. Perhaps most striking are sacred and idyllic landscapes populated by shepherds and wanderers in settings that convey a certain Theocritan, dreamlike quality. As they were in contemporary literature and sculpture, gods and goddesses appear humanized when depicted in mythological scenes. Especially interesting are attempts at showing perspective that paralleled similar innovations in bas-reliefs. The artist frequently used architectural constructions as backgrounds, which were apparently inspired by theatrical settings and scenery. Although they knew about axial perspective, they tended to apply its laws only to buildings and not, consistently at least, to natural elements of the landscape. Generally speaking, landscapes were illusionistic and portrayed a world pulsating with life, filled with opulent color, enlivened by the dramatic use of light and shade.

The Hellenistic Age was important for architecture and town planning because the foundation of many new cities, the enlargement of others, and the rising standard of urban living among the wealthy demanded building and care for the amenities of life on a hitherto unparalleled scale. Except possibly in Egypt, the Near Eastern influence on Hellenistic architecture was slight; its essence remained basically Greek, its characteristics having evolved out of tendencies in building already apparent before Alexander's conquest.

Although there was a strong traditional or conservative element in Hellenistic architecture, it contained possibilities for innovation that were fully realized under the Romans. Hellenistic architects distinguished themselves from their classical predecessors by striving for axial symmetry and scenographic effects and by the first, hesitant attempts to transcend post-and-lintel architecture through the use of arch and vault. The greater size of the monumental buildings and the attention paid to the decoration of their facades and to their settings frequently made Hellenistic architecture seem overly dramatic or theatrical.

So that temples might hold their own in any natural setting, they were conceived of more frequently as isolated monuments forming the central feature of a large, surrounding, paved enclosure, which sometimes was a broad platform mounted by transverse stairways. A similar desire to transcend the landscape was evident in monumental tombs, of which the Mausoleum of Halicarnassus was the most famous prototype. Typically surrounded by a precinct, there were either rectangular structures in the Doric style surmounted by a stepped pyramid or an Ionic building supporting a circular drum and a cone. To devise new decorative effects, architects sometimes created variety by blending Doric and Ionic features and by applying to them the principles of attenuation and entasis, but most strikingly by fully working out the Corinthian order. Hellenistic domestic architecture was also important for having completed the development of the Greek house built around a central open court, or peristyle, which was soon to be adopted and popularized by the Romans.

Urban planning had been known to the Greek world since the days of Hippodamus of Miletus, but it was applied on a much wider scale and more systematically than ever before during the Hellenistic period. The dominant feature of such planning was the adaptation to local terrain of a gridiron pattern of streets. No one Hellenistic architect systematically encouraged this pattern, although many cities may have followed the lead of Alexander's town planner, Deinocrates. Deinocrates made Alexandria an elongated rectangle bisected by a main boulevard called the *Canopic Street,* which was regularly intersected at right angles by smaller side streets. Pergamon provides the most striking, and Priene the most famous, example of the new system. When refounded (ca. 300 B.C.), Pergamon contained a semi-circle of monumental public buildings crowning the crest of a steep hillside, which precluded a checkerboard pattern of streets. The problem was solved by building the monumental quarter of the city on terraces, connected by radial streets from the summit. Hellenistic Priene, a small town of some four thousand population in western Asia Minor, was unusual in that its plan provided for no sweeping scenic vistas, which Hellenistic architects were otherwise so fond of. The main street was only twenty-three feet wide, the side streets barely ten, and the largest open space was the agora or marketplace. The new system of town planning was even taken up in Old Greece, where ancient cities like Sicyon and Thebes were rebuilt on gridiron plans.

The rational arrangement of streets was only part of city planning, and attention was frequently given to the special development of certain quarters for residential, governmental, and commercial purposes. A characteristic by-product of city planning was the greater frequency and detail of municipal by-laws, like those of Pergamon, which regulated the height of buildings, the width of streets, and street cleaning and sometimes even provided for municipal services like water supply and the disposal of sewage, although these civic amenities were exceptional. Advances in military engineering gave cities more sophisticated fortification, and civil engineering provided for an unprecedented development of harbor installations and ports. The most famous was the first lighthouse of antiquity, the great Pharos of Alexandria, a tower four hundred feet high resting on a square base one hundred feet on the side. This monument, most of which survived until the thirteenth century A.D., was duplicated on a smaller scale in other parts of the Greek world.

Science.   The most original Hellenistic contributions to civilization were scientific. Since the Ionian Enlightenment Greek science had been cross-fertilized by many Near Eastern achievements in fields like geometry, astronomy, and medicine, which Greek thinkers in many cases had transformed by providing with a theoretical base. Yet the Near East seems to have given Greece its significant scientific lore before Alexander's conquests, and any new influences from that quarter on later Greek scientists cannot be proved. Although the reasons for the extraordinary development of Hellenistic science are not obvious, it should probably be regarded as the ultimate culmination of a predominantly Greek intellectual phenomenon originating with Thales of Miletus. The circumstances determining the place and time of its flowering were apparently two: the influence of Aristotle and the greater endowment of research that began in the latter part of the fourth century.

As a polymath and pedagogue, Aristotle was the first Hellenistic mind, the initiator of a new intellectual spirit. His systematic approach to knowledge and its organization meant the definite separation of science from other fields like poetry and politics, emphasis on the observation and collection of data, and the introduction of scientific first principles. In its initial phases, his Peripatetic school produced outstanding researchers in many fields, whose fructifying influence spread far beyond Athens even after the Peripatetics themselves limited their interests to history. The personal patronage of scientists by the early Ptolemies and the creation of chairs of science at the Museum tended to make Alexandria its most productive center. Despite the greater material security enjoyed by Alexandrian scientists, much important work was done elsewhere by researchers working independently, and even the beneficial effects of endowments on science, when they did occur, were limited.

Among the essential but auxiliary fields closely related to science was mathematics, particularly geometry, perhaps most congenial to Greek minds traditionally interested in discovering harmonious relationships between numbers and forms. The early Sophists had sanctioned Pythagorean mathematics as part of the curriculum for educated men, but interest in the subject waned after Isocrates enlarged the role of rhetoric. Aristotle prepared the way for the use of mathematics—at least, as a tool for research—by distinguishing among axioms, postulates, and definitions. Both practical and theoretical understanding of the subject culminated after him in the third and second centuries B.C. in the work of brilliant polymaths unequaled in their creativity until the scientific revolution of the seventeenth and eighteenth centuries A.D.

These included Euclid (ca. 310-230), who studied and taught at Alexandria, achieving fame by writing the *Elements* of geometry, probably the most influential textbook of Western civilization. Its value lies not in his having developed any radically new kind of mathematics but rather in the originality and clarity in the systematic organization he gave the propositions of earlier geometers. His younger contemporary, Apollonius of Perga (fl. 240-200), also a famous textbook writer and a client of the Ptolemies, was known as the "Great Geometer" because of his special research in the field of conic sections. The most creative mathematician of antiquity, Archimedes (287-212), worked not at Alexandria but in his native Syracuse. Among other things, he developed a system of infinitesimal calculus, but his broad scientific interests also included basic research in two fields of theoretical physics, statics and hydrostatics, in which he discovered important laws. A figure of only slightly less originality was the polymath Eratosthenes, who, in addition to being a writer, a philologist, and a librarian of the Museum, was also interested in the practical application of mathematics. He was the first mathematical geographer, measuring on a trigonometric basis and with apparently great accuracy the circumference of the earth.

Interest in mathematics was closely related to an interest in astronomy, Archimedes, for example, having also built a kind of planetarium accurate enough to account for eclipses. The influence of Aristotle's school on astronomy was significant, and the most famous Hellenistic astronomer, Aristarchus of Samos, was a student of the Peripatetic physicist Strato. Known as the "ancient Copernicus," Aristarchus went further than his predecessors in conceiving of a heliocentric universe and on a geometrical basis tried to estimate the relative sizes and distances from the earth of the sun and moon. Probably more creative was the mind of Hipparchus, who lived and worked in Egypt in the second century B.C. Because, unlike Aristarchus, he knew trigonometry, he was able to determine very accurately the precession of the equinoxes and the length of the year. Unfortunately for science, however, he held the geocentric theory, which his great prestige canonized for the remainder of antiquity.

Similarly striking advances were made in the fields of biology and medicine, which were no less rooted than mathematics in earlier Greek history. These roots are attested to by the so-called Hippocratic corpus, a collection of predominantly medical cases, dating from the fifth and fourth centuries but compiled under Ptolemaic auspices at Alexandria in about 200 B.C. The corpus also contains observations on animal and even plant life, with a suggested grouping of the former into genera. Aristotle restored the prestige of natural science, which the Platonic school had denigrated in favor of ethics, and organized it as he did mathematics. He apparently wrote widely on subjects related to biology, although some such works attributed to him in antiquity are spurious. The genuine ones, in which he classified many data concerning plants and animals apparently collected by his students, are at least reliable when describing flora and fauna of the Aegean area.

Aristotle's theory of biology was determined by his teleology, his belief that Nature made everything for a purpose, and by his notion that the presence of a nonmaterial "soul" (psyche) was essential for life. Basically he described rather than analyzed nature, and he owed his considerable fame as a biologist to his arrangement of animals by genera and species. He apparently dissected some animals, but never a human body, and while ascertaining exotic trivia like the reproductive habits of certain kinds of squids, a phenomenon not rediscovered until 1851, he failed to trace sense organs and nerves to the brain. Aristotle found a worthy pupil and successor in the field of biology and botany in Theophrastus (372–287), who filled in the details of his master's system of classifying plants and animals. After Theophrastus, however, biology disappeared as an independent field, physiology and anatomy in particular being subordinated to medicine.

About half the medical doctors and researchers known in the Hellenistic era worked at Alexandria and were connected with the Museum, although there were medical schools elsewhere, as at Pergamon. Before important breakthroughs by Ptolemaic doctors, Hippocratic medicine had only primitive ideas of anatomy, physiology, and pathology. It was also largely ignorant of the causes of disease, although a basis had been laid for epidemiology by the connection of sickness with climate. Perhaps the best Hippocratic characteristic was the accurate observation of symptoms and the development of individual diseases, leading to prognosis and treatment, mainly through rest and diatetics rather than the use of drugs.

Alexandrian medicine is usually identified with two scientists of the third century B.C., Herophilus, the founder of anatomy, and Erasistratus, the pioneer physiologist. The extent to which they may have used knowledge gained previously by Egyptians through millennial practices such as mummification and trepanning is unknown. They certainly profited by the freedom, traditional there, to dissect corpses, and they almost certainly were allowed by the government to practice vivisection on condemned criminals. Herophilus standardized autopsy techniques and was the first to measure the pulse, to distinguish the brain as the center of the nervous system, and to advocate the extensive use of drugs in curing disease. Erasistratus, it seems, distinguished clearly between motor and sensory nerves. As a result of experimentation by him and other scientists with the use of new or improved medical instruments like the catheter and with anesthetics, surgery at Alexandria reached a level not reattained until relatively recent times.

The Golden Age of Hellenistic science was concentrated almost entirely in the third century B.C., and important discoveries made thereafter were few. After almost advancing to the threshhold of transforming civilization by realizing medical, technological, and industrial revolutions, Hellenistic scientific creativity waned. Many reasons have been adduced for this abortive development. The advance of Rome on the Greek world, it is alleged, dampened scientific research because the Romans were not interested in speculation or theory that did not have an obvious and immediate practical value. Slavery, it is argued, depressed the costs of labor, so that there was little incentive for entrepreneurs to look to scientists for labor-saving devices in the form of machinery. The Greeks are even accused of having preferred to solve scientific problems by intellect alone and to have enjoyed pure theorizing at the expense of experimentation or practical application of their discoveries. In this respect is often cited the attitude of scientists like Archimedes, who regarded inventions he derived from physics, like steam engines and taximeters, as nothing more than toys. Ancient religion, some believe, played a crucial role in inhibiting scientific research, as suggested by the charges of impiety leveled by some Stoics against Aristarchus because he held that the universe was heliocentric. Frequently mentioned among other contributory factors in the ultimate stagnation of Hellenistic science are the notable failure of the Greeks to develop chemistry, which remained an art bordering on the magical; their lack of precision instruments, which might have given them greater control over experiments; and the limitations imposed on conceptualizing without algebraic notations and methods or a numerical system, like the Arabic, which had a zero sign and a place value for numbers.

None of these arguments satisfactorily explains the phenomenon. The most creative scientific minds in any society, including Nobel Prize winners in our own highly industrialized one, are perhaps more interested in "pure" research than in its application. The Greeks were both natural observers of nature and experimenters, their religion was normally disinterested in science, and even the Romans never actually repressed scientific research. The necessary inhibition by cheap and servile labor on production of machinery seems contradicted by the industrial revolution of the eighteenth and nineteenth centuries in Europe and America, including the invention of the cotton gin in our own slaveholding South. And, finally, the scientists of the Renaissance and early modern times confronted, yet transcended, technological limitations similar to those of the Hellenistic world.

The fact is that no matter how consequential Hellenistic science seems to a modern, scientifically oriented world, it was actually a recessive characteristic of Greek civilization, developing rather in spite of than because of their cultural values. The Hellenistic Greeks themselves regarded it as unimportant, in part because their rhetorically oriented educational system since Isocrates had taught them to appreciate above all belles-lettres, even rudimentary mathematics having barely survived in the curriculum. Hellenistic education was all but impervious to the advance of scientific thought, and it is amazing that so many scientists emerged from it. There was actually little motivation other than intellectual curiosity to become a scientist, as the scientist's social status, save exceptionally under royal patronage, was largely undefined, and scientists scarcely played an important public role anywhere.

Although there was more endowment for research than ever before at the Museum and a few other institutes, community sponsorship of science was unusual, except possibly when it meant the development of engines of war. Funds typically were channeled to more immediate community needs like public works and poor relief; even the Museum, whose support, after all, went mainly to the humanities and philology, decayed along with the Ptolemaic dynasty after 200 B.C. Research libraries, like those at Alexandria and Pergamon, were atypical, and scientists frequently remained rather lonely figures, cut off from possibly fructifying contact with other scholars at the very few well-endowed seats of learning.

Finally, even at its height Greek science actually suffered from attempts to make it popular. Since the beginning of sophistry, handbooks and textbooks had been produced on a wide variety of technical subjects, and science was often so treated during the Hellenistic period. Had those textbooks been written with the expert knowledge and scientific purpose of men like Euclid and Apollonius of Perga, they would perhaps have improved the status of science by broadening its understanding and appreciation by the educated public. Unfortunately, however, they were written by lay compilers, typically literary polymaths and critics with no understanding of original research.

At best, these popularizers appropriated the findings of creative scientists and plausibly represented them in readily digestible commentaries. Their main purpose, however, was merely to convey that smattering of scientific knowledge necessary for a class whose interests were mainly literary. This was no appreciation of science per se, but merely its use as an aid to interpreting scientific allusions in literary classics, so that the compilers themselves showed no preference for the opinions of expert scientists on, say, natural phenomena over those of literary critics or even poets. The popularizers largely determined the kind of scientific knowledge that would be publicized and, hence, survive, and as the very standards determining their choice was unscientific, they had a deleterious effect on the cause of original research.

PART V

THE ROMAN REPUBLIC

21

Early Italy

THE LAND AND ITS PEOPLE

No other state fills so large a place in the history of the world as Rome. It was the achievement of this city to unite all the Mediterranean basin in a great empire under a single government and to unite the nations of this region in many ways. For centuries civilized people from Scotland to Persia paid their taxes into the same treasury, were tried by the same law, were protected by the same armies, and enjoyed a more profound and real peace—the *pax Romana*—than at any other time (map, rear endpaper). This achievement was made possible by geography and able diplomacy, generalship, organization, government, and character. The Roman genius, for example, is best shown in the creation of a body of law, which for its completeness and excellence must be considered one of the greatest legislative works of the human race. After many centuries of development, it is true, the empire declined and finally fell into pieces, but from the fragments great modern states, such as England, France, and Italy, have grown, and its civilization in a modified form has passed into modern life.

The Romans, being farther removed from the influences of the Near East, became civilized later than the Greeks and received most of their improvements from them, but whatever they borrowed they modified to suit their own conditions and thus created a Roman civilization. Just as the history of Greece assumes wider proportions with Alexander's conquest of the ancient Orient, so the history of the entire ancient world becomes a unit as Rome absorbs both Greece and the Orient and expands to the Atlantic Ocean and the North Sea, an accomplishment that throws into relief the failure of the Greeks to form a united state.

Physical Features of Italy. Italy consists of two regions, together more than 90,000 square miles in area, the continental—which extends 70 miles from the Alps to the Apennines and is 320 miles from east to west—and the peninsula, which runs 650 miles in a southeasterly direction between the Mediterranean and the Adriatic seas and is nowhere broader than 125 miles. The northern, or continental, region is essentially a great alluvial plain between the foothills of the Alps and the Apennines. The Po, which is the longest river in Italy, rises in the western Alps and is fed chiefly from Alpine streams and lakes. The Apennines traverse northern Italy south of the Po, then form the backbone of the peninsula, whose shore line exceeds 2,000 miles in length. The fact that these mountains, which rise in places to 9,500 feet, lie nearer the eastern than the western coast makes the eastern slope shorter and steeper, the rivers shorter, and the harbors fewer. The longer slopes on the west terminate in fertile coastal plains; a few rivers, such as the Tiber in central Italy, are navigable; and there are good harbors, particularly at Genoa and Naples and, southward, at Sparta's colony, Tarentum. Unlike Greece, with its clusters of islands, Italy has but three large islands off its coast: Sardinia and Corsica, where the Italians were to meet Carthaginians, and Sicily, whose Greek colonists derived the word *Italia* from the Oscan dialect across the strait (*vitelliu,* calf land). These islands are all that is now left of the land bridge that in geologic times stretched from Europe to Africa.

Continental Italy, the plain and hills of the Po Valley, has a climate not unlike that of central Europe, with four distinct seasons, but the peninsula, in spite of hot, dry summers and rainy winters, also enjoys considerable diversity, because it passes through many degrees of latitude no less than because of the lofty Apennines and the tempering effect of the neighboring seas. Malaria and the absence of rich mineral deposits are disadvantages, which, however, have not prevented the growth of a dense population, for there is a great variety and abundance of natural resources and of useful products in this land: wheat, barley, clay fields, salt from the Tiber marshes, marble, the vine and olive, vegetables, and fine pastures. The Apennines, as the spine of the peninsula, made timber for shipbuilding readily available, and volcanoes on the west, especially in the district around the Bay of Naples known as Campania and in Sicily, enriched the soil.

One of the great facts in the history of the peninsula is that the Alps are passable only at certain points, and even there with difficulty, so that the maintenance of relations with the interior of the continent was not easy, and Italy was compelled to associate with the other countries of the Mediterranean. Yet, the general accessibility of Italy is another great fact in its history, for across the narrow Adriatic is Illyria, Greece lies only a short distance beyond the Ionian Sea, and on the southwest Sicily connects closely with Africa. Hence have come many invaders, and indeed even the Alps, hindrance though they may be to commerce, have often proved a weak barrier against enemies. The early immigrants of diverse race, mingling in friendship and war, stimulated one another to great activity, and, in fact, for centuries Italy formed the western frontier of civilization, drawing to itself the boldest and most enterprising people of the older world and developing intensely the frontier qualities of courage, patience, hardihood, and practical intelligence (map, p. 326).

There were differences in language and customs between one part of early Italy and another, and consequently there grew up a multitude of small independent states, continually warring among themselves; but as life became more settled and communities grew in size, and as a desire for peace developed, the people found the exposed position of their country a positive disadvantage. They were willing, therefore, to accept the supremacy of Rome, as the one state best able to give them protection. Ultimately, however, the Italians discovered that even when they were united, their country was unsafe while neighboring states were free to assail it, and that self-preservation demanded foreign conquest. Thus the accessibility of the country helps to explain at once the political unification of Italy and that of the Mediterranean world. The third and most important task achieved by Rome in her career of empire building was in civilizing her empire, especially the western half, and in this work, too, she was favored by the form and situation of Italy. In part, at least, because the western coast is better supplied than the eastern with harbors, Rome came into closer touch and sympathy with Spain, Gaul, and northwestern Africa than with Greece and the Near East, and the fresh, vital peoples of the West were accordingly far readier than those of the east to adopt her customs, institutions, and ideas.

The Neolithic Age. Italy has been inhabited since Palaeolithic times, and Neanderthal man left traces there. Italy passed into the Neolithic, or New Stone, Age about 3500 B.C., when a short, dark people, belonging to the Mediterranean race, infiltrated, apparently from North Africa. These people enjoyed a typical neolithic culture, with improved stone implements and simple pottery and textiles. Their chief activity was to tend herds of oxen and sheep, to hunt, and to cultivate various grains. They lived in huts and villages and buried their dead in caves or pits.

The Bronze Age. During the late Neolithic and Bronze Ages (1800–1000 B.C.), an Indo-European form of speech was probably brought to the Italian peninsula by invaders perhaps from Switzerland and the upper valley of the Danube. The first wave of newcomers chose as their homes the shores around the northern Italian lakes. As had been their custom in Switzerland, these lake dwellers often built their houses on piles driven into the bottom of the lakes. Other Alpine invaders, about 1500 B.C., penetrated as far as the Po. The soil about their settlements became particularly fertile and has been referred to by modern Italians as *terramara* (plural, *terremare*), a term that is now applied to the early culture itself. The *terremare* people were skilled in the use of bronze, raised cattle, and farmed their lands. They cremated their dead and placed the ashes in urns. During the Bronze Age there were, of course, invasions by still other peoples, particularly by bands of Illyrians from across the Adriatic, who occupied the Venetian plains (the Veneti of the Roman period) and, under the name of Iapygians, the southeast coast of Italy as well. At the same time strong Mycenaean influences reached Sicily.

The Iron Age. Not long after the opening of the Iron Age (shortly before 1000 B.C.), other Indo-European–speaking peoples, infiltrating in the main from across the Adriatic, spread a mosaic of their Italic dialects where they became dominant, roughly in that part of Italy east and southeast of the Tiber River. In historical times the most important of these peoples were, of course, the Latins of the Plain of Latium and the Umbro-Sabellians, including the Samnites, who mainly inhabited the valleys and mountains of the central and southern Appenines, although they later spread to certain coastal areas. In northern Italy, at Villanova (near Bologna), the Iron Age culture was developed early, although the ethnic and linguistic characteristics of the Villanovans are obscure. They lived in villages composed of round huts, made fine weapons of both iron and bronze, and buried the ashes of their dead in distinctive biconical urns. By the sixth century B.C., when the Celts, or Gauls as the Romans called them, entered the valley of the Po, the great

Brenner
Pass
Alps Mts.
L. Como
RAETI
L. Maggiore
VENETI
HISTRIA
L. Garda
Adige R.
ETRUSCANS
Po R.
Adria
ILLYRIA
Alps Mts.
Ticinus R.
Po R.
LIGURES
Apennines
Genoa
Bononia
(Bologna)
Rubicon R.
Ariminum
Gulf of
Genoa
Arno R.
Grimaldi
Caves
Ancona
ADRIATIC SEA
ETRUSCANS
PICENTES
UMBRO
VESTINI
ELBA
SAMNITES
FRENTANI
Tiber R.
CORSICA
SABELLIANS
DAUNII
IAPYGES
ETRUSCANS
Alalia
Tarquinii
Caere
PEUCETII
Roma
Liris R.
VOLSCI
CAMPANIA
Volturnus R.
Capua
Apennines M.
Tarentum
Cumae
Vesuvius M.
MESSAPII
SARDINIA
OSCANS
LUCANIA
TYRRHENIAN
Posidonia
(Paestum)
GREEKS
Gulf of
Tarentum
SEA
ITALIA
GREEKS
GREEKS
CARTHAGINIANS
STROMBOLI
BRUTTIUM
LIPARI IS.
GREEKS
CARTHAGINIANS
AEGATES IS.
ELYMI
Messina
Regium
SICANI
SICULI
Str. of Messina
Carthage
Aetna M.
PANTELLERIA
SICILY
Syracusae

**ITALY
SIXTH
CENTURY B.C.**

AFRICA

MALTA

0   50   100
Miles

migrations by land were over, but in the meantime two other peoples—the Etruscans and the Greeks—had come by sea and seized much of the Italian coast (map, p. 326).

THE ETRUSCANS

The wealthy, luxury-loving, piratical Etruscans are one of the enigmas of history. They have left us an arresting art full of Greek influences and thousands of inscriptions in a Greek alphabet, though the language itself is a non-Indo-European speech apparently also spoken in Asia Minor in the early Iron Age, and save for proper names, it has not been translated. This fact has led to modern controversy concerning their "origins." Despite the linguistic evidence, one school of historians holds that they were aboriginal Italians and that they were historical descendants of the Villanovans, as the archaeological record in north-central Italy, the homeland of both peoples, seems to be evolutionary and does not suggest an intrusion of immigrants. Another school follows Herodotus, who depicted the Etruscans as immigrants into Italy from western Asia Minor. It is probably correct to think of the Etruscans as migrating from western Asia Minor to Italy early in the Iron Age and for a period of several centuries gradually evolving a considerable civilization, which was largely a fusion of native and Greek elements with their own. Because of their superior organization they were able, starting with Tarquinii and Caere near the western coast, to occupy the area between the Tiber and Arno rivers—Etruria or Tuscany, as it is called today. In time, they expanded southward to Latium and Campania—though the Greeks resisted them at Cumae—and northward across the Apennines, where their most important city, Felsina, lay not far from modern Bologna; their seaport, Adria, to the north of the Po, eventually gave its name to the Adriatic Sea.

The height of Etruscan power was reached in the sixth century B.C. The Etruscans even made a treaty with the Carthaginians, and in 535 B.C., because of their fear of Greek competition, the allies expelled the Greeks from their chief colony on Corsica, Alalia. In 509 B.C., however, the Romans drove out the last Etruscan king; in 474 B.C., Hiero of Syracuse defeated an Etruscan fleet before Cumae; and in 438 B.C., the Samnites took Capua, their main Campanian city. By the end of the century, Celtic tribes had deprived them of their northern possessions, so that the Etruscans henceforth were limited to Etruria proper.

Etruscan Culture.   The weakness of the Etruscans lay in their extremely loose federation, for their chief league, that of twelve cities, was religious rather than political, and such expansion as there was sprang from the initiative of individual cities and the elective magistrates of the ruling aristocrats, who, by the sixth century B.C., had displaced the kings and lorded it over their serfs. In their heyday the Etruscan ships controlled the sea that the Greeks named after them, the Tyrrhenian; imported iron from the neighboring island of Elba; and carried on a lively traffic with Greece. Seagoing though they were, the Etruscans were famous also as farmers and raisers of horses and—because of the natural resources of their land,

The Granger Collection

FIGURE 47. Etruscan bronze statuette of a warrior brandishing a lance, 5th century B.C.

such as iron, copper, tin, marble, and timber—for their arts and crafts as well. They paved roads, dug canals for drainage and irrigation, and ruled from lofty hills fortified with massive walls of stone. Their towns were laid out in a regular plan with the two main streets crossing each other at right angles. They produced realistic portraiture; wonderful mirrors, weapons, and other metalwork; a fine black pottery, called *bucchero;* textiles; and interesting temples on a high base and decorated with colored terra-cottas. In plan the temple was almost square, but in contrast to the Greek it had a deep porch, behind which the broad room or temple proper was divided into three compartments, or cellas. Trade with Greece brought strong Hellenic influences into their art and to a limited extent into their religious beliefs, but it was surely the Near East that gave the Etruscans a knowledge both of the arch and vault and of divination. The complicated priestly ritual concerning divination and omens was later inherited by the Romans themselves, who called them collectively *disciplina Etrusca.*

Because of their belief in a future life, the Etruscans, who preferred inhumation to the cremation practiced by the older population, buried their dead in stone sarcophagi, the lids of which were sometimes carved with figures of men or women laden with ornate jewelry. Their chamber tombs superficially recall those of Mycenae. The colorful paintings of these tombs show spirit and originality and often

FIGURE 48. Etruscan
bronze statuette of a rider
and horse, 5th century B.C.

The Granger Collection

suggest the Etruscan love of war, sports, dancing, feasting, and display, as well as
their fear of the evil spirits of the next world. To win the goodwill of the gods in
this one, they practiced human sacrifice. Wherever the Etruscans went, their ideas
and customs were likely to prevail, and the Latins learned from them to interpret
omens, to organize and equip their army, and to build sewers, walls, houses, temples, and cities. The Latins, nevertheless, maintained their own language and national character against these clever immigrants and in the final issue received most
of their foreign influences from the Greeks, even if some of these influences in
actual fact reached them through the Etruscans.

LATIUM

The familiar picture of the founding of Rome has come down to us from the
great poet of Augustan days, Vergil, who told how Aeneas, the son of Venus, escaped from burning Troy and, after many perils and long wanderings, found a
haven at Lavinium on the west coast of Italy. His son, Ascanius, founded Alba
Longa, and a descendant, Rhea, who was a Vestal Virgin, had twin sons, Romulus
and Remus, by Mars, the god of war. Set adrift on the Tiber, the twins were cast
ashore near the Palatine and were nursed by a she-wolf, and in manhood one of
them, Romulus, founded Rome in 753 B.C., as tradition ultimately agreed.

Vergil was not the first to connect the founding of Rome with Troy, for Roman
pride had long required that the city—even though its name is probably Etruscan in
origin—be brought within the orbit of Greece and especially of the tales of Homer,

The Granger Collection

FIGURE 49. Musicians. Detail of wall painting from the Tomb of the Leopards, Tarquinia, c. 470 B.C.

but in actual fact neither Vergil nor his younger contemporary, the historian Livy, had any knowledge of the beginnings of Rome. For the early history of the Eternal City we are dependent chiefly on the evidence of archaeology and on what we can glean from the traditions of noble families and certain religious survivals. Greek historians, especially those in Sicily, give references to early Roman history, but it was not until the end of the fourth century B.C. that the Romans themselves began to make reliable records of their consuls and chief events. When, therefore, the patriotism of conquering Rome demanded a glorious past, the first Roman historians—such as Ennius and Naevius during the Punic Wars, and Fabius Pictor not long afterward—were bewildered by the conflicting and scanty evidence and did not hesitate to invent stories and twist others to the advantage of Rome. Needless to say, our own knowledge of this period is limited.

The literary traditions concerning the founding of Rome and the first 250 years or so of her history have recently been radically challenged by some archaeologists. Suffice it to say here that archaeological evidence does not necessarily contradict the main lines of literary tradition; rather, it supplements that line, and the tradition itself has at least a kernel of historical truth.

Rome's Location. Rome's central position in Italy, allowing her to conquer

The Granger Collection

FIGURE 50. Bronze Etruscan chimera from Arretium (Arezzo), 5th–4th century B.C. Height: 31 1/2 inches.

southward and northward at her convenience, was favorable for ultimate control of the peninsula, whereas in her early period the fact that she was astride the Tiber crossing, the trade route between Etruria and Campania, brought quickening influences into her life, and the inhospitable marshes south of the Tiber long protected her from enterprising Greeks. The Tiber is navigable for fifteen miles from its mouth, where the port of Ostia was later founded, and at the limit of navigation, opposite the Palatine, there is an island that facilitated land traffic. At this point on the left, or eastern, bank of the river are located the famous Seven Hills of Rome: the Capitoline, Palatine, and Aventine, with their spurs, the Quirinal, Viminal, Esquiline, and Caelian; across the river are the Janiculum and Vatican, originally outer defenses but ultimately brought within the city. The hills, which controlled the Tiber passage, attracted early settlers, but the danger of constant floods was a drawback that was not overcome till Etruscan engineers drained the area between the Capitoline and the Palatine; eventually this became the Forum or marketplace.

Archaeological investigations have revealed the first occupation of Rome during the Bronze Age in about 1500 B.C., but this settlement apparently had no continuity with later ones of the Iron Age. These, emerging between the ninth and seventh centuries B.C., were located on the Palatine, Quirinal, Esquiline, and Viminal Hills and attest to at least three separate communities on the site of Rome. That on the Palatine, the site of nuclear Rome, arose about 800 B.C., thus at a date not far from the traditional 753. We are doubtless correct in supposing that the people who

FIGURE 51. Etrusco-Italian rhyton in the shape of a demoniac head, 4th century B.C. Height: 7 1/8 inches.

The Granger Collection

inhabited these settlements represented a cremating Italic folk, called Latins, and an inhuming Sabine stock, who arrived after them, and that as the two amalgamated, they absorbed whatever aborigines they found in the area. Ethnically mixed though they were, and destined to receive Etruscan blood as well, the Romans were nevertheless Latins and akin to the other dwellers of Latium. Latium is a district that extends from the Tiber southward along the coast to the promontory of Circeii and inland to the Apennines. In the mountains south of Circeii, separating Latium from Campania, lived the fierce and hostile Volsci, one of the tribes of the Sabellian-Umbrian group (map, p. 326).

The chief Latin towns, in addition to Rome, were Praeneste, Tibur, and Tusculum, but perhaps because of its reputed age a certain precedence was enjoyed by Alba Longa. This town was situated on the Alban Lake and was the head of a religious league that met annually on the Alban Mount to honor the Latin god Jupiter. When Rome began to expand in the sixth century and conquered Alba Longa, some of these Latin towns founded another, military league, patronized by the goddess Diana, which gradually became a defensive alliance against the rising power of Rome. The first and humble step toward Roman expansion, however, was the creation of a religious festival—that of the Seven Mounts—and the bringing together of the separate communities on the Palatine, Esquiline, and Quirinal and those that

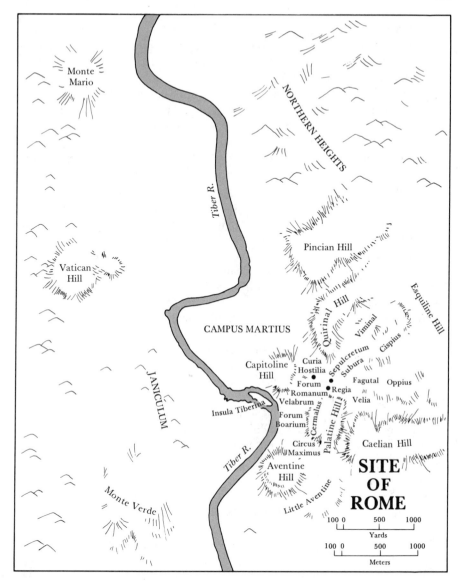

Monte
Mario

NORTHERN HEIGHTS

Tiber R.

Vatican
Hill

Pincian Hill

Esquiline Hill

Quirinal Hill

CAMPUS MARTIUS

Viminal

JANICULUM

Capitoline
Hill

Curia
Hostilia

Sepulcretum

Cispius

Subura

Forum

Fagutal   Oppius

Romanum

Regia

Velabrum

Velia

Insula Tiberina

Cermalus

Palatine Hill

Forum
Boarium

Circus
Maximus

Caelian Hill

Tiber R.

Aventine
Hill

**SITE
OF
ROME**

Little Aventine

Monte Verde

100 0   500   1000
Yards

100 0   500   1000
Meters

had developed on the Viminal and Caelian into a union known as Rome of the Four
Regions, with its citadel (*arx*) on the Capitoline. The sacred boundary of this city,
which was not to include the Aventine until later, was known as the *pomerium* and
was protected by a simple wall.

The Roman Character.   With the growth of Etruscan civilization some Romans
engaged in commerce and industry, but most of the people remained farmers and
shepherds and cultivated their little fields in the rolling plain about the city, which
is known today as the Campagna. As the farmer, clad in his tunic (a loose woolen
garment that reached the knee), followed his bronze-shod plough and yoke of cat-

tle, his narrow mind normally held sober, practical ideas, for he saw nothing of the world beyond the mountains bordering the Latian plain—mountains that inspired him with a feeling of hatred for the enemies who were accustomed to swoop down on his fields. His laborious life—his warfare against famine, pestilence, and neighbors—made him stern, puritanical, and, even in his dealings with the gods, calculating and illiberal. He was strong in the more unsentimental virtues, in dignity, bravery, and energy; he respected the gods and forefathers and, above all, obeyed the laws and ancestral custom (*mos maiorum*).

Simplicity and severity characterized the family and its dwelling. The early house was generally round, with a hole in the thatched roof to carry off the smoke from the hearth in the single room (*atrium*); these houses, incidentally, often served as models for urns to hold the ashes of those who were cremated. The home was sacred, consecrated by the marriage act, and within it lived the guardian deities, the *lares* (who protected the fields) and the *penates* (who watched over the family stores). To them and the other gods the father, in the discharge of his duties (*pietas*), was bound to sacrifice. The father (*pater familias*) had absolute authority (*patria potestas*), even the power of life and death, over his wife and children, his slaves and tenant farmers (*clientes*)—a strict moral school, if we may so describe it, where the wife was respected and shared in the family worship and inheritance, and the young men were disciplined for public life. As the family grew larger in the course of several generations, it often happened that the members, even if widely separated, kept up their social and religious relations with one another in an association known as a clan (*gens*).[1] Small groups of families united in a local community (*curia*), and on certain festal days the men ate together in a common dining hall containing a sacred hearth, on which they kept a fire burning perpetually in honor of Vesta. When war broke out, the members of a *curia* followed their leaders to the front and stood side by side on the field of battle, inspired by kinship and religion to deeds of daring.

THE KINGS OF ROME

Seven kings, according to tradition, ruled Rome in early times: Romulus (a possibly legendary figure), Numa Pompilius, Tullus Hostilius, Ancus Martius, and three others who probably date from the Etruscan conquest (ca. 575-509 B.C.), Lucius Tarquinius Priscus, Servius Tullius, and Lucius Tarquinius Superbus. The Etruscan kings, surely historical personalities, converted the hilltop villages they found into a unified, powerful city. Obscure though these personages are, the fact of the monarchy is proved by the survival in republican days of a priestly office known as king (*rex sacrorum*) and of another office, that of *interrex*, on whom fell the duty if the state was without magistrates, of carrying on the government until elections

---

[1] Members of clans bore the clan name, a personal name, and often a family or honorific name, which distinguished them further. For example, in the case of Publius Cornelius Scipio, Publius is the personal name (*praenomen*) given by his parents, Cornelius is the clan name (*nomen*), and Scipio is the name of his family (*cognomen*), a branch of the Cornelian clan.

were held. The king was commander in war, chief priest, and judge. He appointed
the various officials and, because of the dignity of his office, dressed in an embroidered purple robe and high red shoes; with an eagle-headed scepter in his hand he
sat on an ivory throne, the so-called curule chair. Twelve attendants (*lictors*) carried
the symbols of the king's *imperium,* an axe bound in a bundle of rods (*fasces*).
Although he could decree whippings and executions, his authority was not absolute. He could not name his successor. Son did not follow father to the throne.

   Government and Social Classes.   When the king wished to consult his people on
questions of public interest, such as the possibility of war, his criers went about the
city with oxhorns, calling them to the meeting place (*comitium*). Here the thirty
curiae, ten from each of the three tribes (*Tities, Ramnes,* and *Luceres,* which ultimately became the names of the cavalry corps of the army), met as the assembly, or
comitia curiata, and listened to the king's proposition. Each *curia* cast its own vote,
and a majority of the *curiae* decided the matter. To be binding, however, such a
decision of the assembly had to receive the sanction (the *patrum auctoritas*) of the
senate, the ancient advisory council of elders. The senators (*patres,* "fathers")
ultimately came exclusively from the well-organized, wealthy aristocracy, and the
members of their families and their descendants, known as patricians, filled the
priestly colleges and other offices. The great mass of Romans were called *plebeians,*
and though they were debarred from priesthoods, offices, and senate, they were
personally free and could own property, engage in business, and vote in the popular
assembly. Patricians and plebeians together formed at once the Roman people
(*populus Romanus et Quirites*) and the army. The patricians made up the cavalry
and were followed into battle by plebeians, many of whom had fallen into a state
of clientage to their wealthy patrons. In days of peace, however, the client worked
the land of his noble patron, supported him in public life, and in return received
legal advice and protection, but the relationship of dependency inevitably sharpened the bitter struggle between the social classes of patricians and plebeians that
was long to characterize republican Rome.

   Religion.   It may have been the growing prosperity of Rome that tempted the
Etruscans to Latium. At any rate, it was under the Etruscan kings in the sixth
century that Rome became an important and powerful community. Several Latin
towns were conquered, including even Alba Longa; trade increased to such an
extent that Carthage came within the orbit of Rome; trade guilds of flute players,
smiths, potters, and so on grew up under the patronage of Minerva; fields were
drained, with a corresponding benefit to agriculture, the basis of economic life; the
Forum was drained and the city fortified. There was strong Etruscan influence in
the art and architecture of the temple of Jupiter on the Capitoline, but it was
probably in religious ritual itself that Etruscan influence was most profound. For
example, the Romans took over from Etruria their trinity, though they identified
the chief guardian of the state (Jupiter) and Juno (the patron spirit of women) with
their own deities and retained for them the Latin names. Minerva, the third of the
trinity and goddess of war, skill, and wisdom, kept an Etruscan name. There were,
of course, many other Roman gods, such as Mars, the god of war; Vulcan, the god
of fire and forge; Janus, god of doorways and bridges; and Vesta, the goddess of the

hearth. As the Romans became increasingly aware of Greek civilization, however, they began to identify the gods of Greece with their own. Jupiter was identified with Zeus, Juno with Hera, Minerva with Athena, Mars with Ares, Venus, a garden deity, with Aphrodite, the goddess of love; several Greek gods, such as Apollo, were adopted outright. Roman religion concerned itself primarily with material blessings and had little to do with spiritual needs. In order to win the favor of the gods, the most important thing was the strict observance of ritual; the word *religio* suggests obligation, the necessity of performing duties inspired by fear.

It was the task of the priests to see to the service of the various gods, but certain religious duties were under the supervision of groups, or colleges, of sacred persons, such as the six Vestal Virgins, who attended to the worship of Vesta and preserved the sacred fire of the state in her temple. The college of augurs interpreted for the king the omens (*auspices*) sent by Jupiter, through which he revealed his will regarding the state, in the flight of birds and in thunder and lightning. The Romans borrowed the elements of the *auspices* from Etruria and developed them into a complex system. Because they were intensely religious and obeyed strictly what they believed to be the divine will, it was partly through the *auspices* that the magistrate controlled the people. The college of pontiffs was the principal adviser of the king in religious matters and, as the guardian of the civil and religious law (*ius* and *fas*), drew up the calendar of sacred days. The power of the chief of this college (the *pontifex maximus*) was very great, but it probably did not reflect the union of religious and political authority in the person of the king during the regal period. The fact that many important religious offices were occupied by magistrates doubtless explains why government at Rome did not fall into the hands of priests, as so often happened in the Near East, and the same principle holds for all Roman history.

Overthrow of the Monarchy.   Important as was the Etruscan contribution to the development of Rome, about the year 509 B.C., according to the ancient written tradition, the Latin aristocracy rose up against their last king, Tarquin the Proud, and overthrew him. For a generation or so—down to about 470 B.C., at least—Etruscan cultural influence in Rome remained strong, as attested to archaeologically by the continued presence of Etruscan pottery and other Etruscan artifacts. This influence does not necessarily suggest continued Etruscan political control of the city, as a free Rome would naturally have continued to trade with her culturally more advanced neighbors to the north. Once freed from Etruscan domination, the nobles faced immediately the struggle against the common people in their own state. It was amid these circumstances that the Roman Republic was born.

22

The Expansion and Development of Rome to 265 B.C.

THE EARLY REPUBLIC

Although the details are inexact for the two and a half centuries following the fall of the Roman monarchy, and the dates themselves are largely traditional, there is no doubt that the years were crowded with wars, the successful conclusion of which meant, first, the preservation of Rome itself and, second, the unification of the peninsula under her single rule. These wars helped to determine the character and outcome of the political struggle of the people with the nobles, because the plebeians, ever incited to further expansion by the fruits of conquest and realizing their own growing importance to the military machine, were able to wring greater and greater concessions from the nobility (cf. map, p. 341).

Rome's Neighbors. The downfall of monarchy and the establishment of the republic left Rome exposed to the attacks of her neighbors, especially the Latins, and of the now hostile Etruscans. She was further weakened by dissensions between patricians and plebeians within her own city. But after a brief war the leading Roman statesman of the time, Spurius Cassius, negotiated a perpetual peace with the Latin League (ca. 493 B.C.). His negotiations provided not only for an offensive and defensive alliance but also for an exchange of the private rights of citizenship; that is to say, the right of *commercium* granted Romans and Latins the privilege of carrying on business and owning property in each other's territory, and the right of *conubium* assured legal marriage and inheritance.

It was well that the Romans and Latins had renewed their alliance, for they were soon to begin a long, hard struggle in defense of their property and lives against the hungry tribes of the hills. Year after year the Sabines, descending from their mountain homes, pillaged the Roman territory, and often, too, the Aequi burned farmhouses and drove off the farmers' cattle. Once they trapped a consul and his army in a valley, and according to the famous story, the Senate appointed Cincinnatus dictator in the crisis. The messengers, bearing the commission across the Tiber, found him plowing on his farm. Cincinnatus listened to their message and, leaving his fields, took the command. In sixteen days he was back on his farm, a private citizen once more, but in the interval he had defeated the enemy, captured much booty, and celebrated a triumph—a grand procession that moved along the Sacred Way through the Forum and up the Capitoline to the temple of Jupiter. Though the story is surely more fiction than fact, it does illustrate the simple life of the time, the devotion to duty, and the triumph of a victorious general.

Siege of Veii. For many years Rome carried on war with the Sabines and the Aequi and other mountaineers, named the Volsci, but the incorporation of the nearby Hernici (strategically situated between the Aequi and the Volsci) into the Latin League strengthened the alliance, and by the end of the fifth century Rome had little to fear from raiding bands. About 400 B.C., however, the Romans commenced a war of allegedly epic proportions, the ten-year siege of Veii, an important Etruscan city a dozen miles to the north. Veii had been a rich and civilized city for centuries, very powerful militarily, situated on a strongly fortified height, and controlling an important ferry route across the Tiber. Leading the fight was the Fabian clan, whose estates lay closest to Veii. The propinquity and political influence of Veii were a threat to Rome. At last the great dictator Camillus destroyed the city, sold much of its population into slavery, and doubled the public land of Rome by annexing its territory.

The Gauls Sack Rome (387 B.C.). Veii had received little help in its hour of trial from the other Etruscan cities, partly because of their own loose political organization, but chiefly, no doubt, because they were now faced, on their northern frontier, with a new enemy who had crossed the Alps. These were the Celtic people known as Gauls (see page 277), brave warriors devoted alike to war and drink, and accustomed to fight in dense masses with long, two-edged iron swords; however, they lacked the discipline and the machinery necessary to undertake sustained sieges. They drove the Etruscans from the Po Valley, occupied it themselves permanently—hence the entire area came to be known as Cisalpine Gaul—and then invaded Etruria proper. About eleven miles north of Rome, on a tributary of the Tiber above Fidenae called the Allia, they met a large force of Romans. The Romans had never hesitated to stand up against the wild tribes of the hills, but these fierce northern giants were a new and terrifying experience, and the Romans were routed, some taking refuge in ravaged Veii, while others brought news of impending disaster to Rome. Panic gripped the city, many inhabitants had already fled, and only on the Capitoline were there signs of defiance. The citadel did, indeed, hold out, but the rest of the city was sacked and burned (ca. 387 B.C.). Ever restless and fickle, and worried by threats to their new homeland in the Po Valley, the Gauls ultimately accepted an indemnity and marched off. The Romans, too, returned, and with remarkable perseverance they cleared away the debris and rebuilt their city, but this time they were careful to enclose it with a strong stone wall, which still stands in many places, the so-called Servian Wall.

THE LATIN AND SAMNITE WARS

First Samnite War (343-341 B.C.). The half century following the rebuilding of the city was a period of constant, albeit successful, warfare for the Romans, including an abortive rebellion by some Latin cities against their authority. These cities were defeated by Rome in 358 B.C. Shortly thereafter (ca. 354 B.C.) she took the fateful decision to ally with a non-Latin power.

Because of further danger from the Gauls, the Romans temporarily formed an alliance with Samnium, the most powerful nation in the interior of the peninsula. The Samnites were brave and free, but they were also poor and overpopulated, a race of mountaineers, without cities, wealth, king, or aristocracy. The best solution of their problem, so thought many from time to time, was to raid and occupy the fertile plain of Campania to the west, around the Bay of Naples, but their threat to the wealthy city of Capua brought an appeal to Rome. Thus began the First Samnite War (343-341 B.C.), an inglorious episode in Rome's military history. At the end, the Romans were willing unilaterally to make peace with the Samnites, even abandoning to them some of her own Campanian allies.

The Latin War (340-338 B.C.). Rome's apparent breach of faith in ending hostilities offended the Latins, who had supported the Romans and endured the hazards of war in the belief that they were equal partners. The previous treaty with Samnium had raised questions in their minds, as had Rome's even earlier act of refusing them land confiscated from the Volsci, and therefore they now decided to revolt against a leader that could treat their interests so cavalierly. In the Latin War that followed (340-338 B.C.), Rome enjoyed the advantage that comes to a single city in opposing a loose confederacy, and after one or two fierce battles and a series of sieges, she dissolved the Latin League. In reorganizing Latium and Campania, the Romans for the first time displayed their outstanding political flexibility. Some towns were granted complete Roman citizenship, others partial or potential citizenship rights. Still others had their allied status more fully spelled out. This conglomerate organization was to be the nucleus of Rome's eventual domination of Italy.

Second Samnite War (326-304 B.C.). Rome's consistent successes were due, in part at least, to her superior military organization and equipment. The army by then was a peasant militia, normally obedient, brave, and hardy. It seems to have been inspired, too, with the idea that its struggles were for home and country, in defense of the wealth and civilization of the plain against encroaching barbarism from the mountains. This attitude seems to have been what motivated Rome to attack the Greek city of Naples and to oust the Samnite garrison temporarily controlling it. This attack led to the Second Samnite War (ca. 326-304 B.C.).

At first, Rome was successful, and then the tide turned in favor of Samnium. In 321 B.C. Pontius, the Samnite leader, enticed the Roman consuls with forty thousand men into an ambush at the Caudine Forks, in a valley of the Apennines, and compelled them to surrender. The consuls, in the name of the state, swore to the enemy's terms of surrender, and then the whole army, deprived of its arms, marched under a yoke of three spears in token of their complete and humiliating submission. All were allowed to return home, excepting six hundred cavalrymen, who were detained as hostages.

Rome resumed fighting in 316, and the war dragged on from year to year, but Rome's policy of settling and organizing conquered territory finally bore fruit. The fortress colonies that she established on the border of Samnium, for example, hemmed the enemy in the narrow, mountain valleys, and at the same time the

Romans built a paved road, the Via Appia, from Rome to Capua that provided all-weather communications with Campania. Although the Samnites received help from the Etruscans and the Umbrians, Rome now met with success in all her battles, and the consuls ravaged Etruria and captured the strongholds of Samnium. In 304 B.C., after suffering great losses, the Samnites agreed to renew the former treaty, which had left them free.

Third Samnite War (298-290 B.C.). It was hardly to be expected, however, that so inconclusive a result would long continue, and shortly thereafter the Third Samnite War broke out. The Etruscans, and now the Celts, allied with the Samnites against Rome, which was clearly trying to dominate the peninsula. Rome's strategic geographical position, however, made it possible for her to deal with one enemy at a time, and in a decisive battle at Sentinum in Umbria (295 B.C.), she broke the enemy league. Deserted by their allies, the Samnites held out resolutely for five more years, until Marius Curius Dentatus, the Roman consul, compelled them to sue for peace and accept the status of dependent allies.

The long conflict was now ended. It had begun, at the very opening of the republican period, with strife between the plains and mountains—in border warfare with the Aequi and the Volsci—and it culminated in a long and fierce struggle with Samnium. One can only speculate on what effect these wars had on the manpower and prosperity of Italians in general.

The really astounding thing about Rome is that the more wars she fought, the stronger, the more inexhaustible, she seemed to be. At the same time, it was her great genius, whether by luck or by design, to unite her defeated foes under her and to keep them remarkably loyal. In this way the foundations of empire were laid.

THE CONQUEST OF SOUTHERN ITALY

Tarentum. Magna Graecia was, of course, the home of large numbers of Greeks, who lived in ancient city-states. Much of their life, nevertheless, consisted of quarrels among themselves and with their Italian neighbors, but in addition the Sicilian Greeks and the founding cities of old Greece often interfered in their affairs. One of the richest and most powerful of these cities was Sparta's colony, Tarentum, famous for its harbor, its textiles, pottery, fisheries, and far-flung trade. The Tarentines naturally felt a certain primacy among the Greeks of southern Italy, and they even concluded a treaty with Rome that forbade Roman ships to sail within the Gulf of Tarentum. Tarentum was resentful when the Greeks of Thurii appealed to growing Roman power, rather than to herself, for help against the Lucanians and the Bruttians, and the resentment turned to anger when Rome accepted Thurii, and Locri and Rhegium as well, as allies and placed garrisons in their cities. Not long afterward, a small Roman squadron, in open violation of the treaty, sailed into the gulf, and the Tarentines immediately put to sea, sank several Roman ships, and massacred the crews of others. The Romans sent ambassadors to demand reparation for this and other alleged wrongs, but they were insolently dismissed.

Po R.

Arnus R.

Ariminum

Sena Gallica

Arretium

ETRUSCANS

UMBRAIANS

Firmum

ADRIATIC SEA

Volsini

Ausculum

Castrum Novum

ELBA

Narnia

VESTINI

Cosa

Falero

Radria

Tarquinu

Nopere

Alba Fuceas

Sutrium

Tibuz

Carsioli

Caere

Roma

Praenesta

MARSI

FRENTANI

Ostia

Signia

Ardea

Norba

Fregellas

SAMNITES

APPULIANS

Antium

Setla

Tarracina

Circell

Suesaa

Cales

Minturnae

Beneventum

Sinuesaa

Capus

Saticula

Yenusia

Cumae

Neapolis

HIRPINI

Brundiamm

Tarentuca

Paestum

LUCANIANS

Heraclea

TYRRHENIAN   SEA

Thurli

BRUTTIANS

IONIAN   SEA

Locri

Regium

ROMAN
ITALY
265 B.C.

SICILIA

0   20   40   60   80   100

Miles

Roman territory

Allied territory

Roman colonies

Latin colonies

341

Pyrrhus. Rome found herself at war with a state in the very instep of the peninsula. The Tarentines appealed for aid to the king of Epirus, Pyrrhus, a brilliant but unstable military genius, who responded with an army of twenty-five thousand men, trained in Macedonian fashion, and twenty elephants, newcomers to Italian warfare. His first victory, at Heraclea (280 B.C.), brought him many allies. But his own losses were so great—thus giving rise to the expression, "Pyrrhic victory"—that, though he pushed on to within a few miles of Rome, he was anxious for peace. His ambassador, Cineas, spoke eloquently in the senate, but the old, blind statesman, Appius Claudius Caecus, allegedly cried, "Let Pyrrhus return home, and then we may make peace with him!" The principle, here enunciated, that the interests of Italy were a concern of Rome illustrates the normal Roman policy of making peace only with a defeated enemy and of tying him to Rome by a perpetual treaty. Failing to win his cause by either eloquence or bribery, Cineas returned to Pyrrhus with the report that the Roman Senate was an assembly of kings, The next year, at Asculum, Pyrrhus won yet another victory, but with appalling losses.

In these critical years Rome allied with Carthage, with whom she had had several treaties since early days, and who feared that Pyrrhus might turn his attention to Sicily. This is what Pyrrhus did, for in answer to a call for aid from Syracuse, he crossed over to Sicily and spent four years in war, defeating the Carthaginians of the island and preparing for an invasion of their homeland, when his Greek allies tired of his high-handed methods and deserted. Pyrrhus then withdrew to Italy and after a defeat at Beneventum (275 B.C.) returned to Greece, where he died fighting three years later.

The force that Pyrrhus left behind in Tarentum soon surrendered, and in its place was stationed a Roman garrison. Tarentum and the other Greek cities of southern Italy became Roman allies. Thus, by 265 B.C.—within two and a half centuries of the founding of the republic—Rome was mistress of all Italy south of the Rubicon, a river of northern Italy on the east coast (see map, p. 341).

THE ORGANIZATION OF ROMAN RULE IN ITALY

The Army. The steady and far-seeing guidance of the skilled men who formed the Roman Senate had produced this remarkable achievement, for, even though some of the conquests were accidental and others were the result of defensive wars (which Rome pursued vigorously nonetheless), a pattern of deliberate expansion becomes clearer with the years. The instrument of this policy was, of course, the army. The late monarchic army seems to have consisted of 3,000 heavy infantry and 300 cavalry, recruited equally among the three tribes and organized by centuries of 100 men. Phalanx tactics were the norm. Temporarily abandoned during the early republic, they were reinstated during the fifth century, as the size of the Roman army gradually increased. During the siege of Veii payment for service was introduced, which made possible a thorough change in the military system. Henceforth the citizens, who had been accustomed to short summer campaigns, could serve the entire year, if necessary.

The socially elite arm was the cavalry, drawn from senatorial cadets (and eventually some plebeians) rich enough to afford horses. Such cavalrymen were called *equestrians*. The heavy infantry were the shock troops; those wealthy enough to supply themselves with panoplies of armor were called *the classes*. Light infantry, not so armed and irregularly used, were *below the class*. At some time in the fourth century the organization by phalanx was replaced by more flexible legions of about 4,200 infantry plus cavalry.

The Secret of Rome's Success. Many Greek cities in time of distress appealed for help to Athens or Sparta, but no enduring unity ever resulted from successful intervention. Rome, on the other hand, acted effectively on hearing similar appeals from Italians and created a congomerate state that, among other triumphs, resisted dissolution throughout the long and terrible crisis of the war with Hannibal. Somewhere, in the organization of Roman rule of Italy, lay the formula by which a republican city-state might build a world empire; somehow, in contrast to Athens and Sparta, Rome was creating interest in common Italian welfare. An alliance with Rome could never be broken without war, and when once allied, degradation from independent to dependent status often followed, but Rome was also extraordinarily tolerant of local feeling, customs, and institutions, and peace and trade frequently followed the end of civil strife. In the narrowest sense, part of Rome's success lay in her clever recognition that the local aristocracy would support the power that supported it, but the real secret of success, the whole central idea of Rome's empire building, may be summed up in the word *liberality*. That is to say, those who enjoyed only partial Roman citizenship, or none at all, could look forward to the day when they would be elevated to full citizenship.

Roman Citizens. There were two classes of Roman citizens. The full citizens enjoyed all the privileges and lived, many of them, in Rome itself; still others, however, lived in cities or villages elsewhere in Italy. These communities had their own governments, with magistrates, council, and assembly, and the inhabitants usually had their law cases settled in their local courts and followed their vocations there. As they were Roman citizens, they had the right to go to Rome and vote in the assemblies or present themselves as candidates for office. There were also Roman military colonies, twenty-seven in number, each of which usually consisted of three hundred citizens, with their families, who were placed in a frontier town as a garrison. The full citizens, that is to say, consisted of the people of Rome; cities and villages that were particularly favored by Rome (probably often because of their strategic position, such as Capua and Cumae); and the military colonies, placed in garrisons sometimes beyond the frontier of the actual Roman state.

The other class of Roman citizens was known as *cives sine suffragio* (citizens without the suffrage), for they did not have the right to vote or hold office in Rome, though they did have the private rights (those of *commercium* and *conubium*). Naturally, they fought in the Roman armies. These people lived in *municipia* (municipalities) and had self-government in strictly local affairs. The *municipia* were located in Latium, Etruria, and Campania and represented early Rome's method of preparing for ultimate full citizenship people who either insisted on partial independence or who were not vitally important to her at the moment.

Roman Allies.   Rome also had two classes of allies. The Latin allies were, of course, nearest to the Romans in blood, language, customs, and sympathy. They consisted of the few colonies that had been founded by the old Latin League, certain towns in Latium itself (such as Tibur and Praeneste, which had not received Roman citizenship on the league's dissolution), and the thirty-five Latin colonies founded in all parts of Italy. Romans as well as Latins took part in these foundations, but they were called Latin colonies because all the members had the status of Latin allies. They formed self-governing, almost sovereign states, each bound to Rome by an individual treaty that regulated the relations between the two states. These were the people of the "Latin name" (*nomen Latinum*); the Latin who left a son of military age behind and moved to Rome had an unrestricted right to trade, to buy property there, to intermarry with Romans, and vote as a Roman. The Latin colonies were of a military nature and served as outposts at strategic points; at the same time, they were a means of extending the Latin language and civilization to the natives, while relieving overpopulation and poverty at home.

Rome's other allies were called Italian (*socii Italici*), each of whom, as in the case of the Latins, had its own separate treaty with her. They enjoyed every gradation of privilege. Neither Latins nor Italians paid taxes or tribute to Rome, but all their communities furnished the number of troops fixed by treaty. These troops were not incorporated into the Roman legions but served in separate detachments. Rome furnished subsistence and allowed them to share equally in the booty. The communities on the coast, especially the Greek cities, furnished ships and crews, and all the allies had to equip and pay their own troops. They had no voice, however, in the declaration of war, the general strategy, or the conclusion of treaties.

In her conquest of the Italian peninsula, then, Rome created a league of small states under her leadership. It was a loosely centralized system, directed by Rome and based on common Italian residence and a gradually increasing community of Italian interests.

THE MAGISTRACY, SENATE, AND ASSEMBLY

Domestically, the early republic witnessed periodic social, economic, and ultimately political unrest. The conflict between plebeians and patricians is known as the Struggle Between the Orders, and it must have been clear, almost from the beginning of the republic, that the cooperation of the plebeians, militarily speaking, was so indispensable that they would be able to enforce their demands on the privileged nobility. The Roman respect for law and order was so great, however, that in spite of occasional open strife and much bitterness, the entire struggle was punctuated, most conspicuously, by a series of laws that in the issue, overlong in coming perhaps, gave the Romans democracy, at least on paper. The various laws, together with developing custom, eventually produced a responsible magistracy, regular assemblies, and technical political equality.

The Magistracy.   When the monarchy gave way to the republic in 509 B.C., two consuls[1] with equal power (*imperium*) were elected annually by the curiate assembly in place of the lifelong king. The presence on the earliest consular lists of the names of Etruscans still resident in Rome after the fall of the monarchy and even of plebeians suggests that factional divisions already existed and that, initially at least, the patricians had not yet established a monopoly on office holding. As each consul had the right to veto any public act of the other—a right subsequently enjoyed by some other magistrates—the two colleagues, by checking each other, hindered their office from growing too powerful for the good of the state. In days of peace the consuls generally alternated their rule within the city monthly, but on the battlefield, though it sounds almost incredible, the command of the army usually alternated daily. That the system worked is the best commentary that can be written on it, but its success was probably due, in large part, to the fact that a consul had behind him the experience of many military campaigns; during a critical war or dangerous sedition, however, one of the consuls might nominate to the senate a dictator, who placed the state under martial law and ruled with absolute power. The dictator's term was limited to the period of the emergency, with a maximum of six months.

The consuls had the power of life and death over the soldiers in the field, but in ordinary capital cases they were compelled as judges to grant an appeal to the assembly. The early consuls enjoyed most of the authority of the king, together with his trappings and attendants, such as the curule chair and lictors, but it was the development of other magistracies, occasioned by the growth of state business, that slowly robbed the office of its all-embracing power. As these magistracies came into being and grew—eventually settling themselves into a regular succession, known as the *cursus honorum*—two features that we noted at the outset in connection with the consuls remained: their annuality and their collegiality. Since there was an obvious advantage in permitting a consul to finish a campaign after his term of office had expired, the system of promagistracy was devised during the Second Samnite War, whereby a consul was allowed to continue for an indefinite period "in the place of a consul" (*pro consule*), as it was called.

Not long after the middle of the fifth century, the pressure of war apparently compelled the Romans from time to time to substitute increasingly large boards of military tribunes with consular power—or, more briefly, consular tribunes—for the consuls, but about 366 B.C. they reverted to the annual election of two consuls; henceforth such tribunes were exclusively military officers. But the necessity of having the highest officials continuously ready for the field remained, and a new magistracy, the praetorship, was created (in the usual form of a board or "college") to relieve the consuls of acting as judges in civil cases. Praetors could also command armies and have their own powers extended as propraetors after their normal year in office.

The consuls lost still more of their pristine power when the magistracy was fur-

[1] At first called *praetors.*

ther developed about 443 B.C. by the creation of the censorship. The two censors took over from the consuls the duty of making a register of the citizens and their property and of assigning each man to his tribe and class. They also let out to the highest bidders the privilege of collecting the taxes and attended to the erection of public buildings. The censorship was periodic, for election took place every five years and the incumbents (ordinarily ex-consuls) held office for only eighteen months. In financial matters, too, the consulship lost ground, for the two quaestors, who had originally been appointed by the consuls for the purpose of keeping the treasury, were annually elected by the people from about 450 B.C.; after 421 B.C. there were two additional quaestors who accompanied the army as quartermasters. The supervision of streets and public buildings, markets and public games, fell to the two curule aediles, who were originally patricians.

The Cursus Honorum. Here, then, were the Roman magistracies, so arranged, excepting the censorship, that a man would ordinarily proceed from one to the other: quaestors (at the bottom of the *cursus honorum*), aediles, praetors, consuls, and censors. They all had *potestas* (authority), but only the praetors, consuls, and dictator had *imperium,* the right to command an army, to preside over an assembly, and to try important cases. It was an extraordinary system, designed to bring able men of wide experience to the top, and in combination with the senate it gave Rome tremendous advantages in dealing with the world.

The Senate. All important places of honor and trust during the early republic—military, political, and religious—were filled by patricians, who came to monopolize the senate in the early republic. The senate gained in prestige after the downfall of the monarchy, because as the permanent advisory body of the state it could influence and dominate the consuls, who served only one year and could then be called upon to account to the senate for their administration. By the third century B.C. the senate consisted of 300 members, who were enrolled by the censors from among all office holders of the *cursus honorum,* which meant that their experience was not lost to the state and that they themselves would probably, during their term of office, consult the interests of the body they were about to join. Since the members served for life (unless removed for misconduct), the senate was strongly conservative and class-conscious, and very powerful too, because for a long time the sanction of the patrician senators (the *patrum auctoritas*) was necessary before actions of the public assemblies could become law. After much strife, as we shall see, plebeians gained membership in the senate through office holding; to distinguish them from the patrician senators (*patres*), they were known as the "enrolled" (*conscripti*)—hence the expression *patres conscripti* in addressing the senate.

The Assemblies. It will be recalled that the first assembly of the Roman people was the *comitia curiata,* which the patricians easily dominated, but in the earliest days of the republic it was resolved to create a new assembly, which would not be associated with birth. According to the principle of the Roman military system, the people had been divided into classes by property, each class furnishing a fixed number of centuries, and it was decided to carry this principle over into an assembly that would be exclusively political. The original motive seems to have been to make every citizen's voting power correspond to his worth as a soldier; or, as it might be described, to the completeness of his armor, so that the more property a man possessed, the greater was to be his political influence.

The new assembly was called the *comitia centuriata,* because the citizens were grouped by centuries, ultimately 193 in all, and each century had a single vote. As in the army, they were divided into cavalry (equestrians) and infantry, and the latter were subdivided into five classes according to the amount of their property. Several centuries formed a class, but the centuries themselves varied in size and did not necessarily contain 100 men each; a century of juniors (those liable for military service) was larger than one composed of seniors (the reserves), while that of the landless was by far the largest of all.

Because of its military organization, which must not be confused with its political purpose and function, the centuriate assembly could not gather within the city; it held its meetings, accordingly, outside the *pomerium* in the Campus Martius, and there it elected the magistrates, heard appeals in capital cases, and voted on proposals for laws and wars; its acts, too, needed, for some time, the sanction of the patrician senators to gain the force of law. The cavalry voted first, then the first or wealthiest class, then the other classes in their order till a majority was reached. It will be seen from the following table that the cavalry and the first class formed a majority, so that, if they agreed, they decided the question, and the voting proceeded no further. It rarely happened that all the centuries were called on to vote, and thus it is clear that the more property a man had, the more powerful became his vote.

ORGANIZATION OF THE *COMITIA CENTURIATA*

		Juniors (17–46 years)	Seniors (above 46 years)
I	Class	40 centuries	40 centuries
II	Class	10 centuries	10 centuries
III	Class	10 centuries	10 centuries
IV	Class	10 centuries	10 centuries
V	Class	14 centuries	14 centuries
		84 centuries	84 centuries

	168 centuries
Cavalry (*Equites*)	18 centuries
Substitutes for the killed and wounded	2 centuries
Musicians and workmen	4 centuries
Proletarians	1 century
	193 centuries

The *comitia curiata,* shortly after the formation of the republic, ceased to have real authority, although it continued to meet to sanction the *imperium* of magistrates after their election and to attend to religious formalities.

Perhaps even under the last kings the three old tribes had been abolished and supplanted by nineteen new ones, four urban and fifteen rural. As Roman territory expanded, other rural tribes were created, until there were thirty-five in all (the ultimate number) in 241 B.C. The tribal organization was the basis of the registration of citizens and thus of both taxation and military service. The existence of the tribes surely explains the origin of another assembly, the so-called plebeian council or *concilium plebis*. It was organized by tribes and presided over by tribal leaders called *tribunes* (*tribuni plebis*). Patricians, amounting to a minute portion of the population, were excluded from membership in this council.[1]

In the beginning, the council had no authority over the state, for it was simply a gathering for plebeian business. Measures passed by this body needed the approval of the senate to be binding on all the citizens, including patricians, and were then called *resolutions of the plebs* (*plebi scita*) in contradistinction to the laws (*lex*, pl. *leges*) passed by the centuriate assembly presided over by a magistrate with *imperium*. The council elected the plebeian aediles and tribunes, but the ease with which it could be brought together within the city and the simple method of a mere majority's determining each tribe's vote meant its eventual development into a regular assembly, the chief legislative body at Rome, while the centuriate assembly continued to function primarily for elections.

Here, then, were two sovereign bodies composed of almost the same people—the *comitia centuriata* and the *concilium plebis*—as impossible an arrangement, so it might seem, as the existence of two consuls on the field of battle with equal power; but the Roman respect for law and order permitted the system to work well enough, especially as the custom developed of dividing the two assemblies into elective and legislative bodies. And withal, in the background, stood the senate, something of an enigma and often exercising more power than it was entitled to.

THE GREAT LAWS

The Roman constitution—the magistracies and assemblies and the laws that represent milestones along the way—was hammered out step by step, now more quickly because of the importance of the plebeians to the military effort, now slowly because of the absence of many men on expeditions or because of a crisis that pushed all else into the background. The length of time it took, however, helps to explain its complicated character, as contrasted, for example, with the unified character of a written constitution. The plebeians aimed to win political equality with the patricians, though at the very beginning this must have been a vaguely formulated hope, the immediate business being the correction of obvious wrongs. The plebeians found their leaders from among the rich of their own class, and as the Struggle Between the Orders progressed, the issue was widened to include legal equality in every sphere of life.

---

[1] There was also a tribal assembly (*comitia tributa*) distinct from the plebeian council. Also organized by tribes, it contained both patricians and plebeians and elected certain minor officials. It was never a lawmaking body and may easily be ignored in the following account.

In most respects, the common people lost by the overthrow of the monarchy, for the later kings had shielded them from the oppression of the nobles. Now that the poor no longer had a champion, the patricians began to reduce their clients to the condition of debt slaves. They exacted illegal rents, and if the tenant failed to pay his rent, the amount due was looked on as a debt bearing heavy interest. The creditor had a right to seize the delinquent debtor and to hold him as a slave till he had worked off the debt. If the grievances of poor plebeians were economic, those of the wealthy plebeians, the types of men who became tribunes, were primarily political. They wanted reforms permitting their election to high office, brilliant careers, and senatorial status, in keeping with their wealth and ambition. These wealthy plebeians differed from patricians only in their lack of blue blood.

The Tribunes. The people revolted against such injustice and, according to tradition, marched off across the Tiber to the Janiculum, where they threatened to found a new city (ca. 495 B.C.). Precisely how the problem was resolved is unknown, but the solution could not have been very satisfactory, for the next years witnessed various attempts, particularly by Spurius Cassius, a consul of about 493 B.C., to set up a tyranny, which the patricians harshly suppressed. About 471 B.C., however, the plebeians forced the patricians to assent to the creation of four annual tribal officers of their own. These plebeian tribunes (to be sharply differentiated from the consular tribunes) had the duty of protecting the plebeians and their interests. Their persons were sacred; anyone, even a consul, who injured a tribune or hindered him in the exercise of his duties, might be slain as a man accursed. The law forbade the tribune to be absent from the city overnight and compelled him to keep open house so that the injured and the oppressed might find refuge with him at any hour. The tribunes, moreover, soon won the right to place their bench at the door of the senate, where they could listen to the proceedings within. If a measure under consideration displeased them, they could shout, "Veto" ("I forbid") through the door, and ordinarily the proposal would be dropped. Eventually the tribunes were allowed to sit within the senate, and though, strictly speaking, they were not magistrates, they were officers with *potestas* who had the right to veto all acts of magistrates, senate, and assemblies.

Codification of the Laws (449 B.C.). Up to this time the laws had been unwritten. The patricians, who alone were acquainted with them, handed them down orally from father to son, an exclusive knowledge that they used for the oppression of the plebeians; the patrician judge decided cases in favor of men of his own class, and no plebeian could quote the law as proof of the injustice. The tribunes, therefore, began to urge the codification of the laws in the interest of the common people. The senate yielded, and according to a very likely tradition, a committee was sent to some of the Greek states of southern Italy to study their codes of law. On their return, ten men (*decemvirs*) were elected for one year in place of the consuls for the purpose of drawing up the laws, and the task was completed the following year (449 B.C.) by the consuls, Valerius and Horatius. The new laws were set up in the Forum on twelve wooden tablets and hence became known as the Twelve Tables. They were simple and harsh, but they did at least codify the law of the time. Intermarriage between patricians and plebeians was prohibited, as had already long been the custom; other laws sanctioned debt slavery and gave the father the power of life and death over his son. The Twelve Tables said nothing about legal procedure and thus were scarcely instruments of social justice.

The Canuleian Marriage Law (445 B.C.). The law of the Twelve Tables that forebade marriage between the classes was resented, as a social stigma, by wealthy plebeians. They also looked on intermarriage as a stepping-stone to office; and since the patricians themselves came to favor intermarriage because of their dwindling numbers and wealth, the disability was removed about 445 B.C. by the tribune Canuleius (the *lex Canuleia*).

The Ager Publicus. When the Romans acquired land in war, they leased a small part of it or granted it forthwith to settlers. The larger part, however, was added to the public domain (*ager publicus*), and all who wished might "occupy" it, on condition of paying to the government a percentage of the animals grazed on the land or of the produce. This arrangement seemed sufficiently liberal, except that in actual practice the patricians and the wealthy plebeians alone were able to exercise the privilege. They bought, sold, and bequeathed the land, till in time they came to look on it as their own. The plebeians were determined to end this injustice and at the same time win for themselves admission to all the offices in the state, including the consulship. The whole Struggle Between the Orders came to a head in 367 B.C. when two tribunes, Licinius and Sextius, proposed a series of laws that are associated with their names.

The Licinian-Sextian Laws (367 B.C.). In the political field the Licinian-Sextian laws provided that the recent custom of electing military officers (known as *consular tribunes*) instead of consuls should cease, and that in the future two consuls should regularly be elected, one of whom might be a plebeian. Economic distress was lightened by the provision that interest already paid on a debt was to be deducted from the principal; slavery for debt was then ended or soon afterward. And to solve the agricultural crisis, it was further stipulated that no individual might occupy more than 500 *iugera* (300 acres) of the *ager publicus* nor pasture on it more than 100 cattle or 500 sheep.

The Hortensian Law (287 B.C.). The Licinian-Sextian laws made it inevitable that soon all the magistracies in the state, including both consulships, should be opened to the plebeians. In 300 B.C. the *lex Ogulnia* opened the colleges of pontiffs and augurs to plebeians; and in 287 B.C., which marks the end of the Struggle, the *lex Hortensia* provided that all plebiscites were to be binding on the entire population as laws, whether or not the senate gave its approval. This law, which made the plebeian council a sovereign body, was forced through by the dictator Hortensius, at a time when debt and war with the Samnites had produced sufficient dissatisfaction to cause the plebeians to secede to the Janiculum in order to enforce their demands.

Constitutionally the centuriate assembly and the plebeian council were now free from the senate and were the sovereign power in the state. In form, therefore, the government was a democracy, but in fact it was then oligarchic, for the senate exercised more actual power than ever, composed as it was of the ablest and most experienced men in the state, which made its moral influence irresistible. The senatorial class survived so strongly because it saw, before it was too late, the wisdom of admitting plebeians to its ranks through office holding and marriage. Patrician aristocracy thus gave way to a hybrid oligarchy composed of old and blue-blooded families now intermarried with newly risen rich plebeian ones. This oligarchy was riven at an early date by factionalism and by the manipulation of client voters in the assemblies.

SOCIAL PROGRESS

While the Roman genius was solving constitutional problems, the people themselves grew in the arts of civilization and in wealth, a development that successful conquest made more rapid. The institution of a regular system of coinage[1] was unusually slow, however, especially when one considers the economic importance of Rome and her wide commercial contacts, but this slowness probably indicates that trade was largely in the hands of foreigners; the basis of Roman economy was agriculture, and the interests of the oligarchy centered on land. If the Sextian-Licinian laws are any indication, that oligarchy was already building up large estates.

Public Works. The state, as we have seen, also acquired considerable property through conquest, and some of this wealth was used for public works. For example, Appius Claudius Caecus, during his censorship begun in 312 B.C., built an aqueduct, named after him the Appian Aqueduct, which brought the city plenty of fresh water from the hills about ten miles distant; through a great part of its course, it ran underground. This was the first work of its kind at Rome, but as the city grew through the centuries, larger and longer aqueducts had to be built, and in some of them the water flowed high above the ground in a channel supported by a series of stone arches. We have already mentioned another great work of Appius, also the first of its kind, the Appian Way, which extended from Rome to Capua. It was built to be as straight and level as possible: steep hills were cut through, and marshes and deep valleys were spanned by causeways of stone. The surface was paved with large, flat, durable stones; milestones were set up along the side; and at shorter intervals, other stones were set as aids for mounting on horseback. The example of Appius was followed by other statesmen, till in the course of centuries a network of these roads covered the whole domain ruled by Rome. Their primary object was the rapid movement of armies and military supplies and official letters, but they were free also to the public for travel, commerce, and all other purposes. It was largely by means of such roads that Rome was able to protect the empire she was building up, to govern it, and to bind all parts of it together.

Literature and Religion. From early times, surely, some Roman businessmen and diplomats had learned Greek, but such knowledge was not widespread or, as yet, even historically significant. There were no formal schools, and the upper-class boy learned at his father's knee and by observation of his elders' behavior in the

---

[1] During the Third Samnite War, the Romans circulated bronze bars weighing six pounds (*aes signatum*). The earliest true bronze and silver coins were issued in 269 B.C., the most widely circulated bronze coins being *aes libralis* or *aes grave*.

forum and the law courts. There was thus, strictly speaking, no written literature. The importance of the Twelve Tables to the future development of Roman law must be stressed, but they were too simple to count as literature, and except for a few poems, proverbs, and orations composed by Appius Claudius, the Romans were really without books of their own. Only a few individuals studied Greek literature. From Greece the Romans adopted the god of healing, Aesculapius, for whom they built a shrine on the nearby island in the Tiber. It was customary for sick persons to pass the night in this temple, in the belief that the god would heal them while they slept. There were many festivals to brighten the life of the Romans, particularly the so-called Great Games of harvesttime, the Saturnalia in December, and a crude but vigorous kind of peasant farce combining slapstick and dance, much appreciated by country folk. The surviving sources tend to stress the grim and even harsh side of Roman character. This must surely have been mitigated, for the Romans spent time at lighter pursuits of recreation and, we know, enjoyed a rollicking and even vulgar wit.

Roman Character.   The early Romans were distinguished for their patience and energy, the fruit of a simple life. These qualities became stronger, owing to the care with which the republican government supervised the citizens, for the magistrates had the power to punish not only for crimes but for every offense against order, and even for immorality, including lazy or luxurious habits. All officers enjoyed this authority, but it was the special duty of the censors to see that every citizen subjected himself to the severe discipline prescribed by the state. The father retained his authority over the members of his family and continued to look after his household estate (*res familiaris*). The aim of education in the family and in public life was to repress the freedom of the individual in the interest of the state and to make a nation of brave warriors and dutiful citizens. The highest results of this stern training were reached in the Samnite wars, a period known thereafter as the golden age of virtue and heroism. A citizen of this time was, in the highest degree, obedient to authority, pious, frugal, and generally honest. But though he was willing to sacrifice his life for the good of the state, he was equally ready to enrich himself at the expense of his neighbors; and the wealthy did not hesitate to sell the poor into slavery for debt, till they were forbidden to do so by law.

23

Rome and the Mediterranean (264–133 B.C.)

THE FIRST PUNIC WAR (264–241 B.C.)

Carthage. About 725 B.C. the ancient Phoenician[1] city of Tyre founded Carthage on the northern coast of Africa (map, p. 326). The land was fertile, and the site itself was well situated for trade with East and West, and with Sicily and Italy. In the course of centuries Carthage became wealthy and, as she created an empire on the coasts and islands of the western Mediterranean, a strong political power as well. Her domain included most of the northern coast of Africa, a strip of the western coast beyond Gibraltar, parts of southern Spain and Corsica, all Sardinia, and nearly all Sicily, besides many small islands. In the third century B.C. Carthage was a world power. For the story of her conflict with Rome—the greatest conflict in antiquity—we fortunately possess adequate and reliable accounts from many writers, chiefly Livy, the great Roman historian of the Augustan Age, and Polybius, the distinguished Greek historian who came to Rome in 167 B.C. as a hostage from the Achaean League and became the intimate of many leading Romans.

The Carthaginians ruled a large native Libyan population, but their own government was republican, with an assembly of qualified citizens that elected the two chief magistrates, known as *suffetes,* and the generals. Most of the actual conduct of affairs, however, was in the hands of the senate and the council, composed of members of the leading wealthy families, which accounts for the strongly oligarchic color of their government. Carthage had a large and fine navy and an army of mercenaries, but her ambition was for commercial, rather than political, rule. To further this policy, as Rome gradually assumed a leading position in the western Mediterranean, she concluded several treaties with Rome to regulate their commercial relations. Against Pyrrhus a Roman-Carthaginian alliance was formed for common defense.

Resources of Carthage and Rome. The resources of these two nations were quite

[1] "Punic" in Latin.

different. Carthage, with her magnificent navy, dominated the sea. Her citizens were farmers, landlords, merchants, and artisans. They provided the officer cadres for her armies of mercenary soldiers, who were generally good fighters and loyal when properly led and promptly paid. Italy had a much greater population and could draw on correspondingly greater resources of manpower if called on to fight. Whether Roman, Latin, or Italic, Italians had proved to be hardy, well-disciplined fighters, but in the event perhaps no better at warfare—even when fighting for their own homes—than Punic mercenaries. Their greater weakness was their lack of ships and naval experience, which was to prolong the pending struggle.

Causes of the War.   The underlying cause of the war was simply the conflict of interests between Carthage and Rome. Carthage felt it to her advantage to gain possession of all Sicily, whereas Rome, the leader of Italy and obligated to defend the peninsula, saw in a possibly hostile Sicily a threat to her control. Moreover a clique of influential nobles saw in a Carthaginian war, in which they would be generals, an excellent opportunity to win fame and glory and thus advance their own political careers.

The immediate cause of war lay in the action of certain Campanian mercenaries, known as Mamertini ("Sons of Mars"), who, after they had deserted from the service of the Greek city of Syracuse, seized Messana, killed the men, and divided the women, children, and property among themselves. When Syracuse threatened them, differing factions of the Mamertini appealed for support, some to Carthage and some to Rome. A Carthaginian garrison was introduced into Messina before Rome could react. Suddenly confronted with Punic occupation of a town potentially threatening Italy, the Roman Senate passed the question of what to do to the centuriate assembly. The assembly voted an alliance with the pro-Roman faction, which meant war with Carthage (264 B.C.; map, p. 326).

War in Sicily.   The army that the Romans sent to Sicily defeated Hiero, the able king of Syracuse, and the Carthaginians separately. Messana was taken. The next year (263 B.C.) the Romans attacked Hiero again and agreed to make peace on payment of an indemnity and an alliance with Rome. The Romans and Hiero then turned on the Carthaginians. If, however, the Romans were to drive the Carthaginians from the coastal towns of Sicily and protect their own shores from raids as well, they must have a fleet, and this they lacked. A Carthaginian quinquereme—a warship with five rowers to an oar and accommodating 300 rowers in all and 120 marines—had been stranded and was now used as a model. While the fleet of 120 ships was being built, the crews sat on benches along the shore and practiced rowing in the sand. Then they put to sea under the consul Gaius Duilius and engaged the enemy off Mylae (260 B.C.). The Roman ships were clumsy and the sailors awkward, but they successfully grappled the enemy's vessels to their own, allowing Roman legionaries, as marines, to board the Carthaginian vessels. Thus they gained a decisive victory.

Invasion of Africa.   The Romans then built another great fleet and set sail for Libya. Off Ecnomus on the Sicilian coast they met and defeated a still larger fleet of the enemy (256 B.C.) and afterward they continued on their way to Africa. There, under the consul Marcus Atilius Regulus, they gained victories and captured towns, until a Spartan adventurer, Xanthippus by name, taught the Carthaginians to offer battle in the plain, where they could use their elephants and numerous cavalry to advantage. The result was the destruction of the Roman army and the capture of Regulus, who had been an overconfident and unimaginative general.

At this time the Romans were besieging Lilybaeum on the west coast of Sicily. In 250 B.C. the consul Publius Clodius stole north to Drepana, where he hoped to surprise a Carthaginian fleet, but he suffered an overwhelming defeat instead. Since the Romans still pressed the siege of Lilybaeum, Carthage in 247 sent out a general who was to prove, in himself and his sons, the most dangerous enemy Rome ever met, Hamilcar, surnamed Barca ("Lightning"), a man of genius for war. He occupied Mount Ercte, above Panormus, which was then held by a Roman army. From the harbor beneath him, his light ships harassed the Italian coasts, while from his perch above, he swooped down on the Romans in the neighborhood and as easily retired to the nest, which no enemy dared attack. Three years later he suddenly abandoned this position for Mount Eryx, where he could cooperate with his friends at Drepana, but actually his forces were too small to accomplish much.

The Roman Victory. Rome herself now lacked the resources necessary for sustained effort, but at this juncture the wealthier citizens offered to build 200 warships with their own money. With the new fleet, the consul Lutatius Catulus met a Carthaginian fleet bringing supplies to Sicily and totally defeated it (242 B.C.). As the Carthaginians could carry on the war no longer, the following year they gave Hamilcar full power to make peace. The treaty stipulated that Carthage was to give up Sicily, pay the Romans 3,200 talents[2] within twenty years, and release all prisoners without ransom. Rome now controlled the western Mediterranean, but this control had cost her hundreds of ships and tens of thousands of lives.

Sardinia and Corsica. As Carthage could not pay her mercenaries for their service in war, they mutinied and were joined by the Libyans, who now revolted. While the whole strength of Carthage was engaged in putting down this rebellion (241-238 B.C.), the Romans treacherously seized Sardinia and Corsica, and when Carthage remonstrated, they imposed a heavy fine on her. Utterly exhausted by the mercenary war, Carthage yielded. Rome's motive in seizing the islands was doubtless much the same as in the case of Sicily—the protection of the Italian coasts from Carthaginian attack—and together they became the second Roman province in the same year as Sicily (227 B.C.).

THE ILLYRIAN AND GALLIC WARS (229-219 B.C.)

For some time Italian merchants, trading with Greece, had been plundered by Illyrian pirates. Some had been murdered, others taken captive and held for ransom; after many complaints had come before the Roman government, the senate sent one of its commissions across the Adriatic to Illyria to investigate. The members were mistreated, and thereupon the Romans declared war. In a brief naval

---

[2] About 200,000 pounds of silver.

campaign (229-228 B.C.), they chastised the piratical inhabitants and made them promise to pay tribute. Corcyra and one or two other Greek states became allies of Rome to secure protection from the Illyrians and perhaps, too, from Macedon, which was thus brought within Rome's orbit. At the same time Roman envoys journeyed to the Achaean and Aetolian leagues, confederations of cities in southern and northern Greece, respectively (inset, p. 280). This was Rome's first diplomatic relation with Greece, and she found the Achaeans and Aetolians grateful for the suppression of piracy. Ten years afterward there was a Second Illyrian War (219 B.C.), in which the Romans were likewise successful, but Illyria, though it became a client state of Rome, was not organized as a province until after 167 B.C.

Rome had recently acquired large tracts of land in northern Italy—known as the *ager Gallicus*—in Picenum and along the Umbrian coast, and there was considerable dissatisfaction because, instead of being distributed among the citizens, the land was "occupied" by the wealthy. Against the wishes of the senate, Gaius Flaminius, the tribune of 232 B.C., carried through the plebeian council a law for distributing these public lands among the citizens. The Gauls of the Po Valley saw in the new settlements a menace to their own homes, and in 225 B.C., doubtless reinforced by fresh arrivals of Celts from across the Alps, began war on Rome. Two years later Flaminius, now consul, conducted a campaign that resulted in a complete Roman victory. In 222 B.C. the authority of Rome was extended to the foot of the Alps, and soon afterward to the peninsula of Histria at the head of the Adriatic (cf. map, p. 326).

THE SECOND PUNIC WAR (218–201 B.C.)

Causes of the War. Military defeat, the loss of Sicily, and the treacherous seizure of Sardinia and Corsica were the chief reasons that Hamilcar Barca hated Rome, and it may very well be that the primary motive of his son Hannibal in letting loose on Italy a terrible war was the desire for revenge. And yet, it may be more exact to say that this was the sustaining passion of Hannibal once war began, for the preceding actions of the Barcids do not necessarily prove a deep plot. Probably further conflict between these two dynamic and expanding powers was inevitable under certain circumstances, and this conflict was abetted by Barcid ambitions and personalities.

Carthage in Spain. In any case, Hamilcar Barca probably went to Spain in 237 B.C. for the purpose of creating a new dominion for Carthage—one, perhaps, that might be used years later as a springboard for an invasion of Italy, but chiefly to make up for the loss of Sicily, Sardinia, and Corsica. It was natural enough for him to think of going to Spain, because for centuries Carthage had traded with the Iberian Peninsula, and Carthaginian trading posts and recruiting centers had been created that, moreover, served to exclude rivals to the enhancement of Carthaginian wealth. During nine years Hamilcar built up a Carthaginian province in Spain more by diplomacy than by war; he taught the native tribes to live together in peace under his rule and to develop the resources of their country. He was drowned while besieging a Spanish town in 229 and was succeeded by his son-in-law, Hasdrubal.

Hasdrubal skillfully continued the wise policy of his predecessor in gaining over the tribes and adding them to his empire. When after eight years of such service he was assassinated, the soldiers enthusiastically proclaimed Hannibal, then twenty-five years of age, commander in chief (221 B.C.).

Saguntum. War, however, was to break out in Spain, for Rome's alliances generally had a way of involving her with yet other states, and the ancient and valued treaty with the Greek city of Massilia in southern Gaul was no exception. In 226 B.C. Massilia sent messages to Rome protesting against Hasdrubal's activities in Spain, where Massilia also had interests, and accordingly Rome sent envoys to Spain to investigate. A treaty was drawn up in that year that stipulated that Hasdrubal was not to go north of the river Ebro. At an unknown date, but probably after the Ebro River treaty, Rome informally allied with Saguntum, which lay south of the river. This alliance certainly violated the spirit if not the letter of the treaty with Hasdrubal, as that treaty implied recognition of a Carthaginian sphere of interest south of the Ebro. In 219 B.C., in any case, and despite a Roman protest, Hannibal, in furtherance of his cause, attacked Saguntum, which fell after a siege of eight months. Roman envoys again protested to Carthage and, finding no change of heart, declared war (218 B.C.; rear endpaper).

The Grand Strategy. The grand strategy of Rome was to carry the war to Spain and Africa by land and sea, and Hannibal's was to invade Italy, where he counted on active help from the Gauls and on revolts among Rome's allies. Like Alexander the Great, Hannibal was a military genius, a leader of men, destined never to lose a battle during his expedition. Nevertheless he lost the war, and his life had little influence on history except indirectly: Rome emerged mistress of the western Mediterranean and sure of its strength, and southern Italy was devastated. It is surprising, too, that neither before his departure nor after his arrival in Italy, a land of towns and cities, did Hannibal equip himself with siege machinery. Hannibal's failure to provide for adequate and regular reinforcements was probably his most serious mistake, for he had a powerful land base in Spain, which the Roman rule of the sea could not easily cancel. It must be emphasized, however, that Hannibal received only lukewarm support from his home government.

Hannibal's Invasion of Italy. Hannibal left his brother, another Hasdrubal, behind in Spain to follow later with reinforcements, and he himself, with 40,000 infantry, 9,000 cavalry, and a number of elephants, crossed the Pyrenees into Gaul. He launched his expedition so abruptly that the Roman consul in Sicily, Tiberius Sempronius Longus, dared not set sail for Africa, while the other consul, Publius Cornelius Scipio, had hardly reached Massilia when he heard that Hannibal was across the Rhone. Scipio sent his brother and an army on to Spain to do what damage they could and returned to Italy.

When Hannibal began the ascent of the Alps, the real difficulties of his journey became apparent, for the way was narrow and rough, and the mountaineers rolled stones upon his troops and the long train of pack animals. He reached Italy five months later (in autumn of 218 B.C.), perhaps by way of the Mont Cenis pass, with his army cut in half by the losses. Against him stood a military potential through-

Fototeca Unione

FIGURE 52. Via Latina. One of Rome's most ancient arterial highways, it was used by both Pyrrhus and Hannibal in their attacks on the city.

out Italy of 700,000 infantry and 70,000 cavalry; even so, his own army was full of the spirit of its commander (map, p. 341).

After a light cavalry engagement on the Ticinus River, Scipio withdrew to the south bank of the Po and sought the protection of the hills near the Trebia River. Here his colleague Sempronius joined him with another army and took chief command, for Scipio had been wounded in the previous encounter. In the ensuing battle, the Romans were ambushed in the rear by Hannibal's brother Mago, an impetuous fighter, while the Carthaginian cavalry routed their wings. After a long and desperate struggle, only 10,000 Romans fought their way out; the rest were killed or captured.

This great success led the Gauls to cast in their lot with the victor. Their presence in Hannibal's army made it difficult for many Italians to accept him as any kind of "liberator." Depression ruled Rome, where people spent the winter talking of evil omens. The government, however, took steps to resist the invader and so posted the consuls as to guard the two principal roads between the Po Valley and Rome:

Flaminius was stationed at Arretium in Etruria, and Servilius at Ariminum (map, p. 343). But Hannibal, with amazing topographical knowledge, surprised them by taking an unusual route over the Apennines far to the west, across the marshes north of the Arno River. After a rest, he laid a trap for the Romans. Knowing that Servilius was hurrying from the northeast to the aid of Flaminius, Hannibal coolly marched east past Flaminius. His army was now between the two Roman armies, an enticing bait for Flaminius.

Battle of Lake Trasimene (217 B.C.).   Hannibal's route led him through a narrow pass (Borghetto), along the north shore of Lake Trasimene, into a small plain ringed by mountains. Flaminius marched his entire army of 25,000 men in column from Borghetto into the plain. Never has an army been more completely ambushed and annihilated (217 B.C.). Flaminius was killed, and not long afterward most of the cavalry with Servilius were destroyed. The road to Rome now lay open.

Battle of Cannae (216 B.C.).   In the crisis, the Romans elected Quintus Fabius Maximus dictator; he was to win by his tactics the sobriquet of *Cunctator* (the "Delayer"). Since Hannibal did not attack Rome, but crossed the peninsula to the Adriatic coast and gradually moved southward, living off the land in his progress, Fabius dogged his steps and cut off foraging parties where he could but refused open battle. This policy saved Rome from another defeat that year, but it brought much unpopularity to Fabius, for Hannibal seemed to march and plunder where he liked. Unusual efforts, therefore, were made to levy and train troops for the following summer (216 B.C.) and for what turned out to be the most terrible battle of Roman antiquity. At Cannae, on the Aufidus River in Apulia, 80,000 Romans and allies—under the new consuls, Lucius Aemilius Paulus and Gaius Terentius Varro—faced 50,000 men under Hannibal. Varro, who held the chief command on the day of battle, massed his maniples in a heavy line, in the hope of winning by sheer weight. Hannibal cleverly posted a thin screen of Gauls and Spaniards in front of his center, and these troops slowly withdrew when Varro attacked. But as Varro penetrated into the center, the Libyan infantry on the flanks stood fast, and then Hannibal loosed on the enemy a tempest of cavalry. The Romans and their allies, now surrounded on all sides, were too crowded to keep rank or even to use their weapons, and they fell, losing perhaps 30,000 men. The rest escaped with Varro; the other consul, Aemilius Paulus, eight senators, and many other eminent men, perished. Hannibal was advised to attack Rome immediately, but lacking siege engines, he preferred to encompass its ruin through the revolt of its allies.

Defections from Rome.   At Rome, the senate rose to the occasion, encouraged the people, and posted guards about the city. But the battle of Cannae changed the character of the war. Nearly all the allies of Rome in southern Italy, even including the great cities of Capua and Tarentum, revolted, and on the death of Hiero, king of Syracuse, Sicily also forsook Rome. Philip V, king of Macedon, who had jealously watched Roman interference in the Balkans, allied himself with Hannibal (p. 285). This alliance compelled Rome to counter with friends and alliances of her own— with enemies of Philip, such as the Aetolian League, Sparta, and Pergamum in Asia Minor—and thus once again her orbit was enlarged. The so-called First Macedonian War (215-206 B.C.) Rome fought chiefly through these friends and succeeded in forcing Philip, and his ally, the Achaean League, to agree to peace.

Syracuse, Capua, Tarentum Recovered. Hannibal found that his greatest ob-
stacle in Italy was the fortified Latin colonies, which remained true to Rome and
proved impossible to take. At the same time, he had to protect his Italian friends,
even though his defensive policy gradually wasted his army and robbed him of the
prestige of success, for the Romans followed the example of Fabius and ventured
no more pitched battles. Instead they concentrated on Sicily. After a long siege,
Marcellus took Syracuse, which was defended by the engines of Archimedes, killed
during the subsequent Roman occupation (212 B.C.). Next the Romans surrounded
Capua with three armies. In the hope of diverting part of this force, Hannibal
suddenly marched on Rome, but once again he could accomplish nothing without
adequate siege machinery. Capua fell amid bloody slaughter in 211 B.C., as did
Tarentum, which the Romans took the following year.

War in Spain. The fall of Capua released large numbers of troops for service in
Spain, where affairs had recently taken a bad turn for Rome. By using the system
of promagistracy, which proved more effective than annual commanders, Rome had
kept Gnaeus Scipio and his brother Publius Cornelius Scipio, who had joined him,
for years in Spain, but in 211 B.C. they were both killed in battle by Hasdrubal. It
now looked as if Carthage might win back all Spain, and the Romans decided to
dispatch thither as proconsul Publius Cornelius Scipio, the twenty-five-year-old son
of the dead general of the same name. The only magistracy Scipio had held up to
this time was the aedileship, and it took a special act of the centuriate assembly to
confer the *imperium,* for the first time in history, on a private citizen.

Hasdrubal Invades Italy (208 B.C.). The young commander quickly showed real
genius for warfare, and in 209 B.C. he surprised and captured New Carthage, the
chief city and arsenal of the enemy in Spain. Hasdrubal, however, skillfully eluded
him and, with a large army and supplies, set out by land for Italy to reinforce his
brother. Hannibal desperately needed this help, and Rome as desperately needed to
prevent its arrival. If these two great armies should unite, Rome could have little
hope of victory; her country was drained financially and had been desolated; her
faithful colonies, exhausted by the war, were beginning to refuse aid; and her last
armies were in the field. Fortunately for her, the messengers who bore Hannibal the
news of his brother's coming were captured by the consul Gaius Claudius Nero,
commander of the army in southern Italy opposed to Hannibal. Leaving with a
small force to cover Hannibal, Claudius stole north and united his army with that of
his colleague Marcus Livius Salinator. At the Metaurus River in 207 B.C., the two
consuls surprised and destroyed Hasdrubal and his army. Claudius returned southward with the Carthaginian's head and directed that it be thrown into Hannibal's
camp to inform him of his brother's fate. For two more years Hannibal maintained
himself in southern Italy, during which time Scipio reconquered Spain. Then Scipio
returned to Rome and, after his election to the consulship, set out for Africa.

War in Africa. In obedience to his country's call, Hannibal quit Italy. He left
behind a ravaged southern Italy; he had not lost a battle in fifteen years, though he
had failed to capture many important objectives; and he had maintained himself all
the while in a hostile land, with inadequate reinforcements and little support from
home. In 202 B.C. at Zama, south of Carthage, Hannibal and Scipio met. Scipio

varied the usual Roman formation and placed the maniples in columns with open lanes between, through which the enemy's elephants could rush harmlessly; at a critical moment the Carthaginian mercenaries deserted. Hannibal had suffered his first defeat in a pitched battle, but he was to live on, a potential threat to Rome, for some years, until events forced him to poison himself in Bithynia (182 B.C.).

Peace (201 B.C.). By the terms of the treaty (201 B.C.) that followed the battle of Zama, Carthage agreed to surrender Spain, to pay Rome ten thousand talents, to give up all her elephants and warships except ten triremes,[3] and to wage no war outside of Africa, nor within it without the consent of Rome. This last clause left her a client state, helpless against Rome's ally Masinissa, king of Numidia, who plundered Carthaginian territory as he liked. Meanwhile, in Rome, Scipio celebrated a brilliant triumph and took the title of "Africanus."

THE GREEK EAST (200–133 B.C.)

The defeat of Carthage left Rome free to devote her energy to the remaining Mediterranean states in rapid succession. These were, chiefly, the Antigonid dynasty in Macedonia, the Ptolemaic empire in Egypt, and the Seleucid empire in Asia, which the Romans referred to as Syria; and there were, in addition, the Aetolian and Achaean leagues in Greece, the mercantile island state of Rhodes, and the kingdom of Pergamum in Asia Minor (map, p. 280). Rome did not plot the conquest of the Mediterranean from the beginning but often found in victory an occasion for further war, which was welcomed, more and more openly with time, by the element within the senatorial class that sought to advance their political careers by acquiring military reputations. At other times, however, Rome acted merely from fear of an invasion of Italy or in compliance with treaty obligations.

Second Macedonian War (200–196 B.C.). Philip V of Macedon had used his peace to recover influence over Rome's client states in Illyria and to expand southward into Greece and eastward in the Aegean. This expansion alarmed Pergamum, Athens, and Rhodes, and in 201 B.C. they sent an embassy to Rome accusing Philip of upsetting the balance of power and of preparing an attack on Italy itself. A powerful senatorial faction wished to punish Philip for his alliance with Hannibal, but the general and genuine senatorial feeling was that a dangerous attack on Italy was indeed being planned. The people themselves, however, were war weary, and it was only with effort that the senate forced through the centuriate assembly a declaration for the Second Macedonian War (200–196 B.C.). The issue was decided in 197 B.C. at Cynoscephalae ("Dogs' Heads"), in Thessaly, where the Roman consul Titus Flamininus met Philip. It was a test between legion and phalanx, and the flexible Roman formation, with the help of the excellent Aetolian cavalry, won.

Philip was forced to give up his possessions in Greece and to pay an indemnity. Since, however, it was clear that no power now existed in Greece that was strong enough to launch an attack on Italy, and since the Roman people were anxious not

---

[3] A trireme, the regular warship, consisted of three banks of oarsmen; each man pulled one oar.

to become more deeply involved outside of Italy, Greece was left free. At the Isthmian Festival at Corinth the following spring, proclamation was made by Flamininus of freedom to all the Greeks who had been ruled by Philip. Flamininus was one of an increasingly large number of Romans who had come to respect Greek civilization. The gift of freedom was a fair delusion, however, because the Romans and Greeks interpreted the concept *freedom* differently. By freedom for the Greeks, the Romans meant the conditional freedom of client states, which meant essentially the freedom to follow Rome's lead. The Greeks understood by freedom complete sovereignty, which meant the right to fight among themselves. As their protector and peacemaker, Rome was constantly invited to settle their disputes. This interference was destined soon to destroy their liberty.

Asian War (192-189 B.C.). The confusion caused by the Second Macedonian War gave the able and aggressive king of the Seleucid empire, Antiochus III, called "the Great," an opportunity to overrun Asia Minor and invade Thrace, which had once belonged to his empire. The Aetolians, who were angry that Rome had not allowed them to profit territorially from Philip's defeat, now seized Demetrias (192 B.C.)—a fortress in Thessaly, known, with Chalcis and Corinth, as "the fetters of Greece"—and invited Antiochus to come into Greece and free it from Rome. The Romans, however, drove Antiochus from Europe, and then at Magnesia, in Asia Minor, Lucius Scipio, the brother of Africanus, inflicted an overwhelming defeat on him (190 B.C.). As a result, Antiochus had to pay an indemnity and give up all his possessions north of the Taurus Mountains in southern Asia Minor. Rome left the states of Asia Minor independent, under her general protection.

Rome now compelled the Aetolians, as punishment for their share in the conflict, to accept a formal alliance, not the informal unwritten status as a client. The various states of Greece continued to quarrel among themselves, constantly accusing one another before the Roman Senate and as constantly inviting that body to settle their differences. Accordingly we find one commission of the senate after another going to Greece to arbitrate disputes, both in the interests of the Greeks and in the hope of preventing the formation of a dangerous coalition, for the Romans, at first their protectors, began after the second war with Philip to pose as their masters. Their respect for Greek culture did not prevent these "philhellenes" from encouraging everywhere the growth of political factions (generally among the aristocrats) that would be subservient to Rome.

Third Macedonian War (171-167 B.C.). Such was the state of affairs when Philip died and was succeeded by his son Perseus, who cherished the ambition, perhaps in consort with the Achaean League, of championing Hellas against barbarian Rome. Eumenes II, who as successor of Attalus I was now king of Pergamum, kept Rome informed of Perseus' diplomacy, which threatened to capitalize on the Greek love of independence. To prevent this union, Rome brought on the Third Macedonian War (171-167 B.C.). The principal commander on the Roman side was Lucius Aemilius Paulus, the son of the Aemilius who had died at Cannae, and an honest and able man. He met and conquered Perseus at Pydna, a city of Macedonia, in 168 B.C. Perseus escaped from Pydna but was later captured, and after following with his young children in the triumphal procession of the conqueror, he died in a Roman prison, by either suicide or maltreatment. The Romans divided Macedon into four autonomous republics, which were forbidden all inter-course of *commercium* and *conubium* with one another.

The Romans had been considerate of the Greeks. Now, after Pydna, they prac-ticed another policy. Several scores of cities were sacked in Epirus alone, and tens of thousands of their inhabitants were sold into slavery. At the same time, the Romans began the habit of transporting to Rome vast quantities of loot. Shiploads of furniture, precious metals, and works of art were destined to adorn the homes of important Romans and their city. All this loot, together with other imperial income and the tribute imposed on Macedon, relieved Roman citizens of direct taxation for a long period after 167 B.C.

To punish Rhodes for seeking to arbitrate the quarrel with Perseus, Rome created the free port of Delos, which ruined the trade of the island republic. Nor was there to be real freedom for Greece. Those who had sympathized with Perseus in the war were sent to Rome for trial, while from the Achaean League, one thousand hostages were taken, including Polybius. They were detained sixteen years among the towns of Etruria, until the influence of Polybius secured the release of the three hundred survivors.

When these exiles returned home, they excited Greece against callous Roman domination. The Achaean League became the rallying point of the patriot cause, which was embraced by the poorer masses, many of whom were doubtlessly moti-vated by a desire for social revolution and an improvement in their own economic condition. Accordingly, when Sparta seceded from the league and the Achaeans tried to force it back, Rome not only took the side of Sparta but also decreed the separation of certain other states from the league. Thereupon the Achaeans pre-pared for war with Rome, just as Macedon revolted. The Roman praetor, Metellus, easily suppressed the revolt and united the four Macedonian republics in the prov-ince of Macedonia (148 B.C.). Soon afterward the Achaeans were irretrievably beaten in two battles.

Destruction of Corinth (146 B.C.).   The Roman consul Lucius Mummius who had succeeded to the command, then entered Corinth, killed most of the men he found, and enslaved the remainder of the population (146 B.C.). After plundering the city, he burned it to the ground, while much valuable artistic booty was trans-ported to Rome. The destruction of Corinth was apparently intended to punish the inhabitants for their violent revolt. In this same year another strategic rival, Car-thage, was also destroyed. A century later, however, when the mighty Roman Empire had no more enemies to fear and was trying, instead, to bring back pros-perity to her provinces, both cities were refounded. In the modern excavations at Corinth by the American School of Classical Studies, the buildings of both the Roman and the Greek cities have been brought to light.

More than a century was to pass before all southern Greece became a Roman province under the name Achaea. Meanwhile, all leagues were abolished, and the right to take part in local government was restricted to the wealthy. Those Greeks who had remained loyal to Rome, such as the Spartans, the Athenians, and the Aetolians, continued as independent allies, but the others lost their independence and were placed under the governor of Macedonia.

The Province of Asia.   During the period of the Macedonian and Achaean wars, the protectorate that Rome had acquired over Asia Minor by treaty with Antiochus III continued. The most important state in Asia Minor was the kingdom of Pergamum, whose capital city of the same name was little less famous than Alexandria as a seat of art and culture. The kings were friends of Rome, and the last one, Attalus III, willed his kingdom to Rome on his death (133 B.C.). This extraordinary action may have been inspired by the hope of saving Pergamum from involvement in inevitable war and trouble; if so, it was doomed to disappointment. In any case, it led to the creation of the Roman province of Asia four years later.

THE WEST

Gauls and Ligurians.   The ability and desire of the Romans to carry on many different wars is an outstanding feature of the history of the second century B.C. The Gauls of northern Italy, for example, continued to fight desperately, long after the defeat of Hannibal, and in their struggle they were joined by the hardy Ligurians, who lived in the mountains to the west. Year after year the Roman consuls were baffled and their soldiers slaughtered in conflicts with these tribes, but before the middle of the century resistance was broken, the spirit of the people was crushed, and thousands of Ligurians were transported to empty public lands in Samnium.

War in Spain (154-133 B.C.).   It was in Spain, however, that Rome was destined to wage a long and crucial war, undoubtedly the most unpopular ever waged by the republic. After the defeat of Hannibal, Rome had wrested from Carthage her entire Spanish dominion, and from this territory in 197 B.C. were carved two provinces—Hither and Farther Spain—which were governed by praetors. The Spaniards, however, wanted their freedom, and in any case, they resented the casual brutality of the Roman occupation. They brought on one of the bloodiest and most desperate wars Rome ever waged (154-133 B.C.). The mountaineers were almost unconquerable. At home, it occasionally was impossible to recruit military levies, and tribunes, on occasion, even intervened to stop the draft, thus protecting distressed voters of military age. Failing in arms, the Romans resorted to treachery; they violated treaties and massacred troops who had surrendered under agreement.

The resistance centered in the little town of Numantia, where for many years a few heroic Spaniards held out. The morale and fighting spirit of the Roman troops were low, while the generals themselves were treacherous and incapable. Finally Scipio Aemilianus, the conqueror of Carthage (see p. 365), was given the command, and after restoring strict discipline, he took Numantia and its few survivors (133 B.C.). All Spain was now conquered, excepting a small mountainous district in the northwest. Rome planted few colonies in Spain, but during these years thousands of Italian soldiers either deserted or were discharged from the army at the end of campaigns and settled in the country. They took Spanish wives and mingled with the natives, with the result that the Latin language and civilization spread rapidly over the peninsula, and Spain became thoroughly Romanized.

Destruction of Carthage (146 B.C.).   The war with Hannibal left Rome a legacy of hatred and strife in Africa, no less than in northern Italy and Spain. The treaty with Carthage, it will be recalled, had forbidden her to wage war in her own territory without the consent of Rome, and this clause gave Rome's ally Masinissa, the king of the Numidians, an opportunity to plunder and seize Carthaginian lands. In answer to Carthage's complaints, Rome sent out various commissioners, who were always instructed to side with Masinissa. One of these commissioners was Marcus Porcius Cato, veteran of wars in Spain and a narrow-minded statesman, who convinced himself of the wealth and prosperity of Carthage and reported, on his return, that the city of Hannibal was still a menace to Rome. In fact, he is said to have ended every speech in the Senate, whatever the subject, with the words, "Carthage must be destroyed." His eloquence found a sympathetic hearing among xenophobic senators.

In 151 B.C. a Roman armada set sail for Utica to punish the Carthaginians for their strife with Masinissa. The terrorized Carthaginians were ready for every concession. They handed over, first, three hundred children as hostages and then their arms. Still not satisfied, the consuls told them to leave their city and settle ten miles from the coast. The people finally decided to defend their city to the last drop of blood rather than acquiesce in an arrangement that would rob them forever of their commercial prosperity. Since they had to make new weapons, they converted even the temples into workshops, and the women gave their hair for bowstrings. For three years they repulsed the attackers, and then the Romans, by a special act (since he was not yet eligible for the consulship), elected as consul a vigorous and able commander, Scipio Aemilianus, the son of Aemilius Paulus, who had been adopted into the family of Scipio Africanus. After a terrible siege, Carthage was taken (146 B.C.), the inhabitants were massacred or sold into slavery, the city was plundered and burned, and the land was cursed and made into the Roman province of Africa.

It was less than a century and a half since Rome had embarked on her policy of expansion beyond the borders of Italy, and in another period of equal length, she was to round out her empire so as to include all the countries of the Mediterranean. These years brought with them momentous changes in the character of her government and in the condition of her citizens.

24

Roman Government and Society (264–133 B.C.)

GOVERNMENT AT ROME

Problems Facing Rome. As long as a city-state, like Rome, remained so small that all the citizens could attend the assemblies and take part in public affairs, the government worked well. But the more territory Rome acquired, the more unjust and oppressive became her government, because, having outgrown manageable limits, the new territory was governed more in the private interest of Roman officials than the welfare of the state. In particular, the acquisition of vast wealth outside Italy was producing a class of agricultural capitalists that threatened ruin to the Italian peasantry by the creation of large estates. There were some far-sighted statesmen—such as the consul Gaius Flaminius, who fell at Lake Trasimene—who worked on behalf of the small farmers, but such men were rare.

The immediate need was to adapt the government of a city-state to an empire, to protect the interests of citizen and noncitizen alike; in short to rule the whole for the benefit of all and not merely the oligarchy in Rome. The problems were many, complex, and pressing, and it was the progressive failure to solve them that ultimately produced Caesarism, or one-man rule. The government still consisted, as in the early days, of senate, magistrates, and assemblies. The senate, however, had gained power at the expense of both magistrates and other assemblies, for it was composed of trained executives, generals, and diplomatists—men who had filled offices at home, had commanded armies, and had served on embassies to foreign states. Having once been enrolled on the senate list by the censors, the senators usually held their positions for life, and it was perhaps only natural that an experienced body such as this, which had guided Rome safely through the war with Hannibal and had carried on successful foreign conquest as well, should become supreme. With rare exceptions, the magistrates were obedient to its commands, for they were already senators or hoped soon to be; and few tribunes would interpose a veto, because they had been coopted by the senatorial class, to which they now regularly belonged. The new, tight aristocracy of wealth and office, made up of rich plebeians and the old patricians, might have its own quarrels, but to the outside world it presented a solid front that was rarely pierced by a "new man" (*novus homo*), as the Romans called a person, such as Cato, who was the first of his family

366

to attain high office; in fact, 90 of the 108 consuls between 200 B.C. and 146 B.C. belonged to families who had previously held the office. The inner core of the oligarchy was the "nobility" (*nobilitas*), comprising those families that had produced at least one consul in their history.

Constitutional Development. To win an election, and start one's career through the *cursus honorum* to ultimate honor and riches, was costly and often not free from bribery and corruption. In 180 B.C. the better element in the senate passed the Villian law (*lex Villia annalis*), which unsuccessfully attempted to control abuses. In the future, two years were to intervene between magistracies, and the first office, the quaestorship, was not to be held before the age of twenty-eight. It was not necessary to go on to the aedileship, but an ambitious young man generally did, for here was the profitable opportunity to entertain the people with expensive religious festivals and shows, at his own expense or on borrowed money; in this way he gained their favor and their votes for the higher offices. Thence he went on to the praetorship. There were now four praetors, one of whom, the alien praetor (*praetor peregrinus*), attended to disputes involving foreigners, and the others took charge of civil jurisdiction and served as governors in newly created provinces, but it soon became customary for propraetors and proconsuls to act as governors. From the praetorship, a successful politician advanced to the consulship, and then, after a term in the provinces, the people might show their appreciation by electing him censor. The tribuneship was not regarded as a regular magistracy and hence was not regulated by the Villian Law.

The two principal assemblies were the same as in the past and consisted essentially of the same people. The plebeian council elected the tribunes and certain other officials; it ratified treaties of peace; it received appeals from the judicial dicisions of magistrates in cases involving fines; and it was the chief legislative power. The centuriate assembly elected the higher magistrates, ratified declarations of war, acted as the highest court of appeal in capital cases, and occasionally passed a law. These assemblies, now governing an empire, were easily swayed by respected and skillful senators, who built up strong client factions in the electorate.

If democracy means a government by independent voters, then democracy at Rome was stillborn. The ruling oligarchy cunningly manipulated the voters and successfully minimized their number on election day. The oligarchs saw to it that the sizes of the tribes, the voting units in the plebeian council, were of uneven size. Those farthest from Rome were the largest, which meant that relatively few of the farmers in them would turn up in Rome to vote; the city tribesmen, most likely to vote, had only four of the thirty-five tribal voting units. The centuriate assembly, reorganized on a tribal basis in 241 B.C., was similarly amenable to the control of the oligarchs managing their factions. Furthermore presiding magistrates supervised the agenda, and there was no discussion of issues from the floor. If voting threatened not to go according to a politician's wishes, it was easy for him to find a friendly priest to decree unfavorable omens and postpone the meeting until a proper number of clients could be rounded up to vote as he wished.

Just as striking, perhaps, was the increasing interplay of factions within the governing establishment itself. These were ever-changing alliances of senatorial families, cemented by marriages, that cooperated in mobilizing their clients in assembly to vote for their commonly supported candidates. These factions drew together to prevent the rise to power of an exceptionally brilliant careerist, whose own faction might dwarf the others and monopolize the levers of power. This kind of manipulation actually happened to Scipio Africanus, Hannibal's conqueror, who actually endured ultimate political eclipse after the Second Punic War.

Economic and Social Changes. During the second century B.C., Italian agriculture underwent epochal changes. Peasants of even modest means and farming at subsistence level were the backbone of Rome's armies. Called away constantly to fight abroad, they could not maintain their homesteads and, on demobilization, tended to sell or abandon their farms and drift to the cities to find employment. Such lands were snapped up by senatorial and other entrepreneurs eager to increase their holdings because land was always the safest and most respectable form of investment. From at least the fourth century, they had also been interested in exploiting public domain, which they came to claim as their own by "squatter's rights." Thus large plantations (*latifundia*) developed to give their owners profit, not subsistence. These tended to be worked by slaves, now pouring into Italy from abroad. Independent farming never wholly died out, but the rise of a plantation economy was a striking fact of economic life. Cereal agriculture remained important everywhere, although plantations tended to become more diversified and included grazing ranches and culture of the vine and the olive.

The cities of Italy, like Rome, grew quickly with the peasant influx. For a time, these people found employment on building projects, but such employment was not permanent and was chancy. Because ancient cities, like Rome, never developed a commercial or industrial base to employ large masses, these people tended to live a hand-to-mouth existence as an unemployed or underemployed proletariat, and they became correspondingly demoralized.

At a much higher social level, there arose a subclass within the Roman gentry, what was soon to be called the *equestrian order,* deriving its name from the equestrian (cavalry) centuries of the centuriate assembly. Equestrians of the later republic were essentially those wealthy men who were excluded from political careers by the stranglehold over them exercised by established senatorial families. Like the senators, they invested heavily in estates, and their outlook was properly agrarian and agricultural. A minority of their class, however, took up business and commercial careers because the prohibition on trade and commerce legally applied to senators since a Claudian law of 218 B.C. did not extend to them.

PROVINCIAL ADMINISTRATION

The Provinces. By 133 B.C. Rome ruled most of the territory from central Asia Minor to the Atlantic, a vast area whose conquest and partial organization as provinces may be recapitulated as follows: (1) Sicily, acquired in 241 B.C. and organized as a province in 227 B.C.; (2) Sardinia and Corsica, seized soon after the conquest of Sicily and organized in 227 B.C.; (3) Hither and Farther Spain, acquired in the Second Punic War and organized in 197 B.C.; (5) Cisalpine Gaul, re-conquered early in the second century and organized as a province later; (5) Illyria, acquired in the Third Macedonian War (167 B.C.) and organized later; (6) Macedonia, organized in 148 B.C.; (7) Africa, acquired and organized in 146 B.C.; and (8) Asia, acquired in 133 B.C. and organized as a province in 129 B.C. In addition, there were in Asia and Africa various client states (map, p. 389).

Administration. The plan of administering a province was, on the whole, fair and, if justly adhered to, would not have been oppressive. The status of each province was established by a special charter (*lex provinciae*), which was drawn up by the victorious general and a commission of ten senators, subject to the later approval of the Roman Senate. Within a province there were generally a few communities that were free allies united to Rome by treaty; and there were still others, slightly more numerous, that were declared, not by treaty but by an act of the Roman government, "exempt from tribute and free"; they had substantially the same rights as the allied communities but no guarantee of their continuance. By far the largest number of communities, however, were dependent and provided the taxes of the province. This aggregate of communities formed the province and was subject to the governor. In his work, the governor (a praetor, proconsul, or propraetor) was assisted by a quaestor (his treasurer for receiving the taxes from the collectors), by three lieutenants or legates (*legati*), and by various young men (*comites*), who were glad to pay their own expenses for the experience. The duties of the governor were mainly military and judicial, for he commanded the army in the province and settled disputes at law between Romans as well as the more serious ones between provincials. Each community had its own courts for the trial of its citizens; it retained its own laws and customs, its magistrates, council, and popular assembly, and it was usually free from interference on the part of the governor. In fact, the Roman government did not have a sufficient number of officials for managing the affairs of the communities, even if it had wished, and the idea of taking charge of such local matters had not yet occurred to Rome. During the republic the governor, on assuming office, usually issued an edict, based on those of his predecessors, explaining the legal principles he would follow during his term of office. The foreign affairs of a province were directed by Rome.

Taxation. Theoretically the advantages that came to a province were very great, for peace and prosperity seemed assured. But governors were largely unsupervised, and many of them were proving to be greedily unscrupulous. In addition, a horde of moneylenders (*negotiatores*), bankers, speculators, and traders poured from the capital all over the provinces, and while their Roman citizenship protected them, they unjustly acquired much property in the provinces and reduced the people to debt and misery. A still greater evil, however, lay in Rome's system of letting out ("farming") the collection of taxes to contractors, or publicans (*publicani*). At first the publicans were provincial businessmen, not Roman equestrians, and hence presumably not unsympathetic to the problems of local taxpayers. But even under them, the system of tax farming was open to abuse; it maximized incentives to extortion, as any taxes collected over and above contractual stipulations were the publicans' profit.

The Calpurnian Law (149 B.C.).   Nor did the evil end there, for the governor, who received no salary, expected not to lose but to profit by his command. Some found it wise to make not one but three fortunes during their short term. The first was to pay the debts the governor had incurred on his way through the *cursus honorum,* particularly as aedile, when he had probably borrowed large sums with which to entertain the masses and win their further votes. The second fortune was to satisfy his judges in case of prosectuion on his return to Rome. And the third was to enable him to live in luxury for the remainder of his days. To prevent extortion, the Romans finally passed in 149 B.C. the *lex Calpurnia de repetundis,* which set up a court of fifty senators, presided over by a praetor; but it was a failure, since a group of senators (many of whom had been governors or hoped to be) could not be expected to convict another senator on his return from his province.

INTELLECTUAL DEVELOPMENT

Greek Influence.   It was contact with the Greeks, first in southern Italy and Sicily and then in the homeland, that produced a revolution in the development of Roman civilization. People such as Publius Cornelius Scipio Africanus, the conqueror of Hannibal, and Titus Flamininus, who not much later gave the Greeks their freedom at the Isthmian Festival, were conspicuous philhellenes; and around Scipio Aemilianus there grew up a group that took the lead in advancing Roman education and refinement. Greek philosophy, however, was widely regarded as morally unsettling because it was occasionally skeptical of religious belief. The Romans had little use for epistomology. They did take to Stoicism because it appealed to their own rather uncompromising view of the world.

Cato.   The chief opponent of the new tendencies in Roman life was Marcus Porcius Cato, the conservative, puritanical, close-fisted model of the older Roman virtue. He was a farmer by birth and drew inspiration from the memories of Manius Curius Dentatus, the great farmer-statesman of the good old days, whose modest cottage stood near Cato's father's farm. Accordingly, says Plutarch: "Cato worked with his slaves, in winter wearing a coarse coat without sleeves, in summer nothing but his tunic; and he used to sit at meals with them, eating the same loaf and drinking the same wine. ... When Cato was governor of Sardinia, where former governors had been in the habit of charging their tents, bedding and wearing apparel to the province, and likewise making it pay large sums for their entertainment and that of their friends, he introduced an unheard-of system of economy. He charged nothing to the province, and visited the various cities without a carriage, on foot and alone, attended by one public servant, who carried his robe of state and the vessel for making libations at a sacrifice. With all this, he showed himself so affable and simple to those under his rule, so severe and inexorable in the administration of justice, and so vigilant and careful in seeing that his orders were executed, that the government of Rome was never more feared or more loved in Sardinia than when he ruled that island."

At home Cato assailed with untiring energy the luxury, refinement, and Greek culture represented by the Scipios, and it was chiefly his influence that broke the power of this great family. The nobles feared and hated the red-haired, gray-eyed *novus homo,* who rebuked their follies and sins. During his censorship in 184 B.C., Cato expelled from the senate a number of disreputable members, taxed luxuries unmercifully, administered the public works, and let out the public contracts without favoritism. But his attempts at sumptuary legislation, and the attempts of others in this period (such as the decree of 161 B.C. exiling teachers of rhetoric and philosophy from Rome), were doomed to failure. Cato himself in his old age learned Greek, thus giving added force to Horace's famous line, "Graecia capta ferum victorem cepit" ("Captive Greece took her barbarian conqueror captive").

Latin Literature. Roman acquaintance with Greeks was not limited to contacts in Greek lands, for many Greeks had settled in the capital as traders, while among the thousands of captives were educated Greeks who became the tutors of Roman boys. Still other Greeks came to Rome as envoys, such as Carneades, who was celebrated as the founder of the New Academy in Athens, and Panaetius of Rhodes, whose Stoic philosophy, with its emphasis on principles of valor, appealed to the practical Roman. The distinguished historian Polybius, who was both a friend of Scipio Aemelianus and an admirer of the Roman government, came as a hostage from the Achaean League. It is hardly surprising, then, that a new and vigorous impetus should have been given the development of Latin literature, under Greek influence, at this time. About 220 B.C. Livius Andronicus translated the *Odyssey* into the Saturnian meter (apparently a kind of accentual as distinct from quantitative verse), while Gnaeus Naevius composed plays, for the first time on purely Roman, rather than Greek subjects, and an epic poem on the First Punic War. It was in Plautus (ca. 254–184 B.C.) and Terence (ca. 195–159 B.C.), however, that Roman comedy, based on the Greek New Comedy, reached popular heights.

Poetry, as always, developed more rapidly than prose, and the first great history of Rome from its earliest beginnings was the poetic *Annals* of Ennius (239–169 B.C.), who was later regarded as the father of Latin literature. Ennius also pioneered in the development of a characteristic Latin genre, satire (*satura*), which originally meant discussion of various subjects in a medley of prose and verse.

About 200 B.C. a Roman senator, Fabius Pictor, wrote a prose history of Rome from the early days to the end of the Second Punic War, but he wrote it in Greek, so that the Greeks might better understand the Romans. Another prose history of Rome, covering the period from 264 to 150 B.C., was the *Origins* of Cato, written, of course, in Latin. Cato's *On Agriculture* was an attempt to aid scientific agriculture in Italy; it is the earliest book in Latin prose that has come down to us. Cato gives meticulous advice concerning the growing of vineyards, olive orchards, grain, and vegetables; and in accord with his narrow parsimonious spirit, he explained in detail the harsh treatment to be accorded slaves: they were to be worked hard as long as they were able and then turned out to live or die as best they could.

Religion. In the field of religion, the Roman pantheon was by now thoroughly permeated by the Greek. In times of crisis, new deities were introduced, such as the Phrygian Cybele, or Great Mother, brought in in 205 B.C. Roman puritanism was easily shocked by the rituals of such mystery religions, and the cult of Cybele, which was orgiastic, was soon expelled. Such was also the fate in 186 of the cult of Dionysus, called Bacchus, whose bacchanalian rites seemed both immoral and politically subversive.

Law. The creation of a special praetor, the *praetor peregrinus,* in 241 B.C., to handle cases involving Roman citizens and foreigners governed by other legal systems, illustrated the adaptability of Roman law and its acceptance of the principle of equity, or fairness. The body of law was also supplemented by the legal comments of senators advising their clients, "men learned in the law," or jurisprudents. Such a one was the founder of Roman legal writing, Paetus (ca. 200 B.C.), who became famous for his study of the Twelve Tables. With time, the most momentous contributions to Roman law were the edicts of the various praetors, laying down the principles they would follow during their term.

The City of Rome. Rome now attained a population of several hundred thousand. It was a cosmopolitan place with a great and growing disparity in the living standards of the poor and the rich. The former lived in rickety wooden tenements while the latter were adopting the standards of upper classes in the Greek East, including the habit of living in peristyle houses. The period also saw the beginning of an epochal change in Roman architecture, the use of cement in building, which meant that the Romans could transcend post-and-lintel construction and even shape, rather than merely define, space. In appearance the city became Hellenistic, as Greek building styles were domesticated. Great works of art, looted from Greece, adorned public areas and shaped Roman taste. This taste had always expressed itself in naturalness and realism, in both painting and sculpture. Most artists working in Rome were Greeks, whose own Hellenistic canons easily adopted themselves to the Roman.

25

The Beginning of the Roman Revolution (133–78 B.C.)

THE GRACCHI

The Need of Reform. By the last generation of the second century B.C., thoughtful Romans realized that the state needed reforming. Foremost were problems caused by the abandonment by peasants of their land holdings and the related buildup of the plantation system. Because Roman legionaries had to be landlords, this development meant a grave diminution in the manpower pool available to the military and the consequent drafting of poorer and poorer peasants into the army. The consequences had surfaced during the recent Spanish war, when there had been widespread resistance against the draft. The problems of the urban proletariat were only slightly less pressing. The urban building boom that had employed them until about mid-century had ended, and their situation required remediation. In the background there were other developing problems: the rather anomalous political status of the equestrian order and of Rome's allies in Italy; the problems of provincial government and its corruption; and the latent military demands made on an empire sprawling over three continents.

As it turned out, the institutions of the republic proved unequal to solving these problems. Intermittently, but with increasing frequency, republican institutions were twisted in the direction of one-man rule by the extraordinary or even downright unconstitutional use of traditional offices. This period of domestic strife, and eventual civil war, is frequently called the Era of the Roman Revolution. It witnessed much aggravated factional upheaval within the ruling oligarchy. One group, generally comprising the majority factions in the senate, opposed those reforms that seemed to threaten their own vested interests. They are sometimes called the *Optimates,* or "best men." Their opponents, advocating, by no means disinterestedly, social and economic change, are sometimes called the *Populares.* The translation "People's Party" for the latter is inaccurate, as these leaders of reform, oligarchs themselves to a man, never meant to institute a "grass-roots" democracy and conceived of reform generally in terms of personal political advancement and the enhancement of the power of their own factions.

The first leaders of reform were two brothers, Tiberius and Gaius Gracchus, sons of Tiberius Sempronius Gracchus, who had held the consulship, and of Cornelia, daughter of Scipio Africanus. Thanks to their mother's insistence, Greek tutors instructed them in rhetoric and in the philosophy and political ideas of Hellas. Both brothers served as young men in military and provincial offices, where they won reputations for their ability to pursue the main chance as soldiers and administrators, and perhaps, too, for a genuine sympathy for underdogs.

Tiberius Gracchus.   In 133 B.C., at the age of thirty, and after he had already been quaestor in Spain, Tiberius Gracchus became tribune. His ambitious aim was to eliminate the proletariat, which, as he saw it, involved resettling as many families as possible from the city and refilling the country with hardy peasants. This resettlement would alleviate the crisis of unemployment in the city brought about in part by the recent ending of the boom in public works. By giving these families an opportunity to earn a living, Tiberius hoped not merely to restore their morale but above all to strengthen the army by increasing the number of citizens legally qualified to serve. His aims were clearly conservative. Accordingly, as the member of a faction led by his father-in-law, the dean of the senate, Appius Claudius Pulcher, he proposed to reenact the Licinian Law, which as long ago as 367 B.C. had forbidden anyone to use more than five hundred *jugera* of public land. The provisions of Tiberius' law were very accommodating to the propertied. All public land was in the future to belong to the occupiers, while the surplus over five hundred *jugera* was to be divided among the needy by a commission of three men elected by the plebeian council.

But the rich, who for generations had bought, sold, and bequeathed the *ager publicus* like private property, felt that they were being robbed by Tiberius' bill. When, accordingly, he brought it before the plebeian council, they induced Octavius, a tribune, to veto it, and thus they prevented it from passing. With the advice of Tiberius, the council then deposed the obstinate tribune, and Tiberius' Sempronian Law came into being. Three commissioners—Tiberius; his brother, Gaius; and his father-in-law, Appius Claudius—were elected to supervise its operation. Census figures indicate an increase of seventy-five thousand propertied citizens in subsequent years, but the figures are suspect, and in any case the effect on the census of the Gracchan land reform cannot be measured. The recall of Octavius was a sweeping departure from custom and suggested to rival senatorial factions the danger of a popular assembly dominated by one politician without reference to the normal interplay of oligarchy.

Ever since the days of Gaius Flaminius, the tribune of 232 B.C., dominant senatorial factions had resisted attempts to apportion the public land fairly, so that now their alarm was especially great. When the land law was passed, however, the senate ceased direct opposition; rather, it tried to embarrass the commissioners by refusing them sufficient funds. It was just at this moment that Attalus III of Pergamum died, leaving his kingdom to Rome, whereupon Tiberius declared his intention of appropriating from the new province of Asia whatever money he needed, even though the conduct of financial and foreign affairs had long been prerogatives of the senate. Soon afterward Tiberius offered himself for reelection to the tribunate, another departure from recent custom.

It seemed necessary to Tiberius Gracchus and his friends that he should continue in office in order to secure the enforcement of the land law and the institution of other reforms. The Optimates thought differently. On election day they and their clients and slaves dispersed the council, murdered Tiberius and three hundred of his followers, and threw their bodies into the Tiber. Many times during the previous history of the republic the assembly had committed acts of which the senate had heartily disapproved, but the senate's policy had been to resist by all constitutional means the adoption of such a measure, to yield when legal means of opposition failed, and then, when the excitement of the moment had passed away, to annul the measure quietly. In the present case this course was advised by the consul Scaevola, who as a jurist was most competent to point out the constitutional procedure, but his moderation did not satisfy most senators, who now turned to mob violence at home for putting down a political foe. This was the first, but not the last, time that blood was shed in a political struggle at Rome.

The Latin and Italian Allies. The work of the land commission did not cease with the death of Tiberius Gracchus, for vacancies were filled as they occurred, but a crisis was precipitated when the commissioners challenged the right of certain Italian allies to lands adjoining the *ager publicus.* The Italians appealed to Scipio Aemilianus, the destroyer of Carthage, who intervened on their behalf with the senate, but he died suddenly in 129 before he could help them. When, however, one of the commissioners, Fulvius Flaccus, proposed that Roman citizenship be given the Latin and Italian allies, there was a storm of protest, not only among the senators, who resisted enlarging the electorate, but among the city masses as well, for they had no intention of sharing their benefits with others. The proposal was dropped, to the disappointment of the allies, nor was their pressing problem to be solved by Gaius Gracchus.

Gaius Gracchus. Gaius Gracchus was nine years younger than his brother and had served with him on the land commission. Later on he was quaestor in Sardinia. He was a strident orator and in 124 B.C. stood successfully for the tribunate, to which he was reelected the following year. Gaius turned with vigor to the pressing questions of state, chief of which, as in his brother's day, was the condition of the Roman masses, whom the ruin of agriculture throughout Italy had driven by the thousands into the city. Recently the grain supply had so diminished that relief from the government seemed the only resource against impending famine. Gaius accordingly caused a law to be passed (the *lex frumentaria*) that provided for the monthly distribution of public grain among the citizens at a subsidized price. No new principle was involved, for such relief had long been known in the Greek East, and in fact the senate had often supplied the populace with cheap or free grain, and each noble supported a throng of clients. Although his grain law had much to recommend it in principle, there can be little doubt that Gaius was also motivated by the hope of detaching the people from their patrons and enlisting them in his own clientele.

Gaius Gracchus may have felt that the problem of public lands in Italy had been solved by his brother as well as humanly possible; in any case, he devoted little attention to the matter as such. Within a decade of his death, the commission was abolished, and further encroachment on public lands was forbidden. The overpopulation of Rome, however, still faced Gaius, as it had his brother, and he planned to relieve it by the establishment of commercial and manufacturing colonies at Tarentum, Capua, and elsewhere along the Italian coasts. He also founded a colony, called Junonia, on the old site of Carthage, which represented an entirely new idea of colonizing the provinces with Roman citizens.

The policy of Gaius, apparently, was to restore the well-being of the empire no less than that of Italy, and he did not hesitate to go to the core of the problem and attack senatorial prerogatives. To accomplish this, he also spread his clientele to extend to classes beyond the urban masses. Gaius, for example, welded the equestrians into a politicized class, conscious of its power, when he changed the law concerning provincial extortion. The old law had failed to protect the provinces, for the governors on their return to Rome were tried by a jury of senators, who were unlikely to convict men of their own class for crimes that they themselves had once committed. To put an end to this abuse, Gaius caused a law to be passed that required that the jurors should be equestrians. Its effect, unfortunately, was to give the businessmen of Rome free rein in the provinces, where they could threaten an honest governor with trial on his return to the city if he did not cooperate fully with the rapacious *publicani,* and it was not long before the equestrians were as corrupt as the senators had been. The clientage of the equestrian class was further arrayed on the side of Gaius by his law that provided that the censors should farm out in Rome the tax of 10 per cent on the agricultural produce of Asia; the tribute to be collected was so large that only the biggest corporations could afford to bid, and thus equestrian *publicani,* and not provincial ones, enjoyed a virtual monopoly in Rome's new and rich province. A further blow was struck at senatorial prestige by a law stipulating that the consular provinces were to be designated before the elections, rather than after. The old custom had made it possible for dominant senatorial factions to favor their own candidates by rewarding them with particularly rich plums, but now this privilege was lost.

These and other matters—for example, the passage of a law condemning the murderers of his brother, the construction of roads in Italy, and the erection of granaries in which to store public grain for sale to the people at a reduced rate— were attended to personally by Gaius.

The strategy of the Optimates in dealing with such a man was to enlist the aid of another tribune, Livius Drusus, and suggest to him that he destroy Gaius' clientele by proposing laws even more attractive than his to the people—and then quietly shelving them. The senate also waited for the opportunity to divide its enemies, which arrived when Gaius revived the idea of granting Roman citizenship to the Latins and Latin rights to the Italian allies. Again the electorate were unwilling to have their votes diluted, and the proposal was lost. Gaius' leadership was struck a further blow during his absence at Carthage, where he had gone to supervise the founding of Junonia, for it gave his enemies the chance to circulate unfavorable stories about him. On his return to Rome, he ran for a third term as tribune (122 B.C.) but failed to be reelected. Fearing for his life, Gaius seized the Aventine Hill. The senate ordered the consul Opimius to "see that the state suffer no harm"— this a form of martial law or "decree of last resort" (the *senatus consultum ulti-*

mum) now used for the first time. When Opimius attacked the Gracchans, Gaius commanded a slave to stab him to death, and three thousand of his followers were killed.

Estimate of the Gracchi. Tiberius Gracchus had proposed and carried through one great measure of reform, the use of public lands. Gaius wished to equalize the Italians as nearly as possible with the Romans, to found colonies in Italy and the provinces in order to provide the needy with homes and an honest living, and by founding commercial colonies to reestablish the sources of economic life. These reforms, which aimed at the regeneration of society, might on completion have drawn the poor away from Rome, made the grain laws unnecessary, limited slavery, and rendered Italy prosperous. But the means that the Gracchi chose alarmed the senate; in effect they seemed to make the tribunate a ministry, like the office of general in Periclean Athens, and to give the tribunes vast power, which was to continue from year to year so long as the people in their council willed. Their proposals, conservative and constitutional, did in fact go to the heart of the problems of their day, but they made a great mistake in relying ultimately on the self-interest of the council, and they unduly alienated rival senatorial factions. In death, however, the two brothers became the saints and martyrs of the Populares.

GAIUS MARIUS

The Jugurthine War. The death of Gaius Gracchus restored the dominance of the senatorial establishment, whose incapacity and corruption were soon revealed in North Africa. There the grandson of Rome's former ally Masinissa, Jugurtha by name, after killing the rightful heirs, had usurped the throne of the client state of Numidia. Though the senate intervened, he bought off its embassies one after another, until finally his excesses forced the senate to declare war (111 B.C.), a step heartily favored by the equestrian class. Jugurtha bribed the first commander to withdraw from Africa. When Jugurtha was summoned to Rome to explain matters, he boldly brought about the murder of a man who might have contested his right to the Numidian throne. As a result, it was impossible for him to remain longer in Rome. The war continued, but by corrupting the officers of the second commander sent against him, Jugurtha compelled the surrender of the army and sent it under the yoke.

This state of affairs threatened the neighboring Roman province of Africa, when the energetic consul Quintus Caecilius Metellus took command (109 B.C.). Gaius Marius went with him to Africa as one of his officers. Marius had been born at Arpinum, among the hills of Latium, of an equestrian family, and at an early age had entered the army. Able, and ambitious, he had acquitted himself well as tribune, praetor, and propraetor in Spain. On his return to Rome, he had married Julia, a member of the patrician family of the Caesars, but as a "new man" he was disdained by the nobility. With his help, Metellus disciplined the soldiers in Africa— first and greatest need—and then spent an entire year in a vain attempt to conquer Jugurtha by force or treachery. Another year similarly passed, during which

Marius plotted successfully with equestrian and other backing to win the consulship, and in 107 B.C., despite the senate's wishes, the plebeian council gave him
Metellus' command. Marius, who was a military genius, rapidly besieged and captured one stronghold of the enemy after another and defeated Jugurtha twice in
battle, until finally Lucius Cornelius Sulla, a young patrician who was quaestor
under him, captured Jugurtha by treachery. In 105 B.C. Marius returned to Rome,
where the African king, after gracing the triumph of his conqueror, was put to
death in prison. Numidia was allowed to continue as a client kingdom, with slightly
diminished territory, but the war had suggested the incompetence of the senate.

Invasion of Cimbri and Teutons. An even greater innovation, however, was the
reelection of Marius to the consulship for five years more (104-100 B.C.), when the
terrible threat of invasion from the north caused the Romans to turn to their new
hero. Celtic and Germanic tribes, particularly the Cimbri and the Teutons, had
recently crossed the Rhine and threatened the strip of territory along the southern
coast of Gaul linking Italy with Spain. The Cimbri and the Teutons overwhelmed
various Roman armies sent against them, and in 105 B.C. at Arausio (Orange), they
inflicted the greatest defeat suffered by Rome since Cannae, in which twenty thousand men were lost. The road to Italy was open, but fortunately for the Romans
their enemies spent the next three years in raiding Spain and the interior of Gaul.
This interval gave Marius time to reorganize and train the army, which he equipped
with a better throwing spear (*pilum*). Reelected consul year after year, Marius met
the Teutons, as they were preparing to cross the Alps into Italy, at Aquae Sextiae in
southern Gaul and annihilated them (102 B.C.). The following year he joined his
colleague Quintus Lutatius Catulus, who had not fared well, and slaughtered the
Cimbri at Vercellae, in northern Italy, after they had succeeded in crossing the Alps
(map, rear endpaper).

The Roman Army. The army that gained these great victories had a new character. Always at Rome property holding had been a prerequisite to military service.
Gradually during the third and second centuries, as Rome's wars increased in number and duration, the government had lowered the property qualification, in effect
drafting poorer men, even in occasional crises, the landless. Marius generalized the
conscription of volunteer proletarians, even though the normal draft continued. By
keeping his men long in the service and under careful training, he made them client
soldiers who placed all their hopes in their commander and were ready to follow
him in every undertaking; at the end of their term, moreover, the veterans expected
to be rewarded with bonuses and lands. Marius himself was loyal, but later generals
used client armies to overthrow the republic. In its actual structure, too, Marius
changed and improved the army. He increased the size of the legion to 6,000 men,
divided into ten cohorts of 600 men each, which were further subdivided into
centuries of sixty men, the tactical unit. Over each century stood a noncommis-
sioned officer, a *centurion,* who took great pride in making his company the best in
the legion. The legion itself, with its silver eagle as a standard, had a remarkable
esprit de corps.

Political Strife. Rome had been spared disaster in Africa and an invasion from
the north at the very time when a rebellion of slaves in Sicily and the activities
of Cilician pirates in the eastern Mediterranean had to be suppressed; the latter

achievement ended in the creation of the province of Cilicia (101 B.C.). The senatorial establishment could claim little credit for these victories, the greatest of which had been won by a *novus homo* after the failure of corrupt nobles. During his sixth consulship (100 B.C.), however, Marius, in seeking lands as a reward for his veterans, allied himself with two demagogues, Saturninus, a tribune, and Glaucia, a praetor. These two men aimed to outdo some of the Gracchan reforms, by further lowering the price of grain distributed to the public. When they now suggested the planting of colonies abroad, they met with violent opposition generated in the council by Marius' opponents, but the measures became law. Riot, violence, and murder continued, until the senate called on Marius to restore public order. Reluctantly he armed some of his forces to defend the constitution against his former associates, and after their surrender he placed them and their followers in the Senate house with the intention of treating them in a legal manner. But the mob tore the tiles off the roof and stoned them to death.

Used by the senate against his partisans, Marius missed his destiny, and the fate of Rome passed into other hands. The temporary alliance of the propertied—Optimates and equestrians—to confront the demagogues did not long endure. This was made impossible by the law on extortion, which gave the equestrian juries control over provincial governors. The break between the two upper classes came in 92 B.C., when a charge of extortion was laid against Rutilius Rufus, an upright noble who had restrained the *publicani* during his term in Asia. Convicted though he was, Rutilius actually spent the rest of his life in the province he was supposed to have robbed.

THE ALLIED WAR (90–88 B.C.)

Livius Drusus.   The senate was now faced with the possibility of rebellion by the oppressed Italians. A few liberal Optimates gave thought to the need of reform. The leader of this movement was Marcus Livius Drusus, son of Gaius Gracchus' opponent and a young man of wealth and illustrious family. When he became tribune in 91 B.C., he sponsored colonies and the distribution of cheap grain. Nor did he win popularity among the Optimates by suggesting that the number of the senate be increased to 600 by the enrollment of 300 equestrians, and that future cases of extortion be tried before juries drawn partly from the new senate and partly from the equestrian order. Finally, Drusus met united opposition when he advocated the enfranchisement of Latin and Italian allies. The senate declared his entire work as tribune unconstitutional, perhaps because he had violated a recent law against enacting a measure that contained several different items. This was the so-called Omnibus Law, which aimed at demagogues and provided further that three market days must intervene between the proposal of a bill and the vote on it. Toward the end of his year of office, Drusus, the last of Rome's civilian reformers, was murdered.

The death of Drusus deprived the Italians of their last hope of obtaining their rights by peaceable means. It was not that they wished primarily to vote at Rome, for most of them lived too far away to exercise that privilege, but they did need the protection that citizenship gave. Their soldiers, who had fought so well for Rome, desired humane treatment at the hands of their commanders and immunity from insults and scourging. They also sought the same rights of property and trade that the Romans had always enjoyed.

The Italian Revolt.   Accordingly, in 90 B.C., the Italian allies of central Italy, chiefly the Marsi and the Samnites, revolted and founded a new state, which they called Italia. They selected Corfinium as their capital and patterned their government after that of Rome, with two consuls and a senate; their aim was to annex the whole of Italy, and they gave citizenship to all who joined them in the war for freedom. The struggle that now began between Rome and her allies is called the Allied War. Rome's control of the sea allowed her to obtain reinforcements and supplies at will, but the Italians, who were both numerous and veterans of many a war, fought so successfully that toward the end of the first year Rome felt compelled to grant citizenship to all those who had not revolted. In the next year another law conferred citizenship on those who registered with a Roman praetor within sixty days. These concessions not only prevented the revolt from spreading but so weakened it that, in another year, Rome broke the strength of the allies.

The Italians were now granted Roman citizenship and local municipal government, and the whole Italian nation was organized in one state, with a common Latin language, culture, and law. But the new citizens were dissatisfied because their influence was limited by their enrollment in only eight of the thirty-five tribes, and they continued, therefore, to regard dominant senatorial factions as their enemies.

The Rise of Sulla.   The next domestic conflict came between Marius, who had served as general also during the crisis of the Allied War, and Sulla, who had been his quaestor during the war with Jugurtha. Sulla, patrician though poor, was endowed with a remarkable talent for war, diplomacy, and politics. Success as general in the Allied War brought him the consulship in 88 B.C.

THE FIRST MITHRIDATIC WAR (89–85 B.C.)

Mithridates of Pontus.   Ever since the close of the Asiatic War with Antiochus III in 189 B.C., Rome had enjoyed a protectorate over Asia Minor, but at the time of the war with Jugurtha, the throne of one of the client kingdoms—Pontus, along the southern shore of the Black Sea—came to be filled by a young man who was to prove a dangerous enemy to Rome. This was Mithridates VI Eupator, often styled the Great, a person of physical strength, attractive personality, and genius. A Hellenized Oriental, he remained, in spite of many heroic traits, cunning, unscrupulous, and brutal. Taking advantage of Rome's troubles with Jugurtha, and afterward with her allies, Mithridates rapidly extended his power through conquests and alliances, until he had brought under control nearly all the southern coast of the Black Sea. He constantly tried to interfere in the affairs of Asia Minor, but Rome always succeeded in making him desist. Toward the end of 89 B.C., however, Mithridates boldly decided on war.

So hated were the Roman *publicani* that the inhabitants of the province of Asia welcomed Mithridates as a deliverer, and on an appointed day in 88 B.C., at his order, they massacred all the Italian residents, men, women, and children, several thousand strong. Then his fleet crossed the Aegean to Delos, murdering the Italian commercial colony on the island, and continued to Athens, where revolt had broken out. Rome was threatened with the loss of all her possessions east of the Adriatic, but it was the massacre of Italians in Asia Minor that roused the state to the necessity of immediate action.

Strife in Rome. The senate ordered Sulla, as consul, to proceed to the seat of war, but after his departure from the city, Marius' faction, including many equestrians, contrived to have the command transferred to Marius. This transfer was accomplished by an alliance with the tribune Sulpicius, who was proposing to register the new citizens and freedmen in all thirty-five tribes and stopped at no violence to win his ends. When Sulla learned of the council's action depriving him of his command, he led his army to Rome and settled the question with the sword. The Sulpician laws were repealed, and Sulpicius and many of his adherents were slain, but Marius escaped to Africa. This was a critical moment in the history of the republic, for it was the first time that the army had appeared in politics; the revolution begun so long ago by the Gracchi now found its leaders in generals rather than tribunes. Sulla had turned the army into a revolutionary instrument; after restoring the authority of the senate and decreeing that nothing could be submitted to the assemblies without its consent, Sulla proceeded with his army to the war against Mithridates.

Sulla in the East. With five legions Sulla arrived in Greece, which he robbed of many of its treasures and ravaged brutally. Athens itself was taken (86 B.C.) after a long siege, during which some of its temples were destroyed. Victories at Chaeronea and Orchomenus ended the last resistance of Mithridates' forces in Greece; then, with the aid of his quaestor, Lucius Lucullus, who had a fleet, Sulla invaded Asia Minor, which now fretted under Mithridates' stern rule. Since he was anxious to return to Rome, where the Marians were again in power, Sulla patched up a peace with Mithridates, though no one doubted that the king would break it at the first opportunity. Mithridates was compelled to pay an indemnity and to give up all the conquests he had made at the expense of Rome and her allies, including the province of Asia and the kingdoms of Bithynia and Cappadocia (85 B.C.). Such heavy fines were levied against the Asiatic cities that had aided Mithridates that they were compelled to borrow from Roman moneylenders; these in turn charged an enormous rate of interest, and it was not long before the cities owed six times the amount of the loan.

THE DICTATORSHIP OF SULLA

Cinna and the Populares. No sooner had Sulla left Rome for the war with Mithridates than an armed conflict broke out between the senate and the Marians. The new leader of the Populares was the consul Lucius Cornelius Cinna, who proposed to reenact the law to enroll the Italians equally among the thirty-five tribes, but his colleague Gnaeus Octavius championed the cause of the Optimates and drove him from the city. Cinna quickly gathered an army of Italians, recalled Marius from banishment, and following the example of Sulla, marched against Rome. Marius' exile had made him extremely bitter against the Optimates. With grim determination he promised the Italians their rights. When they finally entered Rome with their bands of Italians, foreigners, and runaway slaves, Marius and Cinna killed Octavius and many other eminent aristocrats; for five days they hunted down their opponents, massacred them, and plundered their property. The Italians won their rights, but this revolution had taken thousands of lives. Soon afterward, Marius, now consul for the seventh time, died (86 B.C.).

Sulla's Return. The revolution had again overthrown the senatorial establishment and placed the Marian Populares at the head of the government. Cinna was reelected to the consulship year after year, and he attempted to be conciliating to other factions. Finally, in 84 B.C., he was murdered by his troops as he was preparing to set out for Macedonia against Sulla. The following year Sulla landed at Brundisium, where he found Gnaeus Pompeius (Pompey) and other young aristocrats eagerly awaiting him. There then began a terrible civil war. The consuls, Carbo and Marius, son of the famous general, had large bodies of troops, particularly from among the new citizens of Samnium and Etruria, but they were not skillful leaders, and at the Colline Gate in Rome they were crushed (82 B.C.). Thousands of prisoners taken in this battle were massacred in cold blood; Carbo fled to Africa; and Marius, who was besieged at Praeneste, committed suicide. Soon all Italy lay at the feet of the conqueror; and the Marians who had escaped to Sicily and Africa were put down by Pompey. The Allied and Civil Wars, with their wholesale destruction of life and property, nearly completed the ruin of Italy, which had long been declining in wealth and population.

Now master of the government, Sulla proceeded coolly to destroy the opponents of his party. Day by day he posted in the Forum a list of his victims ("the proscribed"), whom anyone might slay and thereby earn a reward; a premium was placed on malice, greed, and murder. The goods of the proscribed were confiscated, and their children disenfranchised. The number of persons thus murdered at Rome amounted to thousands, including many senators and equestrians; no one dared shelter a victim, not even children their parents. Many were the victims of private hatred, and many more were killed for the sake of their wealth. At the same time, murder and confiscation were carried on all over Italy; in this way Sulla was able to settle 150,000 of his veterans on the land.

Sulla Dictator. In 82 B.C., Sulla also assumed the office of dictator, which had long been disused, in order that he might bring about a stable government with the Optimates in control. Seven courts were established, each under a praetor and each charged with jurisdiction over a particular class of crimes, but the jurors were to be senators, as they had been before the time of Gaius Gracchus. Since these juries were very large, Sulla raised the number of the Senate from 300 to 600 by adding equestrians who had been his partisans. In order to prevent able men from seeking the tribunate, Sulla ruled that tribunes would be ineligible for higher office. He reduced the effective power of the plebeian council by prohibiting tribunes from submitting legislation to it and in effect ended the practice of having that council sit as a court of law under tribunician presidency. He increased the number of quaestors to twenty and made this office a regular stepping-stone to the senate. Sulla did not disturb the order of offices in the *cursus honorum,* but he insisted on a minimum age for the quaestorship of thirty, for the praetorship of thirty-nine, and for the consulship of forty-two; moreover, he decreed that ten years were to elapse before a man might be reelected to the same office. The election of censors was suspended. The number of praetors was raised to eight, and on the expiration of their year of office these men and the two ex-consuls became promagistrates; that is to say, they went out as governors to the provinces, which now numbered ten with the admission of Cisalpine Gaul as a province. Sulla thus laid the foundation for an imperial civil service, just as his organization of the courts became the framework for the development of criminal law at Rome. The power of provincial governors, it should be emphasized, was limited to their provinces, the consuls were ordinarily restricted to Italy, and the senate was handed the privilege of appointing the commanders for military expeditions abroad. These laws, with the exception of those touching on the assemblies and the tribunate, became a regular part of the constitution.

Sulla's aim was to set up a state dominated by the senate and at the same time protected against demagogues, ambitious generals, and civil war. But the crisis of this generation demanded imagination rather than a rigid conservatism that appealed to a half-real past and left in its wake a passionate desire for revenge. Above all, even if Sulla's constitution had been proof, legally, against one-man rule, the inability to satisfy human longing for peace and prosperity pointed to monarchy as the only apparent solution. With the conviction, however, that his work would be permanent, Sulla abdicated his dictatorship in stages and in 79 B.C. retired to Campania, where he died the following year. He was buried with pomp, but he was hardly in his grave before his government began to totter.

26

The End of the Republic (78–27 B.C.)

THE RISE OF POMPEY

Sulla was the first person in Roman history to enforce his will on the state by means of the army, and after his time the political power fell more and more to generals who were especially designated to deal with a specific crisis. Among the rising officers of the army, Pompey was most fitted to be the heir of Sulla's policy. Vain, pompous, and honorable, Pompey, after his defeat of the Marians in Sicily and Africa, had wrested from Sulla the right to the title of Magnus ("the Great") and the privilege of a triumph upon his return to Rome (79 B.C.).

Sertorius and Pompey in Spain. In the year of Sulla's death (78 B.C.) the consul Marcus Lepidus led an armed attempt to annul much of the dictator's work. The revolt was put down by the other consul, Catulus, but the senate was obliged to call on Pompey for aid. The remnants of Lepidus' troops, under Marcus Perperna, then fled to Spain, where the Marians still held out. The leader of these forces was Quintus Sertorius, who had regarded Sulla as a usurper. Sertorius claimed to represent the true government of Rome and became the hope of the Populares. He was one of the first Romans to sympathize thoroughly with the governed, to make their interests his chief care, and to give them genuine benefits of Latin civilization. In both Hither and Farther Spain he routed the Roman armies sent against him, including that of the consul Quintus Caecilius Metellus. A good general was obviously needed in Spain, and the senate, according to Sulla's arrangements, should have sent thither as proconsul a man who had already been consul. But since it could find no reliable person with this qualification, it gave the proconsulship to Pompey, who was ineligible under the Sullan constitution, having filled not even the quaestorship. No easy conquest awaited Pompey, but Spanish resistance was undermined first by the exactions of Perperna and subsequently by the latter's murder of Sertorius. Finally, after five years (76–71 B.C.), Pompey ended the rebellion.

Spartacus. Pompey returned to Italy just in time to add further laurels to his crown. In 73 B.C. a danger had arisen in the form of a slave revolt. The leader was Spartacus, a gladiator. Gladiatorial exhibitions had apparently originated in Etruria in connection with funeral festivals. Rome, at least, had introduced them from that country; the custom gradually developed for the magistrates to entertain the voters with this brutal sport, and there was a school at Capua in which slaves were trained as gladiators. A Thracian by birth, and a brave, intelligent soldier, Spartacus had been taken prisoner, sold as a slave, and sent to this school. Now, with a few comrades, he struck down the guards and escaped to Mount Vesuvius. Slaves, criminals, and discontented persons of every class flocked to his side till he allegedly had an army of more than seventy thousand men. For two years he defeated Roman armies led by praetors and consuls. Then the praetor Marcus Licinius Crassus defeated and killed him and dispersed his army. Crassus was robbed of full credit, however, for the remnants of Spartacus' forces were met and overwhelmed in northern Italy by Pompey on his return.

Sulla's Constitution Undone.   Crassus, a former legate of Sulla's and a financier grown rich during the proscriptions, now demanded a triumph and the consulship. So did Pompey, even though he was too young for the office and had never held the quaestorship or the praetorship. When the senate hesitated, the two men, who were quite dissimilar, joined forces, appealed to the Populares, and achieved their ends. As consuls (70 B.C.), they undid the work of Sulla: the censorship was restored, which made possible a revision of the senate; the juries henceforth were to be drawn equally from the senate, the equestrians, and a slightly less prosperous class known as the tribunes of the treasury (*tribuni aerarii*); and the tribunate's traditional powers were restored. This reform represented a victory not so much of the Populares as of the army, for the tribunes in the future attached themselves ordinarily to the service of the great military leaders.

The Trial of Verres.   In their determination to reform the juries Pompey and Crassus received ammunition, if any were needed, from the prosecution of Verres, who had been propraetor of Sicily in 73-71 B.C. Verres had robbed the provincials unmercifully of money and works of art, and he stated frankly that the three years' income was intended for himself, his debtors, and the jurors. He had sold justice to the highest bidder, had framed charges against innocent people in order to obtain their property, and had even laid taxes that were greater than the entire value of an estate. The Sicilians hardly expected that a jury of senators would give them more justice than had the equestrians in former days, and in their desperation they turned to Cicero, who had been an honest quaestor in their island during 75 B.C. Marcus Tullius Cicero of Arpinum had been educated in Athens and, now thirty-six years of age, enjoyed a considerable reputation as a pleader. He had just been elected aedile, while his opponent, the defender of Verres, had won the consulship. This was Quintus Hortensius Hortalus, who was the greatest orator of the moment. With remarkable speed and against overwhelming odds, Cicero collected his evidence, brought Verres to trial, and then, instead of making a speech, simply presented the facts. The result was the condemnation of Verres. Cicero later published the full story in his *Orations Against Verres,* which gave in detail the dark picture of provincial corruption.

The Cilician Pirates.   Upon the expiration of his year of office, Pompey decided not to go out as governor to a province, which seemed to promise little in the way of personal advancement, but to wait in Rome for some unusual opportunity. This

FIGURE 53. Marcus
Tullius, Cicero, 106–
43 B.C.

The Granger Collection

was not long in coming. Ever since the collapse of the Rhodian sea power during
the Third Macedonian War, pirates had swarmed over the whole Mediterranean Sea;
they seized cities, attacked Ostia, captured Roman nobles, whom they held for
ransom, and sold free citizens into slavery. The bases of these pirates were in Cilicia
and Crete. By 67 B.C. Metellus had conquered Crete and made it a province, but
even so, the evil continued. The dominant senatorial factions seemed powerless to
cope with the situation, for they were then too suspicious of Pompey to call on
him. When, however, the piratical raids cut off Rome's grain supply and threatened
the city with famine, the tribune Aulus Gabinius proposed in the plebeian council
(67 B.C.) the creation of a single command (with the *imperium* for three years)
over the entire Mediterranean together with a strip of coast fifty miles deep, as far
as Rome's dominion extended. Gabinius, of course, had acted in collusion with
Pompey, and the senate was compelled to acquiesce in the creation of the extraordinary command and Pompey's appointment to it. He was given a fleet of five
hundred ships, twenty-four legates, and a large sum of money. Within three months
Pompey cleared the sea of pirates, destroyed their nests in Cilicia, and settled many
of the survivors as colonists.

The Second Mithridatic War (74-63 B.C.).   Two years and nine months of his
imperium remained, and Pompey, ambitious as ever, intended to capitalize on other

troubles Rome was having in the East. Ever since Sulla had imposed peace terms on Mithridates, the king of Pontus had been preparing for a new war with Rome. The Second Mithridatic War (74-63 B.C.), as it is called, broke out when Nicomedes III, the king of Bithynia, bequeathed his state to Rome. Rome promptly organized it as a province, but Mithridates, who had a powerful fleet and army, also coveted the territory. After several indecisive encounters, the Roman consul Lucius Lucullus, a remarkably skillful general, drove Mithridates from Bithynia and even from Pontus. Mithridates took refuge with his son-in-law Tigranes, the king of Armenia. Lucullus followed and captured the Armenian capital, Tigranocerta, but was prevented from conquering the kingdom by a mutiny of his troops. The tide then began to turn in favor of Mithridates. The equestrian corporations at Rome now saw their chance of replacing Lucullus, whom they hated for having eased the tax burden that Sulla had laid on the province of Asia.

The Manilian Law (66 B.C.).   It was at this juncture, in 66 B.C., that the tribune Gaius Manilius, in furtherance of the wishes of Pompey and the equestrians, carried a law through mob violence that gave the command in the East to Pompey in addition to the tremendous power he already had. Cicero, who was then a praetor and hoped for Pompey's support in his bid for the consulship, delivered a memorable speech, *For the Manilian Law,* which helped to override senatorial opposition. Pompey was equal to his task. He drove Mithridates from Pontus to Armenia and finally to the Crimea.

Most of Pontus was now added to the province of Bithynia, while various sections were attached to allied states, which were in reality clients. Pompey gave much attention to the political organization of the East. He formed a treaty of friendship with the Parthian Empire beyond the Euphrates, and as an added check on Parthia he made Armenia a client kingdom. Tigranes had recently conquered Syria, but Pompey forced him to withdraw (64 B.C.) and made it a Roman province. Thus ended the last shadow of the Seleucid empire. Pompey then entered Judea and, after a siege of three months, took Jerusalem. Some of Judea was added to Syria, but Jerusalem retained its self-government under a high priest who was dependent on Rome. Except for Egypt and a small part of Palestine, Rome now occupied the entire circuit of the Mediterranean with her clients and provinces (map, p. 389).

Pompey's arrangements in the Near East were admirable and promised to bring stability and prosperity to that part of the world, for he avoided the exactions of Sulla. Conscious of his power and laden with booty, Pompey now began his return to Rome.

ROME DURING POMPEY'S ABSENCE

Caesar.   During Pompey's absence in the East, Gaius Julius Caesar began to gain political prominence. Born in 100 B.C., Caesar was a patrician of the Julian *gens,* which traced its ancestry back to gods and heroes, but since he was not rich and, more particularly perhaps, because his wife was Cornelia, the daughter of Cinna, and his aunt, Julia, was the wife of Marius, he naturally associated himself in politics with the Populares. Moreover, he barely escaped the Sullan proscriptions by withdrawing to Rhodes. Later on he returned to Rome and served as quaestor in Farther Spain. In the year 65 B.C. he was aedile, and in 63 *pontifex maximus.*

Another individual gaining prominence was Catiline, a man of high birth and splendid talents, but also ruthless. He appealed to the most desperate men in Italy, such as debtors, the landless, and poor and demoralized men, by offering them a new deal. He ran for consul unsuccessfully and then appeared again at the consular elections of July 64 B.C., the other candidates being Gaius Antonius, a like spirit, and Cicero. Cicero and Antonius were elected consuls for 63 B.C., and the defeated Catiline began to contemplate revolution.

The Conspiracy of Catiline (63 B.C.).   The plan of the anarchists was to cancel debts, murder the consuls, fire the city, and overthrow the government. Cicero, learning of the conspiracy, called on a "concord of the orders," a united front of the senatorial and equestrian classes to stabilize the situation, and he persuaded the senate to pass the "decree of last resort" whereupon Catiline fled to the army he had been preparing in Etruria. The whole tale was unfolded by Cicero, now Rome's greatest orator, in a series of brilliant orations. Catiline was killed in battle, and those of his followers who had remained in Rome were arrested. Cicero urged the senate to condemn them to death, but Caesar advocated a lighter penalty. Marcus Porcius Cato the Younger, a Stoic philosopher and as conservative as his great-grandfather, the famous censor, supported Cicero and the sentence was carried out. The Populares denied the right of the senate to act as a court in such a case and asserted, accordingly, that Cicero had put these men to death without a trial.

Cicero.   Cicero's success in saving the state made him for a time the most eminent man in Rome. The people saluted him as "the father of his country"; and though he was a *novus homo,* the Optimates recognized him as their equal. He was strongly attached to the republican form of government, but the forces opposed to him were overwhelming. Such, in fact, had become the condition of public affairs that the statesman, however grand, appears strangely out of place, for the age of the generals had come; they were the strong men and managed politicians as their puppets. It was vain, therefore, for Cicero to hope that he might make Pompey a defender of the republican constitution.

Pompey's Return to Italy.   Pompey's arrival at Brundisium in 62 B.C. was anxiously watched by everyone at Rome. While both Optimates and Populares claimed him, some feared he might overthrow the government and make himself dictator by means of his client army, as Sulla had done. But believing that his influence sufficed to bring him all the power and honor he needed, Pompey disbanded his army and came to Rome as a private citizen. Although he celebrated a magnificent triumph and distributed large sums of money to his men, he was in other ways bitterly disappointed. The senate, which had always distrusted him, hesitated to sanction his arrangements in the East and to grant lands to his veterans.

It happened, however, that two eminent politicians needed his aid. One was Crassus, who was angered by the senate's refusal, at the behest of Cato the Younger, to lower the amount of money that the *publicani,* his clients, had contracted to pay the treasury from the taxes of the province of Asia, for a poor harvest had rendered

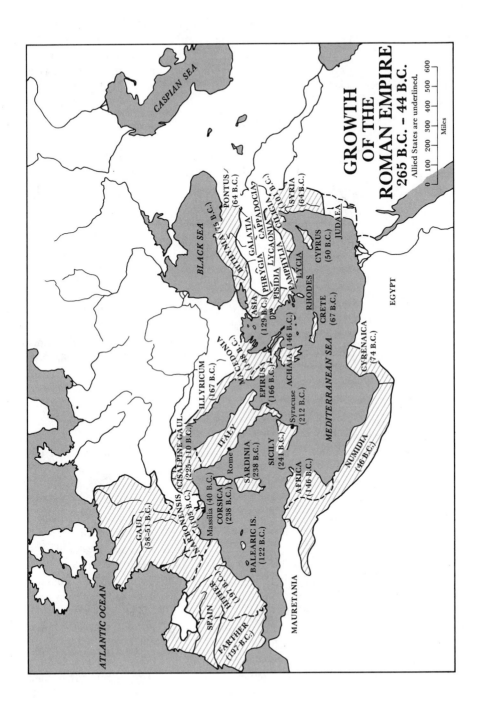

GROWTH OF THE ROMAN EMPIRE 265 B.C. – 44 B.C.

Allied States are underlined.

Miles
0 100 200 300 400 500 600

ATLANTIC OCEAN

CASPIAN SEA

BLACK SEA

MEDITERRANEAN SEA

GAUL (58–51 B.C.)

SPAIN

HITHER (197 B.C.)

FARTHER (197 B.C.)

MAURETANIA

NARBONENSIS (105 B.C.)

Massilia (40 B.C.)

CORSICA (238 B.C.)

SARDINIA (238 B.C.)

BALEARIC IS. (122 B.C.)

CISALPINE GAUL (225–110 B.C.)

ITALY

Rome

SICILY (241 B.C.)

Syracuse (212 B.C.)

AFRICA (146 B.C.)

NUMIDIA (46 B.C.)

ILLYRICUM (167 B.C.)

MACEDONIA (148 B.C.)

EPIRUS (166 B.C.)

ACHAIA (146 B.C.)

CYRENAICA (74 B.C.)

BITHYNIA (75 B.C.)

PONTUS (64 B.C.)

GALATIA

ASIA (129 B.C.)

PHRYGIA

CAPPADOCIA?

LYCAONIA

PISIDIA

PAMPHYLIA

CILICIA (101 B.C.)

LYCIA

RHODES

CRETE (67 B.C.)

SYRIA (64 B.C.)

CYPRUS (50 B.C.)

JUDAEA

EGYPT

their position precarious. The other was Caesar, who in 60 B.C. returned from the propraetorship in Spain to find that the senate refused him a triumph and the consulship. The three men—Pompey, Crassus, and Caesar—though they had little in common, decided to act together for their interests as opposed to the senate. This unofficial union is called the First Triumvirate. Pompey contributed to it his military fame, Crassus the influence of his wealth, and Caesar his popularity with the masses and his commanding intelligence.

THE FIRST TRIUMVIRATE

Caesar Consul (59 B.C.).   According to the agreement reached among the three men, Caesar was elected consul for 59 B.C. He had little difficulty in rewarding Crassus by the remission of one-third of the taxes contracted for the province of Asia, but stiff criticism met his proposals on Pompey's behalf. Caesar's colleague in the consulship was Calpurnius Bibulus, a member of the Optimate faction, who, failing to match the tactics of Caesar's rough-and-ready political clubs, shut himself up in his house and announced that public business could not be transacted because he was watching the skies for omens. Cato was outspoken in his opposition to the triumvirate, and so was Cicero, who several times refused offers to join forces with the triumvirs. Caesar, nevertheless, secured ratification of Pompey's arrangements in the East and obtained lands for his veterans in Campania. Through their tool, Clodius, an unscrupulous patrician who had managed adoption into a plebeian family in order to become tribune, the triumvirs brought about the exile of Cicero on the ground that at the time of Catiline's conspiracy he had put citizens to death without a trial. Cato was removed from the scene by appointment to a commission to organize the province of Cyprus.

Caesar's Gallic Command.   The fate of Rome was firmly in the hands of the triumvirs, and further to strengthen his own position Caesar gave his daughter Julia in marriage to Pompey, who remained, outwardly at least, the most powerful of the three. With amazing foresight Caesar secured for himself the proconsulship in Illyria and Cisalpine Gaul for five years, and Transalpine Gaul (Gallia Narbonensis) on a yearly basis. Since he was appointed to this extraordinary command while he was still consul, he was able legally to raise troops in Italy, and these no doubt were a counterpoise to the potential influence of Pompey's veterans. There may have been those who wondered at Caesar's willingness to seek a command that promised trouble, but this was exactly the kind of position for which he had long been striving. If successful, he would surely have a veteran army devoted to himself, and he would add territory and riches to Rome's dominion, as well as wealth and reputation for himself. During his long absence he wrote frequent accounts of his activities: these became the famous *Commentaries on the Gallic War,* which thrilled the reading public at the time, are a monument to Caesar's skill as a historian, and reveal another facet of his many-sided nature. (See map, p. 392.)

Gaul.   All Gaul, as Caesar said, is divided into three parts; by this he meant non-Roman Gaul or *Gallia comata* (long-haired Gaul), for Gallia Narbonensis, from Lake Geneva along the Mediterranean coast to Spain, was already a Roman prov-

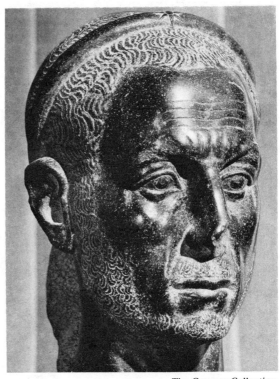

FIGURE 54. Gaius Julius Caesar, 100–44 B.C.

The Granger Collection

ince. Free Gaul was a huge fertile country, with a dense and varied population, which won its living chiefly by agriculture, though trade, metallurgy, pottery, and textile factories formed part of the economy; there were also many strongly forti- fied towns. Broadly speaking, the Aquitanians, who were an Iberian people with a mixture of Celtic blood, occupied the south; the purer Celts were in the center; and in the north, along the lower Rhine, were the Belgian Gauls, who were Celts mixed with Germans. Each of these three groups comprised several independent tribes. The Aquitanians were the most civilized, thanks to the influences radiating from the Greek city of Massilia on the coast and to the many Italian merchants in their midst; the Belgians were the most barbarous and warlike. East of the Rhine were the half-nomadic Germans.

Defeat of the Helvetians (58 B.C.). Several years before Caesar's proconsulship a powerful German tribe, the Suevi, had crossed the Rhine under their chieftain Ariovistus and, having helped the Sequani to defeat the Aedui, who were allies of Rome, had seized some Gallic lands for themselves. This movement was the begin- ning of a Germanic migration, which if unchecked would have thrown Gaul into commotion and might have brought both German and Celtic hordes into Narbo- nensis and even, perhaps, into Italy. A more direct menace to Rome came from the Helvetians, a great Celtic tribe of Switzerland, who in 58 B.C. abandoned their home in the Alps for the broader and more fertile lands of southern Gaul. Caesar,

who at this time had had little experience in command, thus found himself confronted by difficulties and dangers, but the ease with which he overcame everything in his way marked him at once as a great master of the art of war. He quickly gathered his widely scattered forces, enrolled new legions, and inspired his raw recruits with the courage and devotion of veterans. He overtook the Helvetians as they were about to enter Gallia Narbonensis, defeated them, and drove the remnant of their host back to their former home. During this same summer Ariovistus, whom the senate had half-heartedly recognized as a "friend of the Roman people"—in the hope of forestalling trouble—showed further signs of aggression. Caesar accordingly attacked him and compelled him to recross the Rhine. Caesar, quite obviously, did not intend to remain within his provincial confines.

In the following year (57 B.C.), Caesar resolved to subdue the Belgians. While he was approaching their country, the Nervii, who were the most warlike and powerful of the Belgic tribes, fell upon him so fiercely that he could neither form his line nor give orders. Each soldier was left to his own judgment, but the cool courage of the men and the heroism of their commander won the desperate fight. All northern Gaul now submitted.

The Conference at Luca (56 B.C.).   By this time, however, the situation in Rome had become serious, for Pompey and Crassus were no longer friendly, and each viewed Caesar with jealousy. The armed gangs of Clodius, Caesar's tool, fought in the streets with those of the tribune Titus Annius Milo, Pompey's man. In 57 B.C. Cicero was recalled from exile at Pompey's insistence, for he needed the aid of the orator. Cicero received an ovation on his return and soon repaid Pompey by helping to secure his appointment as curator of the grain supply (*curator annonae*) for five years, together with proconsular *imperium* in the Mediterranean. The senate, however, still refused to give Pompey its confidence and support, and each of the triumvirs could see an advantage in reconciling their differences. They accordingly came together, on Caesar's invitation, for a conference in the spring of 56 B.C. at Luca in Cisalpine Gaul. It was there agreed that Pompey and Crassus should be consuls in Hither and Farther Spain and Africa, Crassus in Syria, while Caesar was to have his Gallic command renewed until 50 B.C. These arrangements were carried through, over the objections of Cato and those Optimates who were most strongly devoted to the republican cause. Cicero, aware of his debt to Pompey, grudgingly gave his support to the triumvirs.

Caesar Crosses the Rhine and Invades Britain (55-54 B.C.).   In the summer of 56 B.C., on his return to Gaul, Caesar hastened to Normandy and Brittany where the Veneti, who occupied a strip of the Atlantic coast, threatened trouble. A maritime people, they built their towns on headlands protected by shallow tidewaters and themselves put to sea in clumsy flat-bottomed boats with leather sails. Caesar built a small, light fleet and defeated them. Since the Aquitanians had also submitted, practically all Gaul now owed allegiance to Rome. But it was an uncertain allegiance, made the more so by incursions of Germans from across the Rhine. To strike terror into these people, Caesar crossed the Rhine on his famous bridge (55 B.C.) and later that summer ventured across the English Channel. The Britons, who were largely Celtic, had been aiding their kinsmen in Gaul, and Caesar hoped to stop them. But he had only a small force with him and accomplished little. The next year, however, he landed with thirty thousand men, marched across the Thames, and received the submission of several tribes. The Britons gave hostages and promised tribute, whereupon Caesar, who was aware of the fame and popularity his expeditions had won him in Rome, quit the island; a century was to pass before its real conquest.

Vercingetorix.   The comparative speed with which Caesar had overrun their country convinced the Gallic chieftains of the necessity of burying their individual rivalries and uniting under a leader. This turned out to be Vercingetorix, a young noble, who raised all Gaul in a rebellion that was to tax Caesar's genius to the utmost. Caesar, however, succeeded in cornering Vercingetorix in the fortress of Alesia (near Dijon) and starved him into submission (52 B.C.). By 50 B.C. Gaul was pacified; it was not immediately organized as a province but was placed under the jurisdiction of the governor of Gallia Narbonensis and was subject to tribute and levies of men.

Because Caesar was usually just and mild and humane in his settlement, the Gauls became loyally attached to him. The conquest of Gaul was profoundly significant for the development of the empire. The Gauls retained a large degree of self-government and many of their national institutions. The more warlike spirits enlisted in the Roman armies, while the rest of the population devoted itself to cattle breeding and agriculture. Gold and silver mines were opened, which further helped the economic development of the country. Few Roman colonies were planted among them, but many Italians went there for trade and brought with them ideas from the south. The Gauls opened schools in which Latin language and literature were studied with such zeal and success that ultimately better Latin came to be spoken in Gaul than in Rome. The process of romanization was aided by the chain of military settlements established along the Rhine for the defense of the frontier against the Germans, and naturally civilization took its deepest hold along this line and in the south of the country. Gaul was a great source of strength to Rome in soldiers, food supplies, and taxes, and it helped protect the Rhine frontier from the Germans. Its conquest opened up for the first time northwestern and central Europe to Roman civilization. The immediate significance of the Gallic conquest, however, was that it enabled Caesar to make himself master of the empire.

THE END OF THE FIRST TRIUMVIRATE

Crassus' Death in Syria (53 B.C.). Caesar had been quick to carry out the agreements reached during the conference at Luca in 56 B.C., as far as they touched himself, and so had Crassus. In the year after his consulship Crassus, an old man thirsting for the military glory that his colleagues enjoyed, journeyed to his province of Syria, where he provoked a war with the Parthians (54 B.C.). The Parthian Empire, which had been formed from the Seleucid provinces east of the Euphrates, had received from Pompey a nominal treaty of friendship, but it lay astride rich trade routes and otherwise appealed to Crassus' military ambitions. With a large army Crassus marched into the Mesopotamian desert, but the ten thousand Parthian mounted archers, using the tactics of riding round and round their foe, completely crushed the Roman legions near Carrhae (53 B.C.). Crassus himself was murdered at a parley, a treacherous act that, together with the humiliation of the defeat and the capture of the eagles belonging to the legions, stirred the Romans deeply. Rome was able to save Syria, but for the next three hundred years she was rarely free from anxiety along her eastern frontier.

Pompey's Activities. Crassus' death brought into the forefront the rivalries of the two remaining triumvirs. In spite of the agreement reached at Luca, Pompey had not gone out to his provinces after his consulship—to the two Spains and Africa—but was allowed to govern them through legates. He remained in Italy, instead, to meet the requirements of his appointment to the curatorship of the grain supply. In 54 B.C., moreover, he lost his wife Julia, Caesar's daughter, and this loss freed him from any constraint he may have felt toward his colleague. Cunningly he backed the gangsters used by Clodius in his street fights with Milo, who was now in the service of the Optimates. No consuls could be elected in 54 B.C.; two years later Clodius was slain on the Appian Way by Milo's men; the senate house was burned, there were riots in the city, and once again legislation and elections were impossible. In this way Pompey planned to gain further power from the senate, for order could be restored in the city only by the use of his troops, not all of whom had been dispatched to his provinces. Despite their differences in the past, both Pompey and the Optimates could see the advantage of a rapprochement, since there was no doubting the dangerous strength of Caesar and his popularity with the people. Accordingly, in 52 B.C., Pompey was made sole consul, a very strange office, indeed. He now possessed enormous power, with an army in the provinces and Italy; he also had a fleet and was in charge of the grain supply. He was looked upon, in fact, as the first citizen in the state, or *princeps.*

His position now seemed unassailable. Caesar, on the other hand, had every reason to fear that on the expiration of his Gallic command—the precise date of which is uncertain but was probably sometime in 50 B.C.—he would be prosecuted for his acts as consul in 59 B.C. and as proconsul, for among other things, he had waged unauthorized warfare in Gaul. Cato the Younger insisted in the senate that he would prosecute Caesar for illegal actions. The task before Caesar, therefore, was to enter on another consulship while he was still proconsul and immune from prosecution. Pompey made this ambition impossible by passing a law forbidding an individual to seek a magistracy *in absentia,* but then, fearing that he had gove too far, he exempted Caesar from its provisions. This action led Caesar to feel that he could keep his proconsular *imperium* until the end of 49 B.C. and then, as consul in 48 B.C., secure the ratification of all his acts. In one way or another, however, the Optimates and Pompey persisted in their efforts to deprive Caesar of his favorable position, and it was only through his henchman, the tribune Curio, that Caesar was able to protect himself. Acting on his master's orders, Curio proposed that both Caesar and Pompey should lay down their powers at the same time; Caesar, of course, and most senators accepted the idea, since the latter wished at all costs to avoid civil war, but Pompey, Cato, and their allies refused. Finally, on January 7, 49 B.C., the senate, railroaded by the latter, was persuaded to declare Caesar a public enemy and to pass the "last decree." Pompey was ordered to defend the state. The Caesarian tribunes, Marcus Antonius (Mark Antony) and Quintus Cassius, having interposed their vetoes, fled for their lives to Caesar. The threatened mistreatment of the tribunes gave Caesar, who was spending the winter in Cisalpine Gaul with his army, the pretext of protecting the sacred office.

Civil War. Caesar knew that to bring an army into Italy was a violation of the law and equivalent to a declaration of war on the republic, whereas Pompey enjoyed the moral advantage of occupying a legal position. Still, it was only in appearance that Pompey championed the senate and republican government, for the real question at issue was which of the two men should rule the Roman world. Unless he was to choose surrender and extinction, the only course now open to Caesar was to strike immediately. He discussed the subject with his friends and then, on January 10, 49 B.C., with the exclamation, "Alea jacta est," [1] he crossed the Rubicon, the river that separated his province from Italy.

Caesar in Italy and Spain (49 B.C.). At the head of an army of veterans personally devoted to him and disciplined by the long campaigns in Gaul, Caesar quickly

---

[1] The regular phrase in the Latin games when the dice were thrown. It was too late then to change one's mind; as we might express it, "The die is cast."

marched south. The great popularity that he already enjoyed led various municipalities to welcome him, while his mildness to opponents and his moderation in
relieving distressed debtors and in protecting property won him many adherents
and even made some of Pompey's followers suspect that they had taken the wrong
side. Pompey himself barely escaped being trapped in Italy, and with the consuls
and many senators, who were to embarrass him by their advice, crossed the Adriatic
to Epirus; he was confident that he would rally in the East, where he had long
campaigned, the legions and other resources of war sufficient to his needs. Caesar
did not pursue, for it was necessary first to attach the West firmly to his cause. In
Rome he seized the treasury and set up a temporary government; and then, while
Curio was attacking the Pompeians in Africa, he departed for Spain. The successful
campaign there, which was notable for the capture of Ilerda, brought many Pompeian troops over to his side; and during his return to Italy, Massilia, which had
sympathized with Pompey, was taken. Back in Rome, Caesar held the dictatorship
long enough to ensure his election as consul for 48 B.C. and then, resigning the
dictatorship, turned his thoughts ot Pompey (See map, rear endpaper.)

Caesar's Victories (48-47 B.C.). Although Pompey's fleet commanded the sea,
Caesar was able to transport some of his troops across the Adriatic early in the
winter; the rest followed under Mark Antony in March (48 B.C.). Caesar invested
the port of Dyrrachium but, failing in its capture, marched off to Thessaly, where
he hoped to find supplies. Pompey followed closely; he had more than nine legions,
a force twice as large as Caesar's, and, urged on by his senatorial advisers, decided
to attack him at Pharsalus. This proved to be the decisive battle of the civil war.
Caesar's skill and tactics, no less than the discipline and bravery of his men, won
the day, and Pompey fled to Egypt. Before Caesar could catch up with him in
Alexandria, Pompey was murdered, but Caesar found still other problems awaiting him there. The two rulers of the land—the twenty-year-old Cleopatra and her
younger brother, Ptolemy XIV Dionysus, who was also her husband—were engaged
in a dynastic quarrel. Caesar sided with Cleopatra and established her as monarch,
but he was forced to endure a dangerous siege in Alexandria throughout the winter.
Finally, in June of 47 B.C., Caesar left the charming queen and Egypt for the West.
He marched by way of Syria and Asia Minor, settling the affairs of the provinces as
he passed through. A brief campaign of five days was required to put down the
threat of Pharnaces, the son and successor of Mithridates Eupator. After defeating
him at Zela in Pontus, Caesar sent to Rome his facous dispatch, "Veni, vidi, vici"
("I came, I saw, I conquered").

Caesar's Return to the West. In the autumn of 47 B.C., Caesar reached Italy,
where he had again been elected dictator. It was first necessary to quell rioting in
Rome, which Antony, as his master of the horse, had been unable to handle, and
then put down a mutiny of his veterans, who were impatient to enjoy the fruits of
victory. Some republicans, including Cicero, had accepted the verdict of Pharsalus,
but Cato and many others had gathered in Africa, where with the aid of the Numidian king, Juba, they hoped to uphold the Pompeian cause. Since they presented a
grave danger and had slain his legate, Curio, Caesar crossed to Africa. He received
reinforcements from the king of Mauretania and annihilated the Pompeians at

Thapsus (46 B.C.). In despair of the republic, Cato killed himself at Utica. Caesar then returned to Rome, where he celebrated a monumental triumph in honor of his victories over Gaul, Egypt, Pontus, and Africa. He was now master of the state, with the exception of Spain, where Gnaeus and Sextus Pompey, Pompey's sons, still held out, but in the next year Caesar overwhelmed their forces at Munda.

THE DICTATORSHIP OF CAESAR

The empire over which Caesar had won the mastery extended from the Euphrates River to the Atlantic Ocean and included all the countries that bordered on the Mediterranean Sea. It consisted of a multitude of states, whose status ranged from complete subjection upward through every grade of dependent alliance, while its inhabitants represented many nationalities and languages no less than varied civilizations. It was a loose group of states, held together by the superior power of Rome rather than by common interests or sympathies. The governing state of this empire was in theory a republic, and the chief elements of the government were the senate and the Roman people. In fact, however, the partisan senatorial class and the assemblies no longer represented the Roman citizen body and, having failed to rule and protect the empire, had forfeited the right to leadership. Factional strife had reigned at Rome, and despite the good intentions of many senators, provincial rule had degenerated into robbery and oppression. It would be idle, therefore, to charge Caesar with having destroyed the freedom of the ancient republic. Nor was it possible to go back. The problem before Caesar, rather, was to give the Roman world a better organization, to protect it from foreign and domestic enemies, to redress wrongs, and to create institutions to broaden the base of support of the central government as well as that of the local communities. As in the case of Alexander the Great, Caesar's early death prevented a full unfolding of his plans, but ever since his time Roman Caesars and modern czars and kaisers have been proud to bear his name (See the map, p. 389.)

Caesar's Powers.   To carry through his reforms, it was necessary for Caesar to have autocratic powers, and these he wanted for his own sake as well. In the last analysis his authority rested on his veterans, but it could be given a shadow of legality through appointment to various offices at one and the same time. In 46 B.C., for example, he was appointed dictator for ten years, and in 45 he received the post for life. He was consul several times; his person, like a tribune's, was sacrosanct; as *pontifex maximus* he was head of the state religion, which he manipulated to his own benefit, and as virtual monarch he created magistrates and senators at will. The month in which he was born was renamed Julius (July); he was called "father of his country" and took the title of *imperator* (general). His portrait was stamped on coins, his statue was placed with the kings of Rome and in the temple of Romulus-Quirinus; this association with the gods was in keeping with Hellenistic practice and gave an added prestige to his position. His future acts were ratified in advance. He had the right of appointing half the officials annually, of making peace and war, and of expressing his opinion first in the senate; he also had charge of the treasury

and the sole command of the legions. It is a debatable point whether Caesar wished
ultimately to obtain a permanent monarchy based on the army. Monarchy clearly
implies succession, which he had not provided for by the time of his death. He did
adopt as his son and personal as distinct from political heir his grandnephew, Gaius
Octavius (Octavian), a youth of incredible talent. However he never took the title
rex, and at the feast of the Lupercalia in February 44 B.C., he brushed aside the
crown that Antony offered him.

Caesar's Reforms. Caesar allowed the assemblies little power and made the
senate a mere advisory council. He increased its number from five or six hundred
to seven hundred by admitting equestrians, veterans, and enfranchised Gauls to
strengthen his faction. In order to maintain the enlarged membership of the senate
and to fill the many new posts of government, he increased the number of quaestors from twenty to forty and of praetors from eight to sixteen. Caesar also attacked the evils of provincial administration. He favored fixed annual payments
instead of tax farming to protect provincials, and he appointed able, honest provincial governors and held them strictly to account. The officers whom he appointed
to command the legions under the governor, and the revenue officials, who like
most of the secretariat were slaves and freedmen, saw that his will was everywhere
enforced. The "estates of the Roman people," as the provinces had been called,
were to be cultivated and improved, no longer pillaged. At the same time he prepared a great municipal charter, known as the *Lex Julia Municipalis,* which granted
local autonomy to the towns of Italy and became the model for government in the
new municipalities of the western provinces.

These governmental reforms were imaginative and far-reaching and helped not
only to bind the empire more closely together but to promote its stability and prosperity. Always clement in his acts, Caesar neither engaged in Sullan proscriptions
nor liquidated the assets of creditors through some legal fiction, but he did ease
the burdens of debtors. To lessen the possibility of a revolt by slaves, he decreed
that one-third of the herdsmen and shepherds on Italian ranches should be free
men. The number of those receiving the grain dole was reduced from 320,000 to
150,000; many of his veterans were settled in Italy; and colonies were founded
along the coast of the Black Sea, at Corinth and Carthage, and in Spain. Another
far-reaching change instituted by the facile mind of Caesar touched the calendar.
The Romans had kept their lunar year of 355 days in step with the seasons by
adding an intercalary month periodically, but now Caesar adopted a calendar that
had been devised by the Alexandrian astronomer Sosigenes; it began on January 1
and consisted of three years of 365 days each, with an extra day every fourth year.
The Julian calendar, as it is called, was used by the Western world until 1582, when
Pope Gregory XIII made the slight changes that we now have.

When one considers the multitude and variety of Caesar's reforms, it is difficult
to believe that he was in Rome a total of only sixteen months from the crossing of
the Rubicon to his assassination. But with it all, he had time also to lay far-reaching
plans, which his successors brought to fruition. He planned, for example, a codification of the laws that had been passed by the republic in the previous centuries, and
in the interest of a general tax revision, he proposed an imperial census. Important
steps were taken to make Rome a beautiful, imperial capital, with forums, libraries,

and temples; the Tiber was to be dredged, and Ostia, the port, enlarged; the Pomptine marshes were to be drained; roads were to be built; a canal was to be dug at Corinth.

Caesar's Murder (44 B.C.).   The Optimates were envious of Caesar and longed to regain the privilege of ruling the world; or, as they put it, they hoped to restore the liberties of the ancient republic. A conspiracy of sixty senators, accordingly, was formed against Caesar; among them were the "lean and hungry" Cassius and Marcus Junius Brutus, an impractical scholar and strong republican, whose ancestor had driven the Tarquins from early Rome. Caesar himself was preparing to set out against the troublesome Dacians, in the lower Danubian region, and the Parthians, who had humbled Rome a decade earlier, but when he entered the senate house on the Ides of March (March 15, 44 B.C.), the conspirators gathered around him at the foot of Pompey's statue and, pretending to urge a petition of one of their number, stabbed him to death.

With the possible exception of Alexander the Great and Hannibal, Caesar was the most brilliant military genius the world had thus far produced. He was, too, a master of simple prose, an orator of great clearness and force, and an incessant builder of useful public works. His character was many-sided, his capacity boundless, his personality so warm that it won the passionate devotion of his followers. He was mild to the conquered; and when political enemies laid down their arms, they found him a friend and benefactor. Beginning as an unscrupulous politician, Caesar grew into a great statesman. By taking measures to secure the responsiblity of the provincial governors, he held out to the inhabitants of the empire a picture of a more stable and more prosperous life. The continuance of his policy, however, required a strong executive perpetually in office. Had his plan of establishing absolute rule succeeded, it would have been but a partial solution of the problem of reform, for the problems of absolute rule itself had been illustrated long before among Oriental nations and continued to manifest themselves in the Roman Empire itself for centuries after Caesar's death. Neither Caesar nor any other Roman statesman created institutions by means of which the people of the empire, dispensing with paternal despotism, could safeguard their own interests. The grant of citizenship to the provincials and the admission of representatives of the provinces to the senate would have been a great benefit, and yet even measures of this kind, taken much too late, did not prevent the ultimate decline of the empire.

What Caesar would have accomplished, had he lived, cannot be known, but his murder plunged the empire again into desolating war. In the new struggle the question at issue was not as to the form of government to be adopted; rather, it was what general would succeed to the power of Caesar. It was impossible to hope for a peaceable settlement: as one of Caesar's friends remarked to Cicero, "If Caesar, with all his genius, could not find a way out, who will now?"

THE SECOND TRIUMVIRATE

Caesar's death left the consul Mark Antony at the head of the government. He delivered the funeral oration and read the will, enlarging on and amplifying Caesar's benefits to the people. Its generosity to the citizens stirred them against the murderers, and in their grief they seized Caesar's body and burned it in the Forum. The chief conspirators—or liberators, as they called themselves—hurried away to their provinces in the East. A struggle to the death between them and the adherents of Caesar was inevitable.

Octavian.   The news of his great-uncle's death reached Octavius while he was tarrying at Apollonia in Illyria in readiness for the Parthian war. He was a youth of eighteen, and though his mother and friends warned him against claiming his inheritance and of the rivalry of Antony, he started at once for Italy. As the adopted son and heir of Caesar he took the name Gaius Julius Caesar Octavianus (Octavian), a name that worked like a charm. Caesar's old soldiers flocked to him, but he declined their proposals of support for the time being. In Rome, Octavian promised the people all that Caesar had bequeathed them—chiefly public parks and a sum of money for each citizen—but gave the appearance that he sided politically with the senate, to protect himself against Antony. This show of frank simplicity deceived Cicero, who approved Caesar's assassination though he had had no hand in it; he now declared that the youth stood on the side of the republic. Actually Octavian had no enthusiasm for the cause of the senate, and he coolly outmatched even the political veterans of the capital. In the next months Cicero, as the leader of the senate in its conflict with Antony, delivered against the new factional leader a series of powerful orations, known as *Phillipics,* from their resemblance to the speeches of Demosthenes against Philip of Macedon.

Octavian, Antony, and Lepidus.   At this time, Antony was in Cisalpine Gaul, a province that he had assigned to himself, in spite of the fact that one of the conspirators, Decimus Brutus, had received it from the senate as his own. When Decimus Brutus refused to surrender the command, Antony besieged him in Mutina (43 B.C.). The senate sent the two consuls, Hirtius and Pansa, together with Octavian, to the aid of Decimus Brutus, and in the ensuing battle Antony was defeated, though both consuls were killed; Brutus himself died not much later. After this victory over Antony the senate felt that it could now do without Octavian, who was a mere boy, but he marched on Rome and forced his election as consul. Thus the senate lost the support of Octavian at the very moment when Antony, having met Lepidus, master of the horse when Caesar died, was marching south. Octavian joined them near Bononia, and the three men, with an eye eastward toward Marcus Brutus and Cassius, decided to bury their rivalry. They had at their disposal more than forty-three legions and agreed to make themselves triumvirs with consular power for reestablishing the state. The plebeian council ratified this arrangement, which was to stand for five years: the triumvirs had power to dispose of all magistracies and to issue decrees that should have the force of law. In this way, the Second Triumvirate came officially into being; Antony was the dominant partner, Lepidus hardly more than a name. Partly to avenge Caesar's death, but more particularly because they were in desperate need of funds, the triumvirs filled Rome with their troops and renewed the hideous proscriptions of Sulla. Antony, who hated Cicero, insisted on the great orator's death. Though he was vain and wavering, though the rule of the senate that he championed was no longer fit for the responsibility of empire, in his heart Cicero was a patriot and a friend of liberty and the republic.

Battle of Philippi. The following summer (42 B.C.) Antony and Octavian crossed the Adriatic and led their armies into Macedonia, where Marcus Brutus and Cassius had collected a republican army of eighty thousand men. Two battles were fought near Philippi. After the first, which was indecisive, Cassius killed himself; then Brutus, thoroughly beaten in the second engagement, followed his example (map, rear endpaper).

Division of the Empire. Antony and Octavian now agreed to divide the Roman Empire into eastern and western spheres, where each would enjoy a preponderant influence. Octavian, accordingly, returned to Italy. A pressing duty was to find lands for fifty thousand veterans, and the many confiscations that were necessary to achieve this damaged the Italian economy. This fact, and the recent proscriptions, made Octavian very unpopular. He was also obstructed by Antony's wife and brother, Fulvia and Lucius, until he defeated them at the Etruscan town of Perusia (40 B.C.).

After Philippi, Antony had gone to the East, and at Tarsus in Cilicia he met Cleopatra for the first time. His foremost interest was apparently in getting financial support from her, and after the winter of 40 B.C. he did not see her again for four years. Since the Parthians threatened to overwhelm Syria, Antony proceeded to Italy in search of troops, a lack from which he was always to suffer. He and Octavian met in an atmosphere of mutual suspicion at Brundisium, where it was agreed, nevertheless, that Octavian should have Gaul (Cisalpine Gaul had recently been joined to Italy), Spain, Sardinia, Sicily, and Dalmatia; Antony was to have the lands eastward; Lepidus was given Africa; and each was to enjoy equal power in Italy. The arrangements were formalized by the marriage of Octavian's sister, Octavia, to Antony, whose wife was now dead.

Sextus Pompey. Unfortunately for Antony and Octavian, Pompey's son, Sextus, controlled Sicily and the sea and even threatened Italy with famine, until in 39 B.C. at Misenum Sextus' position was recognized on condition that he provision Rome. It was merely a temporary adjustment of affairs, and in 37 B.C. Antony returned from a trip to the East for a conference with his colleague at Tarentum. There it was agreed to extend the triumvirate, which had actually expired the previous year, to 33 B.C.; Antony gave Octavian 120 warships for his renewed conflict with Sextus Pompey, and in return Octavian promised Antony four legions for the Parthian war, which he cunningly failed to send. Not much later, Sextus Pompey was defeated at sea and died. When Lepidus, moreover, disputed Octavian's claim to Sicily, his troops deserted him, and he was deprived of his command. Octavian was now supreme in the West and assiduously tried to improve his public image through propaganda and attention to affairs of state.

Antony and Cleopatra. Antony, on the other hand, disturbed the Romans by his apparent desire to become an Oriental despot. From Tarentum, Antony went to Syria, where he married Cleopatra at Antioch, and the following year (36 B.C.) he invaded Parthia. He lost many men and was forced to retreat, but he did succeed in overrunning Armenia. This gave him the excuse to celebrate in 34 B.C. a triumph in Alexandria and to present—in the "Donations of Alexandria," as they were called—Rome's eastern possessions to Cleopatra, to the children she had had by him, and to Caesarion, her son by Caesar. Cleopatra duly became "Queen of Kings" and Caesarion, "King of Kings," while Alexander, Ptolemy Philadelphus, and Cleopatra Selene had each a separate kingdom. Antony, who was giving away Roman real estate, remained nominally a Roman magistrate, although in Greece and Asia Minor he was generally regarded as a Hellenistic monarch. He now divorced Octavia.

Octavian was engaging in propaganda and read to the Romans what purported to be Antony's will, in which the East was bequeathed to Cleopatra and her children, and made Antony out to be an unpatriotic weakling, Cleopatra's tool. Then, since the term of the triumvirate had come to an end the previous year, Octavian bound the West to himself by an oath and declared war on Cleopatra (32 B.C.).

Battle of Actium (31 B.C.).   Antony and Cleopatra, thereupon, gathered their forces and proceeded west with a fleet of 500 ships and an army of perhaps 90,000 men. In 31 B.C., Octavian and his extraordinarily able general, Agrippa, having an army of approximately the same size and 400 warships, succeeded in blockading their enemies within the Ambracian Gulf, at Actium off the west coast of Greece. The battle that followed, although famous, was an anticlimax, as few shots were fired. Antony and Cleopatra found it impossible to break the blockade with the mass of their fleet. Cleopatra did manage to slip through the blockade with a small number of ships and her wealth; Antony himself soon followed, but the fleet and the army had no alternative except surrender to Octavian. When Octavian reached Alexandria the next year, first Antony and then Cleopatra, realizing that the end had come, committed suicide. Egypt, with its vast riches, was annexed; and since Greece was to be organized as the province of Achaea, the administrative arrangement of the eastern Mediterranean was now complete. In 29 B.C., Octavian held a magnificent triumph at Rome to celebrate his victories in Europe, Asia, and Africa; and two years later he put aside his extraordinary powers in favor of a new form of government.

The Roman Republic was, in reality, coming to an end. The battle of Actium had placed the destiny of the empire in the hands of an able statesman. The century of revolution that Tiberius Gracchus had inaugurated brought death, suffering, and devastation to a world that yearned for peace. Sulla and Pompey had wielded absolute power, but they lacked the wisdom necessary for creating new and useful institutions. In failing to attract the governing establishment to support his system, Julius Caesar had fallen short of the needs of his time. It remained for his successor, Octavian, to develop a new political organization under which the famous Roman Peace (*Pax Romana*) might flourish through the coming centuries. During forty long years, as Augustus, he rebuilt the Roman world; his reign came to be known as a Golden Age.

27

The Society and Civilization
of the Late Republic

THE SOCIAL AND ECONOMIC BACKGROUND

Economic Deterioration.   Warfare (particularly the Roman struggle with Mithridates and that between contending Roman generals), the exactions of Sulla, the tribute laid on the provinces, the activities of the bankers and *publicani,* and the enormous debt of individual cities—all contributed to the economic ruin of the Eastern provinces during the late republic. Warfare also took its tool in the West, but the ensuing romanization of Gaul and Spain mitigated its effect. The growth of vast estates and the cultivation of grain gave to Africa a somnolent prosperity. The terrible proscriptions and confiscations destroyed life and wealth in Rome itself. The war with Hannibal had begun the economic deterioration of southern Italy, and the subsequent growth of huge estates (*latifundia*) encouraged the small farmer to leave his land. The Gracchi had failed to solve this problem; the city mob remained; and the allotments of land to tens of thousands of veterans further unsettled Italian agriculture and instilled a fear of the future among those who were still untouched.

Italian Recovery.   There were several reasons, however, that Italy was not irrevocably ruined. In the first place, the tribute and the lucrative campaigns [1] brought an enormous amount of money to Italy. Much of this money was invested in land, but a good deal found its way into commerce and industry, so that in actual fact Italy gradually became economically diversified. As a result, Puteoli, because of its location in industrial Campania, supplanted Ostia as Italy's chief port. Bronzes from Capua and Etruria now found a wider market, and so did the fine pottery of Arretium (Arretine ware). Varro tells us that Italy, at the end of the republic, again resembled a garden, from which we must conclude that years of grazing had allowed the soil to recover from its former exhaustion. Even though many of the farms and ranches belonged to the wealthy, whose workers were either slaves or tenant farmers (*coloni*), and though much land had been confiscated for veterans, there were still large numbers of small but prosperous farms, particularly in north-

---

[1] As an example of strictly personal profit, Marcus Brutus charged 48 per cent interest on his loans to Eastern cities, about four times the normal rate.

ern Italy. Their products—grain, wine, olive oil, and woolens—formed the real basis of the Italian economy.

The crippling of Eastern prosperity, moreover, sent many of the ablest men west in search of a new career, and thus the Western provinces, and more particularly Italy, received an influx not only of capable individuals but of various races. There were those who feared that the ancient Italian stock would be swamped by this cosmopolitan population. Many of the newcomers settled in Rome, which as the political capital of the empire afforded unusual opportunities for advancement, but we know little of their life. No ancient writer described their social conditions in detail. Living conditions were certainly primitive for most of them, if we may judge from the archaeological remains, such as the gloomy tenement houses. These were the people who were ever ready to riot in the streets. They supported their patrons, joined political clubs, and insisted on cheap grain and expensive shows. The lot of the free poor was not as happy as that of the freedmen (*liberti*), for the Roman conquests had brought tens of thousands of slaves quite indiscriminately to Italy, and among them were many people of ability. Since manumission was relatively easy—Sulla freed ten thousand slaves, who henceforth were known as Cornelii after his *gens*—the able freedmen worked their way up in the governmental bureaucracy or, as in the case of Cicero's Tiro, became secretaries and managers of estates.

The chief fruits of imperial rule during the late republic went to the members of the senatorial class, who satisfied their pride and ambition in government service and lined their pockets in the provinces, and to the equestrians, who made their fortunes from estates and from business.

Education.   It was conquest, the increase of slavery, provincial exploitation, and the rapid accumulation of wealth that revolutionized the Roman character. The greatness of Rome in the best days of the republic was largely due to the peculiar nature of the Roman family, to its cohesion and traditions. A Roman house of any pretentions, for example, had an alcove, known as the *tablinum,* which contained the family archives, and on each side of this was a recess, or *ala,* where the nobles kept wax masks and other portraits of their ancestors to inspire successive generations to achieve comparable *gloria.* During the early period of the republic, it was the task of parents to train their children at home in the stern, simple virtues that made good soldiers and citizens, and if the increase of wealth brought with it a decline in family traditions, the parents still had the responsibility of planning their children's education. During the late republic, education for the upper classes was formalized outside the home. A boy first attended an elementary school, in which he learned the rudiments of reading, writing, and arithmetic, and then entered a higher school kept by a *grammaticus,* who taught him Greek and Latin literature. The boy read the poems of Naevius and Ennius, the comedies of Plautus and Terence, Homer, Demosthenes, the Greek dramatists, history, oratory, and the Laws of the Twelve Tables; there were schools, too, for girls, though less is known of them. Greek slaves and tutors might provide further education, until finally the young man of means was ready to go to Naples, Athens, Rhodes, or some other Hellenic center of culture to study under the greatest instructors of the day. The youth who wished to enter public life attached himself to an older friend who had work to do in the Forum, and with this practical experience in law and oratory, he combined the further study of theory under a rhetorician. Despite the efforts of Cicero to popularize it, theoretical philosophy was not widely studied, although Stoicism and Epicureanism provided popular styles of life. As in the Greek East, at Rome the core of the educational curriculum consisted of rhetoric and oratory.

Marriage. When he had completed his studies and had reached the age of twenty-five or thirty, most upper-class young men married. The young man arranged the betrothal with the lady's father, since she was probably too young to be consulted in the matter and was, in any case, under parental guardianship. The marriage ceremonies began with a feast and sacrifices in the house of the bride's father and ended in the evening with a procession of youths, torchbearers, musicians, and guests who escorted the bride to her future home, where the groom carried her over the threshold, as it was an ill omen for her to touch the sill with her foot. The newly married pair then ate a sacred cake in the presence of ten witnesses and, if the occasion was important enough, before the chief pontiff and priest of Jupiter. The ceremonies of the evening concluded with a bridal song by the guests, and on the following day the husband gave a marriage feast to his friends.

Though early custom placed the wife in the power of her husband, she went freely into society, attended the theater and public games, taught her children, and sometimes aided her husband in his political career. Her position as mistress of the household commanded respect from the government as well as from society. But if the mother of the Gracchi serves as an excellent example of the older virtues, we may contrast with her, as typical of later sophistication, Clodia, the sister of the political gang leader Clodius, who was noted for her fast pace in society and her vices. Before the end of the republic, indeed, the sacred forms of marriage were giving way to civil contracts made and dissolved at pleasure. Such agreements left the wife in charge of her property and free from her husband's power, but whatever improvement this may have wrought in the condition of women, it was clear proof that the old society centering in the family had come to an end. Divorce grew to be frequent. With the decline of the family, the society of the capital enjoyed increasingly extravagant luxuries and vices.

Palaces and Villas. Fashionable people had their palaces and villas on the Palatine in Rome, in the nearby Campagna, in the Sabine hills, and at Baiae and other seaside resorts of Campania. The care of such a residence required the service of many slaves, and we hear of a man who in the country and city together employed more than four thousand. They were organized, somewhat like an army, in divisions and companies under their several overseers. Each slave had as his special duty some minute part of the household work. Many were needed for the ceremonies attending the admission of guests, many for the care of the baths, bedrooms, kitchen, and dining rooms, as well as for the wardrobes, toilet, and personal service of the various members of the family. On going out the master or mistress was accompanied by a throng of servants, whose number and splendid livery advertised the rank and wealth of their owner. Other companies of slaves spun wool, made clothes, kept the house in repair, and cared for the sick. It is striking that so many persons in a single household could find employment or that the processes of labor could be so minutely portioned out. On the country estates were ploughmen, herdsmen, vinedressers, gardeners, keepers of bees, poultry, and fish, and many other classes of laborers.

Slaves.   Saves not born in the household were obtained by purchase from markets filled by prisoners of war or sometimes by unfortunates caught and sold by pirates or kidnappers. On a single estate might be seen representatives of all nationalities of the known world, particularly the Eastern world. The master had complete power and sometimes treated his slaves with extreme harshness and cruelty. For the slightest offenses he could scourge, torture, or crucify them. In the country the slaves often worked in gangs chained together and slept in crowded, filthy dungeons. Those who were too old or too sickly to work or to put on the market, the master could expose at the shrine of Aesculapius on an island in the Tiber or kill outright. It was this inhumane treatment that provoked Sicilian slave revolts and the insurrection under Spartacus the gladiator.

Freedmen.   From early times it often happened that a slave won his freedom by faithful service or purchased it with his savings. He then became a client of his former master, whose business it was customary for him to help manage. As the number of freedmen increased, the gift of full citizenship was withdrawn, and they were confined to the Latin rights, which meant that they could neither vote nor hold office, although their sons received the franchise. The freedmen formed a large class, socially inferior to freemen, but very enterprising and influential; some of them, after accumulating riches, as is usual among the *nouveaux riches,* became intolerably overbearing. The tendency of emancipation, however, was to break down class feeling and privileges in favor of social and legal equality.

Fashionable Life.   It was the habit of the aristocrat to receive his clients in the early morning, and the larger the number, the more his pride was gratified. Since the ordinary unskilled laborer received a daily pittance as wage, most of which went for food and lodging, many of the visitors had some favor to ask; others, who were candidates for office, sought the rich man's influence. The latter part of the morning might be spent in the senate, the afternoon at exercise. In the early evening the master of a house entertained his friends at dinner or perhaps accepted an invitation to dine out. Romans in the late republican and early imperial periods taxed to the utmost the resources of professional cooks in the preparation of exotic dishes or ransacked the world for rarities with which to please their guests. Their dinners consisted of many and varied courses; they drank costly wines and prolonged their revels till morning, being entertained with music, pantomimes, and dancing girls. Introspective persons—and there were many—seeing the life of society demanding so large a share of their time, were glad to quit Rome for a period of quiet life at Tibur, Laurentum, or some other country retreat.

Death.   When the upper-class Roman died, kinsmen and friends took part in the funeral procession. The dancers, the music, the acting of the mimes (whose leader mimicked the deceased), the wax masks worn by persons dressed to represent the ancestors, and the wailing of hired mourners—all combined to make the ceremony at once solemn and grotesque. A near kinsman pronounced a eulogy on the deceased; the corpse was burned on the funeral pyre, and an urn containing the ashes was deposited in the family tomb.

PHILOSOPHY AND LAW

Rules of Conduct. The puritanical character of many educated Romans found greater satisfaction in philosophies that provided them with rules of conduct than in the imaginative Olympian religion of the Greeks. The common people, with the desperate hope of a happier hereafter, might prefer the mysticism of the emotional Oriental religions, which hordes of eastern slaves and traders and returning soldiers brought with them to Italy. The tendency of philosophy to skim the surface of knowledge, instead of digging down into a study of cause and effect, prevented the growth of healthy experimentation and led to mysticism. When it was discovered that the unaided imagination cannot explain the great truths of life, people turned to things more practical, especially to those systems of thought that pointed the way to right conduct. Cynicism performed a service in its criticism of society, but it was Stoicism that took hold of some of the finest minds of Rome. This philosophy had originally been introduced to Rome by Panaetius and was further developed by a Syrian Greek, Posidonius, who possessed one of the most encyclopedic brains of antiquity. Stoicism taught that virtue alone is sufficient for happiness and that a person should rise above all passions and follow reason. The appeal to self-discipline, with its emphasis on the duty of a public career, pleased the orderly Roman. Epicureanism, on the other hand, offered happiness to the person not interested in politics. It, too, was concerned with ethics and reason and sought the origin of all nature in the movement and combination of atoms, but its emphasis on intellectual pleasure degenerated, under some of its followers, into pure hedonism.[2]

Rules of right conduct, such as these philosophic systems represented, were eagerly studied by the honest Roman. His best ideal was fair play, and with little fear of contradiction he could point to the methods by which his ancestors had built up Roman power in Italy. It was inevitable that this sense of fairness should also manifest itself in the creation of a body of law, which became one of Rome's greatest achievements.

Law. Julius Caesar did not live to undertake the codification of Roman law, as he had planned; this was done at periodic stages after his death. The need for it was acute, not only because of conflicting laws passed by the assemblies through the centuries, but also because it was necessary to bring order to the great principles involved, which had developed with the growth of the Roman frontier and the intellectual horizon of the citizen. Even in monarchical days there had been a distinction between civil and religious law (*ius* and *fas,* p. 336), but it was during the early republic that the civil law, or *ius civile,* received its first great impetus. This was the adoption of the Twelve Tables (p. 349) in 449 B.C. They continued to be the foundation of justice for centuries; as part of their education Roman boys committed them to memory, and in late republican times the jurist Servius Sulpicius Rufus wrote a great commentary on them.

Roman civil law, to which Quintus Mucius Scaevola, the contemporary of Tibe-

---

[2] For a fuller discussion of Stoicism and Epicureanism, see p. 308 ff.

rius Gracchus, gave so much attention, applied to Roman citizens. Its development was due in large part to the praetorship, for it was customary each year for the praetor, on assuming office, to issue an edict that announced the principles he would follow while magistrate; by and large, he adopted the principles of his predecessor, with such changes as seemed advisable. During the late republic, Aulus Ofilius systematized the prators' edicts. Rome, however, ruled many foreign peoples who did not have citizenship, and it was necessary, therefore, to settle fairly the disputes that noncitizens had with one another and with citizens. This task fell in Italy to the praetor for aliens (*praetor peregrinus*) and in the provinces to the governor. Inevitably Rome had to acquaint herself with the customs and laws of the Hellenistic world, and it was discovered that many of these were worth adopting for her own citizens. Within the body of civil law, accordingly, there were general principles that applied to noncitizens as well as citizens, and these were known as the Law of the Nations (*ius gentium*).[3]

LITERATURE AND ART

Hellenic influences had first reached Rome from the Greeks of southern Italy and Sicily, and they grew ever stronger as the custom developed for the sons of Roman nobles to have Greeks as tutors and to follow this tutoring with further study in Athens and Rhodes. Naturally, therefore, Hellenic ideas controlled the intellectual life of the Greco-Roman world. The Roman genius was for political organization, for the temperament of the Romans was realistic and practical. Throughout the years, then, when the political pulse beat high and men spoke their minds freely and assailed one another in the senate, assembly, forum, and courts, Latin prose, especially oratory, reached its peak.

Cicero. The late republic, intellectually speaking, is often referred to as the Age of Cicero. Cicero (106-43 B.C.) was the foremost orator of his day and one of the most famous of all time. His birthplace was Arpinum, a municipality among the hills of southern Latium. While he was still young, his parents moved to Rome, to give their children the best possible education. Receiving his early instruction at home and in private schools, the youth then studied law, heard the eminent orators of the time, took lessons in Greek and Latin rhetoric, and finally went to Athens and Rhodes to complete his preparation as an orator under the greatest instructors of the age. When he returned to Rome, he entered public life and by ability forced his way up through the career of offices. The exclusive circle of nobles had to admit this *novus homo* to an equality with themselves. Through his writings—numerous philosophical works, some poems, fifty-eight orations, and almost nine hundred letters have survived—we know Cicero's character more intimately than that of any other Roman. His own words tell us that he was vain and in politics often wavering, but in these respects he was no worse than any of his contemporaries. His tastes were literary and intellectual, and in spite of weaknesses he could always be found, in great issues, on the side he believed to be right.

---

[3] For a fuller discussion of Roman law, see p. 458 ff.

Cicero's *Orations* unfold an extraordinarily vivid picture of Roman political life. His letters to his friends—especially to Atticus, and to others such as his freedman-secretary, Tiro, in which he speaks candidly of passing events—give a remarkably full and intimate knowledge of the social, moral, and political conditions of the time. When the First Triumvirate all but drove him from politics, Cicero turned to the composition of philosophical works. The soundness of Cicero's character and his desire to raise the standards of the reading public are evinced by his constant choice of the nobler ideas of philosophy in preference to the merely useful and material. In his *Republic* he suggested the idea that a state, when distracted by internal strife like the Roman world of his time, needed the paternal care of its leading citizen, or "Moderator of the Republic." The task of such an official would be to hold the various offices and powers of the state in harmony with one another and to require all to perform their several duties effectively. The government of Augustus later reflected this idea. In general, however, Cicero regarded his philosophical works rather diffidently, admitting that they were unoriginal, merely Greek thought expressed in Latin. These works are nonetheless very important because they frequently are the sole versions of Greek philosophy to have survived and to have been passed down into our civilization. The greatness of Cicero lies chiefly in the fact that he was a literary artist of surpassing genius; his sonorous periods and his incomparable language, vocabulary, and style became the model of later centuries.

History. In an age of action, historical writing was bound to rank with oratory, particularly since it gave its author the opportunity to press his own personal bias. Noble families recorded the deeds of illustrious ancestors, and to give their narratives a brilliant coloring, they filled them with lively stories and startling incidents, however exaggerated and false. One of these romancers was Valerius Antias, who about the time of the Allied War composed his *Annals* of Rome from a strongly aristocratic point of view. A striking contrast with the diffuse rhetoric of Antias is the historical narrative of Caesar, a model of its kind, plain and direct, with a mastery of expression but no pretension to ornament. His *Commentaries* on the Gallic War and the Civil War tell the story of his campaigns and were written—in part, at least—to explain, justify, and further his cause among the Roman people. Factually accurate, Caesar wrote with modesty of his own achievements and generously excused the mistakes or praised the merits of others. Sallust (86-36 B.C.), on the other hand, wrote with a Caesarian bias, and yet his *History,* most of which is unfortunately lost, gave a valuable description of the events following Sulla's death. His *War with Jugurtha* and *Conspiracy of Catiline* analyze the character of society and the motives of conduct. When the great men of Rome began to attract all eyes, a widespread interest developed in biography, but the most famous of these biographers cannot be acquitted of inferior and untrustworthy work. This was Cornelius Nepos (ca. 100-25 B.C.), a Gaul from the Po Valley, whose *Eminent Men* treated distinguished Romans and foreigners in parallel biographies; most of his *Lives* that we still possess are of Greek generals.

Catullus and Lucretius. Within certain fashionable circles of the late republic there lived two great poets. One was Catullus (ca. 87-54 B.C.), from Verona in Cisalpine Gaul, who in his verses hurled some bitter lampoons at Caesar. His particular circle was dominated by Clodia, sister of Clodius, the unscrupulous political leader. Catullus fell madly in love with her and, addressing her as Lesbia, wrote her beautiful and intensely passionate poems, courting, winning, and renouncing a woman who was as promiscuous as she was brilliant. Catullus and his circle called themselves "modernists" (neoterics) and were the first to write Latin love poetry, in meter, style, and subject matter very much influenced by the Alexandrian poets of the Hellenistic Age, like Callimachus (see p. 308).

The other poet, famous for his intensity of purpose, was Lucretius (ca. 99–55 B.C.), whose *On the Nature of Things* (*De Rerum Natura*) is one of the world's greatest poems. It was composed in hexameter verse and sought to explain Creation through the movement of atoms, one of the chief tenets of Epicureanism. Though the poem is materialistic and preaches the mortality of the soul, it reaches great heights of spiritual and philosophical feeling. By scientific means Lucretius sought to free people from superstition and to dispel from their minds all fear of death and the gods.

Varro. Roman authors were eager, of course, to bring their works before the public, and publishers employed slaves in making copies, which were then placed on sale. Cultivated men had private libraries, but it fell to Caesar to plan a large collection of works in Greek and Latin for the use of the general public. He assigned the task of collecting and arranging them to Marcus Terentius Varro (116–27 B.C.), the most learned of the Romans. We know something of Varro's books on the Latin language and on agriculture. Altogether he was the author of seventy-four works, a true encyclopedia, which included all departments of knowledge affecting his own country and race.

Art. In Roman art, as in literature, Hellenistic influences were strong. Greek artists, in their search for commissions, left their homes in the East and migrated to Italy, where they were readily employed on private and public work. They brought portrait sculpture to new heights of realism and decorated the homes of the wealthy with colorful paintings. Victorious generals, moreover, brought back to Rome much art from Greek lands and sometimes added impressive buildings to the city of Rome. Sulla, for example, rebuilt the temple of Jupiter Capitolinus. In 78 B.C. the Tabularium (the public record office) was erected. In the Campus Martius, Pompey built a theater, where comedies and pantomimes were produced; tragedy had long since ceased to be popular. Caesar repaved the Forum Romanum, where after his death a temple to the deified Julius was dedicated. Within the Forum he built the rostra and a law court known as the Basilica Julia, and he began a new forum nearby. In buildings, as in the aqueducts and sewers (for instance, the enlarged *cloaca maxima*) that were constructed at this time, it was customary to use the true arch. Concrete was normally employed; generally it was faced with marble or travertine, a limestone that was displacing the volcanic tufa of earlier days. When the facing consisted of irregular pieces, it was known as *opus incertum,* though in the late Republic a pattern (*opus reticulatum*) was preferred. The city of Rome, with its population of several hundreds of thousands, was a very hectic place. The poor lived in their crowded tenements (*insulae*), seventy feet high, along narrow alleys. Traffic was congested, and fires and street riots, because of the lack of proper supervision and equipment, were frequent.

PART VI

THE ROMAN EMPIRE

28

The Principate of Augustus (27 B.C.– A.D.14)

THE FOUNDATION OF THE PRINCIPATE

Augustus and the First "Act of Settlement." In January 27 B.C., two years after he had celebrated his triumph in honor of his victories in Europe, Asia, and Africa, Octavian, now thirty-five years of age and consul for the seventh time, went before the senate and surrendered the extraordinary powers he had been holding, in order, as he explained, that the republic might be restored. Octavian did not intend to be taken at his word, and the senate knew it. Moving with characteristic caution, he had been methodically planning the development of his power for some three years, and the governing establishment, by then all but identical with his faction, knew what was expected of them. Essentially Octavian had three options. He could rule autocratically, but then perhaps expect Caesar's fate. He could retire, but he was too much the statesman to do so. Or he could devise some other system of government. He took this option and decided to keep essential power in his own hands without touching the republican facade of government. His was a disguised kind of monarchy, authoritarian but not arbitrary, and everybody in the governing establishment knew it.

In January 27 B.C., the senate and the Roman people voted him for ten years a proconsular *imperium* in Spain, Gaul, and Syria, where most of the troops were stationed, making him in effect their commander in chief. His extraordinary proconsular command clearly resembled those of Caesar, Pompey, and Crassus, except that his was all three of them rolled into one. His proconsular command was periodically renewed, and he held it to his death. Simultaneously he was a yearly consul. The action of the senate and the people in granting him these powers in 27 B.C. is frequently called the First Act of Settlement of the Roman Principate. For the next four years, these were the main constitutional powers of his rule, plus his ability to wield what the Romans called *auctoritas,* an untranslatable term that means the rather unquestioned power of elder statesmen to command the obedience of their fellow citizens. Accordingly, from 27 B.C. he was officially called Augustus, the "reverend" or the "consecrated one," with its connotation of divine favor. Moderns insist on easy labels, but it can readily be seen that at the very beginning of his reign, August neither demanded nor received an authority that can be defined in conventional language.

413

FIGURE 55. Augustus,
63 B.C.–14 A.D.

The Granger Collection

In 27 B.C. Augustus left Rome for Spain to subdue the Cantabrians, and he did not return to the capital for three years. His absence gave his new system time to work, and during those three years Augustus and the senate carried on the functions of government in consultation with one another. From the very beginning, then, there was a formal division between emperor and senate, but the division was only formal. Already under Augustus the emperor had the power, and used it, to interfere in any sphere of government, no matter how "senatorial."

The Roman world yearned for peace; it yearned, too, for a return of the old order, or at any rate for a prosperity and security that an ancient past had reputedly held; but it also hated monarchy and feared the absolutism of a Caesar. Though as Octavian he had proved that he could keep pace with his contemporaries in matters of warfare and proscriptions, Augustus now showed a deep awareness of the mentality of the world, for he gave to his rule the semblance of republican legality. Taking into account the sensibilities of the Romans, Augustus professed to derive his authority from the senate and the people, and he disguised his own position in republican forms. Whereas we are likely to speak of him as an emperor, from his title of *imperator,* the Romans preferred to call him by proper republican titulature, applied for example to Pompey, as *princeps,* or "first citizen," and this was the title he himself most often used. Later, in 2 B.C., he was acclaimed *pater patriae,* father of his country, a title that delighted him because it seemed to indicate a wide acceptance of his form of government. It is customary to speak of this particular type of rule as a principate, as it was the *princeps* who gave it its peculiar title.

THE PRINCEPS, SENATE, EQUESTRIANS, AND PLEBS

The Princeps and the "Second Act of Settlement." The Roman principate is sometimes dated from 23 B.C., for it was in that year that Augustus, with his Second Act of Settlement, gave the definitive touches to the system of government in operation since 27 B.C. Having faced an important conspiracy against his regime, perhaps also a split in his faction over succession to his power in the event of his death, and recognizing that annual reelection to the consulship was a shock to republican tradition and in any case fell short of his requirements, Augustus in 23 B.C. surrendered the consulship and received in return tribunician power (*tribunicia potestas*), which gave him control of legislation and hence of civil administration. Because he received this power annually until his death, the custom developed of dating events by the years of his tribunician power. Other authority came to him piecemeal and at later dates. In 19 B.C., for example, he was given consular power in Italy without holding the office, and in 12 B.C., on the death of Lepidus, the old triumvir who had long ago ceased to count, Augustus became *pontifex maximus* for life and thus head of the state religion. The proconsulship and the tribunician power sufficed for military and civil supremacy.

Conservative in nature and deeply aware of the hopes of his subjects, Augustus proposed to keep every republican institution and custom that was possible: the division of the people into senatorial, equestrian, and plebeian orders; the magistrates and the *cursus honorum;* the assembly and the senate. Augustus stood for Rome, its glorious past and its promise of a wonderful future. He proposed, too, that the provinces should be efficiently governed. On the other hand, a repetition of the experience of the late republic, with the rivalries of ambitious generals and their armies, must be avoided by all means; nor did he intend to surrender his own power, which had been won at the cost of civil war. When it came to his personal position within the state, therefore, Augustus resolved to gather to himself every necessary authority for what was, practically, autocratic power, but to receive it, in each instance, from the senate and the people and to bury it as deeply as possible in republican titles; that is to say, he would share the duties of office, as tradition dictated, but would also hold several conventional posts simultaneously.

The Senate. The senate, which was to be Augustus' partner in the vast labor of government, enjoyed an amount of power comparable to what it had had in the republican period, or so it seemed. A *senatus consultum*, for example, no longer expressed the mere opinion of the senate but in effect had the force of law. Just as Augustus had the right to make peace and war, so he was entitled to speak first in the senate, and accordingly the *senatus consulta* represented, in fact, the legislation that he himself preferred. The actual authority of the senate was also reduced by the fact that Augustus, as a magistrate, could issue edicts. Appearances were maintained and with them a limitation on monarchy. So much business affecting the Greco-Roman world came before the senate that Augustus created a small advisory council or cabinet of magistrates and senators to reach a consensus with his establishment before preparing the agenda for senatorial consideration, but he placed special reliance on two intimate friends, Maecenas and Agrippa. The establishment of the senate as a high court of justice represented a new and significant increase in its importance. In an effort to revive the virtues of old, Augustus purged the senate of unworthy persons and set its membership at six hundred. The ultimate fate of the senate was to become a municipal council, but that lay centuries in the future. Certainly, under Augustus, it had the trappings of a glorious past and enough power so that under certain emperors, it became the rallying point of the opposition. The real power of the senate, however, obviously depended on the character of the individual emperor and the degree of independence he chose to give it.

Clearly recognizing that the cooperation of the senate was necessary for the government of a large world that consisted of three ancient cultures—Roman, Greek, and Oriental—Augustus took the obvious step of making life safe and rewarding for the senatorial class. The members of the senate and their families composed this order, which was hereditary, and they had the privilege of wearing a broad purple stripe on their togas, just as August himself wore a purple robe on festive occasions. To maintain one's position and avoid transfer to the lower equestrian order, it was necessary to be worth one million sesterces, but since the civil wars had deprived many otherwise-eligible individuals of their property, Augustus granted them subsidies. The role of the senatorial class was to provide administrators. The *cursus honorum* was still followed, as in republican days, and election to the quaestorship automatically brought membership in the senate. At the conclusion of his journey through the career of offices, a senator might look forward to an important post; for example, he might become city prefect of Rome, an important new post founded by Augustus, or have a responsible office in the government of Italy; it was very likely that he would be awarded a high military command or be invited to serve as Augustus' legate in one of the imperial provinces. These were the frontier provinces, where inevitably the armies and consequently the ultimate basis of power were located. The other provinces, known as senatorial, were the more civilized or romanized, at the same time they were far removed from the scene of possible fighting and in no need of a large armed force, and consequently Augustus left their government to governors elected by the senate and formally responsible to it, and not directly to him.

The Equestrians. The senatorial class was not large enough to attend to the administrative duties of empire. For this it was necessary to call on the special experience of the equestrians, who now found an official outlet for their administrative skill. A career in the imperial civil service—as a financial procurator, for example—meant, moreover, that the equestrians could not fail to become attached to the emperor. It is evident that, under Augustus, the classes at Rome became quite distinct, but it must be emphasized that one could move from class to class, especially if the princeps so desired. Membership in the equestrian class was hereditary, but it was necessary to possess property valued at 400,000 sesterces. Because many of them had experience in business, the equestrians were used chiefly in financial matters, but other civil posts, and even military ones, were open to them. A man might crown his career by becoming prefect of the grain supply at Rome or one of the two prefects of the praetorian guard, the armed force within Rome that originally was Augustus' bodyguard and eventually was able to make or break an emperor. The height of an equestrian's career, at first, however, was the prefecture of Egypt. This great prize did not fall to a senator, for the princeps recognized that his potential opposition lay within the senate, and he dared not allow Rome's granary to come within its grasp.

The Plebs. Within the imperial service there were many lower posts requiring secretarial and financial ability, and these were filled with freedmen and the plebeians. For the populace of Rome, there was also the opportunity to join the army and become a minor officer, but this career was seized chiefly by the people in Italian municipalities. Most citizens in Rome continued to live on subsistence level, and at least 200,000 were supplied with free grain. The popular assemblies continued to meet, the centuriate assembly to elect magistrates, and the plebeian council to make laws, as during the republic. In the long run, however, the autocratic nature of the principate was destined at first to denature and ultimately to destroy the idea of citizen assemblies functioning as electoral or legislative bodies. The election of officials was transferred to the senate by Augustus' immediate successor, and the lawmaking process similarly shifted to the decrees of that body, shaped by the emperor and his cabinet, or to his own magisterial edicts.

Revival of Morality. The various elements in the state were pleased with Augustus: the plebeian might advance according to his ability, the Italian might become a centurion, the equestrian had a recognized career, the senate had survived the civil wars, and the provinces were governed efficiently. Three times during Augustus' principate the doors of the temple of Janus were closed as a sign that peace reigned throughout the empire, and in 13 B.C. the senate celebrated the fact by the erection of an altar of the Augustan Peace (the *ara pacis Augustae*). To inspire all the people and classes of the empire with faith in themselves and their future, Augustus thought it wise to rebuild the moral fabric of society. In 19 B.C. he tried to restrict adultery and to lessen the habit of divorce, and further to reconstitute family life he extended to mothers of three or more children property rights and freedom from the *potestas* of their husbands, and to such fathers preferred advancement in office (A.D. 9). By private example, as well as in his public acts, Augustus sought a return to the values of the past, to patriotism, to the religion of the fathers. To foster this growth, Augustus, in the later years of his principate, allowed his name to be associated with the goddess Roma in a provincial imperial cult. Religion and patriotism were here linked symbolically in a service that, in Italy after his death, was largely in the hands of freedmen known as *Augustales*. The Romans, moreover, now adopted the custom of placing an image of the Genius of Augustus among their *lares,* those protecting deities of the crossings of roads and streets. The idea was to make his genius, or guardian spirit, the center of public worship, and hence willingness to sacrifice to the guardian spirit of the princeps came to be the test of loyalty to the government. It is hardly strange that on his death Augustus, who had refused deification by the Romans while he was alive, should have been placed among the gods. An inscription found in Asia Minor proclaims that "Augustus is the paternal Zeus and the savior of the whole race of man, who fulfills all prayers, even more than we ask. The land and sea enjoy peace; cities flourish; everywhere are harmony and prosperity and happiness."

Augustus, however, did not have to wait till the end of his principate to witness a return of ancient ways. In 17 B.C. Rome celebrated the seventh centenary of its founding, as it was then calculated, and as part of the magnificent ceremonies the poet Horace composed an ode—the famous *Carmen Saeculare*—in which he said, "Now Faith and Peace and Honor and Antique Modesty and neglected Virtue dare return, and Plenty appears in view, rich with her overflowing horn."

THE PROVINCES AND FRONTIERS

The Roman Empire was vast in extent; diverse in race, language, and custom; highly civilized yet thinly populated; and in some areas hardly more than tribal in outlook; but in any case it was regarded by contemporary inhabitants as equivalent to the civilized world. With the exception of the Parthians, civilized people did not relish the thought of living beyond its confines. The administration of the empire produced reform, and no more solid or splendid achievement can be credited to Augustus than his accomplishment in bringing peace, prosperity, and orderly government to the Greco-Roman world. Augustus practiced the same conservatism in the imperial sphere as he did elsewhere. He took the empire as he found it, built on its strength, and controlled abuses. After all, it was an achievement of the highest order to bring peace to a world that had known little but war and to give it just and skillful government in place of rapacious governors. For the blessings he brought the world, said Pliny, "the human race decrees Augustus a civic crown."

For purposes of administration Augustus divided the empire into two large groups of provinces, those that needed legionary forces and those that did not. The former were close to the frontiers, and he proposed to keep them under his personal appointees, since in the last analysis his power rested on the army; the remaining provinces were governed by men elected by the senate. It must not be supposed that Augustus thereupon dismissed the senatorial provinces from his mind; on the contrary, he insisted on efficient government, reviewed their situation from time to time, held the governors liable to the same laws of extortion as applied to the governors of the so-called imperial provinces, and placed them all on salary. At the same time, he used senators in large numbers for the government of the imperial provinces and periodically rendered the senate an account of his administration. Thus there was considerable uniformity in provincial rule, and as far as the titles of officials and their tasks were concerned, there was little change from republican days.

Senatorial Provinces. The governors of the senatorial provinces served one year; they were called *proconsuls* and were chosen by lot from former consuls and praetors. The chief senatorial provinces, representing the inner core of the empire, were Baetica, in southern Spain; Gallia Narbonensis (Provence); Sicily; Macedonia; Achaea; Crete and Cyrene together; Cyprus; Bithynia; Asia; and Africa including Numidia.

Imperial Provinces. The governors of the imperial provinces served as long as the princeps desired, often for many years; their chief test was loyalty to the princeps, but also efficient government. The more important provinces were governed by senators, called *legates,* as Augustus, as a rule, remained in Rome. The governors of the other imperial provinces were known as *procurators,* or occasionally as *prefects,* and were equestrians. The imperial provinces, forming roughly a ring around the empire and counting those created by Augustus, were chiefly Tarraconensis (northwestern Spain); Lusitania (Portugal); Aquitania, Lugdunensis, and Belgica, all in Gaul, with Lugdunum (Lyons) used as a common capital; the Maritime and Cottian Alps; Raetia and Noricum on the Danube; Pannonia (Hungary); Illyria or Dalmatia (along the eastern Adriatic); Moesia (Bulgaria, in part); Sardinia; Galatia and Cilicia in Asia Minor; Syria; and Palestine (added soon after Herod's death in 4 B.C.). A changing frontier, or internal conditions, might alter the status of a province. Egypt was a special case, forming a great prefecture under an equestrian, who was directly responsible to Augustus. (See the map, rear endpaper.)

The Frontiers. Finally, Rome rounded out her frontiers and protected her borders by a system of client kingdoms, such as Mauretania, Thrace, Cappadocia, Lesser Armenia, and Palmyra (in the Syrian desert). These states, which Rome found it convenient not to absorb outright, furnished troops and followed Rome's foreign policy but were otherwise sovereign. The chief threat to the Roman peace lay along the Rhine and the Danube. Parthia, as the only well-organized state outside the empire, was potentially dangerous, but Augustus for a time succeeded in placing a friendly monarch on the throne; the overlordship of Armenia was an endless bone of contention between Rome and Parthia. Rome had little to fear from Arabia, and almost nothing from the Nubians, who lived along Egypt's southern border. Britain still lay outside the Empire.

The Military Establishment. It seems rather extraordinary, in the light of history, that to protect an empire that stretched from the North Sea to the Red Sea, and from the Atlantic to the Euphrates—an area of about 3.5 million square miles—Rome needed a professional standing army of less than 300,000 men. This was due, in the first place, to the favorable political situation; and, secondarily, to such things as Augustus' desire to move the reminders of war to the background, to keep taxes low and the treasury full, and to limit, as far as possible, the enlistment of legionaries to Roman citizens who volunteered for a term of twenty years. There were between eighteen and twenty-eight legions during Augustus' regime—and at the end, twenty-five—each theoretically composed of 6,000 men, all of whom were infantry except for 120 cavalry. Auxiliaries of approximately the same number were attached to the legions; these were provincials who, at the conclusion of twenty-five years' service, received Roman citizenship and perhaps also allotments of land and bonuses. The 9,000 praetorian guards, who were Roman citizens and enlisted for sixteen years, and urban cohorts and the police and fire departments, which were organized in military form, policed Rome. The purpose of the standing navy, which had its main bases at Ravenna and Misenum, was to patrol the Mediterranean and adjacent seas and the frontier rivers.

The Treasury. In order to support the expensive military establishment, Augustus set up a separate military treasury, known as the *aerarium militare;* as the richest man in the world, he contributed to it from his own wealth, while other funds came from a 1 per cent sales tax and a 5 per cent inheritance tax, which was limited to Roman citizens. A 4 per cent tax on the manumission of slaves constituted another indirect tax. The chief direct tax, on land, was paid by the provincials; to ensure that provincial taxation was fair, a census was taken periodically. The regular state treasury, known as the *aerarium Saturni,* derived its income from Italy and the senatorial provinces and was in the charge of the senate. Taxation was not graduated.

The Empire's Chief Military Problem. Although he was not a brilliant military commander, Augustus, after his successful campaigning in Spain, spent the years 22-19 B.C. in the East, his chief purpose being to redeem Rome's honor by recovering the standards lost by Crassus at Carrhae. War with Parthia was avoided, and he accomplished his ends by diplomacy. In the future, however, Augustus was prone to leave active campaigning to his legates. The fundamental military problem before the Roman Empire was to establish a secure frontier in the northeast and the northwest; that is to say, it was necessary to push on to the Danube and the Rhine, or rather, if possible, to the Elbe and even beyond, which would give a much shorter line to defend between the North and Black seas. The first step in this broad strategy was taken in 16 B.C., when Augustus' stepsons, Tiberius and Drusus, conquered the area along the Upper Danube and organized it as the provinces of Raetia and Noricum. Then in 12 B.C. Tiberius conquered eastward and created the provinces of Moesia and Pannonia. Meanwhile Drusus was active in Lower Germany, where he built a series of forts, constructed a fleet, and dug a canal from the Rhine to the Zuider Zee. Deliberately planning each operation, Drusus advanced to the Elbe—an extraordinary feat of arms—but on his return to winter quarters he fatally injured himself by a fall from his horse (9 B.C.). Tiberius hastened to his brother's side, and with a rare devotion brought the body from the depths of the German forest to Rome. It was a great loss to the imperial family, for Drusus was an able man and popular with the army.

Tiberius was likewise the idol of the troops, for he watched over them and shared their hardships, but in 6 B.C. his differences with Augustus came to a head and he retired to Rhodes. After a decade Augustus, who had suffered a series of personal misfortunes, recalled Tiberius and adopted him as his son and successor. Once again

Tiberius' appointment was to Germany. By A.D. 5 he reached the Elbe, and then, just as he was planning to crush the Marcomanni in modern Bohemia and thus eradicate all signs of resistance between the Elbe and the Danube, a terrible revolt broke out in Illyria. The Pannonians, who also were adverse to Roman military service, joined the movement and triggered unpopular conscription in Italy. After three years Tiberius reestablished order, but at this juncture (A.D. 9) the Germans revolted. Their leader was Arminius, a chieftain's son who had received his education in Rome and, like his people, resented the tyrannical rule of the Roman general Publius Quintilius Varus. The Germans ambushed Varus, as he was leading his three legions through the Teutoberg Forest on his way to winter quarters, and annihilated his army. Augustus, his spirit broken, from time to time would cry, "Varus, Varus, give me back my legions."

Tiberius, with Drusus' son, Germanicus, eventually restored peace along the Rhine. But the Elbe, perforce, was abandoned, and the decision not to expand any further, which Augustus at his death called on Rome to respect, was followed in the future. A challenging speculation is to what extent the history of Europe would have been different had Rome succeeded in incorporating and civilizing the great reservoir of Germans who were destined to engulf the empire (map, rear endpaper).

RELIGION, LITERATURE, AND ART

Augustus determined to lead the people back to the simple life of their ancestors, who had made the city great, and to the official Greco-Roman religion, for this, he thought, was the best way to combat new ideas and customs. His law, albeit unsuccessful in the long run, to encourage larger families by giving the parents special privileges was part of this program. For similar reasons he revived the festivals and priestly colleges, became *pontifex maximus,* and permitted the growth throughout the empire of the imperial cult of Roma and Augustus, which identified religion and the state with the princeps; and in Italy he allowed the spread of the worship of the Genius of Augustus. For this same reason, too, he meticulously restored old temples and built new ones. The Secular Games of 17 B.C., for which Horace composed his famous ode, reflected a rebirth of religion and patriotism, of faith and pride.

Livy.   To all this the writers of prose and poetry made their own particular contributions, stirring appeals to the people to lay aside the bitterness of party strife for the blessings of peace. With the encouragement of Augustus and Maecenas, his friend and patron of the arts, the Golden Age of Roman literature aimed to purify and ennoble the present by bringing it the life of the good and great past. Livy (59 B.C.-A.D. 17), from Padua in northern Italy and the most eminent author of prose at this time, wrote an eloquent history of Rome, *From the Founding of the City,* in one hundred and forty-two books, of which only thirty-five survive. Vivid and interesting, they are our chief source for the earlier periods of Roman history. Livy loved what he supposed to be the truth and the right, but he was primarily a stylist rather than an objective or scientifically informed historian. His admiration of law and order and his hatred of violence and vulgarity romanticized the deeds of old, while the vast compass and the stately style of his history helped celebrate Roman government. Other histories—such as those of Dionysius of Halicarnassus and Diodorus of Sicily—and the *Geography* of Strabo were written in Greek, for the Augustan Age had two literatures.

Vergil. The greatest poet of this period, one of the greatest who has ever lived, was Vergil (70-19 B.C.), from Mantua in northern Italy. Inspired by the majesty of Rome, and intensely patriotic, Vergil expressed more perfectly than any other wroter the ideals of Augustan Rome. His principal work, a long epic poem called the *Aeneid* (ca. 26-19 B.C.), tells the story of the wanderings of the Trojan Aeneas and the beginnings of Rome and at the same time glorifies the imperial family, whose descent he traced from the hero of his poem. The lofty style is sustained by high moral aims, which clearly show that the secret of Rome's success lay in *pietas,* a stern regard for duty. The narrative itself is lively and dramatic, graceful and tender, yet moved also by a certain underlying sense of pessimism. Vergil's *Georgics,* on the other hand, (ca. 37-31 B.C.), sing the praises of country life, the affairs of husbandry, the virtues and toil of a day on the farm. Pastoral themes form the subject of the *Eclogues* (ca. 42-38 B.C.), the fourth of which, with its promise of a messianic savior, won Vergil a special place in mediaeval thought as a prophet of the birth of Christ.

Horace and Ovid. Another poet to enjoy the patronage of Maecenas was Horace (65-8 B.C.), who was born in southern Italy of a freedman. Author of polished lyrics—odes, satires, and epistles—Horace was the poet of contentment and common sense. Leave the future to the gods and enjoy your life, he taught. A comfortable villa and some shady nook in the summer, and in winter a roaring fire, good wine, pleasant friends, and a mind free from care make an ideal life. Here was a lesson for the world, after the stormy end of the republic, and succeeding generations as well have found him a source of refreshment and delight. His style frequently owes its inspiration to Greek models, the *Epodes* in particular deriving much from the techniques of Hellenistic poetic genres, especially the epigram. Of the elegiac poets—Propertius, Tibullus, and Ovid—Ovid (43 B.C.-A.D. 17) best represents the attitude that would not be downed, a superficial interest in life and a conviction, one might almost say, that the end of things, rather than the beginning, had been reached. His *Art of Love* is a handbook of seduction, written in defiance of Augustus' moral legislation; the *Fasti* tells of Roman festivals; and the *Metamorphoses* preserves, most fortunately, much of Greek mythology. Ovid got into trouble with Augustus (adultery with one of the emperor's granddaughters is alleged) and spent his last years in exile at Tomi on the Black Sea coast.

Architecture. Art and architecture, no less than literature, did their share to glorify Augustus and imperial Rome. Now, without any question, the capital of the world, Rome was copied throughout the provinces, and it was the rare town that could not boast its forum and temples, its triumphal arches and baths and theaters. In Rome itself Augustus repaired eighty-two temples and rebuilt the Capitoline temple of Jupiter. In the Forum, beside the spot where Caesar's body had been

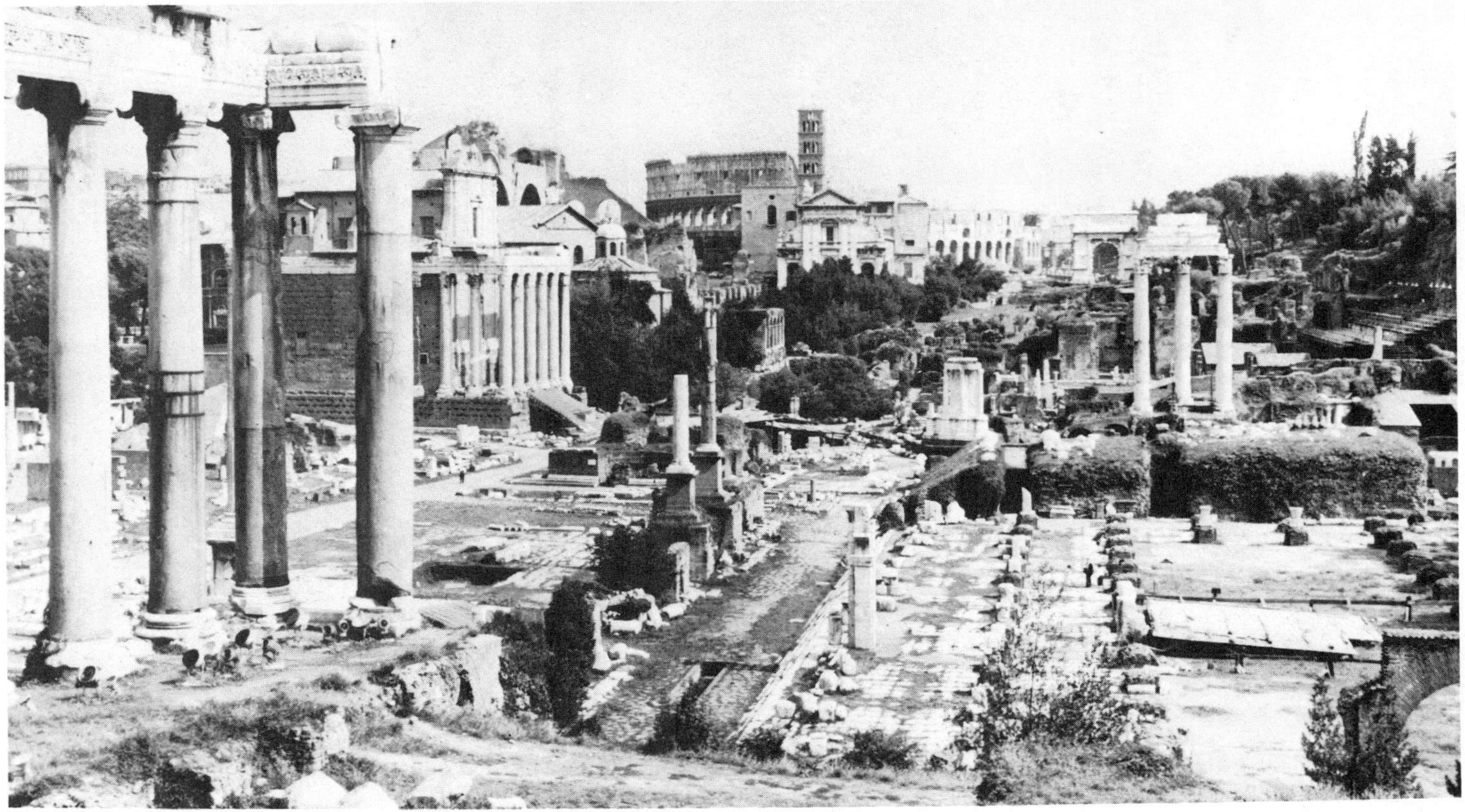

FIGURE 56. The Forum, Rome, as it appears today.

burned, he built a temple of the Divine Julius and, nearby, a temple of Venus Genetrix, the goddess from whom the Julian house traced its descent. Further to associate himself with the gods and to suggest his protective power, Augustus erected on the Palatine, near his own residence, a Greek temple of Apollo, the Averter of Evil, and joined to it libraries for public use. Here, too, was the shrine of Vesta. The new Forum of Augustus, with its monumental arches, was dominated by a temple to another divine ancestor of the imperial family, Mars the Avenger.

It was in the Campus Martius that the greatest building activity of Augustus took place. Here were the mausoleum for the imperial family; the baths of Agrippa; and the Pantheon, which survives today in the vast domed structure rebuilt by the later emperor, Hadrian (p. 453). Agrippa, to whom Augustus delegated much responsibility for the construction of public buildings, erected the Pantheon. The freestone arches of the past could not be used for large structures, because of their thrusts, and therefore solid concrete domes, resting on solid walls, were invented. An excellent concrete was obtained by the mixing of volcanic ash with lime and crushed stones.

Sculpture. Roman art, though reaching out for new forms and ideas, was rooted in its Hellenistic past. Realism was more popular than ever and is illustrated in the portraiture and coins, the gems and metalwork of the period. The Roman loved to decorate arches and other structures with reliefs depicting Rome's past or the important matters of the present. A beautiful example of this attitude, perhaps the most beautiful monument of its day, is the famous Altar of the Augustan Peace.

FIGURE 57. Relief from the *Ara Pacis.* Imperial procession.

Fototeca Unione

FIGURE 58. The "Gemma Augustea" cameo, depicting the glorification of Augustus. Late 1st century B.C.

Richly adorned with flowers and fruit and other details suggesting abundance, the reliefs show Augustus and his family, priests and magistrates, marching in stately procession to the sacrifices in honor of peace. On other panels, representations of Aeneas arriving in Latium, Mother Earth with her babes, and Roma seated on armor add another dimension to the whole by means of myth and allegory. But the *Ara Pacis* does more than glorify the great founder of a new era. It symbolizes one indisputable achievement of a mighty empire, the winning of prosperity and universal peace.

THE SUCCESSION

It was ever on Augustus' mind to secure a peaceful succession.[2] This he did by designating a member of his own family, or, if necessary, by adopting an individual and having him marry into his family; he then provided his heir with proper authority by sharing the tribunician and proconsular powers with him. Thus Augustus

---

[2] Genealogical Table, p. 529.

established the precedent that others followed, but he himself lived so long, though he was never in excellent health, that fate struck down one of his successors after another. In the beginning it was clear that his nephew Marcellus would succeed him, especially since the youth had married Julia, Augustus' daughter by his second wife and his only child. When Marcellus died in 23 B.C., Augustus chose his friend and helper, Agrippa, as his successor and new son-in-law, but Agrippa died in 12 B.C., leaving his sons by Julia, Gaius and Lucius, Augustus' grandsons (among other grandchildren), the closest heirs of his body, whom he chose as his most likely successors.

The boys might need a guardian should Augustus die prematurely, and to give them one the emperor turned to his stepson Tiberius, son of his third wife, the empress Livia, by her ex-husband Tiberius Claudius Nero. Tiberius was forced to divorce his own wife and marry the twice widowed Julia. The pair were uncongenial, and Julia turned out to be an adultress. For this reason and because he realized that the emperor preferred Gaius and Lucius to him as successors, Tiberius withdrew to Rhodes in 6 B.C. Julia's profligacy was subsequently discovered and she was banished. Gaius and Lucius died, and the emperor was thus forced to recall Tiberius in A.D. 4 and to give him powers associated with a successor-designate.

Death of Augustus (A.D. 14).   Augustus died at Nola in Campania on August 19, A.D. 14, an unhappy old man of seventy-five. He had already prepared an account of what he had accomplished—the so-called Deeds of Augustus—and this was set up outside his tomb in the Campus Martius and throughout the empire, for there were few to doubt that he was one of the greatest benefactors of the human race. A copy of this record has been found in Asia Minor at Ancyra (Ankara); it is an important document, needless to say, for understanding a very enigmatic man who brought the world from one era into another.

29

The Early Empire
(A.D. 14–192)

THE JULIO–CLAUDIAN EMPERORS (A.D. 14–68)

Tiberius (14-37). Tiberius was the son of Livia, or Augusta, as Augustus had decreed that his wife should be called, and Tiberius Claudius Nero. Already the stepson, he became also the son-in-law and adopted son of Augustus. The two aristocratic families, now joined together—the Julian and the Claudian—gave Rome her emperors for the next half century.[1] Since the welfare of the entire empire depended in large part on the ability and personality of the princeps, the ancient historians wrote their accounts chiefly in terms of the reigning emperor, his relations with the senate, and his defense of the frontiers. Spicy gossip about life in the capital interested some of these historians, but the principal charge that can be laid against the greatest of them, Tacitus, is his senatorial bias. He left, in his resentment, a one-sided picture that has prejudiced the judgment of posterity.

The choice of emperors became in time a matter for the senate or the armies to decide, but concerning the accession of Tiberius there could be no doubt. His personal connection with Augustus was in itself decisive, even though no formal scheme of hereditary succession had been established, and, moreover, he held the *imperium* and the tribunician and proconsular powers. Accordingly, on the death of Augustus, the senate elected Tiberius emperor (14). As one of his first official acts, he arranged the deification of his predecessor.

Tiberius was fifty-five years of age. Scholarly and peace-loving, he had been compelled by circumstances to spend his youth in government service, commanding armies, and journeying to exposed points of the empire. A popular general and a skillful administrator, he had had unusually wide experience. When, finally, Augustus settled on him as successor, every one else having died, Tiberius found himself immediately engaged in military and civil problems. As emperor, he was surrounded with a multitude of tasks and by a cringing, suspicious senate, which, while shirking responsibility, still longed for the reality of government. Upon his accession he may have been sincere in his request for an excuse from further public service, or at most for a limited share in the government. However that may be, the senate voted

---

[1] Henceforth all dates in the text are A.D., unless otherwise designated. Genealogical Table, p. 529; List of Roman Emperors, pp. 527 ff.

him the *imperium* and tribunician power for life, the former having been granted Augustus in blocks of years only.

Frontiers and Provinces. Immediately after Tiberius' accession, the armies of Illyria and the Rhineland revolted in the hope of winning a shorter term of service, higher pay, and larger bonuses. Drusus, the son of Tiberius, quelled the mutiny in Illyria, while that on the Rhine was put down with difficulty by the commanding general, Germanicus, the son of Tiberius' brother. Germanicus, who was an independent spirit and had already been adopted by Tiberius, hoped to emulate the example of his father, Drusus of German fame, and led his legions across the Rhine and avenged the defeat of Varus. But as Augustus in his will had advised his successors not to extend the boundaries of the empire, Tiberius would not permit his nephew to waste the resources of the government in attempting further conquests and recalled him. The provinces of Upper and Lower Germany were, however, formed on the left bank of the Rhine, and at the same time the three Gallic provinces—Aquitania, Lugdunensis, and Belgica—were separated. No important war disturbed the remainder of Tiberius' reign, for the risings in Gaul (in 21) and Numidia were neither serious nor prolonged. Of far greater contemporary interest was the continuation of reasonably friendly relations with Armenia and Parthia and the transference of Cappadocia from the status of a client kingdom to that of a province.

Administration. Throughout his reign, Tiberius devoted himself to administrative work, and in this he showed remarkable ability. The provinces commanded his particular attention, and in various ways—for example, by rebuilding twelve cities of Asia Minor that had been destroyed by earthquake—he won the respect of the empire. This is not to say that he was popular in Rome itself, for his careful use of public funds was resented. The senate would have preferred to see him pensioning noble spendthrifts, and the populace grumbled because he fed them poorly and provided infrequent shows. Tiberius, however, desired the cooperation of the senate, and as an indication of this, he transferred the election of magistrates from the centuriate assembly to the senate. But relations between senate and emperor were strained; Tiberius was by nature a suspicious and devious man, and the atmosphere at Rome was filled with intrigues and plots, real and imagined. To escape this situation, Tiberius finally, in 27, withdrew to the island of Capri, in the Bay of Naples, and there he remained most of the time until his death. He left the administration of Rome to the city prefect and of the empire to Sejanus, the prefect of the praetorian guard, encamped just outside the city.

Tiberius' Last Years. In 19, Germanicus, his nephew, died mysteriously in the East. Probably he was murdered by Piso, the legate of Syria, but his widow, Agrippina, who was the daughter of Agrippa and Julia (Augustus' daughter), suspected Tiberius. Then Drusus, Tiberius' son and heir, died in 23, allegedly poisoned by Sejanus, who also murdered or exiled Agrippina and her children. Sejanus himself seems to have planned some sort of coup d'état against Tiberius. In any case, the emperor dramatically had his minister arrested and executed in 31.

He enforced rigorously the law of treason (*lex de maiestate*). The first law of treason, dating back to 103 B.C., was amended by either Julius Caesar or Augustus. It embraced conspiracy, libel, and slander against the emperor and adultery with

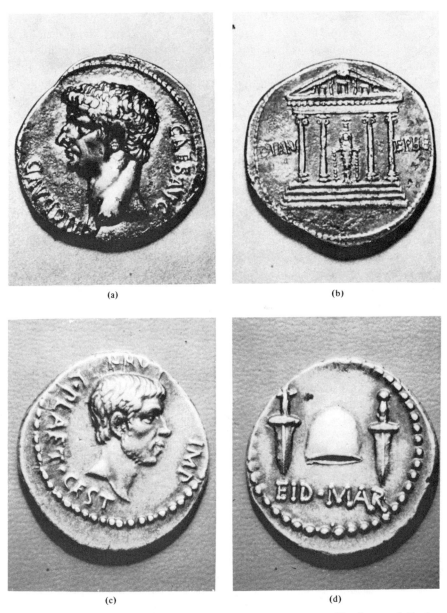

(a)

(b)

(c)

(d)

FIGURE 59. Roman coins. (a) The Emperor Claudius and (b) The Temple of Diana, A.D. 41–45. (c) Bearded head of M. Junius Brutus and (d) Cap of Liberty between two daggers, 43–42 B.C.

a member of his family. It was notoriously open to flexible interpretation by all suspicious emperors, beginning with Tiberius. Having no public prosecutor, Rome had always depended on private informers (*delatores*) for bringing accusations.

Encouraged by Tiberius, these informers caused the death of many persons, not all of whom were guilty. No one felt safe, least of all the senators, who in their haste to please Tiberius condemned men for the most trivial offenses. Tiberius thus grew more and more hateful to the nobility and even to the plebeians. It was not that he was vicious; rather, he was a stern, unsympathetic, and, at the end, thoroughly embittered moralist, unsocial, tactless, and economical, but, withal, an able and conscientious ruler. It is hardly surprising that the senate, piqued by his retirement to Capri and angered by the informers, should have refused to deify him on his death in 37.

Caligula (37-41). The senate conferred imperial powers on Tiberius' grand-nephew Gaius, the surviving son of Germanicus and Agrippina, whom Tiberius had adopted before his death. Gaius is better known to history as Caligula, "Little Boots," a nickname given him by his father's troops in the Rhineland. He was now twenty-five years of age and lost little time in putting to death his only possible rival, Tiberius' grandson. At the opening of his reign, no one could have guessed the inner secrets of his mind. Just as the soldiers had been fond of him as a boy, so now he became a favorite of the senate and the people, who cherished the memory of his father. He won enormous popularity by reducing taxes and spending huge sums on public amusements, but it was not long before he had squandered the surplus left in the treasury by Tiberius. This lack of funds led him to confiscations and murder. His health, it seems, was poor and his mind unsound, so that excitement and dissipation soon made him insane.

Tyranny. Thereafter Caligula's life was a series of extravagant and grotesque caprices. He ruled as an autocrat, without regard to the senate. Whereas Caesar and Augustus had been deified after death, Caligula demanded worship while he still lived, even from the Jews, who because of their religious convictions had been exempted in the past. To emphasize his connections with the gods, he built a bridge from the Palatine to the Capitoline, where the temple of Jupiter was located. In the foreign field he threatened Germany and Britain and annexed Mauretania. Fortunately he did not live long enough to make his tyranny widely felt. In 41 he was killed by some officers of the praetorian guard.

Claudius (41-54). Some senators wished to restore the republic, others wished a continuation of the principate with themselves as candidates for emperor. In the end, the decision rested with the praetorians, whose preferred position depended on the continuance of the present form of government. Their nominee was the uncle of Caligula, Tiberius Claudius Germanicus Caesar, the brother of Germanicus. Exacting from him the promise of a large reward of money, the praetorians forced the senate to salute Claudius as Augustus and to grant him the usual powers. Claudius was fifty-one years of age, grotesque in manners, and lacking dignity, yet possessing a certain as yet hidden shrewdness. Mistakenly considered a learned fool, his reign nevertheless marks the beginning of a new era in imperial history.

Provincial Policy. One of Claudius' certainly more attractive qualities was his open-mindedness in treating Rome's provincial subjects. His own birth in the Gallic city of Lugdunum (Lyons), together with his scholarly training, broadened his political vision as well as his sympathy, so that he rediscovered, so to speak, the secret of Rome's greatness: liberal extension of the citizenship. According to the census of 48, there were seven million Roman citizens in the empire, an increase of more than a million since Augustus' day. Claudius was especially generous in his grant of citizenship to Gauls and allowed some of their nobles to become senators in Rome. He founded many colonies throughout the empire and, unlike Caligula, gave the Jews religious freedom. To provincial administration he devoted careful attention. Mingled with this wisdom was firmness in punishing offenders, in putting down revolts, and in protecting frontiers. One of his generals, the future emperor Vespasian, began the conquest of Britain in 43, occupying the island as far as the Thames. Complete occupation of Britain, however, did not take place for more than a generation. In 44 Mauretania was divided into two provinces, and in 46 the client kingdom of Thrace was annexed (map, rear endpaper).

Domestic Policy. Claudius' domestic policy was marked by humane legislation in favor of slaves. With a view to preventing famine at Rome, he insured importers of grain against loss by storms at sea and dug a new harbor at Ostia, providing it with warehouses and docks. He built roads and two magnificent aqueducts for Rome. Toward the senate Claudius was respectful, though he did not trust it and as censor weeded out some disloyal members. Notwithstanding plots against his life, Claudius restricted the enforcement of the law of treason and the work of informers.

His distrust of senators and equestrians, moreover, led Claudius to give unprecedented power to the freedmen of his household, who functioned as his helpers and secretaries, keeping the accounts, handling his correspondence, and dealing with petitions. Here we have one facet of the development of the famous imperial bureaucracy, with its many secretaries, which became the support of undisguised monarchy. One freedman, Pallas, was appointed secretary of the treasury, which was set up to receive all the funds due the emperor. His rival, Narcissus, was secretary of the imperial correspondence. These freedmen feathered their own nests, of course, and actually sold posts to the highest bidder. Their ascendancy over Claudius was pernicious. But the worst feature of the reign of Claudius was the evil influence of his wives. Messalina, his third, bore him two children, Britannicus and Octavia, but when she became implicated in a plot to overthrow the regime, Claudius, at the suggestion of Narcissus, had her executed. Then, on the advice of Pallas, he married his niece Agrippina the Younger, the daughter of Germanicus and Agrippina. This woman had previously married Gnaeus Domitius Ahenobarbus, by whom she had a son, Domitius. Claudius now adopted the boy as Nero Claudius Caesar and allowed him, at the age of fifteen, to marry his stepsister Octavia. The following year (54), to ensure the accession of her son, Agrippina poisoned Claudius.

Nero (54-68). Sixteen years of age, and utterly inexperienced, Nero became emperor of Rome with the consent of the senate and by a gift to the praetorians. Since he showed more taste for dancing and music than for official work, his first years were marked by good government, which was largely in the hands of the senate. Nero himself was advised by two able men, his tutor Seneca, the Stoic philosopher from Spain, and Burrus, the praetorian prefect. In the beginning, however, he was careful to execute his stepbrother, Brittanicus, a possible rival, and

German Archeological Institute

FIGURE 60. Agrippina the Younger.

then in 59, to allow himself free rein in his revels, he ordered the death of his overly ambitious mother. Not much later he caused the death of his wife, Octavia, and married his mistress, Sabina. These crimes touched only Rome and the empire itself prospered.

Despotism. The personal rule of Nero began in 62, when Burrus died and Seneca retired to private life. It was a capricious despotism, short, and affecting the provinces only near its end. Nero has come for many to personify the degeneration of Rome in taste and morals, for Rome had become, in the words of Tacitus, a place "where all things hideous and shameful from every part of the world find their center and are popular." The current companion of Nero was Tigellinus, the new praetorian prefect, who urged him on in dissipation and the cultivation of his artistic instincts. The conservative element of Rome was scandalized when the emperor appeared in public and gave a musical performance. Convinced of his genius, Nero visited Greece in 66 and was so overcome by the plaudits of a clever people that he granted them freedom from taxation.

The Fire at Rome and the Christians. Nero's extravagance caused a return of terror to Rome's upper classes. To find money for his lavish life, he encouraged informers, executed people, and confiscated their property. Many conspiracies, naturally, were formed against him, and in suppressing one of them, led by the senator Piso, Nero put to death Seneca and his nephew, the poet Lucan. Nevertheless, when the great fire of 64 destroyed more than half of Rome, he was enough the humanitarian to shelter and feed the sufferers and rebuild the city on a grander scale. He also seized the opportunity to erect on the Esquiline Hill his own fabulous Golden House. To find a scapegoat for the conflagration, he accused the Christians of having set it. They were an obscure and unpopular sect known to harbor apocalyptic ideas. His persecution of the Christians, the first in their history, was limited to those within Rome.

Armenia and Britain. Though he later put him to death, Nero was fortunate in his general, Corbulo, to whom the command of the East had been given. The Parthian king, Vologases, wished to place his brother, Tiridates, on the Armenian throne, but this was a threat to Roman prestige; the matter was solved after several years by having Tiridates journey to Rome, where Nero pompously crowned him king of Armenia (63). In Britain, however, more serious trouble stirred. Here the Roman dominion had been extended and included even the island of Mona (Anglesea), the center of the Druid religion. A tribal queen, Boudicca (Boadicea), aroused by Roman brutality, led a general uprising, which resulted in the massacre of thousands of Romans and the destruction of Londinium (London) and the provincial capital of Camulodunum (Colchester). Only with difficulty was the insurrection quelled (60).

Nero's Death. Field army commanders eventually found Nero's capricious tyranny personally threatening. The first general to revolt was Vindex, legate of Gallia Lugdunensis. Though he was put down by Verginius, the governor of Upper Germany, the latter's troops joined the revolt, as did Galba, governor of Hither Spain. A march was begun on Rome. The praetorians deserted Nero, and the senate declared him a public enemy (68). Nero fled the city, and when he realized that all was lost, he ordered a faithful freedman to stab him.

THE YEAR OF THE FOUR EMPERORS (A.D. 68–69)

The Military Basis of Authority. Thus ended the Julio-Claudian line of Roman emperors. Now the military basis of the princeps' authority, once carefully concealed, became all too obvious. The praetorians saluted as emperor the Spanish legate, Sulpicius Galba, an able provincial governor, who was to prove wholly unequal to his new tasks. Tacitus' verdict was that he would have been judged fit to rule had he not ruled. Galba was too indiscreet and obstinate, too severe a disciplinarian, and when he failed to pay the praetorians, they killed him. In January 69, the praetorians selected as emperor Marcus Salvius Otho, once a roisterer in Nero's youthful society. The troops on the Rhine, however, nominated their own general, Aulus Vitellius, the legate of Lower Germany, and marched with him on Rome. Otho was defeated in battle at Cremona in northern Italy and killed himself (April 69). Vitellius, the new emperor, was good-natured, but he was also a sluggard and a glutton. Only a few months remained to Vitellius, for the army of the East had selected its own emperor, Vespasian, the legate of Judea, who was then engaged in a great war against the Jews. Vespasian cut off Rome's grain supply by seizing

Egypt, while the Danubian and other legions marched on Italy. A victory was won at Cremona, Rome was sacked, and Vitellius was killed. Early the next year (70) the new emperor came to Rome to accept from the senate the powers already conferred by the army.

Thus in a little more than twelve months Rome had seen the making of four emperors, all of them the nominees of the soldiers. Says Tacitus, "The fatal secret of the Empire had been discovered, that emperors could be chosen elsewhere than in Rome." It was inevitable that those who protected the empire should claim a voice in selecting the ruler, and that, in the absence of a representative system, the armies, by substituting civil war for the ballot, should take the place of the old republican assemblies. This military revolution had some good results, however, for it ended in setting up an able ruler. Vespasian was the first in a line of emperors trained in the camp, who were to give the empire its most prosperous era; they were capable, experienced, and broad-minded men, uncorrupted by the atmosphere of Rome, though one of them was destined to play the tyrant.

THE FLAVIAN DYNASTY (A.D. 69–96)

Vespasian (69-79). Titus Flavius Vespasianus, who founded the Flavian dynasty, is spoken of as the second founder of the principate. Not only was he a remarkably able ruler, but he gave to his reign certain new and significant characteristics. For example, he took the title *imperator* (largely disused since Augustus' day), which rather candidly admitted the military basis of his power; and he adopted the name Caesar as a symbol of legitimacy. From the beginning, moreover, Vespasian associated his son Titus with himself in the *imperium* and tribunician authority. His action, which was accompanied by the remark that his sons or no one would succeed him, had the advantage of establishing a dynastic succession and of lessening the possibility of war, but the weakness of the principle, whether applied to Rome or to another state, was that it was only through war (or murder) that an unfit ruler could be removed. Clothed though it may have been in constitutional forms, the theory of hereditary military monarchy received great impetus from Vespasian.

Rebellion in Germany and Gaul (69-70). Vespasian came from a Sabine town— the Italian municipality of Reate—of an equestrian family. It was fortunate that he was conscientious and industrious, because Rome was threatened with serious trouble. A Batavian chief, Julius Civilis, led an uprising in Lower Germany, in which he was joined by part of the army of the Rhineland and by some Gallic tribes. Their hope of establishing a Gallic state with its capital at Augusta Treverorum (Trier or Trèves) was destroyed by energetic measures in 70.

Rebellion in Judea (66-70). War in the East antedated Vespasian's reign, for the rebellion in Judea had broken out in 66. The Jews, whether in Judea or Alexandria, were liable neither to military service nor to the obligations of the imperial cult. Rome's supporters in Judea were, as so often happened, the rich, known as the Sadducees. Their rivals, not so prosperous, were religiously conservative Pharisees, but responsibility for the rebellion lay with the Zealots, who felt that their religion forbade them to give political allegiance to Rome. They believed that Yahweh would protect his holy temple, where Caligula had planned to install a statue of himself, and that at the critical moment the Messiah would come to save his people from the oppressor. In 67 Vespasian moved to put down this nationalistic revolt, and on his elevation to the principate, he left the completion of the task to his son Titus. The Jews, who were now besieged in Jerusalem, fought with fanatical zeal, but after five months the temple and Mount Zion were captured (70). Vast numbers of Jews were killed during the war, other thousands taken captive. The destruction of the Temple of Yahweh in Jerusalem had the effect of severing completely the ties between the Christians and cultic Judaism, which ties in any case had been loosening during the preceding generation. The survivors were permitted their previous immunities on payment of a head tax. The arch of Titus still stands in the Roman Forum as a memorial of his victory.

Administration. Although Vespasian, and not the senate, ruled the empire, his reign began a new era of better imperial relations with that body, although he did not tolerate any disrespect from individual senators. As the old republican nobility had either died out or been executed, Vespasian replaced it with new families—the ablest and most loyal he could find—from Italy and the provinces, especially from Gaul and Spain. The equestrians, recruited in like manner, devoted themselves in increasing numbers to the imperial service.

The excesses of Nero and the civil war following his death had emptied the treasury, so that Vespasian was compelled to practice strict economy and to levy new taxes. As censor in 74 he ordered another census of the empire. The resources of the Roman world were so fairly and exactly established that he was able to refill the treasury with surprisingly little friction. This was the more remarkable because, in addition to repairing the damage to Rome caused by the war with Vitellius, he built a temple of peace and created a new forum of his own. Part of the Golden House of Nero was demolished to make room for the Flavian amphitheater, known as the Colosseum; this was finished not much later by Titus, as were some magnificent public baths.

The Provinces. Vespasian supported orderly municipal life throughout the empire as the best means of promoting peace and prosperity. His extension of Roman citizenship, especially among the Spaniards, was accompanied by the grant of Latin rights to all the non-Roman communities of Spain. The whole scheme of provincial administration was examined, with the result that most of the remaining client kingdoms, such as Commagene, were abolished and became provinces or were added to existing ones. The Euphrates and other frontiers were strengthened; a military camp was established at Vindobona (Vienna) on the Danube; and, as a result of the lesson learned in the Gallic rebellion, discipline was restored in the army, and for a time the auxiliaries were stationed in areas far from their homes to lessen the feeling of kinship that they might have for the people they garrisoned. The empire now had about thirty legions (and the usual auxiliaries).

Titus (79-81). The senate deified Vespasian on his death in 79, a stamp of approval that, it was hoped, would inspire other emperors to rule with proper

FIGURE 61. Wall painting from Pompeii.

regard for regular constitutional forms and in the interests of the upper classes. He
was succeeded by his son Titus, "the delight and darling of mankind," as Suetonius
described him. A benevolent ruler, he was exceptionally popular and celebrated the
completion of his public works—the Colosseum and baths—with a hundred days
of games. The chief event of his reign was the eruption of Vesuvius in 79, which
buried under ashes and lava several Campanian towns, notably Pompeii and Herculaneum, whose excavation in modern times has afforded an invaluable opportunity
for the study of ancient life and civilization. In 80 much of Rome was destroyed
by a fire, and during the following year Titus died of a fever.

Domitian (81-96). Titus was succeeded in 81 by his younger brother, Domitian,
a bookish man of about thirty, who lacked much experience in military affairs.
Throughout his reign, nevertheless, Domitian held the government firmly in hand
and appointed able men to command the frontiers and govern the provinces. In
Italy he tried to benefit agriculture by urging that more grain be grown and less
reliance be placed on the cultivation of vineyards. He repaired the damage wrought
by the recent fire at Rome and openly sought the favor of the populace by lavish shows and of the army by increasing its pay, its first raise since the reign of
Augustus.

Tyranny. Domitian was an autocrat by nature, more attached to absolutism
than to the restraining principles of the Augustan principate. He chastised vice with

FIGURE 62. Street scene,
Herculanaeum.

Fototeca Unione

an iron hand and attempted to force on society the austere moral standard of the
early Romans. To effectuate his autocracy, with the senate subservient to him, he
proclaimed himself "perpetual censor," which enabled him to revise the senatorial
lists constantly; and in his egotism, he demanded use of the title "lord and god"
(*dominus et deus*) at his court. When the legate of Upper Germany, Antonius
Saturninus, in 88 boldly called himself *"imperator"*—hoping that with the aid of
the Chatti he could begin a revolt at Mogontiacum (Mainz)—Domitian believed that
many of the Roman nobility were involved in the conspiracy and opened a reign
of terror. The informers returned to power; Christians were persecuted; philosophers were banished from Rome, the Stoics because their teachings insisted on the
rule of the "best man," the Cynics because they advocated anarchy.

    Britain. History composed in the senatorial circle has branded Domitian a ty-
rant, and a tyrant he was in Rome; but the provinces had a different story to tell,
and his reign should probably be termed rather successful. A revolt in Africa was
suppressed. In Britain the father-in-law of Tacitus, Agricola, conquered Wales and
extended the boundary of the province to the highlands of Scotland (Caledonia);
as a protection against raiding tribes, he built a road and forts from Newcastle upon
Tyne to the Solway Firth, a general scheme of defense that was to be followed by
Hadrian and Antoninus Pius. In spite of his demonstrated military ability, Agricola
was refused permission to attack Ireland, on the ground that it would cost too
much, but he did succeed in sailing round the northern tip of Britain, thus confirming its insularity.

    The Rhine and Danube. The greatest danger to Rome, along the Rhine and
the Danube, required Domitian's presence. Vespasian had taken the first step in

protecting the vulnerable angle between the headwaters of the two rivers by incorporating the region of Baden as an imperial domain; the inhabitants became tithe-paying tenants, and hence their lands were known as tithe lands (*agri decumates*). Domitian carried the defense further by building an earthen rampart, 120 miles long, from above Coblenz on the Rhine past Frankfurt and on through Württemberg toward the Danube. Eventually this became the famous *limes* of later Roman history, much longer and more strongly fortified (see the maps, pp. 441, 469). Domitian placed small forts at frequent intervals along his rampart; behind it ran military roads for the rapid movement of troops; to the rear were stone forts and fortified camps, which held large numbers of troops ready for an emergency. Even a small frontier camp was laid out on a regular plan. The professional Roman army was thus being transformed from a striking force into a garrison body. Some of their great camps grew into cities, as their names still indicate; for example, the name Chester, in England, is derived from Latin *castrum,* "camp" (a word that is also found in composition, as in Colchester). The name Cologne represents Colonia Agrippina, one of several Roman frontier colonies that became large cities.

The Dacians. From across the Danube came the greatest threat to the Roman peace. In 85 Decabalus, king of a Thracian tribe known as the Dacians, who dwelled in modern Hungary and Rumania, invaded the province of Moesia and was subsequently joined by the Germanic Marcomanni and Quadi of Bohemia and by a branch of the Oriental Sarmatians, called Iazyges. Domitian did not meet with notable success in his war against the Dacians, for terms of peace were reached (89) by his agreement to give Decebalus an annual subsidy, military engines, and technicians, so that he might resist the tribes behind him. To make the frontier more easily defensible, Domitian divided Moesia into two provinces, Upper and Lower.

Domitian came to an end in 96, when his wife Domitia, fearing for her own safety, induced two praetorian prefects to murder him. The senate ordered that his memory should be cursed and his name stricken from all monuments.

NERVA, TRAJAN, AND HADRIAN (A.D. 96–138)

Nerva (96-98). The senate immediately conferred imperial powers on one of its own members, Marcus Cocceius Nerva, a man over sixty years of age, whose life had been without reproach. Nerva's reign opened the rule of the so-called Five Good Emperors, when the emperors were chosen on the basis of merit rather than birth. This period corresponded with the widest and most prosperous development in the history of Rome.

Monarchy and Liberty. Immediately on assuming office, Nerva operated as a constitutional monarch, not a tyrant, as had been the case of Domitian. He granted the senate a due share in the administration and agreed to put no senator to death without a just trial. Tacitus, who considered earlier emperors either usurpers or tyrants, declared that Nerva had united two things hitherto incompatible, monarchy and liberty. He corrected the worst abuses of the preceding reign and put an end to the law of treason, which Domitian had revived. With considerable justice the government struck coins bearing the legends *Libertas publica* (public liberty) and *Roma renascens* (Rome reborn). Nerva's humanitarianism is reflected in his establishment of a system of poor relief for farmers and paupers' children, which was developed also by his successors. But Nerva, like Titus, was too amiable to be a vigorous ruler, and when he found himself unable to control the praetorians, he adopted as his son Marcus Ulpius Traianus (Trajan), an able general in command of the troops in Upper Germany. Nerva caused Trajan to receive the title of Caesar, the tribunician power, and the proconsular *imperium,* so that on Nerva's death, not long afterward, he succeeded to the principate.

Trajan (98-117). Born in the Roman colony of Italica, Spain, Trajan was the first provincial to become emperor of Rome. Following Nerva's example, this model emperor (as he came to be known) took an oath not to put senators to death without a fair trial. Although he treated the senate respectfully, this did not mean any increase in that body's independence or authority. The whole tendency of government was toward paternalism, or as Pliny approvingly expressed it, "Everything is done according to the will of one man, who for the common interest takes upon himself alone the cares and burdens of all."

Imperial Interference in Municipalities and Provinces. The growing power of the emperor appeared in Italy and the provinces as well as in Rome, for when the finances of a municipium fell into disorder, Trajan sent it a curator to control its accounts. Imperial aid was highly desirable, but in practice the curator gradually usurped authority until, within a century or two, he had deprived the community of self-government. For the moment, however, the curators were a distinct advantage. Trajan turned his attention not only to an improvement of the Italian economy but also to an increase of its population. Accordingly, he founded colonies in Italy and lent the municipia money for the maintenance of poor children. One of the most important acts of his reign was the senatorial decree that permitted a municipium, like a person, to receive bequests.

The provincial governors, following Trajan's habit of placing curators in the municipia, interfered in the administration of towns in their provinces. Many questions, sometimes most minute ones, were, however, referred to Rome, a practice that was to end in the destruction of municipal freedom. For example, when Trajan took over Bithynia from the senate, in order to improve its affairs, the new governor, Pliny, consulted him on such trivial matters as the building of a public bath, the removal of a tomb, and the repair of a sewer. In sum, Trajan's administration was detailed, energetic, just, and humane.

The Dacian Wars. In two wars (101-102, 105-106) Trajan himself differed from Augustus in his ambitious imperialism. He personally subdued Dacia, overthrew Decebalus, and converted his kingdom into a province. The dangerous salient north of the Danube was thereby removed; the Roman technicians, whom Domitian had supplied, were recovered; and the important gold and iron mines of the Carpathian Mountains were added to the imperial economy. Engineers, architects, and workmen built roads and fortresses, which promoted peace and travel. Trajan settled many of his veterans here, while other colonists poured in from Asia Minor and various parts of the empire. The native population either fled the country or adopted the speech and habits of the colonists so thoroughly that Dacia became latinized, and even the name of *Rome* has survived there in the modern *Rumania*.

To commemorate his conquest of Dacia, Trajan built a magnificent forum between the Capitoline and the Quirinal on a spot he had leveled for the purpose by cutting away the ridge that had previously connected the two hills. The chief adornment of the new forum was a marble column more than one hundred feet high, which still stands; it is covered by a spiral band, winding around it from base to summit, and tells in sculptured reliefs the story of the conquest: marches, battles, sieges, the building of camps, the burning of towns, the care of wounds, the slaughter of prisoners, the last scene in the life of Decebalus, and the presentation of his head to the populace of Rome. In the absence of a contemporary literary description of the Dacian wars, Trajan's Column is a historical document of first importance for the campaigns and military habits of both Romans and northern barbarians.

Trajan in the South and East. To win more land for agriculture, Trajan extended the limits of Numidia to the Sahara Desert; garrisons at Thamugadi (Timgad) and Lambaesis kept an eye on the restless tribes and enabled caravans to pass back and forth to Central Africa. Through his legates, Trajan converted the client kingdom of the Nabataean Arabs into a province (106). Eastern trade coming up the Red Sea on its way to Syria caused the city of Petra to reach its greatest heights of prosperity. In 114 Trajan himself took the field in the East, inspired by the example of Alexander the Great. The Parthian king, Osroes, had interfered in the affairs of Armenia, which Rome had looked upon as a vassal state ever since the days of Nero. Trajan found it easy enough to expel the intruder from Armenia and turned the kingdom into a province. Northern Mesopotamia was also made a province, and by 115 Trajan had succeeded in capturing the Parthian capital, Ctesiphon on the Tigris. He continued to the Persian Gulf, but revolts in Egypt and Palestine coincided with a sharp Parthian counterattack, and Trajan abandoned southern Mesopotamia. He died in Cilicia on his way back to Rome (117).

Hadrian (117-138). Just before his death Trajan apparently had adopted as his son Publius Aelius Hadrianus, a kinsman by both blood and marriage, for Hadrian's wife was Trajan's great-niece, Sabina by name. The two men had been rather distant, however, and some at the time believed that the adoption was a fiction invented by Trajan's empress and widow, Plotina, who was Hadrian's partisan. Although born in Italy, Hadrian came, like Trajan, of Roman colonial stock in Spain. He was already well known as an able general and provincial governor, thoroughly experienced in military and administrative affairs. He had, moreover, a broad education, a poet's tastes, and an industrious, curious nature. When Trajan died, the legions of Syria proclaimed Hadrian emperor, an act in which the senate acquiesced.

Travels and Public Works. Of his twenty-one years of rule, Hadrian spent fourteen in traveling through the provinces, from the mountains of Caledonia to the valley of Upper Egypt. His obvious partiality for Greece earned him the not altogether complimentary title of "Greekling." He encouraged and supported the professors of rhetoric and philosophy at Athens, added a large quarter to the city,

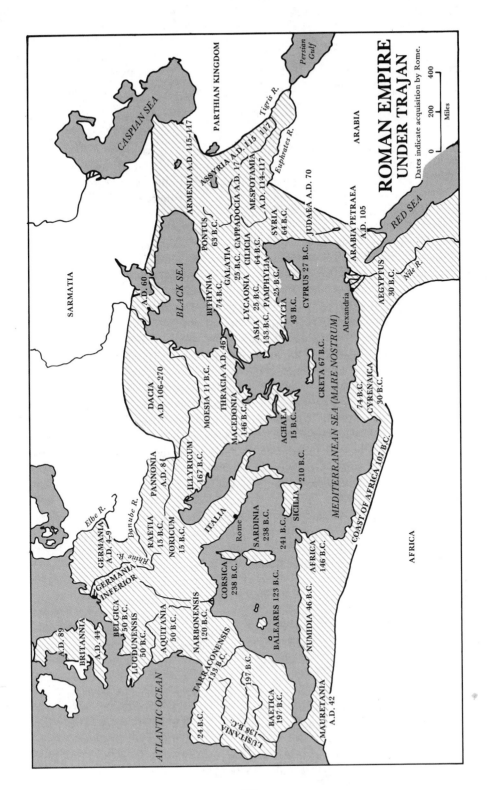

ROMAN EMPIRE
UNDER TRAJAN

Dates indicate acquisition by Rome.

0   200   400

Miles

Persian Gulf

PARTHIAN KINGDOM

CASPIAN SEA

SARMATIA

BLACK SEA

Elbe R.

Danube R.

Rhine R.

ATLANTIC OCEAN

BRITANNIA
A.D. 43

A.D. 44

A.D. 89

BELGICA
50 B.C.

LUGDUNENSIS
50 B.C.

AQUITANIA
50 B.C.

GERMANIA
A.D. 4-9

GERMANIA
INFERIOR

RAETIA
15 B.C.

NORICUM
15 B.C.

PANNONIA
A.D. 8

ILLYRICUM
167 B.C.

DACIA
A.D. 106-270

MOESIA 11 B.C.

THRACIA A.D. 46

ARMENIA A.D. 115-117

ASSYRIA A.D. 115-117

CAPPADOCIA A.D. 17

MESOPOTAMIA
A.D. 114-117

Tigris R.

Euphrates R.

BITHYNIA
74 B.C.

PONTUS
63 B.C.

GALATIA
25 B.C.

LYCAONIA
25 B.C.

CILICIA
64 B.C.

ASIA
133 B.C.

PAMPHYLIA
25 B.C.

LYCIA
43 B.C.

SYRIA
64 B.C.

CYPRUS 27 B.C.

JUDAEA A.D. 70

ARABIA PETRAEA
A.D. 105

ARABIA

RED SEA

AEGYPTUS
30 B.C.

Nile R.

Alexandria

CRETA 67 B.C.

CYRENAICA
74 B.C.
30 B.C.

MEDITERRANEAN SEA (MARE NOSTRUM)

COAST OF AFRICA 107 B.C.

MACEDONIA
146 B.C.

ACHAEA
15 B.C.

ITALIA

Rome

SARDINIA
238 B.C.

CORSICA
238 B.C.

SICILIA
241 B.C.
210 B.C.

BALEARES 123 B.C.

NARBONENSIS
120 B.C.

TARRACONENSIS
139 B.C.

24 B.C.

197 B.C.

LUSITANIA
138 B.C.

BAETICA
197 B.C.

MAURETANIA
A.D. 42

NUMIDIA 46 B.C.

AFRICA
146 B.C.

AFRICA

A.D. 60

and completed the temple of Olympian Zeus, which Peisistratus had begun in the sixth century B.C. In every part of the empire rose temples, theaters, aqueducts, and new foundations, one of which, Adrianople in European Turkey, still bears the emperor's name. In Rome, Hadrian built a temple to Venus and Roma, and his own mausoleum, which became known in the Middle Ages as the Castel Sant'Angelo, while at Tibur (Tivoli) in the Sabine Hills he created a villa that contained reminders of some of the famous buildings and scenes elsewhere in the empire. The travels of Hadrian emphasized the increasing interest of the imperial government in the entire empire and tended to diminish the relative importance of the capital. His division of Italy, outside Rome, into four districts, each under a judge, was the first, if abortive, step toward making it a province and Rome a municipium. Hadrian maintained a respectful attitude to the senate, but, like his predecessors, permitted it little real power.

Frontiers and the Army. Another purpose of Hadrian's travels was to inspect the frontiers. In the furtherance of peace, and to conserve Roman resources, which were seriously strained, he abandoned Trajan's conquests, excepting Dacia and Arabia; Armenia returned to its status of a client kingdom; and the terrible Jewish revolts, which had been the partial cause of Trajan's return from Mesopotamia, were ruthlessly suppressed. In Britain the famous Wall of Hadrian (map, rear endpaper) was built from the mouth of the Tyne to the Solway Firth as a defense against the northern Picts; it consisted, originally, of two parallel moats and walls, with turrets and camps. In Germany a palisade was added to the *limes,* which Domitian had built from the Rhine to the Danube. Hadrian also gave detailed attention to the personnel of the armies and their discipline. The tendency of legions to be recruited provincially, and then locally in the very regions where they were stationed, culminated during his reign, and the defensive and even retrenching nature of his foreign policy accentuated the evolution of Roman armies as relatively immobile garrison forces.

The Civil Service. The amount of administrative business in the hands of the emperor had greatly increased since the days of Augustus. The household staff consisted largely of freedmen as late as Claudius' reign. Subsequent emperors began to substitute equestrians for those freedmen, and the tendency to do so culminated under Hadrian. Whether serving at court or in the financial and administrative machinery of the provinces, the equestrian class was especially identified as the civil service. A complex system of offices had been created, each with its special functions and with regular promotions from the lowest to the highest. The five important secretariats were *a rationibus* (for finance); *a libellis* (for petitions); *ab epistulis* (for correspondence); *a cognitionibus* (for investigations); and *a studiis* (for records). The increase in bureaucracy meant an increase in overhead expenses, to which was added the cost of keeping up the standing army. The prosperous second century could cope with this overhead, but the time was approaching when a flattening or even declining economy could support the administrative and military superstructure only with difficulty.

A vast bureaucracy, such as that which was developing under Hadrian, inevitably delighted in surrounding itself with the trappings of hereditary titles. Thus a senator came to be known as *clarissimus* (most noble), while *vir eminentissimus* (most eminent) was reserved for the praetorian prefects. An equestrian was called *vir perfectissimus* (most perfect) or *vir egregius* (honorable). Hadrian also accentuated the tendency of previous emperors to replace tax farmers by fiscal agents directly responsible to the government, which further increased the size of the civil service.

Jurisprudence.   The highest place in the purely civil service was that of imperial treasurer, but of even greater importance was the praetorian prefect, who stood second only to the emperor himself. Since his duties henceforth were to be judicial as well as military, he was frequently a jurist, and from the class of jurists Hadrian tended to make up his council. The most eminent jurist of the day, Salvius Julianus, codified the praetor's Edicts, which became one of the bases of Roman civil law. This code, under the title Perpetual Edict, henceforth had the authority of law, and was subject to modification only by the emperor. Julianus was the first of those eminent jurists who labored to perfect the civil law.

Conclusion.   By his thorough reforms Hadrian put the machinery of government, as well as the military system, in such order that it continued to run with little repair for a century and a half and was able to see Rome through the terrible ordeal of the third century. Underlying all his work was the devotion of a real servant of the state, a recognition of the principle that the armies, the governors, Rome, and the emperor existed for the welfare of the empire.

Hadrian was a generally benevolent ruler until the very end of his life, when his character was changed, it seems, by a fatal illness. In any case, shortly before his death he began to persecute senators, and feeling against him ran high in the senate when he died.

THE ANTONINES (A.D. 138–192)

Antoninus Pius (138–161).   Toward the end of his life Hadrian adopted as his son and successor Lucius Commodus, and then, on Commodus' sudden death, Titus Aurelius Antoninus, a Roman senator from Nîmes in Narbonese Gaul. Following Hadrian's instructions, Antoninus adopted Commodus' son, Lucius Verus, and Marcus Aurelius Antoninus, a Spanish nephew of Hadrian's wife. When Hadrian died, Antoninus succeeded to the principate as the first emperor from Gaul, and because of his filial devotion in winning deification for Hadrian, despite many senatorial protests, he was called Pius.

A Deceptive Peace.   During his reign, unlike Hadrian, Antoninus Pius remained chiefly in Rome. A man of estimable character, who strove for justice and peace, he advanced the cause of humane legislation. The right of a master to torture his slaves for the purpose of extorting evidence, which Hadrian had already restricted, he limited still further. He also enlarged on the charitable policy of Trajan and set aside an endowment for orphan girls, whom he called Faustinianae, after his wife Faustina. His long and economical reign was prosperous and happy, unmarked by untoward events, but for this he could thank not so much his own ability as the excellent condition in which Hadrian had left the empire. It was a deceptive peace,

however, for on every frontier there were ominous rumblings. Antoninus Pius
adopted a defensive policy against the barbarians, and in Britain he built an earthen
rampart north of Hadrian's Wall, from the Firth of Clyde to the Firth of Forth
(map, rear endpaper). Early in his reign he gave the title of Caesar, and then the
tribunician power and the *imperium*, to his adopted son, Marcus Aurelius, who
became a junior colleague and married the emperor's daughter. In 161, on the death
of Antoninus Pius, Marcus Aurelius became emperor.

Marcus Aurelius (161-180). It is one of the tragic facts of history that this
sensitive Stoic philosopher should have spent his reign in almost constant warfare.
But it was also tragic that at this juncture in history, when civilization was about to
be swept into new currents, a philosopher with little warmth and regard for the
individual should have presided over the empire; energetic and dutiful as he was,
Marcus Aurelius was the living proof that Plato was wrong when he said that humankind would be happy when philosophers were kings (p. 244).

Verus in the East. In general, Marcus Aurelius' administration followed the lines
marked out by his predecessors. One of his first acts was to associate with himself
as colleague Lucius Verus, his brother by adoption, so that for the first time Rome
was ruled by two Augusti, both of whom had equal rights. Marcus Aurelius exercised the greater power, but a certain disinclination for the post, no less than the
pressing problems of state, led him to divide the duties and cares, for the easy
disposition of Antoninus Pius had left him a legacy of troubles. On his accession,
war brewed along the northern and eastern frontiers. In Syria barracks life had
softened the troops, and they were unable to withstand the invasion of the Parthian
king, Vologases III. Marcus Aurelius dispatched Verus to the scene, but Verus, who
was weak and lazy, proceeded to the East in leisurely fashion. Sent off from Rome
in the spring of 162, he took almost a year to reach Antioch. Fortunately, however,
he found good generals awaiting him, the ablest of whom was Avidius Cassius, a
Syrian by birth, but of the old Roman type of severity. Discipline was restored, and
in the course of the war (162-166) the Parthians were driven out, their land was
overrun, and even their capital, Ctesiphon, and Seleucia were captured. As a price
of peace, Rome retained northern Mesopotamia and insisted that Armenia should
once again become a client kingdom.

Plague. Meanwhile a fearful plague, which had started among Cassius' troops at
Seleucia, was raging in the East; and when the troops returned from the war, they
spread the disease over the empire. The army was greatly weakened; and in some
places, as in Italy, a third, or perhaps a half, of the population was carried off. The
plague reduced the revenues and the manpower available to the military, just when
Rome's enemies were growing more formidable and bold. Hard-pressed in their
turn, by restless tribes to the north, they were threatening to overwhelm the defenses of the Danube. The leaders were the Teutonic Marcomanni, Quadi, and
Iazyges, who lived in what are now Bohemia and Moravia.

The Danubian Campaigns. Marcus Aurelius sold imperial treasures to finance the
war (167-175) and, in view of the depleted manpower, recruited the army with
slaves, gladiators and even German mercenaries. Both emperors took the field, but
in 169 Verus died, and Marcus continued the war alone. With considerable bril-

liance he crossed the Danube and defeated the enemy in several campaigns, which were commemorated by a column, reminiscent of Trajan's, set up at Rome. The enemy were forced to surrender their captives and agree to render Rome military service. Large numbers of barbarians were settled as *coloni* on the wastelands of the frontier provinces; advantageous as it was to have them as farmers and soldiers, there was a danger that they might feel closer in sympathy to their kinsmen beyond the empire than to the older inhabitants.

Marcus Aurelius had hurried to bring the war to an end, because a rumor of his death had caused Avidius Cassius to proclaim himself emperor. A campaign in the East was accordingly necessary; after its successful conclusion, and to prevent possible uprisings of the kind in the future, he made his son, Lucius Aelius Aurelius Commodus, his colleague with the title of Augustus. Once more (178-180) the Marcomanni and the Quadi threatened the Danube, and now Marcus Aurelius resolved to invade and annex their lands. Before he was able to accomplish his purpose, he died at Vindobona (Vienna).

Commodus (180-192).   It is a sad commentary on the dynastic principle that the son and successor of Marcus Aurelius, Commodus (180-192), should have had no redeeming virtue, a fact doubtless known to the father, but he scarcely could pass beyond his own family in favor of a capable person. Commodus was weak-minded, cowardly, cruel, sensual, vain, and brutish. He gave up the expedition against the Marcomanni and returned to Rome, where he squandered imperial funds and appeared in the amphitheater as a gladiator and hunter of wild beasts. He looked upon himself as the reincarnation of Hercules and issued coins that showed himself as a god. The empire held together, though ruled by favorites; as discipline in the army declined, brigandage appeared. Finally, a conspiracy was formed against Commodus by the praetorian prefect; Marcia, the emperor's mistress, joined with it, and on the night before Commodus was to take the consulship dressed as a gladia-tor, a wrestler strangled him in his bath. The great age of the empire was ending, and already the seeds of its destruction were accompanied by fresh forces and vital ideas that, after an agonizing struggle, were to transform the old world into the new. The first of these was the Germanic race, which eventually stamped its charac-ter on the empire; and the other was Christianity, which revolutionized the Western world.

30

The Greco-Roman World During the Early Empire

WEAKNESS AMID STRENGTH

Emperor and Senate.   From the days of Augustus until a century after Commodus, the magisterial character of the principate was theoretically preserved by both constitutional and autocratic emperors. But just as the signs of outright monarchy become increasingly visible, so too is there a unity of another sort to the period. Augustus, Vespasian, and the five "good emperors"—different as they were, different as were their problems—would have understood one another and each other's world.

In the early empire a regard for legality and loyalty to the princeps provided this vast world with its cohesion. He came to represent the highest court of appeal, and his wishes, which were often presented to the senate as an address (*oratio*), were automatically ratified and had the force of law. The senate, by the time of Hadrian, contained a large number of provincials, mainly from the Latin West, and certainly was more representative of the empire than hitherto, but it was essentially an advisory body, which helped the emperor with legislation. The Roman assemblies, moreover, had long ceased to exist as formal bodies, although the people might be convoked to acclaim imperial policies.

Municipal Government.   On the other hand, political activity at a municipal level remained vigorous outside Rome; the excavations at Pompeii, for example, show keen and lively interest in local affairs, which was also true of the Greek East. It was the general practice in Italian municipalities, as a whole, to elect an annual board of four magistrates (*quattuorviri*) and one hundred members (*decuriones*) of the curia, or city council, whose business it was to pass the local ordinances. These men were rather well-to-do and were happy to serve without pay in return for the honor, but it became increasingly difficult to find such men later on, when office holding became more expensive to undertake. As in so many other matters, the urbanization of the Roman Empire probably reached its height under Hadrian and his immediate successors. In the West, where rural and tribal life tended to linger, the military camps and colonies of veterans hastened the process of urbanization— each city, as usual, receiving a charter, which settled its rights and government—and even beyond the Rhine, in the *agri decumates*, there were 160 towns, and beyond the Danube, in Dacia, 120. The province of Asia boasted 500 cities.

The Provinces.   The organization of the empire into provinces—and their government—remained much the same under Hadrian as in the past, except that there was greater centralization. There were now forty-five provinces, eleven of which were senatorial, and even the smallest provinces were able, through their councils, to maintain the imperial cult and even occasionally to send embassies to Rome to address the emperor. Romanization meant especially the extension of Greco-Roman civilization to provinces whose population had remained outside classical culture before the advent of the Romans. Romanization in this sense was an organic phenomenon, and as such it was generally not a set, articulate policy of the government. It took place primarily in the cities, and many peasants were scarcely affected by it. The process of romanizing the provinces west of Greece had been rapid, and Gaul became so thoroughly romanized that in many ways it was a second Italy—law-abiding, prosperous, and vigorous enough to provide the empire with some of its finest troops. Indeed, Gaul and Spain also gave Rome eminent poets, scholars, and emperors. The same was coming to be true of other provinces. Along with the progress of culture, individuals and entire communities continued to receive either full Roman citizenship or the slightly inferior Latin rights.

The task of giving the East one civilization had already been accomplished by the Greeks, and theirs was the language of learning, commerce, and diplomacy in the eastern half of the empire. Except for the cities, however, the East tended to be culturally more Oriental than Greek.

The Problem of Rome's Decline.   As we review the early Roman Empire, we see that it was in fact a Greco-Roman world, and that within these two major divisions there was great variety; cantonal life in the West could be matched by temple states and feudal domains in the East. This healthy local diversity was destined to be subject to increasing standardization and uniformity, but under Hadrian and the Antonines, Greco-Roman government and law, architecture and industry, won a high level of prosperity, accompanied by peace. It is true that this prosperous second century was also a period of increasing cultural stagnation, at least within the classical tradition. The factors that create outbursts of intellectual activity are as mysterious as the fact that, with its height, ancient civilization also began its decline. The basic cause of the economic decline that commenced in the second century cannot be discovered in such facile explanations as the exhaustion of the soil. The disease of the ancient world was more complex by far. It must be emphasized that the splendid structure of ancient civilization was built on a primitive foundation, which was marked by technical backwardness. Labor-saving devices were few, and manual labor was held in such contempt that it discouraged the educated classes from turning their minds to applied science. The institution of slavery had little to do with technological backwardness, because, except for relatively limited periods when constant wars and unchecked piracy produced a glut of slaves, free labor was as cheap as slave labor. Under the principate the majority of slaves were bred, and the master had to allow his slaves enough to maintain a wife and family. The abandonment of slave gangs in agriculture in favor of free tenants during the first century suggests that slaves were neither abundant nor cheap; even in mining, slaves gave way either to convicts or to free miners. By the end of the third century there was clearly an acute labor shortage, but economic stimulus produced no inventions.

The opening up of new markets by conquest brought prosperity to Italian manufacture and trade in the first century, but the subsequent decentralization of industry to the provinces checked this boom. Owing to the poverty of the working classes, there was no depth to the market, and prosperity could be maintained only by expansion through further conquests. Trajan attempted this, but the effort proved too great for the resources of the empire, and Hadrian's abandonment of an expansionist policy meant a stabilization and eventual contraction of wealth. The continually increasing overhead expenses of the empire had to be met, and the only means of extracting them from the diminishing resources of the empire was ever-increasing taxation. Since there was no technical advance in production, the growth of large-scale industries and extensive trade did not greatly increase the wealth of the empire. The price of manufactured articles was not reduced by mass production, and their cost to the consumer was increased by the heavy expenses of transport. Conversely, the decentralization of industry to the provinces did not greatly reduce the wealth of the empire; manufactured articles could be produced locally as cheaply, and the cost of transport was saved. In the first century A.D., Italy had profited at the expense of the provinces, and in the second century, the balance was adjusted in the provinces' favor.

It would be easy to exaggerate the importance of manufacture and trade in the economy of the empire. Agriculture was always its basic industry, and the ownership of land the basic source of wealth. The vast majority of the important "middle class" that filled the city councils of the empire and the lower grades of the equestrian order were not enterprising merchants and manufacturers but landowners, living like the senatorial aristocracy on rents, though on a more modest scale. Their fortunes would be unaffected by trade booms or slumps.

We must emphasize, however, that the technological backwardness of the Roman Empire deprived people of incentives and means to economic progress at a critical time, and yet, of course, this was not the cause of the empire's collapse, since technological backwardness had characterized classical antiquity for centuries. For the condition of the Greco-Roman world the upper classes were responsible. The whole atmosphere was unfavorable to technological progress, which would have challenged their privileged position. The leisured class rested—at least, in significant part—first on slavery and subsequently on the tenant farmer. What was needed was not so much an expansion of possible markets as a deepening of them; or rather, the need of the day was to make it possible for the great masses of humanity to share more fully in every aspect of life. It was hardly to be expected that the upper classes would inaugurate a revolution that could only end in the loss of their own special position.

Except in building and engineering, the Roman world suffered from a complete stagnation of technique during the second century A.D., which was especially disastrous for agriculture. We have already said that the decentralization of industry to the provinces rectified an advantage enjoyed previously by Italy and eliminated unnecessary transport. Nevertheless it must be stressed that Roman communications, superior though they were as compared with those of the past, were still rather primitive; another disadvantage from which the economy suffered was the insecurity of credit. The early Roman Empire, however, enjoyed a sound coinage; the most important coins were silver *denarii* and their subdivisions, bronze sesterces. The trouble was that the Oriental trade in luxuries was paid not with Western goods but with coins; hence there was a constant drain of metal from the empire. The unfavorable trade balance led Nero to debase the silver *denarius,* so that *denarii* minted by him and later emperors ceased to circulate in the Orient. Subsequent emperors gradually increased debasement as a means of meeting increased governmental expenditures.

The decentralization of industry to the provinces led ultimately to provincial autarchy, which destroyed the economic unity of the ancient world. As industries moved to the provinces, the tendency developed for them to locate not in towns but in the large, self-sufficing manorial estates or villas. Nevertheless urban culture remained deeply rooted in the East, which helps to explain the survival of the Eastern Empire after the fall of the Western; the intense wave of urbanization that had begun in Hellenistic times was imitated, but never matched, in the West.

The problem of the decline of the Roman Empire will probably be debated as long as history is studied, for it was a complex phenomenon in which many factors interacted, not one of which can be singled out as the prime cause. High on the list of causes of Rome's economic decline must certainly be placed the growth of the bureaucracy and the army and the increase in overhead expenses, with which was coupled subsequently a fall in the available manpower. We have tried to make clear that it is very difficult to say what lay back of Rome's economic, social, cultural, and political decline. Doubtless it was due to a change in mental outlook, to a "failure of nerve," as it has been called, but to account for that change is very difficult.

***The Splendor of the* Pax Romana.** It is an easy guess that few people in the mid-second century were worried by the possibility of incipient decline. A Greek rhetorician of the day, Aelius Aristides, called the whole Roman world a paradise, where men might travel safely from one end of the empire to the other, where, in place of war, cities competed with each other only in their splendor and pleasures. Schools, temples, and gymnasia greeted one everywhere. The condition of the poor did not interest Aristides, nor did he reflect on how much the world had gained in creative achievement, when Greek cities, for example, had vied first with one another and then with Rome. Aristides saw other things, and one can gainsay neither their magnificence nor Rome's greatness in making them possible.

Thanks to the many proscriptions, the emperor owned vast estates. He and other large landowners found it cheaper to lease their property to individuals and corporations, which, in turn, cut it up into small lots and rented them to farmers. These tenants, who were originally free and known as *coloni,* were sharecroppers. Here we have the beginning of a developed tenantry system, which eventually evolved into serfdom.

As we look back on this extraordinary period of history, it is tempting to agree with Gibbon's observation: "If a man were called to fix the period in the history of the world, during which the condition of the human race was most happy and prosperous, he would, without hesitation, name that which elapsed from the death of Domitian to the accession of Commodus. The vast extent of the Roman Empire was governed by absolute power, under the guidance of virtue and wisdom." On the other hand, if we think of the intangibles, Toynbee doubtless expressed a profounder truth when he said: "The Hellenic world lay more or less passive under the pall of the *Pax Romana.*"

ART AND LITERATURE

The Empire's Cities. In its physical aspects the Greco-Roman world did not fall far short of the rhetoric of Aristides. Impressed as the modern visitor to Rome is bound to be, his respect for the mighty Roman Empire is particularly excited by those imposing ruins at the very edge of the ancient provinces: at Bath, a famous watering place once set amid the forests of Britain; Timgad, beside the Sahara Desert, whose military garrison (as was so often the case) grew into a city; Petra,

FIGURE 63. Arena of amphitheater at Capua, a town in Campania, near Naples.

Fototeca Unione

in northern Arabia; Baalbek, the extraordinary show place of Syria; Palmyra, an oasis in the Syrian Desert. There is a similarity to the ruins, as there was, of course, to the towns themselves in the days of their glory, each with its forum, temples, triumphal arches, and basilicas. Wherever Roman rule extended, there followed theaters, amphitheaters, roads, bridges, aqueducts, cisterns, and baths, and the ancient, established cities became ever more magnificent. In particular, Alexandria and Antioch, with their unruly populations were, in effect, great Eastern capitals; their busy trade brought exotic peoples and cargoes from as far away as India and China, and at the same time, as centers of learning, they continued to attract intellectual leaders. Indeed, it was at Antioch that a heretical form of Judaism was systematized and elaborated by Greek philosophy into Christianity.

Architecture at Rome. Rome, which Augustus boasted he had left a city of marble, was, of course, the great city of the empire. There were the palaces of the

FIGURE 64. Street at Leptis Magna (modern Libya).

Fototeca Unione

FIGURE 65. Roman apartment houses, Ostia, the port of Ancient Rome.

Caesars on the Palatine and the imperial forums, around which clustered government buildings, temples, and shops. Here, too, were the basilicas, which were used
as law courts. In general, a basilica had a broad central nave, with perhaps an apse
at one or both ends; the nave and side aisles were separated from each other by
piers, on which rose arches, making the roof higher over the center—light was
admitted through the clerestory that was formed. The masses found their entertainment in a variety of theaters—the Flavian Amphitheater, or Colosseum, had a seating capacity of fifty thousand—and in the public baths (*thermae*), of which there
were more than eight hundred scattered around the city. Some of these baths were
of immense size, such as that of Titus and, of a later date, those of Caracalla and
Diocletian.

A large Roman bath was a social meeting place, with libraries and lecture halls,
gardens and race courses, and rooms for wrestling and boxing. There were also the
hot, warm, and cold pools (*caldarium, tepidarium, frigidarium*); heat was obtained
by a system of hot-air chambers below (hypocausts), whence the warmth was
brought through the walls by vertical and horizontal flue tiles. The best-preserved

FIGURE 66. The Pantheon, Rome.

of all Roman baths, those of Caracalla from the early third century, occupy an area of 270,000 square feet; the central hall measures approximately 170 by 82 feet. One of the most interesting things about the Roman baths is the ability of the ancient architect to bring together a large number of halls, of different sizes and varied heights. Another important fact is the maintenance of the axis in laying out

Roman Orders

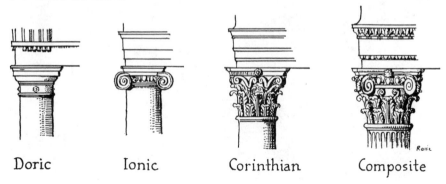

Doric   Ionic   Corinthian   Composite

the plan, which is typical of all Roman architecture, whether in a forum or an ordinary house.

The development of the arch, which made possible the substitution of vaults for flat roofs, was a notable Roman achievement. Large areas could now be covered satisfactorily, and a continuous improvement of the vault resulted in the dome of the Pantheon and the ceilings of the baths of Caracalla.[1] The practical Roman genius was particularly at home in the solution of problems of construction and in building in a vertical direction. Many of their ideas, as we have seen, the Romans took from Greece, but as always they adapted them to their own taste and use. The Doric column, for example, was often left unfluted and rested on a base; the Ionic order was little altered, but the Corinthian, which was never popular in Greece, was widely adopted. The extensive use of concrete, with a brick or other facing, meant that the column and its entablature ceased to have structural significance and became ornamental, being used, for example, as a bracket for the support of vaulting, or to decorate a wall (orders of Greek architecture, p. 142).

Art. In art a number of facets were developed. During the first century the Composite capital, a combination of Ionic and Corinthian, was introduced and used for the first time in Rome on the Arch of Titus. This monument in the Forum commemorated the destruction of Jerusalem. Since Roman art served to reflect public events, historical scenes predominate on the reliefs of this arch and the memorial columns of Trajan and Marcus Aurelius. The reliefs are infused with a remarkable realism, which is also to be found in the portrait sculpture and the coins, whereas the gems and metalwork, the frescoes and mosaics illustrate the Roman gift for detailed work.

Latin Literature. The desire of the emperors to beautify their capital helps to explain the vigor of art during the early empire. There was a corresponding production in literature, which many emperors patronized. The pulse did not beat so high as in the past, however, and the period of the early empire, accordingly, is spoken of as the Silver Age of Latin literature. The great creations of the Augustan Age

---

[1] There were three types of vaulting: semicircular barrel vaults; quadripartite vaulting, formed by the intersection of two barrel vaults; and domical vaulting, as in the Pantheon.

were followed by a singular lull, although in the reign of Tiberius an army officer, Velleius Paterculus, wrote a short *History of Rome* to the year 30. Wordy and pompous, he achieved some accuracy in his statements of fact, but he overflowed with eulogy of Tiberius, like a partisan rather than an objective historian. The same criticism applies to his contemporary Valerius Maximus. The object of his untrustworthy *Memorable Acts and Sayings* seems to have been to supply the youth of the day with material for declamations.

Seneca, Lucan, Petronius. A literary revival took place under Nero. His tutor, Seneca (4 B.C.-A.D. 65), it will be recalled, was a Stoic philosopher and tragedian from Spain. Seneca shared with his age the striving after brilliancy in rhetoric, but nevertheless he gives evidence of the broader and deeper thought that the provinces were bringing to Rome. Another Stoic of this time was the poet Persius, whose *Satires* show him to have been a serious moralist. Seneca's nephew Lucan (39-65) was also a Spaniard and a Stoic philosopher. He composed an epic poem, the *Pharsalia,* on the civil war between Caesar and Pompey. For a time, Lucan stood well at Nero's court, but falling into disfavor, he finished his poem as an ardent republican; later on, he became involved in the conspiracy of Piso and killed himself by order of the emperor. Many writers of this period, considering a simple style insipid, sought to attract attention by rhetorical bombast, far-fetched metaphors, and other unnatural devices, and in this respect, they reflected the educational standards of the day. An exception to the rule is Petronius (died 66), who was known as the creator of the Latin novel. The main episode of his *Satyricon,* "Trimalchio's Dinner," is a coarse, yet entertaining and vigorous satire on the vulgar ways of a rich freedman.

Celsus. Aulus Cornelius Celsus was an important writer on medicine at this time. In reading the following passage on the development and state of medicine, it may be well to bear in mind that Celsus had a profound influence on later ages, and that his book was one of the first to be printed after the invention of printing in the mid-fifteenth century:

"About this same time (300 B.C.) medicine was divided into three parts; one which cured by regimen or diet, one with drugs, and one by hand or external means. The Greeks called the first dietary medicine, the second pharmaceutical, and the third surgical. Now the most famous authorities by far in the field of dietary medicine, in an effort to carry certain aspects of the matter forward, claimed as their own contribution an understanding of how nature works and implied that without this understanding medicine was incomplete and helpless. After these physicians, Serapion (second century B.C.), who was the very first to insist that this theoretical training had nothing to do with actual healing, maintained that healing was accomplished only by long practice and experiment (trial and error). Apollonius and Glaucias and shortly thereafter Heraclides of Tarentum and some other rather important men accepted the doctrine of Serapion and called themselves the experimental physicians. And so it was that the school of medicine which cured by regimen was divided into two parts, for some claimed a skill based on theory and others relied on practice or experiment.

"After Apollonius and Glaucias and Heraclides and their adherents no one made any innovations until the time of Asclepiades who changed the principles of medicine to a considerable degree. Those who professed theoretical medicine explained what it was necessary to understand: first the hidden causes of sickness, then the obvious causes, and after this the natural processes, and finally the inner organs of the body. They were convinced that when pain and various kinds of ailments arise in the internal organs no physician could apply remedies if he did not have their kind of training and understanding. And that is why they said that it was necessary to cut up cadavers and examine their inner vital parts. The theoretical physicians say that the best dissectors were Herophilus and Erasistratus who dissected living convicted prisoners delivered them from the prison by the kings of Alexandria. Herophilus and Erasistratus examined, while the prisoners were still alive, what nature up to that time had kept concealed: the organs' location, color, shape, size, type, hardness, softness, smoothness, junctures, and then the projections and indentations; and, while the prisoners were still alive, the physicians tried to find out if one organ is contained within another or if some organ contains part of another. The theoretical physicians say that, in the case of deep-seated pain, one who does not understand where or what an inner organ is does not know what ails the patient; and they say that the afflicted part cannot be cured by one who does not know what the part is. The theoretical physicians also say that, although most people think so, still it is not cruel to seek cures for all generations of harmless people amid the suffering of condemned criminals—and even of these only a small number is involved.

"Those, on the other hand, who from their tendency to rely on experience, call themselves empirical, cling to the obvious causes of disease as the source which must be understood; the investigation of hidden causes and of natural processes they say is a waste of time because nature cannot be understood and explained. They are convinced that the disagreement of experts on the subject, the disagreement of both philosophers and physicians themselves, demonstrates plainly that nature cannot be understood and explained. Where thorough understanding is lacking, mere conjecture cannot discover a specific remedy. And it must be admitted that theory contributes no more to medicine than does practice. And so many circumstances, which do not have directly to do with the various aspects of healing, still promote healing by stimulating the natural skill of the practitioner. Thus the close observation of nature, although it does not make a physician, still makes a more and more skilled healer of human ills. But medicine needs a theory often enough, even if it does not lie among the unseen causes of disease and among the natural processes. The problem is unsolved; usually both conjecture and experience provide an insufficient answer."[2]

Pliny the Elder, Quintilian, Martial. Under the Flavians fresh life continued to pour in from the provinces. Pliny the Elder (23–79), from Cisalpine Gaul, wrote an encyclopedia known as the *Natural History,* which discussed not only the natural sciences but also geography, medicine, and art. A man of extraordinary industry, he was suffocated by a rain of hot ashes while studying the eruption of Vesuvius

[2] Translated by Arthur Lynch.

that destroyed Pompeii. What Pliny did for science Quintilian (died 95), a native of Spain, did for rhetoric. In an age when form rather than substance mattered, Quintilian nevertheless discoursed delightfully on life and education. His *Institutes of Oratory* could not, of course, come to grips with the political problems of the day, but they do show how a study of rhetoric could train a man both personally and professionally. Another Spaniard, Martial (died 102), wrote brilliant, satirical epigrams, which generally expose the corrupt side of society at the capital.

Tacitus. Martial had been able to write under Domitian because of his fawning flattery of the emperor, but not so Cornelius Tacitus (ca. 55-120), the great historian of the early emperors. On account of Domitian's tyranny, Tacitus had to wait till the reigns of Nerva, Trajan and Hadrian to write, and the unhappy experience colored his estimate of the earlier rulers. On matters of impartiality, and sound judgment, therefore, Tacitus leaves something to be desired, for the satirist occasionally ran away with the historian, and he was also a master of innuendo. But concerning his factual as distinct from interpretive accuracy and his literary artistry there can be no doubt. Beginning with three minor works—an essay on oratory; a fine biography of his father-in-law, Agricola of British fame; and a treatise on the Germans—Tacitus proceeded in his *Annals* and *Histories* to write the history of the Roman Empire from the death of Augustus to that of Domitian. Tacitus tells us that history has a moral purpose. His grand style is typical of the Silver Age, in that the long Ciceronian periods are abandoned in favor of short, concentrated sentences. So, too, commonplace words are avoided, and in their place we find poetic expressions, due to the influence of rhetoric, which sought to break down the boundary between poetry and prose. Tacitus' brevity of expression is as famous as his sententious phrases, which have been quoted ever since. Of Roman conquest he said, "They make a solitude and call it peace"; of the transience of political systems, "Princes die but society is eternal"; on the psychology of power, "The cause of hatred is all the stronger if it is unjust"; "In a community of might concord seldom rules"; "Tyranny is never secure"; "Among the powerful and those greedy of power, serenity is deceptive." In one important respect, however, Tacitus' psychological vision was one-sided, for it was stamped with a thoroughgoing pessimism. A member of the senatorial aristocracy, he bitterly hated the "tyrants" and ignored the blessings the imperial government brought the provinces, this despite his statement that history must be written without preconceived antipathies or sympathies.

Pliny the Younger, Juvenal, Suetonius, Apuleius. Tacitus was the last great writer of classic Latin. His friend Pliny the Younger (62-113), who was a nephew of the naturalist, was an orator and for a time governor of Bithynia. One of his speeches, a eulogy of Trajan, is an example of the tiresome, feeble style of the day, but his polished, sometimes trivial letters are valuable for a study of the times, particularly for Trajan's provincial policy. Juvenal (died 130), on the other hand, was a powerful critic and in his *Satires* attacked the corruption of Roman society. Like Tacitus, he was the originator of many short, memorable sayings. His wish for a sound mind and a sound body (*mens sana in corpore sano*) is still quoted. Less useful than Tacitus but very interesting is the *Lives of the Caesars* from Julius to Domitian, a chaotic mixture of useful facts and foolish gossip, by Hadrian's secretary, Suetonius (75-150). As we review Latin literature of this period, we are impressed with the contributions of provincials. By the time of the Antonines, Africa was well represented, notably in the person of Apuleius, who composed a romance entitled *The Golden Ass*. Another African, the essayist Fronto, who wrote in a turgid, archaistic style, also kept his eyes on Rome's past, as ominous a sign that the process of decay had set in as the fact that many people in Egypt were already looking on themselves as mere tax-paying units and were fleeing the tax gatherers.

Greek Literature and the Second Sophistic. The early Roman Empire continued to have a Greek, no less than a Latin, literature, called the period of the Second Sophistic. The writings of the Apostle Paul, as well as the *Meditations* of the emperor Marcus Aurelius, remind us of the universality of the Greek language. Two officials of Hadrian, Appian and Arrian, wrote important histories, one on Rome's *Civil Wars* and the other on *Alexander the Great,* and their contemporary Pausanias composed a valuable work on the antiquities of Greece. One of the most attractive writers of all time was born at Chaeronea in Boeotia in about 50, the biographer Plutarch, whose *Parallel Lives* of famous Greeks and Romans celebrated the glorious past. Another original genius was Lucian, who was born in Syria in about 125; his *Dialogues* satirize philosophy, religion, and society.

Specialized Works. This large literary output, Greek and Latin, was accompanied by a variety of works on specialized subjects, such as military strategy, agriculture, botany, aqueducts, and science. In the field of medicine, Galen of Pergamum, who was the physician of Marcus Aurelius, wrote many books that influenced later centuries. Hippalus' discovery of the monsoons, which made possible a quick direct sail to India, and the development during the second century of the all-sea route to China, together with other activities of merchants, produced a better understanding of the earth. This subject, and the larger one of the universe itself, attracted various minds, the greatest of whom was Claudius Ptolemy of Alexandria (150). The Ptolemaic conception of both geography and astronomy (where the earth was represented as the center of the universe) was accepted as standard until the time of Copernicus.

The decline of vitality, in general, during the second century affected both the literature and the art. Imitation often took the place of originality, the shallow and the insipid were usually mistaken for thought and imagination, while repetition destroyed the spirit of initiative. And yet, intellectual power remained and continued to manifest itself, particularly in jurisprudence, for which the Romans possessed real genius.[2]

LAW

Introduction. The creative period of Roman law fell, roughly, between 100 B.C. and A.D. 235, and culminated in the Severan dynasty following Commodus. The period of the early principate, in particular, witnessed important developments. The

---

[2] See also pp. 407f.

names of the men who later conducted its practice under the empire are household words in the legal profession, names such as Julian, Papinian, Ulpian, Paul, and Modestine. In their hands Roman law became both sophisticated and humane. Law became a profession at Rome as early as the middle of the third century B.C., but lawyers never approached the character of a caste.

Basic Terms.   There are two basic terms to understand, *ius* (pl. *iura*) and *lex* (pl. *leges*). *Ius* meant a right, both in the sense of something that could be sued for at law and in the sense of a valid defense, if one was sued. But *ius* was also a collective form for all the *iura* that all Roman citizens had, as well as all who had access to a Roman court. In this general sense it was equivalent to "law" as such and had a number of adjectives or phrases attached to it: *ius civile, ius gentium,* and so on. *Lex* was something quite different and much more precise. Only that was *lex* that the *populus Romanus,* formally assembled by a magistrate, ordered. And this *lex* was not *ius* itself, but a source of *ius,* a source of paramount authority.

The Magistrates.   In a community such as Rome, where a differentiated system of courts was developed early, law in any sense can be understood only through the court. The essence of a Roman court was its control by a magistrate, in most instances by a magistrate with *imperium.*

It is this word *imperium* that is the keyword to Roman private, as well as public, law. It meant, probably, "paramount position," and the sense of "command" or "power" is derivative and not original. One of the titles of the first magistrates with *imperium* was *iudex,* the "pointer out" of *ius,* the man who declared where the *ius* lay between two disputants. He would doubtless have asserted that he merely discovered and did not create *ius,* but he soon very definitely and quite consciously did make *ius,* though never arbitrarily or capriciously. This was accomplished by the control exercised by the magistrate over the *legis actio,* the legal procedure established by statute, which was codified by the legislation of the Twelve Tables in the middle of the fifth century B.C.

Process and Procedure.   Procedure was always in the open, and trials were watched by throngs of citizens. It was because this throng was there, and only when the magistrate with *imperium* was fairly sure that their approval would follow, that he ventured openly to modify *ius* by refusing an *actio,* where, strictly speaking, there was no doubt about the *ius* asserted. The magistrate might refuse to entertain an action that was contrary to the *mos maiorum*—ancestral custom—and therefore to the sense of what was right, the *bonum et aequum,* which played so large a part in the development of the law.

It was by acts of this sort that a special source of law arose, the law that was derived from the practice of the magistrate. The "edict," which each new praetor published, contained more and more devices by which the substance of *ius* could be obtained without the time-consuming restrictions of the older law. Supplementary statutes helped less than the flexible activity of the practical magistrate. Indeed, as in our own legal history, statutes often appeared merely to confirm and render precise what the court had long ago done.

The beginnings of a profession of law had been laid by the middle of the third century B.C. The *iuris prudens* was a man who was versed in *ius* and whose services were at the disposal of citizens and magistrates. It was the *iuris prudens* who, as a private citizen, and later as a judge and magistrate, really created the law of Rome as we know it, and it is his exposition of it that forms far the largest part of the compilation of Justinian through which Roman law was transmitted to the medieval and modern world.

Formulary Law. Just as it was the existence of a legal profession that gave Roman law its special character, so it was a remarkable procedure, which displaced the *legis actio,* that enabled it both to fuse the *ius gentium* and the *ius civile* and to adapt itself to a world of the utmost diversity and of a high degree of civilization. This was the procedure *per formulam.* Despite the suggestions of its name, it was to a large extent informal and oral. The succession of pleadings in the *formula* required a sifting and a precision of the dispute between the litigants by the praetor himself, who then turned over the final settling of the dispute to a new kind of *iudex,* a private citizen and not a magistrate, who could and generally did rely on the pronouncements of learned lawyers for a legal decision and on his own common sense and experience for a factual decision.

Now, when *ius*—or rather *iura*—accumulate, as is bound to happen when social and economic life becomes complex, a demand for classification and definition is practically irresistible. It is notorious that in all matters affecting human relations, definitions are extremely difficult. But difficult or hazardous as they are, classification and definition are necessary, if only to enable lawyers to deal at all with the rapidly increasing mass of legal ideas; that is to say, to keep them in mind and discuss them. Definitions and classifications came to the Romans largely through the Stoics, who were much concerned with such matters. It is probably to the Stoic-trained Quintus Mucius, the teacher of Cicero, that we owe the familiar classification in which are listed the law of persons, of things, of obligation, of succession, of procedure, and finally of crimes. Most of the *iura* the Romans knew could be learned in connection with these terms.

Family and Marriage. As far as the law of persons is concerned, we come at once to what may be called the most important figure in the Roman law, the *pater familias.* He was the person in whom all *iura* met. He had all the three forms of status (*caput*). He was free, since a slave could not be a *pater familias.* He was a citizen, since an alien could not be one. And he could acquire and own every type of property and assume every relationship that the law recognized, and to a large extent only he could. The *pater familias* exercised *potestas* over his children and grandchildren. A man became a *pater familias* when his father died, provided that all his other male ancestors were also dead. As for the wife, she could remain within the *potestas* of her father, and if he died, she was free and legally competent.

While marriage was an informal contract, divorce was still more informal and, like all contracts, marriage could be ended by mutual consent; in fact, divorce was possible at the choice of either party. The only check on it was the legal and stringently enforced obligation to restore the dowry (*dos*), which the wife brought to the marriage to help defray the joint expenses of the household.

Ownership. The law of property (*res*) was simplified very early in the history of Rome, and the process of simplification began when the praetorship was created.

The older technicalities were disregarded, although not formally abolished. The most important question in this branch of the law was how the complex of *iura* that we call "ownership," or title, was transferred. It was done by delivery, and when there could be no actual handing over, as in the case of land, by permitting or aiding the new owner to take possession.

Obligations and Contracts. Where the Roman law left its most emphatic mark on the modern systems that are derived from it—the systems in vogue in nearly all the modern world except in the countries where Anglo-Saxon common law prevails—was in the law of obligation. A man became bound in a number of ways to do something, and this bond could be enforced by an *actio,* a suit at law. He became bound either by entering into a contract or by doing some injurious act. In the latter case, what he was bound to do was to make the injury good and in most instances to pay a penalty besides. The contracts, on the other hand, arose out of transactions that sprang from the many associations, economic and social, in which men were necessarily engaged. They were things like sales, leases, partnerships, loans, pledges, and mortgages. Such things fell into various classifications, and people could scarcely fail to be aware that the doing of these things involved a promise and therefore an obligation to do something in the future.

Prosecution. A magistrate had the right of summarily punishing an offense, but in general the matter was managed by permitting any citizen to bring an action against the wrongdoer, asking for his punishment rather than for compensation. The victim of the wrong was preferred as prosecutor, but if he did not come forward anyone else might. In Rome the criminal law entered on a new course by the legislation of Sulla, who prepared what was almost a penal code in which many old categories of offenses were clarified and expanded, and the trial of the cases was referred to a number of panels. The members of a panel, the *iudices,* were something between judges and jurymen. They were judges of both law and fact, and there was no appeal or right of tribunician intercession.

Inheritance. One final group of *iura* was connected with the problems created by the death of the *pater familias.* The ancient law as codified in the Twelve Tables had much to say of that. The succession to the manifold kinds of property of the deceased ought normally to come to the family, the "right heirs." But the *pater familias* early acquired the right to will his property to others. The history of testamentary succession became thereafter an account of the gradual limitation of the right of disposing of property by will. It became necessary to prevent the multiplying of legacies to the total exclusion of the "right heirs"; then, to protect creditors; and finally to provide for members of the family, who, it was felt, ought not to be deprived of all share in the inheritance by an undutiful testator.

Bonum et Aequum. Something must also be said of the general and continuous movement by which technical exactitude and ritual precision, which were highly valued in the early stages, were gradually loosened and humanized for the very reason that seemed to make strictures necessary at first. They were taken to be securities for justice and they became serious obstacles.

The idea of *bonum et aequum* was an almost inevitable inference from the power of the praetor—the magistrate with *imperium*—to qualify the unlimited exercise of an undoubted *ius*. The phrase describes what was "good" or "right" because it was "fair," that is, because it gave each litigant what it was proper for him to have. Whereas the phrase *bonum et aequum* at first was necessarily understood as little more than "in accordance with custom," it soon enough became enlarged to include a growing sense that men of moral integrity do not insist on means of oppressing others, even if they could be justified by literal compliance with the law. This last idea was old enough to have an archaic formulation, "as ought to be done by right-thinking men, acting rightly toward each other." Continually, by their control of the *formula,* praetors pushed cases that plaintiffs sought to have decided by strict law into the field of the *bonum et aequum.* And in the first century of the empire, Celsus, a sharp and practical lawyer with no philosophical pretensions, boldly announced what has become the tritest of Roman law citations, "Law is a device for attaining the *bonum et aequum.*"

It is certainly a most extraordinary result that a vast legal system, developed in a slave economy and against a background of philosophic paganism, should have been, with little adjustment, capable of serving the needs of the Christian societies not only of feudal and Renaissance Europe but, after the turn of the seventeenth century, also of the credit and capitalist economy of our own day. Little as it impinges on our consciousness, Roman law has colored and molded our civilization, perhaps as much as any single element we have derived from those ancient societies out of which we have constructed most of our social and intellectual life.[3]

RELIGION

Rome's Cosmopolitan Population.   Juvenal's statement that the waters of the Orontes had flowed into the Tiber was only slightly exaggerated, for imperial Rome swarmed with Syrians and other peoples of the Near East who had come to the capital for a variety of reasons. Many of them were slaves, or their descendants, and thousands of others were merchants. Still others in Rome had learned of the Near East at first hand as soldiers. The ethnic stock of the city was changing, and at the same time many of these newcomers, by their initiative and industry, rose to a high position in society. Needless to say, they brought their own ideas and outlook on life with them.

While we are apt to speak of the Roman Empire as a Greco-Roman world, the Hellenistic half did, of course, include the ancient Near East, that third great cultural element of antiquity. Now, as in the past, its significant contribution was to be in the field of religion, and now the political unity of the world facilitated the rapid spread of ideas. The soil, moreover, was particularly fertile, not only because so many Orientals had migrated to the West and formed a ready audience, but also because by the second century people everywhere yearned for something new, eagerly seeking faith, not intellectualism.

Philosophy.   This is not to say that the various schools of philosophy did not

---

[3] See also pp. 499f.

continue to exist. For example, Philo, the Jewish philosopher of Alexandria, explained Judaism to his followers during the first century by reference to Greek philosophy, while Dio Chrysostom, the "golden-tongued" orator of the Greeks, preached virtue, but each in his own way was leading philosophy along the road to a union with morality, to an elaboration of the rules of life, rather than toward further speculation. In a sense, too, this was true of Stoicism, with its insistence on the brotherhood of man. Stoicism, as interpreted by a Seneca, might teach people detachment and self-sufficiency and how to live with dignity and die with courage, but its refusal to countenance servility made it politically obnoxious to emperors such as Domitian. Epictetus, the Phrygian freedman, was among the philosophers banished from Rome by him. In his *Meditations,* the emperor-philosopher Marcus Aurelius proclaimed himself a citizen of the world, but his was a modified form of Stoicism, which seemed to think less of a world soul and more of a beneficent Providence.

The New Outlook. Philosophy, however, was not for the masses. Neither was the prosaic old-time religion, except on public occasions when processions in honor of Jupiter and other gods made pleasing spectacles. Emperor worship continued to provide the world with a common, patriotic bond, but it did not satisfy the needs of the heart. What people needed by the second century, or thought they needed, was faith in another world that would be happier than this, which, although peaceful, could seem crassly materialistic.

Eastern Religions. Various religions had been coming out of the East for a long time, that of Magna Mater, the Great Mother, before the days of the war with Hannibal. Another religion to come out of the East long before was that of Isis, whose worship received special impetus from Pompey's soldiers. Its success, however, was due not to its theology or morals (both being quite uncertain) but to its ritual and formulas, which bent the will of heaven and promised future bliss. All Eastern religions had some things in common: they demanded faith; they promised communion with the deity, if the faithful performed certain acts of purification and accepted various symbols; and some even guaranteed eternal life. They grew steadily in popularity and were assured of victory the moment that conditions were ripe. Such a moment was the second century; at least, it was propitious for the beginning of a struggle that was to clear the path for a universal religion as a substitute for the ancient conception of the service of gods and mortals as a civic duty.

Mithraism. A religion that had particular appeal during the second century, and was to be Christianity's chief rival in the next, was a fighting faith that attracted the soldiers engaged in Eastern wars and from them spread westward, as far as the cities and camps of the Rhineland and Britain. This was Mithraism, which had its origin in the Zoroastrian worship of Ahura Mazda. Mithra was not a solar divinity; rather, he was the divine agent of Ahura Mazda, the god of light. In the eternal struggle between the powers of light and darkness, Mithra appeared as the leader of the forces of light, as the god of truth and purity. Women were excluded, but all men—rich and poor, free and slave—were eligible to worship him, and all were treated alike in the underground chapels, where the sacred bull was sacrificed. The faithful formed

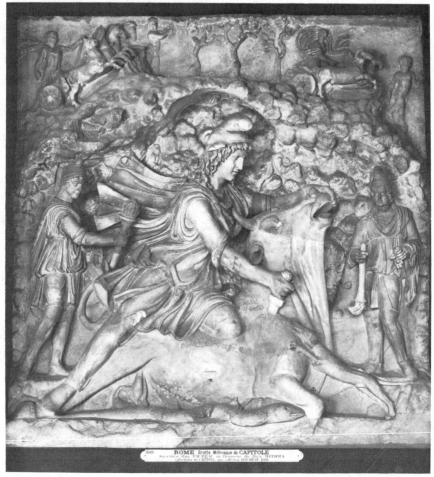

FIGURE 67. A Roman relief showing the sacrifice of a bull in honor of Mithra.

a secret society, with their own watchwords; and all, no doubt, were filled with the certainty of a glorious immortality as they performed the ritual and fasted and moved through the seven degrees of initiation.

Christianity. Those in the West who first listened sympathetically to these religions were chiefly individuals who had their roots in the Near East, and in this respect Christianity was no exception. In the beginning, Christianity was often mistaken for Judaism, and its appeal in Rome, for example, was originally to Jewish slaves. All religions grew under the protection of the imperial government, which tolerated faiths so long as they were not morally offensive or subversive. But Christianity seemingly failed both tests. In so doing, it invited persecution, and yet its certitude and rejection of every compromise added immeasurably to its strength, as did the fact that, instead of claiming some mythical figure as its founder, it could point to a historical figure as the Messiah.

The religion of Jesus of Nazareth, who was born in the reign of Augustus and crucified in that of Tiberius (ca. 30), was destined to revolutionize the West. For the multitude of Greco-Roman gods, or the meticulous ritual of other faiths, it substituted the Father in Heaven; for bloody ceremonies, pure worship; for learning, love and charity, kindness and joy; for law, the Sermon on the Mount; for a selfish, sophisticated life, a life of sacrifice and fellowship. Paul carried it early to the "Gentiles," and Peter preached it even in Rome. Everywhere, and especially in the Eastern cities, the lower classes tended to accept a faith that esteemed the slave equally with the emperor and claimed the humblest on earth as the greatest saints. All who shared in this religion enjoyed the comforting hope of eternal happiness.

Christian Opposition to Established Society. During the first century the followers of Jesus Christ attracted little attention, for Nero's persecution was limited to Christians in Rome and was conceived with the aim of finding scapegoats for the fire that destroyed so much of the city. The learned and the powerful alike considered Christians unworthy of notice, and the government, which protected the public worship of all peoples within the empire, included the Christians with the Jews. But when they discovered that the Christians were a distinct sect, and an increasingly anti-Semitic one at that, the Romans came gradually to regard them as a menace to existing society and government. Unlike the Romans, the Christians were intolerant of all other religions and exceedingly aggressive in making new converts. To keep themselves free from idolatry, they refused to associate with others in public festivities and often in ordinary pleasures, an attitude that won them Tacitus' description of "haters of mankind." Their refusal to worship the Genius of the emperor was naturally construed as impiety and treason, and a religion such as theirs that looked forward to the universal Apocalypse and the end to earthly empires seemed downright subversive. The government, which was always suspicious of secret meetings, could see nothing but danger in those of the Christians, whose church was, in fact, a great secret society with branches in many cities and towns. A class of people, and that in large part an urban lower class of materially dispossessed people, which sometimes advocated the communal ownership of property and objected to military service, seemed to be a threat to society. These were the chief reasons that they were persecuted. Some of them, when accused, obstinately deified the authorities and courted martyrdom. Such conduct widened the chasm between the civil power and the new church, which by the end of the second century had a diocesan organization under bishops. The leaders, too, by wrangling over minute points of doctrine, added further disrepute to their cause.

Persecution of the Christians. At first, some civil authorities occasionally proceeded, accordingly, to punish the Christians for real or imaginary offenses against law and order. In 113 we find Trajan, however, instructing Pliny, the governor of Bithynia, not to hunt them down or to receive anonymous charges against them but to condemn those only who were openly known as Christians and therefore disloyal. Crucial to persecution was the official demand that suspected Christians be tested by having to sacrifice to Rome and the emperor before the authorities. Hadrian discouraged persecution and made informers responsible for any outbreaks their accusations might cause. His successor, the gentle Antoninus Pius, though a restorer of the ancient religion, himself persecuted no one. Nevertheless in his reign popular hatred forced the magistrates in some cities to torture and kill prominent Christians. Under Marcus Aurelius a change came for the worse. As popular dislike of the Christians excited tumults in many cities, especially in the East, he ordered those who confessed the faith to be beaten to death, but otherwise he paid the Christians little attention. Their trouble came chiefly from the people, who regarded them with superstitious hatred. Plague, famine, and other calamities demanded victims, and accordingly riots broke out against them in Lugdunum and elsewhere. Their enemies asserted, on mere rumor, that in their religious meetings the Christians were guilty of gross immorality and feasted on their children. But persecution, instead of helping the empire or its gods, strengthened the new faith and made it more aggressive.

The Early Church. The early Christian congregations met in private homes, indeed, wherever they could, until such time as they were able to build their own basilicas. In the beginning, of course, they had no Christian style to copy, so that in their architecture and other arts they merely followed the Roman phase of Hellenistic art that they observed around them. The subterranean catacombs of Rome, where early Christians were buried (as might be members of any society), have some of our earliest Christian frescoes, but the subjects are so pagan in content that they might be from Pompeii. During the second century a beginning was made of showing Christian subjects—a Good Shepherd or Daniel with his lions—but the scenes and figures are from the Old Testament rather than the New. There were two reasons for this. In the first place, the Old Testament had been translated into Greek at Alexandria long before the Christian era, and its stories were familiar to the Jewish colonies throughout the Roman world. Second, illustrated copies of the Old Testament had been produced at Alexandria and elsewhere and provided themes for the nascent Christian art. It is not until the third century that Christ—a youthful, beardless figure with short hair—begins to appear in frescoes. The excavations at Dura-Europos on the Euphrates show with particular clarity how Greco-Roman art was transformed into something new, involving a shift of content from Greek naturalism to the immaterialism of the East, which marks Christian art. Representations stressing the importance of the spirit and the afterlife became the new theme in art at a time when humankind was confronted with a multitude of problems.

31

The Imperial Crisis and Recovery (A.D. 193–395)

THE MILITARIZATION OF GOVERNMENT: THE SEVERI (A.D. 193–235)

Renewed Emphasis on the Military Basis of Authority. Commodus was strangled the night before he was to take the consulship on January 1, 193. The new year, accordingly, opened propitiously, with Publius Helvius Pertinax the choice of the praetorians. The senate was happy to accept him as emperor, for he was not only a senator himself but also the city prefect and had already proved himself an able military commander under Marcus Aurelius. Pertinax applied himself with energy and success to the restoration of finances and public order, but his habits of economy and severe discipline so displeased the praetorians that they murdered him after three months' rule. Thereupon they offered the throne to the highest bidder, and the opportunity was seized by Marcus Didius Julianus, a wealthy senator, who bought it by a promise to pay the praetorians twenty-five thousand sesterces apiece. So indoctrinated had the troops become with the idea of dynastic succession that, failing a dynasty, civil war was inevitable as in 68. Another broke out in 193 and raged until the strongest general could establish a dynasty of his own. When news of these proceedings reached the troops in Syria, on the Danube, and in Britain, they nominated their own commanders to the office of emperor. Publius Septimius Severus, the legate of Upper Pannonia, who had the best army and was nearest Rome, won the prize. As he approached the capital, his nomination was confirmed by the senate, which had already decreed the death of Julianus.

Septimius Severus (193–211). A member of an equestrian family of romanized Punic stock, Septimius Severus (193–211) was the first emperor born in Africa (at Leptis Magna). He was a firm, clear-headed man who had his own ideas concerning the needs of the empire. One of his first acts was to disband the ungovernable praetorians and to form a new guard of fifteen thousand men from the legions, which by now were largely staffed by provincials. Another key to imperial policy is to be found in the stationing of a legion near Rome, on the Alban Mount. This garrison, even more than Severus' adoption of the title *"imperator,"* signalized the military basis of the monarchy.

Eastern and Western Campaigns.   In order that he might deal separately with the
two rival claimants to the throne, Septimius Severus cunningly offered Clodius
Albinus, the legate of Britain, the title of "Caesar," as if he were to be the successor, and then marched against Gaius Pescennius Niger, the legate of Syria. On
the historic battlefield of Issus, he crushed Niger (194) and proceeded to reassert
Roman authority in northern Mesopotamia and in Osroene, a client state that now
became a province with its capital at Nisibis. During the general restoration of order
in the East, however, an important outpost against the barbarians, Byzantium, was
severely damaged. Severus then turned on Albinus. In 197 the two armies fought at
Lugdunum, which resulted in the death of Albinus and the irreparable devastation
of the greatest city of Gaul. These disturbances gave Vologases IV, the Parthian
king, an opportunity to invade northern Mesopotamia (197-199), but Severus
hurried to the East, relieved the seige of Nisibis, and once again established order
there.

The Army.   For his Parthian campaign Severus had raised three new legions,
which now stood at a total of thirty-three, or 180,000 men; with the auxiliaries,
the army of the empire numbered about 400,000 troops. The auxiliaries, as the
result of a practice that had been building up for a century, included many barbarians, especially Germans, who had been allowed to occupy border districts
of the empire; they formed special contingents known as *numeri* and fought in
their native manner under Roman officers. Because of his dependence on the soldiers, which he openly recognized, Severus increased their pay and allowed them
to marry.

The Frontier Defenses.   Severus also gave much attention to the frontier defenses. A great ditch and wall, with towers and forts, protected North Africa; the
extent of these fortifications was made clear only by aerial photography in the
years following World War II. A series of forts sufficed to protect Asia and the
Danube, which marked the natural northern border. Dacia, however, lay to the
north of the river and had its own *limes;* small sections survive, together with the
wall that protected Moesia at the point where the Danube turns sharply north (see
Mursa and Tomi on the rear endpaper map). The *limes,* which extended for a distance of 350 miles from Rhine to Danube, was strengthened by Severus' son
Caracalla in its Raetian section; here, for more than a hundred miles, a solid stone
wall (four feet thick and six to nine feet high) replaced the earlier wooden palisade.
A determined enemy could, of course, penetrate the *limes,* although the garrisons
in the larger forts and camps to the rear would contain him. The general purpose of
the *limes* was to keep out raiding bands and to control the traffic between the
empire and the barbarian world beyond; this trade, no less than the soldiers themselves, spread Roman civilization far beyond the frontiers. Severus found it necessary to abandon the Wall of Antoninus Pius in Britain because so many troops had
been moved to Gaul by Albinus in his bid for the throne that the Caledonians could
not be controlled. Hadrian's Wall, therefore, was repaired and established as the
new line of defense. It had been designed to resist large hostile forces—not mere
raiding bands—with a garrison stationed at intervals of a mile throughout its extent

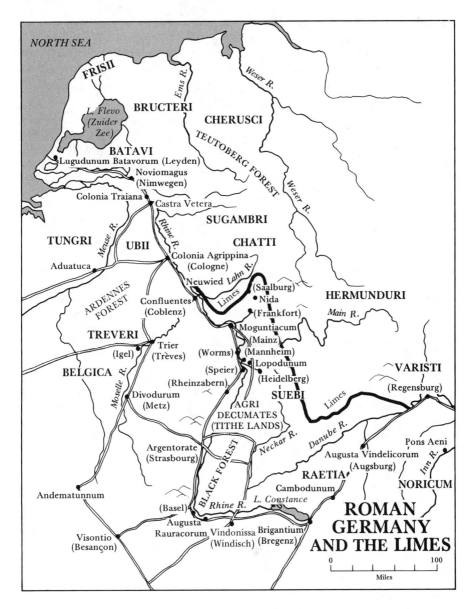

NORTH SEA

FRISII

BRUCTERI

CHERUSCI

Ems R.

Weser R.

L. Flevo
(Zuider
Zee)

BATAVI

TEUTOBERG FOREST

Lugudunum Batavorum (Leyden)

Noviomagus
(Nimwegen)

Colonia Traiana

Castra Vetera

Weser R.

SUGAMBRI

TUNGRI

UBII

CHATTI

Meuse R.

Rhine R.

Aduatuca

Colonia Agrippina
(Cologne)

Neuwied *Lahn R.*

(Saalburg)

HERMUNDURI

ARDENNES
FOREST

Confluentes
(Coblenz)

Limes

Nida

(Frankfort)

Main R.

TREVERI

Trier
(Igel)   (Trèves)

(Worms)

Moguntiacum
(Mainz)

(Mannheim)

BELGICA

Moselle R.

(Speier)
(Rheinzabern)

Lopodunum
(Heidelberg)

SUEBI

Limes

VARISTI

(Regensburg)

Divodurum
(Metz)

AGRI
DECUMATES
(TITHE LANDS)

Neckar R.

Danube R.

Pons Aeni

Inn R.

Argentorate
(Strasbourg)

BLACK FOREST

Augusta Vindelicorum
(Augsburg)

RAETIA

NORICUM

Andematunnum

Cambodunum

(Basel)   *Rhine R.*   L. Constance

Augusta
Visontio   Rauracorum Vindonissa Brigantium
(Besançon)   (Windisch) (Bregenz)

ROMAN
GERMANY
AND THE LIMES

0   100

Miles

of seventy-six miles. The wall itself was eight feet thick and twenty feet high, with fourteen small forts enclosed within it and larger forts and camps to the rear. Severus' sons, Caracalla and Geta, both of whom had been invested with the title of Augustus, accompanied him on the final expedition of his life (208-211), against the restless Caledonians; the emperor died besieging Eboracum (York).

Government.   Among the pressing problems that confronted Septimius Severus on his accession, none was more ominous than the empty treasury. Not only had taxes become oppressively high, but in many places, especially in Egypt, poorer people had long since begun to flee the tax gatherer. A result was that government had no choice but to compel municipal councils to assume the responsibility of paying the local taxes, so that office holding, which had once been sought as an honor, became a burden forced on the rich. Moreover the services rendered by certain groups—such as the colleges or guilds of firemen, bakers, and oil merchants—were considered so important that the individuals were exempted from their regular municipal obligations, in order that they might attend strictly to business; in days not long after the Severi, their services were regarded as public duties (*munera*) that were both obligatory and hereditary. The guilds of shipowners were, of course, closely controlled by the government, for Rome continued to import five million bushels of grain annually from Egypt, about a third of its requirements. The number of those receiving free grain at Rome did not increase appreciably under the empire—and free oil had recently been added to the list—but the number and cost of holidays and spectacles were much greater. Severus also undertook a building program throughout the empire, one memorial of which, his imposing arch, still stands in the Roman Forum. The increasingly large bureaucracy and the army required still more money. Another expense was the imperial post; riders and horses in relays carried official documents and letters over the network of roads.

In order to meet expenses, Severus debased the *denarius,* as emperors had done periodically beginning with Nero. Severus mixed copper and silver in approximately equal proportions, while Caracalla issued a new coin, called the *Antoninianus,* which was supposed to be worth two *denarii* but actually contained only half that value in silver. One windfall came Severus' way. The adherents of his rival, Albinus, had been both numerous and prominent, and accordingly he confiscated their property. A special financial department, known as the *res privata* (privy purse), was set up to look after his new riches, the ancient state treasury (the *aerarium Saturni*) having long since degenerated into a local treasury.

Cosmopolitan Government.   His own provincial origin and that of his wife, Julia Domna—who was the daughter of the priest of the Sun God at Emesa, a Syrian temple state—doubtless influenced Severus' attitude toward provincials in general, particularly those from the East. At least two-thirds of the senate were non-Italian, and most of the most recent members came from Asia Minor, Syria, Egypt, and Africa. Severus also opened many senatorial careers to the sons of centurions and to equestrians, the class he especially favored in administration. These new members of the senate gradually became Italian in outlook; and the prestige of the senatorial class continued, because of both its antiquity and the wealth of its members. Society was becoming more stratified than ever, and already (from ca. 150) the official classes were known as *honestiores,* the common people as *humiliores.* Indeed, the emperor proclaimed his family as sacred and Rome, as a consequence, a sacred city.

Jurisprudence.   Septimius Severus ruled without any regard to the senate, which merely ratified his addresses and thereby gave them the force of law. The center of administrative authority shifted to imperial councils, which gave close attention to the welfare of the provinces and supervised the governors, who were now generally called *praesides,* an increasing number of whom were equestrians, not senators. The praetorian prefect was the most powerful man in the empire after the emperor himself. The task of the praetorian prefect was to preside over the imperial councils if the emperor was absent, to command the military forces in Italy, to try important cases arising in Italy more than one hundred miles from Rome, and to hear appeals from the provinces; the city prefect tried cases arising within one hundred miles of Rome. Papinian was a praetorian prefect at this time; he was perhaps the ablest of Roman jurists, though his younger contemporaries—Paul, Ulpian, and Modestine—were scarcely less eminent. Through them and their associates, Roman law reached the height of development. Order was brought to the mass of past legislation, principles were established, and much in the way of legal theory was adopted from the Hellenistic East. These jurists were also responsible for the adoption of principles that justified autocratic rule. Later jurists did little more than systematize the material already existing. [1]

Caracalla (211-217). The devotion of the armies to the dynastic principle, as well as personal ambition, explains Septimius Severus' decree that he was the son by adoption of Marcus Aurelius. On his death, accordingly, his son Bassianus ascended the throne with the title of Marcus Aurelius Antoninus, but he is better known from the nickname of the Gallic cloak he wore, Caracalla. Caracalla was a brutal spendthrift; nevertheless he occupies a peculiar niche in the history of Rome as the emperor who completed the development of several centuries that brought Italy and the provinces to the same plane. His edict of 212, embodied in the *Constitutio Antoniniana,* or Antonine Constitution, made all the free men of the empire Roman citizens. No special enthusiasm greeted this act, for citizenship now had its burdens; the complete romanization of the provinces meant that the special taxes of citizens would be paid by all. Equally in keeping with Caracalla's autocratic nature was the murder of his brother Geta, who was a possible rival, and of Papinian. In like manner he also tyrannized over the senate and cultivated the work of informers; he also increased the pay of the soldiers and erected huge baths, which rank among the largest monuments of ancient Rome. We are hardly surprised, then, that Caracalla found it necessary to increase taxes and to debase the coinage still further.

Elagabalus (218-222). Two campaigns called Caracalla from Rome: one in the West, where he was able to strengthen the Rhine-Danube defenses; the other in the East, against the Parthians. In 217 a praetorian prefect, Macrinus, had him murdered at Carrhae and reigned in his stead, with his son Diadumenianus, only to be overthrown the following year by Varius Avitus Bassianus. This creature was the grandson of Julia Maesa, the sister of Julia Domna. Through the scheming and ability of Julia Maesa, the Severan dynasty was thus restored, [2] but the new emperor was a mere youth of fourteen, a sensual boy who will perhaps always rank as

---

[1] For a fuller discussion, see pp. 458 ff.
[2] Genealogical Table, p. 529.

the most debauched Roman emperor. He had been priest of the Syrian Sun God Elagabal at Emesa and consequently is known to history as Elagabalus. The new god and his cult were transported to Rome. For four years, while his grandmother ruled on his behalf, Elagabalus indulged himself, until finally the praetorians killed him (222).

Severus Alexander (222-235). His cousin and successor, Severus Alexander, was an amiable youth, mentally gifted and well intentioned, but it was unfortunate that at a time when the duties of the imperial office called loudly for a man of energy and iron, the emperor should have been merely a good-natured dreamer. As Alexander was only fourteen on his accession, the government rested with his mother, Julia Mamaea; she in turn was assisted by Ulpian, the great jurist, who was also a praetorian prefect, and, allegedly, by a council of sixteen senators. Reversing the policy of Septimius Severus and Caracalla, this administration looked to the senate to counteract the growing influence of the army, a policy that marks almost the last appearance of the senate, albeit a feeble one, on the stage of history before its final and complete reduction to the status of a municipal council. Not only in his outward respect for republican traditions, but also in his patronage of education, in his attention to the needs of the poor, and generally in his policy of mildness and justice, Alexander was a faint imitation of "the good emperors." It was impossible, however, to return to the past, and despite all appearances the government remained autocratic.

The Sassanids. Severus Alexander himself was too weak and incompetent to maintain discipline among the soldiers or to defend the empire at the very time when a new danger to the Roman world arose. Ever since the days of Trajan, the Parthian Empire of the Arsacids had slowly declined, but in 227 the Persians suddenly asserted their independence, overthrew the Parthian rule and made the empire Persian, with Ctesiphon as the capital. Artaxerxes (Ardashir), the founder of the new Sassanid dynasty, supported an official revival of Zoroastrianism, the ancient worship of the spirit of Good and Light, against whom darkness and evil forever warred. The ensuing religious fervor strengthened the position of the new monarch, and at the same time, his talent for organization made him a military power.

Since he looked on himself as the successor of the great Cyrus, who had founded the Persian Empire of many centuries ago, Artaxerxes claimed all Asia and ordered Severus Alexander to confine his authority to Europe. An inconclusive war followed, ending superficially to Rome's advantage, but the Eastern menace remained and compelled Rome to mass troops on the Euphrates at the very time when the Alemanni, a Germanic tribe, were threatening invasion. Alexander hurried to Mogontiacum (Mainz), where by diplomacy and bribes he tried to hold off the enemy. But just as the praetorian guards had killed their prefect, Ulpian, some years ago, so now the soldiers, disgusted with Alexander's weak policy, murdered their emperor (235).

The death of Severus Alexander brought the Roman Peace to an end. Only twice since the battle of Actium (31 B.C.) had it been seriously disturbed: in the year of the four emperors (68-69) and in the years immediately following the death of

Commodus (192). For more than two and a half centuries the mighty Roman Empire had provided the civilized world with one blessing it had never enjoyed before; and large areas of that world enjoyed a greater prosperity than ever before or since.

MILITARY ANARCHY (A.D. 235–285)

Civil War, Invasion, and Plague. The murder of Severus Alexander inaugurated a period of anarchy, when for fifty years emperor followed emperor.[3] Not counting a score or more of so-called tyrants—men who unsuccessfully made a bid for the throne—there were not less than twenty-six emperors, only one of whom died a natural death. In the year 260 alone, Gallienus faced eighteen rivals. At the same time, large, organized waves of barbarians—not mere raiding bands—swept over the empire's defenses, often penetrating far into the interior: Saxons sailed against Britain; Berber tribes attacked in Africa; Franks, Alemanni, and other Germanic tribes swarmed across the Rhine; the Quadi and the Marcomanni crossed the Danube; the Carpi, the Sarmatians, and the Vandals overran Dacia and Moesia; the Goths sailed across the Black Sea to ravage Asia Minor; the Herulians sacked Athens; and the Persians menaced the East. As if civil war and invasion were not enough, piracy and brigandage did their share to close lines of communication, stop trade and industry, and carry off movable wealth. Large areas of the empire broke away and set themselves up as independent states, the Christians were regarded as potential traitors—and more than once, as a consequence, were persecuted; and, finally, the dreadful toll of life was greatly increased by a plague, which broke out in 251, raged till 266, and continued for several years thereafter.

The Forces of Destruction. To speak generally, the well-being of the Roman world hitherto had been chiefly due to the wisdom of a line of rulers who had been able to secure the goodwill of the senate and of the population of Rome and the empire, the subordination of the praetorians and the army, and the respect of surrounding peoples. A system cannot be lasting, however, in which so much depends not on continuously directed political activity, but on the accidental succession of able rulers. While the ancient provinces, far removed from the frontiers and enfeebled by centuries of peace, passively bore the burdens of taxation and permitted interference with the liberties of their towns and cities, the populace of Rome rioted if their amusements and food were curtailed. Moreover the interests of the senate often clashed with those of the emperor or the soldiers. The praetorians had been established as a guard of the emperor's person, but they were ready to kill him in order to secure a gift from his successor. Failing a dynasty as in 68 and 193, civil war broke out among the troops. The mutinies and civil wars during the third century are therefore understandable, as no dynasty was established; they can also be explained by the greed of the unruly frontier soldiers, who had lost all contact and community of interest with the interior of the empire and

[3] List of Roman Emperors, p. 527.

were ready to plunder the civilians and enthrone their general in the hope that their own lot would be improved. Though they hated the decurion classes in the cities, they did not hesitate to despoil the peasants whom the city dwellers had also exploited.

A New Governmental Policy Required. To restore order, it was necessary to strengthen the imperial office. As the task of government seemed too great for a single ruler, more than one emperor in the third century shared his duties and honors with a colleague. Again, as the collapse of old institutions exposed the emperor more than ever before to mutiny and assassination, he sought new safe-guards for his person and his authority and became an ever more remote figure. Finally Rome ceased in all but name to be the capital of the empire, as the soldier emperors took up their abode at the posts of danger and issued their decrees from provincial cities. That is to say, some time during the period of military anarchy, the principate that Augustus had founded long ago ceased to be; the senate went down before the soldiers and at last no longer helped to govern or even to invest the emperor with his authority to rule.

Persian Wars. The soldiers who had been responsible for the murder of Severus Alexander elevated their general, a Thracian peasant by the name of Maximinus, to the purple. Maximinus was the first uncouth provincial in history to become emperor of Rome, and although he was a general good enough to ward off invasions from across the frontiers, he was in other ways despotic and cruel. A civilian reac-tion against his terrorism set in, first in Africa, where the proconsul Gordian and his son were proclaimed emperors. They soon lost their lives, however, whereupon the senate rose to the occasion and effected the death of Maximinus. The new emperor, Gordian III (238-244), gave the empire a brief respite, and during his reign the gates of the temple of Janus were closed, for the last recorded time, as a sign of peace. But Gordian was soon compelled by events to hurry eastward, for the Per-sian threat to the empire seemed the most serious at the moment. As he was about to win a victory over the new Sassanid king, Shapur I, son of Artaxerxes, Gordian was murdered by his praetorian prefect, Philip the Arabian. Philip patched up a peace with the Persians but was murdered himself shortly thereafter. As these calamities fell on the civilized world, Goths sailed across the Black Sea and raided Asia Minor and even the Aegean. Many people within the empire thought the Christians responsible for the disasters, and in order to bring these domestic foes out into the open, the emperor Decius (249-251) ordered that everyone through-out the empire should publicly sacrifice to the gods of the state. Many Christians, especially wealthy and conspicuous ones, apostatized their faith, while some stood firm and were martyred.

The Rise of Palmyra. Not much later the emperor Valerian (253-260) resumed the persecution of the Christians, particularly of their bishops and leaders. With his son and colleague, Gallienus (253-268), Valerian also tried to brace the empire against repeated shocks. He himself went to the East, where the Sassanid king, Shapur I, had recently won Armenia. Valerian was treacherously seized by the Persians in a conference and killed, but shortly afterward Odenathus, Rome's client king of Palmyra, defeated Shapur at Carrhae. Gallienus, who was now sole emperor, rewarded Odenathus with the title "Commander of the Romans" (*Dux Romanorum*); the Palmyrene, with his famous wife, Zenobia, then proceeded to create what was in effect an independent state. It came to include Asia Minor and Egypt.

The Gallic Empire.   Gallienus was no more capable of defending the West than the East, and consequently the troops of Gaul revolted and hailed Postumus, their general, as emperor. A new state, known as Imperium Galliarum, was set up (260), with its capital at Augusta Treverorum (Trèves, Trier).

The Empire's Threatened Physical and Economic Ruin.   The economic, no less than the physical, ruin of the empire faced Gallienus. The coinage became so debased that it was practically worthless, trade and industry shrank, prices rose in places twenty times what they had previously been, and people everywhere were compelled to shoulder public duties, this at a moment when the plague was at its height. Taxes for the maintenance of the army (the military *annona*) were paid in kind and were under the general supervision of the praetorian prefects. Additional contributions were demanded from local inhabitants for armies on the march; in spite of the need of military protection, therefore, in so disordered a period, there were few things a community dreaded more than to have an army quartered on it. Gallienus, however, was a man of resource and energy. He stopped the persecution of the Christians, to win as much unity within the empire as possible. To protect himself from senators who might seek the throne, he all but excluded them from a military career. The great commands—the distinction between senatorial and imperial provinces disappeared—were now held by equestrians, many of whom rose from the ranks, and from this class (especially from those who recieved their training in the Danubian provinces) came a series of fine generals and even emperors.

Invasions of Goths and Alemanni.   On the military front Gallienus drove the Goths from Moesia and the Marcomanni from Italy, and in the Balkans, he defeated the Herulians, barbarians who had come from the north and sacked Athens. He settled Goths and Marcomanni in Upper Pannonia and then was forced to return to Italy. At Mediolanum (Milan) he defeated swarms of Alemanni who had crossed the Alps, and not much later he was murdered. The chief contribution to the empire's welfare by his successor, Claudius Gothicus (268-270), was, as his surname suggests, a resounding defeat of the Goths.

Aurelian.   The next emperor was Lucius Domitius Aurelianus (270-275), a humble Illyrian who was to prove the most competent ruler since the days of Septimius Severus. A good general and a strict disciplinarian, with an enviable record as a cavalry commander, Aurelian set about the task of restoring the Roman Empire. Rome's advantage over the barbarian world in the past had consisted in her superior discipline and technical knowledge, but these qualities were disappearing as rapidly as the army itself became barbarized. Moreover, vast spaces, particularly along the frontiers, had been depopulated and resettled with barbarians as *coloni,* and Rome was using more barbarian auxiliaries (*numeri*) to fight barbarians. To cope with the changed situation, the Romans posted militia troops along the frontiers and, like Gallienus, organized mobile forces at strategic points to the rear that could be quickly moved to threatened areas. Since the Persians were especially skillful in the use of cavalry, the Roman foot soldier was equipped with a long sword, which was a better weapon against cavalry than the customary short sword. In addition, Aurelian developed to a high degree of effectiveness the Moorish and other units of cavalry, some of whom were archers; and from Persia was imported the idea of heavy-mailed mounted lancers (cataphracts).

During Aurelian's reign there was no relief from invasions of Sarmatians, Vandals, and other barbarians. The Greco-Roman world was by now accustomed to them and had been looking to its local defenses, those long-forgotten walls that were suddenly put into repair all over the empire. The Mediterranean lands today are full of these silent reminders of the crisis through which civilization once passed, and nowhere more dramatically than at Rome itself, where Aurelian's Wall still stands, twenty feet high, twelve feet thick, and twelve miles in circumference. Almost half a millennium had passed since the last dangerous enemy, Hannibal, had threatened Rome.

The Empire Restored.   The exposed position of Dacia led Aurelian to complete what Gallienus had begun: its abandonment and the creation of a new province of the same name, south of the Danube, carved from parts of Moesia and Thrace. But the real achievement of Aurelian was to regain those large areas that had broken away from the empire. In 271 Zenobia, now a widow, proclaimed Palmyra a kingdom wholly independent of Rome, but in the following year Aurelian took the city and not long afterward, suspecting its loyalty, sacked it. He then marched west and, finding that Tetricus, the new emperor of Gaul, was friendly toward him, completed the unification of the empire. With little exaggeration he called himself "Restorer of the World" (*Restitutor Orbis*).

The Sun God.   Aurelian was not equally successful in administration. He tried, without achieving much, to introduce a sounder currency; and to the Roman masses he gave baked bread instead of grain, as well as salt, pork, and oil. Simple and frugal in his personal habits, in public Aurelian appeared a complete autocrat, surrounded with grand ceremony and protected by the Sun God, whose worship he made an official religion of the empire.

After Aurelian's murder in 275, he was followed in rapid order by half a dozen emperors. When, finally, assassination removed them from the scene (285), the way was clear for an Illyrian general, Diocles, to remake the Roman world.

AUTOCRACY: DIOCLETIAN AND CONSTANTINE (A.D. 285-337)

Diocletian.   The Illyrian officer, Diocles, who was now master of the Roman Empire, chose for himself the name Gaius Valerius Aurelius Diocletianus (285-305). The son of a freedman, Diocletian was, without question, an efficient innovator, blessed with the ability to bring order out of anarchy, but the autocratic government he set up as his particular solution oppressed many of the empire's subjects, some of whom eventually yearned for barbarian invaders and freedom.

Division of Responsibility.   Diocletian recognized that the task of defending the empire from foreign and domestic foes, and of administering it, was too much for

FIGURE 68. The Tetrarchs of Diocletian, St. Mark's, Venice.

The Granger Collection

one man. He therefore hit on an ingenious scheme called the Tetrarchy, whereby he would associate with himself an Augustus, and then each of them would adopt two successors, known as Caesars; on the death or retirement of the Augusti, their Caesars would become Augusti and ·adopt two other Caesars, and so on. Accordingly, Diocletian chose as his fellow Augustus, Valerius Maximianus, a Pannonian general. For his Caesar, Diocletian chose an Illyrian, Gaius Galerius; Maximian chose another Illyrian, Flavius Valerius Constantius; and the Caesars then married daughters of the Augusti. All edicts were issued in the names of the four rulers, for no formal division of the empire was contemplated; a certain precedence was enjoyed by Diocletian, however. It was believed that some such scheme as this, allowing for an orderly succession and permitting no great power to anyone else, would prevent civil war. To protect the empire from foreign invasion, four capitals were selected, each at a strategic point. Because of his love of the East, a land that long ago had accustomed itself to the theory of absolutism, Diocletian chose Nicomedia in Bithynia, and to emphasize his divine right to rule, he adopted the title "Jovius," which, moreover, automatically set him above his colleagues. Under his direct care were Thrace, Asia Minor, Syria, and Egypt. Galerius, his Caesar, took Sirmium as his capital and was in charge of the Balkan and Danubian provinces. Maximian, the other Augustus, adopted "Herculius" as his title and Milan as his capital. He was responsible for Italy, Raetia, Africa, and Spain. Finally, Maximian's Caesar, Constantius, had Trier as his capital and Gaul and Britain as his provinces (see map,

p. 480). Rome, with its glorious traditions and reminders of a republican past, was overlooked except as the historical residence of the senate.

To symbolize their autocracy, the emperors wore diadems and silken robes embroidered with jewels and gold. They assumed the title "Lord" (*Dominus*), and often pictured themselves with patron gods on their coins. In keeping with their new position, the emperors compelled their subjects to prostrate themselves before them and surrounded the throne with the circles of a new nobility of various grades, each attended by its appropriate degree of pomp and ceremony.

Revolts in Gaul and Britain Quelled. The chief military troubles at the beginning were a revolt of Gallic peasants, called Bagaudae, who found their taxes and requisitions unbearable, and a separatist movement in Britain, where a Roman officer named Carausius set himself up as Augustus. But both revolts were subdued, the Frankish and Saxon pirates who were raiding from the North Sea were defeated, and the Alemanni, Franks, and Burgundians who tried to cross the Rhine were repelled.

Organization of the Empire. Fundamental to Diocletian's new administrative policy was the separation of civil and military authority and its assignment to as many persons as possible. Accordingly the provinces were decreased in size and raised in number to over one hundred; even Italy was divided into provinces and taxed. The provinces were grouped into thirteen dioceses. A provincial governor (*praeses*) was responsible to the head (*vicar*) of his diocese. Every official had a sizable office staff (*officium*), and the multiplication of the number of provinces meant a corresponding increase in bureaucracy.

The Edict of Prices (301). Plague, civil war, and barbarian invasion had taken their toll of life, many towns and cities of the empire were much smaller than in the past, trade and industry had shrunk to an intraprovincial scale, and the coinage had lost its value. The high cost of living called for an immediate solution, and in 301 Diocletian issued his famous Edict of Prices, which aimed at setting the maximum price to be charged for all manufactured goods, clothing and food throughout the empire as well as the cost of every form of labor. It proved impossible to enforce the edict, even though death was the penalty of infraction, because it drew no distinction between wholesale and retail prices and failed to consider such things as differences in quality and the variations in supply and demand. Diocletian's failure to reform the currency and control inflation meant that government revenues in coin continued to lose value. As a remedy, the emperor instituted a new tax in kind on agricultural labor and produce (*capitatio–jugatio*). The taxes in kind were generally based on the division of productive land, peasants, and livestock into units of presumably equal tax-paying ability. The total tax was announced annually, and the reassessment of land and workers paying it was revised at first every five (later fifteen) years. Diocletian's new taxation system thus provided the central government with more accurate fiscal information than previously concerning both what it had and what it could expect.

Persecution of the Christians (303). Diocletian's reign is also memorable for the last fierce persecution of the Christians. The Christian Church was now a community as wide as the empire itself. It had survived previous persecutions and possessed the permanence of a state. Pagan and Christian were learning to live together, and the issue no longer lay between them but rather between the state and the church. Perhaps because of his own conservative piety, encouraged by Galerius' rabid anti-Christianity, Diocletian issued an edict in 303 that confiscated all church property, deprived the Christians of their rights as citizens, forbade their worship, and ordered them to sacrifice to the gods of the state. In any case, it was Galerius who enforced the edict with barbaric severity until, in 311, mortally ill and aware that his cruelty had shocked even pagans into becoming Christians, he abandoned the persecution.

Abdication of Diocletian and Maximian. Ill health may explain why Diocletian dicided to abdicate on the twentieth anniversary of his rule, May 1, 305. He withdrew to his palace near Salona (Spalato) in Dalmatia and forced Maximian to retire as well, to his estates in Lucania, or perhaps to a villa in Sicily. A few years later Maximian was executed during a period of civil war, and Diocletian died in his vast palace.

Constantine. The precise scheme of succession, which Diocletian had worked out so laboriously, did indeed raise Galerius and Constantius to the rank of Augustus, but so many quarrels developed over the choice of their successors that in 310 there were five Augusti and no Caesars. Eventually the field narrowed down to two men, Maxentius, the son of Maximian, and Constantine, who had been hailed as Augustus by the troops in Britain after the death (306) of his father, Constantius, at York. Flavius Valerius Aurelius Constantinus (306-337)—Constantine the Great, as he came to be called by Christian writers because of his work on behalf of their religion—was born about 280 at Nish (Naissus), the son of Constantius and his common-law wife, a freedwoman, Helena, a Christian serving maid in a Balkan inn. Capable of cruelty and viciousness, Constantine had wide military experience and bided his time until 312, when at the head of an army of veterans he crossed the Mont Genèvre pass, routed his enemies at Turin and Verona, and pressed on to Rome. The religious influences on his life before 312 are obscure. His father, Constantius, worshiped the Sun God and was said to be sympathetic to Christians. In any case, he enforced only loosely the laws persecuting them under Diocletian. The women in Constantine's family were even then alleged to be practicing Christians themselves. Be that as it may, inspired by a vision of the Christian cross, and the words "By this conquer" (*hoc vince*), Constantine had placed on the shields of his men the labarum—the Christian monogram, an X with a vertical line drawn through it and rounded at the top, so as to represent the first two letters (chi and rho) of *Christ* in Greek. Then, at the Milvian bridge (312), he won against his rival, Maxentius, a victory against overwhelming odds, which had been promised him, so Constantine believed, by the God of the Christians. Now that the promise had been kept, he became a Christian. Admittedly, his Christianity had some ambivalent qualities. He was still titular *pontifex maximus* of the pagan state cult; his coins for some time still bore pagan symbols, particularly of the solar cult; and even the inscription on his arch near the Colosseum attributed his victory of 312 to "inspiration of the Divinity" without specifying that god as Christian. Nevertheless his contemporaries had no doubt about his Christianity.

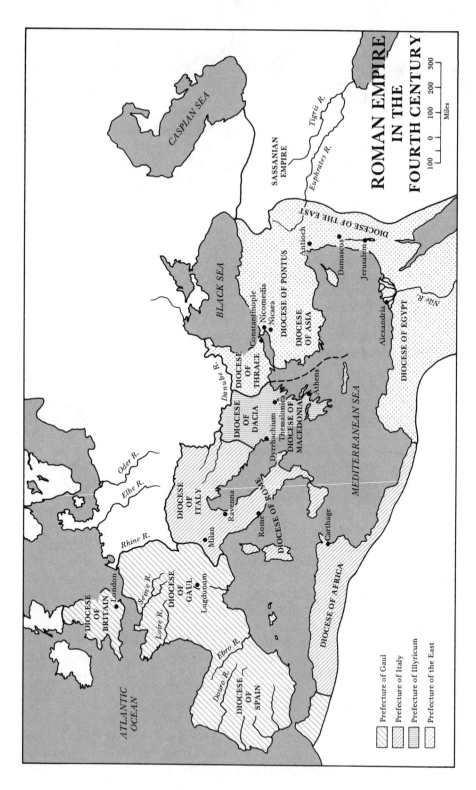

ROMAN EMPIRE
IN THE
FOURTH CENTURY

Miles

100 0 100 200 300

CASPIAN SEA

SASSANIAN
EMPIRE

Tigris R.

Euphrates R.

DIOCESE OF THE EAST

Antioch

Damascus

Jerusalem

BLACK SEA

DIOCESE OF PONTUS

Constantinople
Nicomedia
Nicaea

DIOCESE
OF ASIA

DIOCESE OF EGYPT

Alexandria

Nile R.

Danube R.

DIOCESE
OF
THRACE

DIOCESE
OF
DACIA

Dyrrhachium
Thessalonica
DIOCESE OF
MACEDONIA

Athens

MEDITERRANEAN SEA

Oder R.

Elbe R.

DIOCESE
OF
ITALY

Ravenna

Rome
DIOCESE OF ROME

Rhine R.

Milan

Carthage

DIOCESE OF AFRICA

Seine R.

DIOCESE
OF
GAUL

Lugdunum

London

DIOCESE
OF
BRITAIN

Loire R.

ATLANTIC
OCEAN

Ebro R.

Douro R.

DIOCESE
OF
SPAIN

Prefecture of Gaul

Prefecture of Italy

Prefecture of Illyricum

Prefecture of the East

Foundation of Constantinople (330).   Constantine and Licinianus Licinius, an appointee of Galerius, were now the rulers of the empire. In 313 they met briefly at Milan, where they agreed to legalize Christianity, on the same plane with other religions and restoring to the Christians their civil rights and property. The uneasy peace between the two men finally broke out into open warfare, in which Licinius lost his life. From 324 until his death in 337, Constantine was the sole ruler of the empire. Now that the God of the Christians had restored imperial unity, it was proper that the Roman world should have a Christian capital, and work was immediately begun on the transformation of Byzantium into the City of Constantine. On May 11, 330, Constantinople was dedicated. Situated beside the Golden Horn—its fine harbor on the Bosporus, admirably suited for the fleet and for trade beyond the seas—the new capital was adorned with works of art from the ancient world and strongly fortified against any dangers of the future. From this spot the emperor could easily keep his eye on the two danger lines of the empire, the Euphrates and Danube rivers. Except for a brief interruption in 1204, when the Crusaders took it, this Second Rome stood impregnable for more than a thousand years; but when the Turk did at last come (1453), Constantinople had discharged its chief function in history, and western Europe was ready once again to defend its civilization.

The Council of Nicaea (325).   Constantine saw that unity must be restored within the Church no less than in the State. A religious controversy was dividing the Christians of the East, as not so long before it had those in the West. There the Donatist schism in Africa had compelled the emperor to call together the Synod of Arles (314), the first such gathering in the history of the Church, and to mediate between rival bishops. The present issue concerned the physical nature of Christ. Arius, a presbyter of the Church in Alexandria, maintained that God and the Son were of like substance, but not identical, on the ground that eternal God had created the other two members of the Holy Trinity, the Son and the Spirit; whereas the Bishop of Alexandria, Athanasius, held (as did the West) that they were of the same substance. Arianism so aroused people that in 325 Constantine summoned the bishops of the Church to meet with him at Nicaea in Asia Minor. There an ecumenical council was held, the first in the Church's history, and a creed was agreed on. The orthodox doctrine of Athanasius prevailed, but Arianism continued widespread in the East. Constantine had surely acted like a statesman to try to effect unity within the Church. As he expressed it, the unity of the Church was the condition and guarantee of the prosperity of the empire. The Council of Nicaea was the first gathering that professed to represent the entire Christian world, and as such it added greatly to the power of the Church in its contest with paganism and exalted the position of the clergy.

Organization of the Christian Church.   By the time of Constantine the Church had acquired a considerable organization. Each congregation had its officers: deacons, who cared for the poor; elders, or presbyters, who as the council of the congregation looked after its interests; and an overseer, or bishop, who was the chief of the presbyters. The clergy came to enjoy a privileged position and were freed of taxes and *munera.* As the church of a given city sent out branches to neighboring towns and rural districts, the bishop of the parent community came to have authority over a group of congregations. In Constantine's day some differences of rank and influence among the bishops were already appearing. Those of a province looked for guidance to the highest religious officer of the provincial capital, who, though essentially a bishop, was usually called a *metropolitan* (or, later, an *archbishop*). Above him in dignity were the patriarchs of such important cities as Constantinople, Antioch, and Alexandria, while the Patriarch of Rome was just beginning to acquire the greatest influence of all (see the map, p. 480). It must be emphasized, however, that under Constantine Christianity was not the religion of the state, although it was the favored one of the imperial establishment. It was only on his deathbed, however, by which time Arianism was again in the ascendant and Athanasius was in exile, that Constantine received the sacrament of baptism, from an Arian bishop. Arianism at the time and later was a force to be reckoned with in the imperial household.

The Imperial Court. Constantine's administrative policy was essentially a continuation and refinement of Diocletian's, and since it is not always possible to differentiate between them, it is best to describe their policy together. To begin with, the emperor was an unapproachable autocrat, the elect of God, out of touch with his subjects and surrounded by a multitude of court dignitaries, each with his own pay and grade, jealous of precedence, and anxious for promotion. The equestrian order, in effect, was abolished by the promotion of equestrians en masse into the senatorial order. At the top stood the highest officials, *clarissimi* (most glorious), and just under them the *perfectissimi* (most perfect). The emperor's chief advisers were the Grand Chamberlain, who was in charge of the palace and all its servants; the Count of the Sacred Largesses, who looked after the revenues paid in money; the Count of the Privy Purse, who was responsible for the revenues from the imperial lands; and the Quaestor, minister of justice. Only the emperor could wear a special type of the *paludamentum,* or purple mantle; only he could hold the scepter with its eagle. The highest officials and nobles formed the standing Imperial Consistory, which advised the emperor.

Prefectures and the Bureaucracy. Constantine disbanded the praetorian guard, which had supported Maxentius, but kept the praetorian prefecture as a civil office. Under him the empire began a division into ultimately four great prefectures after his reign: the East, Illyricum, Italy, and Gaul. The praetorian prefects had no military power but were to dispense justice, collect the taxes in kind, and supervise the vicars. They were responsible directly to the emperor.

The many different palace bureaus were under the Master of Offices. He was also in charge of the spies, or *agentes in rebus.* They were ostensibly inspectors of the post and the imperial highways, which of course carried them all over the empire in their undercover work; then, to close their active career, they were assigned as assistants to the provincial governors. The governor, that is to say, had at his elbow a spy busily sending secret reports to the capital. There was no room for free exercise of talent or originiality in a scheme such as this; graft and corruption, rather, were the order of the day. The city masses of Rome and Constantinople occupied a favored position, for they had to be fed and amused. Each of the two cities had its own senate (now a municipal council) and was under a city prefect.

The Army.   The largest expense was the army. The number of legions had grown to sixty, though each was smaller than formerly, and there was also an increase in the cavalry, the auxiliaries, and the fleets. The percentage of barbarians in the armed forces was greater than ever before, and their officers received Roman citizenship. The border garrisons (*limitanei*) now had their own lands for their support, free from the authority of the municipality in which they were located. Such soldiers were essentially peasants under arms, valuable in their way, and to ensure a steady supply, the career was made a hereditary obligation. An officer of such a permanent garrison was known as a *dux* (duke), though the more important ones were called *comites* (counts). It was obviously necessary to provide a large mobile force, stationed at strategic points within the empire, which could be quickly moved to threatened borders. A well-trained and well-equipped field army of 200,000 men was organized, and since the soldiers accompanied the emperor on an expedition, they were called *comitatenses* (companions). Vigorous barbarians along the borders were taken into Roman pay as allies (*foederati*); they continued under their own rulers but were obligated to give military aid. Finally, there were the palatine troops, who officially were based at the palace, though they generally served in the field; and the 3,500 scholarians or imperial bodyguards. The Master of the Horse and the Master of the Foot (Masters of the Soldiers) were directly responsible for the military forces.

The Imperial Economy.   The high cost of army and bureaucracy was destined to crush the Roman world. The primitive economy of the empire was such that when the peasants had paid their taxes and rents to maintain those who did not produce— the soldiers, bureaucrats, and large landowners—they did not have enough left to feed large families. The depopulation caused by war and plague during the third century need not have been more than temporary, but this apparently permanent falling off of population would explain the acute shortage of manpower, which was a major factor in the decline of the empire. And yet the government had to maintain the existing establishment, with its ever-increasing demands for human support.

Constantine reformed the coinage by introducing the *solidus,* containing one-seventy-second of a pound of gold, and the silver *siliqua,* worth one-twenty-fourth of a *solidus.* His currency system was destined to have a long life in the later Byzantine Empire. Because the circulation of these coins was limited to the wealthy, most people continued to use small change of fluctuating and inflated value. For this reason, the government continued to rely on the capitation tax in kind introduced by Diocletian.

In order to discover every possible form of wealth and to tax it, the government took a census regularly. Each year, moreover, an imperial proclamation (*indictio*) announced the amount of taxes to be collected in kind (*annona*), a particularly cruel blow to the farmer, who was thus prevented from taking advantage of a rise in prices. The amount of land a person owned was divided into taxable units, each called a *iugum;* for example, a *iugum* consisted of twenty good acres of arable land, or 225 olive trees, or five acres of vineyard. In addition, the laborers were taxed, one man or two women forming a unit (*caput*). Money taxes were laid on tradesmen, municipal senators, and others for various purposes, and in particular to enable the emperor to distribute a largesse to the army every five years. The taxes, in money and in kind, were not sufficient to meet expenses, so that public duties (*munera*) were required of the population, to keep up the post, to feed and transport the army, and so on. Members of the bureaucracy and the army were free from taxes, and the empire was full of people who hoped to join one or the other. The only other avenues of escape were across the frontiers or into the Church.

Hereditary, Compulsory Service.   To change one's position in life, however, was technically impossible, for the law of *origo* now for the first time systematically bound people to their tasks, which were made hereditary. As a matter of fact, there was a great deal of social mobility, as the laws regulating caste status were only loosely enforced. In an immediate sense, there was a certain justification for the caste system, since the feeding, clothing, and servicing of the empire had to be provided, but the result tended to destroy initiative and life as it had been understood for centuries. The transformation of many free farmers into serfs, which must have been brought about by an imperial decree in the early fourth century (though this decree has not survived), clearly illustrates the process of change. Coloni, who were originally small free farmers and then tenants, were crushed between taxes and *munera* and began a movement from the land. In order to supply the army and the civilian population with their essential needs, the emperor first bound workers on his estates to the soil, and then tenant farmers everywhere. The *colonus* was now a serf, personally free but progressively losing civic rights. He and his children were obligated to cultivate land in their turn and he was included with it when it was sold. There were still, however, many free farmers, especially in the East, who were not bound by serfdom. The old colleges, or guilds, were now also gone, their place was taken by corporations (*corpora*), and their members—tradesmen, artisans, and others—generally found themselves saddled with a hereditary obligation to continue in their careers.

The prosperous "middle class" of former days was also ruined. This section of society provided the municipalities with their councillors (*curiales*), but the custom had developed of making them responsible for the taxes of their communities. When it was discovered that many *curiales* were leaving their posts, this once honorable profession was decreed a hereditary obligation. Yet many of them actually continued to escape into protected castes. The remaining *curiales*, to save themselves from economic disaster, exacted as much as they could from their fellow townsmen and were hated accordingly; it was a common expression that a city had as many tyrants as there were *curiales*.

The Great Landowners.   The only prosperous individuals in the empire were the great landowners, whose fortified villas became centers of country life. The magnates were very powerful and were exempt from the supervision of the municipalities near them, and in return they took over wastelands and made their vast estates as productive as possible. Most of the large landowners throughout the empire were senators, a term that now denoted rank rather than post or function. They were strong enough to shirk their duty to the state and to protect their tenants from injustice and even from imperial tax collectors. For this reason, many freeholders were ready to put themselves under their rich neighbor. He, in turn, was glad to have as many dependents as possible, for they enabled him as well to defy the tax collectors and other imperial officials. The landowners were practically sovereigns and ruled over estates so extensive as to resemble little kingdoms. This was the beginning of manorialism, which was to reach its full development in the Middle Ages.

To speak generally, the dangerous foreign situation, religion, the decline in population, and the financial needs of the state combined to set the social structure of the late Roman Empire. The principal feature of this structure was its legal immobility, which was caused by the inseparable relationship of the head tax and the land tax. The government, that is to say, had to establish a definite stability between land and labor and therefore attached the peasants to the land. As noted, social immobility was never strictly enforced in this state. Some free peasants were able to move, if they did not occupy the same land more than thirty years. In the towns those artisans who were not connected with any public service had some freedom of action, though they were organized in the new corporations and their activities were regulated; their trades were not forcibly hereditary (though in practice that was usually the case), and they might strike for higher wages and intervene in politics. Indeed, even the members of corporations engaged in public services were allowed to find substitutes for themselves; the fact that substitutes could be found shows that the curtailment of freedom and the heavy obligation of membership in the corporations were, in the minds of some, more than compensated for by the security afforded by the corporations. The fabric of society, as it subsequently developed in the Eastern Empire, was in truth ever-changing.

THE LAST YEARS OF THE UNITED EMPIRE (A.D. 337–395)

Diocletian and Constantine, nevertheless, gave the empire a new lease of life, and this was significant, for in the years that remained to the united empire, some of the barbarians across the frontiers gained a respect for Rome's law and new religion.

Constantius II (337–361) and Julian the Apostate (361–363). When Constantine died (337), the troops would recognize only his sons as Augusti; they ruled jointly, until death removed Constantine II and Constans. The surviving son, Constantius, was long occupied with the Sassanid king, Shapur II, who threatened both northern Mesopotamia and Armenia, now a Christian country. Since he had no son of his own, Constantius associated with himself as Caesar his cousin Julian (355). This man had been a Christian, but he had lost his belief in the new religion as he studied classical literature. It was Hellenism, and more particularly Neoplatonism, with its mystical belief in salvation, that appealed to him, and he came to regard Christianity as an absurd religious aberration. Julian, rather surprisingly for a scholar, proved himself a good general and defeated the Franks at Cologne and the Alemanni at Strasbourg. When, however, Constantius summoned to the East some of Julian's finest Gallic troops, civil war was averted only by the timely death of the emperor. Julian himself was killed in 363 during a campaign in the Tigris Valley, but his brief reign is interesting as the last attempt to reassert paganism as the religion of the empire. Julian the Apostate, as he is called, did not persecute Christianity, but he tried to weaken it in various ways. For example, he fought Christianity with its own weapons, by adapting to pagan use its liturgy and preaching, together with its practice of charity. Then, too, under the guise of complete toleration, he favored heretical bishops and decreed that Christians were not to be allowed to teach classical pagan literature. Julian's methods were well calculated to destroy Christianity, and he might have succeeded in his attempt had he lived longer. But with Julian's death all such efforts came to an end, as did the House of Constantine the Great.

Valentinian I and Valens. After the brief reign of Jovian (363-364), the choice of the soldiers fell on a Pannonian officer, Valentinian (364-375), who immediately associated with himself as Augustus his younger brother, Valens (364-378). Leaving Valens to defend the empire along the lower Danube and in the east, Valentinian hastened west, where various dangers threatened. A defeat of the Alemanni in the Black Forest gave him the opportunity to repair the defenses along the Rhine and to create a new fortress at Basileia (Basel). At the same time he sent his general, Theodosius, against the Moors in Africa and against the Scots, Picts, and Saxons in Britain. Valentinian was a superior emperor, measured by the standard of the day. He was tolerant toward various controversies raging within the Christian Church, an attitude, however, that merely allowed feelings to rise to a higher pitch. To protect people against their government (for that is what it amounted to), he set up in the cities "protectors of the community" (*defensores civitatis*). These officials were supposed to defend the weak and ended by oppressing them. Perhaps Valentinian's greatest fault was his uncontrollable temper; in any case, it brought on his death, for during a conference with envoys of the Quadi at Brigetio on the Danube, he burst a blood vessel and died. His son Gratian (367-383), fifteen years of age and already an Augustus, and another son, Valentinian II (375-392), four years old, succeeded him.

Religious Controversy. The chief controversy dividing Christians during this period still was Arianism, which neither the Council of Nicaea nor the return of Athanasius to his see at Alexandria had succeeded in destroying. Although Valentinian himself was orthodox, his lack of interest in dogma and his willingness to let people express their opinions had the effect of fanning the strife. His brother, Valens, on the other hand, was an Arian and persecuted orthodox believers. When, moreover, he found that thousands of people were disappearing into Upper Egypt—some for ascetic reasons; others, in reality, to escape their public obligations—he passed legislation against monasticism.

The Visigoths. Valens also busily defended the Eastern frontiers. The Visigoths, as the Western branch of the Gothic nation was called, were a constant menace, as were their Eastern brothers, the Ostrogoths. The Ostrogoths had built up a considerable kingdom in southern Russia, under Hermanric, and had become Arian Christians; owing to the work of their bishop, Ulfilas, the Scriptures had been translated into Gothic. Both Gothic nations, as well as the other barbarians beyond the frontiers, were now caught up in a series of great migrations, which were to end in the overthrow of the Roman Empire in the West. The fiercest of these nomads were the Mongolian Huns—the Hsiung-nu of the Chinese annals—who in their westward movement conquered first the Alans and then the Ostrogoths. When the

Visigoths saw the fate overhanging them, they appealed to the Romans to be allowed to cross the Danube, without their arms, and to settle in wastelands to the south. The Romans failed, however, to collect their arms and treacherously mistreated them, whereupon the Visigoths revolted. Valens hurried to the rescue as quickly as he could, only to meet his death at Adrianople (378). The Goths were now free to ravage the Balkans.

Theodosius I, The Great (379-395). When he heard of his uncle's death, Gratian appointed Theodosius as a colleague. He was the son of the general who had fought invaders in Africa and Britain; as Theodosius I, "the Great," he was the last emperor from the West (Spain) to rule over a united empire. At the very beginning of his reign, Theodosius was able to subdue the Goths and settle them as allies (*foederati*) on the wastelands south of the Danube, although they kept their own ethnic identity and their kings. The following years saw the murder of Gratian and Valentinian II. When Theodosius himself died (395), his two sons, Arcadius and Honorius, succeeded him and divided the empire between them.

Triumph of Orthodox Christianity. The reign of Theodosius the Great marked the victory of orthodox Christianity. An imperial edict, directed primarily against paganism, finally made Christianity the state religion of the empire. To end religious strife within the Church, Theodosius called together an ecumenical council, the second in its history (381), and persuaded the 150 bishops gathered at Constantinople to adopt a modified version of the Nicene Creed, which is the one still recited in churches today. Although the bishop of Rome, who was called "Pope" (after the Greek word for "father," *pappas*), enjoyed a preeminence over other bishops, nevertheless the outstanding official of the Church at this time was Ambrose, the bishop of Milan. It was Ambrose who wholeheartedly supported Gratian in his persecution of paganism, for now paganism, rather than Christianity, was the object of imperial suppression. Gratian, for example, refused the title of *pontifex maximus,* which was reserved for the head of the old state cults; and he removed the altar and statue of Victory from the senate house at Rome, which as a symbol of the state was particularly venerated by the pagan aristocracy of the senate. One of their number, Symmachus, pleaded with Gratian that "not by one path alone can the Great Mystery be approached," but Gratian had the support of Ambrose and would not relent. Some years later, indeed, the bishop refused Theodosius himself permission to enter his cathedral and excluded him for eight months until he repented of a massacre at Thessalonica, for, he insisted, there were certain moral laws that bound emperors no less than ordinary mortals.

32

The Transition to the Middle Ages (A.D. 395–565)

Division of the Roman Empire.   On the death of Theodosius, his sons, Arcadius and Honorius, divided the Roman Empire formally into an Eastern and a Western half (395). This division in itself might be taken as the end of ancient history, just as the picture of a Christian bishop excluding a Roman emperor from his church seems to symbolize the beginning of Europe's Middle Ages. People at the time, however, were unaware of any abrupt change in the affairs of the world. The Christian Church had long been an established fact; emperors had often before divided their authority, if not the empire, and even now the fiction of a single state was at least maintained; barbarian invasions, and with them changes in the ethnic stock of the empire, had become commonplace. To be sure, the invasions of the next century overwhelmed the Western Empire, and yet might they not prove to be a mere interlude? So long as the Eastern Empire stood, there was always the possibility that the two halves might be rejoined. And this is precisely what Justinian tried to do. Justinian ranks with Constantine as one of the two geniuses of the late empire. In many important respects he belongs to ancient Roman history, but when his partial reconquest of the West failed to endure, humanity, in both East and West, set sail irrevocably on new seas. At that time, the break with the past is so clear that we are justified in saying that one epoch of history had finally closed, if indeed we can say it at all, for every age contains within itself both the old and the germ of the new.

THE GERMANIC INVASIONS OF THE WEST (A.D. 395–476)

Alaric and the Visigoths.   Soon after Theodosius' death, the Visigoths ravaged Greece under their chieftain, Alaric, until Arcadius, emperor of the East, bought his friendship by making him Master of the Soldiers of Epirus. This position gave Alaric the opportunity of supplying his men with arms, so that in a few years he was ready for a more important undertaking, the invasion of Italy. It is a remarkable fact that not only the common soldiers but even the best generals and ministers of the empire were now frequently Germans. Such was Stilicho, a Vandal, who had married a niece of Theodosius and was at this time the guardian and chief general of the worthless Honorius, emperor of the West (395–423). Stilicho and Alaric were well matched, for both were born leaders of men, and both were brave and energetic, with an equal genius for war. But Stilicho had the advantage of Roman organization. Hastily gathering troops from Britain, Gaul, and other parts in the West, he defeated Alaric at Pollentia and Verona and forced him back across the Alps (403).

Honorius, whose chief interest in life was poultry raising, feared that Milan was no longer a safe capital, despite its strategic position in northern Italy, and he removed his residence to the marshes of Ravenna. There he listened to stories about Stilicho's disloyalty, until finally he ordered the Vandal's death (408). As Alaric knew that no able general was left to defend the empire, he crossed the Alps and marched straight for Rome. Afflicted with famine and pestilence, the citizens bought Alaric off by the payment of an enormous ransom. In the following year, he appeared again before the walls, this time demanding whole provinces for the settlement of his men. He appointed his own emperor to displace Honorius, an arrangement that did not last, and then he besieged Rome again.

It was only a few years before this moment, when the Goth was almost at the gates, that the poet Claudian wrote his great eulogy on the Rome of the emperors, the swan song of the Western Empire. It is this Rome, Claudian wrote, who has cared for the human race and given it a common name; who has taken the conquered to her bosom like a mother and called them not subjects but citizens; who has united distant races in the bonds of affection. To the peace that she has brought to us we owe it, every one of us, continued Claudian, that every part of the empire is to us a fatherland; that it matters nothing if we drink of the Rhone or of the Orontes; that we are all one people. That was the last verdict on the Rome of the emperors, it has been remarked, the proudest boast perhaps that any person in any empire has ever made: we are all one people.

The Sack of Rome. For eight hundred years Rome had seen no enemy in her streets, but now (410) the Visigoths burst in and plundered the city. They killed many citizens, but as Christians, who had also, like the Ostrogoths, received their religion from the Arian bishop Ulfilas, they spared the churches and those who took refuge in them. The sack of Rome astonished humankind, for all had supposed the city inviolable, and in her fall they thought they saw the ruin of order in the world. To console them, and particularly the Christians, Saint Augustine wrote his *City of God,* to prove that the community of the Most High would last forever, even though the greatest city of earth had fallen.

The Visigothic Kingdom in Gaul. The Visigoths soon left Rome and wandered southward with their booty, intending to cross to Africa, but while they were making ready, Alaric died. His brother-in-law, Ataulf, succeeded him. This man had once wished to root out the Romans and to replace them with the Visigoths; but as he saw his followers slow in adapting themselves to settled life, he recognized the value of Rome for order and civilization. So far as events permitted, Ataulf henceforth became Rome's champion. He led his people out of Italy, bringing with him Galla Placidia, Honorius' sister, whom he married. From Italy the Visigoths went to Gaul and Spain, which had already been plundered by Vandals, Alans, and Suevi (whose name survives in the modern *Swabia*). After Ataulf's death in 415, Galla Placidia returned to Italy, and many of the Visigoths to Gaul. Here they settled as *foederati* of the Roman Empire—allies obligated to give military aid, but otherwise under their own kings—but later on, they created an independent kingdom, with Toulouse for its capital.

The Vandals.   On the last day of 405, a decade before Ataulf's death, thousands of Vandals crossed the Rhine, whose garrisons had been withdrawn by Stilicho to use against Alaric. The Vandals, joined by Suevi and Alans, ravaged their way through Gaul into Spain. It was here that the Visigoths found them. The Suevi were gradually pressed by the newcomers into the northwest corner of the peninsula, while the Vandals and Alans retired southward. Thus far the Vandals had been driven about from place to place—their history had been an unbroken record of defeats. Now, however, they found their hero king in Gaiseric, under whom they, too, were to appear as a conquering nation. Gaiseric had a cunning, nimble mind, which always hit on the right expedient. Bold, grasping, and persistent, he never lost sight of his ends or of the intricate means that led to them. In addition to his desire to find lands for his men and a kingdom for himself, he sought to humble Rome and, as an Arian Christian, to destroy the orthodox Church. (See map, p. 493.)

The Vandal Kingdom in Africa.   The Vandal chief found his opportunity in Africa. The military governor of Africa was Count Boniface, but he and the Roman government had quarreled. The Western Empire was now ruled by Valentinian III (425–455), nephew of Honorius, though actually the government was in the hands of Galla Placidia, mother of the emperor and now an Augusta, and of Aëtius, the Master of the Soldiers (or Patrician, as the office came to be called). Suspecting Boniface of disloyalty, Placidia ordered him to Rome, but the count turned for revenge to the Vandals and invited them to invade his provinces. Gaiseric, accordingly, crossed to Africa with eighty thousand persons, including women and children (429). In vain the penitent Boniface, who meanwhile had been reconciled to the Roman government, tried to send Gaiseric back. Africa, with its large, fertile estates, was too tempting, and the Vandals occupied the country until the Romans settled them as *foederati* (435). Not content with this accommodation, the Vandals captured Carthage and then built ships and took to piracy, and in 442 the Roman government was forced to recognize them as an independent kingdom. The Sicilian coasts in particular bore the brunt of their "Vandalism." In the year 455, however, Valentinian III was murdered, the last of the dynasty of Theodosius the Great in the West. The new emperor, Petronius Maximus, forced his predecessor's widow to marry him, and when she appealed to the Vandals for revenge, they gladly accepted the invitation. For a fortnight they pillaged Rome and stored in their ships at Ostia all the movable property, together with many captives, including the empress Eudoxia and her daughters. The Roman and the barbarian had indeed exchanged roles. Gaiseric, however, had promised the pope, the great Leo I, to refrain from indiscriminate destruction of buildings, and he kept his word. At the death of Gaiseric (477), the expansion of the Vandal kingdom ceased, but it maintained itself in Africa, the Balearic Islands, Corsica, Sardinia, and part of Sicily, until it was annexed by the Eastern Empire in the next century.

Other Germanic Invasions. While these calamities were falling on the empire of the West, still other Germanic tribes crossed the Rhine to live eventually in Gaul as *foederati*. These were the Burgundians, who settled chiefly in the valley of the Rhone and Saône rivers; the Ripuarian Franks, so called from the fact that they lived on the banks of the Rhine; and the Salian Franks, from the coasts of the North Sea. Britain, however, fared even worse. Roman civilization and Christianity had not taken a deep hold on the island, and consequently when Stilicho recalled the troops from Britain for the protection of Italy, the Britons could not defend themselves against the barbarians who assailed them on every side. Celts from Ireland, Picts from Scotland, Germanic Jutes, Angles, and Saxons overwhelmed them. By the middle of the fifth century, Britain had again become barbarous and pagan. Britain, Africa, and most of Spain had been lost, but the Western Empire still controlled central and southern Gaul. Here Aëtius, Master of the Soldiers and the real power under Valentinian III, maintained imperial authority. Aëtius and the Germanic *foederati* of Gaul were destined to be drawn together by the new great enemy of civilization: Attila the Hun and "Scourge of God."

Attila the Hun. After desolating the provinces of the East and terrorizing Constantinople, the Huns had moved westward to the plains of Hungary and thence to the Rhine. Their king, Attila, attracted to himself men of many races: Germans, Slavs, and even Greeks. Many Hunnish troops were used by Aëtius to maintain Roman power in Gaul, but the amicable relationship between him and Attila was broken when the Hun demanded the hand of Honoria, sister of Valentinian III, and half the Western Empire as her dowry. When this demand was refused, Attila crossed the Rhine and, leaving wasted fields and ruined cities in his path, pressed on to Orleans, which was saved by a combination of Aëtius and the Germanic *foederati* of Gaul under the Visigothic king, Theodoric. As Attila retreated eastward, one of the bloodiest conflicts known to history was fought somewhere between Troyes and Metz, though it is celebrated as the battle of the Mauriac Plain (451). Theodoric fell, but Attila was routed and withdrew across the Rhine.

The next year Attila arrived in Italy on his errand of destruction. Aquileia and many another city were devastated. When it appeared as if Attila would turn on Rome, the Roman pope, Leo, allegedly met him at Lake Garda with the words, "Thus far and no farther," and reminded the Hun of the wrath of God that had stricken Alaric after his sack of the city. This was three years before the same Leo succeeded in softening Gaiseric's plunder of Rome. It is a memorable and challenging picture, this regard of Hun and Vandal for an ancient and beautiful city, even though the presence of troops from the Eastern Empire and hardships among his own men undoubtedly also influenced Attila. The year after his departure from Italy, Attila died (453), and his Hunnish empire broke into pieces.

End of the Western Empire (476). In 454 the emperor of the West, Valentinian III, suspicious of the fame of Aëtius, invited the great commander into the imperial palace and killed him there with his own hand. The following year Valentinian himself was murdered. An able, scheming German, Ricimer, controlled the Western Empire (456-472) for most of the years that were left to it. Though he called himself simply Patrician, he kept the power in his own hands and made and unmade emperors at pleasure. Three years after Ricimer's death, Orestes, an Illyrian, became Patrician and conferred the imperial title on his son Romulus. Romulus Augustulus, the "little Augustus" as he was affectionately called, had ruled only a few months when the Germanic mercenaries in Italy, demanding a third of the land for themselves, deposed him in favor of their leader, Odovacar, whom they made king (October 22, 476). Odovacar compelled the senate to send the purple, with other imperial ornaments, to Constantinople, in token of the reunion of the empire under one head, and the Eastern emperor (Zeno) responded by conferring on Odovacar the title of Patrician.

No one living at the time saw in the event of 476 anything worthy of notice. No one supposed that any part of the empire had fallen. The continuance of the emperors in the East satisfied in some degree a want that Rome had left in the hearts of the barbarians as well as of her native citizens—a longing for a central power that, in the midst of chaos, should stand for law and order throughout the world. Accordingly most men in the West thought of the Eastern emperor as their own. In theory, the event of the year was the reunion of the East and the West under one head; at the same time, it pointed to an accomplished fact, the dissolution of the empire in the West. The happenings of 476 had this important result, that as Italy ceased to be the home of the emperors, the bishop of Rome became the most respected and most influential person in the West: the pope succeeded to the vacant throne of the Augusti.

THE GERMANIC KINGDOMS OF THE WEST (A.D. 476-526)

With the accession of Odovacar (476-493), the entire Western Empire was in the hands of the barbarians. In Gaul and Spain the Romans and Visigoths lived together on good terms, though naturally the Romans, who had been compelled to surrender much of their land (and all that went with it—*coloni,* cattle, and so on), were in an inferior position. Intermarriage between the two peoples was forbidden, and in general, they each had their own laws. In Africa the Vandals persecuted and oppressed their Roman subjects, while in Italy Odovacar continued the Roman system of government (see the map, p. 493).

The Ostrogothic King, Theodoric the Great (493-526). Odovacar was destined, however, to be overthrown by the Ostrogoths. These people had been conquered by the Huns, but on Attila's death they had settled in Pannonia as *foederati* of the Eastern emperor. Zeno, fearing and suspecting his allies, saw that they were anxious to move against Odovacar and gladly bade them farewell. Under their king, Theodoric the Great, the Ostrogoths crossed the Alps, defeated Odovacar in two battles, and killed him. With remarkable tact Theodoric adapted himself to his new position as king of Italy. Though poorly educated himself, he appreciated and encouraged

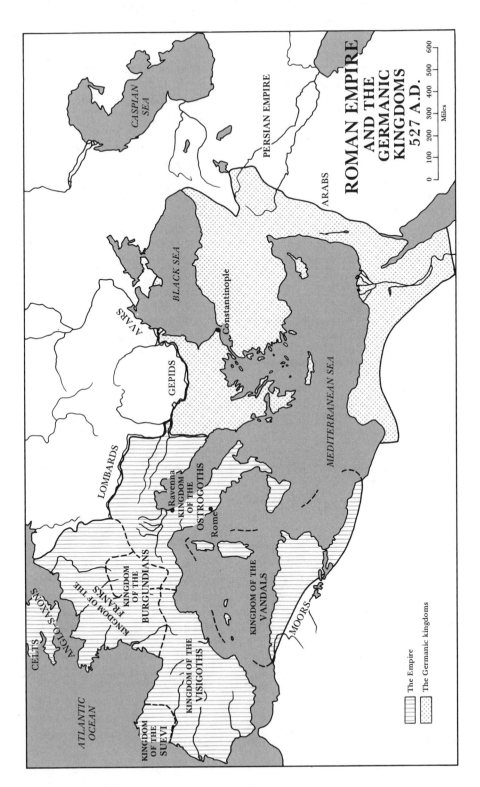

ROMAN EMPIRE
AND THE
GERMANIC
KINGDOMS
527 A.D.

Miles

0   100   200   300   400   500   600

PERSIAN EMPIRE

ARABS

CASPIAN
SEA

BLACK SEA

Constantinople

AVARS

GEPIDS

MEDITERRANEAN SEA

LOMBARDS

Ravenna
KINGDOM
OF THE
OSTROGOTHS

Rome

KINGDOM OF THE
FRANKS

KINGDOM
OF THE
BURGUNDIANS

KINGDOM OF THE
VANDALS

MOORS

ANGLO-SAXONS

CELTS

KINGDOM OF THE
VISIGOTHS

KINGDOM
OF THE
SUEVI

ATLANTIC
OCEAN

☐ The Empire

▦ The Germanic kingdoms

education; a barbarian, he yet knew the value of Roman law and civilization; an Arian, he tolerated the orthodox Christians. He settled his men on the land by setting aside one-third of the imperial estates rather than by confiscating private property. Theodoric, moreover, issued a law code, borrowed from the Roman code, that applied equally to Goths and Romans; the administration of government was patterned after the Roman mode, and Romans filled many of the civil and even some of the military posts. His Master of Offices was the scholar and senator Cassiodorus. Theodoric's capital was at Ravenna, and here he built a palace and churches (p. 493), though he was also careful to repair the ravages of war in Rome and other cities.

The Kingdom of the Franks.   In order to make Italy as secure as possible, Theodoric connected himself by marriages with most of the German kings of the West. He himself married a sister of Clovis, king of the Franks, and his own sister married the Vandal king; one daughter married the Burgundian king; another, the king of the Visigoths. Of all these people, the most important to the history of Europe was Clovis. His life work was to be the founding of a united Frankish kingdom, embracing most of Gaul, together with a part of western Germany; for nearly two and a half centuries after his death, his descendants—known as Merovingians, from Merowig, grandfather of Clovis—continued to rule. In the beginning of his reign, Clovis and his subjects were pagan. But he married the Burgundian princess Clotilda, who belonged to the Roman Church; and when, somewhat later, he convinced himself that her God had helped him to win a battle, he and three thousand of his warriors were baptized into the faith. To appreciate the importance of this event, we must emphasize the fact that while the Romans in what had been the Western Empire were orthodox, the invading Germans, with the exception of a few families like that of Clotilda, were heterodox Arians. The faith of Clovis recommended him both to the Romans and to the Eastern emperor, and the Roman Church encouraged him in his conquest of the heretical Germans. It was this alliance between the Roman Church and the Frankish throne that, under Charlemagne three centuries later, was to refound the empire in the West and give a new character to mediaeval history.

Not long after the death of Clovis in 511, the Eastern emperor, Justin, began a persecution of Arians. Theodoric, accordingly, planned to retaliate in kind by persecuting the orthodox, who, it seemed to him, sympathized with the Eastern Empire. His religious persecution thus had political overtones and accounted for the execution of prominent men, like the renowned philosopher Boethius. But Theodoric died before he was able to carry out his plans in detail (526). No great figure remained in the West; in the East, however, a new and remarkable man sat on the imperial throne, and it was his fortune to reconquer for the empire much that had been lost in the West.

THE EASTERN EMPIRE (A.D. 395–527)

When Arcadius and Honorius, the sons of Theodosius, divided the empire in 395—roughly, by drawing a line from north to south, just east of the heel of Italy

—imperial edicts were published in the names of the two emperors, and in other ways the fiction of a united state was preserved. But the division was a very real one, and in the issue the Western Empire disappeared. The Eastern Roman Empire, on the other hand, lasted more than a thousand years, with only a brief interruption in the thirteenth century. The survival of the imperial government, especially during the chaos of the fifth century, was primarily due to its capacity, despite many faults, to accomplish two great tasks. In the first place, the Eastern emperors were extraordinarily clever in dealing with the barbarians; they purchased their friendship or played one tribe or one chief off against another; and, if necessary, they deflected them westward. Second, the high military command was divided among several Masters of the Soldiers, so that there was a less united military front against the emperors, though much intrigue and strife.

Arcadius (395-408). These generalizations help to explain the survival of the Eastern Empire; they also describe the main activity of government. For example, Arcadius was never strong enough to free himself wholly of powerful personalities— first of the praetorian prefect Rufinus and then of the eunuch Eutropius. At the end of his career Eutropius was forced to seek sanctuary under the high altar of the cathedral when the Bishop of Constantinople, John Chrysostom (the Golden-mouth), was preaching on the text, "Vanity of vanities, all is vanity." The frivolous court life was a special object of the bishop's eloquence, and needless to say, the inhabitants of the empire were heavily taxed to maintain that court, a corrupt and complex bureaucracy, and the armed forces. But when Arcadius reached the end of his life, he could look back on an empire that had remained intact and had survived the invasions of Persians in Syria and Asia Minor and of Alaric and his Visigoths in Thrace, Macedonia, and Thessaly. Doubtless the vitality of Hellenism in the East was the strongest ally in the possession of the empire.

Theodosius II (408-450). Arcadius was succeeded by his son, Theodosius II. Since the new ruler was eight years old, his siter Pulcheria, an austere Christian, acted as regent with the title of Augusta. Some years later she chose as the wife of Theodosius the daughter of a pagan philosopher at Athens, who on her conversion to Christianity took the name of Eudocia. The reign of Theodosius is probably most notable for the issuance in 438 of the Theodosian Code, a collection of imperial laws that was used not only in the East but in the West as well. At this time, too, there began a religious controversy that did not end in certain areas until the Arab conquest of the seventh century. Arianism had been replaced, as a subject of theological debate, by a new question, the nature, or natures, of Christ. Was Christ human and divine, or exclusively divine? The orthodox view accepted the two natures of Christ and was vigorously upheld at Antioch. But Cyril, the patriarch of Alexandria, maintained that the nature of Christ was solely divine, and accordingly those who agreed with him were known as Monophysites. It required two ecumenical councils of the Church—at Ephesus in 431, and at Chalcedon in 451—to settle the question in favor of the orthodox position, which had been supported by the patriarchs of Rome and Constantinople. These religious controversies, more often than not, provided the various bishops with an opportunity to extend their authority, and at the same time they were seized on by depressed people as a means of attacking the government. Thus the Monophysite heresy continued to be popular in Egypt, Palestine, and Syria, where a national reaction against the Greeks was taking place; and indeed the doctrine is held to this day by the Copts.

Development of the Eastern Empire. Though he was a weak and incompetent emperor, Theodosius defended the Eastern frontiers against the Persians; and by payments of gold to the Huns, who looked on the empire as a perpetual source of revenue, he kept Attila quiet after he had ravaged the Balkan provinces (441-443). The death of Theodosius II ended the dynasty of Theodosius the Great in the East. With the reign of Leo I (457-474) we discover another, and very important, reason for the endurance of the Eastern Empire, namely, the reservoir of fine soldiers still available to the government in certain areas. Leo had been chosen emperor by a Master of the Soldiers, an Alan named Aspar, who was supported by the Gothic *foederati.* But in the mountains of southern Asia Minor, there dwelled a warlike and lawless people known as Isaurians, and by hiring them as mercenaries, Leo was able to weaken Aspar's authority. The Gothic *foederati* lived on to plague Leo's son-in-law and successor, Zeno (474-491), who was an Isaurian, and indeed the Isaurian mercenaries were troublesome until the emperor Anastasius (491-518) broke their power. In addition, Anastasius had to fight a war against Persia and to contend with the Slavic Getae and Bulgars who devastated the Balkans.

Anastasius was a strong and wise ruler. He took effective steps against the mercenaries and barbarians, and he tried for religious peace within the empire by adopting a tolerant attitude toward heterodoxy, as he himself was a convinced Monophysite. With the middle classes he gained great popularity by lessening the financial responsibilities of the *curiales,* who were, however, rapidly becoming extinct. His successor was Justin (518-527), a rude Illyrian peasant of the orthodox faith, who made his way to the throne by soldierly ability. Poorly educated himself, he gave his nephew Justinian a thorough education and closely associated him with imperial power. Justinian, virtually co-ruler with his uncle, became so formally in Justin's last year.

JUSTINIAN (527-565 A.D.)

Absolutism. Justinian was a simple Latin peasant from Scupi (Uskub) in Moesia. His wife, Theodora, was a prostitute in her early days, but she became the worthy and imperious partner of a man who loved pwoer and strove to dominate every phase of society. Justinian was so successful in his ambition, and his reign proved so long, that the empire was stamped with its own peculiar character by his genius. Believing in imperial absolutism, Justinian dedicated himself to restoring unity within the Mediterranean world and the Christian Church.

Religious Policy. As a student of Church history, Justinian wrote on theological subjects, and as an autocrat, he determined ecclesiastical policy. In keeping with this policy, he closed those reminders of paganism, the philosophical schools of Athens (529), and sent Christian missionaries as far afield as southern Russia, Arabia, and the Sudan. Justinian's desire to bring about unity within the Church

The Granger Collection

FIGURE 69. Byzantine mosaic in Ravenna of Justinian and his retinue.

was due to his autocratic nature and to his ambition to conquer for the empire the lost provinces of Catholics, for he saw clearly that conquest would be easier with the support of the pope. For this reason, he persecuted the Arians and tried to reconcile the Monophysites to orthodox doctrine, but he ultimately failed, especially because of the growing religious and political bitterness between Greek and Roman, and between Greek and Oriental.

Recovery of the West. The military ambitions of Justinian met similarly with limited success. In 533, when political conditions were unsettled in the West, he sent Belisarius on an expedition against the Vandals in Africa. Belisarius was a commander of considerable genius, but the empire had been so depopulated by wars and invasions that he was able to transport only ten thousand infantry and five thousand cavalry. Nor were many of these soldiers of the ancient type; rather, some were mercenaries raised by individual officers who hired themselves out to the government, and the best among them were the mailed mounted archers (cataphracts). Belisarius, however, won a speedy victory over the Vandals and captured Carthage, though the prosperity of the country was ruined in the process. In 535 he attacked the Ostrogoths, first in Sicily and then in Italy, and took Rome. There the Ostrogothic king, Witiges, besieged him for a year and cut off his water supply by destroying the aqueducts; a thousand years were to pass before these were

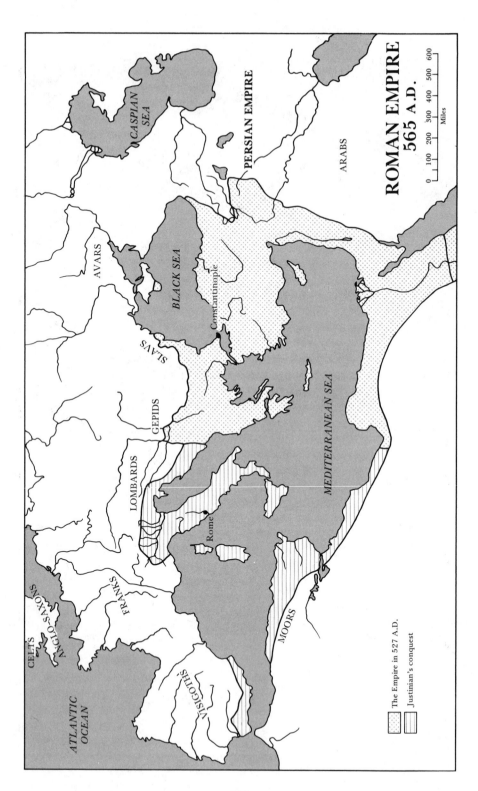

ROMAN EMPIRE
565 A.D.

Miles
0 100 200 300 400 500 600

PERSIAN EMPIRE

ARABS

CASPIAN SEA

AVARS

BLACK SEA

Constantinople

SLAVS

GEPIDS

LOMBARDS

MEDITERRANEAN SEA

FRANKS

Rome

CELTS

ANGLO-SAXONS

ATLANTIC OCEAN

VISIGOTHS

MOORS

The Empire in 527 A.D.

Justinian's conquest

restored. The depopulated city was, in fact, totally abandoned for a while. Belisarius continued in his conquest of the peninsula and, after capturing Ravenna in 540, made Italy a Roman province under a prefect or exarch at Ravenna. At this juncture, he had to return to the East for a war with Persia, and the Goths in Italy, finding the Roman rule oppressive, revolted. Justinian then sent a eunuch, Narses, to Italy with an army of thirty thousand men. Narses was an even more successful general than Belisarius, and after a long, fierce struggle the Goths were driven from Italy (554). Still later, Justinian gained a foothold along the Spanish coast, and the Frankish king acknowledged his leadership.

These conquests (map, p. 498) certainly brought the Western nations into closer contact with Roman civilization, and further impressed upon the minds of the Germans the idea that they, too, were included in the empire. Yet the wars devastated Italy, imperial rule was financially burdensome, and Justinian left Italy without a government strong enough to withstand the next, and last, tribal invasion, that of the Lombards (568).

Eastern Wars. During the struggle for Italy, Justinian had to contend with Slavs, Avars, and Bulgars, who laid waste the Balkans, and at the same time to carry on a war with Persia. Perhaps the gravest weakness of his foreign policy was the relative inattention he paid to the all-important Eastern frontiers, as his primary interest was diverted to the West. In 540 the Persian king, Chosroes I, took the great city of Antioch and transplanted its population.

Codification of Roman Law. A united empire and a universal Church should be accompanied, so Justinian believed, by a common law. The complete codification of the Roman civil law—the *Corpus Juris Civilis* written in Latin—was finally accomplished, and this, Rome's most precious gift to posterity, is doubtless Justinian's greatest achievement. For a thousand years Roman's legal system had been developing along two closely connected lines; statutes and decision. The statutes consisted of the laws of the republic, the edicts of the praetors during the early empire, and the direct legislation of the later emperors. Thus there came to be a great, confused mass of imperial enactments, sorely in need of revision. The second branch of Roman law comprised the decisions of jurists—called *responsa*, because they were given in reply to questions—as to how the statutes should apply to particular cases that had arisen or that might arise. These decisions, filling many volumes, had become hopelessly contradictory and inconsistent. Accordingly, under Justinian's authority, between 528 and 535, Tribonian, an eminent jurist, aided by several associates, drew up the so-called *Corpus Juris Civilis*. It had three parts. The *Codex* (Code) contained a sifted and revised selection of imperial "constitutions"—decisions, decrees, and edicts of the emperors—between the time of Hadrian and that of Justinian. The *Digest* or *Pandects*—much the largest part—contained, in fifty books, selected material from the writings of jurists between 90 B.C. and about A.D. 270. The *Institutes* was an elementary textbook, a treatise on the principles of jurisprudence for the use of students in the law schools of Constantinople, Berytus (Beirut), and Rome. The purpose of the *Novels* (or New Constitutions) which were also issued, was to contain the new statutes enacted after the publication of the code.

Justinian's legislation later modified, remained operative in the Eastern Roman Empire till its downfall in 1453. In the West, the barbarian invasions almost—but not quite—caused it to disappear, but in the twelfth century its study was revived in Bologna. Indeed it was this revival that gave rise to the modern university. From that time on, it became the "imperial law," the "common law of Europe," rapidly crowding out most of the customary local laws, and this process was immensely furthered by the Renaissance of the fifteenth and sixteenth centuries and by Napoleon and his Code. Even in England, where the local feudal law that became our "common law" opposed the most effective resistance of any encountered by this legal invasion, the influence of the legislation of Justinian has been lasting and far-reaching.

The general character of Roman law as we meet it in the *Corpus* is clear enough. The process of testing law by its equitable result had gone on between Celsus (first century A.D.) and the *Corpus,* and "equity" became much more like "humanitarianism" than it had been before. But parallel with this process and to some extent counteracting it was the increasing reliance on severity of administration. The process by *formula* gave way to the "libellary process," which ceased to be oral and became written and documentary, and a whole series of official judges, ranging from lower to higher, intervened between litigants and the final decision of their cause. The most important and most favored of litigants was the imperial treasury— the financial arm of the state—and the *bonum et aequum* was rarely heard when it was the question of a claim of the treasury against a citizen. (Cf. above, pp. 459ff.)

Imperial Administration.   Justinian's close attention to administration had the wholesome effect of limiting corruption, and his willingness to experiment led both to the abolition of the consulship—an unimportant, though dramatic, detail, for the office had been in use a millennium—and to the combination, after a long lapse, of military and civil authority. Like earlier Roman emperors, he was a great builder of roads, fortifications, aqueducts, and other public works. The most splendid of his many churches was the cathedral of the Holy Wisdom (Saint Sophia) at Constantinople (p. 504). During his reign, two Christian missionaries smuggled out of China in hollow canes the eggs of the silkworm; this feat made possible the raising of silkworms and the manufacture of silk goods, especially in Asia Minor and Greece.

The Nika Riot (532).   The large expenses of Justinians's regime—particularly those necessary for war and construction—required ruinous taxation. The praetorian prefect, John of Cappadocia, had the duty of providing the funds, and was famous for his ability to multiply taxes and extort money by fair means or foul. In 532 the citizens of Constantinople found the opportunity to give voice to their feelings about taxation and government in general. It had long been the custom for the population of the capital to divide itself into two factions, the Greens and the Blues, which carried on a bitter rivalry at the time of the horse races in the Hippodrome; in this way the people spent much of the excitement they had once vented in political strife and were still ready to use a riot as a cloak of their real attitude toward the government. On this occasion, a riot developed into an insurrection. Another emperor was set up, and cries of *"Nika"* ("Victory!") filled the streets. Justinian, who held only the palace, was eager to flee the city, but his wife, the Empress Theodora, rallied him with a fiery speech, and the rebellion was mercilessly suppressed.

Justinian died on November 14, 565. Three years later his Italian conquests were overthrown by the Lombard invasion, and the papacy gradually succeeded to power in Italy. Justinian's reign had been so remarkable, however, that the Eastern Roman Empire entered a new phase, which was Greek rather than Latin, though blended with Oriental elements. This was the mediaeval Byzantine Empire, so called from the ancient name of its capital.

33

The Civilization of
the Late Empire

ART

The cultural stagnation that had settled over classical Greco-Roman world during the second century was accelerated by the years of military anarchy of the third and the ensuring economic chaos. Imitation of the past had already sapped originality and the creative spirit; in a period of constant warfare, society's attention was diverted from art, and there was little money available to patronize it. The restoration of stability by Diocletian and Constantine produced a cultural revival, and the vitalizing force of Christianity was to produce ultimately a great art, deeply rooted in the past, and yet at the same time embodying the hopes and ideals of the new religion.

Public Works. Most of the art and architecture of the late empire was done under imperial patronage, the cities then being too poor to sponsor extensive programs of building or civic embillishment. The baths of Diocletian and Constantine at Rome, the basilica at Rome that Maxentius began and Constantine finished, and the palace of Diocletian at Salona in Dalmatia—all are examples of imperial architecture during the late emplire, and all are of stupendous size. Other buildings were erected in Ravenna, Milan, and Constantinople at great cost, but less work was done in the provinces. A vivid proof of the rapid changes in skill and taste is to compare the arch of Septimius Severus in the Roman Forum—which is not so very different from earlier triumphal arches—with that of Constantine near the Colosseum; indeed, one need do no more than look at the sculptures on Constantine's Arch. Those that are realistic have been lifted from monuments of the first and second centuries, whereas the contemporary sculptures abandon respect for the conventions of classic art, leaving the expressionism of the new art free for a naive vivacity in the narration of imperial deeds, which are the subject of the friezes. In their own way, the long lines of single uniform figures point forward to the later mosaics of Ravenna.

Eastern Influences. Realistic portraiture in a classical vein nevertheless lingered on in late imperial coinage and statuary; and the mosaics, particularly those of Africa, continued to picture daily life, but the important artistic contribution of the period was in church architecture. In the fourth century the Roman basilica, with its broad nave and side aisles, was adopted as the model for churches. The interior was decorated with frescoes and mosaics, which were full of symbolism. The figures in late antique art—or early Christian art—left behind the old Greco-Roman notion of nature; the draperies do not seem to contain bodies, and they cast no shadows. The figures are flat, the background has lost its depth, unrelated narrative and description have replaced the Greek understanding of spatial relation in the representation of an event or object. The colors are subtler than hitherto and strive for decorative harmony. The new style can be seen in the Gospel Books that were illustrated in Asia Minor during the sixth century and in the decoration of the churches of Syria and Asia Minor of that period. As Eastern influence in art became stronger, mysticism was translated into symbolism, and narrative into direct, simple action. The East did not like the illusion of depth; it stressed balance and design. Ornament and decoration took the place of restless action and elaborate folds. There were, accordingly, differences in style between East and West, and even within the individual regions, but they tended to coalesce with time, and the greater achievements inspired the artists and architects of later days. For example, Justinian's Church of the Holy Apostles at Constantinople was the source for the eleventh-century Saint-Front at Perigueux, and the sixth-century Church of San Vitale at Ravenna became the model of Charlemagne's imperial chapel at Aachen.

Saint Sophia (532-537). The Church of Saint Sophia (Holy Wisdom) at Constantinople is the greatest architectural achievement of the late Roman Empire; indeed, it is one of the greatest buildings in the world. It was built by Justinian's architects, Anthemius of Tralles and Isidorus of Miletus, between 532 and 537 on the site of a basilica previously erected by Constantine and destroyed in the Nika revolt. It was later partially reconstructed. The outside of the church is majestically impressive, with its masses of vaults and buttresses. The entrance is at the west end through the forecourt, or atrium, and thence through two vestibules (exonarthex and narthex) into the vast interior, 265 feet long by 107 feet wide. This area is crowned by apparently weightless domical vaults and a main dome (supported on pendentives), which is 180 feet high and 107 feet in diameter, with forty small windows. Half domes cover semicircular spaces at the east and west ends; along the north and south are side aisles, two stories high. The domes and half domes enclose an emptiness that appears to be the reality of the building; the impression is given that the interior has been united with all out-of-doors, and thus the Christian ideal of the union of the finite and infinite seems to be realized. The brick core of Saint Sophia is decorated on the inside with beautiful glass mosaics against a golden ground; these cover the vaults and domes, while alabasters, marbles, and other stones decorate the walls. After the Turkish conquest of Constantinople in 1453, Saint Sophia became a mosque, and the mosaics were whitewashed to hide their Christian symbols and inscriptions. The Turkish government has converted the structure into a museum, and today American scholars have returned the mosaics to their pristine glory; those uncovered date chiefly from the tenth century.

FIGURE 70. Saint Sophia, Constantinople.

LITERATURE

So long as the Roman Empire held firmly together, both Greek and Latin continued to be written in East and West, but the divisive influences in the political field affected classical literature, not only by hastening its decline, but also by ultimately restricting the two languages to their original spheres. The decay of pagan letters was accompanied by the rise of a Christian literature, which was based, as were art and architecture, on ancient models.

Pagan Greek Literature. For a decade after the opening of the third century, a Bithynian, Cassius Dio, collected materials for an annalistic *History of Rome,* the composition of which he completed during the next years. Written in Greek, the *History* consisted of eighty books and described the story of Rome from the time of Aeneas to 229, when Dio served as consul with Severus Alexander. Much of this work is preserved and is very useful, though it lacks vigor and imagination. We are able to supplement Dio's *History* with that of Herodian, a third-century Syrian Greek, who wrote a rhetorical, dramatic account of the years 180-238.

Revival of Pagan Religions. It was inevitable that during the disordered third century many minds and pens should turn chiefly to religion. The Oriental cults, the worship of Isis and the Great Mother, and the Mysteries of Eleusis attracted increasingly large numbers of people, as did Mithraism and the Syrian Sun God. The ancient religion of the Olympian gods still appealed to many, particularly to the aristocratic members of the Roman Senate, to whom the symbols of the past meant Roman greatness and salvation.

Neoplatonism. Paganism prospered until Gratian and Theodosius deliberately persecuted it, and indeed it continued until Justinian closed the schools of philosophy at Athens (529). Meanwhile philosophy became, for devotees, a religion, for it abandoned reason and embraced belief. This trend was due primarily to Plotinus, a hellenized Egyptian, who was one of the founders of Neoplatonism in the third century. With Neoplatonism, Greek thought made its last stand against the rising tide of Christianity. Platonic doctrine thus became a religion, a mystical pantheism. Neoplatonism held that it is possible, with the aid of the gods, to free oneself from this world and to commune with the supernatural, because the soul of the mortal is merely a part of the divine soul, to which, through the help of philosophy one can return. Plotinus taught at Rome between 253 and 270, and one of his pupils, Porphyry of Tyre, published his doctrines in groups of nine treatises each—the *Enneads.* Neoplatonic doctrine is reflected in the many surviving philosophical and other tracts of the emperor Julian the Apostate, written in Greek. Julian ranks with Cicero in having left the largest surviving corpus of works to posterity.

Pagan Latin Literature. Pagan Latin literature, like the Greek, contains few notable names. Repetition of age-old themes, unawareness of contemporary life, insistence on form rather than substance, and artificial and archaistic language— each conspired in its own way against creative work. This is the more regrettable, because it has left us with relatively few historical accounts of the late Roman Empire, and these are, in general, poor. The *Historia Augusta,* or *Augustan History,* is a collection of lives of emperors and pretenders from Hadrian to Numerian (117-284), through the biographies from 244 to 253 are missing. The *Historia Augusta* occasionally touches a good source, but on the whole it is exasperatingly fictional. The style lacks literary force, many statements are demonstrably false, and there is an abundance of petty personal details. The work, ostensibly by six authors, was composed in the late fourth century. Another history of limited value is the

Caesares of Aurelius Victor, an African who wrote about 360; it is a short history of Rome from Augustus to Constantius II. In the reign of Valens (364-378) Eutropius wrote a brief history of Rome—entitled *Breviarium ab Urbe Condita*—from the beginning to the year 365. It, too, has little value, but its simple style gives it a certain charm. The last true historian of the ancient world and in fact one of the very best of the historians of Rome, was Ammianus Marcellinus, a Greek of Antioch, who served in the imperial army as a high officer during the late fourth century. He wrote in Rome and in Latin; his work was a continuation of Tacitus and covered the history of Rome from Nerva to the death of Valens (96-378). The only extant books deal with the years 353-378, and they show Ammianus to have been a sound, impartial historian who possessed personal knowledge of the Roman world.

Ausonius and Claudian.   Throughout the late empire, but especially in Alexandria and Gaul, schools and institutions of higher education flourished. Classical literature, some medicine and law, and, above all, rhetoric were studied; the teachers were relieved of *munera* and received high pay. One of the most famous of these teachers was the Latin poet and professor of rhetoric and oratory Ausonius, whose life spanned almost the entire fourth century. Ausonius was the tutor of the future emperor Gratian, who in 379 raised his teacher to the consulate. After the emperor's death, Ausonius retired to Burdigala (Bordeaux), where he composed poems on Roman cities and emperors, on his professional colleagues at Bordeaux, and on other subjects, which shed light on the life of the period. A true lover of nature, Ausonius wrote a deservedly famous poem, the *Mosella,* which gives a charming picture of a journey he once made down the placid Moselle, a river flanked on either side by meadows and villas, vineyards and hills. A young contemporary of Ausonius was an Egyptian Greek, writing in Latin, Claudius Claudianus, who may be described as the last important Roman Poet. Claudian spent his life in Alexandria, Milan, and Rome. A protégé of Stilicho, he was poet laureate of Honorius' court. His verse is pure, classical, and correct—steeped in the antiquarian learning that had characterized the Alexandrian school of poetry for centuries.

Boethius.   One of the most important facts in the history of Europe is that the Christians of the fourth century were able to accept the culture of antiquity—their heritage—without its pagan gods. Had they decided that it was not possible to separate pagan literature from pagan faith, it is highly doubtful that classical civilization would have survived. It was this deliberate acceptance of pagan culture, no less than the triumph of Christianity as the religion of the empire, that spelled the end of pagan literature during the fifth century. Henceforth the authors were Christians; they composed, however, not only sacred writings but also history and the other literary genres. The greatest representative of this profane literature was Boethius, a Roman born about 480; he held various high offices and received the title of Patrician from the Ostrogothic king, Theodoric, but in 524 he was suspected of disloyalty and put to death. While he was in prison awaiting the end, he wrote his treatise *On the Consolation of Philosophy,* the work of a cultivated, intellectual Christian who turned for consolation in his trouble not to faith but to reason. His lifetime project, the translation into Latin of all the works of Plato and Aristotle, was barely begun at the time of his death.

Secular Greek Literature. Procopius. The only truly important figure in secular Greek literature did not appear until the sixth century. He was Procopius, of Caesarea in Palestine, who was a lukewarm Christian. Procopius accompanied Belisarius on his Italian and other campaigns. His *History of the Wars of Justinian* is very valuable for the light it sheds on Belisarius's campaigns in the West and against Persia. He also composed a *Secret History,* which was published after his death and exposed the alleged corruption of Justinian and Theodora.

Christian Greek Literature. Because Christianity had been born in the eastern part of the Roman Empire, it is natural that the first literature concerning the new religion should have been written in Greek. The latter half of the first century witnessed the completion of the New Testament. In the next century, when Christianity had aroused the antagonism of the pagans, there arose a group of defenders, or *apologists,* as they were called. The greatest of these early apologists was Irenaeus, bishop of Lyons at the end of the second century. Irenaeus had been born in Asia Minor, and though a resident of Gaul he wrote in Greek.

Clement and Origen. By the third century, Alexandria had become the greatest intellectual center of Greek Christianity. Clement of Alexandria, one of the first of the Alexandrian Fathers, employed Greek philosophical arguments to defend Christianity; in his *Address to the Greeks* and other writings, he sought to persuade cultivated pagans that in the enlightened realm of culture, paganism and Christianity were not incompatible. Clement left Alexandria for Palestine at the time of Septimius Severus' persecution of the Christians, and was succeeded as a teacher at Alexandria by his pupil Origen (203). Origen was the son of Christian parents and became the greatest apologist for the Christian religion. His *Against Celsus* is a reply to arguments that had been advanced against Christianity in the previous century. Thoroughly educated in Greek philosophy, he was able to coordinate philosophical thought with the faith of the Church. Origen was a prolific author and composed many *Commentaries* on the Bible, but a quarrel with his bishop caused him to move to Caesarea. He was tortured during the persecution of Decius and died three years later at Tyre (253).

The Fourth Century. It was strife—both political and theological—that accounted in large part for the vigor of Christian literature. The duty of defending orthodoxy, in a period of heresies and sectarian differences, called forth eloquent orators, such as Athanasius, the bitter opponent of Arianism, who became bishop of Alexandria in 328; Basil of Caesarea in Cappadocia, who was chiefly instrumental in the development of Greek monasticism; Gregory of Nazianzus in Cappadocia, a learned orator and poet; and, above all, John Chrysostom, who was born at Antioch in the middle of the fourth century and became the Patriarch of Constantinople. The *Church History* of Eusebius is of fundamental importance. Eusebius was a fourth-century bishop of Caesarea in Palestine, and in addition to his *History,* which brought the story of Christianity down to the year 323, he wrote a brief history of the world, known as *Chronicles;* Jerome later translated this history into Latin. Eusebius' *Martyrs of Palestine* describes Diocletian's persecution of the Christians in Palestine and is the only detailed account of provincial persecution to have survived.

Christian Latin Literature. Christian Latin literature began in the second century with Minucius Felix, a Roman convert who defended the faith with all the elegance of classical Latinity. It was in Africa, however, that a real center of Christian Latin literature developed. The first representative of this school, Tertullian (ca. 160-230), wrote in a robust style with little regard for classical traditions. Born at Carthage, Tertullian became a follower of Montanus, a native of Asia Minor who claimed prophetic powers and taught that the Heavenly Jerusalem was shortly to descend to earth. This heresy involved Tertullian in endless controversy with the Church; nevertheless his passionate defense of Christianity marked him as the founder of Western theology. The task of continuing the defense of Christianity was carried on by Tertullian's friend Cyprian, who was chosen bishop of Carthage in the middle of the third century. Cyprian's doctrines were orthodox, and his letters are a valuable source for the developing authority of the bishop of Rome and for the State's attack on the Church. The rather harsh style of the African school of Christian writing was refined by Lactantius (ca. A.D. 300), a philosophical and cultured student of Cicero's writings, into something approaching the elegance of Minucius Felix, a vigorous combination of the classical and Christian styles that was to reach its height in Jerome and Augustine. Lactantius was called by Diocletian to Nicomedia in Bithynia to teach Latin rhetoric, and after his conversion to Christianity, he wrote two important treatises that have survived. One of these, the *Divine Institute,* is a philosophical work in defense of Christianity against paganism; the other, *On the Deaths of the Persecutors,* is an impassioned presentation of the divine government of the world.

Ambrose and Jerome. It is abundantly clear that the necessity of defending orthodoxy from the attacks of heretics, pagans, and the State was partly responsible for the vitality of Christian literature. Ambrose, the famous fourth-century bishop of Milan in the days of Theodosius I, is another example of this necessity, for the threat of the Arian heresy was repelled from Italy by the vigor of his sermons and writings. Ambrose also composed many hymns, which, like those of his contemporary, the Spaniard Prudentius, influenced the music and poetry of the Church. Another controversial writer, and the most learned man of his day, was Jerome (Hieronymus, 335-420), who came from the Pannonian border. It was Jerome's letters, commentaries on the Bible, and other works that helped settle the doctrines of the Christian Church, while his translation of the Old Testament into Latin (made on the order of Pope Damasus) is the basis of the Vulgate, still used by the Catholic Church.

Augustine. With Augustine (354-430) one reaches a pivotal figure in the intellectual history of the early Church. He was born at Tagaste in Africa of a pagan father and a Christian mother. In his youth he followed a Christian heresy known as Manichaeism; founded by a Babylonian priest named Mani, this doctrine emphasized the eternal conflict between the Light and the Dark, between Good and Bad, and God and Man. Augustine was converted to orthodoxy by Ambrose and then became bishop of Hippo in Africa, where he died during the siege of the city by the

Vandals. A theologian and a philosopher, a mystic and a reasoner, Augustine was one of the most influential writers of the Christian Church. His *Confessions* give many details about his personal life, his youth, and his conversion. His *City of God* conforted Christians for Alaric's sack of Rome and refuted the pagan charge that Rome had been destroyed because of neglect of the ancient religion. The City of God, Augustine tells us, is bound to triumph ultimately over earthly government. With these thoughts, we have moved from the ancient into the mediaeval world.

THE CHRISTIAN CHURCH

The decline of the Roman Empire was accompanied by the rise of Christianity, and this, in turn, led to strife with the government, with pagans, and with heretics; at the same time, there developed a regular Church organization and a Christian art and literature. The difference in civilization between the East and the West exercised a profound influence on Christianity. In the East there continued to be much free thought and discussion in the Greek spirit, which in itself invited heresy, whereas Western theologians devoted themselves to matters of doctrine and organization; they felt more deeply the influence of law, impressed on them by Rome. Their doctrine, as it came to differ from that of the East, was less subtle and more simple, systematic, and reasonable. In the East, furthermore, the government exercised greater authority over the Church, for Constantinople was both the seat of the emperor and of a Patriarch; at the same time, the nearby rival patriarchates of Antioch and Alexandria could be closely watched by the state (cf. map, p. 480). There was also rivalry between Constantinople and Rome, but Rome had the advantage of being far removed, and when at last the Western Empire disappeared, priests and bishops, who had long been accustomed to intervene with the government on behalf of the people, were now compelled to stand alone against the barbarians.

The Papacy. These were some of the reasons that the papal office developed an independent role. Its greatness was also due to the ability and wisdom of several early popes—notably Innocent I (402-417) and Leo I (440-461)—who, among other things, were active in charitable work and in sending out missionaries to convert pagans and heretics. The supremacy of the papacy—at least, in the West—was due fundamentally to the belief that God had aided the growth of the Roman Empire as a preparation for Christianity and that on this political basis should be founded a spiritual empire that in time should embrace the whole world. To Western theologians it seemed natural that Rome should be the center of this universal Christian empire, not only because it had so long been the political capital of the world, but more particularly because of the reputed origin of the Christian Church of that city. These theologians believed that Paul and Peter had founded it, and that Peter had been its first bishop. The Roman bishop, accordingly, enjoyed special reverence, for it was understood that Christ had appointed Peter to be head of the Church, on one occasion declaring to him, "And I say unto thee, That thou art Peter, and upon this rock I will build my church" (Matthew 16:18; the word *Peter* means "rock"). The idea was that as the successors of Peter, the bishops, or popes, of Rome also held the headship, and that, receiving the truth by tradition in an unbroken line from the chief apostle, the popes were better able than any others to teach it in its purity.

Saints. The spread of Christianity was most rapid in the cities; indeed, as pagan beliefs remained longest among the rural population, the word *paganus* ("rural") came to be applied to non-Christians. A reason for the rapid growth of Christianity, and one of its greatest merits, was its adaptability to the needs of humankind. For instance, pagan festivals were absorbed into the Christian calendar, Christmas replacing the midwinter feast, Easter the celebration in honor of the spring equinox, and so on. To take a more important example, in accepting the new faith, many converted pagans felt that the infinite God was too great and too distant to pray to directly. There grew up, accordingly, the practice of praying for the intercession of the saints—certain great and good Christians who, having lived especially pure lives, were now with God. It was through the help of the saints that people hoped to receive an answer to their prayers. Statues of the saints and of Christ and the Virgin were set up in the churches, and to them the faithful prayed. By the use of such simple means the Church was able to get and retain a hold on those people to whom some outward symbol seemed essential.

Monasticism. In an effort to attain a life of holiness, many Christians thought it necessary to renounce the world. The desire for an ascetic life first appeared in the East, which had always been given to contemplation, and received a certain impulse from the third-century persecutions. In Egypt such persons often lived as hermits alone in the desert, and in Syria they spent their lives atop pillars. During the fourth century Anthony and Pachomius organized many of these people in Egypt into communities, with their own sets of rules; the members lived together in a large building and possessed land and all other property in common. Men who passed their lives in this way were monks—a word derived from the Greek *monos,* meaning "single"—and their community was a monastery; women who adopted the same form of life were called *nuns,* and their institution was a nunnery or convent. The idea of monasticism spread, first to Palestine, Syria, and Asia Minor. The founder of Greek monasticism was Basil (ca. 360), the bishop of Caesarea in Cappadocia; and then when the custom reached the West, the great organizer of monasteries there was Benedict, who founded Monte Cassino in 520. He also laid down for the monks the three rules of poverty, chastity, and obedience. Although the society to which they belonged might acquire great wealth, the individual monks had to continue poor; the command of chastity required them to remain unmarried; and that of obedience compelled them to submit to the will of their abbot. Members of the order were expected not only to pray but also to labor on the common estate and to read. It was this last injunction that led to the collection of important libraries, for which monks were famous during the Middle Ages. While affording a refuge from the barbarism of the age, monasticism preserved the little learning that remained in the West, taught by example the dignity of labor, and held up a standard of moral and religious life, which was superior to that of the outside world.

Many monasteries of the Benedictine rule were established throughout western Europe. Had it not been for Cassiodorus (ca. 480-575)—the writer who served under Theodoric the Great and subsequently founded a Benedictine monastery in southern Italy that became noted for preserving ancient literature—or for the Celtic refugees who, fleeing from Germanic invaders in Gaul, brought manuscripts with them to Ireland, our knowledge of ancient civilization would be far less than it is.

EPILOGUE

In considering further the decline of antiquity, we must emphasize the apparently contradictory facts that the amazing second century, when humankind was seemingly never more secure in peace, prosperity, and sound government, was culturally increasingly inert. Clearly the manifestations of cultural decline in the classical mainstream reached the surface before any others, but economic collapse was hastened by the growth of bureaucracy under Hadrian and an increase in overhead expenses that the primitive economy could not meet. In order to help the municipalities with their finances, the government had sent them financial supervisors, a well-intentioned move that was to lead to ever greater centralized control. After the Roman world had emerged from the crisis of the third century, during which the cities fought the peasants, and the peasants the army, and the army both of them and the barbarian invaders as well, Diocletian was able to maintain the state only by increasing still further the imperial bureaucracy and centralization. The high taxes and rents necessary to support great numbers of people who were not producers—the members of the army and the bureaucracy, and the large landowners—so crushed the peasants that they were unable to sustain the numbers needed to meet the urgent call for new manpower.

So complicated is the subject of the fall of Rome that it is little wonder that there are almost as many theories as there are writers. The truth is that all the factors we have mentioned, and others that spring to mind, were mere aspects of Rome's decline, and not one of them goes to the roots of the problem. It will be helpful, however, to recall that at the very moment when pagan literature of the late empire suffered eclipse—because it was interested in form rather than substance and appealed to a narrow, educated audience—Christian literature was full of vitality and came to be addressed to common folk as well as scholars.

Chronological Tables

I. PREHISTORY

All dates are approximate

Ramapithecus	14,000,000 B.C.
Australopithecus afarensis (Africanus)	4,000,000 B.C.
Homo habilis	3,500,000 B.C.
Glacial Age	3,000,000–10,000 B.C.
First (Guenz) glaciation	3,000,000 B.C.
Homo erectus	2,000,000 B.C.
Second (Mindel) glaciation	800,000 B.C.
Third (Riss) glaciation	265,000 B.C.
Neanderthal man flourished	86,000–40,000 B.C.
Fourth (Wuerm) glaciation	75,000 B.C.
Homo sapiens	before 70,000 B.C.
Great period of Paleolithic art	30,000–17,000 B.C.
The Forest Folk	14,000–8000 B.C.
Paleolithic period ends	10,000 B.C.
Mesolithic period in Near East	10,000–7,000 B.C.
The first villages	7000 B.C.
Neolithic period in Near East	7000 B.C.
(Chalcolithic period in Near East	5000–3000 B.C.)
Use of metals	5000 B.C.
The Swiss lake villages	4500–2500 B.C.
Megaliths	3500–2000 B.C.
Civilization begins	before 3000 B.C.
Writing	before 3000 B.C.
Bronze Age in Near East	before 3000 B.C.
Iron Age in Near East	before 1000 B.C.

II. SYNCHRONISTIC TABLE

All dates are B.C.

ASIA	EGYPT	GREECE	ROME
Sumerian settlement, ca. 3500	Archaic Age 3100–2685		
Gilgamesh ca. 2700			
Eannatum, ca. 2500	Old Kingdom, 2685–2180		
Sargon of Akkad, ca. 2340			
Ur's supremacy, ca. 2135–2027			
Hammurabi, ca. 1792–1750	Middle Kingdom, 2040–1785		
		Height of Minoan civilization, 1600	
		Height of Mycenaean civilization, 1500–1300	Terremare culture, ca. 1700
Hittite expansion, after 1400	New Kingdom, 1560–1085	Dorian invasion, ca. 1100	
Hittite empire destroyed, after ca. 1200			
Rise of Tyre, after 1000		Middle Age, 1100–750	Etruscan settlement, 10th (?) century
David, ca. 1000–961			
Tiglath-pileser III, 745–727		Colonization, 750–550	Etruscan expansion, 7th and 6th centuries
Ashurbanipal; height of Assyrian civilization, 669–626	Conquered by Assyria, 671 Saïte Period, 663–525		
Destruction of Nineveh, 612		Solon, 594	
Nebuchadnezzar II, 604–562			
Destruction of Jerusalem, 586		Peisistratus, 560–527	
Cyrus the Great, king of Persia, 550–529			

ASIA	EGYPT	GREECE	ROME
Fall of Babylon, 539	Conquered by Persia, 525		Overthrow of monarchy, ca. 509
Darius I, 522–486			
Xerxes, 486–464		Battle of Marathon, 490	
		Battles of Thermopylae, Salamis, Himera, 480	
		Battles of Plataea, Mycale, 479	
		Delian League established, 477	Codification of law, ca. 449
		Athenian Empire established, 448	Capture of Veii, 390
		Peloponnesian War, 431–404	Gallic sack of Rome, 387
		Battle of Leuctra, 371	
		Battle of Mantinea, 362	
		Battle of Chaeronea, 338	Latin War, 340–338
Darius III, 336–330	Conquered by Alexander, 332	Alexander the Great, 336–323	Second Samnite War, 326–304
Fall of Persepolis, 330			
Seleucus I, 305–281	Ptolemy I, 305–285		Lex Hortensia, 287
Antiochus I, 281–261	Ptolemy II, 285–246	Antigonus Gonatas, 276–239	Pyrrhus lands in Italy, 281
Kingdom of Pergamum established, 263		Hiero II of Syracuse, 264–215	First Punic War, 264–241
Antiochus III, the Great, 223–187	Ptolemy IV, 221–203	Philip V, 221–179	Second Punic War, 218–201
		First and Second Macedonian Wars, 215, 200–196	
Battle of Magnesia, 190		Battle of Pydna, 168	
Attalus II of Pergamum, 159–138		Destruction of Corinth, 146	Rome destroys Carthage, 146

III. EARLY MESOPOTAMIA

All dates are B.C. and approximate

Sumerian settlement	3500
Writing	before 3000
Gilgamesh	2700
Royal cemetery, First Dynasty of Ur	2700
Eannatum	2500
Uruinimgina	2355
Lugal Zaggisi	2350
Sargon of Akkad	2340
Naram Sin	2250
The Guti	2150
Gudea	2150
Ur III	2135–2027
Amorite invasion	2000
Hammurabi	1792–1750
Kassite invasion	1550

IV. EGYPT

All dates are B.C. and approximate

Dynasties I–II	3100–2685
Writing	before 3000
Old Kingdom (Dynasties III–IV)	2685–2180
Pyramids of Khufu, Khafre, Menkaure (Fourth Dynasty)	2613–2494
First Intermediate Period	2180–2040
Middle Kingdom (Dynasties VIII–X)	2040–1785
Second Intermediate Period	1785–1560
Hyksos invasion	1674
New Kingdom or Empire (Dynasties XVIII–XX)	1560–1085
Ahmose I	1560–1533
Hatshepsut	1490–1469
Thutmosis III	1490–1436
Amenhotep III	1402–1363
Akhenaten	1363–1347 (?)
Ramses II	1298–1232
Battle of Kadesh	1287
Ramses III	1198–1167
Egypt conquered by Esarhaddon, king of Assyria	671
Saite Period (Dynasty XXVI)	663–525
Egypt conquered by Cambyses, king of Persia	525
Egypt conquered by Alexander the Great	332
Egypt annexed by Rome	30

V. THE HITTITES, SYRIA, AND PALESTINE

All dates are B.C. and approximate

Hittite settlement in Asia Minor	ca. 2000
Expansion under King Suppililiumas	1350
Battle of Kadesh	1287
Treaty between Hattushil and Ramses II	1267
Hittite Empire destroyed	ca. 1200
Developed Phoenician alphabet	11th century
Rise of Tyre	*after* 1000
Phoenician colonization	early first millennium
David, King of Israel and Judah	ca. 1000–961
Solomon	ca. 961–922
Tiglath-pileser III, king of Assyria, takes Damascus	732
Sargon II, king of Assyria, captures Samaria; the Ten Lost Tribes transplanted	722
Nebuchadnezzar, king of Babylon, destroys Jerusalem and carries the population into captivity	586

VI. ASSYRIA AND PERSIA

All dates are B.C.

Assyrian expansion under Ashurnasirpal II	884–859
Tiglath-pileser III	745–727
Capture of Damascus	732
Sargon II	722–705
Capture of Samaria; the Ten Lost Tribes transplanted	722
Sargon's defeat of the Egyptians at Raphia	720
Sennacherib	705–681
Esarhaddon	681–669
Conquest of Egypt	671
Ashurbanipal; height of Assyrian civilization	669–626
Saïte Egypt (Dynasty XXVI)	663–525
Destruction of Nineveh	612
Nebuchadnezzar II, king of the Chaldaean Empire	604–562
Destruction of Jerusalem; its population carried into captivity	586
Treaty between Lydia and Media, setting the Halys as a boundary	585
Croesus, king of Lydia	ca. 560–546
Cyrus the Great, king of Persia	550–529
Cyrus defeats Croesus	546
Conquest of Asiatic Greeks	545
Fall of Babylon	539
Cambyses	529–522
Conquest of Egypt	525

ASSYRIA AND PERSIA *(continued)*

Darius I	522–486
Scythian expedition	513
Revolt of the Ionian Greeks	499–493
Mardonius' expedition; wreck off Mount Athos	492
Expedition of Datis and Artaphernes; battle of Marathon	490
Xerxes	486–464
Battles of Thermopylae and Salamis	480
Battles of Plataea and Mycale	479
Cimon's victory at the Eurymedon River	466
Artaxerxes I	464–424
Peace of Callias	449
Darius II	423–404
Expedition of Cyrus and the Ten Thousand	401
The King's Peace	387
Artaxerxes Ochus	359–338
Darius III	336–330
Battle of Issus	333
Battle of Arbela	331
Persepolis captured by Alexander the Great	330

VII. GREECE

All dates are B.C.

Neolithic age ends	ca. 3000 B.C.
Bronze Age civilization	3rd and 2nd millennia
Height of Minoan civilization	1600
Height of Mycenaean civilization	1500–1300
Fall of Troy	ca. 1250
Dorian invasion	ca. 1100
The Greek Middle Age	ca. 1100–750
Homer	ca. 725–750
First Olympic Games (traditional)	776
Hesiod	seventh century
Colonization	ca. 750–550
Archaic Greek civilization	ca. 750–479
Spartan conquest of Messenia	ca. 730
Synoikismos at Athens	*before* 700
Tyranny	7th and 6th cents.
Draco	ca. 621
Reform of Lycurgus at Sparta	ca. 600 (?)
Solon's archonship at Athens	594
Peisistratus	560–528/7
Croesus of Lydia	ca. 560–546
Beginning of Peloponnesian League	ca. 550

Persian conquest of Asiatic Greeks 545
Aeschylus . . . . ca. 524–456
Pindar. . . . . ca. 522–441
Hippias exiled. 510
Cleisthenes. 508
Ionian Revolt. 499–493
Hipparchus Archon 496/5
Themistocles archon 493–492
Expedition of Mardonius 492
Battle of Marathon 490
Battles of Thermopylae, Artemisium, Salamis. 480
Battle of Himera 480
Battles of Plataea and Mycale. 479
Delian League established 477
Battle of the Eurymedon 466
Ephialtes' reform of the Areopagus. 462
Ostracism of Cimon. 461
Temple of Zeus at Olympia. . . . . ca. 460
Height of Athenian power on land 456
Treasury of Delian League transferred to Athens. 454
Athenian naval expedition to Egypt destroyed 453
Death of Cimon 450
Peace of Callias. 449
Athenian Empire established 448
Collapse of Athenian land empire. 446
The Thirty Years' Peace 445
Ostracism of Thucydides, son of Melesias. 443
Megarian decree 432
Peloponnesian War. 431–404
Archidamian War. 431–421
Death of Pericles. 429
Athens captures Pylos 425
Peace of Nicias 421
Athenian expedition to Melos 416
Athenian expedition to Sicily 415–413
Decelea occupied by Sparta. 413
The Four Hundred at Athens. 411
Recall of Alcibiades. 411
Battle of Arginusae 406
Battle of Aegospotami 405
Fall of Athens. 404
The Thirty Tyrants at Athens 404
Construction of temples on Athenian Acropolis . . . . . . 2nd half of 5th cent.
Period of Athenian dramatists, historians, Socrates . . . . . 2nd half of 5th cent.
Dionysius of Syracuse 405–367
Expedition of Cyrus and the Ten Thousand 401
Death of Socrates 399
King Agesilaus of Sparta in Asia Minor 396
Battle of Cnidus 394

GREECE *(continued)*

The King's Peace   387
Second Athenian Confederacy   377
Battle of Leuctra   371
Battle of Mantinea   362
Philip II of Macedon   359–336
Fall of Chalcidian League   348
Peace of Philocrates   346
Battle of Chaeronea   338
Alexander the Great   336–323
Battle of the Granicus   334
Battle of Issus   333
Siege of Tyre   332
Battle of Arbela   331
Death of Darius   330
Alexander's invasion of Bactria–Sogdiana   329
Alexander's invasion of India   327
Battle of the Hydaspes   326
Alexander's departure from Indus delta   325
Alexander's return to Babylon   323
Lamian War   323
Period of Praxiteles, Demosthenes, Plato, Aristotle . . . . .   4th cent.
Hellenistic Age   323–31
Wars of the Successors   323–276
Agathocles of Syracuse   316–289
The Successors take the title of King   306–305
Ptolemy I   305–283
Seleucus I   305–281
Battle of Ipsus   301
Zeno founds the Stoa   301
Menander and Euclid . . . .   ca. 300
Theocritus, Callimachus, Aristarchus, Archimedes, Eratos-
    thenes . . . .   3rd cent.
Ptolemy II Philadelphus   285–246
Battle of Corupedium   281
Antiochus I   281–261
Pyrrhus in Italy and Sicily   281–275
Invasion of Gauls (Galatians)   279
Antigonus Gonatas   279–239
Chremonidean War   267
Hiero II of Syracuse   264–215
Kingdom of Pergamum established   263
Eumenes I of Pergamum   263–241
Antiochus II   261–247
Seleucus II   247–226
Arsacids of Parthia   247
Ptolemy III Euergetes   246–221

Reform of Agis IV of Sparta	245
Attalus I of Pergamum	241–197
Demetrius II	238–229
Aetolian and Achaean leagues at height	230
Antigonus Doson	229–221
Reforms of Cleomenes at Sparta	226
Seleucus III	226–223
Antiochus III the Great	223–187
Battle of Sellasia. Capture of Sparta	222
Philip V of Macedon	221–179
Ptolemy IV Philopator	221–203
Battle of Raphia	217
First Macedonian War	215–205
Ptolemy V Epiphanes	203–181
Euthydemus, Demetrius, Menander of Bactria	1st half of 2nd cent.
Second Macedonian War	200–197
Battle of Cynoscephalae	197
Eumenes II of Pergamum	197–159
Battle of Magnesia	190
Perseus of Macedon	179–168
Antiochus IV Epiphanes	175–163
Mithridates I of Parthia	171–138
Third Macedonian War	171–167
Battle of Pydna	168
Attalus II of Pergamum	159–138
Macedonia becomes a Roman province	148
Destruction of Corinth	146
Attalus III of Pergamum	138–133
Pergamum becomes the Roman province of Asia	129
Mithridates VI of Pontus	121–63
Syria becomes a Roman province	63
Battle of Actium. Rome wins Egypt	31
Peloponnesus becomes the Roman province of Achaea	27

VIII. ROME [1]

Neolithic age begins	ca. 3500 B.C.
Bronze Age begins	ca. 1800
Terremare civilization	ca. 1700
Iron Age begins	ca. 1000
The Etruscan settlement	10th century (?)
Foundation of Carthage	ca. 725
Greek colonization of southern Italy and Sicily	8th and 7th cents.
Foundation of Rome (traditional)	753
Expansion of the Etruscans	7th and 6th cents.

[1] List of Roman emperors, p. 527.

ROME *(continued)*

Overthrow of the Roman monarchy	ca. 509
Codification of Roman law	ca. 449
Lex Canuleia	445
Capture of Veii	390
The Gauls take Rome	387
Licinian-Sextian Laws	367
Alliance of Rome and Capua	ca. 343
First Samnite War	343–341
The Latin War	340–338
Second Samnite War	326–304
Caudine Forks	321
Appius Claudius censor	312
War with Samnites, Etruscans, Gauls	298–290
Battle of Sentinum	295
Secession of the plebs. *Lex Hortensia*	287
War with Tarentum and Pyrrhus	281–272
Hiero II of Syracuse	264–215
First Punic War	264–241
Battle of Mylae	260
Rome invades Africa	256
First Illyrian War	229–228
Sicily, Sardinia, Corsica organized as provinces	227
Second Illyrian War	220–219
Hannibal attacks Saguntum	219
Second Punic War	218–201
Battle of Lake Trasimene	217
Fabius dictator	217
Battle of Cannae	216
Revolt of Capua	216
First Macedonian War	215–205
Revolt of Syracuse	214
Syracuse taken	212
Capua taken	211
Cornelius Scipio in Spain	210
Battle of the Metaurus	207
Scipio invades Africa	204
Battle of Zama	202
Period of Plautus, Ennius, Terence	
Second Macedonian War	200–196
Battle of Cynoscephalae	197
Hither and Farther Spain organized as provinces	197
War with Antiochus the Great	192–189
Battle of Magnesia	190
Cato censor	184
Lex Villia	180
Third Macedonian War	171–167

Battle of Pydna	168
Lex Calpurnia	149
Macedonia organized as a Roman province	148
Sack of Corinth and Carthage	146
Fall of Numantia	133
Tribunate of Tiberius Gracchus	133
Kingdom of Pergamum bequeathed to Rome	133
Asia organized as a province	129
Tribunate of Gaius Gracchus	123–122
Gallia Narbonensis organized as a province	121
War with Jugurtha	111–105
Consulships of Marius	107, 104–100
Victory over Teutons at Aquae Sextiae	102
Victory over Cimbri at Vercellae	101
Tribunate of Livius Drusus	91
The Allied War	90–88
First Mithridatic War	89–85
Capture of Athens	86
Marius' seventh consulship	86
Sulla returns to Rome	83
Sulla's dictatorship	82–79
Bithynia organized as a province	75
Second Mithridatic War	74–63
Revolt of Spartacus and the gladiators	73–71
Pompey and Crassus consuls	70
Trial of Verres	70
Lex Gabinia	67
Lex Manilia	66
Syria organized as a province	63
Cicero consul	63
Conspiracy of Catiline	63
Period of Varro, Lucretius, Catullus	
The First Triumvirate	60
Caesar's conquest of Gaul	58–51
Cicero exiled	58
Cicero's return	57
Pompey Curator of the Grain Supply	57
The conference at Luca	56
Caesar invades Britain	55–54
Crassus' death at Carrhae	53
Pompey sole consul	52
Civil War begins	49
Battle of Pharsalus	48
Death of Pompey	48
Battle of Thapsus	46
Battle of Munda	45
Caesar's murder	44
The Second Triumvirate	43
Cicero's death	43

ROME *(continued)*

Battle of Philippi	42
Battle of Actium	31
Egypt annexed	30
Peloponnesus organized as the province of Achaea	27
Augustus	27 B.C.–A.D. 14
Augustus' First Act of Settlement	27 B.C.
Augustus' Second Act of Settlement	23 B.C.
Period of Vergil, Horace, Livy, Ovid.	
Rapprochement with Parthia	19 B.C.
Danubian provinces annexed	16–9
Death of Drusus	9 B.C.
Pannonian revolt	A.D. 6–9
Ambush of Varus	9
Tiberius	14–37
Death of Germanicus	19
Tiberius retires to Capri	26
Death of Sejanus	31
Caligula	37–41
Claudius	41–54
Southern Britain organized as a province	43
Nero	54–68
Boudicca's insurrection quelled	60
Tiridates crowned at Rome	63
The fire at Rome	64
Rebellion in Judea	66–70
Period of Seneca, Lucan, Petronius, Pliny the Elder, Quintilian, Martial	
Galba	68–69
Otho, Vitellius	69
Vespasian	69–79
Destruction of Jerusalem	70
Titus	79–81
Pompeii and Herculaneum destroyed	79
Domitian	81–96
Beginning of the German limes	
Dacian Wars	85–89
Nerva	96–98
Period of Pliny the Younger, Plutarch, Tacitus, Juvenal	
Trajan	98–117
Dacian Wars	101–102, 105–106
Parthian War	114–117
Hadrian	117–138
Period of Suetonius	
Antoninus Pius	138–161
Period of Lucian	
Marcus Aurelius	161–180

Lucius Verus	161–169
Parthian War.	162–166
Plague	166
War with the Marcomanni, Quadi, Iazyges	167–175
Revolt of Avidius Cassius	175
Commodus.	180–192
Pertinax and Didius Julianus	193
Septimius Severus	193–211
Pescennius Niger defeated at Issus.	194
Parthian War.	195–196
Clodius Albinus defeated at Lugdunum	197
Parthian War continued	197–199
War in Britain.	208–211
Caracalla	211–217
Geta	211–212
Constitutio Antoniniana	212
Macrinus	217–218
Elagabalus	218–222
Severus Alexander	222–235
Sassanid kingdom established in Persia.	227
Persian War	230–233
War with the Germanic Alemanni.	234–235
Military anarchy	235–285
Maximinus.	235–238
Gordian I, II.	238
Gordian III.	238–244
Philip the Arabian	243–249
Decius.	249–251
Persecution of the Christians	249
Valerian.	253–260
Gallenius	253–268
The Gallic Empire established	260
Plague at its height.	260
The Herulians sack Athens	267
Claudius Gothicus	268–270
Aurelian	270–275
Dacia abandoned.	270
Palmyra revolts.	271
Palmyra taken.	272
Gaul and Britain reconquered	274
Diocletian	285–305
Maximian.	286–305
Galerius and Constantius become Caesars.	293
Edict of Prices	301
Persecution of the Christians	302
Diocletian and Maximian abdicate	305
Wars of succession	306–313
Constantine and Licinus	307–324
Edict of Toleration	311

ROME *(continued)*

"Edict" of Milan 313
Constantine sole emperor 324–337
Council of Nicaea 325
Constantinople founded 330
Constantius 337–360
Julian the Apostate 360–363
Valentinian I 364–375
Valens. 364–378
Valentinian II 375–392
Battle of Adrianople 378
Theodosius I. 379–395
Division of the empire 395
Honorius, western emperor 395–423
Arcadius, eastern emperor. 395–408
Stilicho defeats Alaric and the Visigoths 403
Theodosius II, eastern emperor 408–450
Alaric sacks Rome. 410
Visigoths settle in Gaul and Spain. 412–418
Valentinian III, western emperor 425–455
Aëtius Master of the Soldiers. 427–454
Vandals invade Africa. 429
Theodosian Code. 438
Attila and the Huns defeated at Mauriac Plain. 451
Death of Attila 453
The Vandals sack Rome 455
Ricimer Master of the Soldiers in the West 456–472
Leo I, eastern emperor. 457–474
Zeno, eastern emperor 474–491
Romulus Augustulus, western emperor 475–476
End of the Western Empire 476
Odovacar king in Italy 476–493
Clovis king of the Franks 486–511
Ostrogoths invade Italy. 488
Anastasius, eastern emperor. 491–518
Theodoric the Great. 493–526
Justin, eastern emperor. 518–527
Justinian, eastern emperor. 527–565
The *Corpus Juris Civilis* published. 528–535
Philosophical schools at Athens closed. 529
Saint Sophia built 532–537
Nika riot 532
Africa reconquered 533
Italy and Spain reconquered 535–555
Persians destroy Antioch. 540
Justinian's death 565

List of Roman Emperors

I. FROM AUGUSTUS TO A.D. 395

Augustus	27 B.C.–A.D. 14
Tiberius	A.D. 14–37
Gaius (Caligula)	37–41
Claudius	41–54
Nero	54–68
Galba	68–69
Otho	69
Vitellius	69
Vespasian	69–79
Titus	79–81
Domitian	81–96
Nerva	96–98
Trajan	98–117
Hadrian	117–138
Antoninus Pius	138–161
Marcus Aurelius	161–180
Lucius Verus	161–169
Commodus	180–192
Pertinax	193
Didius Julianus	193
Septimius Severus	193–211
Caracalla	211–217
Geta	211–212
Macrinus	217–218
Diadumenianus	218
Elagabalus	218–222
Severus Alexander	222–235
Maximinus	235–238
Gordian I and Gordian II	238
Balbinus and Pupienus	238
Gordian III	238–244
Philip the Arabian	243–249
Philip Junior	247–249
Decius	249–251
Gallus and Volusianus	251–253
Aemilianus	253
Valerian	253–260
Gallienus	253–268
Claudius Gothicus	268–270
Quintillus	270
Aurelian	270–275
Tacitus	275–276
Florianus	276
Probus	276–282
Carus	282–283

Carinus and Numerianus   283–284
Diocletian   285–305
Maximian.   286–305
Galerius and Constantius I.   305–306
Maxentius   306–312
Galerius, Severus, Constantine I   306–307
Galerius, Licinius, Constantine I.   307–310
Galerius, Licinius, Constantine I, Maximinus Daia   310–311
Constantine I and Licinius.   311–324
Constantine I, sole emperor.   324–337
Constantine II.   337–340
Constans   337–350
Constantius II.   337–361
Julian   361–363
Jovian   363–364
Valentinian I   364–375
Valens.   364–378
Gratian   367–383
Valentinian II.   375–392
Theodosius I.   379–395
Arcadius   383–395
Honorius   393–395

II. WESTERN EMPIRE

Honorius   395–423
Constantius III   421
Valentinian III   423–455
Petronius Maximus   455
Avitus.   455–456
Majorian   457–461
Libius Severus.   461–465
No emperor   465–467
Anthemius.   467–472
Olybrius   472
Glycerius.   473–474
Julius Nepos.   474–475
Romulus Augustulus   475–476

III. EASTERN EMPIRE

Arcadius   395–408
Theodosius II   408–450
Marcian   450–457
Leo I.   457–474
Leo II   474
Zeno.   474–491
Anastasius   491–518
Justin   518–527
Justinian   527–565

Genealogical Tables

I. THE JULIO–CLAUDIAN LINE OF EMPERORS

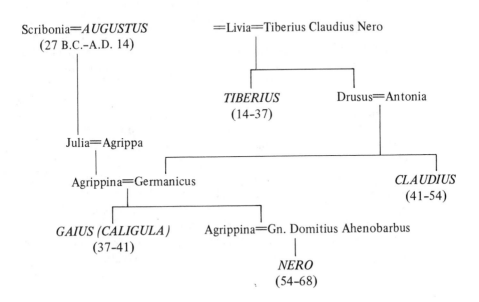

II. THE SEVERI

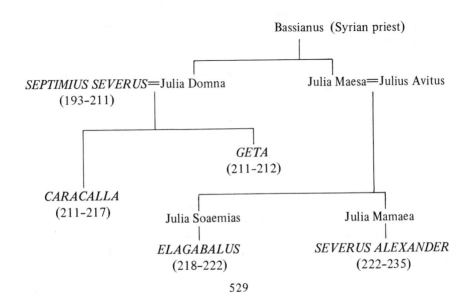

Select Bibliography

This bibliography, consisting of English titles, does not aim at completeness, though it is intended to put the reader on the track of a full bibliography. Full bibliographies and detailed lists of ancient sources will be found in the monumental *Cambridge Ancient History* (3rd ed., 1970), currently being rewritten, and in Marouzeau and Ernst, *L'année philologique*, which appears yearly and summarizes current publications. The importance of art and archaeology to the study of ancient history cannot be overemphasized. Good "picture books" have their own special value, for example, William G. Hayes, *The Scepter of Egypt*, 2 vols. (Metropolitan Museum of Art, New York, 1953-1959); William Stevenson Smith, *Ancient Egypt as Represented in the Museum of Fine Arts*, Boston (4th ed., Boston, 1961); and in general the *Encyclopedia of World Art*, 15 vols. (McGraw-Hill, London, 1959-1968).

Literature, no less than art, reflects the soul of a people. Some of the great literary monuments should be read in their entirety rather than in short extracts, in connection with the study of ancient history. Good translations of most of the Greek and Latin authors may be found in the Loeb Classical Library (Cambridge, Mass.), in progress. The best book containing translations of documents from the ancient Near East (including Sumerian, Babylonian, Assyrian, Hittite, and Egyptian documents) is J. B. Pritchard (Ed.), *Ancient Near Eastern Texts Relating to the Old Testament* (3rd ed., Princeton, N.J., 1969).

I. GENERAL HISTORIES AND WORKS OF REFERENCE

Andrewes, A., *The Greeks* (1967).
Bengtson, H., *Introduction to Ancient History* (6th ed., 1970).
Cambridge Ancient History, I. E. S. Edwards, C. J. Gadd, N. G. L. Hammond, and E. Sollberger (Eds.) (3rd ed., 1970).
Cary, M., *The Geographic Background of Greek and Roman History* (1949).
Cary, M., and E. H. Warmington, *The Ancient Explorers* (1929).
Casson, L., *The Ancient Mariners: Seafarers and Seafighters of the Mediterranean in Ancient Times* (1959).
Casson, L., *Ships and Seamanship in the Ancient World* (1971).
Ehrich, Robert W. (Ed.), *Chronologies in Old World Archeology* (1965).
Finley, M. I., *The Ancient Greeks* (1963).
Finley, M. I. (Ed.), *Slavery in Classical Antiquity* (1968).
Finley, M. I., *The Ancient Economy* (1973).
Garlan, Y., *War in the Ancient World* (1975).
Grant, M., *Ancient History Atlas* (1971).
Hall, H. R. H., *Ancient History of the Near East* (9th ed., 1936).
Hallo, W. W., and W. K. Simpson, *The Ancient Near East: A History* (1971).
Hammond, M., *The City in the Ancient World* (1972).

Kiepert, H., *Atlas Antiquus* (12th ed., 1902).

Kitto, H. D. F., *The Greeks* (1961).

Lloyd, S., *Foundations in the Dust* (1947).

Marrou, H. I., *A History of Education in Antiquity* (1956).

Meiggs, R., and J. B. Bury, *A History of Greece* (4th ed., 1975).

Meyers, J. L., *Mediterranean Culture* (1944).

Neugebauer, O., *The Exact Sciences in Antiquity* (1957).

Nock, A. D., *Conversion* (1933).

Oxford Classical Dictionary (2nd ed., 1970).

Pomeroy, Sarah B., *Goddesses, Whores, Wives, and Slaves: Women in Classical Antiquity* (1975).

Roebuck, C., *The World of Ancient Times* (1966).

Scullard, H. H., and A. A. M. van der Heyden, *A Shorter Atlas of the Classical World* (1967).

Shotwell, J. T., *The History of History* (rev. ed., 1939).

Sinnigen, W. G., and A. E. R. Boak, *A History of Rome to A.D. 565* (6th ed., 1977).

Snowden, B. M., *Blacks in Antiquity* (1970).

Starr, C. G., *A History of the Ancient World* (1965).

Stavely, E. S., *Greek and Roman Voting and Elections* (1972).

Thomson, J. O., *History of Ancient Geography* (1948).

II. PREHISTORY

Braidwood, R. J., *The Near East and the Foundations for Civilization: An Essay in Appraisal of the General Evidence* (1952).

Braidwood, R. J., *Prehistoric Man* (8th ed., 1975).

Burkitt, M. C., *The Old Stone Age* (2nd ed., 1949).

Childe, V. G., *The Dawn of European Civilization* (4th ed., 1948).

Childe, V. G., *Man Makes Himself* (1952).

Childe, V. G., *New Light on the Most Ancient East* (4th ed., 1953).

Childe, V. G., *What Happened in History* (rev. ed., 1954).

Childe, V. G., *The Prehistory of European Society* (1958).

Coon, C. S., *The Origin of Races* (1962).

Finegan, J., *Light from the Ancient East* (2nd ed., 1959).

Gould, S. J., "This View of Life," *Natural History*, Vol. 88 (1979), pp. 46ff.

Hawkes, J., and Sir L. Woolley, *Prehistory and the Beginnings of Civilization*, Vol. 1. Pareti, L., P. Brezzi, and L. Petech, *The Ancient World*, Vol. 2. In *History of Mankind: Cultural and Scientific Development* (1953–1965).

Kroeber, A. L., *Anthropology* (rev. ed., 1948).

Raphael, N., *Prehistoric Cave Paintings* (1946).

Renfrew, C., *Before Civilization* (1973).

Sagan, C., *The Dragons of Eden* (1977).

Trigger, B. G., *Beyond History: The Methods of Prehistory* (1968).

Windels, F., et al., *The Lascaux Cave Paintings* (1950).

Zihlman, A. L., and J. M. Lowenstein, "False Start of the Human Parade," *Natural History*, Vol. 88 (1979), pp. 86ff.

III. EARLY MESOPOTAMIA

Bibby, G., *Looking for Dilmun* (1969).

Bottero, J., et al., *The Near East: The Early Civilizations,* 3 vols. (1967).

Braidwood, R. J., *Prehistoric Man* (8th ed., 1975).

Chiera, E., *They Wrote on Clay* (1956).

Childe, V. G., *New Light on the Most Ancient East* (4th ed., 1953).

Childe, V. G., *What Happened in History* (rev. ed., 1954).

Frankfort, H., et al., *The Intellectual Adventure of Ancient Man* (1946).

Frankfort, H., *Kingship and the Gods* (1948).

Frankfort, H., et al., *Before Philosophy* (1949).

Frankfort, H., *The Birth of Civilization in the Near East* (1950).

Heidel, A., *The Gilgamesh Epic and Old Testament Parallels* (1949).

Kramer, S. N., *Sumerian Mythology* (1944).

Kramer, S. N., *History Begins at Sumer* (1958).

Kramer, S. N., *The Sumerians* (1963).

Mallowan, M. E. L., and D. J. Wiseman (Eds.), *Ur in Retrospect. In Memory of Sir A. Leonard Woolley* (1960).

Mellaart, J., *Earliest Civilizations of the Near East* (1965).

Oppenheim, A. L., *Ancient Mesopotamia: Portrait of a Dead Civilization* (rev. ed., 1977).

Parrot, A., *Sumer: The Dawn of Art* (1961).

Roux, G., *Ancient Iraq* (1966).

Van der Waerden, F., *Science Awakening* (1961).

IV. EGYPT

Aldred, C., *Old Kingdom Art in Ancient Egypt* (1946).

Aldred, C., *Egypt to the End of the Old Kingdom* (1965).

Aldred, C., *Akhenaton* (1968).

Badawy, A., *A History of Egyptian Architecture: The Empire (The New Kingdom)* (1968).

Bell, B., "The Dark Ages in Ancient History. I. The First Dark Age in Egypt," *American Journal of Archaeology,* Vol. 75 (1971), pp. 1ff.

Bell, H. I., *Cults and Creeds in Greco-Roman Egypt* (1953).

Breasted, J. H., *A History of Egypt* (2nd ed., 1935).

Carter, H., and A. C. Mace, *The Tomb of Tut-ankh-Amen,* 3 vols. (1922–1933).

Desroches-Noblecourt, C., *Tutankhamen: Life and Death of a Pharaoh* (1963).

Edwards, I. E. S., *The Pyramids of Egypt* (rev. ed., 1961).

Emery, W. B., *Archaic Egypt* (1961).

Engelbach, R., *Introduction to Egyptian Archeology with Special Reference to the Egyptian Museum, Cairo* (1946).

Frankfort, H., *Ancient Egyptian Religion* (1948).

Gardiner, A. H., *The Attitude of the Ancient Egyptians to Death and the Dead* (1935).

Gardner, Sir A., *Egypt of the Pharaohs* (1961).

Grinsell, L. V., *Egyptian Pyramids* (1947).

Lucas, A., *Ancient Egyptian Materials and Industries* (3rd ed., 1948).

Pendlebury, J. D., *Tell-el-Amarna* (1935).

Petrie, W. M., *Seventy Years in Archaeology* (1932).

Shorter, A. W., *The Egyptian Gods* (1937).

Steindorff, G., and K. C. Seele, *When Egypt Ruled the East* (1957).

Van Seters, J., *The Hyksos: A New Investigation* (1966).

Wilson, J. A., *The Culture of Ancient Egypt* (1956).

Winlock, H. E., *The Rise and Fall of the Middle Kingdom in Thebes* (1947).

V. ASIA MINOR, SYRIA, AND PALESTINE

Albright, W. F., *The Archaeology of Palestine* (rev. ed., 1956).

Albright, W. F., *From the Stone Age to Christianity* (2nd ed., 1957).

Anati, E., *Palestine Before the Hebrews* (1963).

Bright, J., *A History of Israel* (2nd ed., 1972).

Childe, V. G., *The Aryans* (1926).

De Vaux, H., *Ancient Israel: Its Life and Institutions* (1961).

Diringer, D., *The Alphabet* (1948).

Driver, S. R., *Introduction to the Literature of the Old Testament* (1956).

Gray, J., *The Canaanites* (1964).

Gurney, O. R., *The Hittites* (1961).

Lindblom, J., *Prophecy in Ancient Israel* (1962).

Lods, A., *The Prophets and the Rise of Judaism* (1937).

Macalister, L., *The Philistines: Their History and Civilization* (1914).

Margolis, M. L., and A. Marx, *A History of the Jewish People* (1947).

Matthiae, P., "Tell Mardikh: The Archives and Palace," *Archaeology*, Vol. 30 (1977), pp. 244ff.

Meek, T. J., *Hebrew Origins* (1936).

Moscati, S., *Ancient Semitic Civilizations* (1957).

Moscati, S., *The World of the Phoenicians* (1965).

Orlinsky, H. M., *Ancient Israel* (2nd ed., 1960).

Pfeiffer, R. H., *Introduction to the Old Testament* (1941).

Wiseman, D. J. (Ed.), *Peoples of Old Testament Times* (1973).

Wright, G. E. (Ed.), *The Bible and the Ancient Near East* (1960).

Yadin, Y., *The Art of Warfare in Biblical Lands in the Light of Archeology*, 2 vols. (1963).

VI. ASSYRIA AND LATER BABYLONIA

Contenau, G., *Everyday Life in Babylon and Assyria* (1966).

Driver, G. R., and J. C. Miles, *The Assyrian Laws* (1935).

Laessoe, J., *People of Ancient Assyria: Their Inscriptions and Correspondence* (1963).

Mendlesohn, I., *Slavery in the Ancient Near East* (1949).

Oates, D., *Studies in the Ancient History of Northern Iraq* (1968).

Oppenheim, A. L., *Ancient Mesopotamia: Portrait of a Dead Civilization* (rev. ed., 1977).

Orlin, L., *Assyrian Colonies in Cappadocia* (1970).

ASSYRIA AND LATER BABYLONIA *(continued)*

Pallis, S. A., *The Antiquity of Iraq: A Handbook of Assyriology* (1956).
Pfeiffer, R. H., *State Letters of Assyria* (1935).
Saggs, H. W. F., *The Greatness That Was Babylon* (1962).

VII. PERSIA

Cameron, G. G., *History of Early Iran* (1936).
Cameron, G. G., *Persepolis Treasury Tables* (1948).
Colledge, M. A. R., *The Parthians* (1967).
Cullican, W., *The Medes and Persians* (1965).
Herzfeld, E., *Archaeological History of Iran* (1935).
Herzfeld, E., *Iran in the Ancient East* (1941).
Olmstead, A. T., *A History of the Persian Empire* (1948).
Rogers, R. W., *A History of Ancient Persia* (1929).
Ross, E. D., *The Persians* (1930).
Sykes, P. M., *A History of Persia,* 2 vols. (3rd ed., 1930).

VIII. THE AEGEAN AGE

Blegen, C. W., *Troy and the Trojans* (1963).
Blegen, C. W., et al., *Troy: Excavations Conducted by the University of Cincinnati, 1932–1938* (1950–1958).
Blegen, C. W., and N. Rawson, *The Palace of Nestor at Pylos in Western Messenia* (1966).
Chadwick, J., *The Decipherment of Linear B* (1958).
Chadwick, J., *The Mycenaean World* (1976).
Desborough, V. R., *The Last of the Mycenaeans and Their Successors* (1964).
Evans, A. J., *The Palace of Minos at Knossos,* 4 vols. (1921–1935).
Finley, M. I., *The World of Odysseus* (2nd ed., 1977).
Graham, J. W., *The Palaces of Crete* (1962).
Higgins, R. A., *Minoan and Mycenaean Art* (1967).
Hood, M. S., *The Minoans* (1971).
Hutchinson, R. W., *Prehistoric Crete* (1963).
Huxley, G. L., *Achaeans and Hittites* (1960).
Lorimer, H. L., *Homer and the Monuments* (1960).
Marinatos, S., *Crete and Mycenae* (1960).
Mylonas, G. E., *Ancient Mycenae: The Capital City of Agamemnon* (1957).
Mylonas, G., *Mycenae and Mycenaean Civilization* (1966).
Nilsson, M. P., *The Minoan-Mycenaean Religion and Its Survival in Greek Religion* (2nd ed., 1950).
Page, D., *History and the Homeric Iliad* (1959).
Palmer, L. R., *Minoans and Mycenaeans* (2nd ed., 1965).
Pendlebury, J. D. S., *The Archaeology of Crete* (1939).
Platon, C., *Crete* (1966).

Starr, C. G., *The Origins of Greek Civilization* (1961).
Taylor, Lord William, *The Mycenaeans* (1964).
Ventris, M., and J. Chadwick, *Documents in Mycenaean Greek* (1956).
Vermeule, E. T., *Greece in the Bronze Age* (1964).
Wace, A. J. B., *Mycenae: An Archaeological History and Guide* (1949).
Willetts, R. F., *The Civilization of Ancient Crete* (1977).

IX. HELLAS

History

Adcock, F. E., *The Greek and Macedonian Art of War* (1957).
Andrewes, A., *The Greek Tyrants* (1963).
Boardman, J., *The Greeks Overseas* (1964).
Botsford, G. W., and C. A. Robinson, Jr., *Hellenic History* (5th ed., 1969).
Bowra, C. M., *Periclean Athens* (1962).
Burn, A. R., *The Lyric Age of Greece* (1960).
Burn, A. R., *Persia and the Greeks* (1965).
Cary, M., *The Greek World from 323–146 B.C.* (2nd ed., 1963).
Casson, L., *Ancient Mariners* (1959).
Cawkwell, G. L., *Philip of Macedon* (1978).
Conner, W. R., *The New Politicians of Fifth-Century Athens* (1971).
Cook, J. N., *The Greeks in Ionia and the East* (1962).
Day, J. H., and M. H. Chambers, *Aristotle's History of the Athenian Democracy* (1962).
DeLaix, R., *Probouleusis at Athens: A Study of Political Decision-Making* (1973).
Den Boer, W., *Laconian Studies* (1954).
De Romilly, J., *Thucydides and Athenian Imperialism* (1963).
Desborough, V. R. d'A., *The Greek Dark Ages* (1972).
De Ste. Croix, G. E. M., *The Origins of the Peloponnesian War* (1972).
Dunbabin, T., *The Western Greeks* (1948).
Dunbabin, T., *The Greeks and Their Eastern Neighbors* (1957).
Eliot, C. W. J., *The Coastal Demes of Attika* (1962).
Ellis, J., *Philip II and Macedonian Imperialism* (1976).
Ehrenberg, V., *Sophocles and Pericles* (1954).
Ehrenberg, V., *The Greek State* (1960).
Ehrenberg, V., *From Solon to Socrates* (1968).
Finley, M. I., *Ancient Sicily to the Arab Conquest* (1968).
Forrest, W. G., *A History of Sparta, 950–192 B.C.* (1962).
Forrest, W. G., *The Emergence of Greek Democracy* (1966).
Freeman, K., *The Work and Life of Solon* (1926).
Glotz, G., *The Greek City and Its Institutions* (1938).
Gomme, A. W., *Essays in Greek History and Literature* (1937).
Gomme, A. W., *A Historical Commentary on Thucydides* (1945–1956).
Graham, A. J., *Colony and Mother City in Ancient Greece* (1964).
Grote, G., *A History of Greece,* 12 vols. (new ed., 1906).
Grundy, G. B., *The Great Persian War and Its Preliminaries* (1901).
Hammond, N. G. L., *A History of Greece to 322 B.C.* (2nd ed., 1967).
Hammond, N. G., L., *The Classical Age of Greece* (1975).

HELLAS *(continued)*

Havelock, E. A., *The Liberal Temper in Greek Politics* (1957).
Hignett, C., *A History of the Athenian Constitution* (1952).
Hignett, C., *Xerxes' Invasion of Greece* (1962).
Hill, I. T., *The Ancient City of Athens* (1953).
Hopper, H. J., *The Early Greeks* (1976).
Huxley, G. L., *Early Sparta* (1962).
Huxley, G. L., *The Early Ionians* (1966).
Jaeger, W. J., *Demosthenes: The Origin and Growth of His Policy* (1938).
Jones, A. H. M., *Athenian Democracy* (1957).
Kagan, D., *Outbreak of the Peloponnesian War* (1969).
Laistner, M. L. W., *A History of the Greek World from 479 to 323 B.C.* (1936).
Larsen, J. A. O., *Greek Federal States: Their Institutions and History* (1955).
Meiggs, R., *The Athenian Empire* (1972).
Merritt, B. D., H. T. Wade-Gery, and M. F. McGregor, *The Athenian Tribute Lists* (1939–1953).
Parke, H. W., and D. E. W. Wormell, *The Delphic Oracle* (1956).
Pickard-Cambridge, A. W., *Demosthenes and the Last Days of Greek Freedom* (1914).
Rhodes, P. J., *The Athenian Boule* (1972).
Ryder, T. T. B., *Koine Eirene* (1963).
Sinclair, G., *A History of Greek Political Thought* (1951).
Snodgrass, A. M., *The Dark Age of Greece* (1971).
Starr, C. G., *The Origins of Greek Civilization* (1961).
Thompson, H. A., and R. E. Wycherly, *The Agora of Athens* (1972).
Toynbee, A. J., *Some Problems in Greek History* (1972).
Ure, P. N., *The Origin of Tyranny* (1922).
Wade-Gery, H. T., *Essays in Greek History* (1958).
Woodhead, A. G., *Greeks in the West* (1962).

Art, Music, Coinage

Arias, P. E., *A History of Greek Vase Painting* (1962).
Beazley, J. D., *Potter and Painter in Ancient Athens* (1945).
Beazley, J. D., *The Development of Attic Black-Figure* (1951).
Beazley, J. D., *Attic Black-Figure Vase Painters* (1956).
Boardman, J., *Greek Art* (1964).
Carpenter, Rhys, *The Esthetic Basis of Greek Art of the Fifth and Fourth Centuries B.C.* (1959).
Carpenter, R., *Greek Sculpture* (1970).
Cook, R. M., *Greek Painted Pottery* (2nd ed., 1972).
Dinsmoor, W. B., *The Architecture of Ancient Greece* (3rd ed., 1950).
Kraay, C. M., *Greek Coins* (1966).
Lane, A., *Greek Painted Pottery* (1948).
Milne, J. G., *Greek and Roman Coins and the Study of History* (1939).
Richter, G. M. A., *The Sculpture and Sculptors of the Greeks* (3rd ed., 1941).
Richter, G. M. A., *Archaic Greek Art* (1949).
Richter, G. M. A., *The Development of Pictorial Representation from Archaic to Graeco-Roman Times* (1949).

Richter, G. M. A., *Kouroi* (1960).
Richter, G. M. A., *Greek Sculpture* (1970).
Robertson, D. S., *A Handbook of Greek and Roman Architecture* (2nd ed., 1947).
Seltman, C. T., *Masterpieces of Greek Coinage* (1949).
Seltman, C. T., *Greek Coins* (2nd ed., 1955).
Swindler, M. H., *Ancient Painting* (1929).
Von Bothmer, D., *Amazons in Greek Art* (1957).

Literature, Philosophy, Science, Religion, Law

Bieber, M., *The History of the Greek and Roman Theater* (1939).
Bluck, R. S., *Plato's Life and Thought* (1949).
Blum, A. F., *Socrates: The Original and Its Images* (1978).
Bowra, C. M., *Greek Lyric Poetry* (2nd ed., 1961).
Burnet, J., *Early Greek Philosophy* (1962).
Carpenter, R., *Folk Tale, Fiction, and Saga in the Homeric Epics* (1946).
Dodds, E. R., *The Greeks and the Irrational* (1950).
Dover, K. J., *Aristophanic Comedy* (1968).
Edelstein, L., *The Meaning of Stoicism* (1966).
Frazer, J. G., *The Golden Bough* (3rd ed., 1935).
Guthrie, W. K. C., *The Greeks and Their Gods* (1950).
Guthrie, W. K. C., *History of Greek Philosophy* (1971).
Highet, G., *The Classical Tradition* (1949).
Jacoby, F., *Atthis: The Local Chronicles of Ancient Athens* (1949).
Jaeger, W., *Paideia*, 3 vols. (1939–1944).
Jaeger, W., *Aristotle* (1948).
Kirk, G. S., and J. E. Raven, *Presocratic Philosophers* (1960).
Kirkwood, G. M., *A Study of Sophoclean Art* (1958).
Kitto, H. D. F., *Greek Tragedy: A Literary Study* (1954).
Knox, B. M., *The Heroic Temper: Studies in Sophoclean Tragedy* (1964).
Lattimore, R., *Greek Lyrics* (1961).
Murray, G., *The Rise of the Greek Epic* (3rd ed., 1924).
Murray, G., *Aeschylus, The Creator of Tragedy* (1940).
Mylonas, G. E., *Eleusis and the Eleusinian Mysteries* (1961).
Nilsson, M. P., *Greek Popular Religion* (1940).
Nilsson, M. P., *Greek Piety* (1948).
Parke, H. W., *Greek Oracles* (1969).
Parke, H. W., and D. E. W. Wormell, *The Delphic Oracle*, 2 vols. (1956).
Rose, H. J., *Ancient Greek Religion* (1946).
Taylor, A. E., *Socrates* (1933).
Whitman, C., *Sophocles: A Study of Heroic Humanism* (1951).
Whitman, C., *Aristophanes and the Comic Hero* (1964).

Social and Economic Life

Andreades, A. M., *A History of Greek Public Finance* (1933).
Arnheim, M. T. W., *Aristocracy in Greek Society* (1977).
Davies, J. K., *Athenian Propertied Families, 600–300 B.C.* (1971).
Dover, K., *Greek Homosexuality* (1978).
Ehrenberg, V., *The People of Aristophanes* (2nd ed., 1951).
French, A., *The Growth of the Athenian Economy* (1964).

HELLAS *(continued)*

Fustel de Coulanges, N., *The Ancient City* (1956).
Glotz, G., *Ancient Greece at Work* (1926).
Harrison, A. R. W., *The Law of Athens:* (1) *The Family and Property* (1968), (2) *Procedure* (1971).
Hasebroek, J., *Trade and Politics in Ancient Greece* (1933).
Lacey, W. K., *The Family in Classical Greece* (1968).
Michell, H., *The Economics of Ancient Greece* (2nd ed., 1957).
Roebuck, C., *Ionian Trade and Colonization* (1959).
Webster, T. B. L., *Athenian Culture and Society* (1973).
Zimmern, A., *The Greek Commonwealth* (6th ed., 1961).

Warfare

Adcock, F. E., *The Greek and Macedonian Art of War* (1957).
Anderson, J. K., *Military Theory and Practice in the Age of Xenophon* (1970).
Greenhalgh, F. A. L., *Early Greek Warfare* (1971).
Morrison, J. S., and R. T. Williams, *Greek Oared Ships, 900–322 B.C.* (1968).
Parke, H. W., *Greek Mercenaries from the Earliest Times to the Battle of Ipsus* (1933).
Pritchett, W. K., *Ancient Military Practices*, Part 1 (1971).
Pritchett, W. K., *Studies in Ancient Greek Topography*, Part 1 (1971).
Snodgrass, A. M., *Early Greek Arms and Weapons from the End of the Bronze Age to 600 B.C.* (1964).
Snodgrass, A. M., *Arms and Armour of the Greeks* (1967).

Alexander the Great

Fox, J. R., *Alexander the Great* (1973).
Griffith, G. T., (Ed.), *Alexander the Great: The Main Problems* (1966).
Hamilton, J. R., *Alexander the Great* (1973).
Milns, R. D., *Alexander the Great* (1968).
Pearson, L., *The Lost Histories of Alexander the Great* (1968).
Robinson, C. A., Jr., *Alexander the Great* (1948).
Snyder, J. W., *Alexander the Great* (1966).
Tarn, W. W., *Alexander the Great*, 2 vols. (1948).
Wilcken, U., *Alexander* (1967).

X. THE HELLENISTIC AGE

Aalders, G. J. D., *Political Thought in Hellenistic Times* (1975).
Bailey, C., *The Greek Atomists and Epicurus* (1928).
Bell, H. I., *Egypt from Alexander to the Arab Conquest* (1948).
Bevan, E. R., *A History of Egypt Under the Ptolemaic Dynasty* (1927).
Dudley, D. R., *History of Cynicism* (1937).
Ferguson, W. S., *Hellenistic Athens* (1911).
Griffith, G. T., *The Mercenaries of the Hellenistic World* (1935).

Hanfman, G., "Hellenistic Art," *Dumbarton Oaks Papers* (1963), pp. 79ff.
Harris, H. A., *Greek Athletics and the Jews* (1976).
Haverfield, F., *Ancient Town-Planning* (1913).
Heath, T. L., *Manual of Greek Mathematics* (1931).
Jones, A. H. M., *The Greek City from Alexander to Justinian* (1940).
Jouguet, P., *Macedonian Imperialism and the Hellenization of the East* (1928).
More, P. E., *Hellenistic Philosophies* (1923).
Radin, M., *Epicurus* (1949).
Robinson, C. A., Jr., *Federal Unions: The Greek Political Experience* (1941).
Rostovtzeff, M., *Caravan Cities* (1932).
Rostovtzeff, M., *The Social and Economic History of the Hellenistic World,* 3 vols.
    (1941).
Singer, C., *Greek Biology and Greek Medicine* (1922).
Tarn, W. W., *Antigonas Gonatas* (1913).
Tarn, W. W., *The Greeks in Bactria and India* (2nd ed., 1930).
Tarn, W. W., *Hellenistic Military and Naval Developments* (1930).
Tarn, W. W., and G. T. Griffith, *The Hellenistic World* (1951).
Tcherikover, V., *Hellenistic Civilization and the Jews* (1959).
Tod, M. N., *International Arbitration Amongst the Greeks* (1913).
Walbank, F. W., *Philip V of Macedon* (1940).
Walbank, F. W., *Polybius* (1972).
Wycherley, R. E., *How the Greeks Built Cities* (1949).

XI. EARLY ITALY

Alfoeldi, A., *Early Rome and the Latins* (1965).
Banti, L., *The Etruscan Cities and Their Culture* (1973).
Barfeld, L., *Northern Italy Before Rome* (1971).
Boethius, A. et al., *Etruscan Culture, Land and People* (1962).
Gjerstad, E., *Early Rome* (1953–1960).
Momigliano, A., "An Interim Report on the Origins of Rome," *Journal of Roman
    Studies,* Vol. 53 (1963), pp. 95ff.
Pallottino, M., *The Etruscans* (6th ed., 1974).
Pulgram, E., *The Tongues of Italy: Prehistory and History* (1958).
Richardson, E., *The Etruscans, Their Art and Civilization* (1964).
Strong, D., *The Early Etruscans* (1968).
Taylor, L. R., *Local Cults in Etruria* (1925).
Whatmough, J., *The Foundations of Roman Italy* (1937).

XII. ROME

(It will often be found advisable to consult the entries under both republic and
    empire.)

Republic

Adcock, F. E., *The Roman Art of War Under the Republic* (1940).
Astin, A. E., *Scipio Aemilianus* (1967).

ROME *(continued)*

Astin, A. E., *Cato the Censor* (1978).
Badian, E., *Foreign Clientelae (264–70 B.C.)* (1958).
Badian, E., *Roman Imperialism in the Late Republic* (2nd ed., 1968).
Badian, E., *Publicans and Sinners* (1972).
Bernstein, A., *Tiberius Sempronius Gracchus: Tradition and Apostasy* (1978).
Boren, H. C., *The Gracchi* (1968).
Brunt, P. A., *Italian Manpower 225 B.C.–A.D. 14* (1971).
Carney, T. F., *A Biography of C. Marius* (1962).
Cowell, F. R., *Cicero and the Roman Republic* (1948).
Dorey, T. A. (Ed.), *Cicero* (1965).
Gelzer, M., *Caesar: Politician and Statesman* (6th ed., 1968).
Gelzer, M., *The Roman Nobility* (1969).
Grimal, P., *Hellenism and the Rise of Rome* (1968).
Gruen, E. S., *Roman Politics and the Criminal Courts 149–78 B.C.* (1968).
Gruen, E. S., *The Last Generation of the Roman Republic* (1974).
Larsen, J. A. O., *Representative Government in Greek and Roman History* (1966).
Lazenby, J. F., *Hannibal's War: A Military History of the Second Punic War* (1978).
Leach, J., *Pompey the Great* (1978).
Lintott, A. W., *Violence in Republican Rome* (1968).
Marsh, F. B., *The Roman World from 146–30 B.C.* (3rd ed., 1961).
Marshall, B. A., *Crassus: A Political Biography* (1976).
Palmer, R. E. A., *The Archaic Community of the Romans* (1970).
Proctor, D., *Hannibal's March in History* (1971).
Scullard, H. H., *The Roman World from 753–146 B.C.* (3rd ed., 1961).
Scullard, H. H., *Scipio Africanus: Soldier and Politician* (1970).
Scullard, H. H., *Roman Politics (220–150 B.C.)* (2nd ed., 1973).
Smith, R. E., *The Failure of the Roman Republic* (1955).
Syme, R., *The Roman Revolution* (1939).
Taylor, L. R., *Voting Districts of the Roman Republic* (1960).
Taylor, L. R., *Party Politics in the Age of Caesar* (1949).
Taylor, L. R., *Roman Voting Assemblies* (1966).
Wilson, A. J. N., *Emigration from Italy in the Republican Age of Rome* (1966).

The Empire. History

Arnheim, T. W., *The Senatorial Aristocracy in the Later Roman Empire* (1972).
Balsdon, J. P. V. D., *The Emperor Gaius* (1934).
Birley, A., *Marcus Aurelius* (1966).
Birley, A., *Septimius Severus* (1971).
Bowder, D., *The Age of Constantine and Julian* (1978).
Bowersock, G. W., *Julian the Apostate* (1978).
Brown, P., *The World of Late Antiquity* (1971).
Browning, R., *Justinian and Theodora* (1971).
Cary, M., and H. H. Scullard, *History of Rome down to the Reign of Constantine* (3rd ed., 1975).
Crook, J. A., *Consilium Principis* (1955).

Earl, D., *The Age of Augustus* (1968).
Grant, M., *The Climax of Rome* (1968).
Hammond, M., *The Antonine Monarchy* (1959).
Hammond, M., *The Augustan Principate in Theory and Practice* (1968).
Jones, A. H. M., *The Later Roman Empire 284-602*, 3 vols. (1964).
Jones, A. H. M., *The Decline of the Ancient World* (1966).
Jones, A. H. M., *Studies in Roman Government and Law* (1968).
Jones, A. H. M., *Augustus* (1970).
Jones, A. H. M., *The Cities of the Eastern Roman Provinces* (2nd ed., 1971).
Liebeschuetz, J. H. W. G., *Antioch: City and Imperial Administration in the Later Roman Empire* (1972).
Lovick, B., *Tiberius the Politician* (1976).
Macmullen, R., *Constantine* (1970).
Millar, F., *The Roman Empire and Its Neighbors* (1967).
Millar, F., *The Emperor in the Roman World* (31 B.C.-A.D. 337) (1977).
Momigliano, A., *Claudius: The Emperor and His Achievement* (1934).
Ogilvie, R. M., *The Romans and Their Gods in the Age of Augustus* (1969).
Oost, S. I., *Galla Placidia Augusta* (1968).
Rowell, H. T., *Rome in the Augustan Age* (1962).
Salmon, E. T., *The Roman World from 30 B.C.-138 A.D.* (6th ed., 1968).
Scullard, H. H., *From the Gracchi to Nero* (4th ed., 1976).
Sherwin-White, A. N., *Racial Prejudice in Imperial Rome* (1967).
Sieger, R., *Tiberius* (1972).
Sinnigen, W. G., and Boak, A. E. R., *A History of Rome to A.D. 565* (6th ed., 1977).
Todd, M., *The Northern Barbarians, 100 B.C.-A.D. 300* (1975).
Walbank, F. W., *The Awful Revolution: The Decline of the Roman Empire in the West* (1969).
Watson, G. B., *The Roman Soldier* (1969).
Webster, G., *The Roman Imperial Army* (1969).
Wells, C. M., *The German Policy of Augustus* (1972).
Wiseman, T. P., *New Men in the Roman Senate* (1971).
Vogt, J., *The Decline of Rome* (1967).
Yavetz, Z., *Plebs and Princeps* (1969).

The Republic. Art, Music, Coinage

Boethius, A., *Roman and Greek Town Architecture* (1948).
Brown, F. E., *Roman Architecture* (1961).
Encyclopaedia of World Art (1959–1968). Articles: "Etrusco-Italian" (M. Pallottino), "Hellenistic-Roman," (O. Vessberg), "Italo-Roman Folk Art" (G. Mansuelli).
Maiuri, A., *Pompeii* (5th ed., 1948).
Mattingly, H., *The Development of Roman Coinage* (1937).
Nash, E., *A Pictorial Dictionary of Ancient Rome*, 2 vols. (1961–1962).
Richter, G. M. A., *Roman Portraits* (1948).
Richter, G. M. A., *Ancient Italy* (1955).
Robathan, D. M., *The Monuments of Ancient Rome* (1950).
Strong, E., *Art in Ancient Rome*, 2 vols. (2nd ed., 1930).

ROME *(continued)*

Thomsen, R., *Early Roman Coinage*, 3 vols. (1957–1961).
Walters, H. B., *The Art of the Romans* (2nd ed., 1930).

The Empire. Art, Coinage

Anderson, W. J. R. P., and T. Ashby, *The Architecture of Ancient Rome* (1927).
Ashby, T., *The Aqueducts of Ancient Rome* (1935).
Boethius, A., *The Golden House of Nero* (1960).
L'Orange, H. P., *Art Forms and Civic Life in the Late Roman Empire* (1965).
Macdonald, W., *The Architecture of the Roman Empire* (1969).
Maiuri, A., *Roman Painting* (1953).
Mattingly, H., *Roman Coins* (2nd ed., 1960).
Morey, C. R., *Early Christian Art* (1942).
Sutherland, C. H. V., *Coinage in Roman Imperial Policy 31 B.C.–A.D. 68* (1951).
Toynbee, J. M. C., *The Hadrianic School: A Chapter in the History of Greek Art* (1934).

The Republic. Literature, Philosophy, Religion, Science, Law

Adcock, F. E., *Caesar as a Man of Letters* (1956).
Baily, C., *Lucretius* (1947).
Clarke, M. L., *The Roman Mind* (1956).
Crook, J. A., *Law and Life of Rome* (1967).
Dorey, T. A., and D. P. Dudley (Eds.), *Roman Drama* (1965).
Duff, J. W., *A Literary History of Rome from the Origins to the Close of the Golden Age* (reprint, 1953).
Earl, D. C., *The Political Thought of Sallust* (1961).
Edelstein, L., *The Meaning of Stoicism* (1966).
Fraenkel, E., *Horace* (1957).
Frank, T., *Life and Literature in the Roman Republic* (1930).
Hunt, H. A. K., *The Humanism of Cicero* (1954).
Jolowicz, H. F., *Historical Introduction to the Study of Roman Law* (2nd ed., 1952).
Kelly, J. M., *Studies in the Civil Judicature of the Roman Republic* (1976).
Stahl, W., *Roman Science* (1962).
Syme, R. *Sallust* (1964).
Walbank, F., *Polybius* (1972).
Williams, G., *Tradition and Originality in Roman Poetry* (1968).

The Empire. Literature, Philosophy, Religion, Science, Law

Bell, H. I., *Cults and Creeds in Greco-Roman Egypt* (1953).
Bieber, M., *The History of the Greek and Roman Theater* (2nd ed., 1961).
Bonner, S. F., *Education in Ancient Rome* (1977).
Bowersock, G. W., *Greek Sophists in the Roman Empire* (1969).
Cameron, A., *Claudian* (1970).
Cumont, F., *Oriental Religions in Roman Paganism* (reprint, 1956).

Daube, D., *Roman Law* (1969).

Dodds, E. R., *Pagan and Christian in an Age of Anxiety* (1965).

Duff, J. W., *A Literary History of Rome in the Silver Age* (rev. ed., 1969).

Evans, G. A. S., *Procopius* (1972).

Ferguson, J., *The Religions of the Roman Empire* (1970).

Frend, W., *Martyrdom and Persecution in the Early Church* (1967).

Grant, M., *The Jews in the Roman World* (1973).

Grant, R. M., *Gnosticism and Early Christianity* (1959).

Hadas, M., *Stoic Philosophy of Seneca* (1958).

Jaeger, W., *Early Christianity and Greek Paideia* (1961).

Laistner, M. L. W., *The Greater Roman Historians* (1947).

Nicholas, B., *An Introduction to Roman Law* (1962).

Ogilvie, R. H., *The Romans and Their Gods in the Age of Augustus* (1969).

Otis, B., *Vergil: A Study of Civilized Poetry* (1963).

Schulz, F., *Classical Roman Law* (1951).

Scott, K., *The Imperial Cult Under the Flavians* (1936).

Sherwin-White, A. N., *Roman Society and Roman Law in the New Testament* (1963).

Taylor, L. R., *The Divinity of the Roman Emperor* (1931).

Walsh, P. G., *Livy: His Historical Aims and Methods* (1961).

The Republic. Social and Economic Life

Brunt, P. A., *Italian Manpower 225 B.C.-A.D. 14* (1971).

Brunt, P. A., *Social Conflict in the Roman Republic* (1971).

Frank, T., *Economic History of Rome* (2nd ed., 1927).

Heichelheim, F., *An Economic History of the Ancient World*, 2 vols. (1958–1964).

Heitland, W. E., *Agricola* (1931).

Louis, P., *Ancient Rome at Work* (1927).

More, F. G., *The Roman's World* (1936).

Treggiari, S., *Roman Freedmen During the Late Republic* (1969).

The Empire. Social and Economic Life

Balsdon, J. P. V. D., *Roman Women: Their History and Habits* (1962).

Balsdon, J. P. V. D., *Life and Leisure in Ancient Rome* (1969).

Burford, A., *Craftsmen in Greek and Roman Society* (1962).

Charlesworth, M. P., *Trade Routes and Commerce of the Roman Empire* (2nd ed., 1926).

Dill, S., *Roman Society from Nero to Marcus Aurelius* (1905).

Duncan-Jones, R., *The Economy of the Roman Empire* (1974).

Frank, T., *Economic Survey of Ancient Rome*, 5 vols. (1933–1940).

Klausing, R., *The Roman Colonate* (1925).

Loame, H. J., *Industry and Commerce of the City of Rome* (50 B.C.-A.D. 200) (1938).

MacMullen, R., *Enemies of the Roman Order* (1966).

MacMullen, R., *Roman Social Relations* (50 B.C.-284 A.D.) (1973).

Meiggs, R., *Roman Ostia* (2nd ed., 1973).

ROME *(continued)*

Rickman, G. E., *Roman Granaries and Store Buildings* (1971).
Rostovtzeff, N. I., *The Social and Economic History of the Roman Empire,* 2 vols. (2nd ed., 1957).
Warmington, E. H., *The Commerce Between the Roman Empire and India* (1928).
Weaver, P. R. C., *Familia Caesaris: A Social Study of Freedmen and Slaves* (1969).
White, K. D., *Roman Farming* (1970).

Index

A

Abdera, 147
Abraham, 31, 76
Absalom, 78
Abydos, 57
Achaean League, 285ff., 363
Achaemenes, 92
Acropolis, Athenian, 209ff.
Ada, Queen, 260
Adonis, 214
Adrianople, Battle of, 487
Aedile: *see* Magistrates, Roman
Aedui, 391
Aegean Age, 97ff.
Aegean Sea, 99
Aegina, 117ff., 156, 161
Aegospotami, Battle of, 203
Aeolians, 111
Aequi, 337f.
Aerarium militare, 420
Aerarium Saturni, 420, 470
Aeschines, 238
Aeschylus, 149, 174f.
Aesculapius, 352, 406
Aetius, 491f.
Aetolian League, 284ff., 362f.
Africa, Roman province, 365, 369
Agentes in rebus, 482
Ager Gallicus, 356
Ager Publicus, 350, 374
Agis, Spartan king, 262
Agis IV, 287f.
Agora, Athenian, 207f.
Agricola, 437
Agriculture: Prehistoric, 17ff; Sumerian, 32; Babylonian, 37; Egyptian, 49f.; Hittite, 72; Assyrian, 88; Greek, 129; 173f.; Hellenistic, 301f.; Roman, 351, 403f., 448f.
Agri Decumates, 438, 447
Agrippa, 402, 406
Agrippina the Elder, 428
Agrippina the Younger, 431
Ahura Mazda, 152, 463
Akhenaten (Amenhotep IV), 61ff.

Akkad, 27, 31
Alans, 487ff.
Alaric, 488f.
Albinus, 468
Alcibiades, 195ff., 202f.
Alemanni, 472f., 475, 478f., 486
Alexander the Great: source problems, 255ff., education, 256f.; attacks Persia, 258ff.; in Egypt, 261f.; in India, 264; purges, 266; marriages, 266f.; at Opis banquet, 267f.; exiles' decree, 268f.; deification of, 269
Alexander IV, 275f.
Alexandria: founding of, 261, 299, 301, 305f., 315f., and *passim,* Chap. 20; 396, 402, 451, 507
Allies, Roman, 344, 375; Rome's war with, 379f.
Alphabet, invention of, 75; Etruscan, 327
Alps, 324
Altamira, 15
Altar of Peace, 424
Ambrose, St., 487, 508
Amenhotep III, 60f.
Ammianus Marcellinus, 506
Amon-Re, 57
Amorites, 35, 76
Amphictyony, 116
Anabasis, 230, 246
Anastasius, 490
Anaxagoras, 184, 219
Anaximander, 137
Angles, 491
Annona, 483
Anthemius of Tralles, 503
Anthony, St., 510
Antigonid Dynasty, 279, 283ff.
Antigonus Doson, 284, 287
Antigonus Gonatas, 278, 283
Antigonus One-Eyed, 276
Antioch, 289, 301, 401, 451, 499
Antiochus I, 290
Antiochus III, 292; war with Rome, 362
Antipater, 260, 262, 270, 275f.
Antonine Constitution, 471

545

Antoninus Pius, 437, 443f., 465
Antony, Mark, 385, 399ff.; death of, 402
Anu, 27
Apelles, 252
Apollo, 116, 133, 172, 191, 221, 336
Apollonius of Perga, 317
Appian, 458
Appian Way, 351
Appius Claudius Caecus, 351
Apuleius, 458
Arabia, arabs, 27, 84, 270, 442
Aramaeans, 75
Aratus of Sicyon, 284
Arbela, Battle of, 262
Arcadia, 111
Arcadius, 487f., 494f.
Archaeology, importance of, 7
Arches, Roman, 435, 454, 502
Archidamian War, 187ff.
Archidamus, 188
Archimedes, 317, 360
Architecture: archaic Greek, 140f.; Periclean, 209ff.; 315f.; Roman, 422, 451ff.; see also Art.
Archons, 128
Arete, 137, 147, 242f.
Arginusae, 203
Argos, 122, 156, 160, 174
Arianism, 418, 486
Arians, 494
Aristagoras, 154
Aristarchus of Samos, 317, 319
Aristarchus of Samothrace, 305
Aristeides the Just, 160, 168, 172, 194
Aristeides, rhetorician, 449
Aristobulus, 255
Aristocracy, Greek, 115
Aristogeiton, 130
Aristophanes, 185n., 188, 214, 217
Aristotle, 244f., 256f., 307, 316f.
Arius, 481
Ark of the Covenant, 77
Arles, 481
Armenia, 69, 81, 92, 433, 440, 442, 444, 474, 485; kingdom of, 387, 401, 419, 428
Arminius, 412
Army: Babylonian, 57; Egyptian, 56, 59f.; Hittite, 71f.; Assyrian, 83f., 86f.; Persian, 150, 258f.; Greek, 128, 187, 230, 232f.; 233f; Macedonian, 235f., 259ff; Hellenistic, 281f.; Carthaginian, 353; Roman, 342f.;

Roman, Marian reforms of, 378; Roman imperial, 419f., 468, 475, 483
Arrian, 253f., 458
Art: Paleolithic, 14f.; Sumerian, 41; Egyptian, 51f., 56f., 60ff.; Assyrian, 89; Chaldaean, 89f.; Minoan, 101f.; Mycenaean, 106ff.; Persian, 151f.; orientalizing Greek, 138ff.; Periclean, 209ff.; fourth century Greek, 251ff; Hellenistic, 311ff.; Etruscan, 327f.; Roman, 410; Late Roman, 502
Artaphernes, 156
Artaphrenes, 153
Artaxerxes II, 231
Artemisium, 162
Asculepius, 209, 218
Ashur, 82, 86f., 89
Ashurbanipal, 86f.
Asia, province of, 363f.
Asia Minor, 70, 276
Aspar, 496
Assembly, Athenian, 179f.
Assembly, Roman: Curiate, 347; Centuriate, 347; Tribal, 349f.
Assyria, 25; geography of, 81; early history, 82; height of power, 86; fall of, 87; civilization of, 87ff.
Astronomy: Babylonian, 39; Egyptian, 54; Hellenistic, 317f.; Roman, 458
Ataulf, 489f.
Aten, 62f.
Athanasius, 481, 486
Athena, 112, 133, 182, 209
Athens: archaic, 127; fifth century, 178ff.; imperialism of, 181ff.; imperial collapse, 182; revolution at, 202; Periclean society and economy of, 206ff.; drama at, 208ff.; art at, 209; literature, 213; fourth century B.C., 229f.; Second Naval League of, 231; Social War, 237; Hellenistic, 256f.; 381
Athletics, Greek, 133
Athos, Mount, 156
Attalus, Stoa of, 208
Attalus I, 292
Attalus III, 292
Attica, see Athens
Atticus, 409
Attila, 491, 496
Attis (Adonis), 311
Augusta, 427
Augusta Treverorum (Trier), 434, 475

Augustales, 418
Augustine, Saint, 489, 508f.
Augustus, 413ff.; government of, 413–415 and *passim;* succession to, 425f.; death of, 426; *See also* Octavian (Octavius).
Aurelian, 475f.
Aurelius Victor, 505
Aurignacian Man, 13f.
Ausonius, 506
Australopithecus afarensis, 11f.
Avars, 499
Aventine, 331
Avidius Cassius, 444f.

B

Baal, 78
Baalbek, 451
Babylon: civilization of 35ff.; city of, 89; fall of, 93; 147, 262, 270
Babylonia, 27
Babylonian Chronicle, 31
Bacchiadae, 117, 122
Bacchus, 372
Bachylides, 175
Bactria, 93; Hellenistic, 293f.
Bagaudae, 478
Barbarians, Germanic, 473f.
Barsine, 266
Basil of Caesarea, 507, 510
Basilicas, Roman, 410, 452f., 502f.
Bassae, 213
Bath Sheba, 78
Baths, Roman, 452ff., 502
Behistun Rock, 26
Beirut, 73, 499
Belgian Gaul, 391, 428
Belisarius, 497f.
Benedict, St., 610
Beneventum, Battle of, 342
Berbers, 473
Bible, 508
Bithynia, Roman province, 387, 439
Black-figured Greek ware, 138f.
Black Forest, 486
Black Sea, 119f., 174, 184, 230, 380
Blegen, Carl, 109, 112
Boadicea (Boudicca), 433
Boeotia, 106, 111, 167, 181f.
Boethius, 494, 506f.
Boghazkhy, 69, 72
Boniface, St., 490
Bonum et aequum, 461f., 500

Book of the Dead, 57
Bordeaux, 506
Bosporus, 172, 174, 260
Brahmans, 294
Brasidas, 193f.
Brigetio, 486
Britain: Caesar's invasion of, 393; conquest of, 431; 433, 437, 478, 486
Britannicus, 431
Bronze Age, beginning of, 21; in Italy, 325
Brutus, Decimus, 400f., 403n
Brutus, Marcus, 399
Buddha, 274
Bulgars, 499
Burgundians, 478, 491, 494
Byzantine Empire, 501
Byzantium, 120, 171, 468, 481

C

Caesar, Gaius, 426
Caesar, Julius, 387f.; consul, 390; in Gaul, 390f.; dictator, 397ff.; death of, 399; as man of letters, 409
Caesar, Lucius, 426
Caesarea, Cappadocia, 507, 510
Caesarea, Palestine, 507
Cairo, 42
Caledonia, 437, 492
Calendar, 27, 39, 54, 398
Caligula, 430, 435
Callias, Peace of, 182
Callicrates, 209
Callimachus, poet, 308
Callimachus, general, 157
Calpurnian Law, 370
Cambyses, 83, 149
Campagna, 405
Campania, 324, 339, 390, 405
Campus Martius, 347, 410, 424
Camulodunum, 433
Canaan, Canaanites, 73, 77
Cannae, Battle of, 359
Cantabrian, 415
Canuleian Law, 352
Capitoline, 331
Cappadocia, 71; Roman province, 428
Capri, 430
Capua, 327, 339, 343, 376, 403
Caracalla, 461
Carausius, 478
Carbo, 382
Carchemish, 71, 87, 89

Caria, 172, 260
Carneades, 371
Carpathians, 439
Carpi, 473
Carrhae, Battle of, 394; 420, 471, 474
Carthage, 74f., 169, 353f., 364f., 376, 398, 490, 497
Carystos, 172
Caspian Sea, 93, 262
Cassander, 276
Cassiodorus, 511
Cassius Dio, 505
Cassius, Gaius, 399, 401
Cassius, Quintus, 395
Catacombs, Roman, 466
Catal Hüyük, 18
Catiline, 388
Cato the Elder, 365, 370f.
Cato the Younger, 388, 390, 396f.
Catullus, Lucius, 355
Catullus, poet, 409f.
Caudine Forks, Battle of, 339
Celsus, jurist, 462
Celsus, writer, 455f.
Celts (Gauls), 277f., 338; sack Rome, 325, 337
Censor, 345f.,
Ceramaicus, 188, 207, 213
Chaeronea, 239
Chalcedon, Council of, 495
Chalcidice, 120
Chalcis, 117, 174, 362
Chalcolithic Age, 21
Chaldaeans, 85, 87, 89ff
Champollion, 45
Chandragupta, 277
Character, Roman, 352
Chatti, 437
Cheops (Khufu), 51
Chersonese, Thracian, 153, 155, 172
Chester, 438
Chios, 169, 172
Chosroes I, 499
Christianity, 464ff.; Nero persecutes, 465; early art of, 466; persecution of, 474f.; organization of, 481f.; literature of, 507ff.; late Roman, 509ff.
Christians, 432f.; art of, 503; persecution of, 479
Chrysippus, 309
Chrysostom, Dio, 463
Chrysostom, John, 495, 507

Cicero, 224, 385, 387; consul, 388, 393, 396, 400; works of, 408f.
Cilicia, 81, 83, 86, 440
Cilicia, Roman province, 379
Cilician pirates, 386, 387
Cimbri, 378
Cimon, 159, 172f., 178, 180f.
Cincinnatus, 337f.
Cinna, 381f.
Cisalpine Gaul, 338, 369, 383, 390, 395
Cities, Hellenistic, 279f., 301f.; Roman, 343f., 450
Citizens, Roman, 343f.
City Prefect of Rome, 467
City-state, 97, 114f.
Civil service, Roman, 443f.
Civil war, Roman, 395f.
Civilis, 434
Civilization, definition of, 10; beginnings of, 21
Claudian Law, 368
Claudius, 430f.
Claudius Gothicus, 475
Claudius Nero, 426
Claudius Ptolemy, 458
Cleisthenes of Athens, 131f.
Cleisthenes of Sicyon, 122
Cleitus, 260, 264
Clement of Alexandria, 507
Cleomenes, 131, 156
Cleomenes III, 288
Cleon, 191f., 194
Cleopatra VII, 296, 396, 401f.; death of, 402
Cleophon, 202
Cleruchies, Athenian, 172; Ptolemaic, 297
Cloaca Maxima, 410
Clodia, 405, 409
Clodius, 390, 393, 405
Clodius, consul, 355
Clotilda, 494
Clovis, conversion of, 494
Coenus, 265
Coinage: see Art and Economic and Social Background
Colline Gate, 382
Cologne, 438, 485
Colonia Agrippina, 438
Colonization: Phoenician, 73; Greek, 116ff.; Roman, 339, 343
Colosseum, 452
Comitia Centuriata, 347f., 350, 367

Comitia Curiata, 335, 347f.
Comites (Counts), 369
Commagene, 435
Commerce, *see* Trade.
Commercium, 337, 343, 363
Commodus, 443
Concilium plebis, 348ff., 367
Conon, 203, 230
Constans, 485
Constantine the Great, 479–485;
    conversion of, 479, arch of, 502
Constantine II, 485
Constantinople, 481; Council of, 487
Constantius Chlorus, 477ff.
Constantius II, 485
Consul, office of, 345
Copernicus, 317, 458
Coptic, 45
Copts, 496
Corbulo, 433
Corcyra, 120, 184, 192
Corfinum, 380
Corinth, 120; tyranny at, 122; 184;
    destruction of, 363
Corinthian Gulf, 106
Corinthian League, 239ff.
Corinthian War, 230f.
Cornelia, 387
Cornelia, mother of Gracchi, 374
Corporations, Roman, 484
Corpus Iuris Civilis, 499
Corsica, 147, 169, 327, 355, 368
Crassus, 385ff.; death of, 394
Craterus, 275
Cremona, 434
Crete, 71, 99ff.; Roman province, 385
Critias, 205, 230
Croesus, 92, 146f.
Cro-Magnon Man, 13
Ctesiphon, 440, 444, 472
Culture, definition of, 10
Cumae, 119, 327
Curiales, 484
Curius Dentatus, 340
Cursus honorum, 346
Cyaxares, 87, 92
Cybele, 311, 371f.
Cyclades, 111
Cylon, 128
Cynicism, 309
Cynics, 242f.
Cynoscephalae, 361
Cyprian, 508

Cyprus, 18, 73, 106, 154, 171, 174,
    182, 203
Cyrenaics, 242f.
Cyrene, 119n.
Cyril, 495
Cyrus the Great, 146f.
Cyzicus, 202

D

Dacia, 399, 438, 440f., 468, 474
Dalmatia, 479
Damascus, 72, 75, 77, 80, 83, 262
Damasus, Pope, 508
Damonides, 178, 184
Danube River, 69, 258, 419f., 437f.,
    439, 444f.
Darius I, 26, 149ff.
Darius II, 203
Darius III, 259, 261ff.
Dating, relative and absolute, 8; Carbon
    14, 8f.
Datis, 156
David, King, 77g.
Dead Sea, 72
Decabalus, 438ff.
Decelea, 197
Decemvirs, 349
Decius, 91
Deification, of Alexander, 269; of
    Roman emperors, 418
Deioces, 91
Deir el-Bahri
Delatores: *see* Informers
Delian League, 171ff.
Delos, 112, 116, 169, 172, 182, 363,
    381
Delphi, 112, 116, 134, 188, 191
Delta, Egyptian, 42, 54
Demeter, 116, 135f.
Demetrias, 362
Demetrius the Besieger, 276
Demetrius, Bactrian king, 293f.
Democritus, 219
Demosthenes, general, 193, 197
Demosthenes, orator, 238, 249ff.
Dendra, 108
Diadumenianus, 471
Dictaean Cave, 105
Didius Julianus, 467
Digest of Justinian, 499
Dioceses, 478
Diocletian, 476–479

Dionysus, worship of, 136, 209
Dionysius of Syracuse, 233f.
Dipylon, 207
Divination, 39
Divine Julius, Temple of, 424
Djoser, 47
Dodona, 134
Domitia, 438
Domitian, 436ff.
Domitius Ahenobarbus, 431
Domna, 470f.
Donatists, 481
Dorians, 111
Draco, 129
Drama, Greek, origins of, 135; 174ff.
Drepana, 355
Druids, 433
Drusus, brother of Tiberius, 420
Drusus, Marcus Livius, 379
Drusus, son of Tiberius, 428
Duilius, 354
Dur-Sharrukin, 84
Dynasties, Egyptian, 45n.
Dyrrachium, 396

E

Eanna, 31
Eannatum, 29
Ebla, 31
Eboracum, 469
Ecbatana, 91f.
Ecclesia, see Government, Greek
Ecnomus, 354
Economic and Social Background:
   Paleolithic, 14; Neolithic, 19f.;
   Sumerian, 36f.; Babylonian, 37f.;
   Egyptian, 49f.; Hittite, 72;
   Phoenician, 73f.; Minoan, 103;
   Mycenaean, 106f.; Persian, 150f.;
   Etruscan, 327f.; fifth century Greek,
   173f.; fourth century Greek, 227ff.;
   Hellenistic Greek, 300ff.; Roman,
   403ff., 447f., 478, 483f.
Edict of Prices, Diocletian's, 478
Edomites, 77
Education: Babylonian, 39; Egyptian,
   54, Greek, 214f.; Hellenistic, 304;
   Roman, 404f.
Egypt: geography of, 42; historical
   sources of, 44ff.; predynastic, 46;
   archaic, 46f.; Old Kingdom, 47ff.;
   religion, 50; art, 52, First
   Intermediate Period of, 54f.; Middle

Kingdom of, 56ff.; Second
   Intermediate Period of, 58; New
   Kingdom of, 58ff.; Amarna Period
   of, 61ff.; conquered by Assyria, 86;
   Saite Period, 91; Ptolemaic, 294
Elagabalus, 471f.
Elamites, 35
Elba, 327
Elbe River, 420
Eleatics, 137, 218
Eleusinian Mysteries, 135
Eleusis, 112, 128, 183, 207, 505
Elijah, 79
Elisha, 79
Empedocles, 218
En, 27
Enki, 27
Enlil, 27
Ennius, 330, 371
Ensi, 27
Epaminondas, 232f., 235
Ephebes, 304
Ephesus, 141, 154
Ephialtes, 174, 181
Ephor, see Government, Greek
Epic Cycle, 133
Epictetus, 463
Epidamnus, 184
Epirus, 256, 342
Equestrians, 343, 368, 416f., 470, 475,
   482
Erasistratus, 318f.
Eratosthenes, 305
Ercte, Mount, 355
Erech, 27, 31f.
Erechtheum, 212f.
Eretria, 120, 154, 156
Eridu, 27
Eryx, Mount, 355
Esarhaddon, 86
Esquiline, 332
Ethiopia, Ethiopians, 42, 84f.
Etruria, 130, 146, 169, 327f., 403
Etruscans, 36, 327f.
Etruscans, culture of, 327ff.
Euboea, 111, 162, 174, 182
Eubulus, 237f.
Euclid, 317
Eudocia, 495
Eudoxia, 490
Eumenes, 276
Euphrates River, 25f.
Euripides, 185n., 194, 216f., 220, 235
Eurotas, 99, 124

Eurybiades, 168
Eusebius of Caesarea, 507
Euthydemus, 293
Eutropius, 506
Eutropius, eunuch, 495
Evans, Sir Arthur, 101f.

F

Fabius Cunctator, 359
Fabius Pictor, 371
Faustina, 443
Faustinianae, 443
Fayum, 56, 294
Felsina, 327
Fertile Crescent, 18, 25, 72
Festivals, Greek, 133f.
Fidenae, 338
First Peloponnesian War, 183
Firth of Clyde, 444
Firth of Forth, 444
Flamininus, 361f.
Flaminius, 356, 359, 366, 374
Forest Folk, 15f.
Forum: of Augustus, 424; of Caesar, 410; Roman, 452, 502; of Vespasian, 435; of Trajan, 440
Franks, 473, 494, 491
Freedmen, Roman, 406, 431
Frontiers, Roman, 419, 428, 437f., 442, 468, 475
Fronto, 456
Funeral Oration of Pericles, 188ff.

G

Gabinian Law, 386
Gabinius, 386
Gades, 73
Gaiseric, 490f.
Galatia, 278
Galba, 433
Galen, 458
Galerius, 477ff.
Galilee, 72
Galla Placidia, 490
Gallia Comata, 390
Gallia Narbonensis, 378, 390f.
Gallic Empire, 475f.
Gallienus, 474f.
Gandhara, 294
Garda, Lake, 491
Gaul, Gauls, 325, 338, 364, 428, 430, 434, 447, 478; Empire of, 475;

Visigoths in, 488
Gela, 169, 193
Gelon, 161, 169
Genèvre Pass, 479
Genoa, 324
Geometric Art, 114
Germanicus, 420, 428, 430
Germans, Germany, 391f., 421, 428, 430, 434
Gerousia: see Government, Greek
Geta, 469, 471
Getae, 496
Gibbon, Edward, 650
Gilboa, Mount, 77
Gilgamesh Epic, 27, 29f.
Gizeh, 51
Gladiators, 384f.
Glaucia, 379
Golden Horn, 481
Golden House of Nero, 433, 435
Gordian I, 474
Gordian II, 474
Gordian III, 474
Gordium, 260
Gorgias, 220
Gortyn, 124
Goshen, 76
Goths, 473, 475, 487
Gournia, 103
Government: Neolithic, 18f.; Sumerian, 27; Egyptian, 46f., 56, 58f.; Babylonian, 37; Hittite, 71f.; Assyrian, 87f.; Minoan, 103; Greek, 112, 114ff., 124ff., 127ff., 131ff., 159f., 173, 177ff., 183f., 202f., 205, 228f., 235f; Hellenistic, 275, 283, 285f., 287f., 289f., 282, 296f.; Etruscan, 327f.; Carthaginian, 353; Roman, 394f., 343ff., 366ff., 381ff., 385, 413ff., 431, 435, 442f., 446f., 469f., 474, 476ff., 482, 500
Gracchus, Gaius, 375ff.
Gracchus, Tiberius, 374f.
Graii, 119
Granicus, Battle of, 260
Gratian, 484
Great Mother, 505
Greece, geography of, 97.
Gregory of Nazianzus, 507
Gregory XIII, Pope, 398
Grimaldi Cave, 13
Grotefend, Georg, 26
Gudea, 32
Guilds, Roman, 470, 484

Guti, 32f.
Gyges, 87, 91, 122, 146
Gylippus, 197f.
Gymnasiarch, 304
Gymnasium, 304

H

Hadrian, 424, 440ff.
Hadrian's Wall, 437, 442, 444, 468
Hagia Triada, 102f.
Halicarnassus, 223, 315
Halys River, 81, 91
Hamadan, 91
Hamilcar, 169
Hamilcar Barca, 355, 357f.
Hammurabi, 32, 35; Code of, 39f.
Hannibal, 285, 356ff.
Harmhab (Horemhab), 66
Harmodius, 130
Harpagus, 93, 147
Hasdrubal, Hannibal's brother-in-law,
    357; Hannibal's brother, 350
Hatsehpsut, 59f.
Hatti, 69
Hattushil, 67, 71
Hebrews, 75ff.; early history of, 76,
    Covenant, 76; united kingdom, 77;
    divided kingdom, 78f.; liberated by
    Cyrus, 80; Babylonian Captivity of,
    80
Hecataeus, 138, 223f.
Helena, 479
Heliaea, 180
Heliopolis, 56
Helladic Civilization, 106
Hellas, 99
Hellenes, 119
Hellenistic economy and society, 301ff.;
    social instability, 302; culture,
    303ff.; literature, 305
Hellespont, 168, 260
Helots, 124f.
Helvetians, 391
Hephaestion, 265, 269
Hephaestus, Temple of, 207
Hera, 133
Heraclea, Italy, 342
Heracleitus, 137
Hermes
Hernici, 338
Herodotus, 51, 137, 147, 154ff., 162,
    167, 177f., 223f.
Herophilus, 318
Herodian, 505

Herulians, 473, 475
Hesiod, 117, 136
Hezekiah, 86
Hiero, 170
Hieronymus (Jerome), 508
Hieronymus of Cardia, 306
Himera, 119, 169
Hippalus, 458
Hipparchus (tyrant), 130
Hipparchus (scientist), 317
Hippias, son of Peisistratus, 130, 153f.,
    156
Hippias, sophist, 220
Hippo, 508
Hippocrates, 218
Hippocratic corpus, 316
Hippodamus, 183, 315
Hippodrome, at Constantinople, 500
Hiram, 78
Hirtius, 400
Hissarlik, 109
Historia Augusta, 505
History, meaning of, 5
Histria, 356
Hittites, 36, 69ff., 81
Holy Apostles, Church of, 503
Homer, 109, 113f., 133
Homo erectus, 12f.
Homo habilis, 12
Homo sapiens, 13
Honoria, 491
Honorius, 487ff., 494
Horace, 418, 421f.
Horemhab, 66
Hortensian Law, 350
Hortensius, 350
Hortensius Hortalus, 385
Horus, 48, 50
Hoshea, 84
Hsiung-Nu, 486
Hughes, Charles Evans, 5
Huns, 486, 491, 496
Hurrians, 72
Hyksos, 58, 76
Hyperbolus, 195
Hystaspes, 149

I

Illyria, 324, 369, 390, 421, 428
Illyrian and Gallic Wars, by Rome, 355f.
Imbros, 153
Imhotep, 47
Imperium, 345
India, 93, 264f., 294

Indo-Europeans, 69
Indus River, 152, 264f.
Industry: see Economic and Social
    Background and Trade
Informers, 429f., 432, 437, 471
Innana, 27
Innocent I, 509
Inscriptions, importance of, 7
Ionia, 111, 117, 146
Ionian Enlightenment, 136ff.
Ionian Revolt, 154
Ionian Sea, 106, 324
Ionians, 87, 111, 172
Institutes of Justinian, 499
Ipsus, 277f.
Ireland, 437, 491, 511
Irenaeus, 507
Iron, 27, 169
Iron Age, 73; in Italy, 325f.
Irrigation, importance of, 11; 21f.;
    Mesopotamian, 26; Egyptian, 42f.,
    46, 50
Isagoras, 131
Isaiah, 79
Isaurians, 496
Isidorus of Miletus, 503
Isis, 51, 311, 463, 505
Isocrates, 247ff.
Israel, 75, 59; see also Hebrews
Issin, 27, 35
Issus, 261f.
Italia, 324, 380
Italic peoples, 325
Italica, 439
Italy, geography of, 323ff.
Ithaca, 114
Ithome, Mount, 173, 181

J

Jacob, 76
Janiculum, 331, 350
Janus, 335; Temple of, 417, 474
Jarmo, 17
Jason of Pherae, 232
Java, 42
Jaxartes River, 93
Jeremiah, 79
Jericho, 17
Jeroboam, 79
Jerome, 508
Jerusalem, 77f., 79f., 89, 387, 435
Jesse, 77
Jesus, 465
Jews, 431; rebellion of against Rome,

434f., 464; see also Hebrews
John of Cappadocia, 500
Jordan River, 72
Josiah, 87
Juba, 396
Judaea, 387, 434
Judah, 77f.
Judaism, 80, 463f.
Jugurtha, 377f.
Jugurthine War, 377f.
Juktas Mount, 105
Julia, Augustus' daughter, 426
Julia, Caesar's daughter, 390, 394
Julia Domna, 471
Julia Maesa, 471
Julia, Marius' wife, 387
Julian the Apostate, 485f., 505
Julian, jurist, 459
Julianus, 443
Julianus, Didius, 467
Juno, 335
Jupiter, 335; Temple of, 335
Jupiter Capitolinus, Temple of, 410
Juries, Athenian, 180
Jurisprudents, 372
Justin, 494, 496
Justinian, 488, 496–501
Jutes, 491
Juvenal, 457

K

Ka, 51
Kadesh, Battle of, 67, 71
Kamares, 102, 105
Karnak, 59, 67
Kassites, 36, 71, 81
Khafre, 51
Khorsabad, 81, 84
Khufu, 51
Kings, Roman, 334f.
King's Peace, 231
Kish, 31
Kitchen-midden people, 15
Knossos, 101
Korakou, 106
Kouroi, 142ff.

L

Lacedaemonians, 126
Laconia, 124, 174
Lactantius, 508
Lade, 154
Lagash, 29, 32

Lake Dwellers, 20
Lamachus, 196f.
Lambaesis, 440
Land of the Sea, 36
Lanuvium, 329
Lares, 324
Larsa, 27, 35
Lascaux, 14
Latifundia, 368
Latin War, 339
Latins, 325, 329f.
Latium, 329ff.
Laurentum, 406
Laurium, 127, 129, 160, 174, 191, 206
Law: Sumerian, 29, 32; Hammurabi,
    39f.; Egyptian, 46f.; Hittite, 71f.;
    Assyrian, 88; Greek, 116; Roman,
    349f., 372, 407f, 471ff, 443, 458ff.;
    Germanic, 492f.
Leagues: Early Greek, 116; Etruscan,
    327; Latin, 332, 337f., 339, 343.
    See also Achaean League, etc.
Lebanon Mountains, 31, 72
Lemnos, 153
Leo I, Emperor, 496
Leo I, Pope, 491, 496, 509
Leonidas, 162ff.
Leontini, 193
Leotychidas, 169
Lepidus, 400ff., 415
Leptis Magna, 467
Lesbos, 111, 124, 135, 172, 203
Leucippus, 218
Leuctra, Battle of, 232
Levi, 76
Lex de maiestate, 428
Lex frumentaria, 375
Lex Julia municipalis, 398
Lex provinciae, 369
Library of Alexandria, 305
Libya, Libyans, 46, 54, 67
Licinian-Sextian Laws, 350
Licinius, 481
Liguria, 364
Lilybaeum, 355
Limes, Roman, 468f.
Linear A, 103
Linear B, 103, 108, 112f.
Literary remains, importance of, 7
Literature: Sumerian, 33; Babylonian,
    39; Egyptian, 54, 57; Phoenician, 73;
    Assyrian, 88f.; Greek, 113, 134ff.,
    174f., 213ff, 305ff., 371, 408f.,
    421ff., 454ff.; Roman, 351f., 454 ff.,
    504ff.

Livia, 426f.
Livius Andronicus, 371
Livius Drusus, 379
Livy, 330, 353, 421f.
Locri, 340
Locris, 181f.
Lombards, 499, 501
Londinium, 433
London, 433
Luca, Conference of, 393
Lucan, 455
Lucania, 479
Lucian, 458
Lucretius, 410
Lucullus, 387
Lugal, 27
Lugal Zaggisi, 30
Lugdunensis, 428
Lugdunum, 430, 466, 468
Lupercalia, 398
Lutatius Catulus, 355, 378, 384
Lyceum, 245
Lycia, 172
Lycurgus, 127
Lydia, 84, 91, 112, 117f., 146f., 150
Lyons, 430
Lysippus, 252

M

Macedon, Macedonia, 99, 156, 168,
    234ff., 256ff., 283ff., 356, 361f.,
    363
Macedonian Wars, 359, 361ff.
Macrinus, 471
Maecenas, 416, 421f.
Maesa, 471
Magdalenian Art, 14
Magi, 152
Magic: Prehistoric, 15; Egyptian, 57;
    Hebrew, 78, See also Religion.
Magistrates: Roman, 344ff., 366ff.;
    see also Government, Roman.
Maglamosean Swamp, 15f.
Magna Graecia, 119, 174, 233f., 340
Magna Mater, 463
Magnesia, 362
Mago, 358
Mainz, 437
Mallia, 103
Mamaea, 472
Mamertini, 354
Manetho, 45
Mani, 508
Manichaeism, 508

Manilian Law, 387
Manilius, 387
Mantinea, 232f.
Mantua, 422
Marathon, 127, 156ff.
Marcellus, Augustus' nephew, 426; Roman general, 360
Mardonius, 156, 168f.
Marduk, 37ff., 88, 93
Marius, 377ff., 380ff.
Mars, 329, 335; Temple of, 424
Marsi, 380
Martial, 456f.
Masinissa, 365
Massilia (Marseilles), 120, 169, 281, 391, 396
Masters of Soldiers, 494
Mauretania, 396, 430f.
Mausoleum, 253f., 315
Maxentius, 479
Maximian, 477, 479
Maximinus, 474
Medes, 87, 91f.
Media, 81, 86, 89, 91f.
Medicine: Babylonian, 39; Egyptian, 54; Greek, 218; Hellenistic, 318f; Roman, 455f., 458
Mediolanum, 475
Medontidae, 128
Megabazus, 153
Megacles, 128
Megaliths, 20f.
Megara, 117, 181, 183f.
Megaron, 108
Megiddo, 60, 78, 87
Melos, 111, 195
Memnon, 261
Menander, Bactrian King, 294
Menander, comic playwright, 307
Mende, 120n.
Menes, 47
Menkaure, 51
Merovingians, 494
Merowig, 494
Mesolithic Age, 17
Mesopotamia, 25ff; historical sources for, 26
Messalina, 431
Messana, 119, 354
Messenia, 119, 124; revolt of, 173
Metaurus River, 360
Metellus, consul, 377, 384, 386
Metellus, praetor, 363
Methone, 120n.
Metics, Athenian, 207

Meton, 217f.
Metz, 491
Middle Kingdom, Egyptian, 54ff.
Milan, 475, 477, 481, 489, 502
Miletus, 92f., 117, 120, 147f., 154, 174
Milo, 393f.
Miltiades, 155ff., 159
Milvian Bridge, 479
Mimnermus, 135
Minerva, 335
Minoan civilization, 99f.; government, 103; end of, 106
Minos, Palace of, 103
Minucius Felix, 508
Misenum, 401, 420
Mitanni, 69, 80
Mithra, 152, 311, 463f., 505
Mithridatic Wars, 380ff., 387
Mnesicles, 212
Moabites, 77
Modestine, 471
Moeris, Lake, 56
Mona, 433
Monasticism, 510f.
Monophysites, 495, 497
Mont Cénis Pass, 357
Mont Genèvre Pass, 479
Montanus, 508
Monte Cassino, 510
Moors, 486
Moravia, 444
Moselle River, 506
Moses, 76
Mummius, 363
Munda, 397
Munera, 470
Municipalities, 446f.
Museum, 305, 318
Mycale, 169, 171
Mycenae, 106ff.
Mylae, 354
Myron, 177
Myronides, 181
Mytilene, 192

N

Nabataeans, 440
Nabis, 288
Nabonidus, 92
Nabopolassar, 87, 89, 92
Naevius, 330, 371
Nakadeh, 46
Nannar, 38
Naples, 119, 324, 339

Napoleon, 44
Naram Sin, 31f.
Narcissus, 431
Narses, 499
Natufians, 17
Naucratis, 91, 120
Naupactus, 181, 183
Navy: *See* Army.
Naxos, 154, 172, 183n.
Neanderthal Man, 13, 99
Neapolis: *See* Naples.
Nearchus, 265
Nebuchadnezzar, 80, 87, 89
Necho I, 86
Necho II, 87, 97
Nefertiti, 61ff.
Negroes, 17
Neolithic Revolution, 17ff., 325
Neoplatonism, 485, 505
Nepos, 409
Nero, Claudius, consul, 360
Nero, emperor, 431ff.
Nerva, 438f.
Nervii, 392
New Babylonian Empire, 89f.
New Carthage, 360
New Kingdom, Egyptian, 58ff.
"New Men," 366f.
New Testament, 507
Newcastle, 437
Nicaea, Council of, 481, 486
Nicias, 197f.; Peace of, 194
Nicomedes III, 387
Nika Riot, 500f.
Nike, Temple of, 212
Nile River, 42f.
Nineveh, 27, 84ff., 98
Nippur, 27
Nisaea, 183, 193
Nish, 479
Nisibis, 468
Noah, 39
Nola, 426
Nordic people, 17
Noricum, 420
Normandy, 393
North Sea, 419f.
Novels of Justinian, 499
Nubia, 42, 44, 50, 56
Numantia, 364
Numa Pompilius, 334
Numidia, 361, 365, 377f., 440
Nut, 50

O

Octavia, Octavian's sister, 401f.
Octavia, daughter of Claudius, 431
Octavian, 400ff. *See also* Augustus.
Octavius, 374, 382
Odenathus, 474f.
Odeon of Pericles, 209
Odovacar, 492
Odyssey, 113f.
Officia, 482
Ofilius, 408
Ogulnian Law, 350
Old Kingdom, Egyptian, 46ff.
Old Oligarch, 179
Old Testament, 75f.
Oligarchy, Roman, 367
Olympia, 116; Temple at, 176
Olympeion, at Athens, 442
Olympias, 256, 276
Olympus, Mt., 99
Olynthus, 120n.
Opimius, 376f.
Opis, 267
Optimates, 373, and *passim,* Chapters
    25 and 26
Oracles, Greek, 134
Orange, Battle of, 378
Orchomenus, 381
Orestes, 492
Origen, 507
Origo, 484
Orleans, 491
Orphism, 136
Orthagoras, 122
Osiris, 51, 57, 310
Osroene, 468
Osroes, 446
Ostia, 331, 399, 403, 431
Ostracism, 132, 195
Ostrogoths, 486f., 492ff.; conquered by
    Belisarius, 497f.
Otho, 433
Ovid, 422

P

Pachomius, St., 510
Padua, 421
Paestum, 119, 141
Paganism, 505, 510
Paideia, 305

Palaikastro, 103
Palatine, 329f., 405, 424, 452
Paleolithic Age, definition, 10
Paleolithic Age, end of, 16
Pallas, 431
Palmyra, 457, 494f.
Panaetius, 310, 407
Panathenaic festival, 130, 134
Pangaeus, Mt., 172, 174, 184
Panionion, 146
Pannonia, 420
Pansa, 400
Pantheon, 424, 454
Papacy, 509f.
Papinian, 459, 471
Papyri, 7
Parmenio, 240, 258, 263
Parnes, Mt., 205
Parni, 293
Paros, 159, 174
Parthenon, 209f.
Parthia, 93, 293f.
Parthian Empire, 387, 394, 399, 401,
    418ff., 428, 433, 440, 444, 468,
    471f.
Pasargadae, 92
Patriarchs, 509
Paul, Apostle, 458
Paul, jurist, 459, 465, 471
Paulus, general, 362
Pausanias, author, 458
Pausanias, general, 169, 171
Pax Romana, 402, 449ff.
Peace, Thirty Years', 183
Peace, Vespasian's Temple of, 435
Pegae, 181f., 193
Peisistratus, 130f., 134
Peleset, 77
Pella, 235, 240
Peloponnesian League, 127, 161, 173,
    181ff., 184, 187
Peloponnesian War, causes of, 185ff.
Peloponnesus, 99, 111
Penates, 334
Pentacontaetia, 177
Pentelicus, Mt., 127, 174, 206
Pepi I, 47
Pepi II, 47
Perdiccas, King, 184; general and regent,
    270, 275f.
Pergamum (Pergamon), 278, 292f.,
    313, 316, 361, 364, 374
Periander, 122

Pericles, 160, 173, 178, 181, 183, 187;
    Funeral Oration, 188; death of, 191
Pericles the Young, 203
Perioeci, 124
Perperna, 384
Persepolis, 262
Perseus, 362
Persia, 27, 92, 181, 226ff., 258ff.
Persian Empire, 146ff., 230ff., 240
    258ff.
Persian Gulf, 27, 265, 440
Persians, Sassanid period, 472ff., 499
Persis, 149
Persius, 455
Pertinax, 467
Perusia, 401
Peter, St., 465, 509
Petra, 440
Petronius Arbiter, 455
Petronius Maximus, 490
Phaestos, 103
Phaleron, 127, 155, 159, 168
Phaortes, 91
Pharaoh: see Government, Egyptian
Pharisees, 434f.
Pharnaces, 395
Pharsalus, Battle of, 395
Pherae, 249
Phidias, 209f.
Philae, 45
Philaid clan, 155
Philip the Arab, 474
Philip Arrhidaeus, 275
Philip II of Macedon, 235ff.; aggression
    of, 236f.; enters Greece, 238; death
    of, 240, 258
Philip V of Macedon, 284f., 287, 359
Philippi, Battle of, 401
Philistines, 72
Philo, 463
Philosophy: Greek, 136ff., 218ff.;
    Hellenistic, 309; at Rome, 407,
    462f., 505
Philotas, 263
Phocaeans, 120, 147
Phocis, 181f.
Phoenicians, 72ff.
Phormio, 184, 192
Phrygia, 83, 91
Phrynicus, 155
Piankhi, 85
Picts, 442, 486, 491
Pindar, 175f.

Pindus Mts., 99
Piraeus, 127, 155, 171, 181, 183, 188f., 203
Piracy, 386
Piso, 428, 432, 455
Placidia, 490
Plague, at Athens, 189ff.; at Rome, 444, 473
Plataea, 157f., 168f., 171, 183, 187, 192
Plato, 222, 243ff, 505
Plautus, 371
Plebeian Council, 349f.
Plebs, 417
Pleistoanax, 182, 194
Pleistocene Age, 12f.
Pliny the Elder, 456
Pliny the Younger, 439, 457, 469
Plotinus, 505
Plutarch, 182, 185n., 256, 458
Pnyx, 132
Po River, 324f., 338
Pollentia, 489
Polybius, 306, 353, 363, 371
Polycleitus, 213
Polygnotus, 213
Pompeii, 436, 446
Pompey: and the Optimates, 304ff.; 384ff.; returns to Rome, 388f.; 402
Pompey, Sextus, 401
Pomptine Marshes, 399
Pontifex Maximus, 421, 487
Pontius, 339
Pontus, 380f., 387
Populares, 373ff.
Porphyry of Tyre, 505
Porus, 265
Poseidon, 133, 146
Poseidonius, 407
Post, Roman, 470, 482
Postumus, 475
Potidaea, 120n., 122, 184, 187, 192
Pottery: Prehistoric, 6, 20; Sumerian, 27; Egyptian, 46, 50, 52; Minoan, 102f.; Greek, 114, 138; Roman, 403
Praeneste, 332
Praetor: see Magistrates, Roman
Praetor peregrinus, 367
Praetorian Prefect, 471; Prefecture, 482
Praxiteles, 252
Predynastic Egypt, 46
Preglacial man, 11f.

Prehistory, definition, 8
Priene, 316
Princeps, 395, 415ff., 446
Principate of Augustus, 413ff.
Proconsul, 345
Procopius, 507
Prodicus, 220
Propertius, 422
Prophets, Hebrew, 79
Propontis, 153
Propraetor, 345
Propylaea, 212
Proskynesis, 264
Protagoras, 216, 219f.
Provinces, Roman, 368ff., 398, 419f., 439ff., 447, 473f., 478
Prudentius, 508
Psammeticus, 87, 91, 120
Ptah, 50
Ptahhotep, precepts of, 54
Ptolemaic dynasty, 279, 296ff.;
Ptolemy I, 276, 296
Ptolemy II, 296
Ptolemy III, 296
Ptolemy XIV, 396
Publicans, 369
Punic War, First, 353ff.; Second, 356; Third, 388
Punt, 47, 50, 56, 60
Puteoli, 403
Pydna, Battle of, 362
Pylos, 108f., 193f.
Pyramids, The Great, 51f., 57
Pyrrhic War, 392
Pyrrhus, 277, 283, 342, 392
Pythagoras, 137, 217ff.
Pytheas, 306

Q

Quadi, 438, 445, 473, 486
Quaestor: see Magistrates, Roman
Quintilian, 457
Quirinal, 331

R

Races of mankind, 17
Raetia, 420
Ramapithecus, 11
Ramses I, 66
Ramses II, 66
Ramses III, 67

Raphia, 84; Battle of, 296
Ras Shamra, 71
Ravenna, 420, 489, 494, 502
Rawlinson, Sir Henry, 26
Re, 48, 50, 57
Reate, 434
Red-figured Greek pots, 139f.
Red Sea, 27
Regulus, 354f.
Rehoboam, 79
Religion: Prehistoric, 14f.; Sumerian,
    27, 35; Babylonian, 38f.; Egyptian,
    44, 50f., 57, 62ff.; Hittite, 72;
    Hebrew, 76ff.; Assyrian, 88; Greek,
    112, 133f., 214, 310; Roman, 371,
    462; late pagan, 505; see also
    Christianity, Mithra, etc.
Remus, 329
Res Privata, 470
Rhea, 329
Rhegium, 193, 340
Rhine River, 393, 419f., 428
Rhodes, 277, 282, 284; Hellenistic,
    288f; 316, 363, 426
Rhone River, 73, 357, 491
Ricimer, 492
Rim Sin, 35
Roads, Roman, 340, 351, 470, 482;
    see also Royal Road of Persia.
Roman character, 333f.; 362
Roman Empire, division of, 488; end of
    in West, 492; eastern, development
    of, 496
Roman Law, codification of, 499
Rome: founding of, 329f.; location of,
    330f.; character of people, 333f.;
    kings of, 334ff.; regal government,
    335; regal religion, 335f.; overthrow
    of monarchy of, 336; neighbors of,
    337; early Republic, 337ff.; late
    Republic, 373ff.; early Empire,
    413ff.; period of crisis, 467ff.; late
    empire, 476ff.; city of, 372; sacked
    by Alaric, 489; city of, depopulated,
    499
Romulus, 329f.
Romulus Augustulus, 492
Rosetta Stone, 45
Royal Road of Persia, 150
Roxane, 264, 276
Rubicon River, 342, 395
Rufinus, 495
Rumania, 440

Russia, southern, 174
Rutilius Rufus, 379

S

Sabina, 432
Sabines, 332, 337f.
Sacred War, 338
Sadducees, 434
Saguntum, 357
Sahara Desert, 440
Saint Sophia, Church of, 500, 503
Saints, Christian, 510
Sais, 86, 91
Salamis, 167ff.
Salinator, Livius, 360
Sallust, 409
Salona, 479
Samaria, 79
Samnites, 325
Samnite Wars, 338ff.
Samos, 141, 169, 172, 174, 183, 202
Samothrace, Winged Victory of, 313
Samuel, 77
Sanskrit, 69
San Vitale, church of, 503
Saône River, 491
Sappho, 135
Sardinia, annexed by Rome, 355
Sardis, 91, 124, 150, 154, 160
Sargon of Akkad, 31
Sargon II, 80f., 84, 88
Sarmatians, 438, 473, 476
Sassanids, 152, 472f., 474, 499
Satrapies, 149f.
Saturnalia, 352
Saturninus, 379
Saul, 77
Saxons, 461, 473, 478, 486, 491
Scaevola, 375, 407
Schliemann, Heinrich, 107f., 109
Science: Babylonian, 39; Egyptian, 54;
    Ionian, 136ff.; Periclean, 217;
    Hellenistic, 316ff.; Roman, 458
Scione, 120n.
Scipio Aemilianus, 364f., 370, 374
Scipio, Africanus, 360ff., 370, 374
Scipio, Gnaeus, 360
Scipio, Lucius, 362
Scipionic Circle, 370
Scotland, 437, 491
Scots, 486, 491
Sculpture: see Art

Scupi, 496
Scythian Empire, 152
Scythians, 87, 152
Sea Peoples, 67f.
Second Athenian naval league, 231, 237
Second Sophistic, 458
Segesta, 193, 195
Sejanus, 428
Seleuceia on the Tigris, 289, 444
Seleucid dynasty, 279; Empire, 289ff., 361f., 387
Seleucus I, 276, 290
Selinus, 141, 195
Semites, 25; at Ebla, 31
Sempronius Longus, 357f.
Senate, Roman, 346, 350, 366f., 415f., 446, 470, 472
Seneca, 431, 455, 463
Sennacherib, 84, 88
Sentinum, 340
Septimius Severus, 467ff.
Sequani, 391
Serapis, 310
Serfdom, Roman, 484
Sertorius, 384
Servilius, 359
Servius Tullius, 334
Sesostris, III, 56
Sestos, 168, 171
Seti I, 66
Severans, government of, 469f.
Severus Alexander, 472
Sextus Pompey, 401
Shalmaneser III, 83
Shalmaneser V, 84
Shamash, 41
Shapur I, 474
Shapur II, 485
Shuppiluliuma, 71
Shulgi, 33
Sicels, 120
Sicily, 106, 169f., 193, 195ff., 324, 354ff., 359, 368, 385
Sicily, Athenian expedition to, 195ff.
Sicyon, 122, 174
Sidon, 73, 86, 261
Sigeum, 153
Sihwah Oasis, 261f.
Silver Age at Rome, 454
Simonides, 175
Sinai, 44, 47, 56, 76, 78
Sinuhe, 57
Sippas, 31
Sirmium, 477

Skeptics, 308
Skopas, 252
Slave war, Sicily, 378
Slavery: see Economic and Social Background
Smerdis, 149
Society: see Economic and Social Background
Socrates, 117, 185n., 209f., 220ff., 242f.
Sogdiana, 93
Solidus, 483
Solomon, 78
Solon, 129, 147
Solutrean Culture, 14
Solway Firth, 437, 442
Somaliland: see Punt.
Sophistry, 213, 241
Sophists, 219ff.
Sophocles, poet, 147, 183, 215f.
Sophocles, general, 193
Sosigenes, 398
Spain, 73f., 120, 174, 354f., 360, 364, 368f., 384, 393, 396, 413f., 447, 499
Spalato, 479
Sparta, 99, 124ff., 154, 156, 161g., 168g, 171, 181, 183ff., 197, 202f., 229f., 387, 359, 363
Spartacus, 364f.
Sphacteria, 193f.
Sphinx, 52
Spurius Cassius, 337, 349
Stilicho, 489, 491
Stoa of Attalus, 208
Stoicism, 309f., 371, 407, 437, 455, 462
Stonehenge, 21
Strabo, 422
Strasburg, 485
Struggle between the Roman orders, 344f.
Strymon River, 153, 172, 184
Suetonius, 438, 457f.
Suevi, 391, 490
Sulpicius, 381
Sulla, 208, 378, 380ff.; dictator, 382f.; 402, 404
Sumerians, 27ff.
Sun God, Syrian, 476, 505
Sunium, 158
Swiss lake villages, 20
Switzerland, 391
Sybaris, 119
Sybota, 184

Symmachus, 487
Syracuse, 120, 141, 169f., 184, 193,
    197, 233f., 281, 317, 354, 360
Syria, 25, 71f., 261, 289ff., 361, 510;
    Roman province, 387, 394

T

Tabularium, 410
Tacitus, 427, 433f., 437, 457, 465
Tagaste, 508
Tarentum, 119, 324, 340, 359f., 376,
    401
Tarquinii, 327
Tarquinius Priscus, 334
Tarquinius Superbus, 334, 335
Tarsus, 401
Taurus Mts., 31, 69, 72, 83, 362
Taxation, Roman 369
Taygetus, Mt., 124, 126
Technology, 448; see also Economic
    and Social Background and Science
Tegea, 127
Telesippe, 178n.
Tell-el-Amarna, 62ff.
Tempe, 162
Ten Commandments, 76
Ten Lost Tribes, 80
Ten Thousand, march of, 230
Teos, 147
Terence, 371
Terpander, 124
Terremare people, 325
Tertullian, 508
Teshub, 72
Tetrarchy, 477
Tetricus, 476
Teutoberg Forest, Battle of, 421
Teutons, 378
Textiles, Neolithic: 20; see also Art
Thales, 136f., 316
Thaletas, 124
Thames River, 393, 431
Thamugadi, 440
Thapsus, 397
Thasos, 156, 172ff., 183n.
Theagenes, 128
Theater, Greek, 208f.
Thebes, 106, 116, 156, 160, 169, 181,
    187, 205, 230, 239, 258f.; hegemony
    of, 232
Thebes, Egypt, 56f., 58f.
Themistocles, 155ff., 160f., 167f., 171f.
Theocritus, 308

Theodora, 496, 501
Theodoric, 491
Theodoric the Great, 492f., 511
Theodosian Code, 495
Theodosius I, 487
Theodosius II, 495f.
Theognis, 119
Theophrastus, 307, 318
Theoric Fund, 237f.
Thera, 106
Theramenes, 204ff.
Thermopylae, 160ff.
Theseus, 128
Thesmophoria, 207
Thespis, 135
Thessalonica, 487
Thessaly, 99, 106, 111, 156, 160f., 168
Thetes, 179
Thirty Years' Peace, 183ff.
Thrace, 93, 99, 153, 156, 171, 174,
    276f., 476
Thrasybulus, Athenian, 205
Thrasybulus, tyrant, 122
Thucydides, historian, 174, 185ff.,
    196ff., 224ff.
Thucydides, son of Melesias, 183
Thurii, 184, 340
Thutmosis I, 59
Thutmosis III, 59ff.
Tiber River, 324, 329
Tiberius, 420f., 426; reign of, 427ff.
Tibullus, 422
Tibur, 332, 406, 442
Ticinus River, 356
Tigellinus, 432
Tiglath Pileser I, 83
Tiglath Pileser III, 80, 83, 86, 88
Tigranes, 387
Tigranocerta, 387
Tigris River, 25f., 81
Timgad, 440
Tiridates, 433
Tiro, 404, 498
Tiryns, 109
Tissaphernes, 202
Titus, 435f.
Tivoli, 442
Tiye, 61
Tombs, beehive, 107f
Tomi, 422
Tools; Paleolithic, 14; Neolithic, 19;
    see also Art
Toulouse, 490
Toynbee, A., 7, 450

Trade: Neolithic, 20; Sumerian, 27f.;
   Egyptian, 50, 56; Hittite, 72;
   Phoenician, 73f.; Assyrian, 88;
   Mycenaean, 106; Greek, 116ff.,
   227f.; Hellenistic, 300ff.; Roman,
   351, 403f., 448f.; see also Economic
   and Social Background
Trajan, 439ff., 465
Trajan's Column, 440, 454
Transalpine Gaul, 378, 390
Trasimene, Battle of, 359
Trèves: see Trier.
Trives, Roman, 347f., 386f.
Tribonian, 499
Tribunes, consular, 345
Tribunes of the people, 348f., 374ff.
Trier, 434, 375, 377
Troezen, 167, 181f.
Trojan War, 109f.
Troy, 109f., 260
Troyes, 491
Tullus Hostilius, 334
Turin, 479
Tuscany, 327
Tusculum, 332
Tutankhamen, 65ff.
Twelve Tables, 349, 352, 372
Tylissos, 103
Tyne River, 437, 442
Tyrants, Greek, 121ff.
Tyrants, Thirty, 205
Tyre, 73, 86, 89, 261, 353
Tyrrhenian Sea, 327
Tyrtaeus, 124

U

Ugarit (Ras Shamra), 71
Ulfilas, 486, 489
Ulpian, 459, 471f.
Umbro-Sabellians, 325
Umma, 29
Ur, early dynastic, 29; third dynasty at,
   32f.
Ur-Nammu, 32
Urartu, 83
Uruinimgina, 29
Uruk, 27
Uskub, 496
Utica, 73, 365, 397

V

Valens, 486
Valentinian I, 486

Valentinian II, 486
Valentinian III, 490
Valerian, 474
Valerio-Horatian Laws, 349
Valerius Antias, 409
Valerius Maximus, 455
Van, Lake, 83f., 91f.
Vandals, 473, 476, 490f; conquered by
   Belisarius, 497
Vaphio, 108
Varro, author, 403, 410
Varro, consul, 359
Varus, 421, 428
Vases, see Pottery
Vatican, 331
Veii, 338
Velleius Paterculus, 455
Veneti, 393
Ventris, Michael, 103
Venus, 336
Venus and Rome, Temple of, 442
Venus Genetrix, Temple of, 424
Vercellae, 378
Vercingetorix, 393
Vergil, 329f., 422
Verginius, 433
Verona, 409, 479, 489
Verres, 385
Verus, 444
Vespasian, 433f.
Vesta, 335f.
Vestal Virgins, 336
Vesuvius, Mt., 385, 436, 456f.
Via Appia, 340, 351
Vicars, 479
Vienna, 435
Villages, first Neolithic, 17f
Villanova, 325
Villian Law, 367
Viminal, 331
Vindobana, 435, 445
Visigoths, 487f., 488ff., 492
Vitellius, 433f.
Vologases I, 433
Vologases III, 444
Vologases IV, 468
Volsci, 332, 338
Vulcan, 335
Vulgate, 508
Vulture's Stele, 29

W

Wales, 437
Warfare, Hellenistic, 281; see also Army.

Witiges, 497
Writing, beginnings of, 22; 26, 36, 44f., 75, 103, 113, 327
Württemberg, 438

X

Xanthippus, Athenian, 160, 168
Xanthippus, Spartan, 355
Xenophanes, 137, 218
Xenophon, 185n, 203, 222, 230, 246f.
Xerxes, 160ff., 167, 182

Y

Yahweh, 76, 311
Yemen, 84
York, 469, 479
Yueh-chi, 294

Z

Zagros Mts., 25, 81
Zakro, 103
Zama, Battle of, 361
Zancle, 119
Zealots, 435
Zedekiah, 89
Zeno, emperor, 492, 496
Zenobia, 475f.
Zeus, 112, 133
Zeus, Stoa of, and Temple of at Athens, 208; Temple of, at Olympia, 176
Ziggurat, 27
Zion, Mt. 435
Zoroaster, Zoroastrianism, 152, 463f., 472
Zuider Zee, 420